Annual Review of United Nations Affairs

2006/2007

VOLUME I

Edited by
Joachim Müller
and
Karl P. Sauvant

Oceana®
NEW YORK

OXFORD
UNIVERSITY PRESS

Oxford University Press, Inc., publishes works that further Oxford University's objective of excellence in research, scholarship, and education.

Published by Oxford University Press, Inc.
198 Madison Avenue, New York, New York 10016

ISSN: 0066-4340

ISBN: 978-0-19-533728-0 (2006/2007, Volume I)

Note to Readers:

This publication is designed to provide accurate and authoritative information in regard to the subject matter covered. It is based upon sources believed to be accurate and reliable and is intended to be current as of the time it was written. It is sold with the understanding that the publisher is not engaged in rendering legal, accounting, or other professional services. If legal advice or other expert assistance is required, the services of a competent professional person should be sought. Also, to confirm that the information has not been affected or changed by recent developments, traditional legal research techniques should be used, including checking primary sources where appropriate.

(*Based on the Declaration of Principles jointly adopted by a Committee of the American Bar Association and a Committee of Publishers and Associations.*)

SUMMARY TABLE OF CONTENTS

TABLE OF CONTENTS VOLUME I

CHAPTER 1

General Assembly
Sixty-first Session

Note: ARUNA 2006/2007

ARUNA coverage of the UN year

The coverage of the *Annual Review of the United Nations (ARUNA)* follows the "UN year": as a rule, the regular sessions of the General Assembly of the UN begin each year on the third Tuesday in September and last 12 months. The Assembly's Committees normally meet October to December of each year, although the Plenary continues to meet throughout the year, whenever the need arises. (The UN calendar of conferences and meetings for the period covered can be found after the Introduction.) "Life" in the UN is therefore structured from September to September. This volume covers the 61st session of the General Assembly, 12 September 2006 to 17 September 2007. It contains a complete coverage of the outcome of the work of the key organs of the UN.

ARUNA guest author: Professor Edward C. Luck

In this year's edition, the Introduction is written by the ARUNA guest author Edward C. Luck. The author is UN Special Adviser on the Responsibility to Protect and Vice President and Director of Studies at the International Peace Academy. He is on public service leave as Professor of Practice in International and Public Affairs at Columbia University. From 1984 to 1994 he served as President and CEO of the United Nations Association. Mr. Luck is a distinguished international scholar with extensive knowledge of the United Nations system and a superb reputation for academic and practical excellence.

ARUNA concept

ARUNA presents a comprehensive documentation of the work of the United Nations for the time-period covered. Coverage of the UN's six key organs is provided: the General Assembly, the Security Council, the Economic and Social Council (ECOSOC), the Trusteeship Council, the International Court of Justice, and the UN Secretariat. In addition, selected reports of intergovernmental bodies, expert groups and other materials are included. Solely official UN documentation is used.

ARUNA thus occupies a special place in the growing number of publications on the work of the United Nations – it allows readers to obtain an overview of the principal developments in its key organs during the time period covered. This makes it an important reference source for policy-makers and academic researchers.

Description of the chapters contained in ARUNA 2006/2007

The 2006/2007 edition comprises seven chapters:

- Chapter 1 covers the 61st session of the General Assembly. It is introduced by the opening and closing statements of the President of the session, which highlight the main topics and achievements of the UN year under review. This is followed by the agenda of the annual session and the complete set of its resolutions.
- Chapter 2 contains the report of the Security Council, giving a detailed account of the various issues discussed, the documentation considered and the decisions taken by the Security Council during the year under review. This is followed by the resolutions of the Security Council.
- Chapter 3 contains the Report of ECOSOC, comprising three segments. It also reproduces its agenda and makes reference to the resolutions and decisions of the Council.

- Chapter 4 is very short, reflecting the inactive nature of the Trusteeship Council.
- Chapter 5 contains the report of the International Court of Justice and gives details of its jurisdiction, composition and the work undertaken.
- Chapter 6 documents the work of the Secretariat. It starts with the Annual Report of the Secretary-General for the 61st session of the General Assembly. This is followed by a number of reports of various entities of the UN.
- Finally, chapter 7 contains selected reports of intergovernmental bodies, expert groups and the United Nations Secretariat. This includes, in particular, progress reports for the main peacekeeping missions.

We trust that this publication is of use to all those interested in the work of the UN.

ARUNA is edited by Dr. Joachim Müller, Director, World Meteorological Organization, and Dr. Karl P. Sauvant, Executive Director, Columbia Program on International Investment (a joint initiative of The Earth Institute at Columbia University and the Columbia Law School), and Co-Director, Millennium Cities Initiative (e-mail: karlsauvant@gmail.com). The views expressed here do not necessarily reflect those of the institutions with which the editors are affiliated

Overview

The United Nations Year 2006/2007: A new beginning in difficult times

by
Joachim Müller and Karl P. Sauvant*

On 13 October 2006, and on the recommendation of the Security Council, the General Assembly elected Ban Ki-moon, a former Foreign Minister of the Republic of Korea, as the Organization's next Secretary-General. The new Secretary-General had campaigned on the slogan "promise less and deliver more".

Ban Ki-moon took over on 1 January 2007 from Kofi Annan, who left after a ten-year term. Despite the controversies during the last part of his mandate, Annan was widely admired and was considered a difficult act to follow.[1] Moreover, Ban inherited a number of difficult challenges. The internal political dynamics among member states had become more complex during 2006. The bloc of developing countries, organized in the Nonaligned Movement (NAM) and the Group of 77 (G77), considered the ongoing reform process as biased towards reducing their influence. The United States, the most powerful member of the Organization, was unhappy with the pace and direction of the reforms as, in this country's views, they did not address demands in such key areas as human rights, oversight, mandate review, and management reform. Finally, the failure of Security Council reform led to major disappointment among a number of member states hopeful to elevate their position in the Organization.

Ban scored early political points from the developing world with the appointment of a fresh group of senior managers: a Deputy Secretary-General from Tanzania, a Chief of Staff from India, an Under-Secretary-General for Management from Mexico, and a spokesperson from Haiti. Three of those four appointees are women. The Secretary-General was sending a clear signal to developing countries that he would seek to give them a larger voice in the workings of the Secretariat. In parallel, he set out to strengthen relations with the Bush Administration and to establish a less confrontational atmosphere. John R. Bolton, the United States Ambassador to the UN, resigned at the end of 2006 and was replaced by Zalmay Khalilzad. Khalizad took over in April 2007; his previous diplomatic experience included service as the US Ambassador to Iraq and Afghanistan.

New initiatives

One of the first major initiatives introduced by Ban focused on restructuring the UN Secretariat, covering peacekeeping operations and disarmament.[2] With the surge in UN peacekeeping which had reached an unprecedented 100,000 peacekeeping personnel in the field and the expectation that the number could reach 150,000 by the end of 2007, Ban proposed to augment the Department of Peacekeeping Operations (DPKO) with the new Department of Field Support. The new entity would serve as the coordinator for field support needs, including the administration and management of personnel, communication, and information technology, finance, procurement, and logistics in UN peacekeeping operations. DPKO would

* The views expressed here do not necessarily reflect those of the institutions with which the authors are affiliated. They wish to thank Hannelore Hoppe, Olga Sucovic and Tim Wall for comments on an earlier draft.

therefore concentrate on policy planning and implementation, as well as on providing strategic direction for UN peacekeeping activities.

With regard to disarmament, Ban initially proposed to integrate the Department for Disarmament Affairs (DDA) into the Department of Political Affairs (DPA) and to downgrade the head of DDA to the level of Assistant Secretary-General. Both initiatives were met with resistance from member states. Concern was expressed regarding potential overlap and problems in coordination and communication between the two departments responsible for peacekeeping operations. The developing countries, in particular, were strongly opposed to a downgrading of DDA, stressing that any structural change should lead to a strengthening, not weakening, of the UN's work in the field of disarmament, arms control and non-proliferation. Following a round of extensive consultations with member states, the Secretary-General revised his proposals, demonstrating his ability to be flexible and responsive in the face of resistance. This quality has not gone unnoticed by member states, and they reacted more favorably to his ideas.

The General Assembly has hence supported, on 15 March 2007, the proposals for restructuring DPKO and DDA, in Resolutions 61/256 and 61/257, respectively. Yet the General Assembly still requested that the Secretary-General present comprehensive details on the functions and financial, administrative, and budgetary implications of these initiatives. Accordingly, DDA was reconstituted as a separate office in the Secretariat, headed by a "high representative" at the Under-Secretary-General level, reporting directly to the Secretary-General. By maintaining budgetary autonomy and the integrity of the existing structures and functions, the new Office of Disarmament was not too different from the previous department, except that more emphasis was now placed on a strengthened advocacy role of the head of the Office to help mobilize political will to overcome the current stalemate in the field of disarmament.

The Secretary-General also provided new impetus to the reform of the sclerotic personnel system. He stated his intention to institute policies to foster competition for jobs and to eliminate certain employment guarantees. This plan also includes improved annual performance reviews, term limits for new hires of senior officials, and reform of the administration of justice, with the aim of codifying a single standard for disciplinary actions regarding UN staff. Ban publicly made a full disclosure of his personal financial situation and urged his top officials to do the same to demonstrate greater transparency of financial dealings. He also made a quick decision to order an external audit of UNDP, following reports that hard currency transactions in North Korea could have enabled the regime to use such funds for illicit purposes.

Reform efforts carried over to 2007

Ban had inherited a number of ongoing reform initiatives which had seen mixed progress. Progress had been limited on reaching agreement on the terms of reference for the proposed Independent Audit Advisory Committee to strengthen independent oversight. Moreover, the review of over 5,000 mandates approved by the General Assembly, one of the most contentious parts of the 2005 World Summit reform package, was proceeding slowly. Through 2006, the General Assembly's informal consultations on mandate review were marked by intense divisions over the scope and purpose of the exercise. The United States strongly supported the review and, by implication, the potential elimination of mandates, resulting in fearful reactions from states with a vested interest in vulnerable mandates. As a first step, it was decided to examine mandates that were older than five years and had not been renewed; these accounted for only 7 per cent of mandates. The review of those that had been renewed was more contentious, and the process stalled in early 2007. Only in late April 2007 was the review formally re-launched, with reviews taking place according to thematic clusters. At the urging of the NAM and the G77 and China, the review started with the cluster involving drug-control, crime prevention and combating international terrorism – UN activities that are strongly supported by the United States.

The replacement of the Human Rights Commission by the new Human Rights Council in March 2006 had been one of the most visible reform outcomes of the 2005 Millennium Summit.[3] The United States had voted against the establishment of the Council, citing the Council's inadequate mechanisms to ensure credible membership. Subsequently, the United States decided not to run for a seat on the Council, but stated that it would do so in 2007, provided the Council had proven its effectiveness. In March 2007, however, and for the second consecutive year, the Bush Administration did not seek election to the Human Rights Council, alleging that it had an ineffective track record.

The reform of the Security Council, a major preoccupation during the past eight years, was kept under review during 2006, but without coming closer to an agreement. The 2005 World Summit had not managed to resolve this issue. That failure represented a major disappointment in particular for those member states that had hoped to become permanent members, especially Brazil, Germany, India, and Japan. While the issues of expansion and veto privileges were most controversial, even the proposals on the Council's working methods did not garner consensus.

In January 2007, the General Assembly President Sheikha Haya Rashed Al Khalifa appointed a group of five facilitators to consult with member states on Security Council reform. After extensive closed-door consultations, the facilitators issued two reports in April and June 2007, both of which provided an interesting snapshot of the broad spectrum of concerns of member states. The facilitators concluded that, while support for Security Council reform is widespread, deep divisions among countries on how such reform should look is preventing agreement on any permanent changes. There was considerable interest, however, in an intermediary approach that would entail creating a new category of membership in the Security Council, to be reviewed after a given number of years. The main issue, however, was the lack of readiness of member states to move from consultations to negotiations and to agree on a framework for negotiations. In July 2007, Brazil, India, and South Africa announced that they had agreed to work together for permanent seats on the Council under the auspices of the Trilateral Commission of the India-Brazil-South Africa Dialogue Forum (IBSA). The two reports of the facilitators were submitted to the incoming President of the General Assembly, Srgjan Kerim, who is responsible for guiding the ongoing consultations and the negotiation process throughout the 62nd General Assembly session.

Programme focus of the new Secretary-General

During his first months in office, Ban Ki-moon has been quick to formulate his position on a number of key issues, including Darfur, the situation in the Middle East, the Millennium Development Goals, and climate change. He has taken an early stand on addressing the crisis in Darfur, gradually taking on the role of the "world's conscience". On the situation in the Middle East, the new Secretary-General emphasized turning the Quartet – the US, the European Union, Russia, the UN – into a more effective mechanism for resolving the Israeli-Palestinian conflict, and he pledged support for Lebanon's reconstruction following the war in 2006. Ban identified the Millennium Development Goals as one of his major priorities throughout his campaign for the post, and has continued to do so since taking office. In support of that claim, he assembled a working group on Africa and the Millennium Development Goals to serve as "a coalition of the willing" to speed up progress on the goals.

Climate change

Already in early 2007, Ban Ki-moon declared climate change to be a top priority, describing global warming as a threat to the world "as great as modern warfare" and a likely "major driver of war and conflict" in the coming decades. Indeed, subsequent developments indicate that climate change may well become the defining issue of his tenure as Secretary-General. Initial efforts focused on bringing together member states in the negotiations for a successor arrangement to the Kyoto Protocol, aimed at addressing global warming by limiting greenhouse gas emissions. The Protocol and its follow-up are negotiated under the United Nations Framework Convention on Climate Change (UNFCC), which seeks to reduce emissions of greenhouse gases in order to combat global warming. UNFCC was established at the United Nations Conference on Environment and Development (UNCED), informally known as the Earth Summit, held in Rio de Janeiro in 1992.

UNFCC establishes limits on greenhouse gas emissions for individual nations and contains enforcement provisions through treaty updates called Protocols. The Kyoto Protocol requires 36 industrialized countries to cut greenhouse gas emissions by at least 5 per cent below 1990 levels between 2008 and 2012. It allows industrialized countries to meet their targets by trading emission allowances on a newly-created carbon market. The trading system is set to begin in 2008; funds flowing from North to South could reach up to $100 billion over the coming years. The Kyoto Protocol is due to expire at the end of 2012. Post-Kyoto negotiations began in early 2007, with the aim of reaching fundamental agreement by 2009 to allow time for ratification prior to 2012. A series of UNFCCC meetings was planned for the negotiation process, including a major conference in Bali, Indonesia, during December 2007.

Unprecedented interest in climate change by policy makers and the general public was triggered by a report of the Intergovernmental Panel on Climate Change (IPCC)[4] issued on 2 February 2007. IPCC was established by the World Meteorological Organization (WMO) and the United Nations Environment Programme (UNEP) to assess scientific, technical, and socio-economic information relevant to the understanding of climate change, its potential impacts, and options for adaptation and mitigation. For the preparation of the report, IPCC brought together more than 2,000 scientists and experts. They put an end to any doubts about the science side of the debate and about seriousness of the situation. More specifically, the Panel concluded that "warming of the climate system is unequivocal" and that most of the observed increases in temperature are "very likely" due to the increasing concentration of green house gases due to human activities, mostly the burning of fossil fuels and deforestation. It was argued that, without particular emission reduction policies, global temperature may rise by up to 6.4°C (11.5°F) before the end of the century. As a result, the sea level might increase by up to 7 meters (23 feet), accompanied by heavy precipitation events and floods, heat waves, and increased tropical cyclone activities. The impact would be felt everywhere, including cities, with most damage in developing countries. In order to stabilize the atmosphere, emissions would need to be cut by 60 to 80 per cent, implying the need for major investments and fundamental lifestyle changes. This reduction was to be achieved through a new global cap-and-trade system agreed upon among governments in the post-Kyoto negotiations. Essential to success is not only the participation of the United States—which is not a member of the Kyoto Protocol, but is the most important emitter of greenhouse gases—but also the participation of key developing countries, in particular China and India. In October 2007, IPCC and Al Gore Jr., former Vice-President of the United States, were awarded the Nobel Peace Prize "for their efforts to build up and disseminate greater knowledge about man-made climate change, and to lay the foundations for the measures that are needed to counteract such change".[5]

In order to pave the way for the UNFCC to reach an agreement on a post-Kyoto framework during its meeting in Bali in December 2007, the Secretary-General appointed three Special Envoys in May 2007 to facilitate progress in the multilateral climate change negotiations within the UN framework and to prepare a UN high-level meeting on the post-Kyoto treaty on 24 September 2007 at the forthcoming session of the General Assembly. The Special Envoys were Gro Harlem Brundtland, former Prime Minister of Norway and former Chair of the World Commission of Environment and Development; Han Seung-soo, former Minister of Foreign Affairs of the Republic of Korea and former President of the 56th session of the UN General Assembly; and Ricardo Lagos Escobar, former President of Chile. As part of the schedule leading to the September 2007 UN high-level meeting, the General Assembly held its first plenary session devoted exclusively to climate change on 31 July 2007.

Whereas the United Nations had been the central global platform for international cooperation on climate change, a number of preparatory and parallel initiatives emerged. In March, the European Union committed itself to a 20 per cent reduction in greenhouse gas emissions by 2020, and up to 30 per cent if others follow suit. In June 2007, leaders at the Group of Eight (G8) Summit in Heiligendamm, Germany, announced the aim to at least halve global greenhouse gas emissions by 2050. In August 2007, the United States invited members of the G8 and a selected group of countries to a conference on climate change scheduled to be held at the end of September, shortly after the high-level meeting of the General Assembly.

The UN, and in particular the UNFCCC, was widely considered to remain the appropriate forum for negotiating future global action on climate change. In August 2007, a UNFCC meeting in Vienna brought together one thousand representatives from governments, commerce, environmental organizations, and research institutes to set the stage for the major UN conference in Bali during December 2007.

Global issues, development and delivery

Conferences and meetings to foster global norms remain one of the key functions of the UN.[6] Steps towards protecting and promoting human rights and fundamental freedoms included the adoption of the Convention on the Rights of Persons with Disabilities[7], the International Convention for the Protection of All Persons from Enforced Disappearance,[8] and the Declaration on the Rights of Indigenous Peoples[9]. In the development area, the General Assembly approved[10] a strengthening of the Economic and Social Council (ECOSOC) to improve policy and programme coordination. This step included the new mandate of holding an Annual Ministerial

Review of progress on the internationally agreed development goals, including the Millennium Development Goals. The bi-annual Development Cooperation Forum was launched in July 2007 at the ECOSOC meeting and provided a global platform where all stakeholders are able to engage in high-level dialogue on new trends and key policy issues affecting development cooperation. These changes are intended to establish the Council as a central forum for intergovernmental oversight and to provide an assessment of the implementation of the United Nations development agenda. Other milestones in the development area are the midterm review of the Brussels Programme of Action for the Least Developed Countries, and the emergence of new issues, including international migration and development, aid-for-trade, and coherence of the UN system. The operational arm for development and humanitarian relief includes such UN funds and programmes as the United Nations Children's Fund (UNICEF), the United Nations Development Programme (UNDP), the United Nations Population Fund (UNFPA), the United Nations High Commissioner for Refugees (UNHCR), the United Nations Relief and Works Agency for Palestine Refugees in the Near East (UNRWA), and the World Food Programme (WFP).[11] Coordination of activities between the United Nations system organizations, including the specialized agencies, was done in the United Nations System Chief Executive Board (CEB).[12]

Following the 2005 World Summit, the Secretary-General created (in February 2006) a High Level Panel on UN System-wide Coherence in the areas of development, humanitarian assistance, and the environment. The 15-member panel carried out a study of the UN's operational activities and assessed how the UN system works, its comparative advantages, and any areas of overlap among UN agencies. The Panel submitted its report, "Delivering as One",[13] to Secretary-General Kofi Annan in November 2006. Recommendations covered the consolidation of operations at the country level, with one leader, programme, budget, and office. It was further suggested to establish a UN Sustainable Development Board to oversee the One UN Country Programme and a Millennium Development Goal Funding Mechanism to provide multi-year funding for the One UN Country Programme. Other proposals included a Global Leaders' Forum within ECOSOC to upgrade its policy coordination, the strengthening of international environmental governance, and a UN common evaluation system. Finally, the Panel proposed a new UN entity focused on gender equality and womens' empowerment.

Member states gave a ringing endorsement of the Panel's recommendations and offered widespread support for implementing the "One UN" programme. The report was not taken up for formal consideration by the General Assembly, however, until April 2007, when the new Secretary-General issued his own response[14] to the Panel's findings. Ban Ki-moon gave broad support to the recommendations put forth and echoed the Panel's call to overcome the current fragmentation. Rather than "one United Nations", the Secretary-General emphasized "delivering as one" since it was not intended to merge mandates, but to deliver together. This involved the creation of a single Resident Coordinator and integrated programme management and budget control for UN activities at the country level, covering development, humanitarian assistance, and environmental protection. A pilot phase programme was established, involving eight countries (Albania, Cape Verde, Mozambique, Pakistan, Rwanda, Tanzania, Uruguay, and Viet Nam). Consultation about the recommendations of the High-level Panel started in mid-June 2007, including the establishment of a new organizational entity for gender equality and empowerment of women through the consolidation of three existing entities, to be headed by a new Under-Secretary-General.

Political missions, peace-building and peacekeeping

During the current UN year, the Organization responded to regional crises through an expansion of political missions, peace-building, and peacekeeping. Following a dramatic rise during recent years, the number of peace-keepers had increased to over 80,000 by mid-2006. By mid-2007, this figure had grown further to over 100,000 peace-keepers (see box). Major political and peace-building missions include the United Nations Assistance Mission for Iraq (UNAMI), the United Nations Assistance Mission in Afghanistan (NAMA) and the United Nations Mission in Nepal (UNMIN). Other efforts include the United Nations assistance for the establishment of the Special Tribunal for Lebanon in connection with the killing of the former Lebanese Prime Minister Rafiq Hariri.

Peacekeeping operations as of 31 July 2007	
Africa	**Pacekeeper***
MINURSO (Western Sahara)	487
MONUC (Congo)	21,898
UNMIL (Liberia)	16,995
UNMIS (Sudan)	13,755
UNOCI (Cote d'Ivoire)	10,379
UNMEE (Ethiopia and Eritrea)	2,109
Americas	
MINUSTAH (Haiti)	10,389
Asia and the Pacific	
UNMOGIP (India and Pakistan)	109
Europe	
UNFICYP (Cyprus)	1,058
UNMIK (Kosovo)	4,770
UNOMIG (Georgia)	423
UNMIT (East Timor)	3,134
Middle East	
UNDOF (Golan Heights)	1,172
UNIFIL (Lebanon)	14,194
UNTSO (Middle East)	375
Total	**101,247**

Source: United Nations, DPI/1634/Rev.74, August 2007*Including troops, military observers, police, international civilians, local civilians and UN volunteers.

Democratic Republic of Congo

Since 1994, the Congo has experienced ethnic strife and civil war, triggered by a massive inflow of refugees fleeing the Rwandan genocide. This period of conflict was the bloodiest since World War II. Almost three million people died as a result of the fighting. Troops from Zimbabwe, Angola, Namibia, Chad, and Sudan intervened to support the regime in Kinshasa. The United Nations Organization Mission in the Democratic Republic of the

Congo (MONUC) was established by the Security Council in November 1999 to help implement a ceasefire and bring about an agreed process for a political settlement. MONUC is the largest peacekeeping force deployed by the UN, with 21,898 peace-keepers by mid-2007 (as compared to 21,279 in mid-2006).[15]

In July 2006, the Congo held its first multi-party elections since independence in 1960, with no candidate reaching an absolute majority. Joseph Kabila, the young president, secured most votes, with his main opponent, Jean-Pierre Bemba, reaching second place. People died in subsequent fighting between the two factions in the streets of the capital, Kinshasa, before police and MONUC took control of the city. A second round of voting between the two leading candidates was held in October 2006. Rioters destroyed polling stations in Congo's eastern section, and electoral officials organized a revolt over burned ballots in the north. Nevertheless, the presidential vote was called a success. Kabila was declared by the Supreme Court as the legitimate winner. Despite an overall increase in the level of stability, over one million people remained internally displaced in the east of the country. In July 2007, a report by Yakin Erturk, special rapporteur for the UN Human Rights Council, found that extreme sexual violence against women is pervasive in the Congo.

Haiti

Following the collapse of government and widespread violence, the Security Council established the United Nations Stabilization Mission in Haiti (French: *Mission des Nations Unies pour la stabilisation en Haïti*), also known as MINUSTAH. In operation since 2004, MINUSTAH supported the holding of elections and the new Government in establishing strong and sustainable state institutions for governance and the rule of law. The Mission also supported the enhancement of human rights capacity and the coordination of development and humanitarian activities. MINUSTAH included 10,389 peace-keepers in mid-2007, an increase as compared to 9,153 in mid-2006.[16]

By the end of 2006, MINUSTAH continued to struggle for control over the armed gangs, in light of more frequent lynchings and other mob attacks. It maintains an armed checkpoint at the entrance to the shanty town of Cité Soleil. In October of 2006, a group of heavily armed Haitian police were able to enter Cite Soleil for the first time in three years and were able to remain one hour as armored UN troops patrolled the area. The ability of the Haitian police to penetrate the area even for such a short time was seen as a sign of progress. The situation of continuing violence was similar in Port-au-Prince. Ex-soldiers, supporters of the ex-president Jean-Bertrand Aristide, occupied his home against the wishes of the Haitian government.

The mandate of MINUSTAH was extended in early 2007[17] since continued deployment was considered essential at a time when the security capacity of Haiti was still at an early stage of development. MINUSTAH had announced that it would take a tougher stance against gang members. In February 2007, 700 UN troops flooded Cite Soleil, resulting in a major gun battle. On 2 August 2007, Ban Ki-moon arrived in Haiti to assess the role of the UN forces. He visited Cite Soleil, stating that Haiti's largest slum was the most important target for UN peace-keepers in gaining control over the armed gangs. The Haitian president Rene Preval has expressed ambivalent feelings about the UN security presence, stating "if the Haitian people were asked if they wanted the UN forces to leave they would say yes."

Iraq

Sectarian violence and insurgency continue to take a daily toll in lives. Large numbers of people are displaced, both within Iraq and beyond the country's borders. Following the invasion in March 2003 by coalition forces, government authority was transferred to the Iraqi Interim Government in June 2004; a permanent government was elected in October 2005. On 30 December 2006, Saddam Hussein was hanged. More than 140,000 coalition troops remained in Iraq during 2007.

The UN focus in Iraq is on political facilitation and humanitarian assistance. The United Nations Assistance Mission in Iraq (UNAMI) was tasked with promoting national reconciliation, reducing sectarian tension, strengthening national unity, assisting in the holding of elections, supporting the drafting of the Iraqi constitution, and promoting the protection of human rights. Initially set-up by the Security Council in August 2003, the mandate of UNAMI was updated in June 2004[18] with the establishment of the Iraqi Interim Government. In mid-2007, there were nearly 300 UN international staff and 400 national staff serving in Iraq, Kuwait and Jordan.[19] In addition to UNAMI, there are some 16 UN agencies, funds, and offices that constitute the UN Country Team, covering agriculture, food security, environment and natural resources management, education and culture, health and nutrition, infrastructure rehabilitation, refugees, and internally displaced persons. Security represents the greatest implementation constraint, limiting access to many areas. Most international officials working for UN agencies left Baghdad after the UN headquarters were bombed in 2003; UN work now relies mainly on local staff. The suicide bomb attack killed 22 UN staff members, including the Special Representative of the Secretary-General for Iraq, Sergio Vieira de Mello, who was replaced Ashraf Qazi.

In May 2007, an international conference on Iraq was held in the Egyptian city of Sharm el-Sheikh. The meeting was co-chaired by Prime Minister Nuri Al-Maliki of Iraq and Secretary-General Ban Ki-moon and launched the International Compact on Iraq following a year-long preparatory process. The Compact is supported by the World Bank and members of the Compact Preparatory Group. It represents a road map for the next five years with regard to economic and social reforms with the support of the international community, including commitments to promote national dialogue and reconciliation. At the conference, more than 70 nations pledged a total of about US$30 billion towards the recovery of Iraq over the next five years. In order to provide funding for reconstruction and development initiatives, the UN, together with the World Bank, established the International Reconstruction Fund Facility for Iraq (IRFFI). By mid 2007, US$1.2 billion were received, and a total of 152 projects approved. Members of the Paris Club have forgiven 80 per cent of Iraq's debts.

In July 2007, the UN hosted a meeting on the International Compact with Iraq. The meeting in New York noted progress towards establishing unified security forces, legislative actions, and the UN-supported constitutional review process, but also stressed the need for continued support from the international community. In August 2007, the Security Council[20] updated and strengthened the UN mandate in Iraq, establishing responsibilities to advise and assist in areas such as political facilitation, national reconciliation, and the promotion of regional cooperation between Iraq and the other countries of the region. The approval of the International Compact and the Security Council decision on the UN mandate for Iraq indicate that the Organization is edging back into engagement with Iraq. In May 2007, the UN High Commissioner for Refugees announced that international staff would be sent back to Baghdad from Jordan, signaling a willingness to build a bigger support base in Iraq.

Kosovo

The Kosovo conflict ended in 1999 with the UN Security Council placing Kosovo under a transitional UN administration pending a determination of Kosovo's future status. The Council entrusted the United Nations Interim Administration Mission in Kosovo (UNMIK) with sweeping powers to govern Kosovo, whilst Serbia's continued sovereignty over Kosovo was recognized by the international community. NATO has a separate mandate to provide for a safe and secure environment. In May 2001, UNMIK promulgated the Constitutional Framework, which established Kosovo's Provisional Institutions of Self-Government (PISG). Since 2001, UNMIK has been gradually transferring increased governing competencies to the PISG, while reserving for itself some powers that are normally carried out by sovereign states, such as foreign affairs. Kosovo has also established municipal government and an internationally-supervised Kosovo Police Service. In November 2001, the OSCE supervised the first elections for the Kosovo Assembly. UNMIK consisted of 4,770 peace-keepers in mid-2007, as compared to 4,858 in mid-2006.[21]

In February 2006, UN-backed talks began to determine the final status of Kosovo, led by UN Special Envoy Martti Ahtisaari. Kosovo's Albanians, the majority of the province's population, prefer independence, whereas the minority of Kosovo's Serbs is diametrically opposed to independence. In February 2007, Ahtisaari delivered a draft status settlement proposal to leaders in Belgrade and Pristina, as a basis for a draft UN Security Council Resolution which proposes "supervised independence" for the province. As of early July 2007, a draft resolution, backed by the United States, the United Kingdom, and other European members of the Security Council had been rewritten four times to try to accommodate Russian concerns that such a resolution would undermine the principle of state sovereignty. Russia, which holds a veto in the Security Council as one of its five permanent members, had stated that it would not support any resolution that was not acceptable to both Belgrade and Kosovo's Albanians. After many weeks of discussions at the UN, the United States, the United Kingdom, and other members of the Security Council formally discarded the draft resolution based on Ahtisaari's proposal on 20 July 2007, having failed to secure Russian backing. Kosovo's Albanian leaders have reacted by proposing unilateral independence. Violence is feared in the province should the demand for independence not be met.

Rafiq Hariri: Special Tribunal for Lebanon

The Prime Minister of Lebanon Rafiq Hariri was assassinated on 14 February 2005 when explosives were detonated in the Lebanese capital, Beirut. At the request of the Government of Lebanon, the Security Council[22] established an international independent investigation Commission to assist the Lebanese authorities in their investigation of the Hariri assassination. This is the first time that an international court will try individuals for a terrorist crime committed against a specific person.

In October 2005, the Commission issued its initial findings to the Security Council, implicating Syrian and Lebanese officials, with special focus on Syria's military intelligence chief, Assef Shawkat, Syrian President Bashar al-Assad's brother-in-law. The Head of the Commission asked for more time to investigate all leads, and Lebanese politicians have asked to extend the investigative team's duration and charter to include assassinations of other prominent anti-Syrian Lebanese. On 11 January 2006, the Belgian Serge Brammertz, former deputy prosecutor of the International Criminal Court, took over as Commissioner. Since January 2006, talks between UN and Lebanese officials covered the establishment of a tribunal with Lebanese and international involvement to bring suspects in the assassination case to trial. In June 2006, the Commission indicated a definite connection between the Beirut bomb that killed Hariri and 14 other attacks on anti-Syrian Lebanese leaders. The Security Council provided for further review of those related cases by strengthening the mandate of the Commission.[23]

The Middle East conflict of July 2006 halted the Commission's work as the security situation in Lebanon deteriorated.[24] On 6 September 2006, an assassination attempt was made on Samir Shehade, deputy head of the intelligence department in Lebanon's national police force. Shehade had played a key role in a Lebanese probe into the killing of Hariri over the preceeding 18 months. On 13 June 2007, Walid Eido, a lawmaker and a vocal supporter of the tribunal, was also killed.

In February 2007, the UN and Lebanon signed an agreement setting up a Special Tribunal to prosecute the suspected killers of Hariri,[25] and the Security Council extended the mandate of the Commission until 15 June 2008.[26] Ratification of the agreement by the Lebanese parliament was strongly opposed by Syria and its allies in Lebanon. As a result of this deadlock, no vote on the tribunal agreement was taken. Prime Minister Fouad Siniora and the opposition had been in dispute for some months over the current composition of the Government. The opposition considered a resolution of that issue to be a precondition for ending the deadlock on the Special Tribunal.

In May 2007, Prime Minister Fouad Siniora requested the Security Council to put the Special Tribunal into effect under Chapter 7 as a matter of urgency because all domestic options for ratification had been exhausted. In response, the Security Council[27] stated that the agreement setting up the Tribunal would take effect if the Lebanese Parliament would not ratify the establishment of the Tribunal by 10 June 2007. In June 2007, the UN begun formally to establish a Special Tribunal after Lebanon missed the deadline.[28]

In August 2007, the Netherlands offered to host the Special Tribunal for Lebanon. It is likely to take at least one year for the Tribunal to begin operations, as funds have to be raised, judges and other officials have to be appointed and security arrangement for staff, victims, and witnesses have to be determined. In September 2007, Brammertz told the Security Council that evidence obtained so far suggests that a young, male suicide bomber, probably non-Lebanese, detonated up to 1,800 kilograms of explosives inside a van to assassinate Mr. Hariri.[29]

Middle East

In July 2006, war broke out between Israel and the paramilitary forces of Hezbollah, mainly located in southern Lebanon. More than 1,000 people were killed in both countries, and a quarter of Lebanon's population and many Israelis were forced to flee their homes. A UN cease-fire resolution ended the 34-day war on 14 August 2006. The Security Council approved one of the largest peacekeeping missions in the history of the UN[30]. At that time, the UN had two missions in the Middle East, the UN Interim Force in Lebanon (UNIFIL) and the United Nations Disengagement Observer Force (UNDOF). The new UN involvement includes an expanded and enhanced UNIFIL, which was increased from 2,395 peace-keepers in mid-2006 to 14,194 in mid-2007.[31] Along with the UN troops, an equal number of Lebanese army troops were deployed in the south, in the area that borders Israel.

The main task of UNIFIL was to ensure that southern Lebanon could not be used as a base for attacks on Israel. Specifically, the Security Council mandated the cessation of hostilities, the Israeli withdrawal from Lebanon, the disarmament of Hezbollah, the full control of Lebanon by the Lebanese government, and the removal of Hezbollah south of the Litani River, with their replacement by UNIFIL. As of December 2007, hostilities have largely ceased, Israel has withdrawn from Lebanon, and UNIFIL forces are in place. The disarmament of Hezbollah, however, has not been carried out.

Sudan

The decade-long civil war in the south of Sudan ended in January 2005 with the conclusion of a Comprehensive Peace Agreement between the Government of Sudan/National Congress Party in Northern Sudan and the Sudan People's Liberation Movement (SPLM) in Southern Sudan. The United Nations Mission in Sudan (UNMIS) was established to support the implementation of the Agreement, expected to continue through 2011. By mid-2007, UNMIS in southern Sudan consisted of 13,755 peace-keepers, an increase compared to 12,273 by mid-2006.

Just as the civil war in the south of Sudan was reaching a resolution, a new rebellion in the western region of Darfur began in early 2003. In response, the Security Council[32] deployed human rights monitors to report monthly on the situation in Darfur. In addition, a Commission of Inquiry was established. It reported in January 2005 that Sudan forces and allied Janjaweed militias had carried out indiscriminate attacks and committed crimes. Rebel forces in Darfur were considered responsible for possible war crimes. In May 2007, the International Criminal Court (ICC) indicted for crimes against humanity and war crimes former Minister of State for the Interior of the Government of Sudan and current Minister of State for Humanitarian Affairs, Ahmad Haroun, and Janjaweed commander Ali Muhammad Ali Abd-Al-Rahman.

In May 2006, the Sudanese government and Darfur's largest rebel group, the Sudan Liberation Movement (SLM), signed the Darfur Peace Agreement, which aimed at ending the three-year long conflict. More than 200,000 people had been killed, while another two million have been forced to flee their homes. The agreement specified the disarmament of the Janjaweed and the disbandment of the rebel forces, and aimed at establishing a temporal government in which the rebels could take part. The agreement, however, has not been signed by all of the rebel groups.

The Darfur Peace Agreement had been brokered by the African Union with the support of the UN and other partners. It was supervised by the 7,000-strong African Union Mission in Sudan (AMIS). UN humanitarian agencies and their partners, with more than 12,000 humanitarian workers, were leading the largest relief effort in the world in Darfur, in refugee camps in Chad, and in the Central African Republic, aimed at assisting the approximately 4.2 million conflict-affected people in the Darfur crisis. This campaign includes staff from 13 UN agencies, Red Cross/Red Crescent societies, and more than 80 non-governmental organizations (NGOs). Wide-spread violence, however, continued through the region, forcing aid agencies to consider pulling out. Both the Sudanese government and government-sponsored militias launched large offensives against the rebel groups; clashes among the rebel groups also contributed to the violence.

In August 2006, the UN raised the alarm over the crisis in Darfur, and the Secretary General requested the dispatch of UN troops.[33] In November 2006, high-level consultations were held in Addis Ababa, Ethiopia, attended by the Secretary-General, the five Permanent Members of the Security Council, and representatives of the Government of Sudan and the African Union. The Human Rights Council set up in early 2007 a human rights expert group to work with the Sudanese government and the African Union to ensure implementation of the resolutions on Darfur related to human rights. In early June 2007, the Special Envoys on Sudan of the UN and the African Union presented a road map towards peace in Darfur to the Security Council. The roadmap foresees the consolidation of all ongoing peace initiatives, shuttle diplomacy with the non-signatories of the 2006 Darfur Peace Agreement, and, finally, peace negotiations.

In parallel to the increased involvement of the UN, the Organization developed a three-phase approach to augment the African Union Mission in Sudan (AMIS) and deploy an unprecedented AU/UN hybrid peacekeeping operation known as United Nations African Mission in Darfur (UNAMID). Sudan had long resisted the entry of UN peace-keepers in Darfur. Following an intensive diplomacy effort, representatives of the Security Council visited Khartoum in June 2007 to meet with President al-Bashir, securing explicit acceptance of all elements of the hybrid force. Its establishment was approved by the Security Council in July 2007.[34] It has the protection of civilians at its core mandate, as well as contributing to security for humanitarian assistance, monitoring and verifying the implementation of agreements, and assisting an inclusive political process.

This is one of the largest and most complex field operations the UN has ever undertaken. The deployment of the new hybrid force will require a massive logistical effort, especially in providing adequate communications, water, food, supplies, and infrastructure for the mission. In addition to its mission headquarters in El Fasher, UNAMID will have up to 55 deployment locations throughout the three Darfur states. The force, incorporating AMIS, will have some 26,000 peace-keepers at full deployment, including almost 20,000 troops, more than 6,000 police and a significant civilian component. At full strength, UNAMID will become the largest UN peacekeeping mission in history and cost more than $2 billion a year.

UNAMID was to begin deployment in October 2007, to be completed at the beginning of 2008. However, deployment had to be delayed. Anticipated support by the Government of Sudan was not forthcoming. Darfur experienced an escalation of violence, including several attacks and bombardments that have led to the deaths of hundreds of people. The situation became protracted. The United Kingdom and France suggested sanctions against the Sudanese government for the continuing violence in Darfur. The Secretary-General made it clear that the deployment of UNAMID would depend on the Government of Sudan keeping its commitments to provide unconditional support. Moreover, the Secretary-General emphasized that peacekeeping must be accompanied by a political solution to the crisis, a call for the holding of a full-fledged peace conference on Darfur.

West Africa

Liberia had experienced civil war since the early 1990s; 200,000 people were killed and millions others displaced into refugee camps in neighboring countries. The country went through peace negotiations between Liberia's factions, presidential elections, and continuous unrest. In September 2003, the Security Council established the United Nations Mission in Liberia (UNMIL)[35] to help set up a transitional government. UNMIL supported the implementation of the ceasefire agreement and the peace process, humanitarian and human rights activities, and national security reform, including national police training and the formation of a new, restructured military. By mid-2007, the mission included 16,995 peace-keepers, a decrease compared to 17,371 by mid-2006.[36]

President Ellen Johnson-Sirleaf has made great strides in consolidating peace and promoting economic recovery in the country. Her work includes efforts towards lifting timber and diamond sanctions, bolstering public revenues and implementing a poverty reduction strategy. Positive steps were also taken to foster national reconciliation and political inclusiveness in the country. As a result, the Security Council approved measures to draw down UNMIL. The draw-down will take place in multiple stages, resulting in a reduction to 9,750 peace-keepers at the end of 2010. At the request of the Liberian government, former president Charles Taylor was finally extradited by Nigeria to the UN's Sierra Leone tribunal in The Hague, Netherlands, with the trial starting in June 2007. He is the first head of state in Africa to stand trial for war crimes.

In parallel to the fighting in Liberia, a civil war had broken out in Côte d'Ivoire in 2002. Since then, the country has been divided between the government-controlled south and the rebel-held north, the Forces Nouvelles. All Ivorian political forces signed a peace agreement (Linas-Marcoussis Agreement) in January 2003. It provided for the creation of a Government of National Reconciliation and a timetable for new presidential elections, restructuring the defense and security forces, and organizing the regrouping and disarmament of all armed groups. In early 2004, the Security Council established the United Nations Operation in Côte d'Ivoire (UNOCI)[37] to observe and monitor the implementation of the ceasefire agreement of May 3, 2003. By mid-2007, the mission included 10,379 peace-keepers, an increase as compared to 8,659 os of mid-2006.[38]

The mandate of President Laurent Gbagbo had been extended from October 2005 to October 2007. This step became necessary due to the slow progress in the preparation for the presidential elections, which included a new voter-identification scheme and the disarmament, demobilization, and reintegration of militia members. The Ouagadougou Political Agreement, a peace deal between the government and the rebels, was signed in March 2007. Subsequently, Guillaume Soro, leader of the Forces Nouvelles, became Prime Minister. The agreement calls for the creation of a new transitional government, the organization of free and fair presidential elections, the merging of the Forces Nouvelles and the national defense and security forces, the dismantling of the militias and disarming ex-combatants, and the replacement of the "zone of confidence" separating north and south with a green line to be monitored by UNOCI. In August 2007, President Laurent Gbagbo and Prime Minister Guillame Soro held the first "flame of peace" ceremony at which they set fire to stockpiled weapons to launch officially the disarmament process.

*****

The UN and its Secretary-General continue to face a wide range of political, economic, and humanitarian challenges as they enter into the 2007-2008 UN year. Many of them have been on the international agenda for years, defying resolution. In 2006-2007, a new challenge was added which is likely to dominate, if not over-shadow, a number of the existing agenda items, namely the challenge to address climate change effectively. The members of the UN will need all their foresight, good-will, and diplomatic competence to address this threat to the world community.

---

[1] See Chapter VI.A for 'United Nations: Report of the Secretary-General on the Work of the Organization for 2005/2006', A/61/1, 2006.

[2] See Chapter VII.A.5 for 'Secretariat Reform: Peace operations and disarmament, Letter dated 15 February 2007 from the Secretary-General addressed to the President of the General Assembly', A/61/749, 23 February 2007.

[3] See Chapter VI.D for 'United Nations High Commissioner for Human Rights: Report of the High Commissioner for 2006', A/61/36, 2006.

[4] See Chapter VII.A.2 for 'Climate change 2007: the physical science basis, summary for policymakers, Intergovernmental Panel on Climate Change (IPCC)', 2007.

[5] International Panel on Climate Change, The Nobel Peace Prize goes to the IPCC !, www.ipcc.ch, 13 December 2007.

[6] See Calendar of Conferences and Meetings of the United Nations, 12 September 2006 to 17 September 2007.

[7] See Chapter I.D for General Assembly Resolution 61/106, 13 December 2006.

[8] See Chapter I.D for General Assembly Resolution 61/177, 20 December 2006.

[9] See Chapter I.D for General Assembly Resolution 61/295, 13 September 2007.

[10] See Chapter I.D for General Assembly Resolution 61/16, 20 November 2006.

[11] See Chapter VI.B for 'United Nations Children's Fund: Annual Report of the Executive Director for 2006', E/2007/6, 4 December 2006, Chapter VI.C for 'United Nations Development Programme and United Nations Population Fund: Joint Annual Report of the Administrator of UNDP and of the Executive Director of UNFPA for 2006', E/2007/5, 28 November 2006, Chapter VI.E for 'United Nations High Commissioner for Refugees: Report of the High Commissioner for 2005', A/61/12, 2006, Chapter VI.F for 'United Nations Relief and Works Agency for Palestine Refugees in the Near East: Report of the Commissioner General for 1 July 2005 to 30 June 2006', A/61/13, 2006, Chapter VI.G for 'World Food Programme: Annual Report of the Executive Director for 2006', E/2007/14, 19 March 2007.

[12] See Chapter VII.A.1 for 'Annual overview report of the United Nations System Chief Executive Board for Coordination for 2006/2007', E/2007/69, 2007.

[13] See Chapter VII.A.3 for 'Delivering as One: Report of the High-level Panel on United Nations System-wide Coherence in the areas of development, humanitarian assistance and the environment', A/61/586, 20 November 2006.

[14] See Chapter VII.A.4 for 'Delivering as One: Report of the High-level Panel on United Nations System-wide Coherence in the areas of development, humanitarian assistance and the environment, Report of the Secretary-General', A/61/836, 3 April 2007.

[15] See Chapter VII.B.1 for 'Twenty-second report of the Secretary-General on the United Nations Organization Mission in the Democratic Republic of Congo', S/2006/759, 21 September 2006, see Chapter VII.B.2 for 'Twenty-third report of the Secretary-General on the United Nations Organization Mission in the Democratic Republic of the Congo', S/2007/156, 20 March 2007.

[16] See Chapter VII.C.1 for 'Report of the Secretary-General on the United Nations Stabilization Mission in Haiti, 19 December 2006, S/2006/1003, 19 December 2006, Chapter VII.C.2 'Report of the Secretary-General on the United Nations Stabilization Mission in Haiti', S/2007/503, 22 August 2007

[17] See Chapter II.B for Security Council Resolution 1743 (2007), 15 February 2007.

[18] See Chapter 2.2 of ARUNA 2004/2004 for Security Council Resolution 1546 (2004), 8 June 2004.

[19] See Chapter VII.D.1 for 'Report of the Secretary-General pursuant to paragraph 30 of resolution 1546 (2004)', S/2006/706, 1 September 2006, Chapter VII.D.2 for 'Report of the Secretary-General pursuant to paragraph 30 of resolution 1546 (2004)', S/2006/945, 5 December 2006, Chapter VII. D.3 for 'Report of the Secretary-General pursuant to paragraph 30 of resolution 1546 (2004)',

S/2007/126, 7 March 2007, Chapter VII.D.4 for 'Report of the Secretary-General pursuant to paragraph 30 of resolution 1546 (2004)', S/2007/330, 5 June 2007.

[20] See Chapter II.B for Security Council Resolution 1770 (2007), 10 August 2007.

[21] See Chapter VII.E.1 for 'Report of the Secretary-General on the United Nations Interim Administration Mission in Kosovo', S/2006/906, 20 November 2006, Chapter VII.E.2 for 'Report of the Secretary-General on the United Nations Interim Administration Mission in Kosovo', S/2007/134, 9 March 2007, Chapter VII.E.3 for 'Report of the Secretary-General on the United Nations Interim Administration Mission in Kosovo', S/2007/395, 29 June 2007.

[22] See Chapter 2.2 of ARUNA 2004/2005 for Security Council Resolution 1595 (2005), 7 April 2005.

[23] See Chapter 2.2 of ARUNA 2005/2006 for Security Council Resolution 1686 (2006) of 15 June 2006.

[24] See Chapter VII.F.1. for 'Letter dated 25 September 2006 from the Secretary-General addressed to the President of the Security Council: Fifth report of the International Independent Investigation Commission established pursuant to Security Council resolution 1595 (2005), 1636 (2005), 1644 (2005) and 1686 (2006)', S/2006/760, 25 September 2006 (S/2006/760), Chapter VII.F.2 for 'Report of the Secretary-General on the establishment of a special tribunal for Lebanon', S/2006/893, 15 November 2006, Chapter VII.F.3 for 'Letter dated 12 December 2006 from the Secretary-General addressed to the President of the Security Council: Sixth report of the International Independent Investigation Commission established pursuant to Security Council resolutions 1595 (2005), 1636 (2005), 1644 (2005) and 1686 (2006)', S/2006/962, 12 December 2006.

[25] See Chapter VII.F.4 for 'Letter dated 15 March 2007 from the Secretary-General addressed to the President of the Security Council: Sixth report of the International Independent Investigation Commission established pursuant to Security Council resolutions 1595 (2005), 1636 (2005), 1644 (2005) and 1686 (2006)', S/2007/150, 15 March 2007.

[26] See Chapter II.B for Security Council Resolution S/1748 (2007), 27 March 2007.

[27] See Chapter II.B for Security Council Resolution S/1757(2007), 30 May 2007.

[28] See Chapter VII.F.5 for 'Letter dated 12 July 2007 from the Secretary-General addressed to the President of the Security Council: Sixth report of the International Independent Investigation Commission established pursuant to Security Council resolutions 1595 (2005), 1636 (2005), 1644 (2005), 1686 (2006) and 1748 (2007), S/2007/424, 12 July 2007.

[29] See Chapter VII.F.6 for 'Report of the Secretary-General submitted pursuant to Security Council resolution 1757 (2007) of 30 May 2007', S/2007/525, 4 September 2007.

[30] See Chapter 2.2 of ARUNA 2003/2004 for Security Council Resolution S/1559 (2004), 2 September 2004, Chapter 1.4 of ARUNA 2005/2006 for Security Council Resolution 1701 (2006), 14 August 2006.

[31] See Chapter VII.G.1 for 'Report of the Secretary-General on the implementation of resolution 1701 (2006)', S/2006/670, 18 August 2006 (S/2006/670), Chapter VII.G.2 for 'Report of the Secretary-General on the implementation of resolution 1701 (2006)', S/2006/730, 12 September 2006, Chapter VII.G.3 for 'Fourth semi-annual report of the Secretary-General to the Security Council on the implementation of Security Council resolution 1559 (2004)', S/2006/832, 19 October 2006, Chapter VII.G.4 for 'Letter dated 1 December 2006 from the Secretary-General addressed to the President of the Security Council', S/2006/933, 1 December 2006, Chapter VII.G.5 for 'Report of the Secretary-General on the United Nations Disengagement Observer Force (for the period from 10 June 2006 to 1 December 2006)', S/2006/938, 4 December 2006, Chapter VII.G.6 for 'Report of the Secretary-General on the Middle East', S/2006/956, 11 December 2006, Chapter VII.G.7 for 'Report of the Secretary-General on the implementation of resolution 1701 (2006)', S/2007/147, 14 March 2007, Chapter VII.G.8 for 'Fifth semi-annual report of the Secretary-General to the Security Council on the implementation of Security Council resolution 1559 (2004)', S/2007/262, 7 May 2007, Chapter VII.G.9 for 'Report of the Secretary-General on the United Nations Disengagement Observer Force (for the period from 2 December 2006 to 6 June 2007)', S/2007/331, 5 June 2007, Chapter VII.G.10 for 'Report of the Secretary-General on the implementation of resolution 1701 (2006)', S/2007/392, 28 June 2007.

[32] See Chapter 2.2 of ARUNA 2003/2004 for Security Council Resolution 1556 (2004), 30 July 2004.

[33] See Chapter VII.H.1 for 'Report of the Secretary-General on children and armed conflict in the Sudan', S/2006/662, 17 August 2006, Chapter VII.H.2 for 'Report of the Secretary-General on Sudan', S/2006/728, 12 September 2006, Chapter VII.H.3 for 'Monthly report of the Secretary-General on Darfur', S/2006/764, 26 September 2006, Chapter VII.H.4 for 'Monthly report of the Secretary-General on Darfur', S/2006/870, 8 November 2006, Chapter VII.H.5 for 'Monthly report of the Secretary-General on Darfur', S/2006/1041, 28 December 2006, Chapter VII.H.6 for 'Report of the Secretary-General on Sudan', S/2007/42, 15 January 2007, Chapter VII.H.7 for 'Monthly report of the Secretary-General on Darfur', S/2007/104, 13 February 2007, Chapter VII.H.8 for 'Report of the Secretary-General on Sudan', S/2007/213, 17 April 2007, Chapter VII.H.9 for 'Report of the Secretary-General on Darfur', S/2007/462, 27 June 2007, Chapter VII.H.10 for 'Report of the Secretary-General on Sudan', S/2007/500, 20 August 2007.

[34] See Chapter II.B for Security Council Resolution 1769 (2007), 31 July 2007.

[35] See Chapter 2.2 of ARUNA 2003/2004 for Security Council Resolution 1509 (2003), 19 September 2003.

[36] See Chapter VII.I.1 for 'Twelfth progress report of the Secretary-General on the United Nations Mission in Liberia', S/2006/743, 12 September 2006, Chapter VII.I.4 for 'Thirteenth progress report of the Secretary-General on the United Nations Mission in Liberia', S/2006/958, 11 December 2006, Chapter VII.I.6 for 'Fourteenth progress report of the Secretary-General on the United Nations Mission in Liberia', S/2007/151, 15 March 2007, Chapter VII.I.8 for 'Fifteenth progress report of the Secretary-General on the United Nations Mission in Liberia', S/2007/479, 8 August 2007.

[37] See Chapter 2.2 of ARUNA 2003/2004 for Security Council Resolution 1528 (2004), 27 February 2004.

[38] See Chapter VII.I.2 for 'Tenth progress report of the Secretary-General on the United Nations Operation in Côte d'Ivoire', S/2006/821, 17 October 2006, Chapter VII.I. for 'Eleventh progress report of the Secretary-General on the United Nations Operation in Côte d'Ivoire', S/2006/939, 4 December 2006, Chapter VII.I.5 for 'Twelfth progress report of the Secretary-General on the United Nations Operation in Côte d'Ivoire', S/2007/133, 8 March 2007, Chapter VII.I.7 for 'Thirteenth progress report of the Secretary-General on the United Nations Operation in Côte d'Ivoire', S/2007/275, 14 May 2007.

Introduction

The responsible sovereign and the responsibility to protect

by
*Edward C. Luck**

Over its first sixty plus years, the United Nations has been a ceaseless builder and promoter of international principles and norms. Moving from decolonization to development, from disarmament to environmental degradation, and from de-mining to democracy, the world body has endeavored to turn the bold principles and purposes of its Charter into frameworks and agreements to guide behavior both among and within its Member States. Its normative contributions, as a result, have arguably left a deeper and more enduring mark on the way the world conducts its business than have its operational and programmatic ones.

The intricate interplay between the normative and operational dimensions of the UN's work can be seen most vividly in the core realm of human rights and humanitarian affairs. The implementation of these path-breaking norms, first forged in a period of acute East-West tension, has been anything but sure, consistent, or quick. But the ongoing struggle for human decency has, in subtle and dramatic ways, profoundly shaped the global geo-political landscape, as well as the evolving relationship between states and peoples. The latest chapter in this unfolding drama, the 2005 World Summit declaration of the responsibility to protect (RtoP), has proven every bit as contentious and potentially consequential as the earlier normative milestones on which it builds. This Introduction addresses the scope and content of what was agreed at the 2005 Summit, the implications of RtoP for notions of state sovereignty, and some of the conceptual, architectural, and policy challenges facing UN Secretary-General Ban Ki-moon's bold commitment to "operationalizing" the responsibility to protect and translating it "from words to deeds."[1]

What Has, and Has not, Been Agreed

The 2005 Summit, the largest gathering ever of heads of state and government, agreed that states have the responsibility to protect their populations from genocide, war crimes, ethnic cleansing, and crimes against humanity. They unambiguously declared that they "accept this responsibility and will act in accordance with it."[2] For its part, the international community agreed to encourage, help, and assist states in meeting these obligations. The Member States further underscored their responsibility, through the United Nations, "to use appropriate diplomatic, humanitarian and other peaceful means, in accordance with Chapters VI and VIII of the Charter, to help protect populations" from these four violations. When "peaceful means be inadequate and national authorities manifestly fail" to provide such protection, the world leaders pledged "to take collective action in a timely and decisive manner, through the Security Council, in accordance with the Charter, including Chapter VII, on a case-by-case basis and in cooperation with relevant regional organizations as appropriate."

---

* The author is UN Special Adviser on the Responsibility to Protect and Vice President and Director of Studies at the International Peace Academy. He is on public service leave as Professor of Practice in International and Public Affairs at Columbia University. He is grateful for the most helpful substantive comments of Francis Deng and Rachel Davis and, as always, for the invaluable research assistance of Marilyn Messer.

Widely viewed as the cardinal achievement of the Summit, the commitments contained in paragraphs 138 and 139 of the Summit's Outcome Document have been hailed by both UN Secretaries-General Kofi Annan and Ban Ki-moon as a "historic breakthrough."[3] Several Member States, alluding to the nuanced and caveated language of those passages, including paragraph 139's call for the General Assembly "to continue consideration" of RtoP matters, have drawn attention to the continuing differences over the rules for and legitimacy of military intervention or other coercive action for humanitarian purposes.[4]

Both sides of the debate have a point. The assembled heads of state and government in 2005 did not consent to a new norm of armed humanitarian intervention outside of the well established—though too frequently ignored—provisions of the UN Charter concerning the use of force. Indeed, paragraph 139 underscores the importance of utilizing the intergovernmental and Security Council-centered decision-making procedures laid out in the Charter.

Nor is there a consensus on whether RtoP qualifies, at this stage, as an existing or even emerging norm. Six months before the Summit, Secretary-General Kofi Annan, in his *In Larger Freedom* report, endorsed the view of his High-level Panel on Threats, Challenges and Change and the earlier Canadian-initiated International Commission on Intervention and State Sovereignty (ICISS) that there is an "emerging norm that there is a collective responsibility to protect."[5] Secretary-General Ban Ki-moon, on the other hand, has been a bit more deliberate in his choice of terminology than his predecessor, generally referring to RtoP as a "concept", not as a norm.[6] In legal terms, this distinction is an important one. Given how contentious the debate over what was agreed in the Outcome Document remains as of this writing, it would be hard to argue that RtoP has yet reached the status of an international norm. However, over time, UN principles have a way of becoming norms. In essence, the Guiding Principles on Internal Displacement followed a similar, if lower profile, course.[7] This approach could well be RtoP's path in the future, but for now its strength derives largely from the quite extraordinary political commitment embodied in paragraphs 138 and 139 and from the enhancements in policy and procedure they may promise. This, in itself, represents a major step forward. Proponents would do well at this point to consolidate their gains, reinforcing political support for what has been agreed on paper, as well as translating these advances in principle into durable innovations in policy, doctrine, and practice.

Conceptually, RtoP seeks to build bridges. One place where this is needed, as noted above, concerns the well-entrenched notion that there is an inevitable dichotomy between human rights and state sovereignty. To Secretary-General Boutros Boutros-Ghali, there was a need "to find a balance between the needs of good internal governance and the requirements of an ever more interdependent world."[8] As Secretary-General Kofi Annan confided, on the publication of the path-breaking 2001 ICISS report, in his efforts to spur debate on humanitarian intervention he had "sought to develop the idea of two notions of sovereignty: one for States, another for individuals . . . . What is clear is that when the sovereignty of States and the sovereignty of individuals come into conflict, we as an international community need to think hard about how far we will go to defend the former over the latter."[9] RtoP, he later suggested, had produced a new equation, with "human life, human dignity, human rights raised above even the entrenched concept of State sovereignty."[10] Yet, upon further reflection, it seems that RtoP aims to integrate sovereignty and human rights, not to have one triumph over the other. As the continuing concerns of some Member States attest, this marriage of rights and responsibilities remains a troubling and largely theoretical one for some, and it will not be fully consummated without more extensive consultations with the Member States, as well as further discussions with the UN Secretariat, independent experts, and NGOs. As a first step, commentators could usefully devote more attention to what the Outcome Document actually says about the content and scope of RtoP, rather than to what they hoped or feared it might say. As a carefully negotiated multilateral agreement, the words and provisions of paragraphs 138 and 139 already reflect the results of a hard-fought political bridge-building endeavor and should be respected as such.

The 2001 ICISS report, by enunciating and popularizing the notion of a responsibility to protect, provided a singular service, in that it finessed the stale and polarized debate over humanitarian intervention. That latter deabte came to a head at the September 1999 General Assembly debate sparked by a series of provocative speeches by Secretary-General Kofi Annan, who pushed the Member States to find a better alternative to standing by when mass atrocities were unfolding in places like Rwanda, Srebrenica, and Kosovo while divisions within the Security Council were preventing the authorization of effective responsive action.[11] By taking the concept of "sovereignty as responsibility," as developed in the mid-1990s by Francis Deng and his colleagues at the Brookings Institution, a step further,[12] the ICISS panel placed the onus where it properly belongs—on the state itself—with the international community bearing the parallel responsibility of helping the state to meet its abiding responsibilities to the population on its territory, whether citizens, immigrants, or refugees. Like the Outcome Document four years later, the ICISS report recognized that, for both states and the international community, protection begins with prevention.[13] Preventing atrocities in the first place—not responding after the fact militarily—is the far preferable option for both ethical and policy reasons. In this case, what is right and what is feasible happen to coincide.

Unfortunately, however, with little high-level guidance, the post-Summit debate about RtoP lost sight of the actual provisions of paragraphs 138 and 139, unhelpfully drifting back into the familiar, if unproductive and stilted, arguments about humanitarian intervention, Security Council reform, rules for the use of force, and how to organize a military response. While valid and important questions, the over-emphasis on this least likely scenario has largely precluded any sustained public or expert discussion of how to assist states so that they are less likely to start down the path of genocide, war crimes, ethnic cleansing, and crimes against humanity, including through capacity-building efforts implemented by the UN, regional or sub-regional arrangements, or ad hoc groups of well-meaning Member States. Paragraphs 138 and 139 speak of the responsibility of the international community to "encourage," "help," and "assist" states to meet their RtoP obligations, but offer no clue about how to accomplish such feats. Likewise, no blueprints are provided for the call in paragraph 138 for establishing a UN "early warning capability," nor for how timely information generated by the UN's far-flung and multi-layered field presence should be collated, assessed, and channeled to the Secretary-General and, through him or her, to the Security Council and other inter-governmental organs.

For the UN and its Member States, the principle of a responsibility to protect is what is contained in paragraphs 138 and 139 of the Outcome Document, nothing more and nothing less. Some advocates dismiss these provisions as RtoP-lite, because of their caveats about the more muscular options, such as sanctions and military enforcement. Yet, when the largest gathering ever of heads of state and government not only endorses a principle, but also agrees on its scope and content in such detail, then the UN Secretariat, Member State governments, and independent experts and NGOs best give some thought—as Secretary-General Ban Ki-moon has repeatedly urged—to how to give policy and institutional life to those provisions. Otherwise, as he has warned, the UN could once again stand accused of hypocrisy, of being far better at articulating grand ideas than at acting to implement them.[14] Words, once again, would trump deeds.

The Responsible Sovereign

It is often posited, indeed assumed, that there is a deep, inherent, and irreconcilable tension between the notion of a responsibility to protect and the full exercise of sovereignty at the nation state level. Indeed, those most resistant to this new chapter in the evolution in human rights and humanitarian norms are apt to characterize it as an assault on traditional conceptions of state sovereignty. While understandable, such reactions are based on an incomplete understanding both of the contemporary exercise of sovereignty and of the scope and purpose of RtoP. Properly construed, and as expressed in the Outcome Document, RtoP envisions the protection both of vulnerable individuals and groups and of the legitimate sovereignty of the nation state.

The rights of peoples and the prerogatives of the state should be viewed not only as compatible, but as mutually reinforcing in the kind of world envisioned by the UN Charter. The Preamble sees no contradiction in reaffirming "faith in fundamental human rights, in the dignity and worth of the human person, in the equal rights of men and women and of nations large and small." While sovereign equality is the first principle enunciated in the Charter (Article 2 (1)), the record of the founding conference in San Francisco suggests that this phrase was to be understood as a legal term and not as a political or decision-making one. It was to encompass not only juridical equality and respect for sovereignty among states, but also that each state "should, under international order, comply faithfully with its international duties and obligations."[15] The latter soon were to include a raft of human rights obligations under the Genocide Convention and the Universal Declaration of Human Rights, as subsequently elaborated in binding form in the two covenants.

Article 2(7) on the one hand denies the world body authorization "to intervene in matters which are essentially within the domestic jurisdiction of any state" and yet on the other hand goes on to assert that "this principle shall not prejudice the application of enforcement measures under Chapter VII." As Article 34 underlines, the Security Council's powers of investigation extend to "any dispute, or any situation which might lead to international friction or give rise to a dispute," even if there is no evidence of an immediate threat to international peace and security. The purposes of the Organization include "respect for the principle of equal rights and self-determination of peoples," "encouraging respect for human rights and for fundamental freedoms for all without distinction as to race, sex, language, or religion," and serving as "a centre for harmonizing the action of nations in the attainment of these common ends" (Article 1(2) (3) and (4)). As UN Secretary-General Ban Ki-moon has emphasized, "we need competent and responsible states to meet the needs of 'we the peoples' for whom the UN was created."[16]

Strong states are both capable and willing to protect the populations on their territories from genocide, war crimes, ethnic cleansing and crimes against humanity. As the Outcome

Document underscores, the first and foremost role of the international community in fulfilling the RtoP promise is to help them to do so. States, after all, were formed, in large part, to protect their people from external threats and internal disorder, from the chaotic time, according to Thomas Hobbes, "wherein men live without other security, than what their own strength, and their own inventions shall furnish them withal."[17] Such a "miserable condition," in his famous words, provides "no account of time; no arts; no letters; no society; and which is worst of all, continual fear, and danger of violent death; and the life of man, solitary, poor, nasty, brutish, and short." To escape the dire circumstances of chaos, individuals and groups—whether clustered in tribes, clans, or city states—ceded, in an unwritten contract, a portion of their individual and group sovereignty to larger communities in return for some sense of collective security.

Though the greater sovereign generally enjoyed a monopoly on the legitimate use of force—as nation states do today—even groups brought into the fold through conquest enjoyed some level of rights, as well as responsibilities, in the larger society. As Neil MacFarlane and Yuen Foong Khong point out, the "contract" in Hobbes' world would be voided either "if the sovereign threatened the individual with death" or "could no longer fulfill the function for which he or she was given power."[18] In the latter case, according to Hobbes, the sovereign authority "is no longer owed obedience, is no longer indeed a sovereign."[19] Far from Europe and western political traditions, similar views of authority and responsibility, of limits on the arbitrary use of sovereign power, and of the relationship between the individual and the sovereign could be found in Islamic thought, in the practices of the Ottoman Empire, and in Confucianism.[20] The notion that sovereignty is less than absolute, therefore, is neither new nor the product of a single culture or region. In calling for "an integrated approach to human security," Secretary-General Boutros Boutros-Ghali bluntly noted in his 1992 *Agenda for Peace* report that:

> The foundation-stone of this work is and must remain the State. Respect for its fundamental sovereignty and integrity are crucial to any common international progress. The time of absolute and exclusive sovereignty, however, has passed; its theory was never matched by reality.[21]

These are the words, it is worth recalling, of the first Secretary-General to come from Africa or the Arab world. In a similar vein, Alpha Oumar Konare, the Chairperson of the African Union Commission, has championed the principle of "non-indifference" to humanitarian tragedies on the continent.[22]

With sovereignty comes responsibility, with the exercise of that responsibility comes legitimacy, and with legitimacy comes the confidence and sustainability of strong, viable, and modern states. Some states are rich and others poor, some large and others small, some socialist and others capitalist, but they all face this same equation in relation both to their populations and to the international community. As Francis Deng et al. wrote in a prescient 1996 volume, *Security as Responsibility: Conflict Management in Africa*, "living up to the responsibilities of sovereignty becomes in effect the best guarantee of sovereignty."[23] In their view, "by effectively discharging its responsibility for good governance, a state can legitimately claim protection for its national sovereignty."[24] For centuries before the phrase "responsibility to protect" was coined, it was widely recognized that massive violations of human rights in one country could send political ripples across borders.[25] Indeed, the danger of one state intervening in another when it perceives its nationals to be threatened as a vulnerable minority in a neighboring state has been the subject of international agreements and arrangements at least since the sixteenth century.[26] This concern was prominent in the design of the Versailles Treaty and the League of Nations machinery, as well. More recently, in 2000—more than five years before the World Summit—the African Union asserted in its Constitutive Act (Article 4 (h)) "the right of the Union to intervene in a Member State pursuant to a decision of the Assembly in respect of grave circumstances, namely: war crimes, genocide, and crimes against humanity."[27]

So history tells us that when a state commits violations of international human rights and humanitarian norms of the magnitude of those listed in paragraphs 138 and 139 of the Outcome Document (particularly in this age of instantaneous global communications), there are likely to be international repercussions of some sort. At the very least, there will be reputational consequences. Though one should not exaggerate the extent to which repressive leaders have been or would be deterred by reputational concerns, it is remarkable how quick states are to deny or cover-up such atrocities, whether or not they need fear condemnatory resolutions by inter-governmental bodies or the imposition of material sanctions by such groups or individual states.[28] Intrusive and potentially embarrassing monitoring missions are likely to be undertaken by the United Nations, regional bodies, or ad hoc mechanisms under the provisions of conventions and other international agreements to which the state is party. If the transgressions of international norms are widespread, persistent, and aimed at particular ethnic, religious, immigrant, or refugee communities, then popular passions are likely to be raised in neighboring countries, exacerbating relations and posing the risk of increasing tensions and even conflict.

In our inter-connected world, sovereignty cannot equal autarky. All states, even the most isolated ones, choose to engage in a range of ties with neighbors, trading partners, and international institutions. These arrangements necessarily entail some range of promises, commitments, and expectations on all sides. In theory, sovereignty may entail maximizing one's ability to choose, but in real life, states decide, again and again, to limit their own freedom of action in order to gain international agreement on various matters important to them. Today, isolation is neither a rational nor feasible choice for any society. As a result, the 1990s witnessed a historic surge in the quantity and quality of international agreements and institutions, covering any number of sectors of public policy.[29] Some of these covenants were initiated by the developed countries of the North, some by the developing countries of the South, but most reflected a common understanding that the efficient and effective exercise of domestic governance requires growing international cooperation on many fronts at once. It is hard to think of a single important area of national policy in which the exercise of sovereignty does not require a substantial degree of tacit or formal cooperation with other states, whether related to development, trade, security, the environment, health, education, or welfare. More than two decades ago, some of us coined the term "sovereignty gap" to capture this growing reality of contemporary governance.[30] As Stephen Krasner has pointed out, today "while loss of interdependence sovereignty does not necessarily imply anything about domestic sovereignty understood as the organization of authoritative decision making, it does undermine domestic sovereignty comprehended simply as control."[31] On the other hand, he notes, "a state with very limited effective domestic control could still have complete international legal sovereignty. It could still be recognized as a juridical equal by other states, and its representatives could still exercise their full voting rights in international organizations."[32]

If the responsibility to protect is to be considered a challenge to more traditional conceptions of sovereignty, it is hardly alone among UN principles, purposes, and programs. Surely its preventive, capacity-building, and early warning aspects—as discussed above—are no more, and probably less, intrusive than those of international development, environment, trade, or peace-building arrangements. Unlike those other engagements, RtoP does not seek to remodel core national institutions or policy choices; rather, it simply seeks to bolster a state's capacity to avoid the downward slide to anarchy and mass repression. It addresses only the most egregious violations of human rights and humanitarian norms, the kinds of abuses that states consistently deny are either the intent or consequence of their public policies. Even the Outcome Document's references to Chapter VII and possible collective measures are well-embedded in Charter provisions and UN practice, as also noted above. RtoP, therefore, hardly qualifies as a conceptual or strategic revolution in the thinking or practice of contemporary international society. It does qualify as a notable, even historic, political pronouncement because of the global commitments undertaken by Member States in the Outcome Document. But in normative terms, this historic step is better described as evolutionary than as revolutionary. The mark it leaves on state and international practice will depend heavily on how successful UN Secretary-General Ban Ki-moon is in his quest to give it a durable policy expression, both doctrinally and institutionally. As the next section underscores, this will not be an easy task.

Conceptual, Institutional, and Policy Challenges

The World Summit Outcome Document represented a major stride toward the achievement of conceptual clarity for the notion of a responsibility to protect. It underlined that RtoP is well grounded in the existing framework of international law, including the ongoing obligations of Member States under international humanitarian and human rights law, refugee law, and international criminal law. Its scope is to be limited to prevention of (and protection of populations from) genocide, war crimes, ethnic cleansing, and crimes against humanity, rather than seeking to encompass all threats to human dignity and welfare. It is essential that proponents of RtoP resist the sirens' call to stretch the concept beyond recognition or policy utility, as has happened with such disturbing regularity to so many other terms and notions around the UN in years past. If efforts to operationalize RtoP are to have any chance of making a difference to the human condition, their focus must remain narrow and deep. RtoP, it needs to be repeatedly stressed, is not a more palatable term for military intervention or for the North to meddle in the affairs of the South. Its broad appeal stems from its universal quality, its recognition that both individual states and the international community have explicit responsibilities in this realm, and that sorting through how these obligations can best be carried out in a mutually supportive fashion represents one of the prime conceptual, institutional, and policy challenges of our time.

For instance, should RtoP standards and expectations apply only to UN Member States and inter-governmental institutions? In a formal sense, of course, the answer must be affirmative, as states are parties to the conventions on which RtoP is largely based, as well as signatories of the Outcome Document itself. Generally, as well, atrocities of the scale to be addressed by RtoP are undertaken by or with the complicity of governments. Yet terrorists and armed groups may also, at times, aspire to wreak similar havoc on innocent civilians. And states are prone to citing security concerns to explain pronounced declines in their human rights practices, especially given the degree of instability in a number of regions these days. As the

UN has long recognized, it is immensely difficult to resolve security problems and humanitarian emergencies without parallel progress on the political dynamics that have fuelled and sustained them. As of this writing, Darfur and Somalia are prime and sorry cases in point. What lessons can be derived from such hard cases? And has the Outcome Document language made a difference in the way states and international organizations are responding to such situations?

From Nuernberg to the International Criminal Court, it has long been accepted that individuals, not just governments, bear responsibility for the international crimes in which they knowingly and willingly participate. Eliminating impunity has, for more than a decade now, been a key plank in the UN's strategy for prevention and deterrence, as well as for reconciliation after particularly violent conflicts. The UN High Commissioner for Human Rights, Louise Arbour, has suggested that "the responsibility to punish" be added to the ICISS trilogy of the "responsibility to prevent, react, and rebuild."[33] Taking a different tack, non-governmental groups are seeking to organize international networks of individuals pledged not only to refrain from participating in any of the four kinds of violations proscribed by the Outcome Document but also to report on activities that could incite or help organize such acts. Transnational civil society could also play a critical role in helping to turn societies away from such a course, whether through publicity, consciousness-raising, local organizing, or legal action. To date, individuals and NGOs have carried much of the political weight of sustaining support for the concept. So, while the focus of RtoP will remain on governments, the involvement of individuals and groups could prove to be a critical factor in the Secretary-General's efforts to operationalize the concept.

As discussed above, RtoP was not the next step on the humanitarian intervention track laid out so boldly by Kofi Annan in the late 1990s. Its fundamental assumptions were derived, instead, from the path-breaking work on sovereignty as responsibility by Francis Deng and his colleagues earlier in that decade. This second track has three distinct dimensions. The first—that respect for peoples should be seen as an integral part of sovereignty, not as an opposing value—was addressed at length earlier. Second, the international community should assist states in the fulfillment of their responsibilities from the earliest stages, not simply rush in when all else fails. Indeed, the primary responsibility was to help states succeed, not to react once they fail. The failure-reaction cycle featured in humanitarian intervention models was to be replaced, as it was based on the failure of prevention efforts and posed untenable choices for the international community. Third, military intervention should be a secondary option at best, not the centerpiece of the enterprise. While all three points are clearly embodied in the Outcome Document, the second and third raise a series of policy and doctrinal dilemmas that are not easily resolved.

The ethical, legal, political, and policy arguments for proceeding upstream toward early, non-coercive intervention are compelling. Yet there is a risk of widening the scope of inquiry to unmanageable proportions, as such a prevention strategy implies attempting to deal with the lesser and more loosely defined precursors of the four proscribed violations. Incitement, mentioned in paragraph 138, is relatively straightforward. There are no hard and fast rules, however, about which kinds of behavior are most likely to lead down such a destructive path. Nor are the lessons from one case so readily and assuredly applied to the next society. How would prevention for RtoP purposes look different from the efforts at conflict prevention already being pursued by the UN and numerous other actors? The good news, of course, is that such early and non-coercive interventions bear relatively low costs and risks for the UN, its partners, or the Member States. The bad news, however, is that it tends to be hard to assemble political will for such efforts before there are any press or public reports of conscience-shocking atrocities. Capacity-building within states, drawing on best practices domestically and elsewhere as well as on lessons learned from past failures, is a very appealing part of the puzzle. But, again, the knowledge and experiential base for such endeavors remains remarkably thin at this point.

No matter how one tries to recast the terms of the RtoP debate, whether, how, and when to use military force remains a highly contentious issue. To the ICISS panel, military intervention was to be a "last resort," only "justified when every non-military option for the prevention or peaceful resolution of the crisis has been explored, with reasonable grounds for believing lesser measures would not have succeeded."[34] Kofi Annan likewise interpreted the Outcome Document as also consigning the use of force to a last resort.[35] As noted at the outset of this essay, however, paragraph 139 is actually much more nuanced on the subject, eschewing the "last resort" language. Instead, it emphasizes the provisions of Chapter VII of the Charter, which give the Security Council wide latitude in making such momentous decisions. There are sound political and policy reasons for taking the rather flexible stance the Summit chose. One, neither at Dumbarton Oaks, San Francisco, or at any point since have the members of the Security Council, especially the permanent ones, accepted any guidelines, principles, or limitations on their freedom to make political judgments on a case-by-case basis, as long as they are seen as acting within the purposes and principles of the Charter (Article 24 (2)).[36] Two, it makes little policy sense to restrict the Council to any set progression of when it could employ any of the policy tools at its disposal. For example, preventive deployments or an early show of multilateral force might help to dissuade a state from pursuing a destructive course of action. In some cases, the deployment of mixed peacekeeping and humanitarian units, with the even reluctant consent of the host government, might be helpful in enhancing order in an increasingly chaotic situation or in keeping smaller abuses from becoming larger ones.

The Outcome Document quite properly points to the need for a more effective UN early warning system, as well as closer partnerships for the world body with regional and sub-regional organizations. Indeed, more creative thinking ought to be applied to the place of regional and sub-regional arrangements in efforts to monitor and assess local developments—positive or negative—and to mediate problems as they arise. Transnational preventive and capacity-building efforts might also be undertaken, in some cases, on a regional or sub-regional basis. Whether information and assessment sharing can take place on a more regular and candid basis between the global and regional levels remains to be seen. The answer would no doubt vary from place to place and organization to organization, but both the generic and specific questions are certainly worth exploring. The UN itself has enormous information resources, especially in parts of the world experiencing instability and conflict. Getting that information to the Secretary-General, the Security Council, and other relevant intergovernmental organs in a timely and forthcoming fashion has been problematic in the past. A more chronic problem has been the assessment and analysis of the information that is on hand. Over the past two decades, one proposal after another in this regard has grounded on the shoals of inadequate Member State support or, less often, bureaucratic resistance. The Outcome Document offers a fresh basis on which to try once again to give the Secretary-General and the Security Council the kind of world-class analytical support they deserve and the issue demands.

Finally, when all is said and done, the attitude and policies of the Member States will do more to sustain or derail the responsibility to protect than any doctrines or architectural adjustments espoused by the Secretary-General. In this regard, it is worth recalling that decisions of the General Assembly, including of its World Summit, are not binding on the Member States. The Outcome Document does not have the legal status of a negotiated convention or treaty. Yet it may have, and hopefully already is having, a political effect on the way leaders of Member States think about these matters. The political costs of doing nothing when genocide or mass atrocities unfold may be rising, though the process is likely to be slow and uncertain. In Darfur, unlike Rwanda, the Council did not look the other way. Yet its members still failed to find agreement on an effective and timely course of action. The ICISS panel urged the five permanent members of the Security Council to "agree not to apply their veto power, in matters where their vital state interests are not involved, to obstruct the passage of resolutions authorizing military intervention for human protection purposes for which there is otherwise majority support."[37] Louise Arbour, the High Commissioner for Human Rights, recently went much further, raising the prospect of legal consequences "when the exercise or threat of a veto would block action that is deemed necessary by other members to avert genocide, or crimes against humanity."[38] Though the thought of holding Member States legally accountable for the way they choose to vote in inter-governmental bodies seems far-fetched at this point, public pressures and the endorsement of RtoP in the Outcome Document may be raising the political costs for casting a veto in such situations.

By UN standards, RtoP remains in its conceptual and programmatic infancy. Its growth trajectory is uncertain, as its recent articulation by the World Summit has elicited wariness and uncertainty in some quarters along with unbridled enthusiasm in others. Its advocates will need discipline and patience, its detractors a willingness to focus on what has been agreed, not on what they fear the doctrine could become. Fortunately, RtoP's most resilient and realistic supporter is also the best placed: UN Secretary-General Ban Ki-moon. He appears to understand that there is no easy or quick path to operationalizing the responsibility to protect, given the policy dilemmas addressed here. As with so many issues at the UN, the slow, steady path is also the most promising. RtoP, there is reason to believe, is on the right side of history. Now, the trick is to come up with policy initiatives that will help history move a little more quickly and a little more surely.

---

[1] See, for example, his speeches to the Center for Strategic and International Studies in Washington, DC on 16 January 2007 and to the Royal Institute of International Affairs in London on 11 July 2007, as well as his annual address to the General Assembly of 25 September 2007 (U.N. documents SG/SM/10842, SG/SM/11094, and SG/SM/11182, respectively).

[2] U.N. document A/60/L.1, 15 September 2005, p. 31, para. 138. As Louise Arbour, the UN High Commissioner for Human Rights, has underlined, whereas the so-called "right of humanitarian intervention by definition is discretionary," RtoP carries a positive obligation or responsibility for all states. See "Preventing Mass Atrocities: A Conversation with Louise Arbour," Council on Foreign Relations, Washington, DC, 8 June 2007, and her speech, "The Responsibility to Protect as a Duty of Care in International Law and Practice," Trinity College, Dublin, 23 November 2007.

[3] U.N. documents SG/SM/10161 of 12 October 2005 and SG/SM/10842, op. cit.

[4] See, for instance, the interventions of Algeria, Brazil, China, Egypt, and the Russian Federation in the December 2005 Security Council debate on the protection of civilians in armed conflict. None of them refuted the concept of a responsibility to protect, though all called for further discussion of its scope and policy implications. The United States joined a number of other Member States in

stressing "that the primary responsibility for protecting civilians lies with States and their Governments and that international efforts should complement Government efforts rather than assume responsibility for them." UN document S/PV.5319 and Resumption 1, 9 December 2005.

[5] Report of the Secretary-General, *In Larger Freedom: Towards Development, Security and Human Rights for All*, U.N. document A/59/2005, 21 March 2005, p. 35, para. 135.

[6] U.N. documents SG/SM/10842, SG/SM/11094, and SG/SM/11182, op. cit.

[7] See Addendum to the Report of the Representative of the Secretary-General Francis M. Deng to the Human Rights Commission, U.N. document E/CN.4/1998/53/Add.2, 11 February 1998, noted in Commission on Human Rights Resolution 1998/50.

[8] *An Agenda for Peace*, A/47/277, S/24111, 17 June 1992, p. 5, para. 17.

[9] Secretary-General Addresses International Peace Academy Seminar on the Responsibility to Protect, U.N. document SG/SM/8125, 15 February 2002.

[10] World Summit Achieved Concrete, Significant Gains in Human Rights, Rule of Law, Secretary-General Says in Address to Universidade Nova de Lisboa, U.N. document SG/SM/10161, 12 October 2005.

[11] For a handy compilation of his key speeches, see *The Question of Intervention: Statements by the Secretary-General* (New York: United Nations, December 1999). It contains, among others, "Reflections on Intervention," Ditchley Park, United Kingdom, 26 June 1998 and "Two Concepts of Sovereignty," Address to the 54th Session of the UN General Assembly, 20 September 1999.

[12] Francis M. Deng, Sadikiel, Kimaro, Terrence Lyons, Donald Rothschild, and I. William Zartman, *Sovereignty as Responsibility: Conflict Management in Africa* (Washington, D.C.: The Brookings Institution, 1996).

[13] Report of the International Commission on Intervention and State Sovereignty, *The Responsibility to Protect* (Ottawa, Canada: International Development Research Centre, 2001).

[14] Ban Ki-moon, Acceptance Speech on Appointment as the Eighth Secretary-General of the United Nations, 13 October 2006, http://www.un.org/apps/news/infocus/sgspeeches/statments_full.asp?statID=58#.

[15] Ruth B. Russell, *A History of the United Nations Charter: The Role of the United States 1940-1945* (Washington, DC: Brookings Institution Press, 1959), p. 672 and Edward C. Luck, *UN Security Council: Practice and Promise* (London, Routledge, 2006), p. 20.

[16] Ban Ki-moon, Acceptance Speech on Appointment as the Eighth Secretary-General of the United Nations, op. cit.

[17] Thomas Hobbes, *Leviathan* (Oxford: Oxford University Press, 1998), p. 84.

[18] S. Neil MacFarlane and Yuen Foong Khong, *Human Security and the UN: A Critical History* (Bloomington, Indiana: Indiana University Press, 2006), p. 39.

[19] Quoted in ibid.

[20] See, for example, Stephen D. Krasner, *Sovereignty: Organized Hypocrisy* (Princeton: Princeton University Press, 1999), pp. 76-77 and MacFarlane and Khong, op. cit., pp. 30-33.

[21] *An Agenda for Peace*, op. cit., para. 17, p. 5.

[22] See, for example, African Union Press Release on the "Arche de Zoe Affair," Addis Ababa, 7 November 2007 and Said Ida Hassan, "AU Calls for 'Fair' EU/African Economic Agreements," APA, Lisbon, 8 December 2007. In his address at the event launching the AU's Peace and Security Council on 25 May 2004, he called for linking "legality with legitimacy, in the name of the principle of 'non-indifference.'"

[23] Deng, Kimaro, Lyons, Rothschild, and Zartman, *Sovereignty as Responsibility*, op. cit., p. 15.

[24] Ibid., p. 1.

[25] Simon Chesterman, for instance, cites more than four centuries of legal scholarship on wars to assist the oppressed in other countries. See his *Just War or Just Peace?: Humanitarian Intervention and International Law* (Oxford: Oxford University Press, 2001), pp. 13-16.

[26] Friedrich Kratochwil, "Sovereignty as *Dominium*, Is There a Right of Humanitarian Intervention?," in Gene M. Lyons and Michael Mastanduno, eds., *Beyond Westphalia?: State Sovereignty and International Intervention* (Baltimore, MD: Johns Hopkins University Press, 1995), pp. 30-33 and Krasner, op. cit., pp. 103-104.

[27] http://www.africa-union.org/root/au/AboutAU/Constitutive_Act_en.htm. Like the responsibility to protect, the AU clause eschews any assumed linkage between the intervening state(s) and the nationality of those being abused.

[28] For a candid discussion of reputational efforts on behavior, see George W. Downs and Andrea W. Trento, "Conceptual Issues Surrounding the Compliance Gap," in Edward C. Luck and Michael W. Doyle, eds., *International Law and Organization: Closing the Compliance Gap* (Lanham, MD: Rowman and Littlefield, 2004), pp. 21-26.

[29] With this surge in norms and conventions, however, came enormous and continuing compliance shortfalls, in part because of unreliable, missing, or inadequate international monitoring, assessment, and enforcement machinery. See, for example, Edward C. Luck, "Conclusion: Gaps, Commitments, and the Compliance Challenge," James R. Katalikawe, Henry M. Onoria, and Baker G. Williams, "Crises and Conflicts in the African Great Lakes Region: The Problem of Noncompliance with Humanitarian Law," and Jeffrey Herbst, "International Law of War and the African Child: Norms, Compliance, and Sovereignty," in Luck and Doyle, op. cit., pp. 303-330, 121-152, and 185-201, respectively.

[30] Report of the International Panel on UN Management and Decision-Making, United Nations Association of the USA (UNA-USA), in Peter J. Fromuth, ed., *A Successor Vision: The United Nations of Tomorrow* (Lanham, MD: University Press of America for UNA-USA, 1988), pp. 32-33.

[31] Krasner, *Sovereignty: Organized Hypocrisy*, op. cit., p. 13.

[32] Ibid., p. 12.

[33] "A Conversation with Louise Arbour," Council on Foreign Relations, op. cit.

[34] Second Precautionary Principle, International Commission on Intervention and State Sovereignty, *The Responsibility to Protect*, op. cit., p. xii.

[35] U.N. document SG/SM/10161, op. cit.

[36] For a historical and political analysis of this phenomenon, see Edward C. Luck, "A Council for All Seasons: The Creation of the Security Council and Its Relevance Today," in Vaughan Lowe, Adam Roberts, Jennifer Welsh, and Dominik Zaum, eds., *The UN Security Council and War: Evolution of Thought and Practice Since 1945* (Oxford University Press, 2008).

[37] International Commission on Intervention and State Sovereignty, *The Responsibility to Protect*, op. cit., p. xiii.

[38] Louise Arbour, Trinity College, op. cit.

CALENDAR OF CONFERENCES AND MEETINGS OF THE UNITED NATIONS, 12 September 2006 to 17 September 2007

2006

Organ	*Dates (2006)*	*Location*
General Assembly, sixty-first session	12 September–December	New York
UNCITRAL, Working Group on Security Interests	18–22 September	Vienna
Commission on Human Rights, working group of experts on people of African descent	September (1 week)	Geneva
Commission on Human Rights, Working Group on the use of mercenaries	September (1 week)	Geneva
UNCTAD, Working Party on the Medium-term Plan and the Programme Budget	September (5 days)	Geneva
Security Council, Governing Council of the United Nations Compensation Commission established pursuant to Security Council resolution 692 (1991), fifty-third session	September (3 days)	Geneva
UNITAR, Board of Trustees, second part	September (2–3 days)	Geneva
UNRWA, Advisory Commission	September (1 day)	Amman
Committee of Permanent Representatives to UN-Habitat [General Assembly resolution 56/206]	September	Nairobi
UNEP, Committee of Permanent Representatives	September/ October (1 day)	Nairobi
United Nations Staff Pension Committee	September/ October (1 meeting)	New York
Committee on the Rights of the Child, pre-sessional working group	2–6 October	Geneva
WFP, Executive Board, second regular session	18–22 October	Rome
International Narcotics Control Board, eighty-seventh session	30 October–16 November	Vienna
Human Rights Committee, eighty-eighth session	October (3 weeks)	Geneva
Human Rights Committee, Pre-sessional Working Group on Communications	October (1 week)	Geneva
UNHCR, Executive Committee, fifty-seventh session	October (1 week)	Geneva
UNHCR, Executive Committee, fifty-seventh session	October (1 week)	Geneva
United Nations System Chief Executives Board for Coordination, second regular session	October	New York
United Nations Administrative Tribunal	October/ November (5 weeks)	New York

Organ	*Dates (2006)*	*Location*
WFP, Executive Board, second regular session	6–10 November	Rome
Committee against Torture, pre-sessional working group	6–10 November	Geneva
Eighth Annual Conference of the High Contracting Parties to Amended Protocol II to the Convention on Prohibitions or Restrictions on the Use of Certain Conventional Weapons Which May Be Deemed to Be Excessively Injurious or to Have Indiscriminate Effects	6–17 November	Geneva
Annual Meeting, and Third Review Conference, of the States parties to the Convention on Prohibitions or Restrictions on the Use of Certain Conventional Weapons Which May Be Deemed to Be Excessively Injurious or to Have Indiscriminate Effects	6–17 November	Geneva
UNCITRAL, Working Group on Transport Law	6–17 November	Vienna
UNFCCC, Conference of the Parties to the Convention, twelfth session	6–17 November	Bonn
Commission on Human Rights, Working Group on Arbitrary Detention	13–24 November	Geneva
Committee against Torture, thirty-seventh session	13–25 November	Geneva
Committee on Economic, Social and Cultural Rights, thirty-seventh session	13 November–1 December	Geneva
Investments Committee	20 November	New York
Committee on the Exercise of the Inalienable Rights of the Palestinian People, Special Meeting in Observance of the International Day of Solidarity with the Palestinian People	29 November	New York
Sixth Review Conference of the States Parties to the Convention on the Prohibition of the Development, Production and Stockpiling of Bacteriological (Biological) and Toxin Weapons and on Their Destruction	November (3 weeks)	Geneva
Voluntary Fund for Technical Cooperation in the Field of Human Rights, Board of Trustees	November (1 week)	Geneva
Commission on Human Rights, Working Group on Arbitrary Detention	November (1 week)	Geneva
United Nations Pledging Conference for Development Activities	November (1 day)	New York
Ad Hoc Committee of the General Assembly for the Announcement of Voluntary Contributions to the United Nations Relief and Works Agency for Palestine Refugees in the Near East	November (1 meeting)	New York
United Nations Staff Pension Committee	November (1 meeting)	New York
Committee of Experts on the Transport of Dangerous Goods and on the Globally Harmonized System of Classification and Labelling of Chemicals	1–5 December	Geneva
Committee on Economic, Social and Cultural Rights, pre-sessional working group	4–8 December	Geneva

Organ	*Dates (2006)*	*Location*
UNCITRAL, Working Group on Procurement	4–8 December	Vienna
Subcommittee of Experts on the Transport of Dangerous Goods	4–12 December	Geneva
UNCITRAL, Working Group on Insolvency Law	11–15 December	Vienna
Subcommittee of Experts on the Globally Harmonized System of Classification and Labelling of Chemicals	12–14 December	Geneva
Commission on Human Rights, Working Group on Enforced and Involuntary Disappearances	December (2 weeks)	Geneva
UNU, Council, fifty-third session	December (1 week)	Tokyo
Security Council, Governing Council of the United Nations Compensation Commission established pursuant to Security Council resolution 692 (1991), fifty-fourth session	December (3 days)	Geneva
Advisory Committee on the United Nations Programme of Assistance in the Teaching, Study, Dissemination and Wider Appreciation of International Law, fortieth session	December (2 days)	New York
Disarmament Commission, organizational session	December (1–2 days)	New York
Ad Hoc Committee of the General Assembly for the Announcement of Voluntary Contributions to the Programme of the United Nations High Commissioner for Refugees	December (1 meeting)	Geneva
Ad Hoc Committee of the General Assembly for the Announcement of Voluntary Contributions to the Programme of the United Nations High Commissioner for Refugees	December (1 meeting)	Geneva
UNCTAD, Commission on Enterprise, Business Facilitation and Development	December	Geneva
Committee of Permanent Representatives to UN-Habitat	December	Nairobi
UNEP, Committee of Permanent Representatives	December	Nairobi

2007

Organ	*Dates (2007)*	*Location*
Military Staff Committee	12 January, once every fortnight thereafter	New York
UNICEF, Executive Board, first regular session	15–18 January	New York
Committee on the Elimination of Discrimination against Women, thirty-seventh session	15 January–2 February	New York
Economic and Social Council, election of Bureau	17 January	New York
Joint Meeting of the Executive Boards of UNDP/UNFPA, UNICEF and WFP	19 and 22 January	New York
Committee on Non-Governmental Organizations, regular session	22 January–2 February	New York

Organ	*Dates (2007)*	*Location*
UNDP and UNFPA, Executive Board, first regular session	23–26 January	New York
International Narcotics Control Board, eighty-eighth session	29 January–2 February	Vienna
Committee on the Rights of the Child, forty-fourth session	January (3 weeks)	Geneva
Committee on the Rights of the Child, pre-sessional working group	January (1 week)	Geneva
Consultative Committee on the United Nations Development Fund for Women, forty-seventh session	January	New York
UNCTAD, Commission on Investment, Technology and Related Financial Issues	January	Geneva
United Nations Staff Pension Committee	January/February (1 meeting)	New York
Conference on Disarmament, first part	January–March (8 weeks)	Geneva
Committee on the Elimination of Discrimination against Women, Working Group on Communications under the Optional Protocol to the Convention	5–9 February	New York
Committee on the Elimination of Discrimination against Women, pre-sessional working group	5–9 February	New York
UNCITRAL, Working Group on Arbitration	5–9 February	New York
Human Rights Council, Working Group on Situations	5–9 February	Geneva
UNEP, Governing Council, twenty-fourth session	5–9 February	Nairobi
Economic and Social Council, organizational session	6–9 February	New York
Advisory Committee on Administrative and Budgetary Questions	6 February–27 April	New York
Commission for Social Development, forty-fifth session	7–16 February	New York
UNCITRAL, Working Group on Security Interests	12–16 February	New York
Committee on the Peaceful Uses of Outer Space, Scientific and Technical Subcommittee, forty-fourth session	12–23 February	Vienna
ECE, sixty-second session	19–23 February	Geneva
WFP, Executive Board, first regular session	19–23 February	Rome
Committee on the Elimination of Racial Discrimination, seventieth session	19 February–9 March	Geneva
Eleventh Meeting of the States Parties to the Convention on the Rights of the Child	21 February	New York
Intergovernmental preparatory meeting for the fifteenth session of the Commission on Sustainable Development	26 February–2 March	New York
Commission on the Status of Women, fifty-first session	26 February–9 March	New York
Special Committee on Peacekeeping Operations and its Working Group, substantive session	26 February–16 March	New York

Organ	*Dates (2007)*	*Location*
Statistical Commission, thirty-eighth session	27 February–2 March	New York
Investments Committee	February	New York
UNCTAD, Commission on Trade in Goods and Services, and Commodities	February	Geneva
UNCTAD, Commission on Enterprise, Business Facilitation and Development	February	Geneva
United Nations Voluntary Fund for Indigenous Populations, Board of Trustees	February/March (1 week)	Geneva
Special Committee on the Situation with regard to the Implementation of the Declaration on the Granting of Independence to Colonial Countries and Peoples	February/March	New York
Human Rights Committee, Working Group on Communications	5–9 March	New York
United Nations Voluntary Trust Fund on Contemporary Forms of Slavery, Board of Trustees	5–9 March	Geneva
Human Rights Committee, eighty-ninth session	12–30 March	New York
Commission on Narcotic Drugs, fiftieth session	13–22 March	Vienna
Committee of the Whole of the Commission on Narcotic Drugs	13–22 March (4 days)	Vienna
Committee for Development Policy, ninth session	19–23 March	New York
Group of governmental experts on illicit brokering in small arms	19–23 March	New York
ICSC, sixty-fourth session	19–30 March	New York
Commission on the Limits of the Continental Shelf	26–30 March	New York
Committee on the Peaceful Uses of Outer Space, Legal Subcommittee, forty-sixth session	26 March–5 April	Vienna
General Assembly, Fifth Committee, resumed session	March (4 weeks)	New York
UNCTAD, Working Party on the medium-term plan and the programme budget	March (1 week)	Geneva
Advisory Board on Disarmament Matters	March (3 days)	New York
UNITAR, Board of Trustees, forty-fifth session, first part	March (2–3 days)	Geneva
UNEP, Committee of Permanent Representatives	March	Nairobi
Committee of Permanent Representatives to UN-Habitat	March	Nairobi
Security Council, Governing Council of the United Nations Compensation Commission established pursuant to Security Council resolution 692 (1991), sixty-third session	March	Geneva
Committee for the United Nations Population Award	March/April (2 days)	New York
United Nations Staff Pension Committee	March/April (1 meeting)	New York

Organ	*Dates (2007)*	*Location*
Commission on Population and Development, fortieth session	9–13 April	New York
Committee of Experts on Public Administration	9–13 April	New York
Disarmament Commission	9–27 April	New York
United Nations Voluntary Fund for Victims of Torture, Board of Trustees, twenty-sixth session	16–20 April	Geneva
Governing Council of the United Nations Human Settlements Programme, twenty-first session	16–20 April	Nairobi
UNCITRAL, Working Group on Transport Law	16–27 April	New York
United Nations Forum on Forests	16–27 April	New York
Commission on Crime Prevention and Criminal Justice, sixteenth session	17–26 April	Vienna
Commission on Crime Prevention and Criminal Justice, parallel meetings for informal consultations and working groups	17–26 April (12 meetings)	Vienna
Committee on the Protection of the Rights of All Migrant Workers and Members of Their Families	23–27 April	Geneva
Committee on Economic, Social and Cultural Rights, thirty-eighth session	23 April–11 May	Geneva
Economic and Social Council, resumed organizational session	25–26 April	New York
Committee on Information, twenty-ninth session	30 April–11 May	New York
Commission on Sustainable Development, fifteenth session	30 April–11 May	New York
Preparatory Committee for the 2010 Review Conference of the Parties to the Treaty on the Non-Proliferation of Nuclear Weapons, first session	30 April–11 May	New York
Committee against Torture, thirty-eighth session	April/May (3 weeks)	Geneva
Committee against Torture, pre-sessional working group	April/May (1 week)	Geneva
ESCAP, sixty-third session	April (7 days)	Bangkok
Special high-level meetings of the Economic and Social Council with the Bretton Woods institutions, the World Trade Organization and UNCTAD	April (1 day)	New York
United Nations System Chief Executives Board for Coordination, first regular session	April/May	Geneva
International Narcotics Control Board, eighty-ninth session	7–18 May	Vienna
UNFCCC, meetings of subsidiary bodies of the Conference of the Parties to the Convention	7–18 May	Bonn
Committee on Non-Governmental Organizations, resumed session	14–18 May	New York
UNCITRAL, Working Group on Insolvency Law	14–18 May	New York
Permanent Forum on Indigenous Issues	14–25 May	New York

Organ	*Dates (2007)*	*Location*
Committee on the Elimination of Discrimination against Women, thirty-eighth session	14 May–1 June	New York
Committee on the Rights of the Child, forty-fifth session	14 May–1 June	Geneva
Advisory Committee on Administrative and Budgetary Questions	15 May–27 July	New York
UNCITRAL, Working Group on Procurement	21–25 May	New York
Commission on Science and Technology for Development, tenth session	21–25 May	Geneva
United Nations Scientific Committee on the Effects of Atomic Radiation, fifty-fifth session	21 May–1 June	Vienna
Human Rights Council, Subcommission on the Promotion and Protection of Human Rights, Working Group on Minorities	28 May–1 June	Geneva
Committee on Economic, Social and Cultural Rights, pre-sessional working group	28 May–1 June	Geneva
High-level Committee on South-South Cooperation, fifteenth session	29 May–1 June	New York
General Assembly, Fifth Committee, resumed session	May (4 weeks)	New York
Human Rights Council, Working Group on Enforced and Involuntary Disappearances	May (2 weeks)	Geneva
Committee for Programme and Coordination, organizational session	May (1 day)	New York
Investments Committee	May	New York
ECA, Committee of Experts of the Conference of African Ministers of Finance, Planning and Economic Development, twenty-fourth meeting	May	Addis Ababa
ECA, Conference of African Ministers of Finance, Planning and Economic Development, thirty-eighth session of the Commission	May	Addis Ababa
Conference on Disarmament, second part	May/June (7 weeks)	Geneva
International Law Commission, fifty-ninth session	May/June (5 weeks)	Geneva
United Nations Joint Staff Pension Board, Committee of Actuaries	4–6 June	New York
UNICEF, Executive Board, annual session	4–8 June	New York
Group of governmental experts on illicit brokering in small arms	4–8 June	New York
Voluntary Fund for Technical Cooperation in the Field of Human Rights, Board of Trustees	4–8 June	Geneva
Committee on the Rights of the Child, pre-sessional working group	4–8 June	Geneva
WFP, Executive Board, annual session	4–8 June	Rome

Organ	*Dates (2007)*	*Location*
Committee on the Peaceful Uses of Outer Space, fiftieth session	6–15 June	Vienna
Panel of governmental experts on missiles, first session	11–15 June	New York
Human Rights Council, Subcommission on the Promotion and Protection of Human Rights, Working Group on Contemporary Forms of Slavery	11–15 June	Geneva
UNDP and UNFPA, Executive Board, annual session	11–22 June	New York
Committee on Contributions, sixty-seventh session	11–29 June	New York
Committee for Programme and Coordination, forty-seventh session	11 June–6 July	New York
Meeting of persons chairing human rights treaty bodies	18–22 June	Geneva
Meeting of the States Parties to the United Nations Convention on the Law of the Sea	18–29 June	New York
United Nations Commission on International Trade Law, fortieth session	18 June–13 July	Vienna
United Nations Board of Auditors	28–29 June	New York
Security Council, Governing Council of the United Nations Compensation Commission established pursuant to Security Council resolution 692 (1991), sixty-fourth session	June	Geneva
Committee of Permanent Representatives to UN-Habitat	June	Nairobi
Special Committee on the Situation with regard to the Implementation of the Declaration on the Granting of Independence to Colonial Countries and Peoples	June/July (6–8 meetings per week, up to 30 meetings)	New York
Advisory Board on Disarmament Matters	June/July (3–4 days)	New York
UNEP, Committee of Permanent Representatives	June/July (1 day)	Nairobi
United Nations Administrative Tribunal	June/July	Geneva
Open-ended Informal Consultative Process on Ocean Affairs and the Law of the Sea	2–6 July	New York
Human Rights Committee, Working Group on Communications	2–6 July	Geneva
Subcommittee of Experts on the Transport of Dangerous Goods	2–11 July	Geneva
Economic and Social Council, substantive session	2–27 July	Geneva
United Nations Joint Staff Pension Board, Standing Committee	9–13 July	New York
Human Rights Committee, ninetieth session	9–27 July	Geneva
Subcommittee of Experts on the Globally Harmonized System of Classification and Labelling of Chemicals	11–13 July	Geneva
Committee on the Elimination of Discrimination against Women, pre-sessional working group	16–20 July	New York

Organ	*Dates (2007)*	*Location*
Human Rights Council, Subcommission on the Promotion and Protection of Human Rights, Working Group on Indigenous Populations	16–20 July	Geneva
ICSC, sixty-fifth session	16–27 July	New York
Committee on the Elimination of Discrimination against Women, Working Group on Communications under the Optional Protocol to the Convention	18–20 July	New York
Human Rights Council, Subcommission on the Promotion and Protection of Human Rights, intersessional forum on economic, social and cultural rights (Social Forum)	19 and 20 July	Geneva
Committee on the Elimination of Discrimination against Women, thirty-ninth session	23 July–10 August	New York
Committee on the Elimination of Racial Discrimination, seventy-first session	30 July–17 August	Geneva
UNCTAD, Intergovernmental Group of Experts on Competition Law and Policy	July	Geneva
International Law Commission, fifty-ninth session	July/August (5 weeks)	Geneva
International Law Seminar	July/August (3 weeks)	Geneva
Human Rights Council, Subcommission on the Promotion and Protection of Human Rights, fifty-ninth session	July/August (3 weeks)	Geneva
Conference on Disarmament, third part	July/September (7 weeks)	Geneva
Human Rights Council, Subcommission on the Promotion and Protection of Human Rights, Working Group on Communications	13–24 August	Geneva
United Nations Group of Experts on Geographical Names, twenty-fourth session	20 and 31 August	New York
Ninth United Nations Conference on the Standardization of Geographical Names	21–30 August	New York
Commission on the Limits of the Continental Shelf	27–31 August	New York
Human Rights Council, Working Group on Enforced and Involuntary Disappearances	August (2 weeks)	Geneva
Human Rights Council, Working Group on the Use of Mercenaries	August (1 week)	Geneva
UNCITRAL, Working Group on Procurement	3–7 September	Vienna
Advisory Committee on Administrative and Budgetary Questions	4 September–21 December	New York
UNICEF, Executive Board, second regular session	5–7 September	New York
UNDP and UNFPA, Executive Board, second regular session	10–14 September	New York
UNCITRAL, Working Group on Arbitration	10–14 September	Vienna
Committee on the Rights of the Child, forty-sixth session	10–28 September	Geneva

LIST OF ABBREVIATIONS

AAC	African Association of Cartography
AACHD	African Advisory Committee on Health Development
AAF-SAP	African Alternative Framework for Structural Adjustment Programmes for Socio-economic Recovery and Transformation
AAPAM	African Association of Public Administration and Management
AAPSO	Afro-Asian Peoples' Solidarity Organization
AAS	African Academy of Sciences
AATPO	Association of African Trade Promotion Organization
AAU	Association of African Universities
ACARTSOD	African Centre for Applied Research and Training in Social Development
ACC	Administrative Committee on Coordination
ACMAD	African Centre of Meteorological Applications for Development
ACMS	African Centre for Monetary Studies
ACO	African Curriculum Organization
ACP	African, Caribbean and Pacific Group
ACPR	Advisory Committee of Permanent Representatives and Other Representatives Designated by Members of the Commission (ESCAP)
ACU	Asian Clearing Union
ADB	African Development Bank
ADB	Asian Development Bank
ADFIAP	Association of Development Financing Institutions in Asia and the Pacific
AfDB	African Development Bank
AFESD	Arab Fund for Economic and Social Development
AfMF	African Monetary Bank
AFRAND	African Foundation for Research and Development
AFREXIM	African Export-Import Bank
AFSA	African Statistical Association
AGRIS	Agricultural Information System
AHSCP	African Household Survey Capability Programme
AIDF	African Industrial Development Fund
AIDS	Acquired immunodeficiency syndrome
AIHTTR	African Institute for Higher Technical Training and Research
ALO	African Labour Organization
ANC	African National Congress
ANSTI	African Network of Scientific and Technological Institutes
AOAD	Arab Organization for Agricultural Development
AOCRS	African Organization for Cartography and Remote Sensing

APCC	Asian and Pacific Coconut Community
APCTT	Asian and Pacific Centre for Transfer of Technology
APEC	Asia-Pacific Economic Cooperation
APENPLAN	Asian and Pacific Energy Planning Network
APPER	Africa's Priority Programme for Economic Recovery
APPU	Asian Pacific Postal Union
APT	Asia Pacific Telecommunity
ARCC	Africa Regional Coordinating Committee for the Integration of Women in Development Fund
ARCEDEM	African Regional Centre for Engineering Design and Manufacturing
ARCSE	African Regional Centre for Solar Energy
ARCT	African Regional Centre for Technology
ARI	African Rehabilitation Institute for Disabled Persons
ARSAP	Agricultural Requisites Scheme for Asia and the Pacific
ARSC	African Remote Sensing Council
ARSO	African Regional Organization for Standardization
ARSP	African Remote Sensing Programme
AsDB	Asian Development Bank
ASEAN	Association of South-East Asian Nations
ASOEXPO	Association of Export Promotion Organizations of Central America, Panama and the Dominican Republic
ASTIS	African Science and Technology Information System
ASTRO	International Association of State Trading Organizations of Developing Countries
ATRCW	African Training and Research Centre for Women
BADEA	Arab Bank for Economic Development in Africa
BCEAC	Banque centrale des Etats de l'Afrique centrale
BCEAO	Central Bank of West African States
BOAD	West African Development Bank
BPPE	Bureau for Programme Policy and Evaluation
CADIS	Central African Development Information System
CAFRAD	African Centre for Administrative Training and Research for Development
CAMRDC	Central African Mineral Resources Development Centre
CCOP	Committee for Co-ordination of Joint Prospecting for Mineral Resources in Asian Offshore Areas
CD-ROM	Compact disc-read only memory
CDP	Committee for Development Planning
CEAO	Economic Community of West Africa
CEC	Commission of the European Communities

CEPGL	Economic Community of the Great Lakes countries
CERPOD	Centre d'etudes et de recherche sur la population pour le développement
CESAG	Centre africain d'études supérieures de gestion
CFC	Common Fund for Commodities
CGA	Commission of Geodesy for Africa
CGPRT Centre	Regional Coordination Centre for Research and Development of coarse Grains, Pulses, Roots and Tubes Crops in the Humid Tropics of Asia and the Pacific
CIDA	Canadian International Development Agency
CILSS	Permanent Inter-State Committee for Drought Control in the Sahel
CIRDAFRICA	Centre for Integrated Rural Development in Africa
CITYNET	Regional Network of Local Authorities for the Management of Human Settlements
CODESRIA	Council for the Development of Economic and Social Research in Africa
COTAC	ASEAN Committee on Transportation and Communications
CPC	Committee for Programme and Co-ordination
CRTK	Regional Remote Sensing Centre, Kinshasa
CRTO	Regional Remote Sensing Centre, Ouagadougu
CSD	Commission on Sustainable Development
DAM	Department of Administrative and Management
DESD	Department of Economic and Social Development
DHA	Department of Humanitarian Affairs
DPA	Department of Political Affairs
DPI	Department of Public Information
DPO	Department of Peace-Keeping Operations
EC	European Community
ECA	Economic Commission for Africa
ECA-MRAG	Multidisciplinary Regional Advisory Group
ECCAS	Economic Community of Central African States
ECCT	Energy Conservation Center on Thailand
ECDC	Economic Cooperation among Developing Countries
ECE	Economic Commission for Europe
ECLAC	Economic Commission for Latin America and the Caribbean
ECO	Economic Cooperation Organization
ECOSOC	Economic and Social Council of the United Nations
ECOWAS	Economic Community of West African States
EDF	European Development Fund
EDI	Economic Development Institute of the World Bank
EIB	European Investment Bank

EOSG	Executive Office of the Secretary-General
EPOC	ESCAP Pacific Operations Centre
ESADIS	East and Southern African Development Information System
ESAMI	Eastern and Southern African Management Institute
ESAMRDC	Eastern and Southern African Mineral Resources Development Centre
ESCAP	Economic and Social Commission for Asia and the Pacific
ESCWA	Economic and Social Commission for Western Asia
EUROSTAT	Statistical Office of the European Communities
FACC	Federation of African Chambers of Commerce
FADINAP	Fertilizer Advisory, Development and Information Network for Asia and the Pacific
FAO	Food and Agriculture Organization of the United Nations
FAVDO	Forum of African Voluntary Development Organizations
FEMNET	African Women's Development and Communications Network
GATT	General Agreement on Tariffs and Trade
GCA	Global Coalition for Africa
GCCC	Government cash counterpart contribution
GEF	Global Environment Facility
GIS	Geographic information systems
GIS	Geographic information systems
GSP	Generalized system of preferences
Habitat	United Nations Centre for Human Settlement
HRD	Human resource development
IAEA	International Atomic Energy Agency
IATIN	Intra-Arab Information Network
IAWGD	Inter-Agency Working Group on Desertification
ICAO	International Civil Aviation Organization
ICARA	International Conference on Assistance to Refugees in Africa
ICBs	International commodity bodies
ICC	International Chamber of Commerce
ICID	International Commission on Irrigation and Drainage
ICIPE	International Centre for Insect Physiology and Ecology
ICM	Intergovernmental Committee for Migration
ICP	International Comparison Programme
ICPD	International Conference on Population and Development
IDA	International Development Association
IDB	Islamic Development Bank
IDDA	Industrial Development Decade for Africa

IDEP	African Institute for Economic Development and Planning
IDNDR	International Decade for Natural Disaster Reduction
IDRC	International Development Research Centre of Canada
IDWSSD	International Drinking Water Supply and Sanitation Decade
IFA	International Fertilizer Industry Association
IFAD	International Fund for Agricultural Development
IFC	International Finance Corporation
IFORD	Institut de formation et de recherche démographiques
IGADD	Intergovernmental Authority on Drought and Desertification
IGOs	Intergovernmental organizations
IHCPA	International hydrogeological mapping programme for Africa
IHO	International Hydrographic Organization
IJO	International Jute Organization
ILCA	International Livestock Centre for Africa
ILO	International Labour Organization
IMF	International Monetary Fund
IMO	International Maritime Organization
INCB	International Narcotics Control Board
INRO	International Natural Rubber Organization
INSTRAW	International Research and Training Institute for the Advancement of Women
IOC	Indian Ocean Commission
IOMAC	Indian Ocean Marine Affairs Cooperation
IPC	Integrated Programme for Commodities
IPD	International physical distribution
IPF	Indicative Planning Figure
IPOs	Import promotion offices
IPPF	International Planned Parenthood Federation
ISA	International Silk Organization
ISI	International Statistical Institute
ITC	International Trade Centre UNCTAD/GATT
ITL	International trade logistics
ITU	International Telecommunication Union
IUSSP	International Union for the Scientific Study of Population
JAG	Joint Advisory Group on the International Trade centre UNCTAD/GATT
JAIDO	Japan Associate International Development Organization
JASPA	Jobs and Skills Programme for Africa
JICA	Japan International Cooperation Agency

JIU	Joint Inspection Unit
KBO	Kagere Basin Organization
LAS	League of Arab States
LCBC	Lake Chad Basin Commission
LDCs	Least developed countries
LEMIGAS	Oil and Gas Technology Development Centre (of Indonesia)
LPA	Lagos Plan of Action
LWF	Lutheran World Federation
MINENDAF	Conférence des ministres de l'éducation nationale d'Afrique
MNS	Market News Service
MPPM	Maritime policy planning model
MTP	Medium-Term Plan
MU	Maghreb Union
MULPOC	Multinational Programming and Operational Centre
NACP	National Accounts Capability Programme
NADIS	North African Documentation and Information Centre
NAFTA	North American Free Trade Agreement
NATCAPs	National Technical Co-operation Assessments and Programmes
NBA	Niger Basin Authority
NFIS	Network of Fertilizer Information Systems
NGO	Non-Governmental Organization
OAU	Organization of African Unity
OCS	Office of Conference Services
ODA	Official Development Assistance
OECD	Organization for Economic Co-operation and Development
OGS	Office of General Services
OHRM	Office of Human Resource Management
OLA	Office of Legal Affairs
OMVG	Organization for the Development of Gambia River
OMVS	Organization for the Development of Senegal River
OPPBF	Office for Programme Planning, Budget and Finance
OPS	Office for Project Services
PAC	Pan-African Congress of Azania
PACC	Project Appraisal and Clearance Committee
PADIS	Pan-African Documentation and Information System
PANA	Pan-African News Agency
PANAFTEL	Pan-African Telecommunications Network

PEDP	Pacific Energy Development Programme
PMD	Product and market development
POPIN	Population Information Network
PRODEC	Programme for Development Co-operation (Helsinki School of Economics)
PTA	Preferential Trade Area
RANDFORUM	Research and Development Forum for Science-le Development in Africa
RASCOM	Regional African Satellite Communications System
RASDS	Regional Advisory Service in Demographic Statistics
RBA	Regional Bureau for Africa (UNDP)
RBASEP	Regional Bureau for Arab States and European Programmes
RCSSMRS	Regional Centre for Services in Surveying, Mapping and Remote Sensing
RECTAS	Regional Centre for Training in Aerial Surveys
REDP	Regional Energy Development Programme
RIPS	Regional Institute for Population Studies
RMSS	Regional maritime strategy study
RNAM	Regional Network for Agricultural Machinery
RRSP	Regional Remote Sensing Programme
SAARC	South Asian Association for Regional Co-operation
SACEP	South Asian Cooperative Environment Programme
SADC	Southern African Development Community
SADCC	Southern African Development Co-ordination Conference
SAP	Structural Adjustment Programme
SAPAM	Special Action Programme for Administration and Management
SDI	Selective Dissemination of Information
SDRs	Special drawing rights
SEATRADC	Southeast Asia Tin Research and Development Centre
SIAP	Statistical Institute for Asia and the Pacific
SIS	Special Industrial Services
SMEs	Small and medium-sized enterprises
SMF/LDCs	Special Measures Fund for the Least Developed Countries
SOPAC	South Pacific Applied Geoscience Commission
SPC	South Pacific Commission
SPR	Special Programme Resources
SPREP	South Pacific Regional Environment Programme
SSATP	Sub-Saharan Africa Transport Programme
STPA	Statistical Training Programme for Africa
SWMTEP	System-Wide Medium-Term Environment Programme

TCDC	Technical cooperation among developing countries
TCS	Technical consultancy services
TEPCOW	Technical Preparatory Committee of the Whole
TIS	Trade Information Service
TISNET	Regional Trade Information Network
TNCs	Transnational Corporations
TPOs	Trade promotion organizations
UAR	Union of African Railways
UDEAC	Central African Economic and Customs Union
UNAFEI	United Nations Asia and Far East Institute for the Prevention of Crime and the Treatment of Offenders
UNAFRI	United Nations African Institute for the Prevention of Crime and the Treatment of Offenders
UNAIDS	Joint United Nations Programme on HIV/AIDS
UNAVEM	United Nations Angola Verification Mission
UNCDF	United Nations Capital Development Fund
UNCED	United Nations Conference on Environment and Development
UNCHS	United Nations Centre for Human Settlements (Habitat)
UNCPICPUNE	United Nations Conference for the Promotion of International Cooperation in the Peaceful Use of Nuclear Energy
UNCRDA	United Nations Centre for Regional Development
UNCTAD	United Nations Conference on Trade and Development
UNDCP	United Nations International Drug Control Programme
UNDFW	United Nations Development Fund for Women
UNDP	United Nations Development Programme
UNDRO	United Nations Disaster Relief Organization
UNEP	United Nations Environment Programme
UNESCO	United Nations Educational, Scientific and Cultural Organization
UNFPA	United Nations Fund for Population Activities
UNFSSTD	United Nations Financing System for Science and Technology for Development
UNFSTD	United Nations Fund for Science and Technology for Development
UNHCR	United Nations High Commissioner for Refugees
UNHHSF	United Nations Habitat and Human Settlement Foundation
UNICEF	United Nations Children's Fund
UNIDO	United Nations Industrial Development Organization
UNIFEM	United Nations Development Fund for Women
UNIFIL	UN Interim Force in Lebanon
UNITAR	United Nations Institute for Training and Research

UNOG	United Nations Office at Geneva
UNOSOM	United Nations Operation in Somalia
UNOV	United Nations Office at Vienna
UNRFNRE	United Nations Revolving Fund for Natural Resources Exploration
UNRISD	United Nations Research Institute for Social Development
UNRPTC	United Nations Regular Programme of Technical Cooperation
UNRWA	United Nations Relief and Works Agency for Palestine Refugees in the Near East
UNSCO	United Nations Special Coordinator in the Occupied Territories
UNSO	United Nations Sudano-Sahelian Office
UNTACDA	United Nations Transport and Communications Decade in Africa
UNTFAD	United Nations Trust Fund for African Development
UNTNA	Union of National Radio and Television Organization in Africa
UNTSO	United Nations Truce Supervision Organization
UNU	United Nations University
UNV	United Nations Volunteers
UPU	Universal Postal Union
USAID	United States Agency for International Development
WADIS	West African Development Information System
WASME	World Assembly of Small and Medium Enterprises
WFC	World Food Council
WFP	World Food Programme
WFTU	World Federation of Trade Unions
WHO	World Health Organization
WIDER	World Institute for Development Economics Research
WIPO	World Intellectual Property Organization
WMO	World Meteorological Organization
WRI	World Resources Institute
WTO	World Tourism Organization
WWF	World Wildlife Fund

CHAPTER 1

General Assembly Sixty-first Session

1. Address to the General Assembly by Ms. Al-Khalifa, President of the General Assembly, following the opening of the Sixty-first Session, 12 September 2006 (A/61/PV.1)

The meeting was called to order at 10.20 a.m.

I should like first of all to refer to yesterday's commemoration of the 11 September terrorist attacks, which took place five years ago, in 2001. We share the grief of the American people and of the families of the victims.

It is an honour and pleasure for me to preside over the General Assembly at its sixty-first session. I would like to take this opportunity to thank you all for the support and confidence you have placed in me.

I would like to begin by welcoming the Republic of Montenegro, the newest member of the United Nations family. I believe that it will play a valuable role in furthering the work and ideals of the Organization.

Today, the United Nations faces many challenges at all levels and therefore needs the support of the people of the world, just as the people of the world need this Organization, for this is an Organization of hope that is based on commitment, consensus and coexistence. The numerous meetings, discussions and conferences that bring together people from all over the world provide a real platform to exchange experiences and perspectives. This enables us to understand each other better, in order to achieve a global consensus on political, security, economic, environmental and social issues. Only by working together can we translate our commitments into effective actions.

The 2005 world summit was a prime example of this vision. It provided the General Assembly with a clear and wide-ranging reform agenda in the fields of development, international peace and security, human rights and management reforms. Its outcome was indeed a pillar of hope. It confirmed once again the strong and renewed commitment of the world's leaders to the values and principles of the Charter of the United Nations, demonstrating, by their commitment, a solid resolve to implement the Millennium Development Goals.

World leaders' collective vision of a more responsive multilateral approach to the many challenges facing the world will continue to guide our common efforts to build a safer, freer and more prosperous world for all human beings.

The General Assembly at its sixtieth session, under the leadership of President Eliasson, implemented many of the recommendations adopted at the summit, such as the creation of the Peacebuilding Commission and the Human Rights Council, the establishment of the Central Emergency Response Fund and the adoption of resolutions on development, management reform and a Global Counter-Terrorism Strategy.

Here, I should like to congratulate President Eliasson for his tireless efforts to move the reform agenda forward. I commend all Member States for their cooperation and for the spirit of compromise shown throughout the sixtieth session. They worked under intense pressure, and I trust that we can continue to move ahead with the same momentum during this session.

I should also like to pay tribute to the Secretary-General, Kofi Annan, for his tireless efforts in the service of the mission and the ideals of the United Nations during his tenure. He has played a pivotal role in enhancing and strengthening the Organization to meet global challenges and the emerging needs of the world.

It is important that we build upon, broaden and deepen the progress achieved thus far. Our achievements demonstrate the ability of the General Assembly to produce concrete results on important matters that concern the international community. They also demonstrate and confirm the continued importance of the Assembly as the chief deliberative, policymaking and representative organ of the United Nations.

In order to continue playing that role, the General Assembly must continue to evolve and to strive to deliver sustainable solutions to the major challenges of our time. That can take place only within the framework of multilateralism. A well-functioning and proactive multilateral system is in the interest of all nations, particularly at a time when our growing interdependence is the basis for our peaceful coexistence. Multilateralism is the most effective way to ensure our collective peace and security, protect human rights and uphold the rule of law.

I believe that it is the common responsibility of Member States to make the General Assembly and the United Nations as a whole even more effective. As efforts to revitalize the General Assembly are under way, we must not lose sight of the main purpose of those actions: to meet the rising expectations of hundreds of millions of people around the world. We have the challenging task of meeting the expectations of those who are poor, malnourished or illiterate or the victims of disease. We have the challenging task of ensuring their economic and social security, which is just as important as their political and military security. We have the challenging task of liberating them from want while seeking to liberate them from fear.

I should also like to stress that more than half of the world's population—namely, women—typically have less access to health care, employment, decision-making and property ownership. That disparity must be addressed so that both women and men can enjoy the same opportunities, the same rights and the same responsibilities in all aspects of life. To promote gender equality, we need to empower women so that they have more autonomy to lead their lives. To achieve those goals, it is essential that we work closely together so that, together, we can promote human rights and achieve sustainable development.

We cannot confront all these challenges effectively if we do not have peace and security. The United Nations plays a crucial role in responding to the aftermath of natural disasters and maintaining peace and security in areas affected by violent conflict. Regrettably, the recent violence in the Middle East caused heavy casualties on both sides and extensively damaged the Lebanese infrastructure. Today, man-made conflicts are destroying lives and displacing people on a scale sometimes exceeding that of the destructive effects of nature, including floods and hurricanes.

The people of the world have placed an enormous responsibility on our shoulders, as Member States, to identify and address the causes of human conflicts. Only by working together will we be able to defeat the injustices that are at the root of conflicts.

International terrorism is another equally pressing and closely related issue. We must develop and adopt both preventive and defensive measures to combat terrorism. Within that context, I cannot emphasize enough the importance of high-quality education and conscientious media as positive vehicles for nurturing tolerance, compassion and critical thinking.

Now that the Assembly has adopted a resolution on a Global Counter-Terrorism Strategy (resolution 60/288), I hope that during this session we can continue our efforts to successfully reach agreement on a comprehensive convention on terrorism.

As we prepare ourselves to complete the tasks remaining from the previous session, we shall not overlook those recommendations of the 2005 World Summit Outcome (resolution 60/1) that have yet to be fully implemented, such as disarmament and non-proliferation, Security Council reform, mandate review and system-wide coherence. All of these are crucially important agendas. Working together in the spirit of multilateralism to achieve these goals, we can deliver a programme of work to renew, strengthen and update the United Nations.

Reform is a process rather than an event, and we will need to actively pursue work on a variety of pending issues. I trust that Member States will work together to address every issue on its own merits so that progress can be achieved at a steady pace on all the various aspects of the reform agenda.

We, the Member States, must identify our priorities. I will be more than happy to listen to members' views during the general debate and in the months ahead so that, together, we can design an action-oriented and practical workplan.

Before that, we will hold the first ever High-level Dialogue on International Migration and Development. I anticipate that the discussions will underscore the challenges of migration and development and the need for a collective initiative.

The following week, we will hold a High-level Meeting on the midterm comprehensive global review of the implementation of the Programme of Action for the Least Developed Countries for the Decade 2001-2010. It will outline the successes achieved and the obstacles faced by the least developed countries and lay down guidelines for the way forward—actions that need to be taken by the least developed countries, their development partners and the international community as a whole to successfully implement the Programme of Action.

Here, I should like to commend the important role that non-governmental organizations, civil society and the private sector play in the work of the General Assembly. It is my intention to continue to encourage and value their contributions in addressing the many challenges confronting the international community.

Since its inception in 1945, the United Nations has been a global beacon of hope and a global humanitarian necessity. Indeed, world leaders and thinkers had many years before expressed the need for a truly global forum based on high ideals. At the Paris Conference in January 1919, the President of the United States, Woodrow Wilson, called for the creation of an organization that would be the eye of the nations, to keep watch and act on their common interests—an eye that does not slumber, but is everywhere attentive.

Today, should that eye become weary, it is up to us, the Member States, to revitalize and reinforce its role so that our Organization remains the beacon of hope for the peace, prosperity and order of all nations.

2. Statement by Ms. Al-Khalifa, President of the General Assembly, at the closing of the Sixty-first Session, 17 September 2007, (A/61/PV.109)

We have come to the end of the sixty-first session of the General Assembly. It has been an honour and a privilege to work closely with all members. I have presided over a change of leadership in the Secretariat, and we have achieved notable successes in the General Assembly.

During this session, we have worked with determination and consistency, in an open and transparent manner. From my perspective, as the only woman President for a generation, and the first from the Arab world, I have come to see the United Nations as a global family, a family that is becoming ever more interdependent. At times, like all families, some members may have differences of opinion. That is natural in such a large and diverse group. We have many mutual interests, but it is only in the spirit of collective responsibility that we can take further steps to build greater trust and cooperation. We do that best when we all join together in common cause.

Despite the suspicion and mistrust that can at times prevail, members have demonstrated repeatedly that they can rise above their national interests in the service of the common good. It is clear to me, without any doubt, that when we stand united we are stronger; when we pursue our common goals with purpose and determination, the General Assembly makes a real difference and achieves successes sought by the entire world. To do that effectively, we must all accept both our shared responsibilities and our differences. The speed of change in the world around us is accelerating. Over the past year, the world has witnessed many dramatic events; civil wars and human rights abuses continue and have escalated.

Darfur is an ongoing humanitarian crisis; the threat of terrorism continues; natural disasters have increased in frequency and scale. Climate change is no longer a matter of debate; it has become a living reality for many. We truly face a development emergency if we are going to achieve the Millennium Development Goals on time.

Unless we act decisively, the planet will, by 2015, be suffering not less environmental degradation, but more. Feeling forgotten and with misplaced hope, millions of people will still be struggling on less than one dollar a day, and millions of children will still go hungry.

Yet we should not lose hope, for I believe that great hope arises from great hardship. More important, we have the means at our disposal to address and overcome this situation. That is why I made the implementation of the Millennium Development Goals the overarching theme of this session.

Each year the challenges that the multilateral system faces change, and new priorities emerge. The United Nations has at times been slow to react and rise to the occasion. Over the years, the tools we have at our disposal to tackle pressing issues have become less effective. That gap continues to grow. However, during this session of the General Assembly we have added to the list of accomplishments and helped to close that gap. Together we have strengthened the principal organs of the United Nations and have enhanced cooperation among them, as well as with regional organizations.

As stipulated by the Charter of the United Nations, the relationship between the General Assembly and the other principal organs must be founded on complementary, and not on competitiveness. We must therefore continue to develop those relationships in an open, transparent and cooperative manner, so as to strengthen the Organization and better accomplish our common goals.

This year we succeeded in forging good working relationships with the Presidents of the Security Council and the Economic and Social Council. On several occasions, I was invited to address those Councils during their debates. I trust that cooperation will continue in future sessions. In that regard, I would like to call for the implementation of the many resolutions of the General Assembly aimed at the promotion of such transparency and cooperation, in particular resolutions 58/126, 58/316 and 59/313. Going forward, we need to ensure the faithful implementation of those and other resolutions to further enhance partnership among the principal organs.

The revitalization of the General Assembly has been a priority during this session. In addition to adopting a new resolution on the matter, we have also renewed and broadened our engagement with civil society, non-governmental organizations and the private sector.

Another essential component necessary to strengthening the General Assembly is enhancement of the leadership role of the President of the Assembly. The role of the President is not only contingent upon the political and diplomatic skills of the incumbent; it is also based on the support that the Office of the President receives from the Secretariat. It is therefore critical to strengthen the Office of the President of the General Assembly in proportion to the growing responsibilities of the President.

The thematic debates I convened on subjects of development, financing and achieving the Millennium Development Goals (MDGs), gender equality and women's empowerment, civilizations and the challenge for peace, and climate change have boosted our credibility in dealing with important issues on the global agenda. This has been the beginning of a renaissance for the General Assembly. The practice of convening thematic debates on the international priorities of the day has been an essential part of revitalizing the Assembly. I would therefore urge Member States to continue to support those initiatives, both politically and financially.

In announcing a $10 billion fund for the realization of the MDGs during the informal thematic debate on 27 November, the Islamic Development Bank, the newest member of our family, created an outstanding precedent that I hope will continue.

We can all be proud of adopting the landmark Convention on the Rights of Persons with Disabilities (resolution 61/106, annex), the International Convention for the Protection of All Persons from Enforced Disappearance (resolution 61/177, annex) and the Declaration on the Rights of Indigenous Peoples (resolution 61/295, annex). Those are major steps forward in protecting and promoting human rights and fundamental freedoms for all, as well as in reasserting the General Assembly's role as the chief deliberative and policy-making organ of the United Nations.

With the strengthening of the Economic and Social Council, I am confident the Council will more effectively be able to promote global efforts to realize our international development goals. That is both a demanding responsibility and a tremendous opportunity that we must all wholeheartedly support.

We have all reaffirmed the need to reform the Security Council. The status quo is no longer acceptable. During the next session, I hope that the membership will, on the basis of the progress made during the sixty-first session on the positions and proposals of Member States, have the courage to begin discussions on meaningful intergovernmental negotiations. The world of the twenty-first century requires us to make the Security Council more representative, legitimate and effective. It is also incumbent upon us to enhance the Organization so that we can meet the needs of the poor.

The consultations on system-wide coherence have made some progress. They have demonstrated that we are less divided on substance than on the process itself. However, the impasse is not sustainable. We need to take concrete action, as any further delay will only prolong the suffering of the poorest among us.

On the issue of gender equality, the opportunity is now squarely before the Assembly. I hope the proper decisions will be taken.

On other issues, the Assembly has demonstrated its willingness to modernize the Organization to enable it to face the challenges of the twenty-first century. Members have done that by implementing comprehensive reforms to strengthen our role in the areas of peacekeeping and peacebuilding; finalizing consultations recommending concrete options to strengthen international environmental governance; launching and reviewing the implementation of the United Nations Global Counter-Terrorism Strategy; improving the effectiveness of the Peacebuilding Commission and raising new financing for the Peacebuilding Fund—and I would like to thank the Member States that have contributed to the Fund this year, and to express my confidence that the membership at large will continue to raise additional resources in the future sessions—giving the staff of the Organization an effective system to settle disputes and administer justice and strengthening its oversight by creating the Independent Audit Advisory Committee. By adopting a new scale of assessments and finalizing the Capital Master Plan, the Assembly has put the Organization on the right path towards the future.

We have also successfully prepared the ground for important events that will take place during the sixty-session. Those include the high-level dialogue on inter-religious and intercultural understanding, the special commemorative session on children and the high-level dialogue on financing for development.

In this complex and globalized world, there is a larger question that looms over the United Nations. Are we satisfied that the decisions that we take will have a positive impact on the ground to ease the suffering of the many people who are in dire need of our support? In part, the answer is yes, but we need to do much more.

Of course, the United Nations is not a universal cure for the world's problems, though on many issues we have shown the road ahead. Still, we have not silenced our critics. We therefore must remember that it is not they for whom we work to serve, but rather the global public.

I can tell you first hand, from my experience on official visits this year, that this Organization continues—at times against all odds—to work for the common good, to help build a more democratic and prosperous world. While the United Nations can guide the way and point out the futility of military confrontations, ultimately it is the responsibility of sovereign Member States to work out solutions to crises, particularly in the Middle East and Darfur.

More than ever before, we need to focus on the underlying lack of dialogue between civilizations, cultures and nations that is at the core of many of today's problems. The General Assembly concluded during the substantive debate on civilizations that there is a lack of understanding and mutual respect between different parts of the global community. We must tackle these issues squarely, and in doing so, we have to move beyond the outdated mindset that separates the world into donors and recipients, North and South. We live in a new age, with new possibilities and new global players from the South.

Showing the way forward, Gandhi once said that "we must become the change we want to see in the world". Today, for the membership of the United Nations, this means we must match our words with deeds, our rhetoric with action. The promises that States Members of the United Nations have made deserve to be kept. Living up to our promises and achieving the Millennium Development Goals by 2015 is one of the greatest gifts that we could give to humanity, and our future prosperity and stability. We cannot allow our commitments to remain mere pledges; then they remain only words that symbolize our broken promises.

As we close this session, I would like to take this opportunity once again to extend my deepest appreciation to all the Vice-Presidents of the General Assembly during the sixty-first session, and to thank the Chairpersons and the Bureaus of the Main Committees for all their hard work. I would like, in particular, to highlight as well the dedication of all those ambassadors who have chaired or facilitated important consultations, for without their dedicated and skilful efforts I would have nothing to report to the Assembly today.

I also want to extend my sincerest thanks to Secretary-General Ban Ki-moon for his commitment to the principles and ideals of the United Nations, and for his support for the process of reforming this international Organization throughout the last eight months during which I have closely worked with him. I also thank Ms. Asha-Rose Migiro for her continued support of my work on implementing the Millennium Development Goals, particularly in the area of gender equality.

I extend my thanks as well to the Secretariat of the United Nations, particularly the Department for General Assembly and Conference Management.

I also thank the many representatives of civil society and the NGO community, who are such great advocates for a strong United Nations.

Last but not least, I express my great appreciation of and thanks to each member of the team of the presidency of the General Assembly during the sixty-first session, who have represented the diversity of the United Nations through their dedication, hard work, skill and ability.

I wish to take the opportunity to welcome my successor, the President of the General Assembly at its sixty-second session, Mr. Srgjan Kerim. He is an accomplished academic, a leader in the private sector and an experienced diplomat who strongly believes in the United Nations. I have no doubt that the Assembly will extend to him the same cooperation and friendship I have been so privileged to enjoy.

Mr. Secretary-General, Excellencies, distinguished delegates, I would like to thank you once again for all the work you have done over the last year. The challenge before you now is to continue to carry the torch of pluralism forward, to bring light where there is darkness, to bring hope where there is fear. Each of us here today has a responsibility; we are all accountable. Only the passage of time will judge whether we have been successful.

I can pass on this gavel knowing that I have given my all to serve the values and principles of the United Nations. For this honour, privilege and opportunity, I am deeply grateful to all of you. Thank you, farewell, and a Ramadan karim to all of you.

3. Agenda of the Sixty-first Session of the General Assembly, (A/61/251)*

Adopted by the General Assembly at its 2nd plenary meeting, on 13 September 2006

1. Opening of the session by the President of the General Assembly.

2. Minute of silent prayer or meditation.

3. Credentials of representatives to the sixty-first session of the General Assembly:

(a) Appointment of the members of the Credentials Committee;

(b) Report of the Credentials Committee.

4. Election of the President of the General Assembly.[1]

5. Election of the officers of the Main Committees.[1]

6. Election of the Vice-Presidents of the General Assembly.[1]

7. Organization of work, adoption of the agenda and allocation of items: reports of the General Committee.

8. General debate.

A. Maintenance of international peace and security

9. Report of the Security Council.

10. The role of diamonds in fuelling conflict.

11. Prevention of armed conflict.

12. The situation in Central America: progress in fashioning a region of peace, freedom, democracy and development.[2]

13. The situation in the Middle East.

14. Question of Palestine.

15. Zone of peace and cooperation of the South Atlantic.

16. The situation in Afghanistan.

17. The situation in the occupied territories of Azerbaijan.

18. Necessity of ending the economic, commercial and financial embargo imposed by the United States of America against Cuba.

19. Question of Cyprus.[2]

20. Armed aggression against the Democratic Republic of the Congo.[2]

21. Question of the Falkland Islands (Malvinas).[2]

22. The situation of democracy and human rights in Haiti.[2]

23. Armed Israeli aggression against the Iraqi nuclear installations and its grave consequences for the established international system concerning the peaceful uses of nuclear energy, the non-proliferation of nuclear weapons and international peace and security.[2]

24. Consequences of the Iraqi occupation of and aggression against Kuwait.[2]

25. Declaration of the Assembly of Heads of State and Government of the Organization of African Unity on the aerial and naval military attack against the Socialist People's Libyan Arab Jamahiriya by the present United States Administration in April 1986.[2]

26. Report of the Peacebuilding Commission.

27. Protracted conflicts in the GUAM area and their implications for international peace, security and development.

28. University for Peace.

29. Effects of atomic radiation.

30. International cooperation in the peaceful uses of outer space.

31. United Nations Relief and Works Agency for Palestine Refugees in the Near East.

32. Report of the Special Committee to Investigate Israeli Practices Affecting the Human Rights of the Palestinian People and Other Arabs of the Occupied Territories.

33. Comprehensive review of the whole question of peacekeeping operations in all their aspects.

34. Questions relating to information.

35. Information from Non-Self-Governing Territories transmitted under Article 73 *e* of the Charter of the United Nations.

36. Economic and other activities which affect the interests of the peoples of the Non-Self-Governing Territories.

37. Implementation of the Declaration on the Granting of Independence to Colonial Countries and Peoples by the specialized agencies and the international institutions associated with the United Nations.

38. Offers by Member States of study and training facilities for inhabitants of Non-Self-Governing Territories.

39. Implementation of the Declaration on the Granting of Independence to Colonial Countries and Peoples.

40. Permanent sovereignty of the Palestinian people in the Occupied Palestinian Territory, including East Jerusalem, and of the Arab population in the occupied Syrian Golan over their natural resources.

41. Report of the United Nations High Commissioner for Refugees, questions relating to refugees, returnees and displaced persons and humanitarian questions.

B. Promotion of sustained economic growth and sustainable development in accordance with the relevant resolutions of the General Assembly and recent United Nations conferences

42. Report of the Economic and Social Council.

43. Return or restitution of cultural property to the countries of origin.

44. Culture of peace.

45. The role of the United Nations in promoting a new global human order.

46. Follow-up to the outcome of the twenty-sixth special session: implementation of the Declaration of Commitment on HIV/AIDS.

47. Integrated and coordinated implementation of and follow-up to the outcomes of the major United Nations conferences and summits in the economic, social and related fields.

48. 2001-2010: Decade to Roll Back Malaria in Developing Countries, Particularly in Africa.

49. Sport for peace and development.

50. Information and communication technologies for development.

51. Macroeconomic policy questions:

(a) International trade and development;

(b) International financial system and development;

(c) External debt crisis and development;

(d) Commodities.

52. Follow-up to and implementation of the outcome of the International Conference on Financing for Development.

53. Sustainable development:

(a) Implementation of Agenda 21, the Programme for the Further Implementation of Agenda 21 and the outcomes of the World Summit on Sustainable Development;

(b) Follow-up to and implementation of the Mauritius Strategy for the Further Implementation of the Programme of Action for the Sustainable Development of Small Island Developing States;

(c) International Strategy for Disaster Reduction;

(d) Protection of global climate for present and future generations of mankind;

(e) Implementation of the United Nations Convention to Combat Desertification in Those Countries Experiencing Serious Drought and/or Desertification, Particularly in Africa;

(f) Convention on Biological Diversity;

(g) Report of the Governing Council of the United Nations Environment Programme on its ninth special session.

54. Implementation of the outcome of the United Nations Conference on Human Settlements (Habitat II) and strengthening of the United Nations Human Settlements Programme (UN-Habitat).

55. Globalization and interdependence:

(a) Globalization and interdependence;

(b) International migration and development;

(c) Culture and development;

(d) Preventing and combating corrupt practices and transfer of assets of illicit origin and returning such assets, in particular to the countries of origin, consistent with the United Nations Convention against Corruption;

(e) Integration of the economies in transition into the world economy.

56. Groups of countries in special situations:

(a) Third United Nations Conference on the Least Developed Countries;

(b) Specific actions related to the particular needs and problems of landlocked developing countries: outcome of the International Ministerial Conference of Landlocked and Transit Developing Countries and Donor Countries and International Financial and Development Institutions on Transit Transport Cooperation.

57. Eradication of poverty and other development issues:

(a) Implementation of the first United Nations Decade for the Eradication of Poverty (1997-2006);

(b) Industrial development cooperation.

58. Operational activities for development: operational activities for development of the United Nations system.

59. Training and research:

(a) United Nations University;

(b) United Nations Institute for Training and Research.

60. Social development:

(a) Implementation of the outcome of the World Summit for Social Development and of the twenty-fourth special session of the General Assembly;

(b) Social development, including questions relating to the world social situation and to youth, ageing, disabled persons and the family;

(c) United Nations Literacy Decade: education for all;

(d) Follow-up to the International Year of Older Persons: Second World Assembly on Ageing.

61. Advancement of women:

(a) Advancement of women;

(b) Implementation of the outcome of the Fourth World Conference on Women and of the twenty-third special session of the General Assembly.

C. Development of Africa

62. New Partnership for Africa's Development: progress in implementation and international support:

(a) New Partnership for Africa's Development: progress in implementation and international support;

(b) Causes of conflict and the promotion of durable peace and sustainable development in Africa.

D. Promotion of human rights

63. Promotion and protection of the rights of children:

(a) Promotion and protection of the rights of children;

(b) Follow-up to the outcome of the special session on children.

64. Indigenous issues:

(a) Indigenous issues;

(b) Second International Decade of the World's Indigenous People.

65. Elimination of racism and racial discrimination:

(a) Elimination of racism and racial discrimination;

(b) Comprehensive implementation of and follow-up to the Durban Declaration and Programme of Action.

66. Right of peoples to self-determination.

67. Promotion and protection of human rights:

(a) Implementation of human rights instruments;

(b) Human rights questions, including alternative approaches for improving the effective enjoyment of human rights and fundamental freedoms;

(c) Human rights situations and reports of special rapporteurs and representatives;

(d) Comprehensive implementation of and follow-up to the Vienna Declaration and Programme of Action.

68. Report of the Human Rights Council.

E. Effective coordination of humanitarian assistance efforts

69. Strengthening of the coordination of humanitarian and disaster relief assistance of the United Nations, including special economic assistance:

(a) Strengthening of the coordination of emergency humanitarian assistance of the United Nations;

(b) Special economic assistance to individual countries or regions;

(c) Participation of volunteers, "White Helmets", in the activities of the United Nations in the field of humanitarian relief, rehabilitation and technical cooperation for development;

(d) Assistance to the Palestinian people.

F. Promotion of justice and international law

70. Report of the International Court of Justice.

71. Oceans and the law of the sea:

(a) Oceans and the law of the sea;

(b) Sustainable fisheries, including through the 1995 Agreement for the Implementation of the Provisions of the United Nations Convention on the Law of the Sea of 10 December 1982 relating to the Conservation and Management of Straddling Fish Stocks and Highly Migratory Fish Stocks, and related instruments.

72. Report of the International Criminal Tribunal for the Prosecution of Persons Responsible for Genocide and Other Serious Violations of International Humanitarian Law Committed in the Territory of Rwanda and Rwandan Citizens Responsible for Genocide and Other Such Violations Committed in the Territory of Neighbouring States between 1 January and 31 December 1994.

73. Report of the International Tribunal for the Prosecution of Persons Responsible for Serious Violations of International Humanitarian Law Committed in the Territory of the Former Yugoslavia since 1991.

74. Report of the International Criminal Court.

75. Status of the Protocols Additional to the Geneva Conventions of 1949 and relating to the protection of victims of armed conflicts.

76. Consideration of effective measures to enhance the protection, security and safety of diplomatic and consular missions and representatives.

77. Report of the United Nations Commission on International Trade Law on the work of its thirty-ninth session.

78. Report of the International Law Commission on the work of its fifty-eighth session.

79. Report of the Special Committee on the Charter of the United Nations and on the Strengthening of the Role of the Organization.

80. The rule of law at the national and international levels.

G. Disarmament

81. Report of the International Atomic Energy Agency.

82. Reduction of military budgets.

83. Maintenance of international security—good-neighbourliness, stability and development in South-Eastern Europe.

84. Verification in all its aspects, including the role of the United Nations in the field of verification.

85. Developments in the field of information and telecommunications in the context of international security.

86. Role of science and technology in the context of international security and disarmament.

87. Establishment of a nuclear-weapon-free zone in the region of the Middle East.

88. Conclusion of effective international arrangements to assure non-nuclear-weapon States against the use or threat of use of nuclear weapons.

89. Prevention of an arms race in outer space.

90. General and complete disarmament:

(a) Notification of nuclear tests;

(b) Missiles;

(c) Measures to uphold the authority of the 1925 Geneva Protocol;

(d) Mongolia's international security and nuclear-weapon-free status;

(e) Consolidation of peace through practical disarmament measures;

(f) Disarmament and non-proliferation education;

(g) Towards a nuclear-weapon-free world: accelerating the implementation of nuclear disarmament commitments;

(h) Nuclear-weapon-free southern hemisphere and adjacent areas;

(i) Promotion of multilateralism in the area of disarmament and non-proliferation;

(j) Observance of environmental norms in the drafting and implementation of agreements on disarmament and arms control;

(k) Relationship between disarmament and development;

(l) The Hague Code of Conduct against Ballistic Missile Proliferation;

(m) Regional disarmament;

(n) Confidence-building measures in the regional and subregional context;

(o) Transparency and confidence-building measures in outer space activities;

(p) Implementation of the Convention on the Prohibition of the Development, Production, Stockpiling and Use of Chemical Weapons and on Their Destruction;

(q) Nuclear disarmament;

(r) Assistance to States for curbing the illicit traffic in small arms and light weapons and collecting them;

(s) Problems arising from the accumulation of conventional ammunition stockpiles in surplus;

(t) Conventional arms control at the regional and subregional levels;

(u) Follow-up to the advisory opinion of the International Court of Justice on the *Legality of the Threat or Use of Nuclear Weapons*;

(v) Measures to prevent terrorists from acquiring weapons of mass destruction;

(w) Reducing nuclear danger;

(x) Implementation of the Convention on the Prohibition of the Use, Stockpiling, Production and Transfer of Anti-personnel Mines and on Their Destruction;

(y) The illicit trade in small arms and light weapons in all its aspects;

(z) Information on confidence-building measures in the field of conventional arms;

(aa) Transparency in armaments;

(bb) Establishment of a nuclear-weapon-free zone in Central Asia;

(cc) United Nations conference to identify ways of eliminating nuclear dangers in the context of nuclear disarmament;

(dd) Convening of the fourth special session of the General Assembly devoted to disarmament.

91. Review and implementation of the Concluding Document of the Twelfth Special Session of the General Assembly:

(a) United Nations disarmament fellowship, training and advisory services;

(b) United Nations Disarmament Information Programme;

(c) United Nations regional centres for peace and disarmament;

(d) United Nations Regional Centre for Peace, Disarmament and Development in Latin America and the Caribbean;

(e) United Nations Regional Centre for Peace and Disarmament in Asia and the Pacific;

(f) United Nations Regional Centre for Peace and Disarmament in Africa;

(g) Regional confidence-building measures: activities of the United Nations Standing Advisory Committee on Security Questions in Central Africa;

(h) Convention on the Prohibition of the Use of Nuclear Weapons.

92. Review of the implementation of the recommendations and decisions adopted by the General Assembly at its tenth special session:

(a) Advisory Board on Disarmament Matters;

(b) United Nations Institute for Disarmament Research;

(c) Report of the Conference on Disarmament;

(d) Report of the Disarmament Commission.

93. The risk of nuclear proliferation in the Middle East.

94. Convention on Prohibitions or Restrictions on the Use of Certain Conventional Weapons Which May Be Deemed to Be Excessively Injurious or to Have Indiscriminate Effects.

95. Strengthening of security and cooperation in the Mediterranean region.

96. Comprehensive Nuclear-Test-Ban Treaty.

97. Convention on the Prohibition of the Development, Production and Stockpiling of Bacteriological (Biological) and Toxin Weapons and on Their Destruction.

H. Drug control, crime prevention and combating international terrorism in all its forms and manifestations

98. Crime prevention and criminal justice.

99. International drug control.

100. Measures to eliminate international terrorism.

I. Organizational, administrative and other matters

101. Notification by the Secretary-General under Article 12, paragraph 2, of the Charter of the United Nations.

102. Report of the Secretary-General on the work of the Organization.

103. Elections to fill vacancies in principal organs:

(a) Election of five non-permanent members of the Security Council;

(b) Election of eighteen members of the Economic and Social Council.

104. Appointment of the Secretary-General of the United Nations.

105. Elections to fill vacancies in subsidiary organs and other elections:

(a) Election of seven members of the Committee for Programme and Coordination;

(b) Election of thirty members of the United Nations Commission on International Trade Law;

(c) Election of the members of the International Law Commission;

(d) Election of two members of the Organizational Committee of the Peacebuilding Commission;

(e) Election of fourteen members of the Human Rights Council.

106. Appointments to fill vacancies in subsidiary organs and other appointments:

(a) Appointment of members of the Advisory Committee on Administrative and Budgetary Questions;

(b) Appointment of members of the Committee on Contributions;

(c) Confirmation of the appointment of members of the Investments Committee;

(d) Appointment of members of the United Nations Administrative Tribunal;

(e) Appointment of members of the International Civil Service Commission:

(i) Appointment of members of the Commission;

(ii) Designation of the Chairman and the Vice-Chairman of the Commission;

(f) Appointment of members of the Committee on Conferences;

(g) Appointment of the members of the Consultative Committee of the United Nations Development Fund for Women;

(h) Appointment of members of the Joint Inspection Unit.

107. Admission of new Members to the United Nations.

108. Cooperation between the United Nations and regional and other organizations:

(a) Cooperation between the United Nations and the African Union;

(b) Cooperation between the United Nations and the Asian-African Legal Consultative Organization;

(c) Cooperation between the United Nations and the Association of Southeast Asian Nations;

(d) Cooperation between the United Nations and the Black Sea Economic Cooperation Organization;

(e) Cooperation between the United Nations and the Caribbean Community;

(f) Cooperation between the United Nations and the Community of Portuguese-speaking Countries;

(g) Cooperation between the United Nations and the Council of Europe;

(h) Cooperation between the United Nations and the Economic Community of Central African States;

(i) Cooperation between the United Nations and the Economic Cooperation Organization;

(j) Cooperation between the United Nations and the International Organization of la Francophonie;

(k) Cooperation between the United Nations and the Inter-Parliamentary Union;

(l) Cooperation between the United Nations and the Latin American Economic System;

(m) Cooperation between the United Nations and the League of Arab States;

(n) Cooperation between the United Nations and the Organization for the Prohibition of Chemical Weapons;

(o) Cooperation between the United Nations and the Organization for Security and Cooperation in Europe;

(p) Cooperation between the United Nations and the Organization of American States;

(q) Cooperation between the United Nations and the Organization of the Islamic Conference;

(r) Cooperation between the United Nations and the Pacific Islands Forum;

(s) Cooperation between the United Nations and the Preparatory Commission for the Comprehensive Nuclear-Test-Ban Treaty Organization;

(t) Cooperation between the United Nations and the Southern African Development Community.

109. Implementation of the resolutions of the United Nations.

110. Revitalization of the work of the General Assembly.

111. Question of equitable representation on and increase in the membership of the Security Council and related matters.

112. Strengthening of the United Nations system.

113. Follow-up to the outcome of the Millennium Summit.

114. Multilingualism.

115. Financial reports and audited financial statements, and reports of the Board of Auditors:

(a) United Nations;

(b) United Nations Development Programme;

(c) United Nations Children's Fund;

(d) United Nations Relief and Works Agency for Palestine Refugees in the Near East;

(e) United Nations Institute for Training and Research;

(f) Voluntary funds administered by the United Nations High Commissioner for Refugees;

(g) Fund of the United Nations Environment Programme;

(h) United Nations Population Fund;

(i) United Nations Human Settlements Programme;

(j) Fund of the United Nations International Drug Control Programme;

(k) United Nations Office for Project Services;

(l) International Tribunal for the Prosecution of Persons Responsible for Serious Violations of International Humanitarian Law Committed in the Territory of the Former Yugoslavia since 1991;

(m) International Criminal Tribunal for the Prosecution of Persons Responsible for Genocide and Other Serious Violations of International Humanitarian Law Committed in the Territory of Rwanda and Rwandan Citizens Responsible for Genocide and Other Such Violations Committed in the Territory of Neighbouring States between 1 January and 31 December 1994;

(n) Capital master plan.

116. Review of the efficiency of the administrative and financial functioning of the United Nations.

117. Programme budget for the biennium 2006-2007.

118. Programme planning.

119. Improving the financial situation of the United Nations.

120. Administrative and budgetary coordination of the United Nations with the specialized agencies and the International Atomic Energy Agency.

121. Pattern of conferences.

122. Scale of assessments for the apportionment of the expenses of the United Nations.

123. Human resources management.

124. Joint Inspection Unit.

125. United Nations common system.

126. United Nations pension system.

127. Report on the activities of the Office of Internal Oversight Services.

128. Administration of justice at the United Nations.

129. Financing of the International Criminal Tribunal for the Prosecution of Persons Responsible for Genocide and Other Serious Violations of International Humanitarian Law Committed in the Territory of Rwanda and Rwandan Citizens Responsible for Genocide and Other Such Violations Committed in the Territory of Neighbouring States between 1 January and 31 December 1994.

130. Financing of the International Tribunal for the Prosecution of Persons Responsible for Serious Violations of International Humanitarian Law Committed in the Territory of the Former Yugoslavia since 1991.

131. Scale of assessments for the apportionment of the expenses of United Nations peace-keeping operations.

132. Administrative and budgetary aspects of the financing of the United Nations peace-keeping operations.

133. Financing of the United Nations Operation in Burundi.

134. Financing of the United Nations Operation in Côte d'Ivoire.

135. Financing of the United Nations Peacekeeping Force in Cyprus.

136. Financing of the United Nations Organization Mission in the Democratic Republic of the Congo.

137. Financing of the United Nations Mission in East Timor.

138. Financing of the United Nations Mission of Support in East Timor.

139. Financing of the United Nations Mission in Ethiopia and Eritrea.

140. Financing of the United Nations Observer Mission in Georgia.

141. Financing of the United Nations Stabilization Mission in Haiti.

142. Financing of the United Nations Interim Administration Mission in Kosovo.

143. Financing of the United Nations Mission in Liberia.

144. Financing of the United Nations peacekeeping forces in the Middle East:

(a) United Nations Disengagement Observer Force;

(b) United Nations Interim Force in Lebanon.

145. Financing of the United Nations Mission in Sierra Leone.

146. Financing of the United Nations Mission in the Sudan.

147. Financing of the United Nations Mission for the Referendum in Western Sahara.

148. Report of the Committee on Relations with the Host Country.

149. United Nations reform: measures and proposals.

150. International Year of Reconciliation, 2009.

151. Financing of the United Nations Integrated Mission in Timor-Leste.

152. Report of the Secretary-General on the Peacebuilding Fund.

153. Requests for observer status in the General Assembly.

154. Follow-up to the recommendations on administrative management and internal oversight of the Independent Inquiry Committee into the United Nations Oil-for-Food Programme.

---

* Organized under headings corresponding to the priorities of the Organization.

[1] In accordance with rule 30 of the rules of procedure, as amended by resolution 56/509 of 8 July 2002, the General Assembly will hold these elections for its sixty-second session at least three months before the opening of that session.

[2] This item remains on the agenda for consideration upon notification by a Member State.

[3] At its fifty-fifth session, the General Assembly decided that this item should be considered biennially as from the fifty-sixth session (resolution 55/285 of 7 September 2001). The item has been included in the agenda of the sixty-first session as a result of the adoption of resolutions 60/260 of 8 May 2006 and 60/283 of 7 July 2006 and decision 60/551 C of 7 July 2006.

4. Resolutions adopted by the General Assembly at its Sixty-first Session

Resolution 61/1

[without reference to a Main Committee (A/61/L.2)]

61/1. Declaration of the high-level meeting of the sixty-first session of the General Assembly on the midterm comprehensive global review of the implementation of the Programme of Action for the Least Developed Countries for the Decade 2001–2010

The General Assembly,

Having considered the report of the preparatory meeting of experts on the midterm comprehensive global review of the implementation of the Programme of Action for the Least Developed Countries for the Decade 2001–2010, 1 held in New York from 5 to 7 September 2006,

Noting with appreciation the contribution made by the least developed countries and their development partners, the organizations of the United Nations system and other intergovernmental organizations, as well as non-governmental organizations, to the process of the midterm review of the Programme of Action,[2]

Adopts the following Declaration:

Declaration of the high-level meeting of the sixty-first session of the General Assembly on the midterm comprehensive global review of the implementation of the Programme of Action for the Least Developed Countries for the Decade 2001–2010

We, Heads of State and Government and heads of delegations participating in the high-level meeting of the General Assembly on the midterm comprehensive global review of the implementation of the Programme of Action for the Least Developed Countries for the Decade 2001–2010,[2] held on 18 and 19 September 2006:

1. Recommit ourselves to meeting the special needs of the least developed countries by making progress towards the goals of poverty eradication, peace and development through the improvement of the quality of lives of people in the least developed countries and the strengthening of their abilities to build a better future for themselves and develop their countries, as committed to in the Programme of Action for the Least Developed Countries for the Decade 2001–2010;

2. Reaffirm that the Programme of Action constitutes a fundamental framework for a strong global partnership whose goal is to accelerate sustained economic growth, sustainable development and poverty eradication in the least developed countries;

3. Also reaffirm that the primary responsibility for development in the least developed countries rests with those countries themselves, but that their efforts need to be given concrete and substantial international support from Governments and international organizations in a spirit of shared responsibility through genuine partnerships, including with civil society and the private sector;

4. Support the smooth transition strategy developed for the graduation of countries from the list of least developed countries and, in this regard, affirm the need for the international community to render necessary support to the graduation of the least developed countries with a view to averting the disruption of their development projects and programmes and allowing them to continue developing;

5. Stress that the internationally agreed development goals, including the Millennium Development Goals, can be effectively achieved in the least developed countries through, in particular, the timely fulfilment of the seven commitments of the Programme of Action;

6. Note that, while the Programme of Action has, since its adoption, registered some progress in its implementation, at the same time the overall socioeconomic situation in the least developed countries continues to be precarious;

7. Stress that, given current trends, many least developed countries are unlikely to achieve the goals and objectives set out in the Programme of Action;

8. Emphasize, however, that many least developed countries, with the support of their development partners, have, despite many difficulties, produced notable achievements through wide-ranging and far-reaching reforms;

9. Acknowledge the significant efforts by development partners in the implementation of the Programme of Action, also acknowledge that there is more to be done to implement the Programme of Action, in particular in the area of poverty eradication, and recognize that the situation in the least developed countries requires continued attention;

10. Recognize that it is important to achieve the goals and targets of the Programme of Action in a timely manner and, in this regard, welcome the elaboration of the Cotonou Strategy for the Further Implementation of the Programme of Action for the Least Developed Countries for the Decade 2001–2010[3] as an initiative owned and led by least developed countries;

11. Welcome the measures taken by developed and developing countries, as well as by multilateral organizations, to promote South-South cooperation and call upon them to continue to enhance their resources and efforts for capacity-building and development in the least developed countries, including the sharing of best practices in the sustainable development of the least developed countries;

12. Call upon the international community and the United Nations system and its agencies to continue to assist in the implementation of the Programme of Action, taking into account the conclusions of the midterm comprehensive global review;

13. Invite the Economic and Social Council to continue to ensure the annual review of the implementation of the Programme of Action, taking into account the concrete and quantifiable achievements produced in the realization of the agreed objectives.

9th plenary meeting
19 September 2006

[1] A/61/323.

[2] A/CONF.191/13, chap. II.

[3] A/61/117, annex I.

Resolution 61/2

[on the report of the Fifth Committee (A/61/512)]

61/2. Scale of assessments for the apportionment of the expenses of the United Nations: requests under Article 19 of the Charter

The General Assembly,

Having considered chapter V of the report of the Committee on Contributions on its sixty-sixth session,[1]

Reaffirming the obligation of Member States under Article 17 of the Charter of the United Nations to bear the expenses of the Organization as apportioned by the General Assembly,

1. *Reaffirms* its role in accordance with the provisions of Article 19 of the Charter of the United Nations and the advisory role of the Committee on Contributions in accordance with rule 160 of the rules of procedure of the General Assembly;

2. *Also reaffirms* its resolution 54/237 C of 23 December 1999;

3. *Requests* the Secretary-General to continue to bring to the attention of Member States the deadline specified in resolution 54/237 C, including through an early announcement in the *Journal of the United Nations* and through direct communication;

4. *Urges* all Member States requesting exemption under Article 19 of the Charter to submit as much information as possible in support of their requests and to consider submitting such information in advance of the deadline specified in resolution 54/237 C so as to enable the collation of any additional detailed information that may be necessary;

5. *Agrees* that the failure of the Central African Republic, the Comoros, Georgia, Guinea-Bissau, Liberia, the Niger, Somalia and Tajikistan to pay the full minimum amount necessary to avoid the application of Article 19 of the Charter was due to conditions beyond their control;

6. *Decides* that the Central African Republic, the Comoros, Georgia, Guinea-Bissau, Liberia, the Niger, Somalia and Tajikistan should be permitted to vote in the General Assembly until the end of its sixty-first session;

7. *Takes note* of the information provided by the Chargé d'affaires a.i. of the Permanent Mission of Sao Tome and Principe to the United Nations with regard to a request for exemption under Article 19 of the Charter;[2]

8. *Invites* the Government of Sao Tome and Principe to submit appropriate information to the Committee on Contributions if similar circumstances prevail in the future;

9. *Agrees* that the failure of Sao Tome and Principe to pay the full minimum amount necessary to avoid the application of Article 19 of the Charter was due to conditions beyond its control;

10. *Decides* that Sao Tome and Principe should be permitted to vote in the General Assembly until the end of its sixty-first session.

28th plenary meeting
12 October 2006

---

[1] *Official Records of the General Assembly, Sixty-first Session, Supplement No. 11* and corrigendum (A/61/11 and Corr.1).

[2] See A/C.5/61/3, annex.

Resolution 61/3

[without reference to a Main Committee (A/61/L.3)]

61/3. Appointment of the Secretary-General of the United Nations

The General Assembly,

Having considered the recommendation contained in Security Council resolution 1715 (2006) of 9 October 2006,

Appoints Mr. Ban Ki-moon Secretary-General of the United Nations for a term of office beginning on 1 January 2007 and ending on 31 December 2011.

31st plenary meeting
13 October 2006

Resolution 61/4

[without reference to a Main Committee (A/61/L.4 and Add.1)]

61/4. Cooperation between the United Nations and the Black Sea Economic Cooperation Organization

The General Assembly,

Recalling its resolution 54/5 of 8 October 1999, by which it granted observer status to the Black Sea Economic Cooperation Organization, as well as its resolutions 55/211 of 20 December 2000, 57/34 of 21 November 2002 and 59/259 of 23 December 2004, on cooperation between the United Nations and the Black Sea Economic Cooperation Organization,

Recalling also that one of the purposes of the United Nations is to achieve international cooperation in solving international problems of an economic, social or humanitarian nature,

Recalling further the Articles of the Charter of the United Nations that encourage activities through regional cooperation for the promotion of the purposes and principles of the United Nations,

Recalling its Declaration on the Enhancement of Cooperation between the United Nations and Regional Arrangements or Agencies in the Maintenance of International Peace and Security of 9 December 1994,[1]

Recognizing that any dispute or conflict in the region impedes cooperation, and stressing the need to solve such a dispute or conflict on the basis of the norms and principles of international law,

Convinced that the strengthening of cooperation between the United Nations and other organizations contributes to the promotion of the purposes and principles of the United Nations,

Recalling the report of the Secretary-General submitted pursuant to resolution 59/259,[2]

1. *Encourages* efforts within the Black Sea Economic Cooperation Organization to consider ways and means of enhancing the contribution of the Organization to security and stability in the region;

2. *Welcomes* the signing in Athens on 3 December 2004 of the Additional Protocol on Combating Terrorism to the Agreement among the Governments of the Black Sea Economic Cooperation Organization Participating States on Cooperation in Combating Crime, in Particular in its Organized Forms;

3. *Also welcomes* the activities of the Black Sea Economic Cooperation Organization aimed at strengthening regional cooperation in various fields, such as energy, transport, institutional reform and good governance, trade and economic development, banking and finance, communications, agriculture and agro-industry, health care and pharmaceuticals, environmental protection, tourism, science and technology, exchange of statistical data and economic information, collaboration among Customs services, and combating organized crime and illicit trafficking in drugs, weapons and radioactive material, acts of terrorism and illegal migration, or in any other related area;

4. *Encourages* the activities of the Black Sea Economic Cooperation Organization aimed at the elaboration and realization of specific joint regional projects, particularly in the field of transport and energy infrastructure, focused on security of supply of respective services to the economies of the region;

5. *Welcomes* the operationalization and financing of projects by the Project Development Fund of the Black Sea Economic Cooperation Organization to the benefit of the sustainable development of the Black Sea region;

6. *Takes note* of the positive contributions of the Parliamentary Assembly of the Black Sea Economic Cooperation Organization, the Business Council, the Black Sea Trade and Development Bank and the International Centre for Black Sea Studies to the strengthening of multifaceted regional cooperation in the Black Sea area;

7. *Appeals* for greater cooperation between the Black Sea Economic Cooperation Organization and international financial institutions in co-financing feasibility and pre-feasibility studies of the projects in the Black Sea area;

8. *Takes note* of the cooperation between the Black Sea Economic Cooperation Organization and the World Bank and the World Trade Organization and the working contacts with the World Tourism Organization, aimed at promoting the sustainable development of the Black Sea region;

9. *Also takes note* of the importance attached by the Black Sea Economic Cooperation Organization to the strengthening of relations with the European Union, and supports the efforts of the Organization to take concrete steps to advance this cooperation in line with the provisions of the Komotini statement of 23 April 2005, as reinforced by the Chisinau Declaration of 28 October 2005 and the Bucharest statement of 26 April 2006, issued by the Council of Ministers for Foreign Affairs of the States members of the Black Sea Economic Cooperation Organization;

10. *Further takes note* of the cooperation established between the Black Sea Economic Cooperation Organization and other regional organizations and initiatives;

11. *Invites* the Secretary-General to strengthen dialogue with the Black Sea Economic Cooperation Organization with a view to promoting cooperation and coordination between the two secretariats;

12. *Invites* the specialized agencies and other organizations and programmes of the United Nations system to cooperate with the Black Sea Economic Cooperation Organization in order to continue programmes with the Organization and its associated institutions for the achievement of their objectives;

13. *Requests* the Secretary-General to submit to the General Assembly at its sixty-third session a report on the implementation of the present resolution;

14. *Decides* to include in the provisional agenda of its sixty-third session the sub-item entitled "Cooperation between the United Nations and the Black Sea Economic Cooperation Organization".

39th plenary meeting
20 October 2006

---

[1] Resolution 49/57, annex.

[2] A/61/256, part two, sect. XIV.

Resolution 61/5

[without reference to a Main Committee (A/61/L.5 and Add.1)]

61/5. Cooperation between the United Nations and the Asian-African Legal Consultative Organization

The General Assembly,

Recalling its resolutions 36/38 of 18 November 1981, 37/8 of 29 October 1982, 38/37 of 5 December 1983, 39/47 of 10 December 1984, 40/60 of 9 December 1985, 41/5 of 17 October 1986, 43/1 of 17 October 1988, 45/4 of 16 October 1990, 47/6 of 21 October 1992, 49/8 of 25 October 1994, 51/11 of 4 November 1996, 53/14 of 29 October 1998, 55/4 of 25 October 2000, 57/36 of 21 November 2002 and 59/3 of 22 October 2004,

Having considered the report of the Secretary-General on cooperation between the United Nations and the Asian-African Legal Consultative Organization,[1]

Having heard the statement made by the Secretary-General of the Asian-African Legal Consultative Organization on the steps taken by the Consultative Organization to ensure continuing, close and effective cooperation between the two organizations,[2]

Acknowledging in particular the close interaction between the Consultative Organization and the Sixth Committee,

1. *Takes note with appreciation* of the report of the Secretary-General;[1]

2. *Recognizes* the continuing efforts of the Asian-African Legal Consultative Organization towards strengthening the role and function of the United Nations and its various organs in enhancing the rule of law and wider adherence to related international instruments;

3. *Notes with satisfaction* the commendable progress achieved towards enhancing cooperation between the United Nations, its agencies, other international organizations and the Consultative Organization;

4. *Notes with appreciation* the work of the Consultative Organization aimed at strengthening the efforts of the United Nations in respect of issues such as combating corruption,

international terrorism and trafficking in women and children, as well as human rights issues;

5. *Also notes with appreciation* the initiative and efforts the Consultative Organization has undertaken to promote the objectives and principles set out in the United Nations Millennium Declaration, 3 including wider acceptance of treaties deposited with the Secretary-General;

6. *Recommends* that, with a view to promoting close interaction between the Consultative Organization and the Sixth Committee, the consideration of the subitem entitled "Cooperation between the United Nations and the Asian-African Legal Consultative Organization" should be scheduled to coincide with the deliberations of the Committee on the work of the International Law Commission;

7. *Requests* the Secretary-General to submit to the General Assembly at its sixty-third session a report on cooperation between the United Nations and the Consultative Organization;

8. *Decides* to include in the provisional agenda of its sixty-third session the sub-item entitled "Cooperation between the United Nations and the Asian-African Legal Consultative Organization".

39th plenary meeting
20 October 2006

---

[1] A/61/256/Add.1, part five.

[2] See *Official Records of the General Assembly, Sixty-first Session, Plenary Meetings*, 39th meeting (A/61/Pv.39) and Corrigendum.

[3] See resolution 55/2.

Resolution 61/6

[without reference to a Main Committee (A/61/L.6 and Add.1)]

61/6. Cooperation between the United Nations and the Inter-Parliamentary Union

The General Assembly,

Having considered the report of the Secretary-General of 16 August 2006, which takes stock of the broad and substantive cooperation between the United Nations and the Inter-Parliamentary Union over the past two years,[1]

Taking note of the resolutions adopted by the Inter-Parliamentary Union and circulated in the General Assembly and the many activities undertaken by the organization in support of the United Nations,

Welcoming the annual parliamentary hearings at the United Nations as a regular feature of the programme of events held at United Nations Headquarters on the occasion of the sessions of the General Assembly, as well as other specialized parliamentary meetings organized by the Inter-Parliamentary Union in cooperation with the United Nations in the context of major United Nations conferences and events,

Taking into consideration the Cooperation Agreement between the United Nations and the Inter-Parliamentary Union of 1996,[2] which laid the foundation for cooperation between the two organizations,

Recalling the United Nations Millennium Declaration[3] and the 2005 World Summit Outcome,[4] in which Heads of State and Government resolved to strengthen further cooperation between the United Nations and national parliaments through their world organization, the Inter-Parliamentary Union, in all fields of work of the United Nations and for the effective implementation of United Nations reform,

Also recalling its resolution 57/32 of 19 November 2002, in which the Inter-Parliamentary Union was invited to participate in the work of the General Assembly in the capacity of observer, as well as resolutions 57/47 of 21 November 2002 and 59/19 of 8 November 2004,

Taking note of the recommendations contained in the report of the Panel of Eminent Persons on United Nations-Civil Society Relations[5] in regard to engaging parliamentarians more systematically in the work of the United Nations,

1. *Welcomes* the efforts made by the Inter-Parliamentary Union to provide for a greater parliamentary contribution and enhanced support to the United Nations;

2. *Takes note* of the conclusions of the second World Conference of Speakers of Parliament,[6] held at United Nations Headquarters from 7 to 9 September 2005 in conjunction with the 2005 World Summit;

3. *Encourages* the United Nations and the Inter-Parliamentary Union to continue to cooperate closely in various fields, in particular peace and security, economic and social development, international law, human rights, and democracy and gender issues, bearing in mind the significant benefits of cooperation between the two organizations, to which the report of the Secretary-General attests;[1]

4. *Encourages* the Inter-Parliamentary Union to strengthen further its contribution to the work of the General Assembly, including its revitalization, as envisaged in resolution 60/286 of 8 September 2006, and in relation to the newly established bodies such as the Human Rights Council and the Peacebuilding Commission;

5. *Also encourages* the Inter-Parliamentary Union to play an active role in support of the Economic and Social Council, particularly in the implementation of the new functions devolved to the Council by the 2005 World Summit;

6. *Welcomes* the partnership agreement concluded recently between the United Nations Democracy Fund and the Inter-Parliamentary Union, and looks forward to growing cooperation in the realm of democracy and good governance;

7. *Calls for* the further development of the annual parliamentary hearing at the United Nations and other specialized parliamentary meetings in the context of major United Nations meetings as joint United Nations-Inter-Parliamentary Union events;

8. *Also calls for* closer involvement, as appropriate, of the Inter-Parliamentary Union in the elaboration of system-wide strategies for consideration by the United Nations system and the United Nations System Chief Executives Board for Coordination, with a view to ensuring greater and more coherent support by parliaments to the work of the United Nations;

9. *Decides* to include in the provisional agenda of its sixty-third session the sub-item entitled "Cooperation between the United Nations and the Inter-Parliamentary Union".

39th plenary meeting
20 October 2006

[1] See A/61/256, part three.

[2] A/51/402, annex.

[3] See resolution 55/2.

[4] See resolution 60/1.

[5] See A/58/817 and Corr.1.

[6] See A/60/398, annex.

Resolution 61/7

[without reference to a Main Committee (A/61/L.7 and Add.1)]

61/7. Cooperation between the United Nations and the International Organization of la Francophonie

The General Assembly,

Recalling its resolutions 33/18 of 10 November 1978, 50/3 of 16 October 1995, 52/2 of 17 October 1997, 54/25 of 15 November 1999, 56/45 of 7 December 2001, 57/43 of 21 November 2002 and 59/22 of 8 November 2004, as well as its decision 53/453 of 18 December 1998,

Considering that the International Organization of la Francophonie brings together a considerable number of States Members of the United Nations, among which it promotes multilateral cooperation in areas of interest to the United Nations,

Bearing in mind the Articles of the Charter of the United Nations which encourage the promotion of the purposes and principles of the United Nations through regional cooperation,

Bearing in mind also that, according to the Charter of la Francophonie adopted on 23 November 2005 at the Ministerial Conference of la Francophonie, held in Antananarivo, the objectives of the International Organization of la Francophonie are to assist in the establishment and development of democracy, the prevention, management and settlement of conflicts and support for the rule of law and for human rights, the intensification of dialogue between cultures and civilizations, the establishment of closer ties among peoples through mutual knowledge and strengthening of their solidarity through multilateral cooperation activities with a view to promoting the growth of their economies, and the promotion of education and training,

Welcoming the steps taken by the International Organization of la Francophonie to strengthen its ties with the organizations of the United Nations system and with international and regional organizations with a view to attaining its objectives,

Noting with satisfaction the commitment to multilateral cooperation for sustainable development, in particular through education and information technologies, for the purpose of meeting the Millennium Development Goals, undertaken by the Heads of State and

Government of countries using French as a common language, at their eleventh summit, held in Bucharest on 28 and 29 September 2006, and their determination to extend the scope of francophone collaboration and cooperation in order to narrow the digital divide, flight poverty and contribute to the emergence of a more equitable form of globalization that will bring progress, peace, democracy and human rights, in full respect for culture and linguistic diversity, in the interests of the most vulnerable populations and the development of all countries,

Having considered the report of the Secretary-General on the implementation of resolution 59/22,[1]

Noting with satisfaction the substantial progress achieved in cooperation between the United Nations, the specialized agencies and other United Nations bodies and programmes and the International Organization of la Francophonie,

Convinced that strengthening cooperation between the United Nations and the International Organization of la Francophonie serves the purposes and principles of the United Nations,

Noting the desire of the two organizations to consolidate, develop and strengthen the ties that exist between them in the political, economic, social and cultural fields,

1. *Takes note with satisfaction* of the report of the Secretary-General,[1] and welcomes the increasingly close and productive cooperation between the United Nations and the International Organization of la Francophonie;

2. *Notes with satisfaction* that the International Organization of la Francophonie participates actively in the work of the United Nations, to which it makes a valuable contribution;

3. *Notes with great satisfaction* the initiatives taken by the International Organization of la Francophonie in the areas of conflict prevention, the promotion of peace and support for democracy, the rule of law and human rights, in accordance with the commitments reaffirmed at the Ministerial Conference of la Francophonie on Conflict Prevention and Human Security, held on 13 and 14 May 2006 in Saint Boniface, Canada, and commends it on the genuine contribution it makes, in cooperation with the United Nations, in Haiti, the Comoros, Côte d'Ivoire, Burundi, the Democratic Republic of the Congo and the Central African Republic;

4. *Welcomes* the initiation of cooperation between the United Nations and the International Organization of la Francophonie, with the participation of other regional and subregional organizations, as well as non-governmental organizations, in the fields of early warning and conflict prevention, and encourages the pursuit of this initiative with a view to formulating practical recommendations to facilitate the establishment of relevant operational mechanisms, where necessary;

5. *Expresses its gratitude* to the International Organization of la Francophonie for the steps it has taken in recent years to promote cultural and linguistic diversity and dialogue between cultures and civilizations;

6. *Expresses its appreciation* to the Secretary-General of the United Nations and the Secretary-General of the International Organization of la Francophonie for their sustained efforts to strengthen cooperation and coordination between the two organizations, thereby serving their mutual interests in the political, economic, social and cultural fields;

7. *Welcomes* the initiation of cooperation between the International Organization of la Francophonie and the Department of Peacekeeping Operations of the Secretariat with a

view to increasing the number of French-speaking personnel in United Nations peacekeeping operations;

8. *Also welcomes* the fact that the eleventh summit of la Francophonie was devoted to the use of new technologies in the service of education, and calls upon the specialized agencies and the funds and programmes of the United Nations system to enhance their cooperation with the International Organization of la Francophonie in the area of sustainable development;

9. *Further welcomes* the involvement of the countries that use French as a common language, particularly through the International Organization of la Francophonie, in the preparation for, conduct of and follow-up to international conferences organized under United Nations auspices;

10. *Commends* the high-level meetings held periodically between the United Nations Secretariat and the Secretariat of the International Organization of la Francophonie, and advocates the participation of those Secretariats in major meetings of the two organizations;

11. *Expresses its appreciation* to the Secretary-General for including the International Organization of la Francophonie in the periodic meetings he holds with heads of regional organizations, and invites him to continue doing so, taking into account the role played by the International Organization of la Francophonie in conflict prevention and support for democracy and the rule of law;

12. *Notes with satisfaction* the continued collaboration between the United Nations and the International Organization of la Francophonie in the area of electoral monitoring and assistance, and advocates the strengthening of cooperation between the two organizations in that area;

13. *Requests* the Secretary-General of the United Nations, acting in cooperation with the Secretary-General of the International Organization of la Francophonie, to encourage the holding of periodic meetings between representatives of the United Nations Secretariat and representatives of the Secretariat of the International Organization of la Francophonie in order to promote the exchange of information, coordination of activities and identification of new areas of cooperation;

14. *Welcomes* the participation of the International Organization of la Francophonie in the Peacebuilding Commission's work on Burundi, and strongly encourages the International Organization of la Francophonie and the Peacebuilding Commission to continue to cooperate actively;

15. *Invites* the Secretary-General of the United Nations to take the necessary steps, in consultation with the Secretary-General of the International Organization of la Francophonie, to continue to promote cooperation between the two organizations;

16. *Invites* the specialized agencies and the funds and programmes of the United Nations system, as well as the regional commissions, including the Economic Commission for Africa, to collaborate to this end with the Secretary-General of the International Organization of la Francophonie by identifying new synergies in favour of development, in particular in the areas of poverty elimination, energy, sustainable development, education, training and the development of new information technologies;

17. *Requests* the Secretary-General to submit to the General Assembly at its sixty-third session a report on the implementation of the present resolution;

18. *Decides* to include in the provisional agenda of its sixty-third session the sub-item entitled "Cooperation between the United Nations and the International Organization of la Francophonie".

39th plenary meeting
20 October 2006

[1] See A/61/256, part one, sect. XI.

Resolution 61/8

[without reference to a Main Committee (A/61/L.9 and Add.1)]

61/8. Report of the International Atomic Energy Agency

The General Assembly,

Having received the report of the International Atomic Energy Agency for 2005,[1]

Taking note of the statement by the Director General of the International Atomic Energy Agency,[2] in which he provided additional information on the main developments in the activities of the Agency during 2006,

Recognizing the importance of the work of the Agency,

Recognizing also the cooperation between the United Nations and the Agency and the Agreement governing the relationship between the United Nations and the Agency as approved by the General Conference of the Agency on 23 October 1957 and by the General Assembly in the annex to its resolution 1145 (XII) of 14 November 1957,

1. *Takes note with appreciation* of the report of the International Atomic Energy Agency;[1]

2. *Takes note* of resolutions GC(50)/RES/10A on measures to strengthen international cooperation in nuclear, radiation and transport safety and waste management; GC(50)/RES/10B on transport safety; GC(50)/RES/11 on progress on measures to protect against nuclear and radiological terrorism; GC(50)/RES/12 on strengthening of the Agency's technical cooperation activities; GC(50)/RES/13 on strengthening the Agency's activities related to nuclear science, technology and applications, comprising GC(50)/RES/13A on non-power nuclear applications, GC(50)/RES/13B on nuclear power applications and GC(50)/RES/13C on nuclear knowledge; GC(50)/RES/14 on strengthening the effectiveness and improving the efficiency of the safeguards system and application of the Model Additional Protocol; GC(50)/RES/15 on the implementation of the Agreement between the Agency and the Democratic People's Republic of Korea for the application of safeguards in connection with the Treaty on the Non-Proliferation of Nuclear Weapons; GC(50)/RES/16 on the application of Agency safeguards in the Middle East; and decisions GC(50)/DEC/11 on the amendment to article XIV.A of the Statute and GC(50)/DEC/12 on the amendment to article VI of the Statute, adopted on 22 September 2006 by the General Conference of the Agency at its fiftieth regular session;[3]

3. *Reaffirms its strong support* for the indispensable role of the Agency in encouraging and assisting the development and practical application of atomic energy for peaceful uses, in technology transfer to developing countries and in nuclear safety, verification and security;

4. *Appeals* to Member States to continue to support the activities of the Agency;

5. *Requests* the Secretary-General to transmit to the Director General of the Agency the records of the sixty-first session of the General Assembly relating to the activities of the Agency.

43rd plenary meeting
30 October 2006

---

[1] International Atomic Energy Agency, *The Annual Report for 2005* (GC(50)/4); transmitted to the members of the General Assembly by a note by the Secretary-General (A/61/266).

[2] See *Official Records of the General Assembly, Sixty-first Session, Plenary Meetings*, 42nd meeting (A/61/PV.42), and corrigendum.

[3] See International Atomic Energy Agency, *Resolutions and Other Decisions of the General Conference, Fiftieth Regular Session, 18–22 September 2006* (GC(50)/RES/DEC(2006)).

Resolution 61/9

[on the report of the Fifth Committee (A/61/547)]

61/9. Financing of the United Nations Operation in Burundi

The General Assembly,

Having considered the reports of the Secretary-General on the financing of the United Nations Operation in Burundi[1] and the related report of the Advisory Committee on Administrative and Budgetary Questions,[2]

Recalling Security Council resolution 1545 (2004) of 21 May 2004, by which the Council authorized, for an initial period of six months as from 1 June 2004, with the intention to renew it for further periods, the deployment of a peacekeeping operation called the United Nations Operation in Burundi, and the subsequent resolutions by which the Council extended the mandate of the Operation, the latest of which was resolution 1692 (2006) of 30 June 2006, by which the Council extended the mandate of the Operation until 31 December 2006,

Recalling also its resolution 58/312 of 18 June 2004 on the financing of the Operation and its subsequent resolutions thereon, the latest of which was resolution 60/269 of 30 June 2006,

Reaffirming the general principles underlying the financing of United Nations peacekeeping operations, as stated in General Assembly resolutions 1874 (S-IV) of 27 June 1963, 3101 (XXVIII) of 11 December 1973 and 55/235 of 23 December 2000,

Mindful of the fact that it is essential to provide the Operation with the necessary financial resources to enable it to fulfil its responsibilities under the relevant resolutions of the Security Council,

1. *Takes note* of the status of contributions to the United Nations Operation in Burundi as at 30 June 2006,[3] including the contributions outstanding in the amount of 31.1 million United States dollars, representing some 5 per cent of the total assessed contributions, notes with concern that only forty-nine Member States have paid their assessed contributions in full, and urges all other Member States, in particular those in arrears, to ensure payment of their outstanding assessed contributions;

2. *Expresses its appreciation* to those Member States which have paid their assessed contributions in full, and urges all other Member States to make every possible effort to ensure payment of their assessed contributions to the Operation in full;

3. *Expresses concern* at the financial situation with regard to peacekeeping activities, in particular as regards the reimbursements to troop contributors that bear additional burdens owing to overdue payments by Member States of their assessments;

4. *Also expresses concern* at the delay experienced by the Secretary-General in deploying and providing adequate resources to some recent peacekeeping missions, in particular those in Africa;

5. *Emphasizes* that all future and existing peacekeeping missions shall be given equal and non-discriminatory treatment in respect of financial and administrative arrangements;

6. *Also emphasizes* that all peacekeeping missions shall be provided with adequate resources for the effective and efficient discharge of their respective mandates;

7. *Reiterates its request* to the Secretary-General to make the fullest possible use of facilities and equipment at the United Nations Logistics Base at Brindisi, Italy, in order to minimize the costs of procurement for the Operation;

8. *Welcomes* the use of the installation at Entebbe, Uganda, to enhance the efficiency and responsiveness of its logistical support operations for peacekeeping missions in the region;

9. *Endorses* the conclusions and recommendations contained in the report of the Advisory Committee on Administrative and Budgetary Questions,[2] and requests the Secretary-General to ensure their full implementation, subject to the provisions of the present resolution;

10. *Takes note* of the recommendations contained in paragraphs 21, 25 and 27 of the report of the Advisory Committee;

11. *Decides* to establish two National Officer posts for the Human Rights Office and one National Officer post for the Office of the Chief of Administrative Services through redeployment of posts;

12. *Also decides* to establish four general temporary assistance positions (one P-4, one P-2 and two national staff, including one National Officer) for the Conduct and Discipline Team;

13. *Re-emphasizes* the need to refine budgetary assumptions through closer scrutiny of expenditure patterns of the Operation;

14. *Reaffirms* its resolution 59/296 of 22 June 2005, and requests the Secretary-General to ensure the full implementation of its relevant provisions and the relevant provisions of its resolution 60/266 of 30 June 2006;

15. *Requests* the Secretary-General to take all necessary action to ensure that the Operation is administered with a maximum of efficiency and economy;

16. *Also requests* the Secretary-General, in order to reduce the cost of employing General Service staff, to continue efforts to recruit local staff for the Operation against General Service posts, commensurate with the requirements of the Operation;

17. *Welcomes* the efforts of the Operation and its personnel, and looks forward to the successful completion of the mandate of the Operation;

18. *Requests* the Secretary-General to ensure an orderly transition, including the transfer of assets, to the planned follow-on mission—the United Nations Integrated Office in Burundi—and the efficient liquidation of the Operation's assets in accordance with the Operation's exit strategy and liquidation timetables;

19. *Also requests* the Secretary-General to encourage strong coordination between the Operation, the planned follow-on mission and the United Nations country team with a view to ensuring a smooth transition to the planned follow-on mission and to reducing the potential duplication of activities among members of the United Nations country team;

20. *Further requests* the Secretary-General to ensure that the lessons learned from other peacekeeping missions are applied during the Operation's drawdown, liquidation and transition to the planned follow-on mission;

21. *Notes* the additional information on projected expenditure for the Operation for the period from 1 July 2006 to 30 June 2007, amounting to 128,536,700 dollars, provided by the Secretary-General;[4]

Financial performance report for the period from 1 July 2004 to 30 June 2005

22. *Takes note* of the report of the Secretary-General on the financial performance of the Operation for the period from 1 July 2004 to 30 June 2005;[5]

Budget estimates for the period from 1 July 2006 to 30 June 2007

23. *Decides* to appropriate to the Special Account for the United Nations Operation in Burundi the amount of 128,536,700 dollars for the maintenance and administrative liquidation of the Operation for the period from 1 July 2006 to 30 June 2007, inclusive of the amount of 78,959,200 dollars previously authorized by the General Assembly under the terms of its resolution 60/269 for the maintenance of the Operation for the period from 1 July to 31 October 2006, and in addition to the amount of 3,426,800 dollars already appropriated under the terms of the same resolution for the support account for peacekeeping operations and the United Nations Logistics Base at Brindisi, Italy, for the period from 1 July 2006 to 30 June 2007;

Financing of the appropriation for the period from 1 July 2006 to 30 June 2007

24. *Also decides*, taking into account the amount of 40 million dollars already apportioned under the terms of its resolution 60/269 for the maintenance of the Operation for the period from 1 July to 31 October 2006, to apportion among Member States the additional amount of 88,536,700 dollars for the maintenance and administrative liquidation of the Operation

for the period from 1 July 2006 to 30 June 2007, in accordance with the levels updated in its resolution 58/256 of 23 December 2003, and taking into account the scale of assessments for 2006, as set out in its resolution 58/1 B of 23 December 2003, and the scale of assessments for 2007;[6]

25. *Further decides* that, in accordance with the provisions of its resolution 973 (X) of 15 December 1955, there shall be set off against the apportionment among Member States, as provided for in paragraph 24 above, their respective share in the Tax Equalization Fund of the amount of 1,774,600 dollars, representing the estimated additional staff assessment income approved for the Operation for the period from 1 July 2006 to 30 June 2007;

26. *Decides* that, for Member States that have fulfilled their financial obligations to the Operation, there shall be set off against their apportionment, as provided for in paragraph 24 above, their respective share of the additional unencumbered balance in the amount of 115,500 dollars in respect of the financial period ended 30 June 2004, in accordance with the levels updated in its resolution 58/256, and taking into account the scale of assessments for 2004, as set out in its resolution 58/1 B;

27. *Also decides* that, for Member States that have not fulfilled their financial obligations to the Operation, there shall be set off against their outstanding obligations their respective share of the additional unencumbered balance in the amount of 115,500 dollars in respect of the financial period ended 30 June 2004, in accordance with the scheme set out in paragraph 26 above;

28. *Further decides* that, for Member States that have fulfilled their financial obligations to the Operation, there shall be set off against their apportionment, as provided for in paragraph 24 above, their respective share of the unencumbered balance and other income in the total amount of 31,523,100 dollars in respect of the financial period ended 30 June 2005, in accordance with the levels updated in its resolution 58/256, and taking into account the scale of assessments for 2005, as set out in its resolution 58/1 B;

29. *Decides* that, for Member States that have not fulfilled their financial obligations to the Operation, there shall be set off against their outstanding obligations their respective share of the unencumbered balance and other income in the total amount of 31,523,100 dollars in respect of the financial period ended 30 June 2005, in accordance with the scheme set out in paragraph 28 above;

30. *Also decides* that the decrease in the estimated staff assessment income in the amount of 583,800 dollars in respect of the financial period ended 30 June 2005 shall be set off against the credits from the amount of 31,523,100 dollars referred to in paragraphs 28 and 29 above;

31. *Emphasizes* that no peacekeeping mission shall be financed by borrowing funds from other active peacekeeping missions;

32. *Encourages* the Secretary-General to continue to take additional measures to ensure the safety and security of all personnel under the auspices of the United Nations participating in the Operation, bearing in mind paragraphs 5 and 6 of Security Council resolution 1502 (2003) of 26 August 2003;

33. *Invites* voluntary contributions to the Operation in cash and in the form of services and supplies acceptable to the Secretary-General, to be administered, as appropriate, in accordance with the procedure and practices established by the General Assembly;

34. *Decides* to keep under review during its sixty-first session the item entitled "Financing of the United Nations Operation in Burundi".

44th plenary meeting
31 October 2006

---

[1] A/60/612 and A/61/309.

[2] A/61/485.

[3] ST/ADM/SER.B/695, annex XXXIX.

[4] See *Official Records of the General Assembly, Sixty-first Session, Fifth Committee*, 12th meeting (A/C.5/61/SR.12), and corrigendum.

[5] A/60/612.

[6] To be adopted by the General Assembly.

Resolution 61/9

[on the report of the Fifth Committee (A/61/547/Add.2)]

61/9. Financing of the United Nations Operation in Burundi

B[1]

The General Assembly,

Having considered the report of the Secretary-General on the financing of the United Nations Operation in Burundi[2] and the related report of the Advisory Committee on Administrative and Budgetary Questions,[3]

Recalling Security Council resolution 1545 (2004) of 21 May 2004, by which the Council authorized, for an initial period of six months as from 1 June 2004, with the intention to renew it for further periods, the deployment of a peacekeeping operation called the United Nations Operation in Burundi, and the subsequent resolutions by which the Council extended the mandate of the Operation, the last of which was resolution 1692 (2006) of 30 June 2006, by which the Council extended the mandate of the Operation until 31 December 2006,

Recalling also its resolution 58/312 of 18 June 2004 on the financing of the Operation and its subsequent resolutions thereon, the latest of which was resolution 61/9 A of 31 October 2006, and its decision 61/554 of 4 April 2007,

Reaffirming the general principles underlying the financing of United Nations peacekeeping operations, as stated in General Assembly resolutions 1874 (S-IV) of 27 June 1963, 3101 (XXVIII) of 11 December 1973 and 55/235 of 23 December 2000,

1. *Takes note* of the status of contributions to the United Nations Operation in Burundi as at 31 March 2007, including the contributions outstanding in the amount of 18.9 million United States dollars, representing some 2 per cent of the total assessed contributions, notes with concern that only thirty-three Member States have paid their assessed contributions in full, and urges all other Member States, in particular those in arrears, to ensure payment of their outstanding assessed contributions;

2. *Expresses its appreciation* to those Member States which have paid their assessed contributions in full, and urges all other Member States to make every possible effort to ensure payment of their assessed contributions to the Operation in full;

3. *Expresses concern* at the financial situation with regard to peacekeeping activities, in particular as regards the reimbursements to troop contributors that bear additional burdens owing to overdue payments by Member States of their assessments;

4. *Also expresses concern* at the delay experienced by the Secretary-General in deploying and providing adequate resources to some recent peacekeeping missions, in particular those in Africa;

5. *Emphasizes* that all future and existing peacekeeping missions shall be given equal and non-discriminatory treatment in respect of financial and administrative arrangements;

6. *Also emphasizes* that all peacekeeping missions shall be provided with adequate resources for the effective and efficient discharge of their respective mandates;

7. *Endorses* the conclusions and recommendations contained in the report of the Advisory Committee on Administrative and Budgetary Questions,[3] and requests the Secretary-General to ensure their full implementation;

Financial performance report for the period from 1 July 2005 to 30 June 2006

8. *Takes note* of the report of the Secretary-General on the financial performance of the Operation for the period from 1 July 2005 to 30 June 2006;[2]

9. *Decides* that, for Member States that have fulfilled their financial obligations to the Operation, there shall be credited their respective share of the unencumbered balance and other income in the total amount of 69,015,000 dollars in respect of the financial period ended 30 June 2006, in accordance with the levels updated in General Assembly resolution 58/256 of 23 December 2003, and taking into account the scale of assessments for 2006, as set out in its resolution 58/1 B of 23 December 2003;

10. *Encourages* Member States that are owed credits referred to in paragraph 9 above to apply those credits to any accounts where the Member State concerned has outstanding assessed contributions;

11. *Decides* that, for Member States that have not fulfilled their financial obligations to the Operation, there shall be set off against their outstanding obligations their respective share of the unencumbered balance and other income in the total amount of 69,015,000 dollars in respect of the financial period ended 30 June 2006, in accordance with the scheme set out in paragraph 9 above;

12. *Also decides* that the decrease of 2,304,500 dollars in the estimated staff assessment income in respect of the financial period ended 30 June 2006 shall be set off against the credits from the amount of 69,015,000 dollars referred to in paragraphs 9 and 11 above;

13. *Further decides* to include in the provisional agenda of its sixty-second session the item entitled "Financing of the United Nations Operation in Burundi".

104th plenary meeting
29 June 2007

---

[1] Resolution 61/9, in section VI of the *Official Records of the General Assembly, Sixty-first Session, Supplement No. 49* and corrigendum (A/61/49 and A/61/49 (Vol.I)/Corr.1), vol. I, becomes resolution 61/9 A.

[2] A/61/716 and Corr.1.

[3] A/61/852/Add.6.

Resolution 61/10

[without reference to a Main Committee (A/61/L.12 and Add.1)]

61/10. Sport as a means to promote education, health, development and peace

The General Assembly,

Recalling its resolutions 58/5 of 3 November 2003, 59/10 of 27 October 2004 and 60/9 of 3 November 2005, its decision to proclaim 2005 the International Year for Sport and Physical Education to strengthen sport as a means to promote education, health, development and peace, and its resolution 60/1 of 16 September 2005, in which it underlined that sport could foster development and peace and could contribute to an atmosphere of tolerance and understanding,

Taking note with appreciation of the report of the Secretary-General,[1] which includes the Action Plan that serves as an initial road map for a three-year period to expand and strengthen partnerships, sport for development and peace programmes and projects and advocacy and communications activities,

Acknowledging the major role of the Member States and the United Nations system in promoting human development through sport and physical education, through the country programmes,

Acknowledging also that sport and physical education can present opportunities for solidarity and cooperation in order to promote tolerance, a culture of peace, social and gender equality, adequate responses to the special needs of persons with disabilities, intercultural dialogue, social cohesion and harmony,

Recognizing the need for greater coordination of efforts at the international level to facilitate a more effective fight against doping,

Noting the need to further develop a common framework within the United Nations to promote sport for education, health, development and peace, thereby broadening the mission of the Working Group on Sport for Development and Peace of the United Nations Communications Group to establish a policy and communications platform that will define common strategies, policy and programmes to increase coherence and synergies, while simultaneously raising awareness within the United Nations system and among external partners,

Recalling the "Call to Action", which was adopted on 6 December 2005 in Magglingen, Switcherland, at all culminating conference of the International Year for Sport and Physical Education, to promote sport for development and peace among Governments, the United Nations system and international sports organizations,

Taking note with appreciation of the organization in 2006 of the Global Youth Leadership Summit that highlighted the use of the convening power of sport as an entry point towards the achievement of the Millennium Development Goals by 2015,

1. *Appreciates* the appointment of sports celebrities as spokespersons and Goodwill Ambassadors for the United Nations, representing the positive values of sport;

2. *Encourages* the strengthening of cooperation with the International Olympic Committee, the International Paralympic Committee, sports organizations and other partners of the world of sport;

3. *Invites* Member States, the United Nations system, including the governing bodies of the United Nations agencies, sport-related organizations, the media, civil society and the private sector to collaborate to promote greater awareness and action to foster peace and accelerate the attainment of the Millennium Development Goals through sport-based initiatives and to promote the integration of sport for development and peace in the development agenda, by working along the following points, adapted from the Action Plan included in the report of the Secretary-General:[1]

(*a*) Further develop a global framework to strengthen a common vision, define priorities and further raise awareness to promote and mainstream sport for development and peace policies that are easily replicable;

(*b*) Promote and support the integration and mainstreaming of sport for development and peace in development programmes and policies;

(*c*) Promote innovative funding mechanisms and multi-stakeholder arrangements on all levels, on a voluntary basis, including the engagement of sports organizations, civil society, athletes and the private sector;

(*d*) Promote common evaluation and monitoring tools, indicators and benchmarks based on commonly agreed standards;

4. *Invites* Member States to initiate sports programmes to promote gender equality and the empowerment of women;

5. *Invites* Governments and international sports organizations to assist developing countries, in particular the least developed countries, in their capacity-building efforts in sport and physical education, by providing national experiences and best practices, as well as financial, technical and logistic resources for the development of sports programmes;

6. *Encourages* Member States to ratify the International Convention Against Doping in Sport;[2]

7. *Encourages* the Secretary-General to maintain the mandate of Special Adviser on Sport for Development and Peace and to provide guidance on the institutional future of sport for development and peace within the United Nations system;

8. *Invites* Member States to provide voluntary contributions to ensure adequate execution of and follow-up to the activities being implemented by the Office of Sport for Development and Peace in Geneva and in New York;

9. *Requests* the Secretary-General to report to the General Assembly at its sixty-second session on the implementation of the present resolution and on progress at the national, regional and international levels to encourage policies and best practices related to sport for development and peace, under the item entitled "Sport for peace and development".

48th plenary meeting
3 November 2006

[1] A/61/373.

[2] United Nations Educational, Scientific and Cultural Organization, *Records of the General Conference, Thirty-third Session, Paris, 3–21 October 2005*, vol. 1: *Resolutions*, chap. V, resolution 14.

Resolution 61/11

[without reference to a Main Committee (A/61/L.10)]

61/11. Necessity of ending the economic, commercial and financial embargo imposed by the United States of America against Cuba

The General Assembly,

Determined to encourage strict compliance with the purposes and principles enshrined in the Charter of the United Nations,

Reaffirming, among other principles, the sovereign equality of States, non-intervention and non-interference in their internal affairs and freedom of international trade and navigation, which are also enshrined in many international legal instruments,

Recalling the statements of the Heads of State or Government at the Ibero-American Summits concerning the need to eliminate unilateral application of economic and trade measures by one State against another that affect the free flow of international trade,

Concerned at the continued promulgation and application by Member States of laws and regulations, such as that promulgated on 12 March 1996 known as the "Helms-Burton Act", the extraterritorial effects of which affect the sovereignty of other States, the legitimate interests of entities or persons under their jurisdiction and the freedom of trade and navigation,

Taking note of declarations and resolutions of different intergovernmental forums, bodies and Governments that express the rejection by the international community and public opinion of the promulgation and application of measures of the kind referred to above,

Recalling its resolutions 47/19 of 24 November 1992, 48/16 of 3 November 1993, 49/9 of 26 October 1994, 50/10 of 2 November 1995, 51/17 of 12 November 1996, 52/10 of 5 November 1997, 53/4 of 14 October 1998, 54/21 of 9 November 1999, 55/20 of 9 November 2000, 56/9 of 27 November 2001, 57/11 of 12 November 2002, 58/7 of 4 November 2003, 59/11 of 28 October 2004 and 60/12 of 8 November 2005,

Concerned that, since the adoption of its resolutions 47/19, 48/16, 49/9, 50/10, 51/17, 52/10, 53/4, 54/21, 55/20, 56/9, 57/11, 58/7, 59/11 and 60/12, further measures of that nature aimed at strengthening and extending the economic,

1. *Takes note* of the report of the Secretary-General on the implementation of resolution 60/12;[1]

2. *Reiterates its call upon* all States to refrain from promulgating and applying laws and measures of the kind referred to in the preamble to the present resolution, in conformity with their obligations under the Charter of the United Nations and international law, which, inter alia, reaffirm the freedom of trade and navigation;

3. *Once again urges* States that have and continue to apply such laws and measures to take the necessary steps to repeal or invalidate them as soon as possible in accordance with their legal regime;

4. *Requests* the Secretary-General, in consultation with the appropriate organs and agencies of the United Nations system, to prepare a report on the implementation of the present

resolution in the light of the purposes and principles of the Charter and international law and to submit it to the General Assembly at its sixty-second session;

5. *Decides* to include in the provisional agenda of its sixty-second session the item entitled "Necessity of ending the economic, commercial and financial embargo imposed by the United States of America against Cuba".

50th plenary meeting
8 November 2006

[1] A/61/132.

Resolution 61/12

[without reference to a Main Committee (A/61/L.8 and Add.1)]

61/12. Cooperation between the United Nations and the Economic Cooperation Organization

The General Assembly,

Recalling its resolution 48/2 of 13 October 1993, by which it granted observer status to the Economic Cooperation Organization,

Recalling also its previous resolutions on cooperation between the United Nations and the Economic Cooperation Organization, in which it invited various specialized agencies as well as other organizations and programmes of the United Nations system and relevant international financial institutions to join in the efforts to implement the economic programmes and projects of the Economic Cooperation Organization,

Appreciating the technical and financial assistance extended by the United Nations system and the relevant international and regional organizations to the Economic Cooperation Organization for its economic programmes and projects, and encouraging them to continue their support,

Welcoming the endeavours of the Economic Cooperation Organization to consolidate its ties with the United Nations system and the relevant international and regional organizations for the development and promotion of projects in all priority areas,

Expressing its support for the relevant plans and programmes as well as the institutional changes in the Economic Cooperation Organization made with a view to achieving internationally agreed development goals, including those contained in the United Nations Millennium Declaration,[1]

Expressing its grave concern and sympathy over the human casualties caused by the worst natural disasters and their devastating impact on the socio-economic situation in the Economic Cooperation Organization region, which is prone to disasters such as earthquakes, floods and drought,

1. *Takes note with appreciation* of the report of the Secretary-General on the implementation of resolution 59/4 of 22 October 2004,[2] and expresses satisfaction at the mutually beneficial interaction between the United Nations and the Economic Cooperation Organization;

2. *Takes note* of the Baku Declaration, adopted at the ninth Economic Cooperation Organization summit, held in Baku on 5 May 2006, which provides guidelines to the Organization in areas such as trade, transportation, energy, agriculture, industry, health and the environment;

3. *Welcomes* the adoption by the Council of Ministers of the Economic Cooperation Organization at its fifteenth meeting of "ECO Vision 2015" as the basic reference document of the Economic Cooperation Organization, in line with the Millennium Development Goals, inter alia, in which the establishment of a free trade area in the region, facilitation of trade and investment information networking, transportation, the promotion of small- and medium-sized enterprises and utilization of new and renewable technologies are highlighted;

4. *Calls for* the strengthening of technical assistance of the World Trade Organization, the United Nations Conference on Trade and Development and other trade-related United Nations bodies, such as the International Trade Centre UNCTAD/WTO, to States members of the Economic Cooperation Organization, taking into account the fact that the member States are developing countries and countries with economies in transition, some of which are in the process of becoming members of the World Trade Organization and that their access to world markets and increasing intraregional and interregional trade through the implementation of regional trade agreements will boost their efforts to achieve their development goals;

5. *Notes with satisfaction* the implementation of the Programme of Action of the Economic Cooperation Organization Decade of Transport and Communications (1998–2007), which is supported by technical assistance from the Economic and Social Commission for Asia and the Pacific and the United Nations Conference on Trade and Development, especially for the elimination of non-physical barriers on main transit-transport routes of the region;

6. *Welcomes* the signing by most States members of the Economic Cooperation Organization of the Intergovernmental Agreement on the Asian Highway Network, which has been launched under the auspices of the Economic and Social Commission for Asia and the Pacific, and calls upon the member States concerned to contribute to the operationalization of the project by identifying their priority investment projects;

7. *Expresses its appreciation* for the efforts of the Economic Cooperation Organization in developing a regional energy trade with the cooperation and active participation of subregional and international organizations such as the Economic and Social Commission for Asia and the Pacific, the World Bank, the Asian Development Bank and the Islamic Development Bank;

8. *Appreciates* that the Regional Programme for Food Security of the Economic Cooperation Organization has been formulated with the technical and financial assistance of the Food and Agriculture Organization of the United Nations and contributions of the Islamic Development Bank, invites the relevant United Nations bodies, other international organizations and donor agencies to assist the Secretariat of the Economic Cooperation Organization in the efficient implementation of the Regional Programme, which contains eleven regional projects and several national projects, and, in this framework, expresses its appreciation for the signing and launching in early 2006 of the Technical Cooperation Programme for Strengthening Seed Supply in the Economic Cooperation Organization

Region of the Food and Agriculture Organization of the United Nations and the Economic Cooperation Organization;

9. *Notes with satisfaction* the enhancement of cooperation between the United Nations Industrial Development Organization and the Economic Cooperation Organization, especially in such areas as industrial cooperation strategy, the transfer of technology, plans of action for small- and medium-sized enterprises and standardization, and invites the United Nations Industrial Development Organization to continue contributing to relevant activities and projects of the Economic Cooperation Organization;

10. *Expresses its satisfaction* at the identification of new fields of cooperation within the framework of the Economic Cooperation Organization and at establishing a new directorate of human resource and sustainable development to enhance cooperation on such important issues as health, the alleviation of poverty and human and sustainable development, and recommends that all relevant United Nations bodies, including the Division for Sustainable Development of the Department of Economic and Social Affairs of the Secretariat, the World Health Organization, the United Nations Population Fund, the United Nations Development Programme and the Office for the Coordination of Humanitarian Affairs of the Secretariat, extend technical and financial support to the Economic Cooperation Organization in its endeavour to enhance cooperation in the above-mentioned areas;

11. *Welcomes* the signing of memorandums of understanding between the Economic Cooperation Organization and the World Meteorological Organization and the United Nations Environment Programme, and calls for the effective implementation of the memorandums;

12. *Takes note* of the contribution made by the Drug Coordination Control Unit of the Economic Cooperation Organization in compiling and disseminating drug-related data and in organizing training programmes/courses in the field of drug control for the experts of the member States, with the technical and financial assistance of the United Nations Office on Drugs and Crime and the European Union, and invites the donor agencies to assist the Economic Cooperation Organization in funding the projects jointly prepared by the United Nations Office on Drugs and Crime and the Secretariat of the Economic Cooperation Organization;

13. *Welcomes* efforts of the Economic Cooperation Organization towards enabling conditions for Afghanistan to assume a more active role in the region in order to benefit from increased trade and export opportunities, and, while taking note of the valuable contribution of the Economic Cooperation Organization in improving the extent and scope of the reintegration of Afghanistan into regional cooperation schemes, appreciates the operationalization of the Special Fund of the Economic Cooperation Organization to finance some priority projects in Afghanistan, and invites the relevant United Nations agencies, such as the United Nations Development Programme and the United Nations Assistance Mission in Afghanistan, to cooperate with the Secretariat of the Economic Cooperation Organization for the successful implementation of its current programmes and projects and the Plan of Action for the Rehabilitation and Reconstruction of Afghanistan, and of a new plan after its expiry in 2007;

14. *Invites* the United Nations system, its relevant bodies and the international community to continue to provide technical assistance, as appropriate, to the States members of the Economic Cooperation Organization in developing and enhancing their early warning

systems, preparedness, capacity for timely response and rehabilitation, with a view to reducing human casualties and mitigating the socio-economic impact of natural disasters and infectious diseases;

15. *Takes note with appreciation* of the strides made by the Economic Cooperation Organization in the sphere of external relations, and expresses its desire for the strengthening of the Organization's relations with other international/regional organizations through the establishment of a mechanism to accord it the status of observer/dialogue partner and through the activation of contact groups in the relevant international forums;

16. *Requests* the Secretary-General to submit to the General Assembly at its sixty-third session a report on the implementation of the present resolution;

17. *Decides* to include in the provisional agenda of its sixty-third session the sub-item entitled "Cooperation between the United Nations and the Economic Cooperation Organization".

52nd plenary meeting
13 November 2006

[1] See resolution 55/2.

[2] See A/61/256, part two, sect. XV.

Resolution 61/13

[without reference to a Main Committee (A/61/L.14 and Add.1)]

61/13. Cooperation between the United Nations and the Council of Europe

The General Assembly,

Recalling the Agreement between the Council of Europe and the Secretariat of the United Nations signed on 15 December 1951 and the Arrangement on Cooperation and Liaison between the Secretariats of the United Nations and the Council of Europe of 19 November 1971,

Recalling also the 2005 World Summit Outcome, approved at the United Nations summit held in New York from 14 to 16 September 2005, including the section on regional organizations,[1] which provides an incentive to reinforce links between the United Nations and regional organizations such as the Council of Europe,

Welcoming the outcome of the Third Summit of the Council of Europe, held in Warsaw on 16 and 17 May 2005, and the fact that on this occasion the Heads of State and Government encouraged cooperation with the United Nations and the specialized agencies, and committed themselves to achieving the Millennium Developments Goals in Europe, including environmental development,

Welcoming also the increasingly close relations between the United Nations and the Council of Europe,

Welcoming further the report of the Secretary-General on cooperation between the United Nations and the Council of Europe,[2]

1. *Considers* that cooperation with the Council of Europe regarding the protection of human rights, the fight against racism, discrimination, xenophobia and intolerance, the protection of the rights of persons belonging to minorities, the prevention of torture and inhuman or degrading treatment or punishment, the fight against trafficking in human beings and violence against women, as well as the protection and promotion of the rights of the child should be reinforced;

2. *Takes note* of the important role of the European Court of Human Rights, and invites the Human Rights Council and the Office of the United Nations High Commissioner for Human Rights to work closely with the Council of Europe, and in particular its Commissioner for Human Rights, in promoting respect for human rights;

3. *Notes* the contribution of the Council of Europe to the protection and strengthening of democracy, inter alia, through the Forum for the Future of Democracy, and welcomes fruitful cooperation between the United Nations and the Council of Europe in the area of democracy, good governance and education for democratic citizenship and human rights, in particular through the strengthening of links between the United Nations Decade of Education for Sustainable Development and the Council of Europe Project on Education for Democratic Citizenship and Human Rights;

4. *Encourages* the development of cooperation, where appropriate, between the United Nations Peacebuilding Commission and the Council of Europe, with a view to promoting post-conflict re-establishment and consolidation of peace in Europe, with full respect for human rights and the rule of law;

5. *Commends* the ongoing cooperation between the Counter-Terrorism Committee and its Executive Directorate and the Council of Europe, as well as the contribution of the Council of Europe to the implementation of Security Council resolutions 1373 (2001) of 28 September 2001 and 1624 (2005) of 14 September 2005, and calls for the deepening of cooperation in the fight against terrorism, while protecting human rights;

6. *Encourages* cooperation between the two organizations regarding the fight against transnational organized crime, cybercrime, corruption and money-laundering, as well as concerning the promotion of human rights and the rule of law in the information society;

7. *Reiterates its support* for cooperation between the two organizations in the social field, in particular concerning the protection and promotion of the rights and dignity of persons with disabilities, combating poverty and social exclusion and ensuring equal access to social rights for all;

8. *Welcomes* the joint initiatives of the United Nations Educational, Scientific and Cultural Organization and the Council of Europe for the promotion of intercultural dialogue, especially the creation of the Faro Platform of interinstitutional cooperation in 2005, and encourages the continuation of such cooperation, in particular through the European Centre for Global Interdependence and Solidarity of the Council of Europe, and also as regards the promotion of cultural diversity;

9. *Notes* the constructive interest of the Parliamentary Assembly of the Council of Europe in the reform process of the United Nations, and welcomes its proposals for a closer involvement of parliamentarians in the work of the United Nations;

10. *Requests* the Secretaries-General of the United Nations and the Council of Europe to combine their efforts in seeking answers to global challenges, within their respective mandates, and calls upon all relevant United Nations bodies to support the enhancement of cooperation with the Council of Europe in the areas mentioned above;

11. *Decides* to include in the provisional agenda of its sixty-third session the sub-item entitled "Cooperation between the United Nations and the Council of Europe", and requests the Secretary-General to submit to the General Assembly at its sixty-third session a report on cooperation between the United Nations and the Council of Europe in implementation of the present resolution.

52nd plenary meeting
13 November 2006

---

1 Resolution 60/1, para. 170.

2 A/61/256, part one, sect. VI.

Resolution 61/14

[without reference to a Main Committee (A/61/L.17 and Add.1)]

61/14. Cooperation between the United Nations and the League of Arab States

The General Assembly,

Recalling its previous resolutions on cooperation between the United Nations and the League of Arab States,

Having considered the report of the Secretary-General on cooperation between the United Nations and regional and other organizations,[1]

Recalling article 3 of the Pact of the League of Arab States,[2] which entrusts the Council of the League with the function of determining the means whereby the League will collaborate with the international organizations which may be created in the future to guarantee peace and security and organize economic and social relations,

Noting the desire of both organizations to consolidate, develop and enhance further the ties existing between them in the political, economic, social, humanitarian, cultural, technical and administrative fields,

Taking into account the report of the Secretary-General entitled "An Agenda for Peace",[3] in particular section VII concerning cooperation with regional arrangements and organizations, and the "Supplement to an Agenda for Peace",[4]

Convinced of the need for more efficient and coordinated utilization of available economic and financial resources in order to promote the common objectives of the two organizations,

Recognizing the need for the further strengthening of cooperation between the United Nations system and the League of Arab States and its specialized organizations for the realization of the common goals and objectives of the two organizations,

1. *Takes note with satisfaction* of the report of the Secretary-General;[1]

2. *Commends* the continued efforts of the League of Arab States to promote multilateral cooperation among Arab States, and requests the United Nations system to continue to lend its support;

3. *Expresses its appreciation* to the Secretary-General for the follow-up action taken by him to implement the proposals adopted at the meetings between representatives of the Secretariat of the United Nations and other organizations of the United Nations system and the General Secretariat of the League of Arab States and its specialized organizations, including the sectoral meeting in 2005 on the theme "Achieving and financing the Millennium Development Goals and sustainable development in the Arab region" and the general meeting on cooperation held in 2006;

4. *Requests* the Secretariat of the United Nations and the General Secretariat of the League of Arab States, within their respective fields of competence, to intensify further their cooperation for the realization of the purposes and principles embodied in the Charter of the United Nations, the strengthening of international peace and security, economic and social development, disarmament, decolonization, self-determination and the eradication of all forms of racism and racial discrimination;

5. *Requests* the Secretary-General to continue his efforts to strengthen cooperation and coordination between the United Nations and other organizations and agencies of the United Nations system and the League of Arab States and its specialized organizations in order to enhance their capacity to serve the mutual interests and objectives of the two organizations in the political, economic, social, humanitarian, cultural and administrative fields;

6. *Calls upon* the specialized agencies and other organizations and programmes of the United Nations system:

(*a*) To continue to cooperate with the Secretary-General and among themselves, as well as with the League of Arab States and its specialized organizations, in the follow-up of multilateral proposals aimed at strengthening and expanding cooperation in all fields between the United Nations system and the League of Arab States and its specialized organizations;

(*b*) To strengthen the capacity of the League of Arab States and of its institutions and specialized organizations to benefit from globalization and information technology and to meet the development challenges of the new millennium;

(*c*) To step up cooperation and coordination with the specialized organizations of the League of Arab States in the organization of seminars and training courses and in the preparation of studies;

(*d*) To maintain and increase contacts and improve the mechanism of consultation with the counterpart programmes, organizations and agencies concerned regarding projects and programmes in order to facilitate their implementation;

(*e*) To participate whenever possible with organizations and institutions of the League of Arab States in the execution and implementation of development projects in the Arab region;

(*f*) To inform the Secretary-General of the progress made in their cooperation with the League of Arab States and its specialized organizations and, in particular, of the follow-up action taken on the multilateral and bilateral proposals adopted at the previous meetings between the two organizations;

7. *Also calls upon* the specialized agencies and other organizations and programmes of the United Nations system to increase their cooperation with the League of Arab States and its specialized organizations in the priority sectors of energy, rural development, desertification and green belts, training and vocational education, technology, environment, information and documentation, trade and finance, water resources, development of the agricultural sector, empowerment of women, transport, communications and information, promotion of the role of the private sector and capacity-building;

8. *Requests* the Secretary-General of the United Nations, in cooperation with the Secretary-General of the League of Arab States, to encourage periodic consultation between representatives of the Secretariat of the United Nations and of the General Secretariat of the League of Arab States in order to review and strengthen coordination mechanisms with a view to accelerating implementation of, and follow-up action on, the multilateral projects, proposals and recommendations adopted at the meetings between the two organizations;

9. *Recommends* that the United Nations and all organizations of the United Nations system make the greatest possible use of Arab institutions and technical expertise in projects undertaken in the Arab region;

10. *Reaffirms* that, in order to enhance cooperation and for the purpose of the review and appraisal of progress, a general meeting between representatives of the United Nations system and the League of Arab States should be held once every two years and that joint inter-agency sectoral meetings should also be convened on a biennial basis to address priority areas of major importance to the development of Arab States, on the basis of agreement between the United Nations system and the League of Arab States and its specialized organizations;

11. *Also reaffirms* the importance of holding the sectoral meeting between the United Nations and the League of Arab States and its specialized organizations during 2007 and also of holding the general meeting on cooperation between representatives of the secretariats of the organizations of the United Nations system and the General Secretariat of the League of Arab States and its specialized organizations during 2008;

12. *Requests* the Secretary-General to submit to the General Assembly at its sixty-third session a report on the implementation of the present resolution;

13. *Decides* to include in the provisional agenda of its sixty-third session the sub-item entitled "Cooperation between the United Nations and the League of Arab States".

52nd plenary meeting
13 November 2006

---

* Reissued for technical reasons.

[1] A/61/256 and Add.1.

[2] United Nations, *Treaty Series*, vol. 70, No. 241.

[3] A/47/277-S/24111.

[4] A/50/60-S/1995/1.

Resolution 61/15

[without reference to a Main Committee (A/61/L.21 and Add.1)]

61/15. Report of the International Criminal Court

The General Assembly,

Recalling its resolution 60/29 of 23 November 2005 and all its previous relevant resolutions,

Recalling also that the Rome Statute of the International Criminal Court[1] reaffirms the purposes and principles of the Charter of the United Nations,

Emphasizing that justice, especially transitional justice in conflict and post-conflict societies, is a fundamental building block of sustainable peace,

Noting with satisfaction the fact that the International Criminal Court is fully operational and has achieved considerable progress in its analyses, investigations and judicial proceedings in various situations and cases which were referred to it by States parties to the Rome Statute and by the Security Council, in accordance with the Rome Statute,

Recalling that effective cooperation and assistance by States, the United Nations and other international and regional organizations remains essential for the International Criminal Court to carry out its activities,

Welcoming the continuous support given by civil society to the International Criminal Court,

Expressing its appreciation to the Secretary-General for providing effective and efficient assistance to the International Criminal Court in accordance with the Relationship Agreement between the United Nations and the International Criminal Court ("Relationship Agreement"),[2]

Acknowledging the Relationship Agreement as approved by the General Assembly in its resolution 58/318 of 13 September 2004, including paragraph 3 of the resolution with respect to the payment in full of expenses accruing to the United Nations as a result of the implementation of the Relationship Agreement,[3] which provides a framework for continued cooperation between the Court and the United Nations, which could indlude the facilitation by the United Nations of the Court's field activities, and encouraging the conclusion of supplementary arrangements and agreements, as necessary,

Recognizing the role of the International Criminal Court in a multilateral system that aims to end impunity, establish the rule of law, promote and encourage respect for human rights and achieve sustainable peace, in accordance with international law and the purposes and principles of the Charter,

Expressing its appreciation to the International Criminal Court for providing assistance to the Special Court for Sierra Leone and for granting a leave of absence to its Deputy Prosecutor for Investigations to enable him to work for the International Independent Investigation Commission,

Reiterating the historic significance of the adoption of the Rome Statute,

1. *Welcomes* the report of the International Criminal Court for 2005–2006;[4]

2. *Welcomes* the States that have become parties to the Rome Statute of the International Criminal Court[1] in the past year, and calls upon all States from all regions of the world that are not yet parties to the Rome Statute to consider ratifying or acceding to it without delay;

3. *Calls upon* all States that have not yet done so to consider becoming parties to the Agreement on the Privileges and Immunities of the International Criminal Court;[5]

4. *Encourages* States parties to the Rome Statute that have not yet done so to adopt national legislation to implement obligations emanating from the Rome Statute and to cooperate with the International Criminal Court in the exercise of its functions, and recalls the provision of technical assistance by States parties in this respect;

5. *Welcomes* the effective cooperation and assistance provided to the International Criminal Court by States, the United Nations and other international and regional organizations, and calls upon them to continue providing such cooperation and assistance in the future;

6. *Encourages* States to contribute to the Trust Fund established for the benefit of victims of crimes within the jurisdiction of the International Criminal Court, and of the families of such victims, as well as to the Trust Fund for the participation of least developed countries, and acknowledges with appreciation contributions made to both trust funds so far;

7. *Emphasizes* the importance of the full implementation of the Relationship Agreement,[2] which forms a framework for close cooperation between the two organizations and for consultation on matters of mutual interest pursuant to the provisions of that Agreement and in conformity with the respective provisions of the Charter of the United Nations and the Rome Statute, as well as the need for comprehensive information from the Secretary-General with respect to steps taken in the implementation of the Agreement;

8. *Notes* the establishment and operationalization of the International Criminal Court liaison office to United Nations Headquarters, and encourages the Secretary-General to work closely with that office;

9. *Welcomes* the report of the Secretary-General on the work of the Organization,[6] in which reference is made to the important role of the International Criminal Court in advancing the cause of justice and the rule of law;

10. *Recalls* that, by virtue of article 12, paragraph 3, of the Rome Statute, a State which is not a party to the Statute may, by declaration lodged with the Registrar of the International Criminal Court, accept the exercise of jurisdiction by the Court with respect to specific crimes that are mentioned in paragraph 2 of that article;

11. *Notes* the work of the Special Working Group on the Crime of Aggression, which is open to all States on an equal footing, and encourages all States to consider participating actively in the Working Group with a view to elaborating proposals for a provision on the crime of aggression;

12. *Looks forward* to the fifth session of the Assembly of States Parties to the Rome Statute of the International Criminal Court, to be held in The Hague from 23 November to 1 December 2006, as well as the resumed fifth session to be held in New York from 29 to 31 January 2007, and encourages the widest possible participation of States in these proceedings;

13. *Takes note* of the decision of the Assembly of States Parties to the Rome Statute at its fourth session, while recalling that according to article 112, paragraph 6, of the Rome Statute, the Assembly of States Parties shall meet at the seat of the International Criminal Court or at United Nations Headquarters, to hold its sixth session in New York in 2007, and requests the Secretary-General to provide the necessary services and facilities in accordance with the Relationship Agreement and resolution 58/318;

14. *Invites* the International Criminal Court to submit, in accordance with article 6 of the Relationship Agreement, a report on its activities for 2006–2007, for consideration by the General Assembly at its sixty-second session.

56th plenary meeting
20 November 2006

---

[1] United Nations, *Treaty Series*, vol. 2187, No. 38544.

[2] See A/58/874 and Add.1.

[3] Articles 10 and 13 of the Relationship Agreement.

[4] See A/61/217.

[5] *Official Records of the Assembly of States Parties to the Rome Statute of the International Criminal Court, First session, New York, 3–10 September 2002* (United Nations publication, Sales No. E.03.V.2 and corrigendum), part II.E.

[6] *Official Records of the General Assembly, Sixty-first Session, Supplement No. 1* and corrigendum (A/61/1 and Corr.1).

Resolution 61/16

[without reference to a Main Committee (A/61/L.24)]

61/16. Strengthening of the Economic and Social Council

The General Assembly,

Recalling the 2005 World Summit Outcome,[1]

Recalling also its resolutions 45/264 of 13 May 1991, 50/227 of 24 May 1996, 52/12 B of 19 December 1997, 57/270 B of 23 June 2003, 59/250 of 22 December 2004 and 60/265 of 30 June 2006,

Recalling further its resolution 60/180 of 20 December 2005 and Security Council resolution 1645 (2005) of 20 December 2005,

Reaffirming the role that the Charter of the United Nations and the General Assembly have vested in the Economic and Social Council, and recognizing the need for a more effective Council as a principal body for coordination, policy review, policy dialogue and recommendations on issues of economic and social development, as well as for implementation of the international development goals agreed at the major United Nations conferences and summits, including the Millennium Development Goals,

Reaffirming also the commitments to and emphasizing the need to fully implement the global partnership for development set out in the United Nations Millennium Declaration,[2] the Monterrey Consensus of the International Conference on Financing for Development[3] and the Plan of Implementation of the World Summit on Sustainable Development

("Johannesburg Plan of Implementation")[4] and to enhance the momentum generated by the 2005 World Summit in order to operationalize and implement, at all levels, the commitments set out in the outcomes of the major United Nations conferences and summits, including the 2005 World Summit, in the economic, social and related fields,

Reiterating that the Economic and Social Council should continue to strengthen its role as the central mechanism for system-wide coordination and thus promote the integrated and coordinated implementation of and follow-up to the outcomes of the major United Nations conferences in the economic, social and related fields, in accordance with the Charter and relevant General Assembly resolutions, in particular resolutions 50/227 and 57/270 B,

Resolving to accelerate the implementation of the measures and mechanisms defined in its resolution 57/270 B on integrated and coordinated implementation of and follow-up to the outcomes of the major United Nations conferences and summits in the economic and social fields,

Welcoming Economic and Social Council decision 2006/206 of 10 February 2006, entitled "Adapting the work of the Economic and Social Council",

Recalling that the Economic and Social Council should increase its role in overseeing system-wide coordination and the balanced integration of economic, social and environmental aspects of United Nations policies and programmes aimed at promoting sustainable development, and reaffirming that the Commission on Sustainable Development should continue to be the high-level commission on sustainable development within the United Nations system and serve as a forum for consideration of issues related to integration of the three dimensions of sustainable development,

In pursuance of paragraphs 155 and 156 of the 2005 World Summit Outcome,

1. *Decides* to maintain the current segment structure of the substantive session of the Economic and Social Council;

2. *Also decides* that the Economic and Social Council should continue to promote global dialogue, inter alia, through strengthening existing arrangements, including:

(*a*) The special high-level meeting with the Bretton Woods institutions, the World Trade Organization and the United Nations Conference on Trade and Development;

(*b*) An annual high-level policy dialogue with international financial and trade institutions held in the framework of a strengthened high-level segment of the annual substantive session of the Council;

(*c*) A thematic discussion on a theme from economic, social and related fields to be decided by the Council and informed by a report of the Secretary-General;

3. *Further decides* that the biennial high-level Development Cooperation Forum will be held within the framework of the high-level segment of the Economic and Social Council, while stressing the need to preserve the distinct identity of the Forum so as to facilitate high-level participation, with a view to enhancing the implementation of international development cooperation issues affecting the realization of the internationally agreed development goals, including the Millennium Development Goals, and to promote dialogue to find effective ways to support it;

4. *Decides* that the biennial Development Cooperation Forum will be held in alternate years in the framework of the high-level segment of the Economic and Social Council and that it should:

(*a*) Review trends and progress in international development cooperation and give policy guidance and recommendations to promote more effective international development cooperation;

(*b*) Identify gaps and obstacles with a view to making recommendations on practical measures and policy options to enhance coherence and effectiveness and to promote development cooperation for the realization of the internationally agreed development goals, including the Millennium Development Goals;

(*c*) Provide a platform for Member States to exchange lessons learned and share experiences in formulating, supporting and implementing national development strategies;

(*d*) In accordance with the rules of procedure, be open to participation by all stakeholders, including the organizations of the United Nations, the international financial and trade institutions, the regional organizations, civil society and private sector representatives;

5. *Requests* the Economic and Social Council to consider launching the Development Cooperation Forum during the high-level segment of its substantive session of 2007 and thereafter meeting in New York, starting in 2008;

6. *Decides* that the Economic and Social Council should undertake a regular and periodic review and assessment of international economic and development policies and their impact on development;

7. *Requests* the Secretary-General to prepare an analytical background report for consideration by the Development Cooperation Forum;

8. *Decides* that the Economic and Social Council should hold annual ministerial-level substantive reviews as part of its high-level segment, and also decides that such reviews should be conducted by means of a cross-sectoral approach focusing on thematic issues common to the outcomes of the major United Nations conferences and summits in the economic, social and related fields, including the Millennium Development Goals and other internationally agreed development goals, review progress made in the implementation of the outcomes of those conferences and summits and their follow-up processes and assess its impact on the achievement of the goals and targets of the conferences and summits, and in this regard:

(*a*) Recommends that such reviews provide an opportunity for countries to make voluntary national presentations;

(*b*) Requests the Council to urge the functional commissions and other relevant subsidiary bodies and follow-up mechanisms, as appropriate, to contribute, in accordance with their mandates and taking into account their specificity, to the assessment;

(*c*) Recommends that the Council establish a multi-year programme of work for the ministerial-level substantive reviews;

(*d*) Invites the organizations of the United Nations system, including the Bretton Woods institutions and the World Trade Organization, to contribute within their respective mandates to the consideration by the Council;

9. *Requests* the Economic and Social Council to urge the United Nations regional commissions, in collaboration with other regional and subregional organizations and processes, as appropriate, to contribute, within their mandates, to the review of progress made in the implementation of and follow-up to the outcomes of the major United Nations conferences and summits in the economic, social and related fields and to provide input to the discussions of the Council in accordance with its rules of procedure;

10. *Requests* the Secretary-General, when submitting his reports for the high-level segment, to include a concise, analytical section providing an assessment of progress, identifying gaps and obstacles in implementation and making recommendations to overcome those gaps and obstacles for consideration by Member States;

11. *Decides* that the outcome of the high-level segment should be one ministerial declaration;

12. *Also decides* that the Economic and Social Council should support and complement international efforts aimed at addressing humanitarian emergencies, including natural disasters, in order to promote an improved, coordinated response by the United Nations;

13. *Stresses* the importance of the humanitarian affairs segment of the Economic and Social Council in strengthening the coordination and effectiveness of United Nations humanitarian assistance;

14. *Emphasizes* that in addition to the humanitarian affairs segment, the Economic and Social Council should convene ad hoc meetings, in accordance with its rules of procedure, on specific humanitarian emergencies on the request of the affected Member State and following a recommendation of the Bureau, and that such ad hoc meetings should raise awareness and promote the engagement of all stakeholders in support of international relief efforts aimed at addressing those emergencies;

15. *Reaffirms* the role of the Economic and Social Council in providing overall coordination and guidance for operational development programmes and funds on a system-wide basis, including objectives, priorities and strategies in the implementation of the policies formulated by the General Assembly, as well as in concentrating on cross-cutting and coordination issues related to operational activities, in accordance with relevant Assembly resolutions;

16. *Also reaffirms* the importance of the triennial comprehensive policy review of operational activities, through which the General Assembly establishes key system-wide policy orientations for the development cooperation and country-level modalities of the United Nations system;

17. *Recalls* the role of the Economic and Social Council in providing coordination and guidance to the United Nations system to ensure that those policy orientations are implemented on a system-wide basis in accordance with General Assembly resolutions 48/162 of 20 December 1993, 50/227 and 57/270 B;

18. *Expresses concern* that insufficient provision of conference services and substantive support to the meetings of the Economic and Social Council has at times impeded its ability to fulfil its mandate despite its status as a Charter body, and in this regard decides to ensure provision of full and substantive support and conference services to the Council for all meetings necessary to enable it to fulfil its strengthened mandate;

19. *Recognizes* that the Economic and Social Council, as a Charter body, is entitled to convene meetings as and when needed, with full substantive support and conference services, and in

this regard decides that the Council, beginning with its 2007 session, is entitled to convene additional meetings, of up to two weeks, in order to facilitate the fulfilmenr of its newly assigned responsibilities for organizing the annual ministerial reviews and the Development Cooperation Forum, as well as to hold ad hoc meetings, in order to effectively fulfil its mandate under the Charter;

20. *Recalls* its resolution 60/180 on the Peacebuilding Commission that addresses the special needs of countries emerging from conflict towards recovery, reintegration and reconstruction and assists them in laying the foundation for sustainable development, and in this regard reaffirms the importance of interaction between the Economic and Social Council and the Commission;

21. *Underlines* the experience of the Economic and Social Council in the area of post-conflict peacebuilding and the success of its ad hoc advisory groups on countries emerging from conflict, and invites the Peacebuilding Commission to benefit from it;

22. *Reiterates* that the agenda of the Peacebuilding Commission will be based on, inter alia, requests for advice from the Economic and Social Council with the consent of a concerned Member State in exceptional circumstances on the verge of lapsing or relapsing into conflict and of which the Security Council is not seized in accordance with Article 12 of the Charter;

23. *Reiterates its request* to the Peacebuilding Commission to make the outcomes of its discussions, recommendations and other reports available as United Nations documents to, inter alia, the Economic and Social Council;

24. *Decides* to review the implementation of the present resolution at its sixty-fifth session.

56th plenary meeting
20 November 2006

[1] See resolution 60/1.

[2] See resolution 55/2.

[3] *Report of the International Conference on Financing for Development, Monterrey, Mexico, 18–22 March 2002* (United Nations publication, Sales No. E.02.II.A.7), chap. I, resolution 1, annex.

[4] *Report of the World Summit on Sustainable Development, Johannesburg, South Africa, 26 August–4 September 2002* (United Nations publication, Sales No. E.03.II.A.1 and corrigendum), chap. I, resolution 2, annex.

Resolution 61/17

[without reference to a Main Committee (A/61/L.22 and Add.1)]

61/17. International Year of Reconciliation, 2009

The General Assembly,

Bearing in mind the Charter of the United Nations, including the purposes and principles contained therein, and in particular those of saving succeeding generations from the scourge of war, bringing about by peaceful means, and in conformity with the principles of justice and international law, adjustment or settlement of international disputes or situations which might lead to a breach of the peace, and practising tolerance and living together in peace with one another as good neighbours, thus developing friendly relations among nations and promoting international cooperation to resolve international economic, social, cultural and humanitarian issues,

Recognizing that reconciliation processes are particularly necessary and urgent in countries and regions of the world which have suffered or are suffering situations of conflict that have affected and divided societies in their various internal, national and international facets,

Recognizing also that many of the activities of the United Nations system in general and the international community as a whole to support peacekeeping and peacebuilding, conflict prevention, disarmament, sustainable development, the promotion and protection of human rights and dignity, democracy, the rule of law and governance, inter alia, lead to the initiation and development of reconciliation processes,

Aware that dialogue among opponents from positions of respect and tolerance is an essential element of peace and reconciliation,

Aware also that truth and justice are indispensable elements for the attainment of reconciliation and lasting peace,

Bearing in mind the role of the media in reporting on reconciliation processes,

Convinced that the declaration of an international year of reconciliation at the end of the first decade of the new millennium will provide the international community with the opportunity to pursue, with the active involvement of all stakeholders, efforts to develop reconciliation processes, which are necessary to and a condition for the establishment of firm and lasting peace,

1. *Expresses its steadfast determination* to pursue reconciliation processes in those societies that are affected and/or divided by conflicts;

2. *Decides* to proclaim 2009 the International Year of Reconciliation;

3. *Invites* concerned Governments and international and non-governmental organizations to support reconciliation processes among affected and/or divided societies and to plan and implement adequate cultural, educational and social programmes to promote the concept of reconciliation, including by holding conferences and seminars and disseminating information about the issue.

56th plenary meeting
20 November 2006

Resolution 61/18

[without reference to a Main Committee (A/61/L.25 and Add.1)]

61/18. The situation in Afghanistan

The General Assembly,

Recalling its resolutions 60/32 A and B of 30 November 2005 and all its previous relevant resolutions,

Recalling also all relevant Security Council resolutions and statements by the President of the Council on the situation in Afghanistan, in particular the most recent resolutions 1659 (2006) of 15 February 2006, 1662 (2006) of 23 March 2006 and 1707 (2006) of 12 September 2006, as well as the statement by the President of the Council on 26 July 2006,

Expressing its strong commitment to the implementation of the Afghanistan Compact and the annexes thereto,[1] launched at the London Conference on Afghanistan held on 31 January and 1 February 2006, which provide the framework for the partnership between the Government of Afghanistan and the international community,

Reaffirming its strong commitment to the sovereignty, independence, territorial integrity and national unity of Afghanistan, and respecting its multicultural, multi-ethnic and historical heritage,

Recognizing the urgent need to tackle the challenges in Afghanistan, including terrorist threats, the fight against narcotics, the lack of security, in particular in the south and east, the comprehensive nationwide disbandment of illegal armed groups and the development of Afghan Government institutions, including at the subnational level, the strengthening of the rule of law, the acceleration of justice sector reform, the promotion of national reconciliation, without prejudice to the fulfilment of the measures introduced by the Security Council in its resolution 1267 (1999) of 15 October 1999 and other relevant resolutions, and an Afghan-led transitional justice process, the safe and orderly return of Afghan refugees and internally displaced persons, the promotion and protection of human rights and the advancement of economic and social development,

Expressing in this context its deep concern over attacks against both Afghan and foreign nationals committed to supporting the consolidation of peace, stability and development in Afghanistan, in particular United Nations and diplomatic staff, national and international humanitarian and development personnel, Afghan National Security Forces, the International Security Assistance Force, as well as the Operation Enduring Freedom coalition, and noting with concern that the lack of security is causing some organizations to cease or curtail their humanitarian and development work in some parts of Afghanistan,

Recognizing the progress achieved, while nonetheless remaining deeply concerned about the problem of millions of anti-personnel landmines and explosive remnants of war, which constitute a great danger for the population and a major obstacle for the resumption of economic activities and for recovery and reconstruction efforts,

Noting that, despite improvements in building the security sector, increased terrorist attacks caused by the Taliban, Al-Qaida and other extremist groups, in particular in the south and east of Afghanistan over the past months, and the lack of security caused by criminal activity and the illicit production of and trafficking in drugs, remain a serious challenge, threatening the democratic process as well as reconstruction and economic development,

Noting also that the responsibility for providing security and law and order throughout the country resides with the Government of Afghanistan supported by the Assistance Force and the Operation Enduring Freedom coalition, recognizing the institutional progress achieved in this respect, deeply concerned about the recent increase in violence, and stressing the importance of further extending central government authority to all parts of Afghanistan,

Commending the Afghan National Army and the Afghan National Police, the Assistance Force and the Operation Enduring Freedom coalition for their efforts to improve security conditions in Afghanistan,

Acknowledging, in this context, that the Afghan National Army and the Afghan National Police require additional support to enhance their capability, including through the provision of more modern equipment,

Stressing that regional cooperation constitutes an effective means to promote security and development in Afghanistan,

Reaffirming in this context its continued support for the spirit and the provisions of the Bonn Agreement of 5 December 2001,[2] of the Berlin Declaration, including the annexes thereto, of 1 April 2004[3] and of the Afghanistan Compact of 31 January 2006, and pledging its continued support, after the successful completion of the political transition, to the Government and people of Afghanistan as they rebuild their country, strengthen the foundations of a constitutional democracy and resume their rightful place in the community of nations,

Applauding the inauguration of the Afghan National Assembly on 19 December 2005, which completes the Bonn process, as well as the constitution of the provincial councils,

Welcoming the constitution of the national Government, and noting the importance of it being representative of the ethnic diversity of the country and ensuring also the adequate participation of women,

Welcoming also the finalization of the ten-year strategy for justice reform in Afghanistan, and expressing its appreciation for the appointment and confirmation of a highly qualified Supreme Court,

Welcoming further, in this regard, the guarantee of human rights and fundamental freedoms for all Afghans in the new Constitution as a significant step towards an improved situation of human rights and fundamental freedoms, in particular for women and children,

Recalling Security Council resolution 1325 (2000) of 31 October 2000 on women and peace and security, and applauding the progress achieved in the empowerment of women in Afghan politics as historic milestones in the political process, which will help to consolidate durable peace and national stability in Afghanistan, while noting the need to promote the empowerment of women also at the provincial level,

Noting at the same time with concern reports of continued violations of human rights and of international humanitarian law and violent or discriminatory practices, in particular against women and girls, in certain parts of the country, and stressing the need for adherence to international standards of tolerance and religious freedom,

Welcoming the presentation of the interim Afghanistan National Development Strategy[4] and the adoption of the first report on the Millennium Development Goals by the Government of Afghanistan as well as the further efforts of the Government to achieve the Millennium Development Goals,

Welcoming also the continuing and growing ownership of the rehabilitation and reconstruction efforts by the Government of Afghanistan, and emphasizing the crucial need to achieve ownership in all fields of governance and to improve institutional capabilities, including at the provincial level, in order to use aid more effectively,

Expressing its appreciation for the humanitarian assistance work of the international community in the reconstruction and development of Afghanistan, recognizing the necessity of further addressing the slow pace of change in the living conditions of the Afghan people, and noting the need to strengthen the capacity of the Government of Afghanistan to deliver basic services and to promote development,

Welcoming the continuous return of refugees and internally displaced persons, while noting with concern that conditions in parts of Afghanistan are not yet conducive to safe and sustainable returns to some places of origin and that high concentration of returns to major urban areas have placed an extreme burden on limited urban resources,

Aware of the high vulnerability of Afghanistan to natural disasters and harsh climate conditions, in particular drought or flooding,

Expressing its appreciation for the work of the provincial reconstruction teams and of the executive steering committee,

Recognizing that the social and economic development of Afganistan, specifically the development of alternative gainful and sustainable livelihoods in the formal productive sector, is an important element of the successful implementation of the comprehensive Afghan national drug control strategy and depends to a large extent on enhanced international cooperation with the Government of Afghanistan,

Welcoming the launching on 31 January 2006 of the updated National Drug Control Strategy at the London Conference on Afghanistan,[5]

Deeply concerned about the increased cultivation, production of and trafficking in narcotic drugs in Afghanistan, which is undermining stability and security as well as the political and economic reconstruction of Afghanistan and has dangerous repercussions in the region and far beyond, and commending in this context the publication of the updated National Drug Control Strategy and the reaffirmed commitment of the Government of Afghanistan to rid the country of this pernicious production and trade, including by decisive law enforcement measures,

Expressing its appreciation and strong support for the central and impartial role that the Secretary-General and his Special Representative continue to play in the consolidation of peace and stability in Afghanistan, and underlining the coordinating role of the United Nations in continuing to ensure a seamless transition, under Afghan leadership, from humanitarian relief to recovery and reconstruction,

Welcoming, in this context, the establishment of the Joint Coordination and Monitoring Board pursuant to the Afghanistan Compact as an instrument to further improve coordination between the Government of Afghanistan and its international partners and to monitor the implementation of all benchmarks,

Recognizing the need for a continued strong international commitment to humanitarian assistance and for programmes, under the ownership of the Government of Afghanistan, of recovery, rehabilitation and reconstruction, and expressing, at the same time, its appreciation to the United Nations system and to all States and international and non-governmental organizations whose international and local staff continue to respond positively to the humanitarian, transition and development needs of Afghanistan despite increasing security concerns and difficulties of access in certain areas,

1. *Welcomes* the report of the Secretary-General[6] and the recommendations contained therein;

2. *Strongly condemns* the upsurge of violence throughout Afghanistan, in particular in the southern and eastern parts, owing to the increased violent and terrorist activity by the Taliban, Al-Qaida, other extremist groups and those involved in the narcotics trade, which has resulted in increased casualties among Afghan civilians, Afghan National Security

Forces, the International Security Assistance Force and the Operation Enduring Freedom coalition, as well as among the personnel of Afghan and international aid agencies and all other humanitarian workers;

3. *Stresses* the importance of the provision of sufficient security, welcomes the expansion of the presence of the Assistance Force in southern and eastern Afghanistan, and calls upon Member States to continue contributing personnel, equipment and other resources to the Assistance Force and to further develop the provincial reconstruction teams in close coordination with the Government of Afghanistan and the United Nations Assistance Mission in Afghanistan;

4. *Expresses its appreciation* for the work of the Assistance Mission, and welcomes the extension of its presence in additional provinces, which thus ensures that the United Nations fulfils its essential coordinating role, and encourages the Assistance Mission to continue expansion of its presence throughout the country;

5. *Calls upon* the Government of Afghanistan, with the assistance of the international community, including through the Operation Enduring Freedom coalition and the Assistance Force, in accordance with their respective designated responsibilities, to continue to address the threat to the security and stability of Afghanistan posed by the Taliban, Al-Qaida and other extremist groups as well as by criminal violence, in particular violence involving the drug trade;

6. *Urges* the Government of Afghanistan and local authorities to take all possible steps to ensure the safe and unhindered access of United Nations, development and humanitarian personnel to all affected populations;

7. *Strongly condemns* all acts of violence and intimidation, in particular that directed against development and humanitarian personnel and United Nations and associated personnel as well as against Afghan civilians, including women activists, regrets the loss of life and physical harm, and urges the Government of Afghanistan and local authorities to make every effort, in accordance with General Assembly resolution 60/123 of 15 December 2005, to bring to justice the perpetrators of attacks, to ensure the safety, security and free movement of all United Nations, development and humanitarian personnel and to protect the property of the United Nations and of development or humanitarian organizations;

8. *Welcomes* the successful completion of the disarmament, demobilization and reintegration of former Afghan combatants, which started in October 2003;

9. *Also welcomes* the launching of the programme of disbandment of illegal armed groups, and stresses the importance of advancing its full implementation throughout the country under Afghan ownership, while ensuring further coordination and coherence with other relevant efforts regarding security sector reform and community development;

10. *Further welcomes*, in this context, the commitment of the President of Afghanistan to stand firm on the disbandment of illegal armed groups, at the Second Tokyo Conference on Consolidation of Peace in Afghanistan on 5 July 2006, and encourages the Government of Afghanistan to work actively at national, provincial and local levels to advance this commitment;

11. *Welcomes* the development of the new professional Afghan National Army and the Afghan National Police, calls for accelerated efforts to modernize and strengthen both institutions, welcomes the progress made in the creation of a fair and effective justice system as important steps towards the goal of strengthening the Government of Afghanistan, providing security and ensuring the rule of law throughout the country, and urges the international community to continue to support the efforts of the Government of Afghanistan in these areas in a coordinated manner;

12. *Also welcomes* the completion of the disarmament and demobilization of child soldiers in the Afghan Military Forces, stresses the importance of the reintegration of child soldiers and of care for other children affected by war, commends the Government of Afghanistan for its efforts in this regard, and encourages it to continue efforts in coopertation with the United Nations;

13. *Expresses its concern* about the recruitment and use of child soldiers by illegal armed groups in Afghanistan, reiterates the importance of ending the use of children contrary to international law, and welcomes the accession by Afghanistan to the Convention on the Rights of the Child[7] and the two optional protocols thereto;[8]

14. *Urges* the Government of Afghanistan to meet its responsibilities under the Convention on the Prohibition of the Use, Stockpiling, Production and Transfer of Anti-personnel Mines and on Their Destruction,[9] to cooperate fully with the mine action programme coordinated by the United Nations, and to eliminate all existing stocks of anti-personnel landmines;

15. *Recognizes* the completion of the establishment of democratic institutions according to the Bonn process, notes the challenges lying ahead identified in the Afghanistan Compact,[1] and calls upon the international community to continue to provide sustained support;

16. *Notes with concern* the negative impact of the security situation on the enjoyment of human rights, and calls for all parties to fully respect human rights and international humanitarian law throughout Afghanistan and, with the assistance of the Afghan Independent Human Rights Commission and of the Assistance Mission, to fully implement the human rights provisions of the new Afghan Constitution, and commends the commitment of the Government of Afghanistan in this respect;

17. *Calls for* the full respect of the human rights and fundamental freedoms of all, without discrimination of any kind, including on the basis of gender, ethnicity or religion, in accordance with obligations under the Afghan Constitution and international law;

18. *Stresses* the need to ensure respect for the right to freedom of expression and the right to freedom of thought, conscience or belief;

19. *Continues to emphasize* the necessity of investigating allegations of current and past violations of human rights and of international humanitarian law, including violations committed against persons belonging to ethnic and religious minorities, as well as against women and girls, of facilitating the provision of efficient and effective remedies to the victims and of bringing the perpetrators to justice in accordance with international law;

20. *Reiterates* the important role of the Afghan Independent Human Rights Commission in the promotion and protection of human rights and fundamental freedoms, stresses the need to expand its range of operation in all parts of Afghanistan in accordance with the Afghan Constitution, welcomes the adoption by the Government of Afghanistan of the Action Plan on Peace, Justice and Reconciliation, and stresses the importance of judicial accountability of human rights offenders in accordance with national and international law;

21. *Recalls* Security Council resolution 1325 (2000) on women and peace and security, commends the efforts of the Government of Afghanistan to mainstream gender issues and to protect and promote the equal rights of women and men as guaranteed, inter alia, by virtue of its ratification of the Convention on the Elimination of All Forms of Discrimination against Women,[10] and by the Afghan Constitution, welcomes the level of participation of Afghan women in the parliamentary and provincial council elections, including the election

of female candidates to these bodies, and reiterates the continued importance of the full and equal participation of women in all spheres of Afghan life;

22. *Welcomes* the presentation of the interim national action plan for women in Afghanistan currently under consultation and the significant efforts by the Government of Afghanistan to counter discrimination, urges the Government to actively involve all elements of Afghan society, in particular women, in the development and implementation of relief, rehabilitation, recovery and reconstruction programmes, and encourages the collection and use of statistical data on a sex-disaggregated basis to provide information on gender-based violence and accurately track the progress of the full integration of women into the political, economic and social life of Afghanistan;

23. *Recognizes* the significant progress achieved on gender equality in Afghanistan in recent years, and strongly condemns incidents of discrimination and violence against women in Afghanistan, wherever they occur;

24. *Welcomes* the initiative of the Government of Afghanistan to formulate a national plan of action on combating child trafficking, encourages the Government to formulate the plan of action guided by the Protocol to Prevent, Suppress and Punish Trafficking in Persons, Especially Women and Children, supplementing the United Nations Convention against Transnational Organized Crime,[11] and stresses the importance of considering becoming a party to the Protocol;

25. *Urges* the Government of Afghanistan to continue to effectively reform the public administration sector in order to implement the rule of law and to ensure good governance and accountability at both national and local levels, and stresses the importance of meeting the respective benchmarks of the Afghanistan Compact, with the support of the international community;

26. *Encourages* the Government of Afghanistan to vigorously pursue its efforts to establish a more effective, accountable and transparent administration at all levels of Government leading the fight against corruption in accordance with the Afghanistan Compact, and notes with concern the effects of administrative corruption with regard to security, good governance and combating the narcotics industry;

27. *Stresses once again* the need for further progress on a comprehensive judicial reform in Afghanistan, and urges the Government of Afghanistan and the international community to devote resources also to the reconstruction and reform of the prison sector in order to improve respect for the rule of law and human rights therein, while reducing physical and mental health risks to inmates;

28. *Urges* the Government of Afghanistan to address, with the assistance of the international community, the question of claims for land property through a comprehensive land titling programme, including formal registration of all property and improved security of property rights, and welcomes the steps already taken by the Government in this regard;

29. *Welcomes* the presentation of the interim Afghanistan National Development Strategy at the London Conference on Afghanistan,[4] underlines the need to finalize the Strategy as soon as possible, and urges the international community actively to support this process;

30. *Reiterates* the necessity of providing Afghan children with educational and health facilities in all parts of the country, recognizing the special needs of girls, strongly condemns

terrorist attacks on education facilities, and encourages the Government of Afghanistan, with the assistance of the international community, to expand these facilities, to train professional staff and to promote full and equal access to them by all members of Afghan society, including in remote areas;

31. *Expresses its appreciation* to those Governments that continue to host Afghan refugees, acknowledging the huge burden they have so far shouldered in this regard, and reminds them of their obligations under international refugee law with respect to the protection of refugees, the principle of voluntary return and the right to seek asylum and to allow international access for their protection and care;

32. *Urges* the Government of Afghanistan, acting with the support of the international community, to continue and strengthen its efforts to create the conditions for the voluntary, safe, dignified and sustainable return and reintegration of the remaining Afghan refugees and internally displaced persons;

33. *Calls for* the provision of continued international assistance to the large numbers of Afghan refugees and internally displaced persons to facilitate their voluntary, safe and orderly return and sustainable reintegration into society so as to contribute to the stability of the entire country;

34. *Welcomes* the efforts to date of the Afghan authorities to carry out the updated National Drug Control Strategy presented at the London Conference on Afghanistan on 31 January 2006,[5] and urges the Government of Afghanistan to take decisive action, in particular to stop the processing of and trade in drugs, by pursuing the concrete steps set out in the Strategy and in the Afghanistan Compact;

35. *Calls upon* the international community to assist the Government of Afghanistan in carrying out its National Drug Control Strategy, aimed at eliminating the cultivation, production, trafficking in and consumption of illicit drugs, including through increased support for Afghan law enforcement and criminal justice agencies, rural development, demand reduction, the elimination of illicit crops, increasing public awareness and building the capacity of drug control institutions;

36. *Expresses concern* about the recent increase in the cultivation of opium, notes that opium cultivation, and the related drug production and trafficking, pose a serious threat to security, the rule of law and development in Afghanistan, urges the Government of Afghanistan, supported by the international community, to work to mainstream counter-narcotics throughout all the national programmes, commends the efforts of the Government in this regard, and urges it to increase its efforts against opium cultivation;

37. *Encourages* the international community to increasingly channel counter-narcotics funding through the Government of Afghanistan's counter-narcotics trust fund;

38. *Urges* the Government of Afghanistan, while carrying out its National Drug Control Strategy, to promote the development of sustainable livelihoods in the formal production sector as well as other sectors, thus improving substantially the lives, health and security of the people, particularly in rural areas, and calls upon the international community, in cooperation with the Governement, to continue to assist it in this regard;

39. *Supports* the fight against the illicit trafficking in drugs and precursors within Afghanistan and in neighbouring States and countries along trafficking routes, including increased cooperation among them to strengthen anti-narcotic controls to curb the drug flow;

40. *Welcomes* the outcome of the Second Ministerial Conference on Drug Trafficking Routes from Afghanistan, organized by the Government of the Russian Federation in cooperation with the United Nations Office on Drugs and Crime, held in Moscow from 26 to 28 June 2006, [12] within the framework of the Paris Pact initiative, and therefore calls upon States to strengthen international and regional cooperation to counter the threat to the international community posed by the illicit production of and trafficking in drugs;

41. *Also welcomes* the establishment of the Joint Coordination and Monitoring Board for the implementation of the political commitments of the Afghanistan Compact, and expresses its appreciation for the support to the Assistance Mission and the Government of Afghanistan by the international members of the Board;

42. *Endorses* the key principles for cooperation between the Government of Afghanistan and the international community as referred to in the Afghanistan Compact: respect for the pluralistic culture, values and history of Afghanistan, based on Islam; partnership between the Government of Afghanistan, with its sovereign responsibilities, and the international community, with a central and impartial coordinating role for the United Nations; further engagement of participation and aspiration to ownership of the Afghan people; pursuit of fiscal, institutional and environmental sustainability; building of lasting Afghan capacity and effective State and civil society institutions; ensuring balanced and fair allocation of domestic and international resources throughout the country; recognition of equal rights and responsibilities of men and women in all policies; promotion of regional cooperation; and fight against corruption, and ensuring public transparency and accountability;

43. *Commends* the continuing efforts of the signatories of the Kabul Declaration on Good-neighbourly Relations of 22 December 2002[13] to implement their commitments under the Declaration, including, within that framework, those under the Kabul Declaration of 5 December 2005, adopted at the first Regional Economic Cooperation Conference, and furthermore calls upon all other States to respect and support the implementation of those provisions and to promote regional stability;

44. *Welcomes* efforts by the Governments of Afghanistan and its neighbouring partners to foster trust and cooperation with each other, and looks forward, where appropriate, to increasing cooperation between Afghanistan and all its neighbouring and regional partners against the Taliban, Al-Qaida and other extremist groups and in promoting peace and prosperity in Afghanistan, in the region and beyond;

45. *Appreciates* the efforts of the members of the Tripartite Commission, namely, Afghanistan, Pakistan and the United States of America, to continue to address cross-border activities and to broaden its cooperation, welcomes the participation of the Assistance Force, and calls upon the international community to support those efforts;

46. *Invites* all States, intergovernmental and non-governmental organizations providing assistance to Afghanistan to focus on institution-building in a coordinated manner and to ensure that such work complements and contributes to the development of an economy characterized by sound macroeconomic policies, the development of a financial sector that provides services, inter alia, to microenterprises, small and medium-sized enterprises and households, transparent business regulations and accountability;

47. *Encourages* the international community, including all donor nations, to assist the Government of Afghanistan in making capacity-building and human resources development a cross-cutting priority;

48. *Urges* the international community, in accordance with the Afghanistan Compact, to increase the proportion of donor assistance channelled directly to the core budget, as agreed bilaterally between the Government of Afghanistan and each donor, as well as through other more predictable core budget funding modalities in which the Government participates, such as the Afghanistan Reconstruction Trust Fund, the Law and Order Trust Fund and the Counter-Narcotics Trust Fund;

49. *Urgently appeals* to all States, the United Nations system and international and non-governmental organizations to continue to provide, in close coordination with the Government of Afghanistan and in accordance with its national development strategy, all possible and necessary humanitarian, recovery, reconstruction, financial, technical and material assistance for Afghanistan;

50. *Emphasizes* the need to maintain, strengthen and review civil-military relations among international actors, as appropriate, at all levels in order to ensure complementarity of action based on the different mandates and comparative advantages of the humanitarian, development, law enforcement and military actors present in Afghanistan, bearing in mind the central and impartial coordinating role of the United Nations;

51. *Requests* the Secretary-General to report to the General Assembly every six months during its sixty-first session on developments in Afghanistan, as well as on the progress made in the implementation of the present resolution;

52. *Decides* to include in the provisional agenda of its sixty-second session the item entitled "The situation in Afghanistan".

58th plenary meeting 28
November 2006

---

[1] S/2006/90, annex.

[2] Agreement on Provisional Arrangements in Afghanistan Pending the Re-establishment of Permanent Government Institutions (see S/2001/1154).

[3] Available from www.unama-afg.org.

[4] S/2006/105, annex.

[5] S/2006/106, annex.

[6] A/61/326-S/2006/727.

[7] United Nations, *Treaty Series*, vol. 1577, No. 27531.

[8] Ibid., vol. 2171, No. 27531; and ibid., vol. 2173, No. 27531.

[9] Ibid., vol. 2056, No. 35597.

[10] Ibid., vol. 1249, No. 20378.

[11] Resolution 55/25, annex II.

[12] See A/61/208-S/2006/598, annex.

[13] S/2002/1416, annex.

Resolution 61/19

[without reference to a Main Committee (A/61/L.28 and Add.1)]

61/19. Commemoration of the two-hundredth anniversary of the abolition of the transatlantic slave trade

The General Assembly,

Reaffirming the Universal Declaration of Human Rights[1] which proclaimed that no one shall be held in slavery or servitude and that slavery and the slave trade shall be prohibited in all their forms,

Recalling that the transatlantic slave trade, which operated between the fifteenth and late nineteenth centuries, involved the forced transportation of millions of Africans as slaves, mostly from West Africa to the Americas, thereby enriching the imperial powers of the time,

Honouring the memory of those who died as a result of slavery, including through exposure to the horrors of the middle passage and in revolt against and resistance to enslavement,

Recognizing that the slave trade and slavery are among the worst violations of human rights in the history of humanity, bearing in mind particularly their scale and duration,

Deeply concerned that it has taken the international community almost two hundred years to acknowledge that slavery and the slave trade are a crime against humanity and should always have been so,

Recalling that slavery and the slave trade were declared a crime against humanity by the World Conference against Racism, Racial Discrimination, Xenophobia and Related Intolerance, held in Durban, South Africa, from 31 August to 8 September 2001,[2]

Acknowledging that the slave trade and the legacy of slavery are at the heart of situations of profound social and economic inequality, hatred, bigotry, racism and prejudice, which continue to affect people of African descent today,

Recalling paragraphs 98 to 106 of the Durban Declaration,[2] and emphasizing in particular, the importance of the "provision of effective remedies, recourse, redress, and compensatory and other measures at the national, regional and international levels", aimed at countering the continued impact of slavery and the slave trade,

Recognizing the knowledge gap that exists with regard to the consequences created by the slave trade and slavery, and on the interactions, past and present, generated among the peoples of Europe, Africa, Asia and the Americas, including the Caribbean,

Welcoming the work of the International Scientific Committee for the Slave Route Project of the United Nations Educational, Scientific and Cultural Organization, which aims to correct this knowledge gap, and looks forward to its report in due course,

Recalling resolution 28 adopted by the General Conference of the United Nations Educational, Scientific and Cultural Organization at its thirty-first session, proclaiming 2004 the International Year to Commemorate the Struggle against Slavery and its Abolition,[3] and recalling also that 23 August is that Organization's International Day for the Remembrance of the Slave Trade and its Abolition,

Noting that 2007 will mark the two-hundredth anniversary of the abolition of the transatlantic slave trade, which contributed significantly to the abolition of slavery,

1. *Decides* to designate 25 March 2007 as the International Day for the Commemoration of the Two-hundredth Anniversary of the Abolition of the Transatlantic Slave Trade;

2. *Urges* Member States that have not already done so to develop educational programmes, including through school curricula, designed to educate and inculcate in future generations an understanding of the lessons, history and consequences of slavery and the slave trade;

3. *Decides* to convene, on 26 March 2007, a special commemorative meeting of the General Assembly on the two-hundredth anniversary of the abolition of the transatlantic slave trade;

4. *Requests* the Secretary-General to establish a programme of outreach, with the involvement of Member States and civil society, including non-governmental organizations, to appropriately commemorate the two-hundredth anniversary of the abolition of the transatlantic slave trade;

5. *Also requests* the Secretary-General to submit to the General Assembly at its sixty-second session a special report on initiatives taken by States to implement paragraphs 101 and 102 of the Durban Declaration aimed at countering the legacy of slavery and contributing to the restoration of the dignity of the victims of slavery and the slave trade.[2]

59th plenary meeting
28 November 2006

---

[1] Resolution 217 A (III).

[2] See A/CONF.189/12 and Corr.1, chap. I.

[3] See United Nations Educational, Scientific and Cultural Organization, *Records of the General Conference, Thirty-first Session, Paris, 15 October–3 November 2001,* vol. 1 and corrigendum: *Resolutions*, chap. V.

Resolution 61/20

[on the report of the Second Committee (A/61/427)]

61/20. Commemoration of the sixtieth anniversary of the operations of the United Nations Children's Fund

The General Assembly,

Recalling its resolutions 57 (I) of 11 December 1946, by which it established the International Children's Emergency Fund, 417 (V) of 1 December 1950, by which it affirmed the Fund's decision to devote a greater share of its resources to programmes outside Europe, 802 (VIII) of 6 October 1953, by which it changed the name of the organization to the United Nations Children's Fund and removed the time limits from its mandate, 1391 (XIV) of 20 November 1959, in which it saw aid provided by the Fund as a practical way to carry out the aims proclaimed in the Declaration of the Rights of the Child,[1] and 2057 (XX) of 16 December 1965, in which it applauded the award of the Nobel Peace Prize for 1965 to the United Nations Children's Fund,

Recalling also its resolutions 2855 (XXVI) of 20 December 1971, in which it commended the Fund for its very substantial and significant achievements during its twenty-five years of operation, and 51/192 of 16 December 1996, in which it recognized the important contribution of the Fund in promoting the survival, development and protection of children during its first fifty years of operation,

Recalling further its resolutions 33/83 of 15 December 1978 on the International Year of the Child, 44/25 of 20 November 1989 on the Convention on the Rights of the Child, 45/217 of 21 December 1990 on the World Summit for Children and S-27/2 of 10 May 2002 in which it adopted the document entitled "A world fit for children", annexed to that resolution,

1. *Congratulates* the United Nations Children's Fund on the occasion of its sixtieth anniversary;

2. *Commends* the United Nations Children's Fund for the substantial assistance it has provided to programme countries in achieving the Millennium Development Goals and other agreed development goals in the interest of children;

3. *Commends* the staff of the United Nations Children's Fund and the National Committees and other partners for their contributions to the substantial achievements of the Fund;

4. *Commends* Member States, civil society organizations and the private sector for the generous financial support of the activities of the United Nations Children's Fund, and invites them to consider increasing their support to the work of the Fund;

5. *Requests* the President of the General Assembly to convene, in December 2006, a special commemorative meeting of the Assembly devoted to the sixtieth anniversary of the operations of the United Nations Children's Fund.

59th plenary meeting
28 November 2006

[1] See resolution 1386 (XIV).

Resolution 61/21

[on the report of the Fifth Committee (A/61/592)]

61/21. Renovation of the residence of the Secretary-General

The General Assembly,

Having considered the report of the Secretary-General entitled "Renovation of the residence of the Secretary-General: revised estimates to the programme budget for the biennium 2006–2007"[1] and the related report of the Advisory Committee on Administrative and Budgetary Questions,[2]

1. *Takes note* of the report of the Secretary-General;[1]

2. *Endorses* the observations and recommendations of the Advisory Committee on Administrative and Budgetary Questions contained in its report;[2]

3. *Regrets* that the proposal to renovate the residence of the Secretary-General was not submitted as part of the proposed programme budget for the biennium 2006–2007;

4. *Approves* the renovation of the residence of the Secretary-General;

5. *Authorizes* the Secretary-General to enter into commitments up to an amount of 4,490,400 United States dollars under the programme budget for the biennium 2006–2007, comprising 202,500 dollars under section 1, Overall policymaking, direction and coordination, and 4,287,900 dollars under section 32, Construction, alteration, improvement and major maintenance, and to report on expenditures in the context of the second performance report for the biennium 2006–2007;

6. *Requests* the Secretary-General to ensure, to the extent possible, that activities approved under section 32 of the programme budget for the biennium 2006–2007 are completed within the envisaged time schedule;

7. *Also requests* the Secretary-General to ensure that procurement processes related to the project are conducted in a transparent manner and in full compliance with its relevant resolutions on procurement reform;

8. *Further requests* the Secretary-General to ensure that targeted mitigation measures are put in place pursuant to established minimum operating security standards;

9. *Requests* the Secretary-General to expedite the action referred to in paragraph 2 of the report of the Advisory Committee.

59th plenary meeting
28 November 2006

---

[1] A/61/377.

[2] A/61/523.

Resolution 61/22

[without reference to a Main Committee (A/61/L.31 and Add.1)]

61/22. Committee on the Exercise of the Inalienable Rights of the Palestinian People

The General Assembly,

Recalling its resolutions 181 (II) of 29 November 1947, 194 (III) of 11 December 1948, 3236 (XXIX) of 22 November 1974, 3375 (XXX) and 3376 (XXX) of 10 November 1975, 31/20 of 24 November 1976 and all subsequent relevant resolutions, including those adopted by the General Assembly at its emergency special sessions and resolution 60/36 of 1 December 2005,

Recalling also its resolution 58/292 of 6 May 2004,

Having considered the report of the Committee on the Exercise of the Inalienable Rights of the Palestinian People,[1]

Recalling the mutual recognition between the Government of the State of Israel and the Palestine Liberation Organization, the representative of the Palestinian people, as well as the existing agreements between the two sides and the need for full compliance with those agreements,

Recalling also the Quartet road map to a permanent two-State solution to the Israeli-Palestinian conflict,[2]

Recalling further the advisory opinion rendered on 9 July 2004 by the International Court of Justice on the *Legal Consequences of the Construction of a Wall in the Occupied Palestinian Territory,* [3] and recalling also its resolution ES-10/15 of 20 July 2004,

Reaffirming that the United Nations has a permanent responsibility towards the question of Palestine until the question is resolved in all its aspects in a satisfactory manner in accordance with international legitimacy,

1. *Expresses its appreciation* to the Committee on the Exercise of the Inalienable Rights of the Palestinian People for its efforts in performing the tasks assigned to it by the General Assembly, and takes note of its annual report,[1] including the conclusions and valuable recommondations contained in chapter VII thereof;

2. *Requests* the Committee to continue to exert all efforts to promote the realization of the inalienable rights of the Palestinian people, to support the Middle East peace process and to mobilize international support for and assistance to the Palestinian people, and authorizes the Committee to make such adjustments in its approved programme of work as it may consider appropriate and necessary in the light of developments and to report thereon to the General Assembly at its sixty-second session and thereafter;

3. *Also requests* the Committee to continue to keep under review the situation relating to the question of Palestine and to report and make suggestions to the General Assembly, the Security Council or the Secretary-General, as appropriate;

4. *Further requests* the Committee to continue to extend its cooperation and support to Palestinian and other civil society organizations in order to mobilize international solidarity and support for the Palestinian people, particularly during this critical period of humanitarian hardship and financial crisis, with the overall aim of promoting the achievement by the Palestinian people of its inalienable rights and for a peaceful settlement of the question of Palestine, and to continue to involve additional civil society organizations in its work;

5. *Requests* the United Nations Conciliation Commission for Palestine, established under General Assembly resolution 194 (III), and other United Nations bodies associated with the question of Palestine to continue to cooperate fully with the Committee and to make available to it, at its request, the relevant information and documentation which they have at their disposal;

6. *Invites* all Governments and organizations to extend their cooperation to the Committee in the performance of its tasks;

7. *Requests* the Secretary-General to circulate the report of the Committee to all the competent bodies of the United Nations, and urges them to take the necessary action, as appropriate;

8. *Also requests* the Secretary-General to continue to provide the Committee with all the necessary facilities for the performance of its tasks.

63rd plenary meeting
1 December 2006

---

[1] *Official Records of the General Assembly, Sixty-first Session, Supplement No. 35* (A/61/35).

[2] S/2003/529, annex.

[3] See A/ES-10/273 and Corr.1

Resolution 61/23

[without reference to a Main Committee (A/61/L.32)]

61/23. Division for Palestinian Rights of the Secretariat

The General Assembly,

Having considered the report of the Committee on the Exercise of the Inalienable Rights of the Palestinian People,[1]

Taking note in particular of the relevant information contained in chapter V.B of that report,

Recalling its resolution 32/40 B of 2 December 1977 and all subsequent relevant resolutions, including resolution 60/37 of 1 December 2005,

1. *Notes with appreciation* the action taken by the Secretary-General in compliance with its resolution 60/37;

2. *Considers* that the Division for Palestinian Rights of the Secretariat continues to make a useful and constructive contribution by assisting the Committee on the Exercise of the Inalienable Rights of the Palestinian People in the implementation of its mandate;

3. *Requests* the Secretary-General to continue to provide the Division with the necessary resources and to ensure that it continues to carry out its programme of work as detailed in the relevant earlier resolutions, in consultation with the Committee on the Exercise of the Inalienable Rights of the Palestinian People and under its guidance, including, in particular, the organization of international meetings and conferences in various regions with the participation of all sectors of the international community, liaison and cooperation with civil society, the further development and expansion of the documents collection of the United Nations Information System on the Question of Palestine, the preparation and widest possible dissemination of publications and information materials on various aspects of the question of Palestine and the provision of the annual training programme for staff of the Palestinian Authority;

4. *Also requests* the Secretary-General to ensure the continued cooperation of the Department of Public Information and other units of the Secretariat in enabling the Division to perform its tasks and in covering adequately the various aspects of the question of Palestine;

5. *Invites* all Governments and organizations to extend their cooperation to the Division in the performance of its tasks;

6. *Requests* the Division, as part of the observance of the International Day of Solidarity with the Palestinian People on 29 November, to continue to organize, under the guidance of the Committee on the Exercise of the Inalienable Rights of the Palestinian People, an annual exhibit on Palestinian rights or a cultural event in cooperation with the Permanent Observer Mission of Palestine to the United Nations, and encourages Member States to continue to give the widest support and publicity to the observance of the Day of Solidarity.

63rd plenary meeting
1 December 2006

---

[1] *Official Records of the General Assembly, Sixty-first Session, Supplement No. 35* (A/61/35).

Resolution 61/24

[without reference to a Main Committee (A/61/L.33)]

61/24. Special information programme on the question of Palestine of the Department of Public Information of the Secretariat

The General Assembly,

Having considered the report of the Committee on the Exercise of the Inalienable Rights of the Palestinian People,[1]

Taking note in particular of the information contained in chapter VI of that report,

Recalling its resolution 60/38 of 1 December 2005,

Convinced that the worldwide dissemination of accurate and comprehensive information and the role of civil society organizations and institutions remain of vital importance in heightening awareness of and support for the inalienable rights of the Palestinian people,

Recalling the mutual recognition between the Government of the State of Israel and the Palestine Liberation Organization, the representative of the Palestinian people, as well as the existing agreements between the two sides and the need for full compliance with those agreements,

Recalling also the Quartet road map to a permanent two-State solution to the Israeli-Palestinian conflict,[2]

Recalling further the advisory opinion rendered on 9 July 2004 by the International Court of Justice on the *Legal Consequences of the Construction of a Wall in the Occupied Palestinian Territory*,[3]

Reaffirming that the United Nations has a permanent responsibility towards the question of Palestine until the question is resolved in all its aspects in a satisfactory manner in accordance with international legitimacy,

1. *Notes with appreciation* the action taken by the Department of Public Information of the Secretariat in compliance with resolution 60/38;

2. *Considers* that the special information programme on the question of Palestine of the Department is very useful in raising the awareness of the international community concerning the question of Palestine and the situation in the Middle East and that the programme is contributing effectively to an atmosphere conducive to dialogue and supportive of the peace process;

3. *Requests* the Department, in full cooperation and coordination with the Committee on the Exercise of the Inalienable Rights of the Palestinian People, to continue, with the necessary flexibility as may be required by developments affecting the question of Palestine, its special information programme for the biennium 2006–2007, in particular:

(*a*) To disseminate information on all the activities of the United Nations system relating to the question of Palestine, including reports on the work carried out by the relevant United Nations organizations;

(*b*) To continue to issue and update publications on the various aspects of the question of Palestine in all fields, including materials concerning the recent developments in that regard, in particular the efforts for peace;

(*c*) To expand its collection of audio-visual material on the question of Palestine and to continue the production and preservation of such material and the updating of the exhibit in the Secretariat;

(*d*) To organize and promote fact-finding news missions for journalists to the Occupied Palestinian Territory, including East Jerusalem;

(*e*) To organize international, regional and national seminars or encounters for journalists, aiming in particular at sensitizing public opinion to the question of Palestine;

(*f*) To continue to provide assistance to the Palestinian people in the field of media development, in particular to strengthen the annual training programme for Palestinian broadcasters and journalists.

63rd plenary meeting
1 December 2006

[1] *Official Records of the General Assembly, Sixty-first Session, Supplement No. 35* (A/61/35).

[2] S/2003/529, annex.

[3] See A/ES-10/273 and Corr.1.

Resolution 61/25

[without reference to a Main Committee (A/61/L.34)]

61/25. Peaceful settlement of the question of Palestine

The General Assembly,

Recalling its relevant resolutions, including those adopted by its tenth emergency special session,

Recalling also its resolution 58/292 of 6 May 2004,

Recalling further relevant Security Council resolutions, including resolutions 242 (1967) of 22 November 1967, 338 (1973) of 22 October 1973, 1397 (2002) of 12 March 2002, 1515 (2003) of 19 November 2003 and 1544 (2004) of 19 May 2004,

Welcoming the affirmation by the Security Council of the vision of a region where two States, Israel and Palestine, live side by side within secure and recognized borders,

Noting with concern that it has been fifty-nine years since the adoption of resolution 181 (II) of 29 November 1947 and thirty-nine years since the occupation of Palestinian territory, including East Jerusalem, in 1967,

Having considered the report of the Secretary-General submitted pursuant to the request made in its resolution 60/39 of 1 December 2005,[1]

Reaffirming the permanent responsibility of the United Nations with regard to the question of Palestine until the question is resolved in all its aspects in accordance with international law,

Recalling the advisory opinion rendered on 9 July 2004 by the International Court of Justice on the *Legal Consequences of the Construction of a Wall in the Occupied Palestinian Territory*, [2] and recalling also its resolution ES-10/15 of 20 July 2004,

Convinced that achieving a just, lasting and comprehensive settlement of the question of Palestine, the core of the Arab-Israeli conflict, is imperative for the attainment of comprehensive and lasting peace and stability in the Middle East,

Aware that the principle of equal rights and self-determination of peoples is among the purposes and principles enshrined in the Charter of the United Nations,

Affirming the principle of the inadmissibility of the acquisition of territory by war,

Recalling its resolution 2625 (XXV) of 24 October 1970,

Reaffirming the illegality of the Israeli settlements in the Palestinian territory occupied since 1967,

Reaffirming also the illegality of Israeli actions aimed at changing the status of Jerusalem, including measures such as the so-called E-l plan and all other unilateral measures aimed at altering the status of the city and the territory as a whole,

Reaffirming further that the construction by Israel, the occupying Power, of a wall in the Occupied Palestinian Territory, including in and around East Jerusalem, and its associated regime, are contrary to international law,

Expressing deep concern about the Israeli policy of closure and the severe restrictions, including curfews and the permit regime, that continue to be imposed on the movement of persons and goods, including medical and humanitarian personnel and goods, throughout the Occupied Palestinian Territory, including East Jerusalem, and the consequent negative impact on the socio-economic situation of the Palestinian people, which remains that of a dire humanitarian crisis,

Concerned about the continued establishment of Israeli checkpoints in the Occupied Palestinian Territory, including East Jerusalem, and the transformation of several of these checkpoints into structures akin to permanent border crossings inside the Occupied Palestinian Territory, which are severely impairing the territorial contiguity of the Territory and severely undermining efforts to rehabilitate and develop the Palestinian economy,

Affirming once again the right of all States in the region to live in peace within secure and internationally recognized borders,

Recalling the mutual recognition between the Government of the State of Israel and the Palestine Liberation Organization, the representative of the Palestinian people,[3] and the agreements concluded between the two sides and the need for full compliance with those agreements,

Recalling also the endorsement by the Security Council, in resolution 1515 (2003), of the Quartet road map to a permanent two-State solution to the Israeli-Palestinian conflict,[4] and stressing the urgent need for its implementation and compliance with its provisions,

Welcoming the efforts of the Arab Foreign Ministers, demonstrated in the meeting of the Security Council on 21 September 2006, who called for, among other things, a solution to the conflict on the basis of relevant United Nations resolutions, especially from the Security Council, the Arab Peace Initiative and the road map,

Welcoming also the important contribution to the peace process of the United Nations Special Coordinator for the Middle East Peace Process and Personal Representative of the Secretary-General to the Palestine Liberation Organization and the Palestinian Authority, including in the framework of the activities of the Quarter,

Welcoming further the "Stockholm Donor Conference on the Humanitarian Situation in the Palestinian Territories" of 1 September 2006 and encouraging further donor meetings, as well as the establishment of international mechanisms, and in this regard acknowledging the Temporary International Mechanism, to provide assistance to the Palestinian people to alleviate the financial crisis and the dire socio-economic and humanitarian situation being faced by the Palestinian people,

Recognizing the efforts being undertaken by the Palestinian Authority, with international support, to rebuild, reform and strengthen its damaged institutions, and emphasizing the need to preserve the Palestinian institutions and infrastructure,

Expressing its concern over the tragic events that have occurred in the Occupied Palestinian Territory, including East Jerusalem, since 28 September 2000, including the large number of deaths and injuries, mostly among Palestinian civilians, the widespread destruction of public and private Palestinian property and infrastructure, the internal displacement of civilians, and the serious deterioration of the socio-economic and humanitarian conditions of the Palestinian people,

Expressing its grave concern over the repeated military actions in the Occupied Palestinian Territory and the reoccupation of Palestinian population centres by the Israeli occupying forces, and emphasizing in this regard the need for the implementation by both sides of the Sharm el-Sheikh understandings,

Welcoming the Palestinian truce initiative and its acceptance by Israel that came into effect on 26 November 2006, and urging both sides to maintain this truce, which could pave the way for genuine negotiations towards a just resolution to the conflict, and extend it to the West Bank,

Emphasizing the importance of the safety and well-being of all civilians in the whole Middle East region, and condemning all acts of violence and terror against civilians on both sides, including the suicide bombings, the extrajudicial executions and the excessive use of force,

Noting the Israeli withdrawal from within the Gaza Strip and parts of the northern West Bank and the importance of the dismantlement of the settlements therein as a step towards the implementation of the road map,

Stressing the urgent need for sustained and active international involvement, including by the Quartet, to support both parties in revitalizing the peace process towards the resumption and acceleration of direct negotiations between the parties for the achievement of a just, lasting and comprehensive peace settlement, in accordance with the road map,

Welcoming the initiatives and efforts undertaken by civil society in pursuit of a peaceful settlement of the question of Palestine,

Taking note of the findings by the International Court of Justice, in its advisory opinion, including on the urgent necessity for the United Nations as a whole to redouble its efforts to bring the Israeli-Palestinian conflict, which continues to pose a threat to international peace and security, to a speedy conclusion, thereby establishing a just and lasting peace in the region,[5]

1. *Reaffirms* the necessity of achieving a peaceful settlement of the question of Palestine, the core of the Arab-Israeli conflict, in all its aspects, and of intensifying all efforts towards that end;

2. *Also reaffirms* its full support for the Middle East peace process, which began in Madrid, and the existing agreements between the Israeli and Palestinian sides, stresses the necessity for the establishment of a comprehensive, just and lasting peace in the Middle East, and welcomes in this regard the ongoing efforts of the Quartet;

3. *Welcomes* the Arab Peace Initiative adopted by the Council of the League of Arab States at its fourteenth session, held in Beirut on 27 and 28 March 2002;[6]

4. *Calls upon* the parties themselves, with the support of the Quartet and other interested parties, to exert all efforts necessary to halt the deterioration of the situation, to reverse all measures taken on the ground since 28 September 2000 and to immediately resume direct peace negotiations towards the conclusion of a final peaceful settlement on the basis of relevant United Nations resolutions, especially from the Security Council, the Arab Peace Initiative, the terms of reference of the Madrid Conference and the road map;[4]

5. *Calls upon* the Quartet, together with the international community, to take immediate steps, including confidence-building measures between the parties, aimed at stabilizing the situation and restarting the peace process;

6. *Stresses* the need for a speedy end to the reoccupation of Palestinian population centres and for the complete cessation of all acts of violence, including military attacks, destruction and acts of terror;

7. *Also stresses* the need for the immediate implementation of the Sharm el-Sheikh understandings;

8. *Calls upon* both parties to fulfil their obligations in respect of the implementation of the road map by taking parallel and reciprocal steps in this regard, and stresses the importance and urgency of establishing a credible and effective third-party monitoring mechanism, including all members of the Quartet;

9. *Notes* the Israeli withdrawal from within the Gaza Strip and parts of the northern West Bank and the dismantlement of the settlements therein as a step towards the implementation of the road map;

10. *Emphasizes* the need for the parties, with the help of the international community, speedily and fully to resolve all remaining issues in the Gaza Strip, including a durable arrangement for the border crossings, the airport, the construction of the seaport, the removal of the rubble and the establishment of a permanent physical link between the Gaza Strip and the West Bank, and stresses also the need for the full implementation by both parties of the Agreement on Movement and Access and the Agreed Principles for the Rafah Crossing, of 15 November 2005;

11. *Calls upon* Israel, the occupying Power, to comply strictly with its obligations under international law, including international humanitarian law, and that it cease all of its measures that are contrary to international law and unilateral actions in the Occupied Palestinian Territory, including East Jerusalem, that are aimed at altering the character and status of the Territory, including via the de facto annexation of land, and thus at prejudging the final outcome of peace negotiations;

12. *Demands accordingly* that Israel, the occupying Power, comply with its legal obligations under international law, as mentioned in the advisory opinion[2] and as demanded in resolutions ES-10/13 of 21 October 2003 and ES-10/15 of 20 July 2004 and, inter alia, that it immediately cease its construction of the wall in the Occupied Palestinian Territory, including East Jerusalem, and calls upon all States Members of the United Nations to comply with their legal obligations, as mentioned in the advisory opinion;

13. *Reiterates its demand* for the complete cessation of all Israeli settlement activities in the Occupied Palestinian Territory, including East Jerusalem, and in the occupied Syrian Golan, and calls for the full implementation of the relevant Security Council resolutions;

14. *Reaffirms its commitment*, in accordance with international law, to the two-State solution of Israel and Palestine, living side by side in peace and security within recognized borders, based on the pre-1967 borders;

15. *Stresses* the need for:

(*a*) The withdrawal of Israel from the Palestinian territory occupied since 1967;

(*b*) The realization of the inalienable rights of the Palestinian people, primarily the right to self-determination and the right to their independent State;

16. *Also stresses* the need for resolving the problem of Palestine refugees in conformity with its resolution 194 (III) of 11 December 1948;

17. *Urges* Member States to expedite the provision of economic, humanitarian and technical assistance to the Palestinian people and the Palestinian Authority during this critical period to help to alleviate the humanitarian crisis being faced by the Palestinian people, rehabilitate the Palestinian economy and infrastructure and support the rebuilding, restructuring and reform of Palestinian institutions;

18. *Requests* the Secretary-General to continue his efforts with the parties concerned, and in consultation with the Security Council, towards the attainment of a peaceful settlement of the question of Palestine and the promotion of peace in the region and to submit to the General Assembly at its sixty-second session a report on these efforts and on developments on this matter.

63rd plenary meeting
1 December 2006

---

[1] A/61/355-S/2006/748.

[2] See A/ES-10/273 and Corr.1.

[3] See A/48/486-S/26560, annex.

[4] S/2003/529, annex.

[5] See A/ES-10/273 and Corr.1, advisory opinion, para. 161.

[6] A/56/1026-S/2002/932, annex II, resolution 14/221.

Resolution 61/26

[without reference to a Main Committee (A/61/L.35 and Add.1)]

61/26. Jerusalem

The General Assembly,

Recalling its resolution 181 (II) of 29 November 1947, in particular its provisions regarding the City of Jerusalem,

Recalling also its resolution 36/120 E of 10 December 1981 and all subsequent resolutions, including resolution 56/31 of 3 December 2001, in which it, inter alia, determined that all legislative and administrative measures and actions taken by Israel, the occupying Power, which have altered or purported to alter the character and status of the Holy City of Jerusalem, in particular the so-called "Basic Law" on Jerusalem and the proclamation of Jerusalem as the capital of Israel, were null and void and must be rescinded forthwith,

Recalling further the Security Council resolutions relevant to Jerusalem, including resolution 478 (1980) of 20 August 1980, in which the Council, inter alia, decided not to recognize the "Basic Law" on Jerusalem,

Recalling the advisory opinion rendered on 9 July 2004 by the International Court of Justice on the *Legal Consequences of the Construction of a Wall in the Occupied Palestinian Territory*,[1] and recalling resolution ES-10/15 of 20 July 2004,

Expressing its grave concern about any action taken by any body, governmental or non-governmental, in violation of the above-mentioned resolutions,

Expressing its grave concern in particular about the continuation by Israel, the occupying Power, of illegal settlement activities, including the so-called E-1 plan, and its construction of the wall in and around East Jerusalem, and the further isolation of the city from the rest of the Occupied Palestinian Territory, which is having a detrimental effect on the lives of Palestinians and could prejudge a final status agreement on Jerusalem,

Reaffirming that the international community, through the United Nations, has a legitimate interest in the question of the City of Jerusalem and the protection of the unique spiritual, religious and cultural dimensions of the city, as foreseen in relevant United Nations resolutions on this matter,

Having considered the report of the Secretary-General,[2]

1. *Reiterates its determination* that any actions taken by Israel, the occupying Power, to impose its laws, jurisdiction and administration on the Holy City of Jerusalem are illegal and therefore null and void and have no validity whatsoever, and calls upon Israel to cease all such illegal and unilateral measures;

2. *Welcomes* the decision of those States that had established diplomatic missions in Jerusalem to withdraw their missions from the city, in compliance with Security Council resolution 478 (1980);

3. *Stresses* that a comprehensive, just and lasting solution to the question of the City of Jerusalem should take into account the legitimate concerns of both the Palestinian and Israeli sides and should include internationally guaranteed provisions to ensure the freedom

of religion and of conscience of its inhabitants, as well as permanent, free and unhindered access to the holy places by the people of all religions and nationalities;

4. *Requests* the Secretary-General to report to the General Assembly at its sixty-second session on the implementation of the present resolution.

63rd plenary meeting
1 December 2006

[1] See A/ES-10/273 and Corr.1.

[2] A/61/298.

Resolution 61/27

[without reference to a Main Committee (A/61/L.36)]

61/27. The Syrian Golan

The General Assembly,

Having considered the item entitled "The situation in the Middle East",

Taking note of the report of the Secretary-General,[1]

Recalling Security Council resolution 497 (1981) of 17 December 1981,

Reaffirming the fundamental principle of the inadmissibility of the acquisition of territory by force, in accordance with international law and the Charter of the United Nations,

Reaffirming once more the applicability of the Geneva Convention relative to the Protection of Civilian Persons in Time of War, of 12 August 1949, [2] to the occupied Syrian Golan,

Deeply concerned that Israel has not withdrawn from the Syrian Golan, which has been under occupation since 1967, contrary to the relevant Security Council and General Assembly resolutions,

Stressing the illegality of the Israeli settlement construction and other activities in the occupied Syrian Golan since 1967,

Noting with satisfaction the convening in Madrid on 30 October 1991 of the Peace Conference on the Middle East, on the basis of Security Council resolutions 242 (1967) of 22 November 1967, 338 (1973) of 22 October 1973 and 425 (1978) of 19 March 1978 and the formula of land for peace,

Expressing grave concern over the halt in the peace process on the Syrian track, and expressing the hope that peace talks will soon resume from the point they had reached,

1. *Declares* that Israel has failed so far to comply with Security Council resolution 497 (1981);

2. *Also declares* that the Israeli decision of 14 December 1981 to impose its laws, jurisdiction and administration on the occupied Syrian Golan is null and void and has no validity whatsoever, as confirmed by the Security Council in its resolution 497 (1981), and calls upon Israel to rescind it;

3. *Reaffirms its determination* that all relevant provisions of the Regulations annexed to the Hague Convention of 1907,[3] and the Geneva Convention relative to the Protection of Civilian Persons in Time of War,[2] continue to apply to the Syrian territory occupied by Israel since 1967, and calls upon the parties thereto to respect and ensure respect for their obligations under those instruments in all circumstances;

4. *Determines once more* that the continued occupation of the Syrian Golan and its de facto annexation constitute a stumbling block in the way of achieving a just, comprehensive and lasting peace in the region;

5. *Calls upon* Israel to resume the talks on the Syrian and Lebanese tracks and to respect the commitments and undertakings reached during the previous talks;

6. *Demands once more* that Israel withdraw from all the occupied Syrian Golan to the line of 4 June 1967 in implementation of the relevant Security Council resolutions;

7. *Calls upon* all the parties concerned, the co-sponsors of the peace process and the entire international community to exert all the necessary efforts to ensure the resumption of the peace process and its success by implementing Security Council resolutions 242 (1967) and 338 (1973);

8. *Requests* the Secretary-General to report to the General Assembly at its sixty-second session on the implementation of the present resolution.

63rd plenary meeting
1 December 2006

---

[1] A/61/298.

[2] United Nations, *Treaty Series*, vol. 75, No. 973.

[3] See Carnegie Endowment for International Peace, *The Hague Conventions and Declarations of 1899 and 1907* (New York, Oxford University Press, 1915).

Resolution 61/28

[without reference to a Main Committee (A/61/L.27 and Add.1)]

61/28. The role of diamonds in fuelling conflict: breaking the link between the illicit transaction of rough diamonds and armed conflict as a contribution to prevention and settlement of conflicts

The General Assembly,

Recognizing that the trade in conflict diamonds continues to be a matter of serious international concern, which can be directly linked to the fuelling of armed conflict, the activities of rebel movements aimed at undermining or overthrowing legitimate Governments and the illicit traffic in and proliferation of armaments, especially small arms and light weapons,

Recognizing also the devastating impact of conflicts fuelled by the trade in conflict diamonds on the peace, safety and security of people in affected countries, and the systematic and gross human rights violations that have been perpetrated in such conflicts,

Noting the negative impact of such conflicts on regional stability and the obligations placed upon States by the Charter of the United Nations regarding the maintenance of international peace and security,

Recognizing, therefore, that continued action to curb the trade in conflict diamonds is imperative,

Recalling that the elimination of illicit diamonds from legitimate trade is the primary objective of the Kimberley Process,

Bearing in mind the positive benefits of the legitimate diamond trade to producing countries, and underlining the need for continued international action to prevent the problem of conflict diamonds from negatively affecting the trade in legitimate diamonds, which makes a critical contribution to the economies of many of the producing, exporting and importing States, especially developing States,

Noting that the vast majority of rough diamonds produced in the world are from legitimate sources,

Recalling the Charter and all the relevant resolutions of the Security Council related to conflict diamonds, and determined to contribute to and support the implementation of the measures provided for in those resolutions,

Recalling also Security Council resolution 1459 (2003) of 28 January 2003, in which the Council strongly supported the Kimberley Process Certification Scheme[1] as a valuable contribution aganist trafficking in conflict diamonds,

Welcoming the important contribution of the Kimberley Process, which was initiated by African diamond-producing countries,

Noting with satisfaction that the implementation of the Kimberley Process Certification Scheme continues to have a positive impact in reducing the opportunity for conflict diamonds to play a role in fuelling armed conflict and would help to protect legitimate trade and ensure the effective implementation of the relevant resolutions on trade in conflict diamonds,

Recalling its resolutions 55/56 of 1 December 2000, 56/263 of 13 March 2002, 57/302 of 15 April 2003, 58/290 of 14 April 2004, 59/144 of 15 December 2004 and 60/182 of 20 December 2005, in which it called for the development and implementation as well as a periodic review of proposals for a simple, effective and pragmatic international certification scheme for rough diamonds,

Welcoming, in this regard, the implementation of the Kimberley Process Certification Scheme in such a way as not to impede the legitimate trade in diamonds or impose an undue burden on Governments or industry, particularly smaller producers, nor hinder the development of the diamond industry,

Welcoming also the decision of forty-seven Kimberley Process participants, representing seventy-one countries, including the twenty-five members of the European Union represented by the European Commission, to address the problem of conflict diamonds by participating in the Process and implementing the Kimberley Process Certification Scheme,

Welcoming further the important contributions made and that continue to be made by the diamond industry, in particular the World Diamond Council, as well as civil society, to assist international efforts to stop the trade in conflict diamonds,

Welcoming the voluntary self-regulation initiatives for the diamond industry announced by the World Diamond Council, and recognizing that a system of such voluntary self-regulation will contribute, as described in the Interlaken Declaration of 5 November 2002 on the Kimberley Process Certification Scheme for Rough Diamonds,[2] to ensuring the effectiveness of national systems of internal control for rough diamonds,

Appreciating in this regard the decision taken by the plenary meeting of the Kimberley Process, held in Gaborone from 6 to 9 November 2006, based on calls from participants, civil society and the World Diamond Council urging stronger internal control standards for participants, together with measures offering clearer guidance on implementing effective controls from mine to export, stronger government oversight of the diamond industry, and spot checks of industry compliance,

Noting with appreciation that the Kimberley Process has pursued its deliberations on an inclusive basis, involving concerned stakeholders, including producing, exporting and importing States, the diamond industry and civil society, as well as applicants,

Recognizing that State sovereignty should be fully respected and that the principles of equality, matual benefits and consensus should be adhered to,

Recognizing also that the Kimberley Process Certification Scheme, which came into effect on 1 January 2003, will be credible only if all participants have requisite national legislation coupled with effective and credible internal systems of control designed to eliminate the presence of conflict diamonds in the chain of producing, exporting and importing rough diamonds within their own territories, while taking into account that differences in production methods and trading practices, as well as differences in institutional controls thereof, may require different approaches to meeting minimum standards,

1. *Reaffirms its strong and continuing support* for the Kimberley Process Certification Scheme[1] and the Kimberley Process as a whole;

2. *Recognizes* that the Kimberley Process Certification Scheme can help to ensure the effective implementation of relevant resolutions of the Security Council containing sanctions on the trade in conflict diamonds and act as a mechanism for the prevention of future conflicts, and calls for the full implementation of existing Council measures targeting the illicit trade in rough diamonds, particularly conflict diamonds which play a role in fuelling conflict;

3. *Also recognizes* the important contributions that the international efforts to address the problem of conflict diamonds, including the Kimberley Process Certification Scheme, have made to the settlement of conflicts and the consolidation of peace in Angola, the Democratic Republic of the Congo, Liberia and Sierra Leone;

4. *Takes note* of Security Council resolution 1643 (2005) of 15 December 2005 which calls upon the States in the West Africa region that are not participants in the Kimberley Process to intensify their efforts to join the Process, stresses that the widest possible participation in the Kimberley Process Certification Scheme is essential, and encourages all Member States to contribute to the work of the Process by seeking membership, participating actively in the Certification Scheme and complying with its undertakings;

5. *Takes note with appreciation* of the report of the Chair of the Kimberley Process submitted pursuant to resolution 60/182, [3] and congratulates the Governments, the regional economic integration organization, the diamond industry and civil society participating in the

Process for contributing to the development, implementation and monitoring of the Kimberley Process Certification Scheme;

6. *Notes* the decision of the General Council of the World Trade Organization of 15 May 2003 granting a waiver with respect to the measures taken to implement the Kimberley Process Certification Scheme, effective from 1 January 2003 to 31 December 2006, [4] and the decision of the General Council of 17 November 2006 granting an extension of the waiver until 31 December 2012;[5]

7. *Notes with satisfaction* that in line with paragraph 7 of its resolution 60/182, the preliminary development of "footprints" that characterize diamond production from Côte d'Ivoire has been undertaken, and encourages expeditious commencement of further work to develop similar footprints for other diamond producers;

8. *Notes with appreciation* the contribution of the Kimberley Process in preparing a detailed assessment of the volume of rough diamonds produced in and exported from Côte d'Ivoire as requested by Security Council resolution 1643 (2005) and, recognizing the cooperation between the Process and the United Nations Operation in Côte d'Ivoire, calls for the full implementation of the resolution on the subject of illicit diamond production in Côte d'Ivoire adopted by the plenary meeting of the Process held in Moscow from 15 to 17 November 2005, and encourages continued cooperation between the Process and the United Nations in tackling this issue;

9. *Also notes with appreciation* the action taken by the Kimberley Process to address concerns raised in the context of the report of the Group of Experts on Côte d'Ivoire submitted to the Security Council involving allegations that Ivorian diamonds were entering legitimate trade through third countries;[6]

10. *Welcomes* the establishment of a new Working Group of the Kimberley Process on Artisanal Alluvial Production under the chairmanship of Angola, which will address issues of particular concern to artisanal alluvial producers and further contribute to the implementation of the existing declaration on improving internal controls over alluvial diamond production, and encourages potential donors to provide capacity-building assistance to further the effective implementation of the Kimberley Process Certification Scheme;

11. *Notes with appreciation* the contribution of the Kimberley Process and of its Chair to the work of the Security Council Committee established pursuant to resolution 1521 (2003) concerning Liberia, including the submission of a report on the results of the Kimberley Process expert mission to Liberia, as well as the progress made by Liberia towards putting in place the necessary internal controls and other requirements in order to satisfy the minimum requirements of the Process pursuant to Council resolution 1521 (2003), welcomes the contributions of the United Nations Mission in Liberia, the United States of America and other donors to these efforts, and encourages all those in a position to assist Liberia, to do so;

12. *Also notes with appreciation* the conclusions of the three-year review of the Kimberley Process Certification Scheme and the recommendations adopted by the plenary meeting of the Kimberley Process held in Gaborone and notes that the timely implementation of these recommendations will strengthen and consolidate the Process, and therefore encourages the timely implementation of those recommendations;

13. *Recognizes* that the peer review mechanism and the collection and submission of statistical data are critical monitoring tools, essential for effective implementation of the Kimberley Process Certification Scheme, and in this respect:

(*a*) Welcomes the important progress made in the implementation of the peer review mechanism in the Kimberley Process Certification Scheme, encourages all remaining participants to receive voluntary review visits, and notes with appreciation the intention of the Kimberley Process to commence a second round of review visits in 2007;

(*b*) Also welcomes the progress made towards the collection and submission of statistical reports on the production of and trade in rough diamonds, encourages all of the Kimberley Process participants to enhance the quality of data, and to this end applauds the decision of the plenary meeting held in Gaborone to release Kimberley Process summary data on trade and production, by value and volume, and certificate counts for 2004 and 2005 data;

14. *Notes with appreciation* the assistance and capacity-building efforts extended by various donors, and encourages other donors to provide financial and technical expertise to Kimberley Process participants to help them to develop tighter monitoring and control measures;

15. *Acknowledges with great appreciation* the important contribution that Botswana, as Chair of the Kimberley Process in 2006, has made to the efforts to curb the trade in conflict diamonds, and welcomes the succession of the European Community as Chair and India as Vice-Chair of the Process for 2007;

16. *Requests* the Chair of the Kimberley Process to submit a report on the implementation of the Process to the General Assembly at its sixty-second session;

17. *Decides* to include in the provisional agenda of its sixty-second session the item entitled "The role of diamonds in fuelling conflict".

64th plenary meeting
4 December 2006

---

[1] See A/57/489.

[2] Ibid., annex 2.

[3] A/61/589, annex.

[4] World Trade Organization, document WT/L/518. Available from http://docsonline.wto.org.

[5] World Trade Organization, document G/C/W/559/Rev.1. Available from http://docsonline. wto.org.

[6] See S/2006/735.

Resolution 61/29

[on the report of the Sixth Committee (A/61/450)]

61/29. Criminal accountability of United Nations officials and experts on mission

The General Assembly,

Recalling its resolution 59/281 of 29 March 2005, in which it endorsed the recommendation in paragraph 56 of the report of the Special Committee on Peacekeeping Operations[1] that the Secretary-General make available to the United Nations membership a comprehensive report on the issue of sexual exploitation and abuse in United Nations peacekeeping operations,

Noting that the Secretary-General, on 24 March 2005, transmitted to the President of the General Assembly a report of his Adviser concerning sexual exploitation and abuse by United Nations peacekeeping personnel,[2]

Recalling its resolution 59/300 of 22 June 2005 endorsing the recommendation of the Special Committee on Peacekeeping Operations[3] that a group of legal experts be established to provide advice on the best way to proceed so as to ensure that the original intent of the Charter of the United Nations can be achieved, namely that United Nations staff and experts on mission would never be effectively exempt from the consequences of criminal acts committed at their duty station, nor unjustly penalized, in accordance with due process,

Noting the report of the Group of Legal Experts established by the Secretary-General pursuant to resolution 59/300,[4]

Convinced of the need for the United Nations to take strong and effective steps in this regard,

1. *Decides* to establish an Ad Hoc Committee, open to all States Members of the United Nations or members of specialized agencies or of the International Atomic Energy Agency, for the purpose of considering the report of the Group of Legal Experts, in particular its legal aspects;

2. *Decides also* that the Ad Hoc Committee shall meet from 9 to 13 April 2007;

3. *Requests* the Secretary-General to provide the Ad Hoc Committee with the necessary facilities for the performance of its work;

4. *Requests* the Ad Hoc Committee to report on its work to the General Assembly at its sixty-second session;

5. *Decides* to include in the provisional agenda of its sixty-second session the item entitled "Criminal accountability of United Nations officials and experts on mission".

64th plenary meeting
4 December 2006

---

[1] See *Official Records of the General Assembly, Fifty-ninth Session, Supplement No. 19* (A/59/19/Rev.1), part one, chap. III, sect. D.

[2] See A/59/710.

[3] See *Official Records of the General Assembly, Fifth-ninth Session, Supplement No. 19* (A/59/19/Rev.1), part two, chap. II, sect. N.

[4] See A/60/980.

Resolution 61/30

[on the report of the Sixth Committee (A/61/451)]

61/30. Status of the Protocols Additional to the Geneva Conventions of 1949 and relating to the protection of victims of armed conflicts

The General Assembly,

Recalling its resolutions 32/44 of 8 December 1977, 34/51 of 23 November 1979, 37/116 of 16 December 1982, 39/77 of 13 December 1984, 41/72 of 3 December 1986, 43/161 of 9 December 1988, 45/38 of 28 November 1990, 47/30 of 25 November 1992, 49/48 of 9 December 1994, 51/155 of 16 December 1996, 53/96 of 8 December 1998, 55/148 of 12 December 2000, 57/14 of 19 November 2002 and 59/36 of 2 December 2004,

Having considered the report of the Secretary-General,[1]

Thanking Member States and the International Committee of the Red Cross for their contribution to the report of the Secretary-General,

Reaffirming the continuing value of established humanitarian rules relating to armed conflicts and the need to respect and ensure respect for those rules in all circumstances within the scope of the relevant international instruments, pending the earliest possible termination of such conflicts,

Stressing the possibility of making use of the International Humanitarian Fact-Finding Commission in relation to an armed conflict, pursuant to article 90 of Protocol I[2] to the Geneva Conventions of 1949,[3]

Stressing also the possibility for the International Humanitarian Fact-Finding Commission to facilitate, through its good offices, the restoration of an attitude of respect for the Geneva Conventions and Protocol I,

Stressing further the need to consolidate the existing body of international humanitarian law through its universal acceptance and the need for wide dissemination and full implementation of such law at the national level, and expressing concern about all violations of the Geneva Conventions and the Additional Protocols,[4]

Noting with satisfaction the increasing number of national commissions and other bodies involved in advising authorities at the national level on the implementation, dissemination and development of international humanitarian law,

Noting with appreciation the meetings of representatives of those bodies organized by the International Committee of the Red Cross to facilitate the sharing of concrete experience and the exchange of views on their roles and on the challenges they face,

Mindful of the role of the International Committee of the Red Cross in offering protection to the victims of armed conflicts,

Noting with appreciation the continuing efforts of the International Committee of the Red Cross to promote and disseminate knowledge of international humanitarian law, in particular the Geneva Conventions and the Additional Protocols,

Recalling that the Twenty-eighth International Conference of the Red Cross and Red Crescent stressed the need to reinforce the implementation of and respect for international humanitarian law,

Welcoming the entry into force of the Protocol on Explosive Remnants of War to the Convention on Prohibitions or Restrictions on the Use of Certain Conventional Weapons Which May be Deemed to Be Excessively Injurious or to Have Indiscriminate Effects (Protocol V),[5]

Noting the adoption, on 8 December 2005, of the Protocol additional to the Geneva Conventions of 12 August 1949, and relating to the Adoption of an Additional Distinctive Emblem (Protocol III),

Welcoming the significant debate generated by the recent publication of the study on Customary International Humanitarian Law by the International Committee of the Red Cross, and looking forward to further constructive discussion on the subject,

Calling upon Member States to disseminate knowledge of international humanitarian law as widely as possible, and calling upon all parties to armed conflict to apply international humanitarian law,

Recalling the entry into force, on 9 March 2004, of the second Protocol[6] to the 1954 Hague Convention, and appreciating the ratifications received so far,

Acknowledging the fact that the Rome Statute of the International Criminal Court,[7] which entered into force on 1 July 2002, includes the most serious crimes of international concern under international humanitarian law, and that the Statute, while recalling that it is the duty of every State to exercise its criminal jurisdiction over those responsible for such crimes, shows the determination of the international community to put an end to impunity for the perpetrators of such crimes and thus to contribute to their prevention,

Acknowledging also the usefulness of discussing in the General Assembly the status of instruments of International humanitarian law relevant to the protection of victims of armed conflicts,

1. *Welcomes* the universal acceptance of the Geneva Conventions of 1949,[3] and notes the trend towards a similarly wide acceptance of the two Additional Protocols of 1977;[4]

2. *Calls upon* all States parties to the Geneva Conventions that have not yet done so to consider becoming parties to the Additional Protocols at the earliest possible date;

3. *Calls upon* all States that are already parties to Protocol I,[2] or those States not parties, on becoming parties to Protocol I, to make the declaration provided for under article 90 of that Protocol and to consider making use, where appropriate, of the services of the International Humanitarian Fact-Finding Commission in accordance with the provisions of article 90 of Protocol I;

4. *Calls upon* all States that have not yet done so to consider becoming parties to the Convention for the Protection of Cultural Property in the Event of Armed Conflict[8] and the two Protocols thereto, and to other relevant treaties on international humanitarian law relating to the protection of victims of armed conflict;

5. *Calls upon* all States parties to the Protocols Additional to the Geneva Conventions to ensure their wide dissemination and full implementation;

6. *Notes with appreciation* the Declaration and Agenda for Humanitarian Action adopted by the Twenty-eighth International Conference of the Red Cross and Red Crescent, which noted that all States must take national measures to implement international humanitarian law, including training of the armed forces and making this law known among the general public, as well as the adoption of legislation to punish war crimes in accordance with their international obligations;

7. *Affirms* the necessity of making the implementation of international humanitarian law more effective;

8. *Welcomes* the advisory service activities of the International Committee of the Red Cross in supporting efforts made by Member States to take legislative and administrative action to implement international humanitarian law and in promoting the exchange of information on those efforts between Governments;

9. *Also welcomes* the increasing number of national commissions or committees for the implementation of international humanitarian law and for promoting the incorporation of treaties on international humanitarian law into national law and disseminating the rules of international humanitarian law;

10. *Calls upon* States to consider becoming parties to the Optional Protocol to the Convention on the Rights of the Child on the involvement of children in armed conflict;[9]

11. *Requests* the Secretary-General to submit to the General Assembly at its sixty-third session a report on the status of the Additional Protocols relating to the protection of victims of armed conflicts, as well as on measures taken to strengthen the existing body of international humanitarian law, inter alia, with respect to its dissemination and full implementation at the national level, based on information received from Member States and the International Committee of the Red Cross;

12. *Decides* to include in the provisional agenda of its sixty-third session the item entitled "Status of the Protocols Additional to the Geneva Conventions of 1949 and relating to the protection of victims of armed conflicts".

64th plenary meeting
4 December 2006

1 A/61/222 and Add.1.

2 United Nations, *Treaty Series*, vol. 1125, No. 17512.

3 Ibid., vol. 75, Nos. 970-973.

4 Ibid., vol. 1125, Nos. 17512 and 17513.

5 See CCW/MSP/2003/3, annex V, appendix II.

6 United Nations, *Treaty Series*, vol. 2253, No. 3511.

7 Ibid., vol. 2187, No. 38544.

8 Ibid., vol. 249, No. 3511.

9 Ibid., vol. 2173, No. 27531.

Resolution 61/31

[on the report of the Sixth Committee (A/61/452)]

61/31. Consideration of effective measures to enhance the protection, security and safety of diplomatic and consular missions and representatives

The General Assembly,

Having considered the report of the Secretary-General,[1]

Conscious of the need to develop and strengthen friendly relations and cooperation among States,

Convinced that respect for the principles and rules of international law governing diplomatic and consular relations is a basic prerequisite for the normal conduct of relations among States and for the fulfilment of the purposes and principles of the Charter of the United Nations,

Alarmed by the recent acts of violence against diplomatic and consular representatives, as well as against representatives of international intergovernmental organizations and officials of such organizations, which have endangered or taken innocent lives and seriously impeded the normal work of such representatives and officials,

Expressing sympathy for the victims of such illegal acts,

Concerned at the failure to respect the inviolability of diplomatic and consular missions and representatives,

Recalling that, without prejudice to their privileges and immunities, it is the duty of all persons enjoying such privileges and immunities to respect the laws and regulations of the receiving State,

Recalling also that diplomatic and consular premises must not be used in any manner incompatible with the functions of diplomatic and consular missions,

Emphasizing the duty of States to take all appropriate measures as required by international law, including measures of a preventive nature, and to bring offenders to justice,

Welcoming measures already taken by States to this end in conformity with their international obligations,

Convinced that the role of the United Nations, which includes the reporting procedures established pursuant to General Assembly resolution 35/168 of 15 December 1980 and further elaborated in subsequent Assembly resolutions, is important in promoting efforts to enhance the protection, security and safety of diplomatic and consular missions and representatives,

1. *Takes note* of the report of the Secretary-General;[1]

2. *Strongly condemns* acts of violence against diplomatic and consular missions and representatives, as well as against missions and representatives of international intergovernmental organizations and officials of such organizations, and emphasizes that such acts can never be justified;

3. *Urges* States to strictly observe, implement and enforce the applicable principles and rules of international law governing diplomatic and consular relations, including during a period of armed conflict, and, in particular, to ensure, in conformity with their international obligations, the protection, security and safety of the missions, representatives and officials mentioned in paragraph 2 above officially present in territories under their jurisdiction, including practical measures to prohibit in their territories illegal activities of persons, groups and organizations that encourage, instigate, organize or engage in the perpetration of acts against the security and safety of such missions, representatives and officials;

4. *Also urges* States to take all appropriate measures at the national and international levels to prevent any acts of violence against the missions, representatives and officials mentioned in paragraph 2 above, including during a period of armed conflict, and to ensure, with the participation of the United Nations where appropriate, that such acts are fully investigated with a view to bringing offenders to justice;

5. *Recommends* that States cooperate closely through, inter alia, contacts between the diplomatic and consular missions and the receiving State with regard to practical measures designed to enhance the protection, security and safety of diplomatic and consular missions and representatives and with regard to the exchange of information on the circumstances of all serious violations thereof;

6. *Urges* States to take all appropriate measures, in accordance with international law, at the national and international levels, to prevent any abuse of diplomatic or consular privileges and immunities, in particular serious abuses, including those involving acts of violence;

7. *Recommends* that States cooperate closely with the State in whose territory abuses of diplomatic and consular privileges and immunities may have occurred, including by exchanging information and providing assistance to its juridical authorities in order to bring offenders to justice;

8. *Calls upon* States that have not yet done so to consider becoming parties to the instruments relevant to the protection, security and safety of diplomatic and consular missions and representatives;

9. *Calls upon* States, in cases where a dispute arises in connection with a violation of their international obligations concerning the protection of the missions or the security of the representatives and officials mentioned in paragraph 2 above, to make use of the means available for peaceful settlement of disputes, including the good offices of the Secretary-General, requests the Secretary-General, when he deems it appropriate, to offer his good offices to the States directly concerned;

10. *Requests*:

(*a*) All States to report to the Secretary-General as promptly as possible serious violations of the protection, security and safety of diplomatic and consular missions and representatives as well as missions and representatives with diplomatic status to international intergovernmental organizations;

(*b*) The State in which the violation took place — and, to the extent possible, the State where the alleged offender is present — to report to the Secretary-General as promptly as possible on measures taken to bring the offender to justice and eventually to communicate, in accordance with its laws, the final outcome of the proceedings against the offender, and to report on measures adopted with a view to preventing a repetition of such violations;

(*c*) The States so reporting to consider using or taking into account the guidelines prepared by the Secretary-General;[2]

11. *Requests* the Secretary-General:

(*a*) To send, without delay, a circular note to all States reminding them of the request contained in paragraph 10 above;

(*b*) To circulate to all States, upon receipt, the reports received by him pursuant to paragraph 10 above, unless the reporting State requests otherwise;

(*c*) To draw the attention, when appropriate, of the States directly concerned to the reporting procedures provided for in paragraph 10 above, when a serious violation has been reported pursuant to subparagraph 10 (*a*) above;

(*d*) To address reminders to States where such violations have occurred if reports pursuant to subparagraph 10 (*a*) above or follow-up reports pursuant to subparagraph 10 (*b*) above have not been made within a reasonable period of time;

12. *Also requests* the Secretary-General to invite States, in the circular note referred to in paragraph 11 (*a*) above, to inform him of their views with respect to any measures needed or already taken to enhance the protection, security and safety of diplomatic and consular missions and representatives as well as missions and representatives with diplomatic status to international intergovernmental organizations;

13. *Further requests* the Secretary-General to submit to the General Assembly at its sixty-third session a report containing:

(*a*) Information on the state of ratification of, and accessions to, the instruments referred to in paragraph 8 above;

(*b*) A summary of the reports received and views expressed pursuant to paragraphs 10 and 12 above;

14. *Invites* the Secretary-General to include in his report to the General Assembly any views he may wish to express on the matters referred to in paragraph 13 above;

15. *Decides* to include in the provisional agenda of its sixty-third session the item entitled "Consideration of effective measures to enhance the protection, security and safety of diplomatic and consular missions and representatives".

64th plenary meeting
4 December 2006

---

[1] A/61/119 and Add.1 and 2.

[2] A/42/485, annex.

Resolution 61/32

[on the report of the Sixth Committee (A/61/453)]

61/32. Report of the United Nations Commission on International Trade Law on the work of its thirty-ninth session

The General Assembly,

Recalling its resolution 2205 (XXI) of 17 December 1966, by which it established the United Nations Commission on International Trade Law with a mandate to further the progressive harmonization and unification of the law of international trade and in that respect to bear in mind the interests of all peoples, in particular those of developing countries, in the extensive development of international trade,

Reaffirming its belief that the progressive modernization and harmonization of international trade law, in reducing or removing legal obstacles to the flow of international trade, especially those affecting the developing countries, would contribute significantly to universal economic cooperation among all States on a basis of equality, equity and common interest and to the elimination of discrimination in international trade and, thereby, to the well-being of all peoples,

Having considered the report of the Commission on the work of its thirty-ninth session,[1]

Reiterating its concern that activities undertaken by other bodies in the field of international trade law without adequate coordination with the Commission might lead to undesirable duplication of efforts and would not be in keeping with the aim of promoting efficiency, consistency and coherence in the unification and harmonization of international trade law,

Reaffirming the mandate of the Commission, as the core legal body within the United Nations system in the field of international trade law, to coordinate legal activities in this field, in particular to avoid duplication of efforts, including among organizations formulating rules of international trade, and to promote efficiency, consistency and coherence in the modernization and harmonization of international trade law, and to continue, through its secretariat, to maintain close cooperation with other international organs and organizations, including regional organizations, active in the field of international trade law,

1. *Takes note with appreciation* of the report of the United Nations Commission on International Trade Law on the work of its thirty-ninth session;[1]

2. *Commends* the Commission for the finalization and adoption of revised articles[2] of the Model Law on International Commercial Arbitration of the United Nations Commission on International Trade Law[3] on the form of the arbitration agreement and interim measures, and of the recommendation regarding the interpretation of article II, paragraph 2, and article VII, paragraph 1,[4] of the Convention on the Recognition and Enforcement of Foreign Arbitral Awards, done at New York, 10 June 1958;[5]

3. *Also commends* the Commission for the approval of the substance of the recommendations of the draft legislative guide on secured transactions, which has been designed to facilitate secured financing, thus promoting increased access to low-cost credit and enhancing national and international trade;

4. *Welcomes* the progress made by the Commission in its work on a revision of its Model Law on Procurement of Goods, Construction and Services,[6] and on a draft instrument on transport law, and endorses the decision of the Commission to take up new topics in the areas of arbitration and insolvency law;

5. *Endorses* the efforts and initiatives of the Commission, as the core legal body within the United Nations system in the field of international trade law, aimed at increasing coordination of and cooperation on legal activities of international and regional organizations active in the field of international trade law, as well as promoting the rule of law at the national and international levels in this field, and in this regard appeals to relevant international and regional organizations to coordinate their legal activities with those of the Commission, to avoid duplication of efforts and to promote efficiency, consistency and coherence in the modernization and harmonization of international trade law;

6. *Reaffirms* the importance, in particular for developing countries, of the work of the Commission concerned with technical assistance and cooperation in the field of international trade law reform and development, and in this connection:

(*a*) Welcomes the initiatives of the Commission towards expanding, through its secretariat, its technical assistance and cooperation programme;

(*b*) Expresses its appreciation to the Commission for carrying out technical assistance and cooperation activities in Belarus, Benin (for the United Nations Conference on Trade and Development/World Trade Organization International Trade Centre seminar), Colombia, Egypt, the Republic of Korea, Singapore, Slovakia and Switzerland (for the United Nations Conference on Trade and Development/World Trade Organization International Trade Centre symposium on multilateral trade treaties and developing countries) and for providing assistance with legislative drafting in the field of international trade law to China, Georgia, Greece, Malaysia, Peru, Rwanda (through the joint project with the International Law Institute), Serbia, Slovenia and the former Yugoslav Republic of Macedonia, and to the Commonwealth Telecommunications Organisation;

(*c*) Expresses its appreciation to the Governments whose contributions enabled the technical assistance and cooperation activities to take place, and appeals to Governments, the relevant bodies of the United Nations system, organizations, institutions and individuals to make voluntary contributions to the United Nations Commission on International Trade Law Trust Fund for Symposia and, where appropriate, to the financing of special projects, and otherwise to assist the secretariat of the Commission in carrying out technical assistance activities, in particular in developing countries;

(*d*) Reiterates its appeal to the United Nations Development Programme and other bodies responsible for development assistance, such as the World Bank and regional development banks, as well as to Governments in their bilateral aid programmes, to support the technical assistance programme of the Commission and to cooperate and coordinate their activities with those of the Commission, in the light of the relevance and importance of the work and programmes of the Commission to the implementation of the United Nations development agenda, including the achievement of the Millennium Development Goals;

7. *Takes note with regret* that, since the thirty-sixth session of the Commission, no contributions have been made to the trust fund established to provide travel assistance to developing countries that are members of the Commission, at their request and in consultation with the Secretary-General,[7] stresses the need for contributions to the trust fund in order to increase expert representation from developing countries at sessions of the Commission and its working groups, necessary to build local expertise and capacities in the field of international trade law in those countries to facilitate the development of international trade and the promotion of foreign investment, and reiterates its appeal to Governments, the relevant bodies of the United Nations system, organizations, institutions and individuals to make voluntary contributions to the trust fund;

8. *Decides*, in order to ensure full participation by all Member States in the sessions of the Commission and its working groups, to continue, in the competent Main Committee during the sixty-first session of the General Assembly, its consideration of granting travel assistance to the least developed countries that are members of the Commission, at their request and in consultation with the Secretary-General;

9. *Recalls* that the responsibility for the work of the Commission lies with the meetings of the Commission and its intergovernmental working groups, and stresses in this regard that information should be provided regarding meetings of experts, which bring an essential contribution to the work of the Commission;

10. *Recalls* its resolutions on partnerships between the United Nations and non-State actors, in particular the private sector,[8] and in this regard encourages the Commission to further

explore different approaches to the use of partnerships with non-State actors in the implementation of its mandate, in particular in the area of technical assistance, in accordance with the applicable principles and guidelines and in cooperation and coordination with other relevant offices of the Secretariat, including the Global Compact Office;

11. *Reiterates its request* to the Secretary-General, in conformity with the General Assembly resolutions on documentation-related matters,[9] which, in particular, emphasize that any reduction in the length of documents should not adversely affect either the quality of the presentation or the substance of the documents, to bear in mind the particular characteristics of the mandate and work of the Commission in implementing page limits with respect to the documentation of the Commission;

12. *Requests* the Secretary-General to continue providing summary records of the meetings of the Commission relating to the formulation of normative texts;

13. *Recalls* its resolution approving the establishment of the *Yearbook of the United Nations Commission on International Trade Law*, with the aim of making the work of the Commission more widely known and readily available,[10] expresses its concern regarding the timeliness of the publication of the *Yearbook*, and requests the Secretary-General to explore options to facilitate the timely publication of the *Yearbook*;

14. *Stresses* the importance of bringing into effect the conventions emanating from the work of the Commission for the global unification and harmonization of international trade law, and to this end urges States that have not yet done so to consider signing, ratifying or acceding to those conventions;

15. *Welcomes* the preparation of digests of case law relating to the texts of the Commission, such as a digest of case law relating to the United Nations Convention on Contracts for the International Sale of Goods[11] and a digest of case law relating to the Model Law on International Commercial Arbitration of the United Nations Commission on International Trade Law,[3] with the aim of assisting in dissemination of information on those texts and promoting their use, enactment and uniform interpretation;

16. *Welcomes also* the decision of the Commission to hold, in the context of its fortieth session in 2007, a congress on international trade law in Vienna, with a view to reviewing the results of the past work of the Commission as well as related work of other organizations active in the field of international trade law, assessing current work programmes and considering topics and areas for future work, and acknowledges the importance of holding such a congress for the coordination and promotion of activities aimed at the modernization and harmonization of international trade law;

17. *Recalls* its resolutions affirming the importance of high-quality, user-friendly and cost-effective United Nations websites and the need for their multilingual development, maintenance and enrichment,[12] commends the restructured website of the Commission in the six official languages of the United Nations, and welcomes the continuous efforts of the Commission to maintain and improve its website in accordance with the applicable guidelines.

64th plenary meeting
4 December 2006

---

[1] *Official Records of the General Assembly, Sixty-first Session, Supplement No. 17* (A/61/17).

[2] Ibid., chap. IV, para. 181, and annex I.

[3] Ibid., *Fortieth Session, Supplement No. 17* (A/40/17), annex I.

[4] Ibid., *Sixty-first Session, Supplement No. 17* (A/61/17), chap. IV, para. 181, and annex II.

[5] United Nations, *Treaty Series*, vol. 330, No. 4739.

[6] *Official Records of the General Assembly, Forty-ninth Session, Supplement No. 17* and corrigendum (A/49/17 and Corr.1), annex I.

[7] Resolution 48/32, para. 5.

[8] Resolutions 55/215, 56/76, 58/129 and 60/215.

[9] Resolutions 52/214, sect. B, 57/283 B, sect. III, and 58/250, sect. III.

[10] Resolution 2502 (XXIV), para. 7.

[11] United Nations, *Treaty Series*, vol. 1489, No. 25567.

[12] Resolutions 52/214, sect. C, para. 3; 55/222, sect. III, para. 12; 56/64 B, sect. X; 57/130 B, sect. X; 58/101 B, sect. V, paras. 61–76; 59/126 B, sect. V, paras. 76–95; and 60/109 B, sect. IV, paras. 66–80.

Resolution 61/33

[on the report of the Sixth Committee (A/61/453)]

61/33. Revised articles of the Model Law on International Commercial Arbitration of the United Nations Commission on International Trade Law, and the recommendation regarding the interpretation of article II, paragraph 2, and article VII, paragraph 1, of the Convention on the Recognition and Enforcement of Foreign Arbitral Awards, done at New York, 10 June 1958

The General Assembly,

Recognizing the value of arbitration as a method of settling disputes arising in the context of international commercial relations,

Recalling its resolution 40/72 of 11 December 1985 regarding the Model Law on International Commercial Arbitration,[1]

Recognizing the need for provisions in the Model Law to conform to current practices in international trade and modern means of contracting with regard to the form of the arbitration agreement and the granting of interim measures,

Believing that revised articles of the Model Law on the form of the arbitration agreement and interim measures reflecting those current practices will significantly enhance the operation of the Model Law,

Noting that the preparation of the revised articles of the Model Law on the form of the arbitration agreement and interim measures was the subject of due deliberation and extensive consultations with Governments and interested circles and would contribute significantly to the establishment of a harmonized legal framework for a fair and efficient settlement of international commercial disputes,

Believing that, in connection with the modernization of articles of the Model Law, the promotion of a uniform interpretation and application of the Convention on the Recognition and Enforcement of Foreign Arbitral Awards, done at New York, 10 June 1958,[2] is particularly timely,

1. *Expresses its appreciation* to the United Nations Commission on International Trade Law for formulating and adopting the revised articles of its Model Law on International Commercial Arbitration on the form of the arbitration agreement and interim measures, the text of which is contained in annex I to the report of the United Nations Commission on International Trade Law on the work of its thirty-ninth session,[3] and recommends that all States give favourable consideration to the enactment of the revised articles of the Model Law, or the revised Model Law on International Commercial Arbitration of the United Nations Commission on International Trade Law, when they enact or revise their laws, in view of the desirability of uniformity of the law of arbitral procedures and the specific needs of international commercial arbitration practice;

2. *Also expresses its appreciation* to the United Nations Commission on International Trade Law for formulating and adopting the recommendation regarding the interpretation of article II, paragraph 2, and article VII, paragraph 1, of the Convention on the Recognition and Enforcement of Foreign Arbitral Awards, done at New York, 10 June 1958,[2] the text of which is contained in annex II to the report of the United Nations Commission on International Trade Law on the work of its thirty-ninth session;[3]

3. *Requests* the Secretary-General to make all efforts to ensure that the revised articles of the Model Law and the recommendation become generally known and available.

64th plenary meeting
4 December 2006

---

[1] *Official Records of the General Assembly, Fortieth Session, Supplement No. 17* (A/40/17), annex I.

[2] United Nations, *Treaty Series*, vol. 330, No. 4739.

[3] *Official Records of the General Assembly, Sixty-first Session, Supplement No. 17* (A/61/17).

Resolution 61/34

[on the report of the Sixth Committee (A/61/454)]

61/34. Report of the International Law Commission on the work of its fifty-eighth session

The General Assembly,

Having considered the report of the International Law Commission on the work of its fifty-eighth session,[1]

Emphasizing the importance of furthering the codification and progressive development of international law as a means of implementing the purposes and principles set forth in the Charter of the United Nations and in the Declaration on Principles of International Law concerning Friendly Relations and Cooperation among States in accordance with the Charter of the United Nations,[2]

Recognizing the desirability of referring legal and drafting questions to the Sixth Committee, including topics that might be submitted to the International Law Commission for closer examination, and of enabling the Sixth Committee and the Commission to enhance further their contribution to the progressive development of international law and its codification,

Recalling the need to keep under review those topics of international law which, given their new or renewed interest for the international community, may be suitable for the progressive development and codification of international law and therefore may be included in the future programme of work of the International Law Commission,

Welcoming the holding of the International Law Seminar, and noting with appreciation the voluntary contributions made to the United Nations Trust Fund for the International Law Seminar,

Stressing the usefulness of focusing and structuring the debate on the report of the International Law Commission in the Sixth Committee in such a manner that conditions are provided for concentrated attention to each of the main topics dealt with in the report and for discussions on specific topics,

Wishing to enhance further, in the context of the revitalization of the debate on the report of the International Law Commission, the interaction between the Sixth Committee as a body of governmental representatives and the Commission as a body of independent legal experts, with a view to improving the dialogue between the two bodies,

Welcoming initiatives to hold interactive debates, panel discussions and question time in the Sixth Committee, as envisaged in resolution 58/316 of 1 July 2004 on further measures for the revitalization of the work of the General Assembly,

1. *Takes note* of the report of the International Law Commission on the work of its fifty-eighth session,[1] and recommends that the Commission continue its work on the topics in its current programme, taking into account the comments and observations of Governments, whether submitted in writing or expressed orally in debates in the General Assembly;

2. *Expresses its appreciation* to the International Law Commission for the work accomplished at its fifty-eighth session, in particular for the following accomplishments:

(*a*) The completion of the second reading of the draft articles on diplomatic protection;

(*b*) The completion of the second reading of the draft principles on the allocation of loss in the case of transboundary harm arising out of hazardous activities under the topic "International liability for injurious consequences arising out of acts not prohibited by international law (International liability in case of loss for transboundary harm arising out of hazardous activities)";

(*c*) The completion of the first reading of the draft articles on the law of transboundary aquifers under the topic "Shared natural resources";

(*d*) The completion of the work on "Unilateral acts of States" by the adoption of the Guiding Principles applicable to unilateral declarations of States capable of creating legal obligations;

(*e*) The completion by its Study Group of the report and the conclusions on the topic "Fragmentation of international law: difficulties arising from diversification and expansion of international law";

3. *Takes note* of the Guiding Principles applicable to unilateral declarations of States capable of creating legal obligations under the topic "Unilateral acts of States", contained in paragraph 176 of the report of the International Law Commission[1] and commends their dissemination;

4. *Also takes note* of the forty-two conclusions of the Commission's Study Group on the topic "Fragmentation of international law: difficulties arising from diversification and expansion of international law", contained in paragraph 251 of the report of the International Law Commission, together with the analytical study[3] on which they were based;

5. *Draws the attention* of Governments to the importance for the International Law Commission of having their views on the various aspects involved in the topics on the agenda of the Commission identified in chapter III of its report, including in particular on the draft articles and commentaries on the law of transboundary aquifers;[4]

6. *Invites* Governments to provide to the International Law Commission, as requested in chapter III of its report,[5] information on legislation and practice regarding the topic "The obligation to extradite or prosecute (*aut dedere aut judicare*)";

7. *Takes note* of the decision of the International Law Commission to include five topics[6] in its long-term programme of work;

8. *Invites* the International Law Commission to continue taking measures to enhance its efficiency and productivity and to consider making proposals to that end;

9. *Encourages* the International Law Commission to continue taking cost-saving measures at its future sessions without prejudice to the efficiency of its work;

10. *Takes note* of paragraph 270 of the report of the International Law Commission, and decides that the next session of the Commission shall be held at the United Nations Office at Geneva from 7 May to 8 June and from 9 July to 10 August 2007;

11. *Welcomes* the enhanced dialogue between the International Law Commission and the Sixth Committee at the sixty-first session of the General Assembly, stresses the desirability of further enhancing the dialogue between the two bodies, and in this context encourages, inter alia, the continued practice of informal consultations in the form of discussions between the members of the Sixth Committee and the members of the Commission attending the sixty-second session of the Assembly;

12. *Encourages* delegations, during the debate on the report of the International Law Commission, to adhere as far as possible to the structured work programme agreed to by the Sixth Committee and to consider presenting concise and focused statements;

13. *Encourages* Member States to consider being represented at the level of legal adviser during the first week in which the report of the International Law Commission is discussed in the Sixth Committee (International Law Week) to enable high-level discussions on issues of international law;

14. *Requests* the International Law Commission to continue to pay special attention to indicating in its annual report, for each topic, any specific issues on which expressions of views by Governments, either in the Sixth Committee or in written form, would be of particular interest in providing effective guidance for the Commission in its further work;

15. *Takes note* of paragraphs 271 to 274 of the report of the International Law Commission with regard to cooperation with other bodies, and encourages the Commission to continue the implementation of article 16, paragraph (*e*), and article 26, paragraph 1 and 2, of its statute in order to further strengthen cooperation between the Commission and other bodies concerned with international law, having in mind the usefulness of such cooperataion;

16. *Notes* that the International Law Commission, in accordance with article 25, paragraph 1, of its statute, envisages a meeting during its fifty-ninth session with United Nations experts in the field of human rights, including representatives from human rights treaty bodies, in order to hold a discussion on issues relating to human rights treaties;

17. *Also notes* that consulting with national organizations and individual experts concerned with international law may assist Governments in considering whether to make comments and observations on drafts submitted by the International Law Commission and in formulating their comments and observations;

18. *Reaffirms* its previous decisions concerning the indispensable role of the Codification Division of the Office of Legal Affairs of the Secretariat in providing assistance to the International Law Commission;

19. *Approves* the conclusions reached by the International Law Commission in paragraphs 262 to 267 of its report, and reaffirms its previous decisions concerning the documentation and summary records of the Commission;[7]

20. *Notes with appreciation* the expansion of the website of the International Law Commission[8] to include all its documentation, and welcomes the continuous efforts of the Codification Division to maintain and improve the website;

21. *Expresses the hope* that the International Law Seminar will continue to be held in connection with the sessions of the International Law Commission and that an increasing number of participants, in particular from developing countries, will be given the opportunity to attend the Seminar, and appeals to States to continue to make urgently needed voluntary contributions to the United Nations Trust Fund for the International Law Seminar;

22. *Requests* the Secretary-General to provide the International Law Seminar with adequate services, including interpretation, as required, and encourages him to continue considering ways to improve the structure and content of the Seminar;

23. *Also requests* the Secretary-General to forward to the International Law Commission, for its attention, the records of the debate on the report of the Commission at the sixty-first session of the General Assembly, together with such written statements as delegations may circulate in conjunction with their oral statements, and to prepare and distribute a topical summary of the debate, following established practice;

24. *Requests* the Secretariat to circulate to States, as soon as possible after the conclusion of the session of the International Law Commission, chapter II of its report containing a summary of the work of that session, chapter III containing the specific issues on which the views of Governments would be of particular interest to the Commission and the draft articles adopted on either first or second reading by the Commission;

25. *Recommends* that the debate on the report of the International Law Commission at the sixty-second session of the General Assembly commence on 29 October 2007.

64th plenary meeting
4 December 2006

---

[1] *Official Records of the General Assembly, Sixty-first Session, Supplement No. 10* (A/61/10).

[2] Resolution 2625 (XXV), annex.

[3] A/CN.4/L.682 and Corr.1 and Add.1.

[4] *Official Records of the General Assembly, Sixty-first Session, Supplement No. 10* (A/61/10), paras. 75 and 76.

[5] Ibid., paras. 26–33.

[6] Immunity of State officials from foreign criminal jurisdiction; Jurisdictional immunity of international organizations; Protection of persons in the event of disasters; Protection of personal data in the transborder flow of information; and Extraterritorial jurisdiction.

[7] See resolutions 32/151, para. 10, and 37/111, para. 5, and all subsequent resolutions on the annual reports of the International Law Commission to the General Assembly.

[8] www.un.org/law/ilc.

Resolution 61/35

[on the report of the Sixth Committee (A/61/454)]

61/35. Diplomatic protection

The General Assembly,

Having considered chapter IV of the report of the International Law Commission on the work of its fifty-eighth session,[1] which contains the draft articles on diplomatic protection,[2]

Noting that the Commission decided to recommend to the General Assembly the elaboration of a convention on the basis of the draft articles on diplomatic protection,[3]

Emphasizing the continuing importance of the codification and progressive development of international law, as referred to in Article 13, paragraph 1 (*a*), of the Charter of the United Nations,

Noting that the subject of diplomatic protection is of major importance in the relations of States,

Taking into account views and comments expressed in the Sixth Committee on chapter IV on diplomatic protection of the report of the Commission,[4]

1. *Expresses its appreciation* to the International Law Commission for its continuing contribution to the codification and progressive development of international law;

2. *Takes note* of the draft articles on diplomatic protection, presented by the Commission,[2] and invites Governments to submit comments concerning the recommendation by the Commission to elaborate a convention on the basis of these articles;[3]

3. *Decides* to include in the provisional agenda of its sixty-second session an item entitled "Diplomatic protection".

64th plenary meeting
4 December 2006

[1] *Official Records of the General Assembly, Sixty-first Session, Supplement No. 10* (A/61/10).

[2] Ibid., para. 49.

[3] Ibid., para. 46.

[4] Ibid., para. 50.

Resolution 61/36

[on the report of the Sixth Committee (A/61/454)]

61/36. Allocation of loss in the case of transboundary harm arising out of hazardous activities

The General Assembly,

Recalling that the International Law Commission at its fifty-third session[1] completed the draft articles on prevention of transboundary harm from hazardous activities and recommended to the General Assembly the elaboration of a convention on the basis of the draft articles,

Recalling also its resolution 56/82 of 12 December 2001,

Having considered chapter V of the report of the Commission on the work of its fifty-eighth session,[2] which contains the draft principles on the allocation of loss in the case of transboundary harm arising out of hazardous activities,

Noting that the Commission decided to recommend to the General Assembly that it endorse the draft principles by a resolution and urge States to take national and international action to implement them,[3]

Emphasizing the continuing importance of the codification and progressive development of international law, as referred to in Article 13, paragraph 1 (*a*), of the Charter of the United Nations,

Noting that the questions of prevention of transboundary harm from hazardous activities and allocation of loss in the case of such harm are of major importance in the relations of States,

Taking into account views and comments expressed in the Sixth Committee on chapter V of the report of the Commission on international liability in case of loss from transboundary harm arising out of hazardous activities[3] of the report of the Commission at its fifty-eighth session,

1. *Expresses its appreciation* to the International Law Commission for its continuing contribution to the codification and progressive development of international law;

2. *Takes note* of the principles on the allocation of loss in the case of transboundary harm arising out of hazardous activities, presented by the Commission, the text of which is annexed to the present resolution, and commends them to the attention of Governments;

3. *Decides* to include in the provisional agenda of its sixty-second session an item entitled "Consideration of prevention of transboundary harm from hazardous activities and allocation of loss in the case of such harm".

64th plenary meeting
4 December 2006

---

[1] *Official Records of the General Assembly, Fifty-sixth Session, Supplement No. 10* and corrigendum (A/56/10 and Corr.1), paras. 91, 94 and 97.

[2] Ibid., *Sixty-first Session, Supplement No. 10* (A/61/10).

[3] Ibid., para. 63.

Annex

Principles on the allocation of loss in the case of transboundary harm arising out of hazardous activities

The General Assembly,

Reaffirming Principles 13 and 16 of the Rio Declaration on Environment and Development,

Recalling the draft articles on the Prevention of Transboundary Harm from Hazardous Activities,

Aware that incidents involving hazardous activities may occur despite compliance by the relevant State with its obligations concerning prevention of transboundary harm from hazardous activities,

Noting that as a result of such incidents other States and/or their nationals may suffer harm and serious loss,

Emphasizing that appropriate and effective measures should be in place to ensure that those natural and legal persons, including States, that incur harm and loss as a result of such incidents are able to obtain prompt and adequate compensation,

Concerned that prompt and effective response measures should be taken to minimize the harm and loss which may result from such incidents,

Noting that States are responsible for infringements of their obligations of prevention under international law,

Recalling the significance of existing international agreements covering specific categories of hazardous activities and stressing the importance of the conclusion of further such agreements,

Desiring to contribute to the development of international law in this field,

...

Principle 1
Scope of application

The present draft principles apply to transboundary damage caused by hazardous activities not prohibited by international law.

Principle 2
Use of terms

For the purposes of the present draft principles:

(*a*) "damage" means significant damage caused to persons, property or the environment; and includes:

(i) loss of life or personal injury;

(ii) loss of, or damage to, property, including property which forms part of the cultural heritage;

(iii) loss or damage by impairment of the environment;

(iv) the costs of reasonable measures of reinstatement of the property, or environment, including natural resources;

(v) the costs of reasonable response measures;

(*b*) "environment" includes natural resources, both abiotic and biotic, such as air, water, soil, fauna and flora and the interaction between the same factors, and the characteristic aspects of the landscape;

(*c*) "hazardous activity" means an activity which involves a risk of causing significant harm;

(*d*) "State of origin" means the State in the territory or otherwise under the jurisdiction or control of which the hazardous activity is carried out;

(*e*) "transboundary damage" means damage caused to persons, property or the environment in the territory or in other places under the jurisdiction or control of a State other than the State of origin;

(*f*) "victim" means any natural or legal person or State that suffers damage;

(*g*) "operator" means any person in command or control of the activity at the time the incident causing transboundary damage occurs.

Principle 3
Purposes

The purposes of the present draft principles are:

(*a*) to ensure prompt and adequate compensation to victims of transboundary damage; and

(*b*) to preserve and protect the environment in the event of transboundary damage, especially with respect to mitigation of damage to the environment and its restoration or reinstatement.

Principle 4
Prompt and adequate compensation

1. Each State should take all necessary measures to ensure that prompt and adequate compensation is available for victims of transboundary damage caused by hazardous activities located within its territory or otherwise under its jurisdiction or control.

2. These measures should include the imposition of liability on the operator or, where appropriate, other person or entity. Such liability should not require proof of fault. Any conditions, limitations or exceptions to such liability shall be consistent with draft principle 3.

3. These measures should also include the requirement on the operator or, where appropriate, other person or entity, to establish and maintain financial security such as insurance, bonds or other financial guarantees to cover claims of compensation.

4. In appropriate cases, these measures should include the requirement for the establishment of industry-wide funds at the national level.

5. In the event that the measures under the preceding paragraphs are insufficient to provide adequate compensation, the State of origin should also ensure that additional financial resources are made available.

Principle 5
Response measures

Upon the occurrence of an incident involving a hazardous activity which results or is likely to result in transboundary damage:

(*a*) the State of origin shall promptly notify all States affected or likely to be affected of the incident and the possible effects of the transboundary damage;

(*b*) the State of origin, with the appropriate involvement of the operator, shall ensure that appropriate response measures are taken and should, for this purpose, rely upon the best available scientific data and technology;

(*c*) the State of origin, as appropriate, should also consult with and seek the cooperation of all States affected or likely to be affected to mitigate the effects of transboundary damage and if possible eliminate them;

(*d*) the States affected or likely to be affected by the transboundary damage shall take all feasible measures to mitigate and if possible to eliminate the effects of such damage;

(*e*) the States concerned should, where appropriate, seek the assistance of competent international organizations and other States on mutually acceptable terms and conditions.

Principle 6
International and domestic remedies

1. States shall provide their domestic judicial and administrative bodies with the necessary jurisdiction and competence and ensure that these bodies have prompt, adequate and effective remedies available in the event of transboundary damage caused by hazardous activities located within their territory or otherwise under their jurisdiction or control.

2. Victims of transboundary damage should have access to remedies in the State of origin that are no less prompt, adequate and effective than those available to victims that suffer damage, from the same incident, within the territory of that State.

3. Paragraphs 1 and 2 are without prejudice to the right of the victims to seek remedies other than those available in the State of origin.

4. States may provide for recourse to international claims settlement procedures that are expeditious and involve minimal expenses.

5. States should guarantee appropriate access to information relevant for the pursuance of remedies, including claims for compensation.

Principle 7
Development of specific international regimes

1. Where, in respect of particular categories of hazardous activities, specific global, regional or bilateral agreements would provide effective arrangements concerning compensation,

response measures and international and domestic remedies, all efforts should be made to conclude such specific agreements.

2. Such agreements should, as appropriate, include arrangements for industry and/or State funds to provide supplementary compensation in the event that the financial resources of the operator, including financial security measures, are insufficient to cover the damage suffered as a result of an incident. Any such funds may be designed to supplement or replace national industry-based funds.

Principle 8
Implementation

1. Each State should adopt the necessary legislative, regulatory and administrative measures to implement the present draft principles.

2. The present draft principles and the measures adopted to implement them shall be applied without any discrimination such as that based on nationality, domicile or residence.

3. States should cooperate with each other to implement the present draft principles.

Resolution 61/37

[on the report of the Sixth Committee (A/61/455)]

61/37. Commemoration of the sixtieth anniversary of the International Court of Justice

The General Assembly,

Mindful that, in accordance with Article 2, paragraph 3, of the Charter of the United Nations, all Members shall settle their international disputes by peaceful means in such a manner that international peace and security, and justice, are not endangered,

Bearing in mind the Declaration on Principles of International Law concerning Friendly Relations and Cooperation among States in accordance with the Charter of the United Nations[1] and the Manila Declaration on the Peaceful Settlement of International Disputes,[2]

Recognizing the need for universal adherence to and implementation of the rule of law at both the national and international levels,

Recalling that the International Court of Justice is the principal judicial organ of the United Nations, and reaffirming its authority and independence,

Noting that 2006 marks the sixtieth anniversary of the inaugural sitting of the International Court of Justice,

Noting with appreciation the special commemorative event held at The Hague in April 2006 to celebrate the anniversary,

1. *Solemnly commends* the International Court of Justice for the important role that it has played as the principal judicial organ of the United Nations over the past sixty years in adjudicating disputes among States, and recognizes the value of its work;

2. *Expresses its appreciation* to the Court for the measures adopted to operate an increased workload with maximum efficiency;

3. *Stresses* the desirability of finding practical ways and means to strengthen the Court, taking into consideration, in particular, the needs resulting from its workload;

4. *Encourages* States to continue considering recourse to the Court by means available under its Statute, and calls upon States that have not yet done so to consider accepting the jurisdiction of the Court in accordance with its Statute;

5. *Calls upon* States to consider means of strengthening the Court's work, including by supporting the Secretary-General's Trust Fund to Assist States in the Settlement of Disputes through the International Court of Justice on a voluntary basis, in order to enable the Fund to carry on and to strengthen its support to the countries which submit their disputes to the Court;

6. *Stresses* the importance of promoting the work of the International Court of Justice, and urges that efforts be continued through available means to encourage public awareness in the teaching, study and wider dissemination of the activities of the Court in the peaceful settlement of disputes, in view of both its judiciary and advisory functions.

64th plenary meeting
4 December 2006

---

[1] Resolution 2625 (XXV), annex.

[2] Resolution 37/10, annex.

Resolution 61/38

[on the report of the Sixth Committee (A/61/455)]

61/38. Report of the Special Committee on the Charter of the United Nations and on the Strengthening of the Role of the Organization

The General Assembly,

Recalling its resolution 3499 (XXX) of 15 December 1975, by which it established the Special Committee on the Charter of the United Nations and on the Strengthening of the Role of the Organization, and its relevant resolutions adopted at subsequent sessions,

Recalling also its resolution 47/233 of 17 August 1993 on the revitalization of the work of the General Assembly,

Recalling further its resolution 47/62 of 11 December 1992 on the question of equitable representation on and increase in the membership of the Security Council,

Taking note of the report of the Open-ended Working Group on the Question of Equitable Representation on and Increase in the Membership of the Security Council and Other Matters related to the Security Council,[1]

Recalling the elements relevant to the work of the Special Committee contained in its resolution 47/120 B of 20 September 1993,

Recalling also its resolution 51/241 of 31 July 1997 on the strengthening of the United Nations system and its resolution 51/242 of 15 September 1997, entitled "Supplement to an Agenda for Peace", by which it adopted the texts on coordination and the question of sanctions imposed by the United Nations, which are annexed to that resolution,

Concerned about the special economic problems confronting certain States arising from the carrying out of preventive or enforcement measures taken by the Security Council against other States, and taking into account the obligation of Members of the United Nations under Article 49 of the Charter of the United Nations to join in affording mutual assistance in carrying out the measures decided upon by the Council,

Recalling the right of third States confronted with special economic problems of that nature to consult the Security Council with regard to a solution of those problems, in accordance with Article 50 of the Charter,

Recalling also that the International Court of Justice is the principal judicial organ of the United Nations, and reaffirming its authority and independence,

Noting the adoption of the revised working papers on the working methods of the Special Committee,

Taking note of the report of the Secretary-General on the *Repertory of Practice of United Nations Organs* and the *Repertoire of the Practice of the Security Council*,[2]

Taking note also of paragraphs 106 to 110, 176 and 177 of the 2005 World Summit Outcome,[3]

Mindful of the decision of the Special Committee, in which it expressed its readiness to engage, as appropriate, in the implementation of any decisions that may be taken at the High-level Plenary Meeting of the sixtieth session of the General Assembly in September 2005 that concern the Charter and any amendments thereto,[4]

Recalling the provisions of its resolutions 50/51 of 11 December 1995, 51/208 of 17 December 1996, 52/162 of 15 December 1997, 53/107 of 8 December 1998, 54/107 of 9 December 1999, 55/157 of 12 December 2000, 56/87 of 12 December 2001, 57/25 of 19 November 2002, 58/80 of 9 December 2003 and 59/45 of 2 December 2004,

Recalling also its resolution 60/23 of 23 November 2005,

Having considered the report of the Special Committee on the work of its session held in 2006,[5]

Noting with appreciation the work done by the Special Committee to encourage States to focus on the need to prevent and to settle peacefully their disputes which are likely to endanger the maintenance of international peace and security,

1. *Takes note* of the report of the Special Committee on the Charter of the United Nations and on the Strengthening of the Role of the Organization;[5]

2. *Decides* that the Special Committee shall hold its next session from 7 to 14 and 16 February 2007;

3. *Notes with appreciation* the adoption, as a decision, of the working methods of the Special Committee, contained in paragraph 72 of its 2006 report;[5]

4. *Requests* the Special Committee, at its session in 2007, in accordance with paragraph 5 of General Assembly resolution 50/52 of 11 December 1995:

(*a*) To continue its consideration of all proposals concerning the question of the maintenance of international peace and security in all its aspects in order to strengthen the role of the United Nations, and, in this context, to consider other proposals relating to the maintenance of international peace and security already submitted or which may be submitted to the Special Committee at its session in 2007;

(*b*) To continue to consider, on a priority basis and in an appropriate substantive manner and framework, the question of the implementation of the provisions of the Charter of the United Nations related to assistance to third States affected by the application of sanctions under Chapter VII of the Charter based on all of the related reports of the Secretary-General[6] and the proposals submitted on the question;

(*c*) To keep on its agenda the question of the peaceful settlement of disputes between States;

(*d*) To consider, as appropriate, any proposal referred to it by the General Assembly in the implementation of the decisions of the High-level Plenary Meeting of the sixtieth session of the Assembly in September 2005 that concern the Charter and any amendments thereto;

(*e*) To continue to consider, on a priority basis, ways and means of improving its working methods and enhancing its efficiency with a view to identifying widely acceptable measures for future implementation;

5. *Invites* the Special Committee at its session in 2007 to continue to identify new subjects for consideration in its future work with a view to contributing to the revitalization of the work of the United Nations;

6. *Notes* the readiness of the Special Committee to provide, within its mandate, such assistance as may be sought at the request of other subsidiary bodies of the General Assembly in relation to any issues before them;

7. *Requests* the Special Committee to submit a report on its work to the General Assembly at its sixty-second session;

8. *Recognizes* the important role of the International Court of Justice, the principal judicial organ of the United Nations, in adjudicating disputes among States and the value of its work, as well as the importance of having recourse to the Court in the peaceful settlement of disputes, and requests the Secretary-General to distribute, in due course, the advisory opinions requested by the principal organs of the United Nations as official documents of the United Nations;

9. *Commends* the Secretary-General for the progress made in the preparation of studies of the *Repertory of Practice of United Nations Organs*, including the increased use of the internship programme of the United Nations and the wider cooperation with academic institutions for this purpose, as well as the progress made towards updating the *Repertoire of the Practice of the Security Council*;

10. *Calls upon* the Secretary-General to continue his efforts towards updating the two publications;

11. *Reiterates* the responsibility of the Secretary-General for the quality of the *Repertory of Practice of United Nations Organs* and the *Repertoire of the Practice of the Security Council* and, in particular, with regard to the *Repertoire of the Practice of the Security Council*, requests the Secretary-General to continue to follow the modalities outlined in paragraphs 102 to 106 of his report of 18 September 1952;[7]

12. *Recognizes* the desirability of making available electronically the *Repertory of Practice of United Nations Organs* and the *Repertoire of the Practice of the Security Council* in all their respective language versions;

13. *Reiterates its call* for voluntary contributions to the trust fund for the updating of the *Repertoire of the Practice of the Security Council*, as well as the trust fund for the elimination of the backlog in the *Repertory of Practice of United Nations Organs*, and the sponsoring, on a voluntary basis, and at no cost to the United Nations, of associate experts to assist in the updating of the two publications;

14. *Requests* the Secretary-General to submit a report on both the *Repertory of Practice of United Nations Organs* and the *Repertoire of the Practice of the Security Council* to the General Assembly at its sixty-second session;

15. *Also requests* the Secretary-General to submit to the Special Committee for its consideration the information referred to in paragraph 12 of his report on implementation of the provisions of the Charter of the United Nations related to assistance to third States affected by the application of sanctions,[8] on modalities, technical procedures and guidelines on coordination of technical assistance available to third States affected by the implementation of sanctions, as well as a possible methodology for assessing the adverse consequences actually incurred by third States, in the report mentioned in paragraph 16 below;

16. *Further requests* the Secretary-General to submit a report on the implementation of the provisions of the Charter of the United Nations related to assistance to third States affected by the application of sanctions to the General Assembly at its sixty-second session, under the item entitled "Report of the Special Committee on the Charter of the United Nations and on the Strengthening of the Role of the Organization";

17. *Decides* to include in the provisional agenda of its sixty-second session the item entitled "Report of the Special Committee on the Charter of the United Nations and on the Strengthening of the Role of the Organization".

64th plenary meeting
4 December 2006

---

[1] *Official Records of the General Assembly, Sixtieth Session, Supplement No. 47* (A/60/47).

[2] A/61/153.

[3] See resolution 60/1.

[4] *Official Records of the General Assembly, Sixtieth Session, Supplement No. 33* (A/60/33), para. 77.

[5] Ibid., *Sixty-first Session, Supplement No. 33* (A/61/33).

[6] A/48/573-S/26/705, A/49/356, A/50/60-S/1995/1, A/50/361, A/50/423, A/51/317, A/52/308, A/53/312, A/54/383 and Add.1, A/55/295 and Add.1, A/56/303, A/57/165 and Add.1, A/58/346, A/59/334 and A/60/320.

[7] A/2170.

[8] A/61/304.

Resolution 61/39

[on the report of the Sixth Committee (A/61/456)]

61/39. The rule of law at the national and international levels

The General Assembly,

Reaffirming its commitment to the purposes and principles of the Charter of the United Nations and international law, which are indispensable foundations of a more peaceful, prosperous and just world, and reiterating its determination to foster strict respect for them and to establish a just and lasting peace all over the world,

Reaffirming also that human rights, the rule of law and democracy are interlinked and mutually reinforcing and that they belong to the universal and indivisible core values and principles of the United Nations,

Reaffirming further the need for universal adherence to and implementation of the rule of law at both the national and international levels and its solemn commitment to an international order based on the rule of law and international law, which together with the principles of justice, is essential for peaceful coexistence and cooperation among States,

Convinced that the advancement of the rule of law at the national and international levels is essential for the realization of sustained economic growth, sustainable development, the eradication of poverty and hunger and the protection of all human rights and fundamental freedoms, and acknowledging that collective security depends on effective cooperation, in accordance with the Charter and international law, against transnational threats,

Reaffirming the duty of all States to refrain in their international relations from the threat or use of force in any manner inconsistent with the purposes and principles of the United Nations and to settle their international disputes by peaceful means in such a manner that international peace and security, and justice, are not endangered, and calling upon States that have not yet done so to consider accepting the jurisdiction of the International Court of Justice in accordance with its Statute,

Convinced that the promotion of and respect for the rule of law at the national and international levels, as well as justice and good governance, should guide the activities of the United Nations and of its Member States,

1. *Requests* the Secretary-General to seek the views of Member States on matters pertaining to the issues addressed in the present resolution and to submit a report thereon at its sixty-second session;

2. *Also requests* the Secretary-General to prepare an inventory of the current activities of the various organs, bodies, offices, departments, funds and programmes within the United Nations system devoted to the promotion of the rule of law at the national and international levels for submission at its sixty-third session, and to submit an interim report thereon to the General Assembly for its consideration at its sixty-second session;

3. *Further requests* the Secretary-General, after having sought the views of Member States, to prepare and submit, at its sixty-third session, a report identifying ways and means for strengthening and coordinating the activities listed in the inventory to be prepared pursuant to paragraph 2 above, with special regard to the effectiveness of assistance that may be

requested by States in building capacity for the promotion of the rule of law at the national and international levels;

4. *Urges* the Secretary-General, as a matter of priority, to submit the report on the establishment of a rule of law assistance unit within the Secretariat, in conformity with paragraph 134 (*e*) of the 2005 World Summit Outcome;[1]

5. *Decides* to include in the provisional agenda of its sixty-second session the item entitled "The rule of law at the national and international levels", and recommends that, as from the sixty-second session and after consultations among Member States, the Sixth Committee annually choose one or two sub-topics to facilitate a focused discussion for the subsequent session, without prejudice to the consideration of the item as a whole.

64th plenary meeting
4 December 2006

[1] See resolution 60/1.

Resolution 61/40

[on the report of the Sixth Committee (A/61/457)]

61/40. Measures to eliminate international terrorism

The General Assembly,

Guided by the purposes and principles of the Charter of the United Nations,

Reaffirming the United Nations Global Counter-Terrorism Strategy in all its aspects adopted on 8 September 2006,[1] enhancing the overall framework for the efforts of the international community to effectively counter the scourge of terrorism in all its forms and manifestations,

Recalling the Declaration on the Occasion of the Fiftieth Anniversary of the United Nations,[2]

Recalling also the United Nations Millennium Declaration,[3]

Recalling further the 2005 World Summit Outcome,[4] and reaffirming in particular the section on terrorism,

Recalling the Declaration on Measures to Eliminate International Terrorism, contained in the annex to General Assembly resolution 49/60 of 9 December 1994, and the Declaration to Supplement the 1994 Declaration on Measures to Eliminate International Terrorism, contained in the annex to resolution 51/210 of 17 December 1996,

Recalling also all General Assembly resolutions on measures to eliminate international terrorism, and Security Council resolutions on threats to international peace and security caused by terrorist acts,

Convinced of the importance of the consideration of measures to eliminate international terrorism by the General Assembly as the universal organ having competence to do so,

Deeply disturbed by the persistence of terrorist acts, which have been carried out worldwide,

Reaffirming its strong condemnation of the heinous acts of terrorism that have caused enormous loss of human life, destruction and damage, including those which prompted the adoption of General Assembly resolution 56/1 of 12 September 2001, as well as Security Council resolutions 1368 (2001) of 12 September 2001, 1373 (2001) of 28 September 2001 and 1377 (2001) of 12 November 2001, and those that have occurred since the adoption of the latter resolution,

Recalling the strong condemnation of the atrocious and deliberate attack against the headquarters of the United Nations Assistance Mission for Iraq in Baghdad on 19 August 2003 in General Assembly resolution 57/338 of 15 September 2003 and Security Council resolution 1502 (2003) of 26 August 2003,

Affirming that States must ensure that any measure taken to combat terrorism complies with all their obligations under international law and adopt such measures in accordance with international law, in particular international human rights, refugee and humanitarian law,

Stressing the need to strengthen further international cooperation among States and among international organizations and agencies, regional organizations and arrangements and the United Nations in order to prevent, combat and eliminate terrorism in all its forms and manifestations, wherever and by whomsoever committed, in accordance with the principles of the Charter, international law and the relevant international conventions,

Noting the role of the Security Council Committee established pursuant to resolution 1373 (2001) concerning counter-terrorism in monitoring the implementation of that resolution, including the taking of the necessary financial, legal and technical measures by States and the ratification or acceptance of the relevant international conventions and protocols,

Mindful of the need to enhance the role of the United Nations and the relevant specialized agencies in combating international terrorism, and of the proposals of the Secretary-General to enhance the role of the Organization in this respect,

Mindful also of the essential need to strengthen international, regional and subregional cooperation aimed at enhancing the national capacity of States to prevent and suppress effectively international terrorism in all its forms and manifestations,

Reiterating its call upon States to review urgently the scope of the existing international legal provisions on the prevention, repression and elimination of terrorism in all its forms and manifestations, with the aim of ensuring that there is a comprehensive legal framework covering all aspects of the matter,

Emphasizing that tolerance and dialogue among civilizations, and enhancing interfaith and intercultural understanding, are among the most important elements in promoting cooperation and success in combating terrorism, and welcoming the various initiatives to this end,

Reaffirming that no terrorist act can be justified in any circumstances,

Recalling Security Council resolution 1624 (2005) of 14 September 2005, and bearing in mind that States must ensure that any measure taken to combat terrorism complies with their obligations under international law, in particular international human rights, refugee and humanitarian law,

Taking note of the recent developments and initiatives at the international, regional and subregional levels to prevent and suppress international terrorism, including those of, inter alia, the African Union, the ASEAN Regional Forum, the Asia-Pacific Economic Cooperation, the Association of Southeast Asian Nations, the Bali Counter-Terrorism Process, the Central American Integration System, the Collective Security Treaty Organization, the Common Market for Eastern and Southern Africa, the Cooperation Council for the Arab States of the Gulf, the Council of Europe, the Economic Community of West African States, the Euro-Mediterranean Partnership, the European Free Trade Association, the European Union, the Group of Eight, the Intergovernmental Authority on Development, the International Maritime Organization, the International Civil Aviation Organization, the League of Arab States, the Movement of Non-Aligned Countries, the North Atlantic Treaty Organization, the Organization for Economic Cooperation and Development, the Organization for Security and Cooperation in Europe, the Organization of American States, the Organization of the Islamic Conference, the Pacific Islands Forum, the Shanghai Cooperation Organization, the Southern African Development Community and the World Customs Organization,

Noting regional efforts to prevent, combat and eliminate terrorism in all its forms and manifestations, wherever and by whomsoever committed, including through the elaboration of and adherence to regional conventions,

Recalling its decision in resolutions 54/110 of 9 December 1999, 55/158 of 12 December 2000, 56/88 of 12 December 2001, 57/27 of 19 November 2002, 58/81 of 9 December 2003, 59/46 of 2 December 2004 and 60/43 of 8 December 2005 that the Ad Hoc Committee established by General Assembly resolution 51/210 of 17 December 1996 should address, and keep on its agenda, the question of convening a high-level conference under the auspices of the United Nations to formulate a joint organized response of the international community to terrorism in all its forms and manifestations,

Recalling also the Final Document of the Fourteenth Conference of Heads of State or Government of Non-Aligned Countries, adopted in Havana on 16 September 2006, which reiterated the collective position of the Movement of Non-Aligned Countries on terrorism and reaffirmed its previous initiative[5] calling for an international summit conference under the auspices of the United Nations to formulate a joint organized response of the international community to terrorism in all its forms and manifestations, as well as other relevant initiatives,

Aware of its resolutions 57/219 of 18 December 2002, 58/187 of 22 December 2003, 59/191 of 20 December 2004 and 60/158 of 16 December 2005,

Having examined the report of the Secretary-General,[6] the report of the Ad Hoc Committee established by resolution 51/210[7] and the oral report presented by the Chairman of the Working Group established by the Sixth Committee during the sixty-first session of the General Assembly,[8]

1. *Strongly condemns* all acts, methods and practices of terrorism in all its forms and manifestations as criminal and unjustifiable, wherever and by whomsoever committed;

2. *Calls upon* all Member States, the United Nations and other appropriate international, regional and subregional organizations to implement the United Nations Global Counter-Terrorism Strategy[1] in all its aspects at the international, regional, subregional and national levels without delay, including through mobilizing resources and expertise;

3. *Recalls* the pivotal role of the General Assembly in following up the implementation and updating of the Strategy, and in this regard also recalls its invitation to the Secretary-General to contribute to the future deliberations of the General Assembly, and requests the Secretary-General when doing so to provide information on relevant activities within the Secretariat to ensure overall coordination and coherence in the counter-terrorism efforts of the United Nations system;

4. *Reiterates* that criminal acts intended or calculated to provoke a state of terror in the general public, a group of persons or particular persons for political purposes are in any circumstances unjustifiable, whatever the considerations of a political, philosophical, ideological, racial, ethnic, religious or other nature that may be invoked to justify them;

5. *Reiterates its call upon* all States to adopt further measures in accordance with the Charter of the United Nations and the relevant provisions of international law, including international standards of human rights, to prevent terrorism and to strengthen international cooperation in combating terrorism and, to that end, to consider in particular the implementation of the measures set out in paragraphs 3 (*a*) to (*f*) of resolution 51/210;

6. *Also reiterates its call upon* all States, with the aim of enhancing the efficient implementation of relevant legal instruments, to intensify, as and where appropriate, the exchange of information on facts related to terrorism and, in so doing, to avoid the dissemination of inaccurate or unverified information;

7. *Reiterates its call upon* States to refrain from financing, encouraging, providing training for or otherwise supporting terrorist activities;

8. *Urges* States to ensure that their nationals or other persons and entities within their territory that wilfully provide or collect funds for the benefit of persons or entities who commit, or attempt to commit, facilitate or participate in the commission of terrorist acts are punished by penalties consistent with the grave nature of such acts;

9. *Reminds* States of their obligations under relevant international conventions and protocols and Security Council resolutions, including Security Council resolution 1373 (2001), to ensure that perpetrators of terrorist acts are brought to justice;

10. *Reaffirms* that international cooperation as well as actions by States to combat terrorism should be conducted in conformity with the principles of the Charter, international law and relevant international conventions;

11. *Recalls* the adoption of the International Convention for the Suppression of Acts of Nuclear Terrorism,[9] the Amendment to the Convention on the Physical Protection of Nuclear Material,[10] the Protocol of 2005 to the Convention for the Suppression of Unlawful Acts against the Safety of Maritime Navigation[11] and the Protocol of 2005 to the Protocol for the Suppression of Unlawful Acts against the Safety of Fixed Platforms Located on the Continental shelf,[12] and urges all States to consider, as a matter of priority, becoming parties to these instruments;

12. *Urges* all States that have not yet done so to consider, as a matter of priority, and in accordance with Security Council resolution 1373 (2001), and Council resolution 1566 (2004) of 8 October 2004, becoming parties to the relevant conventions and protocols as referred to in paragraph 6 of General Assembly resolution 51/210, as well as the International Convention for the Suppression of Terrorist Bombings,[13] the International Convention for the Suppression of the Financing of Terrorism,[14] the International Convention for the Suppression of Acts of Nuclear Terrorism, and the Amendment to the Convention on the

Physical Protection of Nuclear Material, and calls upon all States to enact, as appropriate, the domestic legislation necessary to implement the provisions of those conventions and protocols, to ensure that the jurisdiction of their courts enables them to bring to trial the perpetrators of terrorist acts, and to cooperate with and provide support and assistance to other States and relevant international and regional organizations to that end;

13. *Urges* States to cooperate with the Secretary-General and with one another, as well as with interested intergovernmental organizations, with a view to ensuring, where appropriate within existing mandates, that technical and other expert advice is provided to those States requiring and requesting assistance in becoming parties to and implementing the conventions and protocols referred to in paragraph 12 above;

14. *Notes with appreciation and satisfaction* that, consistent with the call contained in paragraphs 9 and 10 of resolution 60/43, a number of States became parties to the relevant conventions and protocols referred to therein, thereby realizing the objective of wider acceptance and implementation of those conventions;

15. *Reaffirms* the Declaration on Measures to Eliminate International Terrorism and the Declaration to Supplement the 1994 Declaration on Measures to Eliminate International Terrorism, and calls upon all States to implement them;

16. *Calls upon* all States to cooperate to prevent and suppress terrorist acts;

17. *Urges* all States and the Secretary-General, in their efforts to prevent international terrorism, to make the best use of the existing institutions of the United Nations;

18. *Requests* the Terrorism Prevention Branch of the United Nations Office on Drugs and Crime in Vienna to continue its efforts to enhance, through its mandate, the capabilities of the United Nations in the prevention of terrorism, and recognizes, in the context of the United Nations Global Counter-Terrorism Strategy and Security Council resolution 1373 (2001), its role in assisting States in becoming parties to and implementing the relevant international conventions and protocols relating to terrorism, including the most recent among them, and in strengthening international cooperation mechanisms in criminal matters related to terrorism, including through national capacity-building;

19. *Welcomes* the publication by the Secretariat of the second edition of *International Instruments related to the Prevention and Suppression of International Terrorism*,[15] prepared by the Codification Division of the Office of Legal Affairs of the Secretariat pursuant to paragraph 10 (*a*) of the Declaration on Measures to Eliminate International Terrorism, in English and French, and considers it useful to examine the possibility of having future editions issued in all official languages;

20. *Invites* regional intergovernmental organizations to submit to the Secretary-General information on the measures they have adopted at the regional level to eliminate international terrorism, as well as on intergovernmental meetings held by those organizations;

21. *Notes* the progress attained in the elaboration of the draft comprehensive convention on international terrorism during the meetings of the Ad Hoc Committee established by General Assembly resolution 51/210 of 17 December 1996 and the Working Group established by the Sixth Committee during the sixty-first session of the General Assembly, and welcomes continuing efforts to that end;

22. *Decides* that the Ad Hoc Committee shall, on an expedited basis, continue to elaborate the draft comprehensive convention on international terrorism, and shall continue to discuss the item included in its agenda by General Assembly resolution 54/110 concerning the question of convening a high-level conference under the auspices of the United Nations;

23. *Decides also* that the Ad Hoc Committee shall meet on 5, 6 and 15 February 2007 in order to fulfil the mandate referred to in paragraph 22 above;

24. *Requests* the Secretary-General to continue to provide the Ad Hoc Committee with the necessary facilities for the performance of its work;

25. *Requests* the Ad Hoc Committee to report to the General Assembly at its sixty-first session in the event of the completion of the draft comprehensive convention on international terrorism;

26. *Also requests* the Ad Hoc Committee to report to the General Assembly at its sixty-second session on progress made in the implementation of its mandate;

27. *Decides* to include in the provisional agenda of its sixty-second session the item entitled "Measures to eliminate international terrorism".

64th plenary meeting
4 December 2006

---

[1] Resolution 60/288.

[2] See resolution 50/6.

[3] See resolution 55/2.

[4] See resolution 60/1.

[5] See A/53/667-S/1998/1071, annex I, paras. 149–162.

[6] A/61/210 and Add.1 and 2. See also A/61/178.

[7] *Official Records of the General Assembly, Sixty-first Session, Supplement No. 37* (A/61/37).

[8] Ibid., *Sixty-first Session, Sixth Committee,* 10th meeting (A/C.6/61/SR.10), and corrigendum.

[9] Resolution 59/290, annex.

[10] Adopted on 8 July 2005 by the Conference to Consider Proposed Amendments to the Convention on the Physical Protection of Nuclear Material.

[11] Adopted on 14 October 2005 by the Diplomatic Conference on the Revision of the SUA Treaties (LEG/CONF.15/21).

[12] Adopted on 14 October 2005 by the Diplomatic Conference on the Revision of the SUA Treaties (LEG/CONF.15/22).

[13] United Nations, *Treaty Series*, vol. 2149, No. 37517.

[14] Ibid., vol. 2178, No. 38349.

[15] United Nations publication, Sales No. E.03.V.9.

Resolution 61/41

[on the report of the Sixth Committee (A/61/461)]

61/41. Report of the Committee on Relations with the Host Country

The General Assembly,

Having considered the report of the Committee on Relations with the Host Country,[1]

Recalling Article 105 of the Charter of the United Nations, the Convention on the Privileges and Immunities of the United Nations,[2] the Agreement between the United Nations and the United States of America regarding the Headquarters of the United Nations[3] and the responsibilities of the host country,

Recalling also that, in accordance with paragraph 7 of General Assembly resolution 2819 (XXVI) of 15 December 1971, the Committee should consider, and advise the host country on, issues arising in connection with the implementation of the Agreement between the United Nations and the United States of America regarding the Headquarters of the United Nations,

Recognizing that effective measures should continue to be taken by the competent authorities of the host country, in particular to prevent any acts violating the security of missions and the safety of their personnel,

1. *Endorses* the recommendations and conclusions of the Committee on Relations with the Host Country contained in paragraph 86 of its report;[1]

2. *Considers* that the maintenance of appropriate conditions for the normal work of the delegations and the missions accredited to the United Nations and the observance of their privileges and immunities, which is an issue of great importance, are in the interest of the United Nations and all Member States, and requests the host country to continue to solve, through negotiations, problems that might arise and to take all measures necessary to prevent any interference with the functioning of missions; and urges the host country to continue to take appropriate action, such as training of police, security, customs and border control officers, with a view to maintaining respect for diplomatic privileges and immunities and if violations occur to ensure that such cases are properly investigated and remedied, in accordance with applicable law;

3. *Notes* the problems experienced by some permanent missions in connection with the implementation of the Parking Programme for Diplomatic Vehicles[4] and shall remain seized of the matter, with a view to continuing to maintain the proper implementation of the Parking Programme in a manner that is fair, non-discriminatory, effective and therefore consistent with international law, and also notes the decision of the Committee to conduct another review of the implementation of the Programme during the sixty-first session of the General Assembly and, subject to its outcome, will proceed accordingly;

4. *Requests* the host country to consider removing the remaining travel restrictions, notes that during the reporting period some travel restrictions previously imposed by the host country on staff of certain missions and staff members of the Secretariat of certain nationalities were removed, and, in this regard, notes the positions of affected States as reflected in the report of the Committee, of the Secretary-General and of the host country;

5. *Notes* that the Committee anticipates that the host country will enhance its efforts to ensure the issuance, in a timely manner, of entry visas to representatives of Member States, pursuant to article IV, section 11, of the Agreement between the United Nations and the United States of America regarding the Headquarters of the United Nations[3] to travel to New York on United Nations business; and notes that the Committee anticipates that the host country will enhance efforts to facilitate participation, including visa issuance, of representatives of Member States in other United Nations meetings as appropriate;

6. *Notes also* that a number of delegations have requested shortening the time frame applied by the host country for issuance of entry visas to representatives of Member States, since this time frame poses difficulties for the full-fledged participation of Member States in United Nations meetings;

7. *Expresses its appreciation* for the efforts made by the host country, and hopes that the issues raised at the meetings of the Committee will continue to be resolved in a spirit of cooperation and in accordance with international law;

8. *Affirms* the importance of the Committee being in a position to fulfil its mandate and meet on short notice to deal with urgent and important matters concerning the relations between the United Nations and the host country, and in that connection requests the Secretariat and the Committee on Conferences to accord priority to requests from the Committee on Relations with the Host Country for conference-servicing facilities for meetings of that Committee that must be held while the General Assembly and its Main Committees are meeting, without prejudice to the requirements of those bodies and on an "as available" basis;

9. *Requests* the Secretary-General to remain actively engaged in all aspects of the relations of the United Nations with the host country;

10. *Requests* the Committee to continue its work in conformity with General Assembly resolution 2819 (XXVI);

11. *Decides* to include in the provisional agenda of its sixty-second session the item entitled "Report of the Committee on Relations with the Host Country".

64th plenary meeting
4 December 2006

---

1 *Official Records of the General Assembly, Sixty-first Session, Supplement No. 26* (A/61/26).

2 Resolution 22 A (I).

3 See resolution 169 (II).

4 A/AC.154/355, annex.

Resolution 61/42

[on the report of the Sixth Committee (A/61/462)]

61/42. Observer status for the OPEC Fund for International Development in the General Assembly

The General Assembly,

Wishing to promote cooperation between the United Nations and the OPEC Fund for International Development,

1. *Decides* to invite the OPEC Fund for International Development to participate in the sessions and the work of the General Assembly in the capacity of observer;

2. *Requests* the Secretary-General to take the necessary action to implement the present resolution.

64th plenary meeting
4 December 2006

Resolution 61/43

[on the report of the Sixth Committee (A/61/462)]

61/43. Observer status for the Indian Ocean Commission in the General Assembly

The General Assembly,

Wishing to promote cooperation between the United Nations and the Indian Ocean Commission,

1. *Decides* to invite the Indian Ocean Commission to participate in the sessions and the work of the General Assembly in the capacity of observer;

2. *Requests* the Secretary-General to take the necessary action to implement the present resolution.

64th plenary meeting
4 December 2006

Resolution 61/44

[on the report of the Sixth Committee (A/61/462)]

61/44. Observer status for the Association of Southeast Asian Nations in the General Assembly

The General Assembly,

Wishing to promote cooperation between the United Nations and the Association of Southeast Asian Nations,

1. *Decides* to invite the Association of Southeast Asian Nations to participate in the sessions and the work of the General Assembly in the capacity of observer;

2. *Requests* the Secretary-General to take the necessary action to implement the present resolution.

64th plenary meeting
4 December 2006

Resolution 61/45

[without reference to a Main Committee (A/61/L.16 and Add.1)]

61/45. International Decade for a Culture of Peace and Non-Violence for the Children of the World, 2001–2010

The General Assembly,

Bearing in mind the Charter of the United Nations, including the purposes and principles contained therein, and especially the dedication to saving succeeding generations from the scourge of war,

Recalling the Constitution of the United Nations Educational, Scientific and Cultural Organization, which states that, "since wars begin in the minds of men, it is in the minds of men that the defences of peace must be constructed",

Recalling also its previous resolutions on a culture of peace, in particular resolution 52/15 of 20 November 1997 proclaiming 2000 the International Year for the Culture of Peace, resolution 53/25 of 10 November 1998 proclaiming the period 2001–2010 the International Decade for a Culture of Peace and Non-Violence for the Children of the World, and resolutions 56/5 of 5 November 2001, 57/6 of 4 November 2002, 58/11 of 10 November 2003, 59/143 of 15 December 2004 and 60/3 of 20 October 2005,

Reaffirming the Declaration[1] and Programme of Action[2] on a Culture of Peace, recognizing that they serve, inter alia, as the basis for the observance of the Decade, and convinced that the effective and successful observance of the Decade throughout the world will promote a culture of peace and non-violence that benefits humanity, in particular future generations,

Recalling the United Nations Millennium Declaration,[3] which calls for the active promotion of a culture of peace,

Taking note of Commission on Human Rights resolution 2000/66 of 26 April 2000 entitled "Towards a culture of peace",[4]

Taking note also of the report of the Secretary-General on the International Decade for a Culture of Peace and Non-Violence for the Childeren of the World,[5] including paragraph 28 thereof, which indicates that each of the ten years of the Decade will be marked with a different priority theme related to the Programme of Action,

Noting the relevance of the World Summit on Sustainable Development, held in Johannesburg, South Africa, from 26 August to 4 September 2002, the International Conference on Financing for Development, held in Monterrey, Mexico, from 18 to 22 March 2002, the special session of the General Assembly on children, held in New York from 8 to 10 May 2002, the World Conference against Racism, Racial Discrimination, Xenophobia and Related Intolerance, held in Durban, South Africa, from 31 August to 8 September 2001, and the United Nations Decade for Human Rights Education, 1995–2004, for the International Decade for a Culture of Peace and Non-Violence for the Children of the World, 2001–2010, as well as the need to implement, as appropriate, the relevant decisions agreed upon therein,

Recognizing that all efforts made by the United Nations system in general and the international community at large for peacekeeping, peacebuilding, the prevention of conflicts, disarmament, sustainable development, the promotion of human dignity and human rights, democracy, the rule of law, good governance and gender equality at the national and international levels contribute greatly to the culture of peace,

Noting that its resolution 57/337 of 3 July 2003 on the prevention of armed conflict could contribute to the further promotion of a culture of peace,

Taking into account the "Manifesto 2000" initiative of the United Nations Educational, Scientific and Cultural Organization promoting a culture of peace, which has so far received over seventy-five million signatures of endorsement throughout the world,

Taking note with appreciation of the report of the Director-General of the United Nations Educational, Scientific and Cultural Organization on the implementation of resolution 60/3,[6]

Taking note of the 2005 World Summit Outcome adopted on 16 September 2005 at the High-level Plenary Meeting of the General Assembly,[7]

Welcoming the establishment of the Peacebuilding Commission,

1. *Reiterates* that the objective of the International Decade for a Culture of Peace and Non-Violence for the Children of the World, 2001–2010, is to strengthen further the global movement for a culture of peace following the observance of the International Year for the Culture of Peace in 2000;

2. *Invites* Member States to continue to place greater emphasis on and expand their activities promoting a culture of peace and non-violence, in particular during the Decade, at the national, regional and international levels and to ensure that peace and non-violence are fostered at all levels;

3. *Commends* the United Nations Educational, Scientific and Cultural Organization for recognizing the promotion of a culture of peace as the expression of its fundamental mandate, and encourages it, as the lead agency for the Decade, to strengthen further the activities it has undertaken for promoting a culture of peace, including the dissemination of the Declaration[1] and Programme of Action[2] on a Culture of Peace and related materials in various languages across the world;

4. *Also commends* the relevant United Nations bodies, in particular the United Nations Children's Fund, the United Nations Development Fund for Women and the University for Peace, for their activities in further promoting a culture of peace and non-violence, including the promotion of peace education and activities related to specific areas identified in the Programme of Action, and encourages them to continue and further strengthen and expand their efforts;

5. *Encourages* the Peacebuilding Commission to promote a culture of peace and non-violence for children in its activities;

6. *Encourages* the appropriate authorities to provide education, in children's schools, that includes lessons in mutual understanding, tolerance, active citizenship, human rights and the promotion of a culture of peace;

7. *Commends* civil society, including non-governmental organizations and young people, for their activities in further promoting a culture of peace and non-violence, including through their campaign to raise awareness on a culture of peace, and notes the progress achieved by more than seven hundred organizations in more than one hundred countries;

8. *Encourages* civil society, including non-governmental organizations, to further strengthen its efforts in furtherance of the objectives of the Decade, inter alia, by adopting its own programme of activities to complement the initiatives of Member States, the organizations of the United Nations system and other international and regional organizations;

9. *Encourages* the involvement of the mass media in education for a culture of peace and non-violence, with particular regard to children and young people, including through the planned expansion of the Culture of Peace News Network as a global network of Internet sites in many languages;

10. *Welcomes* the efforts made by the United Nations Educational, Scientific and Cultural Organization to continue the communication and networking arrangements established during the International Year for providing an instant update of developments related to the observance of the Decade;

11. *Invites* Member States to observe 21 September of each year as the International Day of Peace, as a day of global ceasefire and non-violence, in accordance with resolution 55/282 of 7 September 2001;

12. *Invites* Member States, as well as civil society, including non-governmental organizations, to continue providing information to the Secretary-General on the observance of the Decade and the activities undertaken to promote a culture of peace and non-violence;

13. *Appreciates* the participation of Member States in the day of plenary meetings to review progress made in the implementation of the Declaration and Programme of Action and the observance of the Decade at its midpoint;

14. *Requests* the Secretary-General to explore enhancing mechanisms for the implementation of the Declaration and Programme of Action;

15. *Also requests* the Secretary-General to submit to the General Assembly at its sixty-second session a report on the implementation of the present resolution;

16. *Decides* to include in the provisional agenda of its sixty-second session the item entitled "Culture of peace".

64th plenary meeting
4 December 2006

---

[1] Resolution 53/243 A.

[2] Resolution 53/243 B.

[3] See resolution 55/2.

[4] See *Official Records of the Economic and Social Council, 2000, Supplement No. 3* and corrigendum (E/2000/23 and Corr.1), chap. II, sect. A.

[5] A/56/349.

[6] See A/61/175.

[7] See resolution 60/1.

Resolution 61/46

[without reference to a Main Committee (A/61/L.13 and Add.1)]

61/46. Cooperation between the United Nations and the Association of Southeast Asian Nations

The General Assembly,

Bearing in mind the aims and purposes of the Association of Southeast Asian Nations, as enshrined in the Bangkok Declaration of 8 August 1967,[1] in particular the maintenance of close and beneficial cooperation with existing international and regional organizations with similar aims and purposes,

Recalling its resolution 59/5 of 22 October 2004 on cooperation between the United Nations and the Association,

Noting with appreciation the report of the Secretary-General on cooperation between the United Nations and the Association,[2]

Noting with satisfaction that the activities of the Association are consistent with the purposes and principles of the United Nations,

Welcoming the ongoing efforts that strengthen the cooperation between the United Nations system and the Association,

Welcoming also the participation of the Association in the high-level meetings between the United Nations and regional organizations, as well as the collaboration between the Association and the Economic and Social Commission for Asia and the Pacific to promote dialogue and cooperation among regional organizations in Asia and the Pacific,

1. *Welcomes* the holding of the Second Association of Southeast Asian Nations-United Nations Summit at United Nations Headquarters on 13 September 2005, chaired jointly by Prime Minister Dato' Seri Abdullah Ahmad Badawi of Malaysia, the rotating Chair of the Association of Southeast Asian Nations Standing Committee and the Secretary-General of the United Nations, and attended by the leaders of the Association, as well as the heads of various United Nations agencies, funds and programmes;

2. *Acknowledges* the commitment of the leaders of the Association and the Secretary-General of the United Nations to further broaden cooperation between the Association and the United Nations, in the areas mentioned in the joint communiqué of the Second Association of Southeast Asian Nations-United Nations Summit;[3]

3. *Continues to encourage* both the United Nations and the Association to further strengthen and expand their areas of cooperation;

4. *Welcomes* the Association as an observer in the General Assembly;

5. *Encourages* the United Nations and the Association to convene Association of Southeast Asian Nations-United Nations summits regularly;

6. *Commends* the President of the General Assembly, the Secretary-General of the United Nations and the Ministers for Foreign Affairs of the States members of the Association for their efforts to hold regular meetings, on an annual basis, with the presence of the Secretary-General

of the Association, during the regular session of the Assembly, with a view to further strengthening the cooperation between the United Nations and the Association;

7. *Takes note* of the efforts of the Association to hold meetings with other regional organizations at the fringes of the sessions of the General Assembly to promote cooperation in support of multilateralism;

8. *Requests* the Secretary-General to submit to the General Assembly at its sixty-third session a report on the implementation of the present resolution;

9. *Decides* to include in the provisional agenda of its sixty-third session the sub-item entitled "Cooperation between the United Nations and the Association of Southeast Asian Nations".

65th plenary meeting
4 December 2006

[1] United Nations, *Treaty Series*, vol. 1331, No. 22341.

[2] See A/61/256, part one, sect. III.

[3] A/61/517, annex.

Resolution 61/47

[without reference to a Main Committee (A/61/L.18 and Add.1)]

61/47. Cooperation between the United Nations and the Preparatory Commission for the Comprehensive Nuclear-Test-Ban Treaty Organization

The General Assembly,

Taking note of the report of the Secretary-General on cooperation between the United Nations and the Preparatory Commission for the Comprehensive Nuclear-Test-Ban Treaty Organization,[1]

Taking note also of the report of the Executive Secretary of the Preparatory Commission for the Comprehensive Nuclear-Test-Ban Treaty Organization,[2]

Decides to include in the provisional agenda of its sixty-third session the sub-item entitled "Cooperation between the United Nations and the Preparatory Commission for the Comprehensive Nuclear-Test-Ban Treaty Organization".

65th plenary meeting
4 December 2006

[1] See A/61/256, part four.

[2] See A/61/184.

Resolution 61/48

[without reference to a Main Committee (A/61/L.20/Rev.1 and Add.1)]

61/48. Cooperation between the United Nations and the Pacific Islands Forum

The General Assembly,

Recalling its resolutions 49/1 of 17 October 1994 and 59/20 of 8 November 2004,

Welcoming the ongoing efforts towards closer cooperation between the United Nations and the Pacific Islands Forum and its associated institutions,

Bearing in mind that the Pacific Islands Forum, established in 1971, promotes regional cooperation and integration among its members through trade, investment, economic development and political and international affairs, to achieve their shared goals of economic growth, sustainable development, good governance and security,

Recalling the importance of the internationally agreed development goals set out in the United Nations Millennium Declaration,[1] the Monterrey Consensus of the International Conference on Financing for Development,[2] the Plan of Implementation of the World Summit on Sustainable Development ("Johannesburg Plan of Implementation")[3] and the Mauritius Strategy for the Further Implementation of the Programme of Action for the Sustainable Development of Small Island Developing States ("Mauritius Strategy for Implementation"),[4]

Taking note of the special circumstances pertaining to the continued presence of radioactive contaminants in certain Pacific Islands Forum nations,[5]

Recalling that one of the purposes of the United Nations is to achieve international cooperation in addressing international problems of an economic, social, cultural or humanitarian character,

Reaffirming the commitment of leaders at the 2005 World Summit, and bearing in mind the call thereat for a stronger relationship between the United Nations and regional and subregional organizations,

Affirming the need to strengthen the cooperation that already exists between entities of the United Nations system and the Pacific Islands Forum in the areas of peace and security, sustainable development, environmental protection and good governance,

Noting that many Pacific Islands Forum nations depend upon the continued existence of sustainable marine ecosystems,

Welcoming the support and assistance given by the United Nations towards the maintenance of peace and security in the Pacific Islands Forum region,

Taking note of the Communiqué of the Thirty-seventh Pacific Islands Forum, held at Nadi, Fiji, on 24 and 25 October 2006,[5]

Mindful of the need for coordinated and effective utilization of available resources in pursuing the common objectives of the two organizations,

Having considered the report of the Secretary-General on cooperation between the United Nations and regional and other organizations,[6]

1. *Takes note* of the report of the Secretary-General,[6] in particular part one, section XII, on cooperation between the United Nations and the Pacific Islands Forum, and encourages further such cooperation;

2. *Notes with satisfaction* that regular consultations continue at all levels between the United Nations and the Secretariat of the Pacific Islands Forum, including participation at the annual consultations between the Secretary-General and heads of regional organizations;

3. *Invites* the Secretary-General of the United Nations to take the necessary measures, in consultation with the Secretary-General of the Pacific Islands Forum, to promote and expand cooperation and coordination between the two secretariats in order to increase the capacity of the organizations to attain their common objectives;

4. *Welcomes* the ongoing work of various international organizations and United Nations agencies, funds and programmes in advancing knowledge in the key strategic areas related to governance, security, economic growth, trade and sustainable development, as well as in the implementation of the internationally agreed development goals, including those contained in the United Nations Millennium Declaration,[1] in the Pacific island countries;

5. *Recognizes* the challenges that Pacific island countries are facing in combating the HIV/AIDS pandemic, and in this regard urges the international community, including the United Nations system, to support Pacific island countries in their efforts to implement the Political Declaration on HIV/AIDS, adopted by the General Assembly at its sixtieth session on 2 June 2006,[7] including the commitment to set, in 2006, ambitious national targets that reflected the urgent need to scale up significantly towards the goal of universal access to comprehensive prevention programmes, treatment, care and support by 2010;

6. *Urges* Governments and all relevant international and regional organizations, the Economic and Social Council, United Nations funds, programmes and regional economic commissions, specialized agencies, international financial institutions and the Global Environment Facility, as well as other intergovernmental organizations and major groups, to take timely actions to support Pacific island countries in their efforts to ensure the effective implementation of and follow-up to the Johannesburg Declaration on Sustainable Development,[8] the Johannesburg Plan of Implementation[3] and the Mauritius Strategy for Implementation;[4]

7. *Notes* the importance of the United Nations Global Counter-Terrorism Strategy adopted on 8 September 2006,[9] and in this regard calls for the support of the United Nations system and other international partners in assisting Pacific island countries in their efforts to implement it;

8. *Welcomes* the ongoing efforts of the Pacific Islands Forum to promote, primarily through the Regional Security Committee, law enforcement cooperation, the rule of law and regional peace and security, including combating all types of terrorism, in implementing the core United Nations treaties on anti-terrorism, anti-money-laundering, transnational crime and the financing of terrorism;

9. *Requests*, in this regard, that the United Nations continue to assist the Pacific Islands Forum in facilitating among its members the timely implementation of relevant United Nations mandates, and invites States to contribute to the Biketawa Trust Fund, which is administered by the Pacific Islands Forum for confidence-building measures and conflict prevention;

10. *Welcomes* the significant efforts of the Pacific Islands Forum in enhancing peace and security in the region, including through the Regional Assistance Mission to Solomon Islands;

11. *Notes with appreciation* the role of the United Nations in the Bougainville peace process in Papua New Guinea and the steady progress being made by the parties;

12. *Welcomes* the establishment of the Peacebuilding Commission and the Peacebuilding Fund, and calls upon the Secretary-General and other relevant actors to give consideration to using these and other mechanisms to support post-conflict peacebuilding activities, reconstruction and institution-building efforts in Pacific island countries, particularly on the island of Bougainville and in Solomon Islands;

13. *Requests* that the Department of Political Affairs of the Secretariat and the United Nations Development Programme, in cooperation with the Pacific Islands Forum, promote joint cooperative needs assessment missions in the region to determine additional support to enhance peacebuilding and reconciliation processes and to complement the activities of regional missions and mechanisms;

14. *Calls upon* the international community to provide, where appropriate, technical and financial support to Pacific island countries in combating the illicit traffic in small arms and light weapons through, inter alia, the implementation of the Programme of Action to Prevent, Combat and Eradicate the Illicit Trade in Small Arms and Light Weapons in All Its Aspects;[10]

15. *Notes* the importance of the United Nations field presence in Pacific island countries for enhancing the cooperation with the United Nations system and its development agencies needed to implement the internationally agreed development goals, including the Millennium Development Goals and the Mauritius Strategy for Implementation;

16. *Welcomes*, in this regard, the endorsement by the Secretary-General of the establishment of an expanded and joint in-country presence of the United Nations in Kiribati, the Marshall Islands, Micronesia (Federated States of), Nauru, Palau, Solomon Islands, Tuvalu and Vanuatu;

17. *Expresses*, in this regard, its appreciation for the support and cooperation of the Pacific Islands Forum members in fulfilling host-country obligations and other operational modalities;

18. *Notes* the efforts of the United Nations, in cooperation with the Pacific Islands Forum, in respect of considering ways to assist Nauru, and in this regard calls upon the United Nations system to support implementation of the Republic of Nauru preparatory assistance project of the United Nations Development Programme as well as that country's national sustainable development strategy;

19. *Also notes* the participation of Pacific leaders at the special session of the Economic and Social Commission for Asia and the Pacific held in Jakarta on 10 April 2006, and takes note of the project "Enhancing Pacific connectivity";[11]

20. *Welcomes* the adoption of the Pacific Plan by Pacific Islands Forum leaders at the Thirty-sixth Pacific Islands Forum, in Madang, Papua New Guinea, during the leaders' Forum Retreat on 26 October 2005, which is aimed at enhancing regional integration and cooperation among its members and cooperation with the international community, including the United Nations system;

21. *Also welcomes* the leadership role of the Pacific Islands Forum in furthering the implementation of the 1995 Agreement for the Implementation of the Provisions of the United Nations Convention on the Law of the Sea of 10 December 1982 relating to the Conservation and Management of Straddling Fish Stocks and Highly Migratory Fish Stocks,[12] particularly in

the convening of the negotiations for, and the adoption of, the Convention on the Conservation and Management of Highly Migratory Fish Stocks in the Western and Central Pacific Ocean;

22. *Further welcomes* the decision to convene the Pacific regional seminar on decolonization in Nadi, Fiji, from 28 to 30 November 2006;

23. *Urges* the United Nations to support Pacific island countries in pursuing initiatives for enhancing South-South cooperation among themselves and also with other developing countries;

24. *Takes note* of the steps taken by the Pacific Islands Forum to solidify its partnership with non-State actors in the region in promoting governance and sustainable development issues;

25. *Recognizes* the burden placed on small States by growing international reporting requirements, and encourages the investigation of innovative reporting modalities, including regional reporting, where appropriate;

26. *Calls upon* the Office of the United Nations High Commissioner for Human Rights to provide technical support to Pacific Islands Forum members to contribute to the regional efforts in promoting awareness and knowledge of all international human rights treaties and instruments;

27. *Requests* the Secretary-General to submit to the General Assembly at its sixty-third session a report on the implementation of the present resolution;

28. *Decides* to include in the provisional agenda of its sixty-third session the sub-item entitled "Cooperation between the United Nations and the Pacific Islands Forum".

65th plenary meeting
4 December 2006

---

[1] See resolution 55/2.

[2] *Report of the International Conference on Financing for Development, Monterrey, Mexico, 18–22 March 2002* (United Nations publication, Sales No. E.02.II.A.7), chap. I, resolution 1, annex.

[3] *Report of the World Summit on Sustainable Development, Johannesburg, South Africa, 26 August–4 September 2002* (United Nations publication, Sales No. E.03.II.A.1 and corrigendum), chap. I, resolution 2, annex.

[4] *Report of the International Meeting to Review the Implementation of the Programme of Action for the Sustainable Development of Small Island Developing States, Port Louis, Mauritius, 10–14 January 2005* (United Nations publication, Sales No. E.05.II.A.4 and corrigendum), chap. I, resolution 1, annex II.

[5] See A/61/558, annex.

[6] A/61/256 and Add.1.

[7] Resolution 60/262, annex.

[8] *Report of the World Summit on Sustainable Development, Johannesburg, South Africa, 26 August–4 September 2002* (United Nations publication, Sales No. E.03.II.A.1 and corrigendum), chap. I, resolution 1, annex.

[9] Resolution 60/288.

[10] See *Report of the United Nations Conference on the Illicit Trade in Small Arms and Light Weapons in All Its Aspects, New York, 9–20 July 2001* (A/CONF.192/15), chap. IV, para. 24.

[11] See A/61/256, para. 89.

[12] United Nations, *Treaty Series*, vol. 2167, No. 37924.

Resolution 61/49

[without reference to a Main Committee (A/61/L.26 and Add.1)]

61/49. Cooperation between the United Nations and the Organization of the Islamic Conference

The General Assembly,

Recalling its resolutions 37/4 of 22 October 1982, 38/4 of 28 October 1983, 39/7 of 8 November 1984, 40/4 of 25 October 1985, 41/3 of 16 October 1986, 42/4 of 15 October 1987, 43/2 of 17 October 1988, 44/8 of 18 October 1989, 45/9 of 25 October 1990, 46/13 of 28 October 1991, 47/18 of 23 November 1992, 48/24 of 24 November 1993, 49/15 of 15 November 1994, 50/17 of 20 November 1995, 51/18 of 14 November 1996, 52/4 of 22 October 1997, 53/16 of 29 October 1998, 54/7 of 25 October 1999, 55/9 of 30 October 2000, 56/47 of 7 December 2001, 57/42 of 21 November 2002 and 59/8 of 22 October 2004,

Recalling also its resolution 3369 (XXX) of 10 October 1975, by which it decided to invite the Organization of the Islamic Conference to participate in the sessions and the work of the General Assembly and of its subsidiary organs in the capacity of observer,

Welcoming the efforts of the Secretary-General of the Organization of the Islamic Conference in strengthening the role of the Organization in conflict prevention, confidence-building, peacekeeping, conflict resolution and post-conflict rehabilitation in member States as well as in conflict situations involving Muslim communities,

Noting the adoption by the third extraordinary session of the Islamic Summit Conference, held in Mecca, Saudi Arabia, on 7 and 8 December 2005, of the Ten-Year Programme of Action,[1]

Having considered the report of the Secretary-General on cooperation between the United Nations and regional and other organizations,[2]

Taking into account the desire of the two organizations to continue to cooperate closely in the political, economic, social, humanitarian, cultural and scientific fields and in their common search for solutions to global problems, such as question relating to international peace and security, disarmament, self-determination, the promotion of a culture of peace through dialogue and cooperation, decolonization, fundamental human rights and economic and social development,

Recalling the Articles of the Charter of the United Nations that encourage activities through regional cooperation for the promotion of the purposes and principles of the United Nations,

Noting the strengthening of cooperation between the United Nations, its funds and programmes and the specialized agencies and the Organization of the Islamic Conference, its subsidiary organs and its specialized and affiliated institutions,

Noting also the encouraging progress made in the ten priority areas of cooperation between the two organizations and their respective agencies and institutions, as well as in the identification of other areas of cooperation between them,

Convinced that the strengthening of cooperation between the United Nations and other organizations of the United Nations system and the Organization of the Islamic Conference and its organs and institutions contributes to the promotion of the purposes and principles of the United Nations,

Welcoming the results of the general meeting of the organizations and agencies of the United Nations system and the Organization of the Islamic Conference and its subsidiary organs and specialized and affiliated institutions, held in Rabat from 11 to 13 July 2006, and the fact that these meetings are now being held every two years, with the next one scheduled for 2008, and also welcoming the memorandum of understanding on technical cooperation in the field of human rights between the Office of the United Nations High Commissioner for Human Rights and the Organization of the Islamic Conference signed at the Rabat meeting,

Welcoming also the issuance of a joint statement in Doha on 25 February 2006 by the Secretaries-General of the United Nations, the Organization of the Islamic Conference and the League of Arab States, together with the representatives of Qatar, Spain and Turkey, in the context of the Alliance of Civilizations, committing themselves to formulate a joint strategy to promote tolerance and mutual respect,

Welcoming further the close and multifaceted cooperation between the organizations and specialized institutions of the United Nations and the Organization of the Islamic Conference with a view to strengthening the capacities of the two organizations in addressing challenges to development and social progress,

Noting with appreciation the determination of the two organizations to strengthen further the existing cooperation by developing specific proposals in the designated priority areas of cooperation, as well as in the political field,

1. *Takes note with satisfaction* of the report of the Secretary-General;[2]

2. *Urges* the United Nations system to cooperate with the Organization of the Islamic Conference in areas of mutual interest, as appropriate;

3. *Notes with satisfaction* the active participation of the Organization of the Islamic Conference in the work of the United Nations towards the realization of the purposes and principles embodied in the Charter of the United Nations;

4. *Requests* the United Nations and the Organization of the Islamic Conference to continue to cooperate in their common search for solutions to global problems, such as questions relating to international peace and security, disarmament, self-determination, promotion of a culture of peace through dialogue and cooperation, decolonization, human rights and fundamental freedoms, terrorism, emergency relief and rehabilitation, social and economic development and technical cooperation;

5. *Welcomes* the efforts of the United Nations and the Organization of the Islamic Conference to continue to strengthen cooperation between the two organizations in areas of common concern and to review and explore innovative ways and means of enhancing the mechanisms of such cooperation;

6. *Welcomes with appreciation* the continuing cooperation between the United Nations and the Organization of the Islamic Conference in the fields of peacemaking, preventive diplomacy, peacekeeping and peacebuilding, and notes the close cooperation between the two organizations in reconstruction and development in Afghanistan, Bosnia and Herzegovina and Sierra Leone;

7. *Welcomes* the efforts of the secretariats of the two organizations to strengthen information exchange, coordination and cooperation between them in areas of mutual interest in the political field and to develop practical modalities of such cooperation;

8. *Also welcomes* the periodic high-level meetings between the Secretary-General of the United Nations and the Secretary-General of the Organization of the Islamic Conference, as well as between senior secretariat officials of the two organizations, and encourages their participation in important meetings of the two organizations;

9. *Encourages* the specialized agencies and other organizations of the United Nations system to continue to expand their cooperation with the subsidiary organs and specialized and affiliated institutions of the Organization of the Islamic Conference, in particular by negotiating cooperation agreements, and through necessary contacts and meetings of the respective focal points for cooperation in priority areas of interest to the United Nations and the Organization of the Islamic Conference;

10. *Urges* the United Nations and other organizations of the United Nations system, especially the lead agencies, to provide increased technical and other forms of assistance to the Organization of the Islamic Conference and its subsidiary organs and specialized and affiliated institutions in order to enhance cooperation;

11. *Expresses its appreciation* to the Secretary-General for his continued efforts to strengthen cooperation and coordination between the United Nations and other organizations of the United Nations system and the Organization of the Islamic Conference and its subsidiary organs and specialized and affiliated institutions to serve the mutual interests of the two organizations in the political, economic, social, cultural, humanitarian and scientific fields;

12. *Requests* the Secretary-General to report to the General Assembly at its sixty-third session on the state of cooperation between the United Nations and the Organization of the Islamic Conference;

13. *Decides* to include in the provisional agenda of its sixty-third session the sub-item entitled "Cooperation between the United Nations and the Organization of the Islamic Conference".

65th plenary meeting
4 December 2006

---

[1] A/60/633-S/2005/826, annex III.

[2] A/61/256 and Add.1.

Resolution 61/50

[without reference to a Main Committee (A/61/L.29 and Add.1)]

61/50. Cooperation between the United Nations and the Caribbean Community

The General Assembly,

Recalling its resolutions 46/8 of 16 October 1991, 49/141 of 20 December 1994, 51/16 of 11 November 1996, 53/17 of 29 October 1998, 55/17 of 7 November 2000, 57/41 of 21 November 2002 and 59/138 of 10 December 2004,

Bearing in mind the provisions of Chapter VIII of the Charter of the United Nations on the existence of regional arrangements or agencies for dealing with such matters relating to the maintenance of international peace and security as are appropriate for regional action and other activities consistent with the purposes and principles of the United Nations,

Bearing in mind also the assistance given by the United Nations towards the maintenance of peace and security in the Caribbean region,

Recalling the signing, on 27 May 1997, by the Secretary-General of the United Nations and the Secretary-General of the Caribbean Community of a cooperation agreement between the secretariats of the two organizations,

Bearing in mind that, in its resolutions 54/225 of 22 December 1999, 55/203 of 20 December 2000, 57/261 of 20 December 2002 and 59/230 of 22 December 2004, it recognized the importance of adopting an integrated management approach to the Caribbean Sea area in the context of sustainable development,

Bearing in mind also that in the United Nations Millennium Declaration, adopted by resolution 55/2 of 8 September 2000, Heads of State and Government resolved to address the special needs of small island developing States by implementing the Barbados Programme of Action[1] and the outcome of the twenty-second special session of the General Assembly[2] rapidly and in full,

Noting that the World Summit on Sustainable Development considered the specific issues and problems facing small island developing States,[3] taking note in this regard of the Monterrey Consensus of the International Conference on Financing for Development,[4] and noting the outcome of the International Meeting to Review the Implementation of the Programme of Action for the Sustainable Development of Small Island Developing States,[5]

Noting also that the Caribbean region is the second most hazard-prone region in the world and is frequently exposed to devastating hazards including earthquakes, floods, hurricanes and volcanic eruptions,

Noting further that the Caribbean region has been hard hit, and in some cases devastated, by hurricanes in the recent past, and concerned that their frequency, intensity and destructive power continue to pose a challenge to the development of the region,

Noting that the Declaration of Commitment on HIV/AIDS adopted by the General Assembly in resolution S-26/2 of 27 June 2001 recognized the Caribbean region as having the second-highest rate of infection after sub-Saharan Africa and that the region therefore needs special attention and assistance from the international community,

Noting also the commitment undertaken by the international community in the Political Declaration on HIV/AIDS, adopted by the High-level Meeting on HIV/AIDS on 2 June 2006, to assist low- and middle-income countries in achieving universal access to comprehensive HIV/AIDS prevention programmes, treatment, care and support by 2010,[6]

Affirming the need to strengthen the cooperation that already exists between entities of the United Nations system and the Caribbean Community in the areas of economic and social development, as well as the areas of political and humanitarian affairs,

Convinced of the need for the coordinated utilization of available resources to promote the common objectives of the two organizations,

Having considered the report of the Secretary-General on cooperation between the United Nations and regional and other organizations,[7]

1. *Takes note* of the report of the Secretary-General,[7] in particular part one, section IV, on the Caribbean Community, as well as efforts to strengthen cooperation;

2. *Calls upon* the Secretary-General of the United Nations, in association with the Secretary-General of the Caribbean Community, as well as the relevant regional organizations, to continue to assist in furthering the development and maintenance of peace and security within the Caribbean region;

3. *Invites* the Secretary-General to continue to promote and expand cooperation and coordination between the United Nations and the Caribbean Community in order to increase the capacity of the two organizations to attain their objectives;

4. *Urges* the specialized agencies and other organizations and programmes of the United Nations system to cooperate with the Secretary-General of the United Nations and the Secretary-General of the Caribbean Community in order to initiate, maintain and increase consultations and programmes with the Caribbean Community and its associated institutions in the attainment of their objectives, with special attention to the areas and issues identified at the third general meeting between representatives of the Caribbean Community and its associated institutions and of the United Nations system, held in New York on 12 and 13 April 2004, as set out in the report of the Secretary-General, as well as in resolutions 54/225, 55/2, 55/203 and S-26/2 and the decisions of the World Summit on Sustainable Development,[3] and the International Meeting to Review the Implementation of the Programme of Action for the Sustainable Development of Small Island Developing States,[5] as well as the Monterrey Consensus of the International Conference on Financing for Development;[4]

5. *Invites* the organizations of the United Nations system as well as Member States to increase financial and other assistance to the countries of the Caribbean Community to help to implement the priorities of the Caribbean Regional Strategic Framework for HIV/AIDS, which sets out realistic targets for reducing the rate of new infections, raising the quality and coverage of care, treatment and support and building institutional capacity, and to cope with the problems and the burden caused by the HIV/AIDS pandemic;

6. *Invites* the Secretary-General to consider utilizing a strategic programming framework modality to strengthen the coordination and cooperation between the two secretariats as well as between the United Nations field offices and the Caribbean Community;

7. *Calls upon* the United Nations, the specialized agencies and other organizations and programmes of the United Nations system to assist the countries of the Caribbean in addressing the social and economic consequences of the vulnerability of Caribbean economies and the challenges that this poses for achieving the Millennium Development Goals and the goal of sustainable development;

8. *Reaffirms* the objective of strengthening the implementation of the Mauritius Strategy for the Further Implementation of the Programme of Action for the Sustainable Development of Small Island Developing States,[5] including through the mobilization of financial and technological resources, as well as capacity-building programmes;

9. *Welcomes* the initiatives of Member States in assisting in the cooperation between the United Nations and the Caribbean Community, and encourages their continuing efforts;

10. *Recommends* that the fourth general meeting between representatives of the Caribbean Community and its associated institutions and of the United Nations system be held in the Caribbean in early 2007 in order to review and appraise progress in the implementation of the agreed areas and issues and to hold consultations on such additional measures and procedures as may be required to facilitate and strengthen cooperation between the two organizations;

11. *Requests* the Secretary-General to submit to the General Assembly at its sixty-third session a report on the implementation of the present resolution;

12. *Decides* to include in the provisional agenda of its sixty-third session the sub-item entitled "Cooperation between the United Nations and the Caribbean Community".

65th plenary meeting
4 December 2006

---

[1] Programme of Action for the Sustainable Development of Small Island Developing States (*Report of the Global Conference on the Sustainable Development of Small Island Developing States, Bridgetown, Barbados, 25 April–6 May 1994* (United Nations publication, Sales No. E.94.I.18 and corrigenda), chap. I, resolution 1, annex II).

[2] See resolution S-22/2.

[3] See *Report of the World Summit on Sustainable Development, Johannesburg, South Africa, 26 August–4 September 2002* (United Nations publication, Sales No. E.03.II.A.1 and corrigendum).

[4] *Report of the International Conference on Financing for Development, Monterrey, Mexico, 18–22 March 2002* (United Nations publication, Sales No. E.02.II.A.7), chap. I, resolution 1, annex.

[5] See *Report of the International Meeting to Review the Implementation of the Programme of Action for the Sustainable Development of Small Island Developing States, Port Louis, Mauritius, 10–14 January 2005* (United Nations publication, Sales No. E.05.II.A.4 and corrigendum).

[6] See resolution 60/262, annex.

[7] A/61/256 and Add.1.

Resolution 61/51

[without reference to a Main Committee (A/61/L.37 and Add.1)]

61/51. Cooperation between the United Nations and the Southern African Development Community

The General Assembly,

Recalling its resolution 37/248 of 21 December 1982 and all other relevant General Assembly resolutions and decisions on the promotion of cooperation between the United Nations and the Southern African Development Community, including resolutions 57/44 of 21 November 2002 and 59/140 of 15 December 2004 and decision 56/443 of 21 December 2001,

Recalling also its resolution 59/49 of 2 December 2004, in which it decided to invite the Community to participate in its sessions and its work in the capacity of observer,

Recognizing that cooperation between the Community and the United Nations system has continued to deepen,

Commending States members of the Community for demonstrating continued commitment to deeper and more formal arrangements for cooperation among themselves towards regional integration,

Welcoming the continued commitment made by the States members of the Community to deepen democracy, human rights, good governance and sound economic management,

Expressing satisfaction over continued efforts to bring peace to the Democratic Republic of the Congo, launched by the Community in collaboration with the African Union, the United Nations and other entities, and recognizing that the recent elections undertaken in the Democratic Republic of the Congo to end the current transition period by the establishment of elected institutions at all levels are an essential element of the peace process,

Noting with concern that the HIV/AIDS pandemic has reached crisis proportions in the region, and that other communicable diseases, such as malaria and tuberculosis, are having far-reaching social and economic consequences,

Expressing concern over the persistent natural disasters in countries of the region,

Welcoming the efforts of the Community to make southern Africa a landmine-free zone,

Recognizing the important role that women play in the development of the region,

Recognizing also the important role of civil society and the private sector in the development of the region,

1. *Takes note* of the report of the Secretary-General on cooperation between the United Nations and regional and other organizations;[1]

2. *Expresses its appreciation* to the United Nations funds and programmes as well as the international community for the assistance given to the Southern African Development Community;

3. *Welcomes* the decision of the Heads of State and Government of the Southern African Development Community at the summit held in Maseru on 17 and 18 August 2006 to convene a conference on poverty and development, to which the international community will be invited;

4. *Also welcomes* the progress made by the Community on gender and development towards achieving the target of 30 per cent representation of women in decision-making, and its commitment to the new target of 50 per cent;

5. *Notes with satisfaction* the commitment of States members of the Community to scale up the implementation of regional economic integration through, inter alia, the launching of a free trade area by 2008 and the preparations for a custom union by 2010;

6. *Expresses its support* for the economic reforms being implemented by States members of the Community, in pursuance of their shared vision of creating a strengthened regional economic community through deeper economic integration;

7. *Calls upon* the international community to strengthen support for the measures taken by the Community in fighting HIV and AIDS, as well as other communicable diseases such as malaria and tuberculosis, including commitments on the follow-up to the outcome of the

twenty-sixth special session of the General Assembly, and the implementation of the Declaration of Commitment on HIV/AIDS;[2]

8. *Recognizes* the vulnerability of the Community subregion to natural disasters, and in this regard calls upon the international community to provide the required assistance to strengthen the Community's disaster preparedness and early-warning capacity;

9. *Urges* the United Nations, its related bodies and the international community to continue to support the Community in building its capacity in negotiations on trade;

10. *Appeals* to the international community and to relevant organizations and bodies of the United Nations system to continue providing financial, technical and material assistance to the Community to support its efforts to fully implement the Regional Indicative Strategic Development Plan and the New Partnership for Africa's Development[3] as well as towards the achievement of other internationally agreed development goals, including the Millennium Development Goals;

11. *Appeals* to the United Nations, its related bodies and the international community to continue to assist and support the Community in its demining activities, and welcomes the progress made so far by its member States;

12. *Calls upon* the international community, in particular the United Nations system, to continue to contribute to the promotion of peace and stability in the Democratic Republic of the Congo and to assist in the rehabilitation and economic reconstruction of that country;

13. *Also calls upon* the international community to continue to assist the Democratic Republic of the Congo through the provision of humanitarian, financial and material assistance to alleviate the suffering of the Congolese people, in particular the children, women and the elderly, and calls upon the Government of the Democratic Republic of the Congo to implement economic and social policies and programmes that will improve the lives of the people of the Democratic Republic of the Congo;

14. *Urges* the United Nations funds and programmes and the international community to continue to provide technical assistance to national vulnerability assessment committees that have been established in the States members of the Community;

15. *Calls upon* the international community to support the efforts of the Community in capacity-building and in addressing the new challenges, opportunities and consequences presented to the economies in the region arising from the process of globalization and liberalization;

16. *Requests* the Secretary-General, in consultation with the Executive Secretary of the Community, to enhance contacts aimed at promoting and harmonizing further cooperation between the United Nations and the Community;

17. *Also requests* the Secretary-General to submit to the General Assembly at its sixty-third session a report on cooperation between the United Nations and the Southern African Development Community.

65th plenary meeting
4 December 2006

---

[1] A/61/256 and Add.1.

[2] Resolution S-26/2, annex.

[3] A/57/304, annex.

Resolution 61/52

[without reference to a Main Committee (A/61/L.15/Rev.1 and Add.1)]

61/52. Return or restitution of cultural property to the countries of origin

The General Assembly,

Reaffirming the relevant provisions of the Charter of the United Nations,

Recalling its resolutions 3026 A (XXVII) of 18 December 1972, 3148 (XXVIII) of 14 December 1973, 3187 (XXVIII) of 18 December 1973, 3391 (XXX) of 19 November 1975, 31/40 of 30 November 1976, 32/18 of 11 November 1977, 33/50 of 14 December 1978, 34/64 of 29 November 1979, 35/127 and 35/128 of 11 December 1980, 36/64 of 27 November 1981, 38/34 of 25 November 1983, 40/19 of 21 November 1985, 42/7 of 22 October 1987, 44/18 of 6 November 1989, 46/10 of 22 October 1991, 48/15 of 2 November 1993, 50/56 of 11 December 1995, 52/24 of 25 November 1997, 54/190 of 17 December 1999, 56/97 of 14 December 2001 and 58/17 of 3 December 2003,

Recalling also its resolution 56/8 of 21 November 2001, in which it proclaimed 2002 the United Nations Year for Cultural Heritage,

Recalling further the Convention for the Protection of Cultural Property in the Event of Armed Conflict, adopted at The Hague on 14 May 1954,[1] and the two Protocols thereto, adopted in 1954 and 1999,

Recalling the Convention on the Means of Prohibiting and Preventing the Illicit Import, Export and Transfer of Ownership of Cultural Property, adopted on 14 November 1970 by the General Conference of the United Nations Educational, Scientific and Cultural Organization,[2]

Recalling also the Convention concerning the Protection of the World Cultural and Natural Heritage, adopted on 16 November 1972 by the General Conference of the United Nations Educational, Scientific and Cultural Organization,[3]

Recalling further the Convention on Stolen or Illegally Exported Cultural Objects, adopted in Rome on 24 June 1995 by the International Institute for the Unification of Private Law,[4]

Taking note of the adoption of the Convention on the Protection of the Underwater Cultural Heritage by the General Conference of the United Nations Educational, Scientific and Cultural Organization on 2 November 2001,[5]

Noting the adoption of the Convention for the Safeguarding of the Intangible Cultural Heritage by the General Conference of the United Nations Educational, Scientific and Cultural Organization on 17 October 2003[6] and the Convention on the Protection and Promotion of the Diversity of Cultural Expressions by the General Conference of the United Nations Educational, Scientific and Cultural Organization on 20 October 2005,[7]

Noting also the adoption of the United Nations Convention on Jurisdictional Immunities of States and Their Property on 2 December 2004,[8] as it might apply to cultural property,

Recalling the Medellin Declaration for Cultural Diversity and Tolerance and the Plan of Action on Cultural Cooperation, adopted at the first Meeting of the Ministers of Culture of the Movement of Non-Aligned Countries, held in Medellin, Colombia, on 4 and 5 September 1997,[9]

Noting the adoption of the Universal Declaration on Cultural Diversity and the Action Plan for its implementation, adopted by the General Conference of the United Nations Educational, Scientific and Cultural Organization on 2 November 2001,[5]

Welcoming the report of the Secretary-General submitted in cooperation with the Director-General of the United Nations Educational, Scientific and Cultural Organization,[10]

Aware of the importance attached by some countries of origin to the return of cultural property that is of fundamental spiritual and cultural value to them, so that they may constitute collections representative of their cultural heritage,

Expressing concern about the illicit traffic in cultural property and its damage to the cultural heritage of nations,

Expressing concern also about the loss, destruction, removal, theft, pillage, illicit movement or misappropriation of and any acts of vandalism or damage directed against cultural property, in particular in areas of armed conflict, including territories that are occupied, whether such conflicts are international or internal,

Recalling Security Council resolution 1483 (2003), adopted on 22 May 2003, in particular paragraph 7 relating to the restitution of the cultural property of Iraq,

1. *Commends* the United Nations Educational, Scientific and Cultural Organization and the Intergovernmental Committee for Promoting the Return of Cultural Property to its Countries of Origin or its Restitution in Case of Illicit Appropriation on the work they have accomplished, in particular through the promotion of bilateral negotiations, for the return or restitution of cultural property, the preparation of inventories of movable cultural property and the implementation of the Object-ID standard related thereto, as well as for the reduction of illicit traffic in cultural property and the dissemination of information to the public;

2. *Calls upon* all relevant bodies, agencies, funds and programmes of the United Nations system and other relevant intergovernmental organizations to work in coordination with the United Nations Educational, Scientific and Cultural Organization, within their mandates and in cooperation with Member States, in order to continue to address the issue of return or restitution of cultural property to the countries of origin and to provide appropriate support accordingly;

3. *Welcomes* the adoption by the General Conference of the United Nations Educational, Scientific and Cultural Organization on 17 October 2003 of the Declaration concerning the Intentional Destruction of Cultural Heritage;[6]

4. *Reaffirms* the importance of the Convention on the Means of Prohibiting and Preventing the Illicit Import, Export and Transfer of Ownership of Cultural Property,[2] as well as the Convention on Stolen or Illegally Exported Cultural Objects of the International Institute for the Unification of Private Law,[4] and of their implementation, and invites Member States that have not already done so to consider becoming parties to these Conventions;

5. *Recognizes* the importance of the Convention on the Protection of the Underwater Cultural Heritage[5] and the Convention on the Protection and Promotion of the Diversity of Cultural Expressions,[7] notes that these Conventions have still not entered into force, and invites Member States that have not already done so to consider becoming parties to these Conventions;

6. *Also recognizes* the importance of the United Nations Convention on Jurisdictional Immunities of States and Their Property,[8] notes that this Convention has still not entered into force, and invites Member States that have not already done so to consider becoming parties to the Convention;

7. *Reaffirms* the importance of the principles and provisions of the Convention for the Protection of Cultural Property in the Event of Armed Conflict,[1] and of their implementation, and invites Member States that have not already done so to become parties to the Convention;

8. *Also reaffirms* the importance of the Second Protocol to the Convention, adopted at The Hague on 26 March 1999, and of its implementation, and invites all States parties to the Convention that have not already done so to consider becoming parties to the Second Protocol;

9. *Welcomes* the most recent efforts made by the United Nations Educational, Scientific and Cultural Organization for the protection of the cultural heritage of countries in conflict, including the safe return to those countries of cultural property and other items of archaeological, historical, cultural, rare scientific and religious importance that have been illegally removed, and calls upon the international community to contribute to these efforts;

10. *Urges* Member States to introduce effective national and international measures to prevent and combat illicit trafficking in cultural property, including special training for police, customs and border services;

11. *Invites* Member States, in cooperation with the United Nations Educational, Scientific and Cultural Organization, to continue to draw up systematic inventories of their cultural property, as well as to work towards the creation of a database of their national cultural legislation, in particular in electronic format;

12. *Welcomes* the launch of the Cultural Heritage Laws Database of the United Nations Educational, Scientific and Cultural Organization in 2005, and invites Member States to provide their legislation in electronic format for inclusion in the database, to provide regular updates to the database and to promote it;

13. *Reaffirms* the efforts of the United Nations Educational, Scientific and Cultural Organization to promote the use of identification systems, in particular the application of the Object-ID standard, and to encourage the linking of identification systems and existing databases, including the one developed by Interpol, to allow for the electronic transmission of information in order to reduce illicit trafficking in cultural property, and encourages the United Nations Educational, Scientific and Cultural Organization to make further efforts in this regard in cooperation with Member States, where appropriate;

14. *Recognizes* the revision of the Statutes of the Intergovernmental Committee for Promoting the Return of Cultural Property to its Countries of Origin or its Restitution in Case of Illicit Appropriation to include mediation and conciliation processes, and invites Member States to consider the possibility of using such processes as appropriate;

15. *Welcomes* the development of the model export certificate for cultural objects by the United Nations Educational, Scientific and Cultural Organization and the World Customs Organization as a tool to combat illicit trafficking in cultural property, and invites Member

States to consider adopting the model export certificate as their national export certificate, in accordance with domestic law and procedures;

16. *Notes* the decision taken in resolution 45, adopted on 20 October 2005 by the General Conference of the United Nations Educational, Scientific and Cultural Organization at its thirty-third session, that the subject of cultural objects displaced in connection with the Second World War should be the subject of a non-binding standard-setting instrument;[7]

17. *Recognizes* the public awareness and increased mobilization and action in favour of heritage values that was achieved in 2002, the United Nations Year for Cultural Heritage, and calls upon the international community and the United Nations to continue to cooperate with the United Nations Educational, Scientific and Cultural Organization on the basis of that work;

18. *Welcomes* the endorsement of the International Code of Ethics for Dealers in Cultural Property by the General Conference of the United Nations Educational, Scientific and Cultural Organization on 16 November 1999,[11] which was adopted in January 1999 by the Intergovernmental Committee for Promoting the Return of Cultural Property to its Countries of Origin or its Restitution in Case of Illicit Appropriation, and invites those who deal with trade in cultural property and their associations, where they exist, to encourage the implementation of the Code;

19. *Recognizes* the importance of the creation, by the General Conference of the United Nations Educational, Scientific and Cultural Organization, of the International Fund for the Return of Cultural Property to its Countries of Origin or its Restitution in Case of Illicit Appropriation, launched in November 2000, and encourages the United Nations Educational, Scientific and Cultural Organization to continue to promote the Fund and render it operational;

20. *Requests* the Secretary-General to cooperate with the United Nations Educational, Scientific and Cultural Organization in its efforts to bring about the attainment of the objectives of the present resolution;

21. *Also requests* the Secretary-General, in cooperation with the Director-General of the United Nations Educational, Scientific and Cultural Organization, to submit to the General Assembly at its sixty-fourth session a report on the implementation of the present resolution;

22. *Decides* to include in the provisional agenda of its sixty-fourth session the item entitled "Return or restitution of cultural property to the countries of origin".

65th plenary meeting
4 December 2006

---

[1] United Nations, *Treaty Series*, vol. 249, No. 3511.

[2] Ibid., vol. 823, No. 11806.

[3] Ibid., vol. 1037, No. 15511.

[4] Available from www.unidroit.org.

[5] See United Nations Educational, Scientific and Cultural Organization, *Records of the General Conference, Thirty-first Session, Paris, 15 October–3 November 2001*, vol. 1 and corrigendum: *Resolutions*.

[6] Ibid., *Thirty-second Session, Paris, 29 September–17 October 2003*, vol. 1: *Resolutions*.

[7] Ibid., *Thirty-third Session, Paris, 3–21 October 2005*, vol. 1: *Resolutions*.

[8] Resolution 59/38, annex.

[9] A/52/432, annexes I and II.

[10] See A/61/176.

[11] See United Nations Educational, Scientific and Cultural Organization, *Records of the General Conference, Thirtieth Session, Paris, 26 October–17 November 1999*, vol. 1: *Resolutions*.

Resolution 61/53

[on the report of the First Committee (A/61/387)]

61/53. Maintenance of international security — good-neighbourliness, stability and development in South-Eastern Europe

The General Assembly,

Recalling the purposes and principles of the Charter of the United Nations and the Final Act of the Conference on Security and Cooperation in Europe, signed in Helsinki on 1 August 1975,

Recalling also the United Nations Millennium Declaration[1] and the 2005 World Summit Outcome,[2]

Recalling further its previous resolutions on the subject, including resolution 59/59 of 3 December 2004,

Welcoming with appreciation the continuing cooperation among countries in the region of South-Eastern Europe on issues related to security, economy, trade, transport, energy, cross-border cooperation, human rights and justice and home affairs,

Welcoming the Republic of Montenegro as the 192nd State Member of the United Nations,

Reiterating the importance of the South-East European Cooperation Process for further enhancing regional cooperation and stability, which constitutes one of the main elements of the Stabilization and Association Process, and welcoming the positive results of the South-East European Cooperation Process summit meeting, held in Thessaloniki, Greece, on 4 May 2006,

Recalling the conclusions reached at the Summit of the European Council, held in Thessaloniki, Greece, on 19 and 20 June 2003, the decisions of the European Council on the principles, priorities and conditions contained in the European Partnerships with all countries of the Stabilization and Association Process and the outcome of the meeting held in Salzburg, Austria, of Ministers for Foreign Affairs on the European Union Stabilization and Association Process, confirming that the future of the Western Balkans lies in the European Union,

Noting the progress made by the countries of the region, including those of the Stabilization and Association Process, in fulfilling the criteria for membership in the European Union and, in this context, the start of the accession negotiations of Croatia and Turkey, the former Yugoslav Republic of Macedonia becoming a candidate country for membership in the European Union, the signing of the Stabilization and Association Agreement with Albania and the opening of the negotiations for a stabilization and association agreement with Bosnia and Herzegovina and Montenegro, as well as resuming stabilization and association agreement negotiations with Serbia, pending full cooperation with the International Tribunal for the Former Yugoslavia,

Stressing the role and responsibility of the United Nations Interim Administration Mission in Kosovo, supported by the Organization for Security and Cooperation in Europe and the European Union, and of the North Atlantic Treaty Organization and its Kosovo Force for further promotion of stability in the region, and noting the Council of the European Union's joint action establishing a European Union planning team,

Reaffirming the validity of the Agreement for the delineation of the borderline between the former Yugoslav Republic of Macedonia and Serbia and Montenegro, signed in Skopje on 23 February 2001,[3] and encouraging the parties to the Agreement and inviting all the parties involved in the process of settlement of the future status of Kosovo to respect the Agreement, to cooperate fully and to prepare for its timely implementation,

Emphasizing the crucial importance of strengthening regional efforts in South-Eastern Europe on arms control, demining, disarmament and confidence-building measures and non-proliferation of weapons of mass destruction, and noting that, in spite of ongoing efforts, the illicit trade in small arms and light weapons in all its aspects persists in some parts of the region,

Reaffirming its support for all regional initiatives on combating the illicit proliferation of small arms and light weapons, including the activities undertaken at the national level for their collection and destruction,

Mindful of the importance of national, regional and international activities aimed at the creation of peace, security, stability, democracy, cooperation and economic development and the observance of human rights and good-neighbourliness in South-Eastern Europe,

Reaffirming its determination that all nations should live together in peace with one another as good neighbours,

1. *Reaffirms* the need for full observance of the Charter of the United Nations;

2. *Calls upon* all States, the relevant international organizations and the appropriate organs of the United Nations to respect and support all the principles of the Charter and the commitments of the Organization for Security and Cooperation in Europe and through further development of regional arrangements, as appropriate, to eliminate threats to international peace and security and to help to prevent conflicts in south-Eastern Europe, which can lead to the violent disintegration of States;

3. *Acknowledges* the positive results achieved so far by the countries of the region, urges them to invest further efforts in consolidating South-Eastern Europe as a region of peace, security, stability, democracy, the rule of law, cooperation and economic development and for the promotion of good-neighbourliness and the observance of human rights, thus contributing to the maintenance of international peace and security and enhancing the prospects for sustained development and prosperity for all peoples in the region as an integral part of Europe, and recognizes the role of the United Nations, the Organization for Security and Cooperation in Europe and the European Union in successfully promoting regional disarmament;

4. *Supports* the countries of the region in their determination to gradually take over ownership and responsibility for regional cooperation by a phased evolution of the Stability Pact for South-Eastern Europe into a more regionally owned, streamlined and effective regional cooperation framework as set out at the Stability Pact's Regional Table meeting on 30 May 2006 in Belgrade;

5. *Stresses* that every effort should be made to achieve a negotiated settlement in line with Security Council resolution 1244 (1999) of 10 June 1999 and the contact group guiding principles; emphasizes the importance of the implementation of the standards for Kosovo; and fully supports the work of the Special Envoy of the Secretary-General and his team on the Kosovo status talks;

6. *Rejects* the use of violence in pursuit of political aims, and stresses that only peaceful political solutions can assure a stable and democratic future for South-Eastern Europe;

7. *Stresses* the importance of good-neighbourliness and the development of friendly relations among States, and calls upon all States to resolve their disputes with other States by peaceful means, in accordance with the Charter;

8. *Urges* the strengthening of relations among the States of South-Eastern Europe on the basis of respect for international law and agreements, in accordance with the principles of good-neighbourliness and mutual respect;

9. *Recognizes* the efforts of the international community, and in particular those of the European Union, the Stability Pact for South-Eastern Europe and other contributors, as well as of the South-East European Cooperation Process as an authentic voice of the region, in promoting the long-term process of democratic and economic development of the region;

10. *Calls upon* all States to intensify cooperation with and render all necessary assistance to the International Tribunal for the Prosecution of Persons Responsible for Serious Violations of International Humanitarian Law Committed in the Territory of the Former Yugoslavia since 1991 to bring all at-large indictees to surrender to the Tribunal in line with Security Council resolutions 1503 (2003) of 28 August 2003 and 1534 (2004) of 26 March 2004;

11. *Stresses* the importance of enhanced regional cooperation for the development of the South-Eastern European States in the priority areas of infrastructure, transport, trade, energy and environment, as well as in other areas of common interest, and welcomes the Treaty establishing the Energy Community, the establishment of the Regional Cooperation Council and the negotiations for the simultaneous enlargement and amendment of the Central European Free Trade Agreement;

12. *Also stresses* that the further rapprochement of the South-Eastern European States with the Euro-Atlantic institutions will favourably influence the security, political and economic situation in the region, as well as good-neighbourly relations among the States;

13. *Emphasizes* the importance of continuous regional efforts and intensified dialogue in South-Eastern Europe aimed at arms control, disarmament and confidence-building measures, as well as strengthening cooperation and undertaking appropriate measures at the national, subregional and regional levels against the proliferation of weapons of mass destruction and to prevent all acts of terrorism;

14. *Recognizes* the seriousness of the problem of anti-personnel mines and explosive remnants of war in some parts of South-Eastern Europe, welcomes in this context the efforts of the countries in the region and of the international community in support of mine action, and encourages States to join and support these efforts;

15. *Urges* all States to take effective measures against the illicit trade in small arms and light weapons in all its aspects and to help programmes and projects aimed at the collection and safe destruction of surplus stocks of small arms and light weapons, and stresses the importance of closer cooperation among States, inter alia, in crime prevention, combating terrorism, trafficking in human beings, organized crime and corruption, drug trafficking and money-laundering;

16. *Calls upon* all States and the relevant international organizations to communicate to the Secretary-General their views on the subject of the present resolution;

17. *Decides* to include in the provisional agenda of its sixty-third session the item entitled "Maintenance of international security — good-neighbourliness, stability and development in South-Eastern Europe".

67th plenary meeting
6 December 2006

---

1 See resolution 55/2.

2 See resolution 60/1.

3 A/56/60-S/2001/234, annex.

Resolution 61/54

[on the report of the First Committee (A/61/389)]

61/54. Developments in the field of information and telecommunications in the context of international security

The General Assembly,

Recalling its resolutions 53/70 of 4 December 1998, 54/49 of 1 December 1999, 55/28 of 20 November 2000, 56/19 of 29 November 2001, 57/53 of 22 November 2002, 58/32 of 8 December 2003, 59/61 of 3 December 2004 and 60/45 of 8 December 2005,

Recalling also its resolutions on the role of science and technology in the context of international security, in which, inter alia, it recognized that scientific and technological developments could have both civilian and military applications and that progress in science and technology for civilian applications needed to be maintained and encouraged,

Noting that considerable progress has been achieved in developing and applying the latest information technologies and means of telecommunication,

Affirming that it sees in this process the broadest positive opportunities for the further development of civilization, the expansion of opportunities for cooperation for the common good of all States, the enhancement of the creative potential of humankind and additional improvements in the circulation of information in the global community,

Recalling, in this connection, the approaches and principles outlined at the Information Society and Development Conference, held in Midrand, South Africa, from 13 to 15 May 1996,

Bearing in mind the results of the Ministerial Conference on Terrorism, held in Paris on 30 July 1996, and the recommendations that it made,[1]

Bearing in mind also the results of the World Summit on the Information Society, held in Geneva from 10 to 12 December 2003 (first phase) and in Tunis from 16 to 18 November 2005 (second phase),[2]

Noting that the dissemination and use of information technologies and means affect the interests of the entire international community and that optimum effectiveness is enhanced by broad international cooperation,

Expressing its concern that these technologies and means can potentially be used for purposes that are inconsistent with the objectives of maintaining international stability and security and may adversely affect the integrity of the infrastructure of States to the detriment of their security in both civil and military fields,

Considering that it is necessary to prevent the use of information resources or technologies for criminal or terrorist purposes,

Noting the contribution of those Member States that have submitted their assessments on issues of information security to the Secretary-General pursuant to paragraphs 1 to 3 of resolutions 53/70, 54/49, 55/28, 56/19, 57/53, 58/32, 59/61 and 60/45,

Taking note of the reports of the Secretary-General containing those assessments,[3]

Welcoming the initiative taken by the Secretariat and the United Nations Institute for Disarmament Research in convening an international meeting of experts in Geneva in August 1999 on developments in the field of information and telecommunications in the context of international security, as well as its results,

Considering that the assessments of the Member States contained in the reports of the Secretary-General and the international meeting of experts have contributed to a better understanding of the substance of issues of international information security and related notions,

Bearing in mind that the Secretary-General, in fulfilment of resolution 58/32, established in 2004 a group of governmental experts, which, in accordance with its mandate, considered existing and potential threats in the sphere of information security and possible cooperative measures to address them and conducted a study on relevant international concepts aimed at strengthening the security of global information and telecommunications systems,

Taking note of the report of the Secretary-General on the Group of Governmental Experts on Developments in the Field of Information and Telecommunications in the Context of International Security, prepared on the basis of the results of the Group's work,[4]

1. *Calls upon* Member States to promote further at multilateral levels the consideration of existing and potential threats in the field of information security, as well as possible measures to limit the threats emerging in this field, consistent with the need to preserve the free flow of information;

2. *Considers* that the purpose of such measures could be served through the examination of relevant international concepts aimed at strengthening the security of global information and telecommunications systems;

3. *Invites* all Member States to continue to inform the Secretary-General of their views and assessments on the following questions:

(*a*) General appreciation of the issues of information security;

(*b*) Efforts taken at the national level to strengthen information security and promote international cooperation in this field;

(*c*) The content of the concepts mentioned in paragraph 2 above;

(*d*) Possible measures that could be taken by the international community to strengthen information security at the global level;

4. *Requests* the Secretary-General, with the assistance of a group of governmental experts, to be established in 2009 on the basis of equitable geographical distribution, to continue to study existing and potential threats in the sphere of information security and possible cooperative measures to address them, as well as the concepts referred to in paragraph 2 above, and to submit a report on the results of this study to the General Assembly at its sixty-fifth session;

5. *Decides* to include in the provisional agenda of its sixty-second session the item entitled "Developments in the field of information and telecommunications in the context of international security".

67th plenary meeting
6 December 2006

[1] See A/51/261, annex.

[2] See A/C.2/59/3 and A/60/687.

[3] A/54/213, A/55/140 and Corr.1 and Add.1, A/56/164 and Add.1, A/57/166 and Add.1, A/58/373, A/59/116 and Add.1, A/60/95 and Add.1 and A/61/161.

[4] A/60/202.

Resolution 61/55

[on the report of the First Committee (A/61/390)]

61/55. Role of science and technology in the context of international security and disarmament

The General Assembly,

Recognizing that scientific and technological developments can have both civilian and military applications and that progress in science and technology for civilian applications needs to be maintained and encouraged,

Concerned that military applications of scientific and technological developments can contribute significantly to the improvement and upgrading of advanced weapons systems and, in particular, weapons of mass destruction,

Aware of the need to follow closely the scientific and technological developments that may have a negative impact on international security and disarmament, and to channel scientific and technological developments for beneficial purposes,

Cognizant that international transfers of dual-use as well as high-technology products, services and know-how for peaceful purposes are important for the economic and social development of States,

Also cognizant of the need to regulate such transfers of dual-use goods and technologies and high technology with military applications through multilaterally negotiated, universally applicable, non-discriminatory guidelines,

Expressing its concern about the growing proliferation of ad hoc and exclusive export control regimes and arrangements for dual-use goods and technologies, which tend to impede the economic and social development of developing countries,

Recalling that in the final document of the Fourteenth Conference of Heads of State or Government of Non-Aligned Countries, held in Havana on 15 and 16 September 2006,[1] it was again noted with concern that undue restrictions on exports to developing countries of material, equipment and technology for peaceful purposes persisted,

Emphasizing that internationally negotiated guidelines for the transfer of high technology with military applications should take into account the legitimate defence requirements of all States and the requirements for the maintenance of international peace and security, while ensuring that access to high-technology products and services and know-how for purpose is not denied,

1. *Affirms* that scientific and technological progress should be used for the benefit of all mankind to promote the sustainable economic and social development of all States and to safeguard international security, and that international cooperation in the use of science and technology through the transfer and exchange of technological know-how for peaceful purposes should be promoted;

2. *Invites* Member States to undertake additional efforts to apply science and technology for disarmament-related purposes and to make disarmament-related technologies available to interested States;

3. *Urges* Member States to undertake multilateral negotiations with the participation of all interested States in order to establish universally acceptable, non-discriminatory guidelines for international transfers of dual-use goods and technologies and high technology with military applications;

4. *Encourages* United Nations bodies to contribute, within existing mandates, to promoting the application of science and technology for peaceful purposes;

5. *Decides* to include in the provisional agenda of its sixty-third session the item entitled "Role of science and technology in the context of international security and disarmament".

67th plenary meeting
6 December 2006

---

[1] A/61/472-S/2006/780, annex I.

Resolution 61/56

[on the report of the First Committee (A/61/391)]

61/56. Establishment of a nuclear-weapon-free zone in the region of the Middle East

The General Assembly,

Recalling its resolutions 3263 (XXIX) of 9 December 1974, 3474 (XXX) of 11 December 1975, 31/71 of 10 December 1976, 32/82 of 12 December 1977, 33/64 of 14 December 1978, 34/77 of 11 December 1979, 35/147 of 12 December 1980, 36/87 A and B of 9 December 1981, 37/75 of 9 December 1982, 38/64 of 15 December 1983, 39/54 of 12 December 1984, 40/82 of 12 December 1985, 41/48 of 3 December 1986, 42/28 of 30 November 1987, 43/65 of 7 December 1988, 44/108 of 15 December 1989,

45/52 of 4 December 1990, 46/30 of 6 December 1991, 47/48 of 9 December 1992, 48/71 of 16 December 1993, 49/71 of 15 December 1994, 50/66 of 12 December 1995, 51/41 of 10 December 1996, 52/34 of 9 December 1997, 53/74 of 4 December 1998, 54/51 of 1 December 1999, 55/30 of 20 November 2000, 56/21 of 29 November 2001, 57/55 of 22 November 2002, 58/34 of 8 December 2003, 59/63 of 3 December 2004 and 60/52 of 8 December 2005 on the establishment of a nuclear-weapon-free zone in the region of the Middle East,

Recalling also the recommendations for the establishment of such a zone in the Middle East consistent with paragraphs 60 to 63, and in particular paragraph 63 *(d)*, of the Final Document of the Tenth Special Session of the General Assembly,[1]

Emphasizing the basic provisions of the above-mentioned resolutions, which call upon all parties directly concerned to consider taking the practical and urgent steps required for the implementation of the proposal to establish a nuclear-weapon-free zone in the region of the Middle East and, pending and during the establishment of such a zone, to declare solemnly that they will refrain, on a reciprocal basis, from producing, acquiring or in any other way possessing nuclear weapons and nuclear explosive devices and from permitting the stationing of nuclear weapons on their territory by any third party, to agree to place their nuclear facilities under International Atomic Energy Agency safeguards and to declare their support for the establishment of the zone to deposit such declarations with the Security Council for consideration, as appropriate,

Reaffirming the inalienable right of all States to acquire and develop nuclear energy for peaceful purposes,

Emphasizing the need for appropriate measures on the question of the prohibition of military attacks on nuclear facilities,

Bearing in mind the consensus reached by the General Assembly since its thirty-fifth session that the establishment of a nuclear-weapon-free zone in the Middle East would greatly enhance international peace and security,

Desirous of building on that consensus so that substantial progress can be made towards establishing a nuclear-weapon-free zone in the Middle East,

Welcoming all initiatives leading to general and complete disarmament, including in the region of the Middle East, and in particular on the establishment therein of a zone free of weapons of mass destruction, including nuclear weapons,

Noting the peace negotiations in the Middle East, which should be of a comprehensive nature and represent an appropriate framework for the peaceful settlement of contentious issues in the region,

Recognizing the importance of credible regional security, including the establishment of a mutually verifiable nuclear-weapon-free zone,

Emphasizing the essential role of the United Nations in the establishment of a mutually verifiable nuclear-weapon-free zone,

Having examined the report of the Secretary-General on the implementation of resolution 60/52,[2]

1. *Urges* all parties directly concerned to consider seriously taking the practical and urgent steps required for the implementation of the proposal to establish a nuclear-weapon-free zone in the region of the Middle East in accordance with the relevant resolutions of the General Assembly, and, as a means of promoting this objective, invites the countries concerned to adhere to the Treaty on the Non-Proliferation of Nuclear Weapons;[3]

2. *Calls upon* all countries of the region that have not done so, pending the establishment of the zone, to agree to place all their nuclear activities under International Atomic Energy Agency safeguards;

3. *Takes note* of resolution GC(50)/RES/16, adopted on 22 September 2006 by the General Conference of the International Atomic Energy Agency at its fiftieth regular session, concerning the application of Agency safeguards in the Middle East;[4]

4. *Notes* the importance of the ongoing bilateral Middle East peace negotiations and the activities of the multilateral Working Group on Arms Control and Regional Security in promoting mutual confidence and security in the Middle East, including the establishment of a nuclear-weapon-free zone;

5. *Invites* all countries of the region, pending the establishment of a nuclear-weapon-free zone in the region of the Middle East, to declare their support for establishing such a zone, consistent with paragraph 63 *(d)* of the Final Document of the Tenth Special Session of the General Assembly,[1] and to deposit those declarations with the Security Council;

6. *Also invites* those countries, pending the establishment of the zone, not to develop, produce, test or otherwise acquire nuclear weapons or permit the stationing on their territories, or territories under their control, of nuclear weapons or nuclear explosive devices;

7. *Invites* the nuclear-weapon States and all other States to render their assistance in the establishment of the zone and at the same time to refrain from any action that runs counter to both the letter and the spirit of the present resolution;

8. *Takes note* of the report of the Secretary-General;[2]

9. *Invites* all parties to consider the appropriate means that may contribute towards the goal of general and complete disarmament and the establishment of a zone free of weapons of mass destruction in the region of the Middle East;

10. *Requests* the Secretary-General to continue to pursue consultations with the States of the region and other concerned States, in accordance with paragraph 7 of resolution 46/30 and taking into account the evolving situation in the region, and to seek from those States their views on the measures outlined in chapters III and IV of the study annexed to the report of the Secretary-General of 10 October 1990[5] or other relevant measures, in order to move towards the establishment of a nuclear-weapon-free zone in the Middle East;

11. *Also requests* the Secretary-General to submit to the General Assembly at its sixty-second session a report on the implementation of the present resolution;

12. *Decides* to include in the provisional agenda of its sixty-second session the item entitled "Establishment of a nuclear-weapon-free zone in the region of the Middle East".

67th plenary meeting
6 December 2006

---

[1] Resolution S-10/2.

[2] A/61/140 (Part I).

[3] United Nations, *Treaty Series*, vol. 729, No. 10485.

[4] See International Atomic Energy Agency, *Resolutions and Other Decisions of the General Conference, Fiftieth Regular Session, 18–22 September 2006* (GC(50)/RES/DEC(2006)).

[5] A/45/435.

Resolution 61/57

[on the report of the First Committee (A/61/392)]

61/57. Conclusion of effective international arrangements to assure non-nuclear-weapon States against the use or threat of use of nuclear weapons

The General Assembly,

Bearing in mind the need to allay the legitimate concern of the States of the world with regard to ensuring lasting security for their peoples,

Convinced that nuclear weapons pose the greatest threat to mankind and to the survival of civilization,

Welcoming the progress achieved in recent years in both nuclear and conventional disarmament,

Noting that, despite recent progress in the field of nuclear disarmament, further efforts are necessary towards the achievement of general and complete disarmament under effective international control,

Convinced that nuclear disarmament and the complete elimination of nuclear weapons are essential to remove the danger of nuclear war,

Determined to abide strictly by the relevant provisions of the Charter of the United Nations on the non-use of force or threat of force,

Recognizing that the independence, territorial integrity and sovereignty of non-nuclear-weapon States need to be safeguarded against the use or threat of use of force, including the use or threat of use of nuclear weapons,

Considering that, until nuclear disarmament is achieved on a universal basis, it is imperative for the international community to develop effective measures and arrangements to ensure the security of non-nuclear-weapon States against the use or threat of use of nuclear weapons from any quarter,

Recognizing that effective measures and arrangements to assure non-nuclear-weapon States against the use or threat of use of nuclear weapons can contribute positively to the prevention of the spread of nuclear weapons,

Bearing in mind paragraph 59 of the Final Document of the Tenth Special Session of the General Assembly,[1] the first special session devoted to disarmament, in which it urged the nuclear-weapon States to pursue efforts to conclude, as appropriate, effective arrangements to assure non-nuclear-weapon States against the use or threat of use of nuclear weapons, and desirous of promoting the implementation of the relevant provisions of the Final Document,

Recalling the relevant parts of the special report of the Committee on Disarmament[2] submitted to the General Assembly at its twelfth special session,[3] the second special session devoted to disarmament, and of the special report of the Conference on Disarmament submitted to the Assembly at its fifteenth special session,[4] the third special session devoted to disarmament, as well as the report of the Conference on its 1992 session,[5]

Recalling also paragraph 12 of the Declaration of the 1980s as the Second Disarmament Decade, contained in the annex to its resolution 35/46 of 3 December 1980, which states, inter alia, that all efforts should be exerted by the Committee on Disarmament urgently to negotiate with a view to reaching agreement on effective international arrangements to assure non-nuclear-weapon States against the use or threat of use of nuclear weapons,

Noting the in-depth negotiations undertaken in the Conference on Disarmament and its Ad Hoc Committee on Effective International Arrangements to Assure Non-Nuclear-Weapon States against the Use or Threat of Use of Nuclear Weapons,[6] with a view to reaching agreement on this question,

Taking note of the proposals submitted under the item in the Conference on Disarmament, including the drafts of an international convention,

Taking note also of the relevant decision of the Thirteenth Conference of Heads of State or Government of Non-Aligned Countries, held at Kuala Lumpur on 24 and 25 February 2003,[7] which was reiterated at the Fourteenth Conference of Heads of State or Government of Non-Aligned Countries, held at Havana on 15 and 16 September 2006,[8] as well as the relevant recommendations of the Organization of the Islamic Conference,

Taking note further of the unilateral declarations made by all the nuclear-weapon States on their policies of non-use or non-threat of use of nuclear weapons against the non-nuclear-weapon States,

Noting the support expressed in the Conference on Disarmament and in the General Assembly for the elaboration of an international convention to assure non-nuclear-weapon States against the use or threat of use of nuclear weapons, as well as the difficulties pointed out in evolving a common approach acceptable to all,

Taking note of Security Council resolution 984 (1995) of 11 April 1995 and the views expressed on it,

Recalling its relevant resolutions adopted in previous years, in particular resolutions 45/54 of 4 December 1990, 46/32 of 6 December 1991, 47/50 of 9 December 1992, 48/73 of 16 December 1993, 49/73 of 15 December 1994, 50/68 of 12 December 1995, 51/43 of 10 December 1996, 52/36 of 9 December 1997, 53/75 of 4 December 1998, 54/52 of 1 December 1999, 55/31 of 20 November 2000, 56/22 of 29 November 2001, 57/56 of 22 November 2002, 58/35 of 8 December 2003, 59/64 of 3 December 2004 and 60/53 of 8 December 2005,

1. *Reaffirms* the urgent need to reach an early agreement on effective international arrangements to assure non-nuclear-weapon States against the use or threat of use of nuclear weapons;

2. *Notes with satisfaction* that in the Conference on Disarmament there is no objection, in principle, to the idea of an international convention to assure non-nuclear-weapon States against the use or threat of use of nuclear weapons, although the difficulties with regard to evolving a common approach acceptable to all have also been pointed out;

3. *Appeals* to all States, especially the nuclear-weapon States, to work actively towards an early agreement on a common approach and, in particular, on a common formula that could be included in an international instrument of a legally binding character;

4. *Recommends* that further intensive efforts be devoted to the search for such a common approach or common formula and that the various alternative approaches, including, in particular, those considered in the Conference on Disarmament, be explored further in order to overcome the difficulties;

5. *Also recommends* that the Conference on Disarmament actively continue intensive negotiations with a view to reaching early agreement and concluding effective international agreements to assure the non-nuclear-weapon States against the use or threat of use of nuclear weapons, taking into account the widespread support for the conclusion of an international convention and giving consideration to any other proposals designed to secure the same objective;

6. *Decides* to include in the provisional agenda of its sixty-second session the item entitled "Conclusion of effective international arrangements to assure non-nuclear-weapon States against the use or threat of use of nuclear weapons".

67th plenary meeting
6 December 2006

---

[1] Resolution S-10/2.

[2] The Committee on Disarmament was redesignated the Conference on Disarmament as from 7 February 1984.

[3] *Official Records of the General Assembly, Twelfth Special Session, Supplement No. 2* (A/S-12/2), sect. III.C.

[4] Ibid., *Fifteenth Special Session, Supplement No. 2* (A/S-15/2), sect. III.F.

[5] Ibid., *Forty-seventh Session, Supplement No. 27* (A/47/27), sect. III.F.

[6] Ibid., *Forty-eighth Session, Supplement No. 27* (A/48/27), para. 39.

[7] See A/57/759-S/2003/332, annex I.

[8] See A/61/472-S/2006/780, annex I.

Resolution 61/58

[on the report of the First Committee (A/61/393)]

61/58. Prevention of an arms race in outer space

The General Assembly,

Recognizing the common interest of all mankind in the exploration and use of outer space for peaceful purposes,

Reaffirming the will of all States that the exploration and use of outer space, including the Moon and other celestial bodies, shall be for peaceful purposes and shall be carried out for the benefit and in the interest of all countries, irrespective of their degree of economic or scientific development,

Reaffirming also the provisions of articles III and IV of the Treaty on Principles Governing the Activities of States in the Exploration and Use of Outer Space, including the Moon and Other Celestial Bodies,[1]

Recalling the obligation of all States to observe the provisions of the Charter of the United Nations regarding the use or threat of use of force in their international relations, including in their space activities,

Reaffirming paragraph 80 of the Final Document of the Tenth Special Session of the General Assembly,[2] in which it is stated that in order to prevent an arms race in outer space, further measures should be taken and appropriate international negotiations held in accordance with the spirit of the Treaty,

Recalling its previous resolutions on this issue, and taking note of the proposals submitted to the General Assembly at its tenth special session and at its regular sessions, and of the recommendations made to the competent organs of the United Nations and to the Conference on Disarmament,

Recognizing that prevention of an arms race in outer space would avert a grave danger for international peace and security,

Emphasizing the paramount importance of strict compliance with existing arms limitation and disarmament agreements relevant to outer space, including bilateral agreements, and with the existing legal regime concerning the use of outer space,

Considering that wide participation in the legal regime applicable to outer space could contribute to enhancing its effectiveness,

Noting that the Ad Hoc Committee on the Prevention of an Arms Race in Outer Space, taking into account its previous efforts since its establishment in 1985 and seeking to enhance its functioning in qualitative terms, continued the examination and identification of various issues, existing agreements and existing proposals, as well as future initiatives relevant to the prevention of an arms race in outer space,[3] and that this contributed to a better understanding of a number of problems and to a clearer perception of the various positions,

Noting also that there were no objections in principle in the Conference on Disarmament to the re-establishment of the Ad Hoc Committee, subject to re-examination of the mandate contained in the decision of the Conference on Disarmament of 13 February 1992,[4]

Emphasizing the mutually complementary nature of bilateral and multilateral efforts in the field of preventing an arms race in outer space, and hoping that concrete results will emerge from those efforts as soon as possible,

Convinced that further measures should be examined in the search for effective and verifiable bilateral and multilateral agreements in order to prevent an arms race in outer space, including the weaponization of outer space,

Stressing that the growing use of outer space increases the need for greater transparency and better information on the part of the international community,

Recalling, in this context, its previous resolutions, in particular resolutions 45/55 B of 4 December 1990, 47/51 of 9 December 1992 and 48/74 A of 16 December 1993, in which, inter alia, it reaffirmed the importance of confidence-building measures as a means conducive to ensuring the attainment of the objective of the prevention of an arms race in outer space,

Conscious of the benefits of confidence- and security-building measures in the military field,

Recognizing that negotiations for the conclusion of an international agreement or agreements to prevent an arms race in outer space remain a priority task of the Ad Hoc Committee and that the concrete proposals on confidence-building measures could form an integral part of such agreements,

Noting with satisfaction the constructive, structured and focused debate on the prevention of an arms race in outer space at the Conference on Disarmament in 2006,

1. *Reaffirms* the importance and urgency of preventing an arms race in outer space and the readiness of all States to contribute to that common objective, in conformity with the provisions of the Treaty on Principles Governing the Activities of States in the Exploration and Use of Outer Space, including the Moon and Other Celestial Bodies;[1]

2. *Reaffirms its recognition*, as stated in the report of the Ad Hoc Committee on the Prevention of an Arms Race in Outer Space, that the legal regime applicable to outer space does not in and of itself guarantee the prevention of an arms race in outer space, that the regime plays a significant role in the prevention of an arms race in that environmen, that there is a need to consolidate and reinforce that regime and enhance its effectiveness and that it is important to comply strictly with existing agreements, both bilateral and multilateral;

3. *Emphasizes* the necessity of further measures with appropriate and effective provisions for verification to prevent an arms race in outer space;

4. *Calls upon* all States, in particular those with major space capabilities, to contribute actively to the objective of the peaceful use of outer space and of the prevention of an arms race in outer space and to refrain from actions contrary to that objective and to the relevant existing treaties in the interest of maintaining international peace and security and promoting international cooperation;

5. *Reiterates* that the Conference on Disarmament, as the sole multilateral disarmament negotiating forum, has the primary role in the negotiation of a multilateral agreement or agreements, as appropriate, on the prevention of an arms race in outer space in all its aspects;

6. *Invites* the Conference on Disarmament to complete the examination and updating of the mandate contained in its decision of 13 February 1992[4] and to establish an ad hoc committee as early as possible during its 2007 session;

7. *Recognizes*, in this respect, the growing convergence of views on the elaboration of measures designed to strengthen transparency, confidence and security in the peaceful uses of outer space;

8. *Urges* States conducting activities in outer space, as well as States interested in conducting such activities, to keep the Conference on Disarmament informed of the progress of bilateral and multilateral negotiations on the matter, if any, so as to facilitate its work;

9. *Decides* to include in the provisional agenda of its sixty-second session the item entitled "Prevention of an arms race in outer space".

67th plenary meeting
6 December 2006

[1] Resolution 2222 (XXI), annex.

[2] Resolution S-10/2.

[3] *Official Records of the General Assembly, Forty-ninth Session, Supplement No. 27* (A/49/27), sect. III.D (para. 5 of the quoted text).

[4] CD/1125.

Resolution 61/59

[on the report of the First Committee (A/61/394)]

61/59. Missiles

The General Assembly,

Recalling its resolutions 54/54 F of 1 December 1999, 55/33 A of 20 November 2000, 56/24 B of 29 November 2001, 57/71 of 22 November 2002, 58/37 of 8 December 2003 and 59/67 of 3 December 2004 and its decision 60/515 of 8 December 2005,

Reaffirming the role of the United Nations in the field of arms regulation and disarmament and the commitment of Member States to take concrete steps to strengthen that role,

Realizing the need to promote regional and international peace and security in a world free from the scourge of war and the burden of armaments,

Convinced of the need for a comprehensive approach towards missiles, in a balanced and non-discriminatory manner, as a contribution to international peace and security,

Bearing in mind that the security concerns of Member States at the international and regional levels should be taken into consideration in addressing the issue of missiles,

Underlining the complexities involved in considering the issue of missiles in the conventional context,

Expressing its support for the international efforts against the development and proliferation of all weapons of mass destruction,

1. *Takes note* of the report of the Secretary-General on the issue of missiles in all its aspects, submitted pursuant to resolution 59/67;[1]

2. *Decides* to include in the provisional agenda of its sixty-second session the item entitled "Missiles".

67th plenary meeting
6 December 2006

[1] A/61/168.

Resolution 61/60

[on the report of the First Committee (A/61/394)]

61/60. Convening of the fourth special session of the General Assembly devoted to disarmament

The General Assembly,

Recalling its resolutions 49/75 I of 15 December 1994, 50/70 F of 12 December 1995, 51/45 C of 10 December 1996, 52/38 F of 9 December 1997, 53/77 AA of 4 December 1998, 54/54 U of 1 December 1999, 55/33 M of 20 November 2000, 56/24 D of 29 November 2001, 57/61 of 22 November 2002 and 59/71 of 3 December 2004, as well as its decisions 58/521 of 8 December 2003, 60/518 of 8 December 2005 and 60/559 of 6 June 2006,

Recalling also that, there being a consensus to do so in each case, three special sessions of the General Assembly devoted to disarmament were held in 1978, 1982 and 1988 respectively,

Bearing in mind the Final Document of the Tenth Special Session of the General Assembly, adopted by consensus at the first special session devoted to disarmament,[1]

Bearing in mind also the ultimate objective of general and complete disarmament under effective international control,

Taking note of paragraph 80 of the Final Document of the Fourteenth Conference of Heads of State or Government of Non-Aligned Countries, held at Havana on 15 and 16 September 2006,[2] which supported the convening of the fourth special session of the General Assembly devoted to disarmament, which would offer an opportunity to review, from a perspective more in tune with the current international situation, the most critical aspects of the process of disarmament and to mobilize the international community and public opinion in favour of the elimination of nuclear and other weapons of mass destruction and of the control and reduction of conventional weapons,

Recalling the United Nations Millennium Declaration, adopted by the Heads of State and Government during the Millennium Summit of the United Nations, held in New York from 6 to 8 September 2000,[3] in which they resolved "to strive for the elimination of weapons of mass destruction, particulary nuclear weapons, and to keep all options open for achieving this aim, including the possibility of convening an international conference to identify ways of eliminating nuclear dangers",

Reiterating its conviction that a special session of the General Assembly devoted to disarmament can set the future course of action in the fields of disarmament, arms control, non-proliferation and related international security matters,

Emphasizing the importance of multilateralism in the process of disarmament, arms control, non-proliferation and related international security matters,

Taking note of the report of the Open-ended Working Group to consider the objectives and agenda, including the possible establishment of the preparatory committee, for the fourth special session of the General Assembly devoted to disarmament,[4]

1. *Decides* to establish an open-ended working group, working on the basis of consensus, to consider the objectives and agenda, including the possible establishment of the preparatory

committee, for the fourth special session of the General Assembly devoted to disarmament, taking note of the paper presented by the Chairman of Working Group II during the 1999 substantive session of the Disarmament Commission[5] and the written proposals and views submitted by Member States as contained in the working papers presented during the three substantive sessions of the Open-ended Working Group in 2003[6] as well as the reports of the Secretary-General regarding the views of Member States on the objectives, agenda and timing of the fourth special session of the General Assembly devoted to disarmament;[7]

2. *Requests* the Open-ended Working Group to hold an organizational session in order to set the date for its substantive sessions in 2007 and to submit a report on its work, including possible substantive recommendations, before the end of the sixty-first session of the General Assembly;

3. *Requests* the Secretary-General, within existing resources, to provide the Open-ended Working Group with the necessary assistance and services as may be required to discharge its tasks;

4. *Decides* to include in the provisional agenda of its sixty-second session the item entitled "Convening of the fourth special session of the General Assembly devoted to disarmament".

67th plenary meeting
6 December 2006

---

[1] Resolution S-10/2.

[2] A/61/472-S/2006/780, annex I.

[3] See resolution 55/2.

[4] A/57/848.

[5] *Official Records of the General Assembly, Fifty-fourth Session, Supplement No. 42* (A/54/42), annex II.

[6] See A/AC.268/2003/WP.2.

[7] A/55/130 and Add.1, A/56/166 and A/57/120.

Resolution 61/61

[on the report of the First Committee (A/61/394)]

61/61. Measures to uphold the authority of the 1925 Geneva Protocol

The General Assembly,

Recalling its previous resolutions on the subject, in particular resolution 59/70 of 3 December 2004,

Determined to act with a view to achieving effective progress towards general and complete disarmament under strict and effective international control,

Recalling the long-standing determination of the international community to achieve the effective prohibition of the development, production, stockpiling and use of chemical and biological weapons as well as the continuing support for measures to uphold the authority of the Protocol for the Prohibition of the Use in War of Asphyxiating, Poisonous or Other Gases, and of Bacteriological Methods of Warfare, signed at Geneva on 17 June 1925,[1] as expressed by consensus in many previous resolutions,

Emphasizing the necessity of easing international tension and strengthening trust and confidence between States,

1. *Takes note* of the note by the Secretary-General;[2]

2. *Renews its previous call* to all States to observe strictly the principles and objectives of the Protocol for the Prohibition of the Use in War of Asphyxiating, Poisonous or Other Gases, and of Bacteriological Methods of Warfare,[1] and reaffirms the vital necessity of upholding its provisions;

3. *Calls upon* those States that continue to maintain reservations to the 1925 Geneva Protocol to withdraw them;

4. *Requests* the Secretary-General to submit to the General Assembly at its sixty-third session a report on the implementation of the present resolution.

67th plenary meeting
6 December 2006

[1] League of Nations, *Treaty Series*, vol. XCIV (1929), No. 2138.

[2] A/61/116.

Resolution 61/62

[on the report of the First Committee (A/61/394)]

61/62. Promotion of multilateralism in the area of disarmament and non-proliferation

The General Assembly,

Determined to foster strict respect for the purposes and principles enshrined in the Charter of the United Nations,

Recalling its resolution 56/24 T of 29 November 2001 on multilateral cooperation in the area of disarmament and non-proliferation and global efforts against terrorism and other relevant resolutions, as well as its resolutions 57/63 of 22 November 2002, 58/44 of 8 December 2003, 59/69 of 3 December 2004 and 60/59 of 8 December 2005 on the promotion of multilateralism in the area of disarmament and non-proliferation,

Recalling also the purpose of the United Nations to maintain international peace and security and, to that end, to take effective collective measures for the prevention and removal of threats to the peace and for the suppression of acts of aggression or other breaches of the peace, and to bring about by peaceful means, and in conformity with the principles of justice and international law, adjustment or settlement of international disputes or situations which might lead to a breach of the peace, as enshrined in the Charter,

Recalling further the United Nations Millennium Declaration,[1] which states, inter alia, that the responsibility for managing worldwide economic and social development, as well as threats to international peace and security, must be shared among the nations of the world and should be exercised multilaterally and that, as the most universal and most representative organization in the world, the United Nations must play the central role,

Convinced that, in the globalization era and with the information revolution, arms regulation, non-proliferation and disarmament problems are more than ever the concern of all countries in the world, which are affected in one way or another by these problems and, therefore, should have the possibility to participate in the negotiations that arise to tackle them,

Bearing in mind the existence of a broad structure of disarmament and arms regulation agreements resulting from non-discriminatory and transparent multilateral negotiations with the participation of a large number of countries, regardless of their siza and power,

Aware of the need to advance further in the field of arms regulation, nonproliferation and disarmament on the basis of universal, multilateral, nondiscriminatory and transparent negotiations with the goal of reaching general and complete disarmament under strict international control,

Recognizing the complementarity of bilateral, plurilateral and multilateral negotiations on disarmament,

Recognizing also that the proliferation and development of weapons of mass destruction, including nuclear weapons, are among the most immediate threats to international peace and security which need to be dealt with, with the highest priority,

Considering that the multilateral disarmament agreements provide the mechanism for States parties to consult one another and to cooperate in solving any problems which may arise in relation to the objective of, or in the application of, the provisions of the agreements and that such consultations and cooperation may also be undertaken through appropriate international procedures within the framework of the United Nations and in accordance with the Charter,

Stressing that international cooperation, the peaceful settlement of disputes, dialogue and confidence-building measures would contribute essentially to the creation of multilateral and bilateral friendly relations among peoples and nations,

Being concerned at the continuous erosion of multilateralism in the field of arms regulation, non-proliferation and disarmament, and recognizing that a resort to unilateral actions by Member States in resolving their security concerns would jeopardize international peace and security and undermine confidence in the international security system as well as the foundations of the United Nations itself,

Noting that the Fourteenth Conference of Heads of State or Government of Non-Aligned Countries, held at Havana on 15 and 16 September 2006, welcomed the adoption of General Assembly resolution 60/59 on the promotion of multilateralism in the area of disarmament and non-proliferation, and underlined the fact that multilateralism and multilaterally agreed solutions, in accordance with the Charter, provide the only sustainable method of addressing disarmament and international security issues,

Reaffirming the absolute validity of multilateral diplomacy in the field of disarmament and non-proliferation, and determined to promote multilateralism as an essential way to develop arms regulation and disarmament negotiations,

1. *Reaffirms* multilateralism as the core principle in negotiations in the area of disarmament and non-proliferation with a view to maintaining and strengthening universal norms and enlarging their scope;

2. *Also reaffirms* multilateralism as the core principle in resolving disarmament and non-proliferation concerns;

3. *Urges* the participation of all interested States in multilateral negotiations on arms regulation, non-proliferation and disarmament in a non-discriminatory and transparent manner;

4. *Underlines* the importance of preserving the existing agreements on arms regulation and disarmament, which constitute an expression of the results of international cooperation and multilateral negotiations in response to the challenges facing mankind;

5. *Calls once again upon* all Member States to renew and fulfil their individual and collective commitments to multilateral cooperation as an important means of pursuing and achieving their common objectives in the area of disarmament and non-proliferation;

6. *Requests* the States parties to the relevant instruments on weapons of mass destruction to consult and cooperate among themselves in resolving their concerns with regard to cases of non-compliance as well as on implementation, in accordance with the procedures defined in those instruments, and to refrain from resorting or threatening to resort to unilateral actions or directing unverified noncompliance accusations against one another to resolve their concerns;

7. *Takes note* of the report of the Secretary-General containing the replies of Member States on the promotion of multilateralism in the area of disarmament and non-proliferation, submitted pursuant to resolution 60/59;[2]

8. *Requests* the Secretary-General to seek the views of Member States on the issue of the promotion of multilateralism in the area of disarmament and non-proliferation and to submit a report thereon to the General Assembly at its sixty-second session;

9. *Decides* to include in the provisional agenda of its sixty-second session the item entitled "Promotion of multilateralism in the area of disarmament and nonproliferation".

67th plenary meeting
6 December 2006

---

[1] See resolution 55/2.

[2] A/61/114.

Resolution 61/63

[on the report of the First Committee (A/61/394)]

61/63. Observance of environmental norms in the drafting and implementation of agreements on disarmament and arms control

The General Assembly,

Recalling its resolutions 50/70 M of 12 December 1995, 51/45 E of 10 December 1996, 52/38 E of 9 December 1997, 53/77 J of 4 December 1998, 54/54 S of 1 December 1999, 55/33 K of 20 November 2000, 56/24 F of 29 November 2001, 57/64 of 22 November 2002, 58/45 of 8 December 2003, 59/68 of 3 December 2004 and 60/60 of 8 December 2005,

Emphasizing the importance of the observance of environmental norms in the preparation and implementation of disarmament and arms limitation agreements,

Recognizing that it is necessary to take duly into account the agreements adopted at the United Nations Conference on Environment and Development, as well as prior relevant agreements, in the drafting and implementation of agreements on disarmament and arms limitation,

Taking note of the report of the Secretary-General submitted pursuant to resolution 60/60,[1]

Mindful of the detrimental environmental effects of the use of nuclear weapons,

1. *Reaffirms* that international disarmament forums should take fully into account the relevant environmental norms in negotiating treaties and agreements on disarmament and arms limitation and that all States, through their actions, should contribute fully to ensuring compliance with the aforementioned norms in the implementation of treaties and conventions to which they are parties;

2. *Calls upon* States to adopt unilateral, bilateral, regional and multilateral measures so as to contribute to ensuring the application of scientific and technological progress within the framework of international security, disarmament and other related spheres, without detriment to the environment or to its effective contribution to attaining sustainable development;

3. *Welcomes* the information provided by Member States on the implementation of the measures they have adopted to promote the objectives envisaged in the present resolution;[1]

4. *Invites* all Member States to communicate to the Secretary-General information on the measures they have adopted to promote the objectives envisaged in the present resolution, and requests the Secretary-General to submit a report containing this information to the General Assembly at its sixty-second session;

5. *Decides* to include in the provisional agenda of its sixty-second session the item entitled "Observance of environmental norms in the drafting and implementation of agreements on disarmament and arms control".

67th plenary meeting
6 December 2006

[1] A/61/113.

Resolution 61/64

[on the report of the First Committee (A/61/394)]

61/64. Relationship between disarmament and development

The General Assembly,

Recalling that the Charter of the United Nations envisages the establishment and maintenance of international peace and security with the least diversion for armaments of the world's human and economic resources,

Recalling also the provisions of the Final Document of the Tenth Special Session of the General Assembly concerning the relationship between disarmament and development,[1] as well as the adoption on 11 September 1987 of the Final Document of the International Conference on the Relationship between Disarmament and Development,[2]

Recalling further its resolutions 49/75 J of 15 December 1994, 50/70 G of 12 December 1995, 51/45 D of 10 December 1996, 52/38 D of 9 December 1997, 53/77 K of 4 December 1998, 54/54 T of 1 December 1999, 55/33 L of 20 November 2000, 56/24 E of 29 November 2001, 57/65 of 22 November 2002, 59/78 of 3 December 2004 and 60/61 of 8 December 2005, and its decision 58/520 of 8 December 2003,

Bearing in mind the Final Document of the Twelfth Conference of Heads of State or Government of Non-Aligned Countries, held in Durban, South Africa, from 29 August to 3 September 1998,[3] and the Final Document of the Thirteenth Ministerial Conference of the Movement of Non-Aligned Countries, held in Cartagena, Colombia, on 8 and 9 April 2000,[4]

Mindful of the changes in international relations that have taken place since the adoption on 11 September 1987 of the Final Document of the International Conference on the Relationship between Disarmament and Development, including the development agenda that has emerged over the past decade,

Bearing in mind the new challenges for the international community in the field of development, poverty eradication and the elimination of the diseases that afflict humanity,

Stressing the importance of the symbiotic relationship between disarmament and development and the important role of security in this connection, and concerned at increasing global military expenditure, which could otherwise be spent on development needs,

Recalling the report of the Group of Governmental Experts on the relationship between disarmament and development[5] and its reappraisal of this significant issue in the current international context,

1. *Stresses* the central role of the United Nations in the disarmament-development relationship, and requests the Secretary-General to strengthen further the role of the Organization in this field, in particular the high-level Steering Group on Disarmament and Development, in order to assure continued and effective coordination and close cooperation between the relevant United Nations departments, agencies and sub-agencies;

2. *Requests* the Secretary-General to continue to take action, through appropriate organs and within available resources, for the implementation of the action programme adopted at the 1987 International Conference on the Relationship between Disarmament and Development;[2]

3. *Urges* the international community to devote part of the resources made available by the implementation of disarmament and arms limitation agreements to economic and social development, with a view to reducing the ever-widening gap between developed and developing countries;

4. *Encourages* the international community to achieve the Millennium Development Goals and to make reference to the contribution that disarmament could provide in meeting them

when it reviews its progress towards this purpose in 2006, as well as to make greater efforts to integrate disarmament, humanitarian and development activities;

5. *Encourages* the relevant regional and subregional organizations and institutions, non-governmental organizations and research institutes to incorporate issues related to the relationship between disarmament and development in their agendas and, in this regard, to take into account the report of the Group of Governmental Experts on the relationship between disarmament and development;[5]

6. *Requests* the Secretary-General to report to the General Assembly at its sixty-second session on the implementation of the present resolution;

7. *Decides* to include in the provisional agenda of its sixty-second session the item entitled "Relationship between disarmament and development".

67th plenary meeting
6 December 2006

---

[1] See resolution S-10/2.

[2] United Nations publication, Sales No. E.87.IX.8.

[3] A/53/667-S/1998/1071, annex I.

[4] A/54/917-S/2000/580, annex.

[5] See A/59/119.

Resolution 61/65

[on the report of the First Committee (A/61/394)]

61/65. Towards a nuclear-weapon-free world: accelerating the implementation of nuclear disarmament commitments

The General Assembly,

Recalling its resolution 60/56 of 8 December 2005,

Expressing its grave concern at the danger to humanity posed by the possibility that nuclear weapons could be used,

Reaffirming that nuclear disarmament and nuclear non-proliferation are mutually reinforcing processes requiring urgent irreversible progress on both fronts,

Mindful of the contribution of the final report of the Weapons of Mass Destruction Commission,[1]

Recalling the decisions and the resolution on the Middle East of the 1995 Review and Extension Conference of the Parties to the Treaty on the Non-Proliferation of Nuclear Weapons[2] and the Final Document of the 2000 Review Conference of the Parties to the Treaty on the Non-Proliferation of Nuclear Weapons,[3]

Recalling also the unequivocal undertaking by the nuclear-weapon States to accomplish the total elimination of their nuclear arsenals, leading to nuclear disarmament, in accordance with commitments made under article VI of the Treaty on the Non-Proliferation of Nuclear Weapons,[4]

Urging States parties to exert all possible efforts to ensure a successful and productive preparatory process for the 2010 Review Conference of the Parties to the Treaty on the Non-Proliferation of Nuclear Weapons,

1. *Continues to emphasize* the central role of the Treaty on the Non-Proliferation of Nuclear Weapons[4] and its universality in achieving nuclear disarmament and nuclear non-proliferation, and calls upon all States parties to respect their obligations;

2. *Reaffirms* that the outcome of the 2000 Review Conference of the Parties to the Treaty on the Non-Proliferation of Nuclear Weapons sets out the agreed process for systematic and progressive efforts towards nuclear disarmament;[3]

3. *Reiterates its call upon* the nuclear-weapon States to accelerate the implementation of the practical steps towards nuclear disarmament that were agreed upon at the 2000 Review Conference, thereby contributing to a safer world for all;

4. *Calls upon* all States to comply fully with all commitments made regarding nuclear disarmament and nuclear non-proliferation and not to act in any way that may compromise either cause or that may lead to a new nuclear arms race;

5. *Again calls upon* all States parties to spare no effort to achieve the universality of the Treaty on the Non-Proliferation of Nuclear Weapons, and urges India, Israel and Pakistan, which are not yet parties to the Treaty, to accede to it as non-nuclear-weapon States promptly and without conditions;

6. *Condemns* the announced nuclear-weapon test by the Democratic People's Republic of Korea on 9 October 2006, all nuclear-weapon tests by States that are not yet parties to the Treaty on the Non-Proliferation of Nuclear Weapons and any further nuclear-weapon test by any State whatsoever, and urges the Democratic People's Republic of Korea to rescind its announced withdrawal from the Treaty;

7. *Decides* to include in the provisional agenda of its sixty-second session the item entitled "Towards a nuclear-weapon-free world: accelerating the implementation of nuclear disarmament commitments" and to review the implementation of the present resolution at that session.

67th plenary meeting
6 December 2006

---

[1] *Weapons of Terror: Freeing the World of Nuclear, Biological and Chemical Arms* (United Nations publication, Sales No. E.06.I.17).

[2] See *1995 Review and Extension Conference of the Parties to the Treaty on the Non-Proliferation of Nuclear Weapons, Final Document, Part I* (NPT/CONF.1995/32 (Part I) and Corr.2), annex.

[3] *2000 Review Conference of the Parties to the Treaty on the Non-Proliferation of Nuclear Weapons, Final Document*, vols. I–III (NPT/CONF.2000/28 (Parts I–IV)).

[4] United Nations, *Treaty Series*, vol. 729, No. 10485.

Resolution 61/66

[on the report of the First Committee (A/61/394)]

61/66. The illicit trade in small arms and light weapons in all its aspects

The General Assembly,

Recalling its resolutions 56/24 V of 24 December 2001, 57/72 of 22 November 2002, 58/241 of 23 December 2003, 59/86 of 3 December 2004 and 60/81 of 8 December 2005,

Emphasizing the importance of the continued and full implementation of the Programme of Action to Prevent, Combat and Eradicate the Illicit Trade in Small Arms and Light Weapons in All Its Aspects, adopted by the United Nations Conference on the Illicit Trade in Small Arms and Light Weapons in All Its Aspects,[1]

Welcoming the efforts by Member States to submit, on a voluntary basis, national reports on their implementation of the Programme of Action,

Noting with satisfaction regional and subregional efforts being undertaken in support of the implementation of the Programme of Action, and commending the progress that has already been made in this regard, including tackling both supply and demand factors that are relevant to addressing the illicit trade in small arms and light weapons,

Recognizing the efforts undertaken by non-governmental organizations in the provision of assistance to States for the implementation of the Programme of Action,

Recalling that, as part of the follow-up to the United Nations Conference on the Illicit Trade in Small Arms and Light Weapons in All Its Aspects, it was agreed that meetings of States should be convened on a biennial basis to consider the national, regional and global implementation of the Programme of Action,[2]

Reiterating the significance of the adoption of the International Instrument to Enable States to Identify and Trace, in a Timely and Reliable Manner, Illicit Small Arms and Light Weapons,[3]

Recognizing that illicit brokering in small arms and light weapons is a serious problem that the international community should address urgently, and in this regard welcoming the decision of the General Assembly to establish a group of governmental experts to consider further steps to enhance international cooperation in preventing, combating and eradicating illicit brokering in small arms and light weapons,

Taking note of the report of the Secretary-General on the implementation of resolution 60/81,[4]

Welcoming the fact that the United Nations Conference to Review Progress Made in the Implementation of the Programme of Action to Prevent, Combat and Eradicate the Illicit Trade in Small Arms and Light Weapons in All Its Aspects,[5] held from 26 June to 7 July 2006, highlighted the importance of implementing the Programme of Action in the activities of the international community to prevent, combat and eradicate the illicit trade in small arms and light weapons in all its aspects, beyond 2006,

1. *Encourages* all initiatives, including those of the United Nations, other international organizations, regional and subregional organizations, nongovernmental organizations and civil society, for the successful implementation of the Programme of Action to Prevent, Combat and Eradicate the Illicit Trade in Small Arms and Light Weapons in All Its Aspects,[1]

and calls upon all Member States to contribute towards the continued implementation of the Programme of Action;

2. *Regrets* the fact that the United Nations Conference to Review Progress Made in the Implementation of the Programme of Action was not able to conclude an outcome document;[5]

3. *Calls upon* all States to implement the International Instrument to Enable States to Identify and Trace, in a Timely and Reliable Manner, Illicit Small Arms and Light Weapons,[3] among others, through the provision of information to the Secretary-General on the name and contact information of the national points of contact and on national marking practices related to markings used to indicate country of manufacture and/or country of import, as applicable;

4. *Decides* that, as stipulated in the Programme of Action, the next biennial meeting of States to consider the national, regional and global implementation of the Programme of Action shall be held no later than in 2008, in New York;

5. *Also decides* that the meeting of States to consider the implementation of the International Instrument to Enable States to Identify and Trace, in a Timely and Reliable Manner, Illicit Small Arms and Light Weapons, shall be held within the framework of the biennial meeting of States;

6. *Recalls* that the group of governmental experts, established to consider further steps to enhance international cooperation in preventing, combating and eradicating illicit brokering in small arms and light weapons is to submit a report on the outcome of its study to the General Assembly at its sixty-second session;

7. *Emphasizes* the fact that initiatives by the international community with respect to international cooperation and assistance remain essential and complementary to national implementation efforts, as well as to those at the regional and global levels;

8. *Continues to encourage* all such initiatives, including regional and subregional ones, to mobilize resources and expertise to promote the implementation of the Programme of Action and to provide assistance to States in its implementation;

9. *Encourages* States to submit national reports on their implementation of the Programme of Action and to include in such reports information on their implementation of the International Instrument to Enable States to Identify and Trace, in a Timely and Reliable Manner, Illicit Small Arms and Light Weapons in accordance with these instruments, and requests the Secretary-General to collate and circulate such data and information provided by States;

10. *Also encourages* States to share information on national experiences relating to best practices in the implementation of the Programme of Action;

11. *Requests* the Secretary-General to report to the General Assembly at its sixty-second session on the implementation of the present resolution;

12. *Decides* to include in the provisional agenda of its sixty-second session the item entitled "The illicit trade in small arms and light weapons in all its aspects".

67th plenary meeting
6 December 2006

[1] See *Report of the United Nations Conference on the Illicit Trade in Small Arms and Light Weapons in All Its Aspects, New York, 9–20 July 2001* (A/CONF.192/15), chap. IV, para. 24.

[2] Ibid., sect. IV, para. 1 (*b*).

[3] A/60/88 and Corr.2, annex; see also decision 60/519.

[4] See A/61/288.

[5] See A/CONF.192/2006/RC/9.

Resolution 61/67

[on the report of the First Committee (A/61/394)]

61/67. Declaration of a fourth disarmament decade

The General Assembly,

Recalling its previous resolutions on arms control, disarmament and nonproliferation, in particular those relating to its declaration of the First, Second and Third Disarmament Decades,[1]

Reaffirming the validity of the Final Document of the Tenth Special Session of the General Assembly,[2] the first special session devoted to disarmament,

Recalling the conclusion of the Secretary-General in his latest report to the General Assembly on the work of the Organization, inter alia, that if ever there was a time to break the deadlock in multilateral negotiations and bring disarmament back into the limelight of the international agenda, it is now,[3]

Seriously concerned at the current disarmament, non-proliferation and international security climate,

Recognizing the urgent need to mobilize concerted and more intensive global efforts to reverse the current trend in the field of arms control, disarmament and non-proliferation, including, where appropriate, indicative targets for accelerating attainment of the objectives of general and complete disarmament under effective international control,

Conscious of the role that a fourth disarmament decade could play in the mobilization of such global efforts to meet current and emerging challenges in the area of arms control, disarmament, non-proliferation and international security,

Directs the Disarmament Commission, at its 2009 substantive session, to prepare elements of a draft declaration of the 2010s as the fourth disarmament decade and to submit them for consideration by the General Assembly at its sixty-fourth session.

67th plenary meeting
6 December 2006

[1] Resolutions 2602 E (XXIV), 35/46 and 45/62 A.

[2] Resolution S-10/2.

[3] See *Official Records of the General Assembly, Sixty-first Session, Supplement No. 1* and corrigendum (A/61/1 and Corr.1), para. 95.

Resolution 61/68

[on the report of the First Committee (A/61/394)]

61/68. Implementation of the Convention on the Prohibition of the Development, Production, Stockpiling and Use of Chemical Weapons and on Their Destruction

The General Assembly,

Recalling its previous resolutions on the subject of chemical weapons, in particular resolution 60/67 of 8 December 2005, adopted without a vote, in which it noted with appreciation the ongoing work to achieve the objective and purpose of the Convention on the Prohibition of the Development, Production, Stockpiling and Use of Chemical Weapons and on Their Destruction,[1]

Determined to achieve the effective prohibition of the development, production, acquisition, transfer, stockpiling and use of chemical weapons and their destruction,

Noting with satisfaction that, since the adoption of resolution 60/67, six additional States have ratified the Convention or acceded to it, bringing the total number of States parties to the Convention to one hundred and eighty,

Reaffirming the importance of the outcome of the First Special Session of the Conference of the States Parties to Review the Operation of the Chemical Weapons Convention, including the Political Declaration,[2] in which the States parties reaffirmed their commitment to achieving the objective and purpose of the Convention, and the final report,[3] which addressed all aspects of the Convention and made important recommendations on its continued implementation,

1. *Emphasizes* that the universality of the Convention on the Prohibition of the Development, Production, Stockpiling and Use of Chemical Weapons and on Their Destruction[1] is fundamental to the achievement of its objective and purpose and acknowledges progress made in the implementation of the action plan for the universality of the Convention, and calls upon all States that have not yet done so to become parties to the Convention without delay;

2. *Underlines* the fact that the Convention and its implementation contribute to enhancing international peace and security, and emphasizes that its full, universal and effective implementation will contribute further to that purpose by excluding completely, for the sake of all humankind, the possibility of the use of chemical weapons;

3. *Stresses* that the full and effective implementation of all provisions of the Convention, including those on national implementation (article VII) and assistance and protection against chemical weapons (article X), constitutes an important contribution to the efforts of the United Nations in the global fight against terrorism in all its forms and manifestations;

4. *Also stresses* the importance to the Convention that all possessors of chemical weapons, chemical weapons production facilities or chemical weapons development facilities, including previously declared possessor States, should be among the States parties to the Convention, and welcomes progress to that end;

5. *Reaffirms* the obligation of the States parties to the Convention to destroy chemical weapons and to destroy or convert chemical weapons production facilities within the time limits provided for by the Convention;

6. *Notes* that the effective application of the verification system builds confidence in compliance with the Convention by States parties;

7. *Stresses* the importance of the Organization for the Prohibition of Chemical Weapons in verifying compliance with the provisions of the Convention as well as in promoting the timely and efficient accomplishment of all its objectives;

8. *Urges* all States parties to the Convention to meet in full and on time their obligations under the Convention and to support the Organization for the Prohibition of Chemical Weapons in its implementation activities;

9. *Welcomes* progress made in the national implementation of the plan of action on the implementation of article VII obligations and commends the States parties and the Technical Secretariat for assisting other States parties, on request, with the implementation of the follow-up to the plan of action regarding article VII obligations, and urges States parties that have not fulfilled their obligations under article VII to do so without further delay, in accordance with their constitutional processes;

10. *Reaffirms* the importance of article XI provisions relating to the economic and technological development of States parties and recalls that the full, effective and non-discriminatory implementation of those provisions contributes to universality, and also reaffirms the undertaking of the States parties to foster international cooperation for peaceful purposes in the field of chemical activities of the States parties and the importance of that cooperation and its contribution to the promotion of the Convention as a whole;

11. *Notes with appreciation* the ongoing work of the Organization for the Prohibition of Chemical Weapons to achieve the objective and purpose of the Convention, to ensure the full implementation of its provisions, including those for international verification of compliance with it, and to provide a forum for consultation and cooperation among States parties, and also notes with appreciation the substantial contribution of the Technical Secretariat and the Director-General to the continued development and success of the Organization;

12. *Welcomes* the decision of the Conference of the States Parties at its tenth session approving the appointment of Mr. Rogelio Pfirter as the Director-General of the Technical Secretariat of the Organization for the Prohibition of Chemical Weapons;[4]

13. *Also welcomes* the beginning of preparatory work by the States parties on the substance of the Second Special Session of the Conference of the States Parties to Review the Operation of the Chemical Weapons Convention;

14. *Draws attention* to the tenth anniversary of the entry into force of the Convention, on 29 April 2007, which provides a special occasion to publicly renew commitment to the multilateral treaty system and to the objective and purpose of the Convention, and takes note of the unveiling in The Hague on 9 May 2007 of a permanent memorial to all victims of chemical weapons;

15. *Welcomes* the cooperation between the United Nations and the Organization for the Prohibition of Chemical Weapons within the framework of the Relationship Agreement

between the United Nations and the Organization, in accordance with the provisions of the Convention;

16. *Decides* to include in the provisional agenda of its sixty-second session the item entitled "Implementation of the Convention on the Prohibition of the Development, Production, Stockpiling and Use of Chemical Weapons and on Their Destruction".

67th plenary meeting
6 December 2006

---

[1] United Nations, *Treaty Series*, vol. 1974, No. 33757.

[2] See Organization for the Prohibition of Chemical Weapons, document RC-1/3.

[3] Ibid., document RC-1/5.

[4] Ibid., document C-10/DEC.7.

Resolution 61/69

[on the report of the First Committee (A/61/394)]

61/69. Nuclear-weapon-free southern hemisphere and adjacent areas

The General Assembly,

Recalling its resolutions 51/45 B of 10 December 1996, 52/38 N of 9 December 1997, 53/77 Q of 4 December 1998, 54/54 L of 1 December 1999, 55/33 I of 20 November 2000, 56/24 G of 29 November 2001, 57/73 of 22 November 2002, 58/49 of 8 December 2003, 59/85 of 3 December 2004 and 60/58 of 8 December 2005,

Recalling also the adoption by the Disarmament Commission at its 1999 substantive session of a text entitled "Establishment of nuclear-weapon-free zones on the basis of arrangements freely arrived at among the States of the region concerned",[1]

Determined to pursue the total elimination of nuclear weapons,

Determined also to continue to contribute to the prevention of the proliferation of nuclear weapons in all its aspects and to the process of general and complete disarmament under strict and effective international control, in particular in the field of nuclear weapons and other weapons of mass destruction, with a view to strengthening international peace and security, in accordance with the purposes and principles of the Charter of the United Nations,

Recalling the provisions on nuclear-weapon-free zones of the Final Document of the Tenth Special Session of the General Assembly,[2] the first special session devoted to disarmament,

Stressing the importance of the treaties of Tlatelolco,[3] Rarotonga,[4] Bangkok[5] and Pelindaba[6] establishing nuclear-weapon-free zones, as well as the Antarctic Treaty,[7] to, inter alia, achieve a world entirely free of nuclear weapons,

Underlining the value of enhancing cooperation among the nuclear-weapon-free-zone treaty members by means of mechanisms such as joint meetings of States parties, signatories and observers to those treaties,

Noting the adoption of the Declaration of Santiago de Chile by the Governments of the States members of the Agency for the Prohibition of Nuclear Weapons in Latin America and the Caribbean and the States parties to the Treaty of Tlatelolco, during the nineteenth regular session of the General Conference of the Agency, held in Santiago on 7 and 8 November 2005,[8]

Recalling the applicable principles and rules of international law relating to the freedom of the high seas and the rights of passage through maritime space, including those of the United Nations Convention on the Law of the Sea,[9]

1. *Welcomes* the continued contribution that the Antarctic Treaty[7] and the treaties of Tlatelolco,[3] Rarotonga,[4] Bangkok[5] and Pelindaba[6] are making towards freeing the southern hemisphere and adjacent areas covered by those treaties from nuclear weapons;

2. *Also welcomes* the ratification by all original parties of the Treaty of Rarotonga, and calls upon eligible States to adhere to the Treaty and the protocols thereto;

3. *Further welcomes* the efforts towards the completion of the ratification process of the Treaty of Pelindaba, and calls upon the States of the region that have not yet done so to sign and ratify the Treaty, with the aim of its early entry into force;

4. *Calls upon* all concerned States to continue to work together in order to facilitate adherence to the protocols to nuclear-weapon-free-zone treaties by all relevant States that have not yet adhered to them;

5. *Welcomes* the steps taken to conclude further nuclear-weapon-free-zone treaties on the basis of arrangements freely arrived at among the States of the region concerned, and calls upon all States to consider all relevant proposals, including those reflected in its resolutions on the establishment of nuclear-weapon-free zones in the Middle East and South Asia;

6. *Also welcomes* the signing of the Treaty on a Nuclear-Weapon-Free Zone in Central Asia, in Semipalatinsk, Kazakhstan, on 8 September 2006;

7. *Affirms its conviction* of the important role of nuclear-weapon-free zones in strengthening the nuclear non-proliferation regime and in extending the areas of the world that are nuclear-weapon-free, and, with particular reference to the responsibilities of the nuclear-weapon States, calls upon all States to support the process of nuclear disarmament and to work for the total elimination of all nuclear weapons;

8. *Welcomes* the progress made on increased collaboration within and between zones at the first Conference of States Parties and Signatories to Treaties that Establish Nuclear-Weapon-Free Zones, held in Tlatelolco, Mexico, from 26 to 28 April 2005, at which States reaffirmed their need to cooperate in order to achieve their common objectives;

9. *Congratulates* the States parties and signatories to the treaties of Tlatelolco, Rarotonga, Bangkok and Pelindaba, as well as Mongolia, for their efforts to pursue the common goals envisaged in those treaties and to promote the nuclear-weapon-free status of the southern hemisphere and adjacent areas, and calls upon them to explore and implement further ways and means of cooperation among themselves and their treaty agencies;

10. *Encourages* the competent authorities of the nuclear-weapon-free-zone treaties to provide assistance to the States parties and signatories to those treaties so as to facilitate the accomplishment of the goals;

11. *Decides* to include in the provisional agenda of its sixty-second session the item entitled "Nuclear-weapon-free southern hemisphere and adjacent areas".

67th plenary meeting
6 December 2006

---

[1] *Official Records of the General Assembly, Fifty-fourth Session, Supplement No. 42* (A/54/42), annex I.

[2] Resolution S-10/2.

[3] United Nations, *Treaty Series*, vol. 634, No. 9068.

[4] See *The United Nations Disarmament Yearbook*, vol. 10: 1985 (United Nations publication, Sales No. E.86.IX.7), appendix VII.

[5] United Nations, *Treaty Series*, vol. 1981, No. 33873.

[6] A/50/426, annex.

[7] United Nations, *Treaty Series*, vol. 402, No. 5778.

[8] See A/60/678.

[9] United Nations, *Treaty Series*, vol. 1833, No. 31363.

Resolution 61/70

[on the report of the First Committee (A/61/394)]

61/70. 2010 Review Conference of the Parties to the Treaty on the Non-Proliferation of Nuclear Weapons and its Preparatory Committee

The General Assembly,

Recalling its resolution 2373 (XXII) of 12 June 1968, the annex to which contains the Treaty on the Non-Proliferation of Nuclear Weapons,[1]

Noting the provisions of article VIII, paragraph 3, of the Treaty regarding the convening of review conferences at five-year intervals,

Recalling the outcomes of the 1995 Review and Extension Conference of the Parties to the Treaty on the Non-Proliferation of Nuclear Weapons[2] and of the 2000 Review Conference of the Parties to the Treaty,[3]

Recalling also the decision of the 2000 Review Conference of the Parties to the Treaty on improving the effectiveness of the strengthened review process for the Treaty,[4] which reaffirmed the provisions in the decision on strengthening the review process for the Treaty, adopted by the 1995 Review and Extension Conference of the Parties to the Treaty,[5]

Recalling further that the 2005 Review Conference of the Parties to the Treaty, held from 2 to 27 May 2005,[6] was unable to produce a consensus substantive outcome on the review of the implementation of the provisions of the Treaty,

Noting the decision on strengthening the review process for the Treaty, in which it was agreed that review conferences should continue to be held every five years, and noting that, accordingly, the next review conference should be held in 2010,

Recalling the decision of the 2000 Review Conference that three sessions of the Preparatory Committee should be held in the years prior to the review conference,[4]

1. *Takes note* of the decision of the parties to the Treaty on the Non-Proliferation of Nuclear Weapons,[1] following appropriate consultations, to hold the first session of the Preparatory Committee in Vienna from 30 April to 11 May 2007;

2. *Requests* the Secretary-General to render the necessary assistance and to provide such services, including summary records, as may be required for the 2010 Review Conference of the Parties to the Treaty on the Non-Proliferation of Nuclear Weapons and its Preparatory Committee.

67th plenary meeting
6 December 2006

---

[1] See also United Nations, *Treaty Series*, vol. 729, No. 10485.

[2] See *1995 Review and Extension Conference of the Parties to the Treaty on the Non-Proliferation of Nuclear Weapons, Final Document, Part I* (NPT/CONF.1995/32 (Part I) and Corr.2).

[3] See *2000 Review Conference of the Parties to the Treaty on the Non-Proliferation of Nuclear Weapons, Final Document*, vols. I–III (NPT/CONF.2000/28 (Parts I–IV)).

[4] Ibid., vol. I (NPT/CONF.2000/28 (Parts I and II), part I).

[5] *1995 Review and Extension Conference of the Parties to the Treaty on the Non-Proliferation of Nuclear Weapons, Final Document, Part I* (NPT/CONF.1995/32 (Part I) and Corr.2), annex, decision 1.

[6] See NPT/CONF.2005/DC/1.

Resolution 61/71

[on the report of the First Committee (A/61/394)]

61/71. Assistance to States for curbing the illicit traffic in small arms and light weapons and collecting them

The General Assembly,

Recalling its resolution 60/71 of 8 December 2005 on assistance to States for curbing the illicit traffic in small arms and collecting them,

Deeply concerned by the magnitude of human casualty and suffering, especially among children, caused by the illicit proliferation and use of small arms and light weapons,

Concerned by the negative impact that the illicit proliferation and use of those weapons continue to have on the efforts of States in the Sahelo-Saharan subregion in the areas of poverty eradication, sustainable development and the maintenance of peace, security and stability,

Bearing in mind the Bamako Declaration on an African Common Position on the Illicit Proliferation, Circulation and Trafficking of Small Arms and Light Weapons, adopted at Bamako on 1 December 2000,[1]

Recalling the report of the Secretary-General entitled "In larger freedom: towards development, security and human rights for all",[2] in which he emphasized that States must strive just as hard to eliminate the threat of illicit small arms and light weapons as they do to eliminate the threat of weapons of mass destruction,

Taking note of the International Instrument to Enable States to Identify and Trace, in a Timely and Reliable Manner, Illicit Small Arms and Light Weapons, adopted in 2005,[3]

Welcoming the expression of support in the 2005 World Summit Outcome for the implementation of the Programme of Action to Prevent, Combat and Eradicate the Illicit Trade in Small Arms and Light Weapons in All its Aspects,[4]

Welcoming also the adoption, at the thirtieth ordinary summit of the Economic Community of West African States, held in Abuja in June 2006, of the Convention on Small Arms and Light Weapons, Their Ammunition and Other Related Materials, in replacement of the moratorium on the importation, exportation and manufacture of small arms and light weapons in West Africa,[5]

Welcoming further the decision taken by the Economic Community to establish a Small Arms Unit responsible for advocating appropriate policies and developing and implementing programmes, as well as the establishment of the Economic Community's Small Arms Control Programme, launched on 16 June 2006 in Bamako, in replacement of the Programme for Coordination and Assistance for Security and Development,

Taking note of the latest report of the Secretary-General on assistance to States for curbing the illicit traffic in small arms and light weapons and collecting them and the illicit trade in small arms and light weapons in all its aspects,[6]

Welcoming, in that regard, the decision of the European Union to significantly support the Economic Community in its efforts to combat the illicit proliferation of small arms and light weapons,

Recognizing the important role that civil society organizations play, in raising public awareness, in efforts to curb the illicit traffic in small arms and light weapons,

Taking note of the report of the United Nations Conference to Review Progress Made in the Implementation of the Programme of Action to Prevent, Combat and Eradicate the Illicit Trade in Small Arms and Light Weapons in All Its Aspects, held in New York from 26 June to 7 July 2006,[7]

1. *Commends* the United Nations and international, regional and other organizations for their assistance to States for curbing the illicit traffic in small arms and light weapons and collecting them;

2. *Encourages* the Secretary-General to pursue his efforts in the context of the implementation of General Assembly resolution 49/75 G of 15 December 1994 and the recommendations of the United Nations advisory missions, aimed at curbing the illicit circulation of small arms and light weapons and collecting them in the affected States that so request, with the support of the United Nations Regional Centre for Peace and Disarmament in Africa and in close cooperation with the African Union;

3. *Encourages* the international community to support the implementation of the Economic Community of West African States Convention on Small Arms and Light Weapons, Their Ammunition and Other Related Materials;

4. *Encourages* the countries of the Sahelo-Saharan subregion to facilitate the effective functioning of national commissions to combat the illicit proliferation of small arms and light weapons, and, in that regard, invites the international community to lend its support wherever possible;

5. *Encourages* the collaboration of civil society organizations and associations of in the efforts of the national commissions to combat the illicit traffic in small arms and light

weapons and in the implementation of the Programme of Action to Prevent, Combat and Eradicate the Illicit Trade in Small Arms and Light Weapons in All Its Aspects;[8]

6. *Also encourages* cooperation among State organs, international organizations and civil society in supporting programmes and projects aimed at combating the illicit traffic in small arms and light weapons and collecting them;

7. *Calls upon* the international community to provide technical and financial support to strengthen the capacity of civil society organizations to take action to help to combat the illicit trade in small arms and light weapons;

8. *Invites* the Secretary-General and those States and organizations that are in a position to do so to continue to provide assistance to States for curbing the illicit traffic in small arms and light weapons and collecting them;

9. *Requests* the Secretary-General to continue to consider the matter and to report to the General Assembly at its sixty-second session on the implementation of the present resolution;

10. *Decides* to include in the provisional agenda of its sixty-second session the item entitled "Assistance to States for curbing the illicit traffic in small arms and light weapons and collecting them".

67th plenary meeting
6 December 2006

---

[1] A/CONF.192/PC/23, annex.

[2] A/59/2005.

[3] A/60/88 and Corr.2, annex; see also decision 60/519.

[4] See resolution 60/1, para. 94.

[5] A/53/763-S/1998/1194, annex.

[6] A/61/288.

[7] A/CONF.192/2006/RC/9.

[8] See *Report of the United Nations Conference on the Illicit Trade in Small Arms and Light Weapons in All Its Aspects, New York, 9–20 July 2001* (A/CONF.192/15), chap. IV, para. 24.

Resolution 61/72

[on the report of the First Committee (A/61/394)]

61/72. Problems arising from the accumulation of conventional ammunition stockpiles in surplus

The General Assembly,

Mindful of contributing to the process initiated within the framework of the United Nations reform to make the Organization more effective in maintaining peace and security by giving it the resources and tools it needs for conflict prevention, peaceful resolution of disputes, peacekeeping, post-conflict peacebuilding and reconstruction,

Underlining the importance of a comprehensive and integrated approach to disarmament through the development of practical measures,

Taking note of the report of the Group of Experts on the problem of ammunition and explosives,[1]

Recalling the recommendation contained in paragraph 27 of the report submitted by the Chairman of the Open-ended Working Group to Negotiate an International Instrument to Enable States to Identify and Trace, in a Timely and Reliable Manner, Illicit Small Arms and Light Weapons, namely, to address the issue of small arms and light weapons ammunition in a comprehensive manner as part of a separate process conducted within the framework of the United Nations,[2]

Noting with satisfaction the work and measures pursued at the regional and subregional levels with regard to the issue of conventional ammunition,

Recalling its decision 59/515 of 3 December 2004 and its resolution 60/74 of 8 December 2005, by which it decided to include the issue of conventional ammunition stockpiles in surplus in the agenda of its sixty-first session,

1. *Encourages* all interested States to assess, on a voluntary basis, whether, in conformity with their legitimate security needs, parts of their stockpiles of conventional ammunition should be considered to be in surplus, and recognizes that the security of such stockpiles must be taken into consideration and that appropriate controls with regard to the security and safety of stockpiles of conventional ammunition are indispensable at the national level in order to eliminate the risk of explosion, pollution or diversion;

2. *Appeals* to all interested States to determine the size and nature of their surplus stockpiles of conventional ammunition, whether they represent a security risk, if appropriate, their means of destruction, and whether external assistance is needed to eliminate this risk;

3. *Encourages* States in a position to do so to assist interested States within a bilateral framework or through international or regional organizations, on a voluntary and transparent basis, in elaborating and implementing programmes to eliminate surplus stockpiles or to improve their management;

4. *Encourages* all Member States to examine the possibility of developing and implementing, within a national, regional or subregional framework, measures to address accordingly the illicit trafficking related to the accumulation of such stockpiles;

5. *Requests* the Secretary-General to seek the views of Member States regarding the risks arising from the accumulation of conventional ammunition stockpiles in surplus and regarding national ways of strengthening controls on conventional ammunition, and to submit a report to the General Assembly at its sixty-second session;

6. *Decides* to address the issue of conventional ammunition stockpiles in surplus in a comprehensive manner;

7. *Requests* the Secretary-General to establish a group of governmental experts to consider, commencing no later than 2008, further steps to enhance cooperation with regard to the issue of conventional ammunition stockpiles in surplus, and to transmit the report of the group of experts to the General Assembly for consideration at its sixty-third session;

8. *Decides* to include this issue in the provisional agenda of its sixty-third session.

67th plenary meeting
6 December 2006

[1] See A/54/155.

[2] A/60/88 and Corr.2.

Resolution 61/73

[on the report of the First Committee (A/61/394)]

61/73. United Nations study on disarmament and non-proliferation education

The General Assembly,

Recalling its resolutions 55/33 E of 20 November 2000, 57/60 of 22 November 2002 and 59/93 of 3 December 2004,

Welcoming the report of the Secretary-General on disarmament and nonproliferation education,[1] in which the Secretary-General reported on the implementation of the recommendations contained in the United Nations study on disarmament and non-proliferation education,[2]

Emphasizing that the Secretary-General concludes in his report that efforts need to be continued to implement the recommendations of the study and follow the good examples of how they are being implemented to stimulate even further long-term results,

Desirous of stressing the urgency of promoting concerted international efforts at disarmament and non-proliferation, in particular in the field of nuclear disarmament and non-proliferation, with a view to strengthening international security and enhancing sustainable economic and social development,

Conscious of the need to combat the negative effects of cultures of violence and complacency in the face of current dangers in this field through long-term programmes of education and training,

Remaining convinced that the need for disarmament and non-proliferation education has never been greater, especially on the subject of weapons of mass destruction, but also in the field of small arms and light weapons, terrorism and other challenges to international security and the process of disarmament, as well as on the relevance of implementing the recommendations contained in the United Nations study,

Recognizing the importance of the role of civil society, including non-governmental organizations, in the promotion of disarmament and non-proliferation education,

1. *Expresses its appreciation* to the Member States, the United Nations and other international and regional organizations, civil society and non-governmental organizations, which, within their purview, implemented the recommendations made in the United Nations study,[2] as discussed in the report of the Secretary-General reviewing the implementation of the recommendations,[1] and encourages them once again to continue applying those recommendations and reporting to the Secretary-General on steps taken to implement them;

2. *Requests* the Secretary-General to prepare a report reviewing the results of the implementation of the recommendations and possible new opportunities for promoting disarmament and non-proliferation education, and to submit it to the General Assembly at its sixty-third session;

3. *Also requests* the Secretary-General to utilize electronic means to the fullest extent possible in the dissemination, in as many official languages as feasible, of information related to that report and any other information that the Department for Disarmament Affairs of the Secretariat gathers on an ongoing basis in regard to the implementation of the recommendations of the United Nations study;

4. *Decides* to include in the provisional agenda of its sixty-third session the item entitled "Disarmament and non-proliferation education".

67th plenary meeting
6 December 2006

[1] A/61/169 and Add.1.

[2] A/57/124.

Resolution 61/74

[on the report of the First Committee (A/61/394)]

61/74. Renewed determination towards the total elimination of nuclear weapons

The General Assembly,

Recalling the need for all States to take further practical steps and effective measures towards the total elimination of nuclear weapons, with a view to achieving a peaceful and safe world free of nuclear weapons, and renewing the determination to do so,

Noting that the ultimate objective of the efforts of States in the disarmament process is general and complete disarmament under strict and effective international control,

Recalling its resolution 60/65 of 8 December 2005,

Convinced that every effort should be made to avoid nuclear war and nuclear terrorism,

Reaffirming the crucial importance of the Treaty on the Non-Proliferation of Nuclear Weapons[1] as the cornerstone of the international nuclear disarmament and non-proliferation regime, and expressing regret over the lack of agreement on substantive issues at the Review Conference of the Parties to the Treaty on the Non-Proliferation of Nuclear Weapons, as well as over the elimination of references to nuclear disarmament and non-proliferation in the World Summit Outcome[2] in 2005, the year of the sixtieth anniversary of the atomic bombings in Hiroshima and Nagasaki, Japan,

Recalling the decisions and the resolution of the 1995 Review and Extension Conference of the Parties to the Treaty on the Non-Proliferation of Nuclear Weapons[3] and the Final Document of the 2000 Review Conference of the Parties to the Treaty,[4]

Recognizing that the enhancement of international peace and security and the promotion of nuclear disarmament are mutually reinforcing,

Reaffirming that further advancement in nuclear disarmament will contribute to consolidating the international regime for nuclear non-proliferation and thereby ensuring international peace and security,

Expressing deep concern regarding the growing dangers posed by the proliferation of weapons of mass destruction, inter alia, nuclear weapons, including that caused by proliferation networks,

Condemning the nuclear test proclaimed by the Democratic People's Republic of Korea on 9 October 2006,

1. *Reaffirms* the importance of all States parties to the Treaty on the Non-Proliferation of Nuclear Weapons[1] complying with their obligations under all the articles of the Treaty;

2. *Stresses* the importance of an effective Treaty review process, and calls upon all States parties to the Treaty to work together to ensure that the first session of the Preparatory Committee in 2007 is held constructively, in order to facilitate the successful outcome of the 2010 Review Conference of the Parties to the Treaty on the Non-Proliferation of Nuclear Weapons;

3. *Reaffirms* the importance of the universality of the Treaty, and calls upon States not parties to the Treaty to accede to it as non-nuclear-weapon States without delay and without conditions, and pending their accession to refrain from acts that would defeat the objective and purpose of the Treaty as well as to take practical steps in support of the Treaty;

4. *Encourages* further steps leading to nuclear disarmament, to which all States parties to the Treaty are committed under article VI of the Treaty, including deeper reductions in all types of nuclear weapons, and emphasizes the importance of applying irreversibility and verifiability, as well as increased transparency in a way that promotes international stability and undiminished security for all, in the process of working towards the elimination of nuclear weapons;

5. *Encourages* the Russian Federation and the United States of America to implement fully the Treaty on Strategic Offensive Reductions,[5] which should serve as a step for further nuclear disarmament, and to undertake nuclear arms reductions beyond those provided for by the Treaty, while welcoming the progress made by nuclear-weapon States, including the Russian Federation and the United States, on nuclear arms reductions;

6. *Encourages* States to continue to pursue efforts, within the framework of international cooperation, contributing to the reduction of nuclear-weapons-related materials;

7. *Calls for* the nuclear-weapon States to further reduce the operational status of nuclear weapons systems in ways that promote international stability and security;

8. *Stresses* the necessity of a diminishing role for nuclear weapons in security policies to minimize the risk that these weapons will ever be used and to facilitate the process of their total elimination, in a way that promotes international stability and based on the principle of undiminished security for all;

9. *Urges* all States that have not yet done so to sign and ratify the Comprehensive Nuclear-Test-Ban Treaty[6] at the earliest opportunity with a view to its early entry into force, stresses the importance of maintaining existing moratoriums on nuclear-weapon test explosions pending the entry into force of the Treaty, and reaffirms the importance of the continued development of the Comprehensive Nuclear-Test-Ban Treaty verification regime, including the international monitoring system, which will be required to provide assurance of compliance with the Treaty;

10. *Calls upon* the Conference on Disarmament to immediately resume its substantive work to its fullest, considering the developments of this year in the Conference;

11. *Emphasizes* the importance of the immediate commencement of negotiations on a fissile material cut-off treaty and its early conclusion, and calls upon all nuclear-weapon States and States not parties to the Treaty on the Non-Proliferation of Nuclear Weapons to declare moratoriums on the production of fissile material for any nuclear weapons or other nuclear explosive devices pending the entry into force of the Treaty;

12. *Calls upon* all States to redouble their efforts to prevent and curb the proliferation of nuclear and other weapons of mass destruction and their means of delivery;

13. *Stresses* the importance of further efforts for non-proliferation, including the universalization of the International Atomic Energy Agency comprehensive safeguards agreements and Model Protocol Additional to the Agreement(s) between State(s) and the International Atomic Energy Agency for the Application of Safeguards approved by the Board of Governors of the International Atomic Energy Agency on 15 May 1997[7] and the full implementation of Security Council resolution 1540 (2004) of 28 April 2004;

14. *Encourages* all States to undertake concrete activities to implement, as appropriate, the recommendations contained in the report of the Secretary-General on the United Nations study on disarmament and non-proliferation education, submitted to the General Assembly at its fifty-seventh session,[8] and to voluntarily share information on efforts they have been undertaking to that end;

15. *Encourages* the constructive role played by civil society in promoting nuclear non-proliferation and nuclear disarmament.

67th plenary meeting
6 December 2006

---

[1] United Nations, *Treaty Series*, vol. 729, No. 10485.

[2] See resolution 60/1.

[3] See *1995 Review and Extension Conference of the Parties to the Treaty on the Non-Proliferation of Nuclear Weapons, Final Document, Part I* (NPT/CONF.1995/32 (Part I) and Corr.2), annex.

[4] *2000 Review Conference of the Parties to the Treaty on the Non-Proliferation of Nuclear Weapons, Final Document*, vols. I–III (NPT/CONF.2000/28 (Parts I–IV)).

[5] See CD/1674.

[6] See resolution 50/245.

[7] International Atomic Energy Agency, INFCIRC/540 (Corrected).

[8] A/57/124.

Resolution 61/75

[on the report of the First Committee (A/61/394)]

61/75. Transparency and confidence-building measures in outer space activities

The General Assembly,

Recalling its resolution 60/66 of 8 December 2005,

Reaffirming that the prevention of an arms race in outer space would avert a grave danger to international peace and security,

Conscious that further measures should be examined in the search for agreements to prevent an arms race in outer space, including the weaponization of outer space,

Recalling, in this context, its previous resolutions, including resolutions 45/55 B of 4 December 1990 and 48/74 B of 16 December 1993, which, inter alia, emphasize the need for increased transparency and confirm the importance of confidence-building measures as a means conducive to ensuring the attainment of the objective of the prevention of an arms race in outer space,

Recalling also the report of the Secretary-General of 15 October 1993 to the General Assembly at its forty-eighth session, the annex to which contains the study by governmental experts on the application of confidence-building measures in outer space,[1]

Noting the constructive debate which the Conference on Disarmament held on this subject in 2006,

1. *Invites* all Member States to submit to the Secretary-General before its sixty-second session concrete proposals on international outer space transparency and confidence-building measures in the interest of maintaining international peace and security and promoting international cooperation and the prevention of an arms race in outer space;

2. *Requests* the Secretary-General to submit to the General Assembly at its sixty-second session a report with an annex containing concrete proposals from Member States on international outer space transparency and confidence-building measures;

3. *Decides* to include in the provisional agenda of its sixty-second session the item entitled "Transparency and confidence-building measures in outer space activities".

67th plenary meeting
6 December 2006

---

1 A/48/305 and Corr.1.

Resolution 61/76

[on the report of the First Committee (A/61/394)]

61/76. Consolidation of peace through practical disarmament measures

The General Assembly,

Recalling its resolutions 51/45 N of 10 December 1996, 52/38 G of 9 December 1997, 53/77 M of 4 December 1998, 54/54 H of 1 December 1999, 55/33 G of 20 November 2000, 56/24 P of 29 November 2001 and 57/81 of 22 November 2002, its decision 58/519 of 8 December 2003 and its resolution 59/82 of 3 December 2004 entitled "Consolidation of peace through practical disarmament measures",

Convinced that a comprehensive and integrated approach towards certain practical disarmament measures often is a prerequisite to maintaining and consolidating peace and security and thus provides a basis for effective post-conflict peacebuilding; such measures include collection and responsible disposal, preferably through destruction, of weapons obtained through illicit trafficking or illicit manufacture as well as of weapons and ammunition declared by competent national authorities to be surplus to requirements, particularly with regard to small arms and light weapons, unless another form of disposition or use has been officially authorized and provided that such weapons have been duly marked and registered; confidence-building measures; disarmament, demobilization and reintegration of former combatants; demining; and conversion,

Noting with satisfaction that the international community is more than ever aware of the importance of such practical disarmament measures, especially with regard to the growing problems arising from the excessive accumulation and uncontrolled spread of small arms and light weapons, including their ammunition, which pose a threat to peace and security and reduce the prospects for economic development in many regions, particularly in post-conflict situations,

Stressing that further efforts are needed in order to develop and effectively implement programmes of practical disarmament in affected areas as part of disarmament, demobilization and reintegration measures so as to complement, on a case-by-case basis, peacekeeping and peacebuilding efforts,

Taking note with appreciation of the report of the Secretary-General on prevention of armed conflict,[1] which, inter alia, refers to the role which the proliferation and the illicit transfer of small arms and light weapons play in the context of the build-up and sustaining of conflicts,

Taking note of the statement by the President of the Security Council of 31 August 2001[2] underlining the importance of practical disarmament measures in the context of armed conflicts, and, with regard to disarmament, demobilization and reintegration programmes, emphasizing the importance of measures to contain the security risks stemming from the use of illicit small arms and light weapons,

Taking note also of the report of the Secretary-General prepared with the assistance of the Group of Governmental Experts on Small Arms[3] and, in particular, the recommendations contained therein, as an important contribution to the consolidation of the peace process through practical disarmament measures,

Welcoming the work of the Coordinating Action on Small Arms, which was established by the Secretary-General to bring about a holistic and multidisciplinary approach to this complex and multifaceted global problem and to cooperate with non-governmental organizations in the implementation of practical disarmament measures,

Welcoming also the reports of the First and Second Biennial Meetings of States to Consider the Implementation of the Programme of Action to Prevent, Combat and Eradicate the Illicit Trade in Small Arms and Light Weapons in All Its Aspects, held in New York from 7 to 11 July 2003[4] and from 11 to 15 July 2005,[5] respectively, as well as the report of the Open-ended Working Group to Negotiate an International Instrument to Enable States to Identify and Trace, in a Timely and Reliable Manner, Illicit Small Arms and Light Weapons,[6]

1. *Stresses* the particular relevance of the "Guidelines on conventional arms control/limitation and disarmament, with particular emphasis on consolidation of peace in the context of General Assembly resolution 51/45 N", adopted by the Disarmament Commission by consensus at its 1999 substantive session;[7]

2. *Takes note* of the report of the Secretary-General on the consolidation of peace through practical disarmament measures, submitted pursuant to resolution 59/82,[3] and once again encourages Member States as well as regional arrangements and agencies to lend their support to the implementation of recommendations contained therein;

3. *Emphasizes* the importance of including in United Nations-mandated peacekeeping missions, as appropriate and with the consent of the host State, practical disarmament measures aimed at addressing the problem of the illicit trade in small arms and light weapons in conjunction with disarmament, demobilization and reintegration programmes aimed at former combatants, with a view to promoting an integrated comprehensive and effective weapon management strategy that would contribute to a sustainable peacebuilding process;

4. *Welcomes* the activities undertaken by the Group of Interested States, and invites the Group to continue to promote, on the basis of lessons learned from previous disarmament and peacebuilding projects, new practical disarmament measures to consolidate peace, especially as undertaken or designed by affected States themselves, regional and subregional organizations as well as United Nations agencies;

5. *Encourages* Member States, including the Group of Interested States, to continue to lend their support to the Secretary-General, relevant international, regional and subregional organizations, in accordance with Chapter VIII of the Charter of the United Nations, and non-governmental organizations in responding to requests by Member States to collect and destroy small arms and light weapons, including their ammunition, in post-conflict situations;

6. *Welcomes* the synergies within the multi-stakeholder process, including Governments, the United Nations system, regional and subregional organizations and institutions as well as non-governmental organizations in support of practical disarmament measures and the Programme of Action to Prevent, Combat and Eradicate the Illicit Trade in Small Arms and Light Weapons in All Its Aspects,[8] in particular, inter alia, through the Coordinating Action on Small Arms;

7. *Thanks* the Secretary-General for his report on the implementation of resolution 59/82,[3] taking into consideration the activities of the Group of Interested States in this regard;

8. *Welcomes* the report of the Secretary-General on disarmament and nonproliferation education,[9] as well as his report on the United Nations Disarmament Information Programme;[10]

9. *Requests* the Secretary-General to submit to the General Assembly at its sixty-third session a report on the implementation of practical disarmament measures, taking into consideration the activities of the Group of Interested States in this regard;

10. *Decides* to include in the provisional agenda of its sixty-third session the item entitled "Consolidation of peace through practical disarmament measures".

67th plenary meeting
6 December 2006

---

[1] A/55/985-S/2001/574 and Corr.1.

[2] S/PRST/2001/21; see *Resolutions and Decisions of the Security Council, 1 January 2001–31 July 2002.*

[3] A/61/288.

[4] A/CONF.192/BMS/2003/1.

[5] A/CONF.192/BMS/2005/1.

[6] A/60/88 and Corr.2.

[7] *Official Records of the General Assembly, Fifty-fourth Session, Supplement No. 42* (A/54/42), annex III.

[8] See *Report of the United Nations Conference on the Illicit Trade in Small Arms and Light Weapons in All Its Aspects, New York, 9–20 July 2001* (A/CONF.192/15), chap. IV, para. 24.

[9] A/61/169 and Add.1.

[10] A/61/215.

Resolution 61/77

[on the report of the First Committee (A/61/394)]

61/77. Transparency in armaments

The General Assembly,

Recalling its resolutions 46/36 L of 9 December 1991, 47/52 L of 15 December 1992, 48/75 E of 16 December 1993, 49/75 C of 15 December 1994, 50/70 D of 12 December 1995, 51/45 H of 10 December 1996, 52/38 R of 9 December 1997, 53/77 V of 4 December 1998, 54/54 O of 1 December 1999, 55/33 U of 20 November 2000, 56/24 Q of 29 November 2001, 57/75 of 22 November 2002, 58/54 of 8 December 2003 and 60/226 of 23 December 2005 entitled "Transparency in armaments",

Continuing to take the view that an enhanced level of transparency in armaments contributes greatly to confidence-building and security among States and that the establishment of the United Nations Register of Conventional Arms[1] constitutes an important step forward in the promotion of transparency in military matters,

Welcoming the consolidated report of the Secretary-General on the Register,[2] which includes the returns of Member States for 2005,

Welcoming also the response of Member States to the request contained in paragraphs 9 and 10 of resolution 46/36 L to provide data on their imports and exports of arms, as well as available background information regarding their military holdings, procurement through national production and relevant policies,

Welcoming further the inclusion by some Member States of their transfers of small arms and light weapons in their annual report to the Register as part of their additional background information,

Noting the focused discussion on transparency in armaments that took place in the Conference on Disarmament in 2006,

Stressing that the continuing operation of the Register and its further development should be reviewed in order to secure a Register that is capable of attracting the widest possible participation,

1. *Reaffirms its determination* to ensure the effective operation of the United Nations Register of Conventional Arms,[1] as provided for in paragraphs 7 to 10 of resolution 46/36 L;

2. *Endorses* the report of the Secretary-General on the continuing operation of the Register and its further development,[3] and the recommendations ensuing from the consensus report of the 2006 group of governmental experts contained therein;

3. *Decides* to adapt the scope of the Register in conformity with the recommendations contained in the report of the Secretary-General on the continuing operation of the Register and its further development;

4. *Calls upon* Member States, with a view to achieving universal participation, to provide the Secretary-General, by 31 May annually, with the requested data and information for the Register, including nil reports if appropriate, on the basis of resolutions 46/36 L and 47/52 L, the recommendations contained in paragraph 64 of the 1997 report of the Secretary-General

on the continuing operation of the Register and its further development,[4] the recommendations contained in paragraph 94 of the 2000 report of the Secretary-General and the appendices and annexes thereto,[5] the recommendations contained in paragraphs 112 to 114 of the 2003 report of the Secretary-General[6] and the recommendations contained in paragraphs 123 to 127 of the 2006 report of the Secretary-General;[3]

5. *Invites* Member States in a position to do so, pending further development of the Register, to provide additional information on procurement through national production and military holdings and to make use of the "Remarks" column in the standardized reporting form to provide additional information such as types or models;

6. *Also invites* Member States in a position to do so to provide additional background information on transfers of small arms and light weapons on the basis of the optional standardized reporting form, as adopted by the 2006 group of governmental experts,[7] or by any other methods they deem appropriate;

7. *Reaffirms its decision*, with a view to further development of the Register, to keep the scope of and participation in the Register under review and, to that end:

(*a*) Recalls its request to Member States to provide the Secretary-General with their views on the continuing operation of the Register and its further development and on transparency measures related to weapons of mass destruction;

(*b*) Requests the Secretary-General, with a view to the three-year cycle regarding review of the Register, to ensure that sufficient resources are made available for a group of governmental experts to be convened in 2009 to review the continuing operation of the Register and its further development, taking into account the work of the Conference on Disarmament, the views expressed by Member States and the reports of the Secretary-General on the continuing operation of the Register and its further development;

8. *Requests* the Secretary-General to implement the recommendations contained in his 2000, 2003 and 2006 reports on the continuing operation of the Register and its further development and to ensure that sufficient resources are made available for the Secretariat to operate and maintain the Register;

9. *Invites* the Conference on Disarmament to consider continuing its work undertaken in the field of transparency in armaments;

10. *Reiterates its call upon* all Member States to cooperate at the regional and subregional levels, taking fully into account the specific conditions prevailing in the region or subregion, with a view to enhancing and coordinating international efforts aimed at increased openness and transparency in armaments;

11. *Requests* the Secretary-General to report to the General Assembly at its sixty-second session on progress made in implementing the present resolution;

12. *Decides* to include in the provisional agenda of its sixty-third session the item entitled "Transparency in armaments".

67th plenary meeting
6 December 2006

[1] See resolution 46/36 L.

[2] A/61/159 and Corr.1 and 2 and Add.1 and Add.1/Corr.1.

[3] A/61/261.

[4] A/52/316 and Corr.2.

[5] A/55/281.

[6] A/58/274.

[7] A/61/261, annex I.

Resolution 61/78

[on the report of the First Committee (A/61/394)]

61/78. Nuclear disarmament

The General Assembly,

Recalling its resolution 49/75 E of 15 December 1994 on a step-by-step reduction of the nuclear threat, and its resolutions 50/70 P of 12 December 1995, 51/45 O of 10 December 1996, 52/38 L of 9 December 1997, 53/77 X of 4 December 1998, 54/54 P of 1 December 1999, 55/33 T of 20 November 2000, 56/24 R of 29 November 2001, 57/79 of 22 November 2002, 58/56 of 8 December 2003, 59/77 of 3 December 2004 and 60/70 of 8 December 2005 on nuclear disarmament,

Reaffirming the commitment of the international community to the goal of the total elimination of nuclear weapons and the establishment of a nuclear-weapon-free world,

Bearing in mind that the Convention on the Prohibition of the Development, Production and Stockpiling of Bacteriological (Biological) and Toxin Weapons and on Their Destruction of 1972[1] and the Convention on the Prohibition of the Development, Production, Stockpiling and Use of Chemical Weapons and on Their Destruction of 1993[2] have already established legal regimes on the complete prohibition of biological and chemical weapons, respectively, and determined to achieve a nuclear weapons convention on the prohibition of the development, testing, production, stockpiling, loan, transfer, use and threat of use of nuclear weapons and on their destruction, and to conclude such an international convention at an early date,

Recognizing that there now exist conditions for the establishment of a world free of nuclear weapons, and stressing the need to take concrete practical steps towards achieving this goal,

Bearing in mind paragraph 50 of the Final Document of the Tenth Special Session of the General Assembly,[3] the first special session devoted to disarmament, calling for the urgent negotiation of agreements for the cessation of the qualitative improvement and development of nuclear-weapon systems, and for a comprehensive and phased programme with agreed time frames, wherever feasible, for the progressive and balanced reduction of nuclear weapons and their means of delivery, leading to their ultimate and complete elimination at the earliest possible time,

Reaffirming the conviction of the States parties to the Treaty on the Non-Proliferation of Nuclear Weapons[4] that the Treaty is a cornerstone of nuclear nonproliferation and nuclear disarmament and the importance of the decision on strengthening the review process for the Treaty, the decision on principles and objectives for nuclear non-proliferation and disarmament, the decision on the extension of the Treaty and the resolution on the Middle East, adopted by the 1995 Review and Extension Conference of the Parties to the Treaty on the Non-Proliferation of Nuclear Weapons,[5]

Stressing the importance of the thirteen steps for the systematic and progressive efforts to achieve the objective of nuclear disarmament leading to the total elimination of nuclear weapons, as agreed to by the States parties in the Final Document of the 2000 Review Conference of the Parties to the Treaty on the Non-Proliferation of Nuclear Weapons,[6]

Reiterating the highest priority accorded to nuclear disarmament in the Final Document of the Tenth Special Session of the General Assembly and by the international community,

Reiterating its call for an early entry into force of the Comprehensive Nuclear-Test-Ban Treaty,[7]

Noting with appreciation the entry into force of the Treaty on the Reduction and Limitation of Strategic Offensive Arms (START I),[8] to which Belarus, Kazakhstan, the Russian Federation, Ukraine and the United States of America are States parties,

Noting with appreciation also the entry into force of the Treaty on Strategic Offensive Reductions ("the Moscow Treaty") between the United States of America and the Russian Federation[9] as a significant step towards reducing their deployed strategic nuclear weapons, while calling for further irreversible deep cuts in their nuclear arsenals,

Noting with appreciation further the unilateral measures taken by the nuclear-weapon States for nuclear arms limitation, and encouraging them to take further such measures,

Recognizing the complementarity of bilateral, plurilateral and multilateral negotiations on nuclear disarmament, and that bilateral negotiations can never replace multilateral negotiations in this respect,

Noting the support expressed in the Conference on Disarmament and in the General Assembly for the elaboration of an international convention to assure non-nuclear-weapon States against the use or threat of use of nuclear weapons, and the multilateral efforts in the Conference on Disarmament to reach agreement on such an international convention at an early date,

Recalling the advisory opinion of the International Court of Justice on the *Legality of the Threat or Use of Nuclear Weapons*, issued on 8 July 1996,[10] and welcoming the unanimous reaffirmation by all Judges of the Court that there exists an obligation for all States to pursue in good faith and bring to a conclusion negotiations leading to nuclear disarmament in all its aspects under strict and effective international control,

Mindful of paragraph 64 of the Final Document of the Ministerial Meeting of the Coordinating Bureau of the Movement of Non-Aligned Countries, held in Putrajaya, Malaysia, on 29 and 30 May 2006,[11]

Recalling paragraph 70 and other relevant recommendations in the Final Document of the Fourteenth Conference of Heads of State or Government of Non-Aligned Countries, held in Havana on 15 and 16 September 2006,[12] calling upon the Conference on Disarmament to establish, as soon as possible and as the highest priority, an ad hoc committee on nuclear disarmament and to commence negotiations on a phased programme for the complete elimination of nuclear weapons with a specified time framework,

Reaffirming the specific mandate conferred upon the Disarmament Commission by the General Assembly, in its decision 52/492 of 8 September 1998, to discuss the subject of nuclear disarmament as one of its main substantive agenda items,

Recalling the United Nations Millennium Declaration,[13] in which Heads of State and Government resolved to strive for the elimination of weapons of mass destruction, in particular nuclear weapons, and to keep all options open for achieving this aim, including the possibility of convening an international conference to identify ways of eliminating nuclear dangers,

Reaffirming that, in accordance with the Charter of the United Nations, States should refrain from the use or threat of use of nuclear weapons in settling their disputes in international relations,

Seized of the danger of the use of weapons of mass destruction, particularly nuclear weapons, in terrorist acts and the urgent need for concerted international efforts to control and overcome it,

1. *Recognizes* that, in view of recent political developments, the time is now opportune for all the nuclear-weapon States to take effective disarmament measures with a view to achieving the elimination of these weapons;

2. *Reaffirms* that nuclear disarmament and nuclear non-proliferation are substantively interrelated and mutually reinforcing, that the two processes must go hand in hand and that there is a genuine need for a systematic and progressive process of nuclear disarmament;

3. *Welcomes and encourages* the efforts to establish new nuclear-weapon-free zones in different parts of the world on the basis of agreements or arrangements freely arrived at among the States of the regions concerned, which is an effective measure for limiting the further spread of nuclear weapons geographically and contributes to the cause of nuclear disarmament;

4. *Recognizes* that there is a genuine need to diminish the role of nuclear weapons in strategic doctrines and security policies to minimize the risk that these weapons will ever be used and to facilitate the process of their total elimination;

5. *Urges* the nuclear-weapon States to stop immediately the qualitative improvement, development, production and stockpiling of nuclear warheads and their delivery systems;

6. *Also urges* the nuclear-weapon States, as an interim measure, to de-alert and deactivate immediately their nuclear weapons and to take other concrete measures to reduce further the operational status of their nuclear-weapon systems;

7. *Reiterates its call upon* the nuclear-weapon States to undertake the step-by-step reduction of the nuclear threat and to carry out effective nuclear disarmament measures with a view to achieving the total elimination of these weapons;

8. *Calls upon* the nuclear-weapon States, pending the achievement of the total elimination of nuclear weapons, to agree on an internationally and legally binding instrument on a joint undertaking not to be the first to use nuclear weapons, and calls upon all States to conclude an internationally and legally binding instrument on security assurances of non-use and non-threat of use of nuclear weapons against non-nuclear-weapon States;

9. *Urges* the nuclear-weapon States to commence plurilateral negotiations among themselves at an appropriate stage on further deep reductions of nuclear weapons as an effective measure of nuclear disarmament;

10. *Underlines* the importance of applying the principle of irreversibility to the process of nuclear disarmament, and nuclear and other related arms control and reduction measures;

11. *Underscores* the importance of the unequivocal undertaking by the nuclear-weapon States, in the Final Document of the 2000 Review Conference of the Parties to the Treaty on the Non-Proliferation of Nuclear Weapons, to accomplish the total elimination of their nuclear arsenals leading to nuclear disarmament, to which all States parties are committed under article VI of the Treaty,[14] and the reaffirmation by the States parties that the total elimination of nuclear weapons is the only absolute guarantee against the use or threat of use of nuclear weapons;[15]

12. *Calls for* the full and effective implementation of the thirteen steps for nuclear disarmament contained in the Final Document of the 2000 Review Conference;[6]

13. *Urges* the nuclear-weapon States to carry out further reductions of nonstrategic nuclear weapons, based on unilateral initiatives and as an integral part of the nuclear arms reduction and disarmament process;

14. *Calls for* the immediate commencement of negotiations in the Conference on Disarmament on a non-discriminatory, multilateral and internationally and effectively verifiable treaty banning the production of fissile material for nuclear weapons or other nuclear explosive devices on the basis of the report of the Special Coordinator[16] and the mandate contained therein;

15. *Urges* the Conference on Disarmament to agree on a programme of work that includes the immediate commencement of negotiations on such a treaty with a view to their conclusion within five years;

16. *Calls for* the conclusion of an international legal instrument or instruments on adequate security assurances to non-nuclear-weapon States;

17. *Also calls for* the early entry into force and strict observance of the Comprehensive Nuclear-Test-Ban Treaty;[7]

18. *Expresses its regret* that the 2005 Review Conference of the Parties to the Treaty on the Non-Proliferation of Nuclear Weapons was unable to achieve any substantive result and that the 2005 World Summit Outcome adopted by the General Assembly[17] failed to make any reference to nuclear disarmament and nuclear nonproliferation;

19. *Also expresses its regret* that the Conference on Disarmament was unable to establish an ad hoc committee to deal with nuclear disarmament at its 2006 session, as called for in General Assembly resolution 60/70;

20. *Reiterates its call upon* the Conference on Disarmament to establish, on a priority basis, an ad hoc committee to deal with nuclear disarmament early in 2007 and to commence negotiations on a phased programme of nuclear disarmament leading to the eventual total elimination of nuclear weapons;

21. *Calls for* the convening of an international conference on nuclear disarmament in all its aspects at an early date to identify and deal with concrete measures of nuclear disarmament;

22. *Requests* the Secretary-General to submit to the General Assembly at its sixty-second session a report on the implementation of the present resolution;

23. *Decides* to include in the provisional agenda of its sixty-second session the item entitled "Nuclear disarmament".

67th plenary meeting
6 December 2006

[1] Resolution 2826 (XXVI), annex.

[2] United Nations, *Treaty Series*, vol. 1974, No. 33757.

[3] Resolution S-10/2.

[4] United Nations, *Treaty Series*, vol. 729, No. 10485.

[5] See *1995 Review and Extension Conference of the Parties to the Treaty on the Non-Proliferation of Nuclear Weapons, Final Document, Part I* (NPT/CONF.1995/32 (Part I) and Corr.2), annex.

[6] See *2000 Review Conference of the Parties to the Treaty on the Non-Proliferation of Nuclear Weapons, Final Document*, vol. I (NPT/CONF.2000/28 (Parts I and II)), part I, section entitled "Article VI and eighth to twelfth preambular paragraphs", para. 15.

[7] See resolution 50/245.

[8] *The United Nations Disarmament Yearbook*, vol. 16: 1991 (United Nations publication, Sales No. E.92.IX.1), appendix II.

[9] See CD/1674.

[10] A/51/218, annex; see also *Legality of the Threat or Use of Nuclear Weapons, Advisory Opinion, I.C.J. Reports 1996*, p. 226.

[11] A/60/1002-S/2006/718, annex I.

[12] A/61/472-S/2006/780, annex I.

[13] See resolution 55/2.

[14] *2000 Review Conference of the Parties to the Treaty on the Non-Proliferation of Nuclear Weapons, Final Document*, vol. I (NPT/CONF.2000/28 (Parts I and II)), part I, section entitled "Article VI and eighth to twelfth preambular paragraphs", para. 15:6.

[15] Ibid., section entitled "Article VII and the security of non-nuclear-weapon States", para. 2.

[16] CD/1299.

[17] See resolution 60/1.

Resolution 61/79

[on the report of the First Committee (A/61/394)]

61/79. Information on confidence-building measures in the field of conventional arms

The General Assembly,

Guided by the purposes and principles enshrined in the Charter of the United Nations,

Bearing in mind the contribution of confidence-building measures in the field of conventional arms, adopted on the initiative and with the agreement of the States concerned, to the improvement of the overall international peace and security situation,

Convinced that the relationship between the development of confidence-building measures in the field of conventional arms and the international security environment can also be mutually reinforcing,

Considering the important role that confidence-building measures in the field of conventional arms can also play in creating favourable conditions for progress in the field of disarmament,

Recognizing that the exchange of information on confidence-building measures in the field of conventional arms contributes to mutual understanding and confidence among Member States,

1. *Welcomes* all confidence-building measures in the field of conventional arms already undertaken by Member States as well as the information on such measures voluntarily provided;

2. *Encourages* Member States to continue to adopt confidence-building measures in the field of conventional arms and to provide information in that regard;

3. *Also encourages* Member States to continue the dialogue on confidence-building measures in the field of conventional arms;

4. *Welcomes* the establishment of the electronic database containing information provided by Member States, and requests the Secretary-General to keep the database updated and to assist Member States, at their request, in the organization of seminars, courses and workshops aimed at enhancing the knowledge of new developments in this field;

5. *Decides* to include in the provisional agenda of its sixty-third session the item entitled "Information on confidence-building measures in the field of conventional arms".

67th plenary meeting
6 December 2006

Resolution 61/80

[on the report of the First Committee (A/61/394)]

61/80. Regional disarmament

The General Assembly,

Recalling its resolutions 45/58 P of 4 December 1990, 46/36 I of 6 December 1991, 47/52 J of 9 December 1992, 48/75 I of 16 December 1993, 49/75 N of 15 December 1994, 50/70 K of 12 December 1995, 51/45 K of 10 December 1996, 52/38 P of 9 December 1997, 53/77 O of 4 December 1998, 54/54 N of 1 December 1999, 55/33 O of 20 November 2000, 56/24 H of 29 November 2001, 57/76 of 22 November 2002, 58/38 of 8 December 2003, 59/89 of 3 December 2004 and 60/63 of 8 December 2005 on regional disarmament,

Believing that the efforts of the international community to move towards the ideal of general and complete disarmament are guided by the inherent human desire for genuine peace and security, the elimination of the danger of war and the release of economic, intellectual and other resources for peaceful pursuits,

Affirming the abiding commitment of all States to the purposes and principles enshrined in the Charter of the United Nations in the conduct of their international relations,

Noting that essential guidelines for progress towards general and complete disarmament were adopted at the tenth special session of the General Assembly,[1]

Taking note of the guidelines and recommendations for regional approaches to disarmament within the context of global security adopted by the Disarmament Commission at its 1993 substantive session,[2]

Welcoming the prospects of genuine progress in the field of disarmament engendered in recent years as a result of negotiations between the two super-Powers,

Taking note of the recent proposals for disarmament at the regional and subregional levels,

Recognizing the importance of confidence-building measures for regional and international peace and security,

Convinced that endeavours by countries to promote regional disarmament, taking into account the specific characteristics of each region and in accordance with the principle of undiminished security at the lowest level of armaments, would enhance the security of all States and would thus contribute to international peace and security by reducing the risk of regional conflicts,

1. *Stresses* that sustained efforts are needed, within the framework of the Conference on Disarmament and under the umbrella of the United Nations, to make progress on the entire range of disarmament issues;

2. *Affirms* that global and regional approaches to disarmament complement each other and should therefore be pursued simultaneously to promote regional and international peace and security;

3. *Calls upon* States to conclude agreements, wherever possible, for nuclear non-proliferation, disarmament and confidence-building measures at the regional and subregional levels;

4. *Welcomes* the initiatives towards disarmament, nuclear non-proliferation and security undertaken by some countries at the regional and subregional levels;

5. *Supports and encourages* efforts aimed at promoting confidence-building measures at the regional and subregional levels to ease regional tensions and to further disarmament and nuclear non-proliferation measures at the regional and subregional levels;

6. *Decides* to include in the provisional agenda of its sixty-second session the item entitled "Regional disarmament".

67th plenary meeting
6 December 2006

[1] See resolution S-10/2.

[2] *Official Records of the General Assembly, Forty-eighth Session, Supplement No. 42* (A/48/42), annex II.

Resolution 61/81

[on the report of the First Committee (A/61/394)]

61/81. Confidence-building measures in the regional and subregional context

The General Assembly,

Guided by the purposes and principles enshrined in the Charter of the United Nations,

Recalling its resolutions 58/43 of 8 December 2003, 59/87 of 3 December 2004 and 60/64 of 8 December 2005,

Recalling also its resolution 57/337 of 3 July 2003 entitled "Prevention of armed conflict", in which it calls upon Member States to settle their disputes by peaceful means, as set out in Chapter VI of the Charter, inter alia, by any procedures adopted by the parties,

Recalling further the resolutions and guidelines adopted by consensus by the General Assembly and the Disarmament Commission relating to confidence-building measures and their implantation at the global, regional and subregional levels,

Considering the importance and effectiveness of confidence-building measures taken at the initiative and with the agreement of all States concerned and taking into account the specific characteristics of each region, since such measures can contribute to regional stability,

Convinced that resources released by disarmament, including regional disarmament, can be devoted to economic and social development and to the protection of the environment for the benefit of all peoples, in particular those of the developing countries,

Recognizing the need for meaningful dialogue among States concerned to avert conflict,

Welcoming the peace processes already initiated by States concerned to resolve their disputes through peaceful means bilaterally or through mediation, inter alia, by third parties, regional organizations or the United Nations,

Recognizing that States in some regions have already taken steps towards confidence-building measures at the bilateral, subregional and regional levels in the political and military fields, including arms control and disarmament, and noting that such confidence-building measures have improved peace and security in those regions and contributed to progress in the socio-economic conditions of their people,

Concerned that the continuation of disputes among States, particularly in the absence of an effective mechanism to resolve them through peaceful means, may contribute to the arms race and endanger the maintenance of international peace and security and the efforts of the international community to promote arms control and disarmament,

1. *Calls upon* Member States to refrain from the use or threat of use of force in accordance with the purposes and principles of the Charter of the United Nations;

2. *Reaffirms its commitment* to the peaceful settlement of disputes under Chapter VI of the Charter, in particular Article 33, which provides for a solution by negotiation, enquiry, mediation, conciliation, arbitration, judicial settlement, resort to regional agencies or arrangements or other peaceful means chosen by the parties;

3. *Reaffirms* the ways and means regarding confidence- and security-building measures set out in the report of the Disarmament Commission on its 1993 session;[1]

4. *Calls upon* Member States to pursue these ways and means through sustained consultations and dialogue, while at the same time avoiding actions which may hinder or impair such a dialogue;

5. *Urges* States to comply strictly with all bilateral, regional and international agreements, including arms control and disarmament agreements, to which they are party;

6. *Emphasizes* that the objective of confidence-building measures should be to help strengthen international peace and security and be consistent with the principle of undiminished security at the lowest level of armaments;

7. *Encourages* the promotion of bilateral and regional confidence-building measures, with the consent and participation of the parties concerned, to avoid conflict and prevent the unintended and accidental outbreak of hostilities;

8. *Requests* the Secretary-General to submit a report to the General Assembly at its sixty-second session containing the views of Member States on confidence-building measures in the regional and subregional context;

9. *Decides* to include in the provisional agenda of its sixty-second session the item entitled "Confidence-building measures in the regional and subregional context".

67th plenary meeting
6 December 2006

[1] *Official Records of the General Assembly, Forty-eighth Session, Supplement No. 42* (A/48/42), annex II, sect. III.A.

Resolution 61/82

[on the report of the First Committee (A/61/394)]

61/82. Conventional arms control at the regional and subregional levels

The General Assembly,

Recalling its resolutions 48/75 J of 16 December 1993, 49/75 O of 15 December 1994, 50/70 L of 12 December 1995, 51/45 Q of 10 December 1996, 52/38 Q of 9 December 1997, 53/77 P of 4 December 1998, 54/54 M of 1 December 1999, 55/33 P of 20 November 2000, 56/24 I of 29 November 2001, 57/77 of 22 November 2002, 58/39 of 8 December 2003, 59/88 of 3 December 2004 and 60/75 of 8 December 2005,

Recognizing the crucial role of conventional arms control in promoting regional and international peace and security,

Convinced that conventional arms control needs to be pursued primarily in the regional and subregional contexts since most threats to peace and security in the post-cold-war era arise mainly among States located in the same region or subregion,

Aware that the preservation of a balance in the defence capabilities of States at the lowest level of armaments would contribute to peace and stability and should be a prime objective of conventional arms control,

Desirous of promoting agreements to strengthen regional peace and security at the lowest possible level of armaments and military forces,

Noting with particular interest the initiatives taken in this regard in different regions of the world, in particular the commencement of consultations among a number of Latin American countries and the proposals for conventional arms control made in the context of South Asia, and recognizing, in the context of this subject, the relevance and value of the Treaty on Conventional Armed Forces in Europe,[1] which is a cornerstone of European security,

Believing that militarily significant States and States with larger military capabilities have a special responsibility in promoting such agreements for regional security,

Believing also that an important objective of conventional arms control in regions of tension should be to prevent the possibility of military attack launched by surprise and to avoid aggression,

1. *Decides* to give urgent consideration to the issues involved in conventional arms control at the regional and subregional levels;

2. *Requests* the Conference on Disarmament to consider the formulation of principles that can serve as a framework for regional agreements on conventional arms control, and looks forward to a report of the Conference on this subject;

3. *Requests* the Secretary-General, in the meantime, to seek the views of Member States on the subject and to submit a report to the General Assembly at its sixty-second session;

4. *Decides* to include in the provisional agenda of its sixty-second session the item entitled "Conventional arms control at the regional and subregional levels".

67th plenary meeting
6 December 2006

---

[1] CD/1064.

Resolution 61/83

[on the report of the First Committee (A/61/394)]

61/83. Follow-up to the advisory opinion of the International Court of Justice on the *Legality of the Threat or Use of Nuclear Weapons*

The General Assembly,

Recalling its resolutions 49/75 K of 15 December 1994, 51/45 M of 10 December 1996, 52/38 O of 9 December 1997, 53/77 W of 4 December 1998, 54/54 Q of 1 December 1999, 55/33 X of 20 November 2000, 56/24 S of 29 November 2001, 57/85 of 22 November 2002, 58/46 of 8 December 2003, 59/83 of 3 December 2004 and 60/76 of 8 December 2005,

Convinced that the continuing existence of nuclear weapons poses a threat to all humanity and that their use would have catastrophic consequences for all life on Earth, and recognizing that the only defence against a nuclear catastrophe is the total elimination of nuclear weapons and the certainty that they will never be produced again,

Reaffirming the commitment of the international community to the goal of the total elimination of nuclear weapons and the creation of a nuclear-weapon-free world,

Mindful of the solemn obligations of States parties, undertaken in article VI of the Treaty on the Non-Proliferation of Nuclear Weapons, [1] particularly to pursue negotiations in good faith on effective measures relating to cessation of the nuclear-arms race at an early date and to nuclear disarmament,

Recalling the principles and objectives for nuclear non-proliferation and disarmament adopted at the 1995 Review and Extension Conference of the Parties to the Treaty on the Non-Proliferation of Nuclear Weapons,[2]

Emphasizing the unequivocal undertaking by the nuclear-weapon States to accomplish the total elimination of their nuclear arsenals leading to nuclear disarmament, adopted at the 2000 Review Conference of the Parties to the Treaty on the Non-Proliferation of Nuclear Weapons,[3]

Recalling the adoption of the Comprehensive Nuclear-Test-Ban Treaty in its resolution 50/245 of 10 September 1996, and expressing its satisfaction at the increasing number of States that have signed and ratified the Treaty,

Recognizing with satisfaction that the Antarctic Treaty[4] and the treaties of Tlatelolco,[5] Rarotonga,[6] Bangkok,[7] Pelindaba[8] and Semipalatinsk,[9] as well as Mongolia's nuclear-weapon-free status, are gradually freeing the entire southern hemisphere and adjacent areas covered by those treaties from nuclear weapons,

Stressing the importance of strengthening all existing nuclear-related disarmament and arms control and reduction measures,

Recognizing the need for a multilaterally negotiated and legally binding instrument to assure non-nuclear-weapon States against the threat or use of nuclear weapons,

Reaffirming the central role of the Conference on Disarmament as the sole multilateral disarmament negotiating forum, and regretting the lack of progress in disarmament negotiations, particularly nuclear disarmament, in the Conference during its 2006 session,

Emphasizing the need for the Conference on Disarmament to commence negotiations on a phased programme for the complete elimination of nuclear weapons with a specified framework of time,

Expressing its regret over the failure of the 2005 Review Conference of the Parties to the Treaty on the Non-Proliferation of Nuclear Weapons to reach agreement on any substantive issues,

Expressing its deep concern at the lack of progress in the implementation of the thirteen steps to implement article VI of the Treaty on the Non-Proliferation of Nuclear Weapons agreed to at the 2000 Review Conference of the Parties to the Treaty,[10]

Desiring to achieve the objective of a legally binding prohibition of the development, production, testing, deployment, stockpiling, threat or use of nuclear weapons and their destruction under effective international control,

Recalling the advisory opinion of the International Court of Justice on the *Legality of the Threat or Use of Nuclear Weapons,* issued on 8 July 1996,[11]

Taking note of the relevant portions of the report of the Secretary-General relating to the implementation of resolution 60/76,[12]

1. *Underlines once again* the unanimous conclusion of the International Court of Justice that there exists an obligation to pursue in good faith and bring to a conclusion negotiations leading to nuclear disarmament in all its aspects under strict and effective international control;

2. *Calls once again upon* all States immediately to fulfil that obligation by commencing multilateral negotiations leading to an early conclusion of a nuclear weapons convention prohibiting the development, production, testing, deployment, stockpiling, transfer, threat or use of nuclear weapons and providing for their elimination;

3. *Requests* all States to inform the Secretary-General of the efforts and measures they have taken on the implementation of the present resolution and nuclear disarmament, and requests the Secretary-General to apprise the General Assembly of that information at its sixty-second session;

4. *Decides* to include in the provisional agenda of its sixty-second session the item entitled "Follow-up to the advisory opinion of the International Court of Justice on the *Legality of the Threat or Use of Nuclear Weapons*".

67th plenary meeting
6 December 2006

[1] United Nations, *Treaty Series*, vol. 729, No. 10485.

[2] *1995 Review and Extension Conference of the Parties to the Treaty on the Non-Proliferation of Nuclear Weapons, Final Document, Part I* (NPT/CONF.1995/32 (Part I) and Corr.2), annex, decision 2.

[3] *2000 Review Conference of the Parties to the Treaty on the Non-Proliferation of Nuclear Weapons, Final Document*, vol. I (NPT/CONF.2000/28 (Parts I and II)), part I, section entitled "Article VI and eighth to twelfth preambular paragraphs", para. 15:6.

[4] United Nations, *Treaty Series*, vol. 402, No. 5778.

[5] Ibid., vol. 634, No. 9068.

[6] See *The United Nations Disarmament Yearbook*, vol. 10: 1985 (United Nations publication, Sales No. E.86.IX.7), appendix VII.

[7] United Nations, *Treaty Series*, vol. 1981, No. 33873.

[8] A/50/426, annex.

[9] Treaty on a Nuclear-Weapon-Free Zone in Central Asia.

[10] See *2000 Review Conference of the Parties to the Treaty on the Non-Proliferation of Nuclear Weapons, Final Document*, vol. I (NPT/CONF.2000/28 (Parts I and II)), part I, section entitled "Article VI and eighth to twelfth preambular paragraphs", para. 15.

[11] A/51/218, annex; see also *Legality of the Threat or Use of Nuclear Weapons, Advisory Opinion, I.C.J. Reports 1996*, p. 226.

[12] A/61/127 and Add.1.

Resolution 61/84

[on the report of the First Committee (A/61/394)]

61/84. Implementation of the Convention on the Prohibition of the Use, Stockpiling, Production and Transfer of Anti personnel Mines and on Their Destruction

The General Assembly,

Recalling its resolutions 54/54 B of 1 December 1999, 55/33 V of 20 November 2000, 56/24 M of 29 November 2001, 57/74 of 22 November 2002, 58/53 of 8 December 2003, 59/84 of 3 December 2004 and 60/80 of 8 December 2005,

Reaffirming its determination to put an end to the suffering and casualties caused by anti-personnel mines, which kill or maim hundreds of people every week, mostly innocent and defenceless civilians, including children, obstruct economic development and reconstruction, inhibit the repatriation of refugees and internally displaced persons and have other severe consequences for years after emplacement,

Believing it necessary to do the utmost to contribute in an efficient and coordinated manner to facing the challenge of removing anti-personnel mines placed throughout the world and to assure their destruction,

Wishing to do the utmost in ensuring assistance for the care and rehabilitation, including the social and economic reintegration, of mine victims,

Welcoming the entry into force, on 1 March 1999, of the Convention on the Prohibition of the Use, Stockpiling, Production and Transfer of Anti-personnel Mines and on Their Destruction,[1] and noting with satisfaction the work undertaken to implement the Convention and the substantial progress made towards addressing the global landmine problem,

Recalling the first to sixth meetings of the States parties to the Convention held in Maputo (1999),[2] Geneva (2000),[3] Managua (2001),[4] Geneva (2002),[5] Bangkok (2003)[6] and Zagreb (2005),[7] and the First Review Conference of the States Parties to the Convention, held in Nairobi (2004).[8]

Recalling also the seventh meeting of the States parties to the Convention, held in Geneva from 18 to 22 September 2006, at which the international community monitored progress and supported continued application of the Nairobi Action Plan 2005–2009 [9] and established priorities to achieve further progress towards ending, for all people and for all time, the suffering caused by antipersonnel mines,

Noting with satisfaction that additional States have ratified or acceded to the Convention, bringing the total number of States that have formally accepted the obligations of the Convention to one hundred and fifty-one,

Emphasizing the desirability of attracting the adherence of all States to the Convention, and determined to work strenuously towards the promotion of its universalization,

Noting with regret that anti-personnel mines continue to be used in conflicts around the world, causing human suffering and impeding post-conflict development,

1. *Invites* all States that have not signed the Convention on the Prohibition of the Use, Stockpiling, Production and Transfer of Anti-personnel Mines and on Their Destruction[1] to accede to it without delay;

2. *Urges* all States that have signed but have not ratified the Convention to ratify it without delay;

3. *Stresses* the importance of the full and effective implementation of and compliance with the Convention, including through the continued implementation of the Nairobi Action Plan 2005–2009;[9]

4. *Urges* all States parties to provide the Secretary-General with complete and timely information as required under article 7 of the Convention in order to promote transparency and compliance with the Convention;

5. *Invites* all States that have not ratified the Convention or acceded to it to provide, on a voluntary basis, information to make global mine action efforts more effective;

6. *Renews its call upon* all States and other relevant parties to work together to promote, support and advance the care, rehabilitation and social and economic reintegration of mine victims, mine risk education programmes and the removal and destruction of anti-personnel mines placed or stockpiled throughout the world;

7. *Urges* all States to remain seized of the issue at the highest political level and, where in a position to do so, to promote adherence to the Convention through bilateral, subregional, regional and multilateral contacts, outreach, seminars and other means;

8. *Invites and encourages* all interested States, the United Nations, other relevant international organizations or institutions, regional organizations, the International Committee of the Red Cross and relevant non-governmental organizations to participate in the eighth meeting of the States parties to the Convention, to be held in Jordan from 18 to 22 November 2007, and in the intersessional work programme established at the first meeting of the States parties and further developed at subsequent meetings of the States parties;

9. *Requests* the Secretary-General, in accordance with article 11, paragraph 2, of the Convention, to undertake the preparations necessary to convene the next meeting of the States parties and, on behalf of the States parties and in accordance with article 11, paragraph 4, of the Convention, to invite States not parties to the Convention, as well as the United Nations, other relevant international organizations or institutions, regional organizations, the International Committee of the Red Cross and relevant non-governmental organizations to attend the eighth meeting of the States parties as observers;

10. *Decides* to remain seized of the matter.

67th plenary meeting
6 December 2006

---

[1] United Nations, *Treaty Series*, vol. 2056, No. 35597.

[2] See APLC/MSP.1/1999/1.

[3] See APLC/MSP.2/2000/1.

[4] See APLC/MSP.3/2001/1.

[5] See APLC/MSP.4/2002/1.

[6] See APLC/MSP.5/2003/5.

[7] See APLC/MSP.6/2005/5.

[8] See APLC/CONF/2004/5 and Corr.1.

[9] Ibid., part III.

Resolution 61/85

[on the report of the First Committee (A/61/394)]

61/85. Reducing nuclear danger

The General Assembly,

Bearing in mind that the use of nuclear weapons poses the most serious threat to mankind and to the survival of civilization,

Reaffirming that any use or threat of use of nuclear weapons would constitute a violation of the Charter of the United Nations,

Convinced that the proliferation of nuclear weapons in all its aspects would seriously enhance the danger of nuclear war,

Convinced also that nuclear disarmament and the complete elimination of nuclear weapons are essential to remove the danger of nuclear war,

Considering that, until nuclear weapons cease to exist, it is imperative on the part of the nuclear-weapon States to adopt measures that assure non-nuclear-weapon States against the use or threat of use of nuclear weapons,

Considering also that the hair-trigger alert of nuclear weapons carries unacceptable risks of unintentional or accidental use of nuclear weapons, which would have catastrophic consequences for all mankind,

Emphasizing the imperative need to adopt measures to avoid accidental, unauthorized or unexplained incidents arising from computer anomaly or other technical malfunctions,

Conscious that limited steps relating to de-alerting and de-targeting have been taken by the nuclear-weapon States and that further practical, realistic and mutually reinforcing steps are necessary to contribute to the improvement in the international climate for negotiations leading to the elimination of nuclear weapons,

Mindful that a diminishing role for nuclear weapons in the security policies of nuclear-weapon States would positively impact on international peace and security and improve the conditions for the further reduction and the elimination of nuclear weapons,

Reiterating the highest priority accorded to nuclear disarmament in the Final Document of the Tenth Special Session of the General Assembly1 and by the international community,

Recalling that in the advisory opinion of the International Court of Justice on the *Legality of the Threat or Use of Nuclear Weapons*,[2] it is stated that there exists an obligation for all States to pursue in good faith and bring to a conclusion negotiations leading to nuclear disarmament in all its aspects under strict and effective international control,

Recalling also the call in the United Nations Millennium Declaration[3] to seek to eliminate the dangers posed by weapons of mass destruction and the resolve to strive for the elimination of weapons of mass destruction, particularly nuclear weapons, including the possibility of convening an international conference to identify ways of eliminating nuclear dangers,

1. *Calls for* a review of nuclear doctrines and, in this context, immediate and urgent steps to reduce the risks of unintentional and accidental use of nuclear weapons, including through de-alerting and de-targeting of nuclear weapons;

2. *Requests* the five nuclear-weapon States to take measures towards the implementation of paragraph 1 above;

3. *Calls upon* Member States to take the necessary measures to prevent the proliferation of nuclear weapons in all its aspects and to promote nuclear disarmament, with the objective of eliminating nuclear weapons;

4. *Takes note* of the report of the Secretary-General submitted pursuant to paragraph 5 of General Assembly resolution 60/79 of 8 December 2005;[4]

5. *Requests* the Secretary-General to intensify efforts and support initiatives that would contribute towards the full implementation of the seven recommendations identified in the report of the Advisory Board on Disarmament Matters that would significantly reduce the risk of nuclear war,[5] and also to continue to encourage Member States to endeavour to create conditions that would allow the emergence of an international consensus to hold an international conference as proposed in the United Nations Millennium Declaration,[3] to identify ways of eliminating nuclear dangers, and to report thereon to the General Assembly at its sixty-second session;

6. *Decides* to include in the provisional agenda of its sixty-second session the item entitled "Reducing nuclear danger".

67th plenary meeting
6 December 2006

[1] Resolution S-10/2.

[2] A/51/218, annex; see also *Legality of the Threat or Use of Nuclear Weapons, Advisory Opinion, I.C.J. Reports 1996*, p. 226.

[3] See resolution 55/2.

[4] A/61/127 and Add.1.

[5] See A/56/400, para. 3.

Resolution 61/86

[on the report of the First Committee (A/61/394)]

61/86. Measures to prevent terrorists from acquiring weapons of mass destruction

The General Assembly,

Recalling its resolution 60/78 of 8 December 2005,

Recognizing the determination of the international community to combat terrorism, as evidenced in relevant General Assembly and Security Council resolutions,

Deeply concerned by the growing risk of linkages between terrorism and weapons of mass destruction, and in particular by the fact that terrorists may seek to acquire weapons of mass destruction,

Cognizant of the steps taken by States to implement Security Council resolution 1540 (2004) on the non-proliferation of weapons of mass destruction, adopted on 28 April 2004,

Welcoming the adoption, by consensus, of the International Convention for the Suppression of Acts of Nuclear Terrorism on 13 April 2005,[1]

Welcoming also the adoption, by consensus, of amendments to strengthen the Convention on the Physical Protection of Nuclear Material[2] by the International Atomic Energy Agency on 8 July 2005,

Noting the support expressed in the Final Document of the Fourteenth Conference of Heads of State or Government of Non-Aligned Countries, held in Havana on 15 and 16 September 2006,[3] for measures to prevent terrorists from acquiring weapons of mass destruction,

Noting also that the Group of Eight, the European Union, the Regional Forum of the Association of Southeast Asian Nations and others have taken into account in their deliberations the dangers posed by the acquisition by terrorists of weapons of mass destruction, and the need for international cooperation in combating it,

Acknowledging the consideration of issues relating to terrorism and weapons of mass destruction by the Advisory Board on Disarmament Matters,[4]

Taking note of the relevant resolutions adopted by the General Conference of the International Atomic Energy Agency at its fiftieth regular session,[5]

Taking note also of the 2005 World Summit Outcome adopted on 16 September 2005 at the High-level Plenary Meeting of the sixtieth session of the General Assembly[6] and the adoption of the United Nations Global Counter-Terrorism Strategy on 8 September 2006,[7]

Taking note further of the report of the Secretary-General submitted pursuant to paragraphs 3 and 5 of resolution 60/78,[8]

Mindful of the urgent need for addressing, within the United Nations framework and through international cooperation, this threat to humanity,

Emphasizing that progress is urgently needed in the area of disarmament and non-proliferation in order to help to maintain international peace and security and to contribute to global efforts against terrorism,

1. *Calls upon* all Member States to support international efforts to prevent terrorists from acquiring weapons of mass destruction and their means of delivery;

2. *Appeals* to all Member States to consider signing and ratifying the International Convention for the Suppression of Acts of Nuclear Terrorism[1] in order to bring about its early entry into force;

3. *Urges* all Member States to take and strengthen national measures, as appropriate, to prevent terrorists from acquiring weapons of mass destruction, their means of delivery and materials and technologies related to their manufacture, and invites them to inform the Secretary-General, on a voluntary basis, of the measures taken in this regard;

4. *Encourages* cooperation among and between Member States and relevant regional and international organizations for strengthening national capacities in this regard;

5. *Requests* the Secretary-General to compile a report on measures already taken by international organizations on issues relating to the linkage between the fight against terrorism and the proliferation of weapons of mass destruction, to seek the views of Member States on additional relevant measures for tackling the global threat posed by the acquisition by terrorists of weapons of mass destruction and to report to the General Assembly at its sixty-second session;

6. *Decides* to include in the provisional agenda of its sixty-second session the item entitled "Measures to prevent terrorists from acquiring weapons of mass destruction".

67th plenary meeting
6 December 2006

---

[1] Resolution 59/290, annex.

[2] United Nations, *Treaty Series*, vol. 1456, No. 24631.

[3] A/61/472-S/2006/780, annex I.

[4] See A/59/361.

[5] See International Atomic Energy Agency, *Resolutions and Other Decisions of the General Conference, Fiftieth Regular Session, 18–22 September 2006* (GC(50)/RES/DEC(2006)).

[6] See resolution 60/1.

[7] Resolution 60/288.

[8] A/61/171 and Add.1.

Resolution 61/87

[on the report of the First Committee (A/61/394)]

61/87. Mongolia's international security and nuclear-weapon-free status

The General Assembly,

Recalling its resolutions 53/77 D of 4 December 1998, 55/33 S of 20 November 2000, 57/67 of 22 November 2002 and 59/73 of 3 December 2004,

Recalling also the purposes and principles of the Charter of the United Nations, as well as the Declaration on Principles of International Law concerning Friendly Relations and Cooperation among States in accordance with the Charter of the United Nations,[1]

Bearing in mind its resolution 49/31 of 9 December 1994 on the protection and security of small States,

Proceeding from the fact that nuclear-weapon-free status is one of the means of ensuring the national security of States,

Convinced that the internationally recognized status of Mongolia will contribute to enhancing stability and confidence-building in the region as well as promote Mongolia's security by strengthening its independence, sovereignty and territorial integrity, the inviolability of its borders and the preservation of its ecological balance,

Taking note of the adoption by the Mongolian parliament of legislation defining and regulating Mongolia's nuclear-weapon-free status[2] as a concrete step towards promoting the aims of nuclear non-proliferation,

Bearing in mind the joint statement of the five nuclear-weapon States on security assurances to Mongolia in connection with its nuclear-weapon-free status[3] as a contribution to implementing resolution 53/77 D as well as their commitment to Mongolia to cooperate in the implementation of the resolution, in accordance with the principles of the Charter,

Noting that the joint statement has been transmitted to the Security Council by the five nuclear-weapon States,

Mindful of the support expressed for Mongolia's nuclear-weapon-free status by the Heads of State and Government of Non-Aligned Countries at the Thirteenth Conference of Heads of State or Government of Non-Aligned Countries, held in Kuala Lumpur on 24 and 25 February 2003[4] and the Fourteenth Conference, held in Havana on 15 and 16 September 2006,[5]

Noting that the States parties and signatories to the Treaties of Tlatelolco,[6] Rarotonga,[7] Bangkok[8] and Pelindaba[9] and the State of Mongolia expressed their recognition and full support of Mongolia's international nuclear-weapon-free status at the first Conference of States Parties and Signatories to Treaties that Establish Nuclear-Weapon-Free Zones, held in Tlatelolco, Mexico, from 26 to 28 April 2005,[10]

Noting also other measures taken to implement resolution 59/73 at the national and international levels,

Welcoming Mongolia's active and positive role in developing peaceful, friendly and mutually beneficial relations with the States of the region and other States,

Having considered the report of the Secretary-General on Mongolia's international security and nuclear-weapon-free status,[11]

1. *Takes note* of the report of the Secretary-General on the implementation of resolution 59/73;[11]

2. *Expresses its appreciation* to the Secretary-General for the efforts to implement resolution 59/73;[12]

3. *Endorses and supports* Mongolia's good-neighbourly and balanced relationship with its neighbours as an important element of strengthening regional peace, security and stability;

4. *Welcomes* the efforts made by Member States to cooperate with Mongolia in implementing resolution 59/73, as well as the progress made in consolidating Mongolia's international security;

5. *Invites* Member States to continue to cooperate with Mongolia in taking the necessary measures to consolidate and strengthen Mongolia's independence, sovereignty and territorial integrity, the inviolability of its borders, its independent foreign policy, its economic security and its ecological balance, as well as its nuclear-weapon-free status;

6. *Appeals* to the Member States of the Asia and Pacific region to support Mongolia's efforts to join the relevant regional security and economic arrangements;

7. *Requests* the Secretary-General and relevant United Nations bodies to continue to provide assistance to Mongolia in taking the necessary measures mentioned in paragraph 5 above;

8. *Requests* the Secretary-General to report to the General Assembly at its sixty-third session on the implementation of the present resolution;

9. *Decides* to include in the provisional agenda of its sixty-third session the item entitled "Mongolia's international security and nuclear-weapon-free status".

67th plenary meeting
6 December 2006

[1] Resolution 2625 (XXV), annex.

[2] See A/55/56-S/2000/160.

[3] A/55/530-S/2000/1052, annex.

[4] See A/57/759-S/2003/332, annex I.

[5] See A/61/472-S/2006/780, annex I.

[6] United Nations, *Treaty Series*, vol. 634, No. 9068.

[7] See *The United Nations Disarmament Yearbook*, vol. 10: 1985 (United Nations publication, Sales No. E.86.IX.7), appendix VII.

[8] United Nations, *Treaty Series*, vol. 1981, No. 33873.

[9] A/50/426, annex.

[10] See A/60/121, annex III.

[11] A/61/164.

[12] Ibid., sect. III.

Resolution 61/88

[on the report of the First Committee (A/61/394)]

61/88. Establishment of a nuclear-weapon-free zone in Central Asia

The General Assembly,

Recalling its resolutions 52/38 S of 9 December 1997, 53/77 A of 4 December 1998, 55/33 W of 20 November 2000 and 57/69 of 22 November 2002, and its decisions 54/417 of 1 December 1999, 56/412 of 29 November 2001, 58/518 of 8 December 2003, 59/513 of 3 December 2004 and 60/516 of 8 December 2005,

Convinced that the establishment of nuclear-weapon-free zones contributes to the achievement of general and complete disarmament, and emphasizing the importance of internationally recognized treaties on the establishment of such zones in different regions of the world in the strengthening of the non-proliferation regime,

Considering that the establishment of a nuclear-weapon-free zone in Central Asia on the basis of arrangements freely arrived at among the States of the region[1] constitutes an important step towards strengthening the nuclear non-proliferation regime, promoting cooperation in the peaceful uses of nuclear energy and in the environmental rehabilitation of territories affected by radioactive contamination, and enhancing regional and international peace and security,

Considering also the establishment of a nuclear-weapon-free zone in Central Asia as an effective contribution to combating international terrorism and preventing nuclear materials and technologies from falling into the hands of non-State actors, primarily terrorists,

Reaffirming the universally recognized role of the United Nations in the establishment of nuclear-weapon-free zones,

1. *Welcomes* the signing of the Treaty on a Nuclear-Weapon-Free Zone in Central Asia in Semipalatinsk, Kazakhstan, on 8 September 2006;

2. *Notes* the readiness of the Central Asian countries to continue consultations with the nuclear-weapon States on a number of provisions of the Treaty;

3. *Decides* to include in the provisional agenda of its sixty-third session the item entitled "Establishment of a nuclear-weapon-free zone in Central Asia".

67th plenary meeting
6 December 2006

[1] Kazakhstan, Kyrgyzstan, Tajikistan, Turkmenistan and Uzbekistan.

Resolution 61/89

[on the report of the First Committee (A/61/394)]

61/89. Towards an arms trade treaty: establishing common international standards for the import, export and transfer of conventional arms

The General Assembly,

Guided by the purposes and principles enshrined in the Charter of the United Nations, and reaffirming its respect for and commitment to international law,

Recalling its resolutions 46/36 L of 9 December 1991, 51/45 N of 10 December 1996, 51/47 B of 10 December 1996, 56/24 V of 24 December 2001 and 60/69 and 60/82 of 8 December 2005,

Recognizing that arms control, disarmament and non-proliferation are essential for the maintenance of international peace and security,

Reaffirming the inherent right of all States to individual or collective self-defence in accordance with Article 51 of the Charter,

Acknowledging the right of all States to manufacture, import, export, transfer and retain conventional arms for self-defence and security needs, and in order to participate in peace support operations,

Recalling the obligations of all States to fully comply with arms embargoes decided by the Security Council in accordance with the Charter,

Reaffirming its respect for international law, including international human rights law and international humanitarian law, and the Charter,

Taking note of and encouraging relevant initiatives, undertaken at the international, regional and subregional levels between States, including those of the United Nations, and of the role played by non-governmental organizations and civil society, to enhance cooperation, improve information exchange and transparency and implement confidence-building measures in the field of responsible arms trade,

Recognizing that the absence of common international standards on the import, export and transfer of conventional arms is a contributory factor to conflict, the displacement of people, crime and terrorism, thereby undermining peace, reconciliation, safety, security, stability and sustainable development,

Acknowledging the growing support across all regions for concluding a legally binding instrument negotiated on a non-discriminatory, transparent and multilateral basis, to establish common international standards for the import, export and transfer of conventional arms,

1. *Requests* the Secretary-General to seek the views of Member States on the feasibility, scope and draft parameters for a comprehensive, legally binding instrument establishing common international standards for the import, export and transfer of conventional arms, and to submit a report on the subject to the General Assembly at its sixty-second session;

2. *Also requests* the Secretary-General to establish a group of governmental experts, on the basis of equitable geographical distribution, informed by the report of the Secretary-General submitted to the General Assembly at its sixty-second session, to examine, commencing in 2008, the feasibility, scope and draft parameters for a comprehensive, legally binding instrument establishing common international standards for the import, export and transfer of conventional arms, and to transmit the report of the group of experts to the Assembly for consideration at its sixty-third session;

3. *Further requests* the Secretary-General to provide the group of governmental experts with any assistance and services that may be required for the discharge of its tasks;

4. *Decides* to include in the provisional agenda of its sixty-second session an item entitled "Towards an arms trade treaty: establishing common international standards for the import, export and transfer of conventional arms".

67th plenary meeting
6 December 2006

Resolution 61/90

[on the report of the First Committee (A/61/395)]

61/90. United Nations regional centres for peace and disarmament

The General Assembly,

Recalling its resolution 60/83 of 8 December 2005 regarding the maintenance and revitalization of the three United Nations regional centres for peace and disarmament,

Recalling also the reports of the Secretary-General on the United Nations Regional Centre for Peace and Disarmament in Africa,[1] the United Nations Regional Centre for Peace and Disarmament in Asia and the Pacific[2] and the United Nations Regional Centre for Peace, Disarmament and Development in Latin America and the Caribbean,[3]

Reaffirming its decision, taken in 1982 at its twelfth special session, to establish the United Nations Disarmament Information Programme, the purpose of which is to inform, educate and generate public understanding and support for the objectives of the United Nations in the field of arms control and disarmament,[4]

Bearing in mind its resolutions 40/151 G of 16 December 1985, 41/60 J of 3 December 1986, 42/39 D of 30 November 1987 and 44/117 F of 15 December 1989 on the regional centres for peace and disarmament in Nepal, Peru and Togo,

Recognizing that the changes that have taken place in the world have created new opportunities as well as posed new challenges for the pursuit of disarmament, and, in this regard, bearing in mind that the regional centres for peace and disarmament can contribute substantially to understanding and cooperation among States in each particular region in the areas of peace, disarmament and development,

Noting that in paragraph 146 of the Final Document of the Twelfth Conference of Heads of State or Government of the Non-Aligned Countries, held at Durban, South Africa, from 29 August to 3 September 1998, the Heads of State or Government welcomed the decision adopted by the General Assembly on maintaining and revitalizing the three regional centres for peace and disarmament in Nepal, Peru and Togo,[5]

1. *Reiterates* the importance of the United Nations activities at the regional level to increase the stability and security of its Member States, which could be promoted in a substantive manner by the maintenance and revitalization of the three regional centres for peace and disarmament;

2. *Reaffirms* that, in order to achieve positive results, it is useful for the three regional centres to carry out dissemination and educational programmes that promote regional peace and security and that are aimed at changing basic attitudes with respect to peace and security and disarmament so as to support the achievement of the purposes and principles of the United Nations;

3. *Appeals* to Member States in each region and those that are able to do so, as well as to international governmental and non-governmental organizations and foundations, to make voluntary contributions to the regional centres in their respective regions to strengthen their activities and initiatives;

4. *Emphasizes* the importance of the activities of the regional branch of the Department for Disarmament Affairs of the Secretariat;

5. *Requests* the Secretary-General to provide all necessary support, within existing resources, to the regional centres in carrying out their programmes of activities;

6. *Decides* to include in the provisional agenda of its sixty-second session the item entitled "United Nations regional centres for peace and disarmament".

67th plenary meeting
6 December 2006

[1] A/61/137.

[2] A/61/163.

[3] A/61/157.

[4] See *Official Records of the General Assembly, Twelfth Special Session, Plenary Meetings*, 1st meeting, paras. 110 and 111.

[5] See A/53/667-S/1998/1071, annex I.

Resolution 61/91

[on the report of the First Committee (A/61/395)]

61/91. United Nations disarmament fellowship, training and advisory services

The General Assembly,

Having considered the report of the Secretary-General,[1]

Recalling its decision, contained in paragraph 108 of the Final Document of the Tenth Special Session of the General Assembly,[2] the first special session devoted to disarmament, to establish a programme of fellowships on disarmament, as well as its decisions contained in annex IV to the Concluding Document of the Twelfth Special Session of the General Assembly,[3] the second special session devoted to disarmament, in which it decided, inter alia, to continue the programme,

Noting that the programme continues to contribute significantly to developing greater awareness of the importance and benefits of disarmament and a better understanding of the concerns of the international community in the field of disarmament and security, as well as to enhancing the knowledge and skills of fellows, allowing them to participate more effectively in efforts in the field of disarmament at all levels,

Noting with satisfaction that the programme has trained a large number of officials from Member States throughout its twenty-eight years of existence, many of whom hold positions of responsibility in the field of disarmament within their own Governments,

Recognizing the need for Member States to take into account gender equality when nominating candidates to the programme,

Recalling all the annual resolutions on the matter since the thirty-seventh session of the General Assembly, in 1982, including resolution 50/71 A of 12 December 1995,

Believing that the forms of assistance available to Member States, in particular to developing countries, under the programme will enhance the capabilities of their officials to follow ongoing deliberations and negotiations on disarmament, both bilateral and multilateral,

1. *Reaffirms* its decisions contained in annex IV to the Concluding Document of the Twelfth Special Session of the General Assembly[3] and the report of the Secretary-General[4] approved by the Assembly in its resolution 33/71 E of 14 December 1978;

2. *Expresses its appreciation* to all Member States and organizations that have consistently supported the programme throughout the years, thereby contributing to its success, in particular to the Governments of Germany and Japan for the continuation of extensive and highly educative study visits for the participants in the programme, and to the Government of the People's Republic of China for organizing a study visit for the fellows in the area of disarmament;

3. *Expresses its appreciation* to the International Atomic Energy Agency, the Organisation for the Prohibition of Chemical Weapons, the Preparatory Commission for the Comprehensive Nuclear-Test-Ban Treaty Organization and the Monterey Institute of International Studies for having organized specific study programmes in the field of disarmament in their respective areas of competence, thereby contributing to the objectives of the programme;

4. *Commends* the Secretary-General for the diligence with which the programme has continued to be carried out;

5. *Requests* the Secretary-General to continue to implement annually the Geneva-based programme within existing resources and to report thereon to the General Assembly at its sixty-third session;

6. *Decides* to include in the provisional agenda of its sixty-third session the item entitled "United Nations disarmament fellowship, training and advisory services".

67th plenary meeting
6 December 2006

---

[1] A/61/130 and Corr.1.

[2] Resolution S-10/2.

[3] *Official Records of the General Assembly, Twelfth Special Session, Annexes*, agenda items 9-13, document A/S-12/32.

[4] A/33/305.

Resolution 61/92

[on the report of the First Committee (A/61/395)]

61/92. United Nations Regional Centre for Peace, Disarmament and Development in Latin America and the Caribbean

The General Assembly,

Recalling its resolutions 41/60 J of 3 December 1986, 42/39 K of 30 November 1987 and 43/76 H of 7 December 1988 on the United Nations Regional Centre for Peace, Disarmament and Development in Latin America and the Caribbean, with headquarters in Lima,

Recalling also its resolutions 46/37 F of 9 December 1991, 48/76 E of 16 December 1993, 49/76 D of 15 December 1994, 50/71 C of 12 December 1995, 52/220 of 22 December 1997, 53/78 F of 4 December 1998, 54/55 F of 1 December 1999, 55/34 E of 20 November 2000, 56/25 E of 29 November 2001, 57/89 of 22 November 2002, 58/60 of 8 December 2003, 59/99 of 3 December 2004 and 60/84 of 8 December 2005,

Recognizing that the Regional Centre has continued to provide substantive support for the implementation of regional and subregional initiatives and has intensified its contribution to the coordination of United Nations efforts towards peace, disarmament and the promotion of economic and social development,

Welcoming the report of the Secretary-General,[1] which, inter alia, concludes that the Regional Centre has continued to provide assistance to States in the Latin American and Caribbean region in the implementation of regional initiatives in the areas of peace, disarmament and development and that during the period under review such assistance was provided in the area of practical disarmament, such as weapons destruction and training courses; the preparation of national reports on weapons-related instruments; the creation of mechanisms to facilitate the implementation of disarmament treaties; and the provision of forums for discussion among States to facilitate their reaching common positions on disarmament and non-proliferation issues, and welcoming also the Centre's initiation of the process of transferring to the African region its knowledge and best practices in the area of training courses for the law enforcement community on the prevention of illicit firearms trafficking,

Recalling the report of the Group of Governmental Experts on the relationship between disarmament and development,[2] referred to in General Assembly resolution 59/78 of 3 December 2004, which is of utmost interest with regard to the role that the Regional Centre plays in promoting the issue in the region in pursuit of its mandate to promote economic and social development related to peace and disarmament,

Noting that security and disarmament issues have always been recognized as significant topics in Latin America and the Caribbean, the first inhabited region in the world to be declared a nuclear-weapon-free zone,

Welcoming the support provided by the Regional Centre to strengthening the nuclear-weapon-free zone established by the Treaty for the Prohibition of Nuclear Weapons in Latin America and the Caribbean (Treaty of Tlatelolco),[3] as well as to promoting and assisting the ratification and implementation of existing multilateral agreements related to weapons of mass destruction and to promoting peace and disarmament education projects during the period under review,

Bearing in mind the important role that the Regional Centre can play in promoting confidence-building measures, arms control and limitation, disarmament and development at the regional level,

Bearing in mind also the importance of information, research, education and training for peace, disarmament and development in order to achieve understanding and cooperation among States,

Recognizing the need to provide the three United Nations regional centres for peace and disarmament with sufficient financial resources and cooperation for the planning and implementation of their programmes of activities,

1. *Reiterates its strong support* for the role of the United Nations Regional Centre for Peace, Disarmament and Development in Latin America and the Caribbean in the promotion of United Nations activities at the regional level to strengthen peace, stability, security and development among its member States;

2. *Expresses its satisfaction and congratulates* the Regional Centre for the activities carried out in the last year in the areas of peace, disarmament and development, and requests the Centre to take into account the proposals to be submitted by the countries of the region in promoting confidence-building measures, arms control and limitation, transparency, disarmament and development at the regional level;

3. *Expresses its appreciation* for the political support and financial contributions to the Regional Centre, which are essential for its continued operation;

4. *Appeals* to Member States, in particular those within the Latin American and Caribbean region, and to international governmental and non-governmental organizations and foundations to make and to increase voluntary contributions to strengthen the Regional Centre, its programme of activities and the implementation thereof;

5. *Invites* all States of the region to continue to take part in the activities of the Regional Centre, proposing items for inclusion in its programme of activities and making greater and better use of the potential of the Centre to meet the current challenges facing the international community with a view to fulfilling the aims of the Charter of the United Nations in the areas of peace, disarmament and development;

6. *Recognizes* that the Regional Centre has an important role in the promotion and development of regional initiatives agreed upon by the countries of Latin America and the Caribbean in the field of weapons of mass destruction, in particular nuclear weapons, and conventional arms, including small arms and light weapons, as well as in the relationship between disarmament and development;

7. *Encourages* the Regional Centre to further develop activities in the important area of disarmament and development;

8. *Highlights* the conclusion contained in the report of the Secretary-General that, through its activities, the Regional Centre has demonstrated its role as a viable regional actor in

assisting States in the region to advance the cause of peace, disarmament and development in Latin America and the Caribbean;[4]

9. *Requests* the Secretary-General to provide the Regional Centre with all necessary support, within existing resources, so that it may carry out its programme of activities in accordance with its mandate;

10. *Also requests* the Secretary-General to report to the General Assembly at its sixty-second session on the implementation of the present resolution;

11. *Decides* to include in the provisional agenda of its sixty-second session the item entitled "United Nations Regional Centre for Peace, Disarmament and Development in Latin America and the Caribbean".

67th plenary meeting
6 December 2006

---

[1] A/61/157.

[2] See A/59/119.

[3] United Nations, *Treaty Series*, vol. 634, No. 9068.

[4] See A/61/157, para. 49.

Resolution 61/93

[on the report of the First Committee (A/61/395)]

61/93. United Nations Regional Centre for Peace and Disarmament in Africa

The General Assembly,

Mindful of the provisions of Article 11, paragraph 1, of the Charter of the United Nations stipulating that a function of the General Assembly is to consider the general principles of cooperation in the maintenance of international peace and security, including the principles governing disarmament and arms limitation,

Recalling its resolutions 40/151 G of 16 December 1985, 41/60 D of 3 December 1986, 42/39 J of 30 November 1987 and 43/76 D of 7 December 1988 on the United Nations Regional Centre for Peace and Disarmament in Africa, and its resolutions 46/36 F of 6 December 1991 and 47/52 G of 9 December 1992 on regional disarmament, including confidence-building measures,

Recalling also its resolutions 48/76 E of 16 December 1993, 49/76 D of 15 December 1994, 50/71 C of 12 December 1995, 51/46 E of 10 December 1996, 52/220 of 22 December 1997, 53/78 C of 4 December 1998, 54/55 B of 1 December 1999, 55/34 D of 20 November 2000, 56/25 D of 29 November 2001, 57/91 of 22 November 2002, 58/61 of 8 December 2003, 59/101 of 3 December 2004 and 60/86 of 8 December 2005,

Aware of the important role that the Regional Centre can play in promoting confidence-building and arms-limitation measures at the regional level, thereby promoting progress in the area of sustainable development,

Taking note of the report of the Secretary-General,[1] in which he stated that the Regional Centre continued to operate under enormous uncertainty owing to a persistent decline in voluntary contributions in support of its activities,

Concerned that the activities and staffing of the Regional Centre have been reduced in view of the limited resources at its disposal,

Deeply concerned that, as noted in the report of the Secretary-General, the future of the Regional Centre looks bleak, as there is no foreseeable reliable source of funding that would ensure its operational sustainability,

Bearing in mind the efforts undertaken to mobilize the necessary resources for the operational costs of the Regional Centre,

Conscious of the need to review the mandate and programmes of the Regional Centre in the light of developments in the field of peace and security in Africa since its establishment,

Taking into account the need to establish close cooperation between the Regional Centre and the Peace and Security Council of the African Union, in particular its institutions in the field of peace, disarmament and security, as well as with relevant United Nations bodies and programmes in Africa for greater effectiveness,

Recalling that the General Assembly, in its resolution 60/86, requested the Secretary-General to establish, within existing resources, a consultative mechanism of interested States, in particular African States, for the reorganization of the United Nations Regional Centre for Peace and Disarmament in Africa, and to report thereon to the Assembly at its sixty-first session,

1. *Notes* that the year 2006 commemorates the twentieth anniversary of the establishment of the United Nations Regional Centre for Peace and Disarmament in Africa in Lomé;

2. *Notes with satisfaction* the establishment by the Secretary-General of the Consultative Mechanism for the Reorganization of the United Nations Regional Centre for Peace and Disarmament in Africa and its work aimed at enabling the Centre to effectively fulfil its mandate in responding to the demands and needs of Africa in the field of peace and disarmament;

3. *Requests* the Consultative Mechanism to continue its work, including reviewing the mandate and programmes of the Regional Centre in the light of developments in the field of peace and security in Africa since its establishment, with a view to identifying concrete measures to revitalize the Centre;

4. *Urges* all States, as well as international governmental and nongovernmental organizations and foundations, to make voluntary contributions in order to strengthen the programmes and activities of the Regional Centre and facilitate their implementation;

5. *Requests* the Secretary-General to continue to provide the necessary support to the Regional Centre for better achievements and results;

6. *Also requests* the Secretary-General to facilitate close cooperation between the Regional Centre and the African Union, in particular in the areas of peace, security and development, and to continue to provide assistance towards stabilizing the financial situation of the Centre;

7. *Appeals in particular* to the Regional Centre, in cooperation with the African Union, regional and subregional organizations and the African States, to take steps to promote the

consistent implementation of the Programme of Action to Prevent, Combat and Eradicate the Illicit Trade in Small Arms and Light Weapons in All Its Aspects;[2]

8. *Requests* the Secretary-General to report to the General Assembly at its sixty-second session on the implementation of the present resolution;

9. *Decides* to include in the provisional agenda of its sixty-second session the item entitled "United Nations Regional Centre for Peace and Disarmament in Africa".

67th plenary meeting
6 December 2006

---

[1] A/61/137.

[2] See *Report of the United Nations Conference on the Illicit Trade in Small Arms and Light Weapons in All Its Aspects, New York, 9-20 July 2001* (A/CONF.192/15), chap. IV, para. 24.

Resolution 61/94

[on the report of the First Committee (A/61/395)]

61/94. United Nations Regional Centre for Peace and Disarmament in Asia and the Pacific

The General Assembly,

Recalling its resolutions 42/39 D of 30 November 1987 and 44/117 F of 15 December 1989, by which it established the United Nations Regional Centre for Peace and Disarmament in Asia and renamed it the United Nations Regional Centre for Peace and Disarmament in Asia and the Pacific, with headquarters in Kathmandu and with the mandate of providing, on request, substantive support for the initiatives and other activities mutually agreed upon by the Member States of the Asia-Pacific region for the implementation of measures for peace and disarmament, through appropriate utilization of available resources,

Taking note of the report of the Secretary-General,[1] in which he expresses his belief that the mandate of the Regional Centre remains valid and that the Centre has been a useful instrument for fostering a climate of cooperation for peace and disarmament in the region,

Noting that trends in the post-cold-war era have emphasized the function of the Regional Centre in assisting Member States as they deal with new security concerns and disarmament issues emerging in the region,

Commending the useful activities carried out by the Regional Centre in encouraging regional and subregional dialogue for the enhancement of openness, transparency and confidence-building, as well as the promotion of disarmament and security through the organization of regional meetings, which has come to be widely known within the Asia-Pacific region as "the Kathmandu process",

Expressing its appreciation to the Regional Centre for its organization of meetings, conferences and workshops in the region, held in Kyoto, Japan, from 17 to 19 August 2005; Busan, Republic of Korea, from 1 to 3 December 2005; Bali, Indonesia, on 21 and 22 December 2005; Bangkok, Thailand, from 17 to 19 May 2006; and Beijing, People's Republic of China, on 12 and 13 July 2006,

Welcoming the activities of the Regional Centre in the promotion of disarmament and non-proliferation education in the Asia-Pacific region, as recommended in the United Nations study on disarmament and non-proliferation eductaion,[2]

Noting the important role of the Regional Centre in assisting region-specific initiatives of Member States,

Appreciating highly the overall support that Nepal has extended as the host nation of the headquarters of the Regional Centre,

1. *Reaffirms its strong support* for the forthcoming operation and further strengthening of the United Nations Regional Centre for Peace and Disarmament in Asia and the Pacific;

2. *Underlines* the importance of the Kathmandu process as a powerful vehicle for the development of the practice of region-wide security and disarmament dialogue;

3. *Expresses its appreciation* for the continuing political support and voluntary financial contributions to the Regional Centre, which are essential for its continued operation;

4. *Appeals* to Member States, in particular those within the Asia-Pacific region, as well as to international governmental and non-governmental organizations and foundations, to make voluntary contributions, the only resources of the Regional Centre, to strengthen the programme of activities of the Centre and the implementation thereof;

5. *Requests* the Secretary-General, taking note of paragraph 6 of General Assembly resolution 49/76 D of 15 December 1994, to provide the Regional Centre with the necessary support, within existing resources, in carrying out its programme of activities;

6. *Urges* the Secretary-General to complete, without any further delay, the internal procedure for finalizing the host country agreement and the related memorandum of understanding and to ensure the physical operation of the Regional Centre from Kathmandu within six months of the date of signature of the host country agreement and to enable the Centre to function effectively;

7. *Requests* the Secretary-General to report to the General Assembly at its sixty-second session on the implementation of the present resolution;

8. *Decides* to include in the provisional agenda of its sixty-second session the item entitled "United Nations Regional Centre for Peace and Disarmament in Asia and the Pacific".

67th plenary meeting
6 December 2006

---

1 A/61/163.

2 A/57/124.

Resoluion 61/95

[on the report of the First Committee (A/61/395)]

61/95. United Nations Disarmament Information Programme

The General Assembly,

Recalling its decision taken in 1982 at its twelfth special session, the second special session devoted to disarmament, by which the World Disarmament Campaign was launched,[1]

Bearing in mind its resolution 47/53 D of 9 December 1992, in which it decided, inter alia, that the World Disarmament Campaign should be known thereafter as the "United Nations Disarmament Information Programme" and the World Disarmament Campaign Voluntary Trust Fund as the "Voluntary Trust Fund for the United Nations Disarmament Information Programme",

Recalling its resolutions 51/46 A of 10 December 1996, 53/78 E of 4 December 1998, 55/34 A of 20 November 2000, 57/90 of 22 November 2002 and 59/103 of 3 December 2004,

Welcoming the report of the Secretary-General,[2]

1. *Takes note with appreciation* of the report of the Secretary-General,[2] in which he underlines that the website of the United Nations Disarmament Information Programme has grown exponentially in content and specialization and is being used by a greater number of Member States and other users;

2. *Commends* the Secretary-General for his efforts to make effective use of the limited resources available to him in disseminating as widely as possible, including by electronic means, information on arms limitation and disarmament to Governments, the media, non-governmental organizations, educational communities and research institutes, and in carrying out a seminar and conference programme;

3. *Stresses* the importance of the Programme as a significant instrument in enabling all Member States to participate fully in the deliberations and negotiations on disarmament in the various United Nations bodies, in assisting them in complying with treaties, as required, and in contributing to agreed mechanisms for transparency;

4. *Commends with satisfaction* the launch of the first online version of *The United Nations Disarmament Yearbook*, the 2004 edition, by the Department for Disarmament Affairs of the Secretariat, together with the 2002 and 2003 archival editions;

5. *Notes with appreciation* the cooperation of the Department of Public Information of the Secretariat and its information centres in pursuit of the objectives of the Programme;

6. *Recommends* that the Programme continue to inform, educate and generate public understanding of the importance of multilateral action and support for it, including action by the United Nations and the Conference on Disarmament, in the field of arms limitation and disarmament, in a factual, balanced and objective manner, and that it focus its efforts:

(*a*) To continue to publish in all official languages *The United Nations Disarmament Yearbook*, the flagship publication of the Department for Disarmament Affairs;

(*b*) To continue to maintain the disarmament website as a part of the United Nations website and to produce versions of the site in as many official languages as feasible;

(*c*) To continue to intensify United Nations interaction with the public, principally non-governmental organizations and research institutes, to help further an informed debate on topical issues of arms limitation, disarmament and security;

(*d*) To continue to organize discussions on topics of interest in the field of arms limitation and disarmament with a view to broadening understanding and facilitating an exchange of views and information among Member States and civil society;

7. *Recognizes* the important support received from some Governments for the Voluntary Trust Fund for the United Nations Disarmament Information Programme, and invites once again all Member States to make further contributions to the Fund with a view to sustaining a strong outreach programme;

8. *Takes note* of the recommendations contained in the report of the Secretary-General,[3] which reviews the implementation of the recommendations made in the 2002 study on disarmament and non-proliferation education;[4]

9. *Requests* the Secretary-General to submit to the General Assembly at its sixty-third session a report covering both the implementation of the activities of the Programme by the United Nations system during the previous two years and the activities of the Programme contemplated by the system for the following two years;

10. *Decides* to include in the provisional agenda of its sixty-third session the item entitled "United Nations Disarmament Information Programme".

67th plenary meeting
6 December 2006

[1] See *Official Records of the General Assembly, Twelfth Special Session, Plenary Meetings*, 1st meeting, paras. 110 and 111.

[2] A/61/215.

[3] A/61/169 and Add.1.

[4] A/57/124.

Resolution 61/96

[on the report of the First Committee (A/61/395)]

61/96. Regional confidence-building measures: activities of the United Nations Standing Advisory Committee on Security Questions in Central Africa

The General Assembly,

Bearing in mind the purposes and principles of the United Nations and its primary responsibility for the maintenance of international peace and security in accordance with the Charter of the United Nations,

Recalling its resolutions 43/78 H and 43/85 of 7 December 1988, 44/21 of 15 November 1989, 45/58 M of 4 December 1990, 46/37 B of 6 December 1991, 47/53 F of 15 December 1992, 48/76 A of 16 December 1993, 49/76 C of 15 December 1994, 50/71 B of 12 December 1995, 51/46 C of 10 December 1996, 52/39 B of 9 December 1997, 53/78 A of 4 December 1998, 54/55 A of 1 December 1999, 55/34 B of 20 November 2000, 56/25 A of 29 November 2001, 57/88 of 22 November 2002, 58/65 of 8 December 2003, 59/96 of 3 December 2004 and 60/87 of 8 December 2005,

Considering the importance and effectiveness of confidence-building measures taken at the initiative and with the participation of all States concerned and taking into account the specific characteristics of each region, since such measures can contribute to regional stability and to international peace and security,

Convinced that the resources released by disarmament, including regional disarmament, can be devoted to economic and social development and to the protection of the environment for the benefit of all peoples, in particular those of the developing countries,

Recalling the guidelines for general and complete disarmament adopted at its tenth special session, the first special session devoted to disarmament,

Convinced that development can be achieved only in a climate of peace, security and mutual confidence both within and among States,

Bearing in mind the establishment by the Secretary-General on 28 May 1992 of the United Nations Standing Advisory Committee on Security Questions in Central Africa, the purpose of which is to encourage arms limitation, disarmament, non-proliferation and development in the subregion,

Recalling the Brazzaville Declaration on Cooperation for Peace and Security in Central Africa,[1] the Bata Declaration for the Promotion of Lasting Democracy, Peace and Development in Central Africa[2] and the Yaoundé Declaration on Peace, Security and Stability in General Africa,[3]

Bearing in mind resolutions 1196 (1998) and 1197 (1998), adopted by the Security Council on 16 and 18 September 1998 respectively, following its consideration of the report of the Secretary-General on the causes of conflict and the promotion of durable peace and sustainable development in Africa,[4]

Emphasizing the need to strengthen the capacity for conflict prevention and peacekeeping in Africa,

Recalling the decision of the fourth ministerial meeting of the Standing Advisory Committee in favour of establishing, under the auspices of the Office of the United Nations High Commissioner for Human Rights, a subregional centre for human rights and democracy in Central Africa at Yaoundé,

Noting with satisfaction the efforts being made by the countries members of the Economic Community of Central African States to promote peace and security in their subregion, including the convening in N'Djamena, at the initiative of the current Chairman of the Central African Economic and Monetary Community, of two extraordinary sessions of the Conference of Heads of State of the Central African Economic and Monetary Community, for the purpose of considering the risk of destabilization in Chad,

Recalling the Brazzaville Declaration of 2 September 2005 on the situation between the Democratic Republic of the Congo and the Republic of Rwanda,[5]

Taking note of the successful completion of electoral processes in Chad, the Democratic Republic of the Congo, Gabon and Sao Tome and Principe,

Recognizing the importance of disarmament, demobilization and reintegration programmes in strengthening peace, political stability and reconstruction, especially in post-conflict situations,

1. *Takes note* of the report of the Secretary-General on regional confidence-building measures, which deals with the activities of the United Nations Standing Advisory Committee on Security Questions in Central Africa in the period since the adoption by the General Assembly of its resolution 60/87;[6]

2. *Reaffirms its support* for efforts aimed at promoting confidence-building measures at the regional and subregional levels in order to ease tensions and conflicts in Central Africa and to further sustainable peace, stability and development in the subregion;

3. *Encourages* the States members of the Economic Community of Central African States to pursue their efforts to promote peace and security in their subregion;

4. *Notes with satisfaction* that the Democratic Republic of the Congo and Rwanda are pursuing their efforts to strengthen their bilateral relations;

5. *Strongly appeals* to the international community to provide all necessary support for the smooth functioning of the electoral process in the Democratic Republic of the Congo;

6. *Appeals* to the international community to support the efforts undertaken by the States concerned to implement disarmament, demobilization and reintegration programmes;

7. *Reaffirms its support* for the programme of work of the Standing Advisory Committee adopted at the organizational meeting of the Committee, held at Yaoundé from 27 to 31 July 1992;

8. *Notes with satisfaction* the progress made by the Standing Advisory Committee in implementing its programme of work for the period 2005–2006;[6]

9. *Emphasizes* the importance of providing the States members of the Standing Advisory Committee with the essential support they need to carry out the full programme of activities which they adopted at their ministerial meetings;

10. *Welcomes* the creation of a mechanism for the promotion, maintenance and consolidation of peace and security in Central Africa, known as the Council for Peace and Security in Central Africa, by the Conference of Heads of State and Government of the countries members of the Economic Community of Central African States, held at Yaoundé on 25 February 1999, and requests the Secretary-General to give his full support to the effective realization of that important mechanism;

11. *Emphasizes* the need to make the early warning mechanism in Central Africa operational so that it will serve, on the one hand, as an instrument for analysing and monitoring political situations in the States members of the Standing Advisory Committee with a view to preventing the outbreak of future armed conflicts and, on the other hand, as a technical body through which the member States will carry out the programme of work of the Committee, adopted at its organizational meeting held at Yaoundé in 1992, and requests the Secretary-General to provide it with the assistance necessary for it to function properly;

12. *Requests* the Secretary-General and the United Nations High Commissioner for Human Rights to continue to provide their full assistance for the proper functioning of the Subregional Centre for Human Rights and Democracy in Central Africa;

13. *Requests* the Secretary-General, pursuant to Security Council resolution 1197 (1998), to provide the States members of the Standing Advisory Committee with the necessary support for the implementation and smooth functioning of the Council for Peace and Security in Central Africa;

14. *Also requests* the Secretary-General to support the establishment of a network of parliamentarians with a view to the creation of a subregional parliament in Central Africa;

15. *Requests* the Secretary-General and the United Nations High Commissioner for Refugees to continue to provide increased assistance to the countries of Central Africa for coping with the problems of refugees and displaced persons in their territories;

16. *Thanks* the Secretary-General for having established the Trust Fund for the United Nations Standing Advisory Committee on Security Questions in Central Africa;

17. *Appeals* to Member States and to governmental and non-governmental organizations to make additional voluntary contributions to the Trust Fund for the implementation of the programme of work of the Standing Advisory Committee;

18. *Thanks* the Secretary-General for sending a multidisciplinary mission from 8 to 22 June 2003 for the purpose of undertaking an assessment of the priority needs of the region and challenges confronting it in the areas of peace, security, economic development, human rights and HIV/AIDS, and in the humanitarian field;

19. *Requests* the Secretary-General to continue to provide the States members of the Standing Advisory Committee with assistance to ensure that they are able to carry on their efforts;

20. *Calls upon* the Secretary-General to submit to the General Assembly at its sixty-second session a report on the implementation of the present resolution;

21. *Decides* to include in the provisional agenda of its sixty-second session the item entitled "Regional confidence-building measures: activities of the United Nations Standing Advisory Committee on Security Questions in Central Africa".

67th plenary meeting
6 December 2006

---

[1] A/50/474, annex I.

[2] A/53/258-S/1998/763, annex II, appendix I.

[3] A/53/868-S/1999/303, annex II.

[4] A/52/871-S/1998/318.

[5] A/60/393-S/2005/616, annex.

[6] A/61/365.

Resolution 61/97

[on the report of the First Committee (A/61/395)]

61/97. Convention on the Prohibition of the Use of Nuclear Weapons

The General Assembly,

Convinced that the use of nuclear weapons poses the most serious threat to the survival of mankind,

Bearing in mind the advisory opinion of the International Court of Justice of 8 July 1996 on the *Legality of the Threat or Use of Nuclear Weapons*,[1]

Convinced that a multilateral, universal and binding agreement prohibiting the use or threat of use of nuclear weapons would contribute to the elimination of the nuclear threat and to the climate for negotiations leading to the ultimate elimination of nuclear weapons, thereby strengthening international peace and security,

Conscious that some steps taken by the Russian Federation and the United States of America towards a reduction of their nuclear weapons and the improvement in the international climate can contribute towards the goal of the complete elimination of nuclear weapons,

Recalling that paragraph 58 of the Final Document of the Tenth Special Session of the General Assembly[2] states that all States should actively participate in efforts to bring about conditions in international relations among States in which a code of peaceful conduct of nations in international affairs could be agreed upon and that would preclude the use or threat of use of nuclear weapons,

Reaffirming that any use of nuclear weapons would be a violation of the Charter of the United Nations and a crime against humanity, as declared in its resolutions 1653 (XVI) of 24 November 1961, 33/71 B of 14 December 1978, 34/83 G of 11 December 1979, 35/152 D of 12 December 1980 and 36/92 I of 9 December 1981,

Determined to achieve an international convention prohibiting the development, production, stockpiling and use of nuclear weapons, leading to their ultimate destruction,

Stressing that an international convention on the prohibition of the use of nuclear weapons would be an important step in a phased programme towards the complete elimination of nuclear weapons, with a specified framework of time,

Noting with regret that the Conference on Disarmament, during its 2006 session, was unable to undertake negotiations on this subject as called for in General Assembly resolution 60/88 of 8 December 2005,

1. *Reiterates its request* to the Conference on Disarmament to commence negotiations in order to reach agreement on an international convention prohibiting the use or threat of use of nuclear weapons under any circumstances;

2. *Requests* the Conference on Disarmament to report to the General Assembly on the results of those negotiations.

67th plenary meeting
6 December 2006

---

[1] A/51/218, annex; see also *Legality of the Threat or Use of Nuclear Weapons, Advisory Opinion, I.C.J. Reports 1996,* p. 226.

[2] See resolution S-10/2.

Resolution 61/98

[on the report of the First Committee (A/61/396)]

61/98. Report of the Disarmament Commission

The General Assembly,

Having considered the report of the Disarmament Commission,[1]

Recalling its resolutions 47/54 A of 9 December 1992, 47/54 G of 8 April 1993, 48/77 A of 16 December 1993, 49/77 A of 15 December 1994, 50/72 D of 12 December 1995, 51/47 B of 10 December 1996, 52/40 B of 9 December 1997, 53/79 A of 4 December 1998, 54/56

A of 1 December 1999, 55/35 C of 20 November 2000, 56/26 A of 29 November 2001, 57/95 of 22 November 2002, 58/67 of 8 December 2003, 59/105 of 3 December 2004 and 60/91 of 8 December 2005,

Considering the role that the Disarmament Commission has been called upon to play and the contribution that it should make in examining and submitting recommendations on various problems in the field of disarmament and in the promotion of the implementation of the relevant decisions adopted by the General Assembly at its tenth special session,

1. *Takes note* of the report of the Disarmament Commission;[1]

2. *Reaffirms* the validity of its decision 52/492 of 8 September 1998, concerning the efficient functioning of the Disarmament Commission;

3. *Decides* to adopt the following additional measures for improving the effectiveness of the Disarmament Commission's methods of work:

(*a*) The Chairpersons and Vice-Chairpersons of the Commission and its subsidiary bodies should be elected at an organizational session of the Commission, if possible at least three months before the beginning of the substantive session; the regional groups should, accordingly, present their candidates as soon as possible to ensure that such elections take place within that time frame;

(*b*) Member States are encouraged to adopt the draft agenda of the substantive session of the Commission as early as possible at the organizational meetings of the Commission;

(*c*) Member States are encouraged to present their national working documents to the Commission as early as possible before the beginning of the substantive session to facilitate deliberation in the meetings ahead;

(*d*) The Commission should make efforts to strengthen dialogue with other bodies of the disarmament machinery of the United Nations, that is, the First Committee of the General Assembly and the Conference on Disarmament;

(*e*) The Commission is encouraged to invite, as appropriate, experts on disarmament, including those at the United Nations Institute for Disarmament Research, for discussions at its plenary meetings;

(*f*) The Secretariat is requested to improve the Commission section of the United Nations website to provide better communication and up-to-date information about the work of the Commission, and in particular to make available in a timely manner the information and documentation relevant to the Commission's deliberations;

4. *Reaffirms* the mandate of the Disarmament Commission as the specialized, deliberative body within the United Nations multilateral disarmament machinery that allows for in-depth deliberations on specific disarmament issues, leading to the submission of concrete recommendations on those issues;

5. *Also reaffirms* the importance of further enhancing the dialogue and cooperation between the First Committee, the Disarmament Commission and the Conference on Disarmament;

6. *Requests* the Disarmament Commission to continue its work in accordance with its mandate, as set forth in paragraph 118 of the Final Document of the Tenth Special Session of

the General Assembly,[2] and with paragraph 3 of Assembly resolution 37/78 H of 9 December 1982, and to that end to make every effort to achieve specific recommendations on the items on its agenda, taking into account the adopted "Ways and means to enhance the functioning of the Disarmament Commission";[3]

7. *Recommends* that the Disarmament Commission continue the consideration of the following items at its 2007 substantive session:

(*a*) Recommendations for achieving the objective of nuclear disarmament and non-proliferation of nuclear weapons;

(*b*) Practical confidence-building measures in the field of conventional weapons;

8. *Requests* the Disarmament Commission to meet for a period not exceeding three weeks during 2007, namely from 9 to 27 April, and to submit a substantive report to the General Assembly at its sixty-second session;

9. *Requests* the Secretary-General to transmit to the Disarmament Commission the annual report of the Conference on Disarmament,[4] together with all the official records of the sixty-first session of the General Assembly relating to disarmament matters, and to render all assistance that the Commission may require for implementing the present resolution;

10. *Also requests* the Secretary-General to ensure full provision to the Disarmament Commission and its subsidiary bodies of interpretation and translation facilities in the official languages and to assign, as a matter of priority, all the necessary resources and services, including verbatim records, to that end;

11. *Decides* to include in the provisional agenda of its sixty-second session the item entitled "Report of the Disarmament Commission".

67th plenary meeting
6 December 2006

---

[1] *Official Records of the General Assembly, Sixty-first Session, Supplement No. 42* (A/61/42).

[2] Resolution S-10/2.

[3] A/CN.10/137.

[4] *Official Records of the General Assembly, Sixty-first Session, Supplement No. 27* (A/61/27).

Resolution 61/99

[on the report of the First Committee (A/61/396)]

61/99. Report of the Conference on Disarmament

The General Assembly,

Having considered the report of the Conference on Disarmament,[1]

Convinced that the Conference on Disarmament, as the sole multilateral disarmament negotiating forum of the international community, has the primary role in substantive negotiations on priority questions of disarmament,

Recognizing the need to conduct multilateral negotiations with the aim of reaching agreement on concrete issues,

Recalling, in this respect, that the Conference has a number of urgent and important issues for negotiation,

Taking note of active discussions held on the programme of work during the 2006 session of the Conference, as duly reflected in the report and the records of the plenary meetings,

Taking note also of increased deliberations of the Conference due to the constructive contribution of its member States, focused structured debates on all agenda items including with the participation of experts from capitals, and cooperation between all six Presidents of the Conference in the 2006 session,

Taking note further of significant contributions made during the 2006 session to promote substantive discussions on issues on the agenda, as well as of discussions held on other issues that could also be relevant to the current international security environment,

Stressing the urgent need for the Conference to commence its substantive work at the beginning of its 2007 session,

Recognizing the address of the Secretary-General of the United Nations, as well as the addresses of Ministers for Foreign Affairs and other high-level officials, as expressions of support for the endeavours of the Conference and its role as the sole multilateral disarmament negotiating forum,

Bearing in mind the importance of efforts towards revitalization of the disarmament machinery, including the Conference,

Recognizing the importance of continuing consultations on the question of the expansion of the Conference membership,

1. *Reaffirms* the role of the Conference on Disarmament as the sole multilateral disarmament negotiating forum of the international community;

2. *Calls upon* the Conference to further intensify consultations and explore possibilities with a view to reaching an agreement on a programme of work;

3. *Takes note* of the strong collective interest of the Conference in commencing substantive work as soon as possible during its 2007 session;

4. *Welcomes* the decision of the Conference to request its current President and the incoming President to conduct consultations during the intersessional period and, if possible, to make recommendations, taking into account all relevant proposals, including those submitted as documents of the Conference, views presented and discussions held, and to endeavour to keep the membership of the Conference informed, as appropriate, of their consultations, as contained in paragraph 28 of its report;[1]

5. *Requests* all States members of the Conference to cooperate with the current President and successive Presidents in their efforts to guide the Conference to the early commencement of substantive work in its 2007 session;

6. *Requests* the Secretary-General to continue to ensure the provision to the Conference of adequate administrative, substantive and conference support services;

7. *Requests* the Conference to submit a report on its work to the General Assembly at its sixty-second session;

8. *Decides* to include in the provisional agenda of its sixty-second session the item entitled "Report of the Conference on Disarmament".

67th plenary meeting
6 December 2006

[1] *Official Records of the General Assembly, Sixty-first Session, Supplement No. 27* (A/61/27).

Resolution 61/100

[on the report of the First Committee (A/61/398)]

61/100. Convention on Prohibitions or Restrictions on the Use of Certain Conventional Weapons Which May Be Deemed to Be Excessively Injurious or to Have Indiscriminate Effects

The General Assembly,

Recalling its resolution 60/93 of 8 December 2005,

Recalling with satisfaction the adoption and the entry into force of the Convention on Prohibitions or Restrictions on the Use of Certain Conventional Weapons Which May Be Deemed to Be Excessively Injurious or to Have Indiscriminate Effects,[1] and its amended article 1,[2] and the Protocol on Non-Detectable Fragments (Protocol I),[1] the Protocol on Prohibitions or Restrictions on the Use of Mines, Booby Traps and Other Devices (Protocol II)[1] and its amended version,[3] the Protocol on Prohibitions or Restrictions on the Use of Incendiary Weapons (Protocol III)[1] and the Protocol on Blinding Laser Weapons (Protocol IV),[4]

Recalling the decision of the Second Review Conference of the States Parties to the Convention on Prohibitions or Restrictions on the Use of Certain Conventional Weapons Which May Be Deemed to Be Excessively Injurious or to Have Indiscriminate Effects to establish an open-ended group of governmental experts with two separate coordinators on explosive remnants of war and on mines other than anti-personnel mines,[2]

Recalling also the role played by the International Committee of the Red Cross in the elaboration of the Convention and the Protocols thereto, and welcoming the particular efforts of various international, non-governmental and other organizations in raising awareness of the humanitarian consequences of explosive remnants of war,

1. *Calls upon* all States that have not yet done so to take all measures to become parties, as soon as possible, to the Convention on Prohibitions or Restrictions on the Use of Certain Conventional Weapons Which May Be Deemed to Be Excessively Injurious or to Have Indiscriminate Effects[1] and the Protocols thereto, as amended, with a view to achieving the widest possible adherence to these instruments at an early date, and so as to ultimately achieve their universality;

2. *Calls upon* all States parties to the Convention that have not yet done so to express their consent to be bound by the Protocols to the Convention and the amendment extending the scope of the Convention and the Protocols thereto to include armed conflicts of a non-international character;

3. *Welcomes with satisfaction* the adoption of the Protocol on Explosive Remnants of War (Protocol V) [5] at the Meeting of the States Parties to the Convention held in Geneva on 27 and 28 November 2003 and its entry into force on 12 November 2006, and calls upon the States that have not yet done so to become parties to the Protocol as soon as possible;

4. *Notes* the decision of the Meeting of the States Parties that the Working Group on Mines Other Than Anti-Personnel Mines would continue its work in 2006 with the mandate to consider all proposals on mines other than anti-personnel mines put forward since the establishment of the Group of Governmental Experts, and to conduct meetings of military experts to provide advice, with the aim of elaborating appropriate recommendations on this issue for submission to the Third Review Conference in 2006;[6]

5. *Also notes* the decision of the Meeting of the States Parties that the Working Group on Explosive Remnants of War would continue its work in 2006 with the mandate to continue to consider, including through participation of legal experts, the implementation of existing principles of international humanitarian law and to further study, on an open-ended basis, with particular emphasis on meetings of military and technical experts, possible preventive measures aimed at improving the design of certain specific types of munitions, including sub-munitions, with a view to minimizing the humanitarian risk of these munitions becoming explosive remnants of war, and to report on the work done to the Third Review Conference in 2006;[6]

6. *Further notes* the decision of the Meeting of the States Parties that the President-designate should continue to undertake consultations during the intersessional period on possible options with respect to promoting compliance with the Convention and the Protocols thereto, taking into account proposals put forward, and report on the work done to the Third Review Conference in 2006;[6]

7. *Expresses support* for the work conducted by the Group of Governmental Experts, and encourages the President-designate and the Coordinators of the Group to continue their work in preparation for the Third Review Conference, in accordance with the mandates and decisions for 2006, with the aim of achieving a successful Third Review Conference from 7 to 17 November 2006;

8. *Expresses support* for conducting a thorough review at the Third Review Conference of the scope, operation, status and implementation of the Convention and of the Protocols thereto as amended;

9. *Expresses support* for the decisions of the Group of Governmental Experts to recommend to the Third Review Conference a plan of action to promote universality of the Convention and the Protocols thereto, a declaration on the entry into force of Protocol V on explosive remnants of war, as well as sponsorship programme;

10. *Notes* that, in conformity with article 8 of the Convention, the Review Conference may consider any proposal for amendments to the Convention or the Protocols thereto as well as any proposal for additional protocols relating to other categories of conventional weapons not covered by existing Protocols to the Convention;

11. *Requests* the Secretary-General to render the necessary assistance and to provide such services, including summary records, as may be required for the Eighth Annual Conference of the High Contracting Parties to Amended Protocol II to the Convention on 6 November 2006 and for the Third Review Conference, and for any possible continuation of work after the Conference, should the States parties deem it appropriate;[7]

12. *Also requests* the Secretary-General, in his capacity as depositary of the Convention and the Protocols thereto, to continue to inform the General Assembly periodically, by electronic means, of ratifications and acceptances of and accessions to the Convention, its amended article 1,[2] and the Protocols thereto;

13. *Decides* to remain seized of the matter.

67th plenary meeting
6 December 2006

---

[1] United Nations, *Treaty Series*, vol. 1342, No. 22495.

[2] See CCW/CONF.II/2 and Corr.1, part II.

[3] CCW/CONF.I/16 (Part I), annex B.

[4] Ibid., annex A.

[5] See CCW/MSP/2003/3, appendix II.

[6] See CCW/MSP/2005/2 and Corr.1.

[7] In accordance with the proposed programme budget for the biennium 2006–2007: part II, Political affairs (sect. 4, Disarmament) (A/60/6 (sect. 4)), para. 4.25 (a) (iii) a.

Resolution 61/101

[on the report of the First Committee (A/61/399)]

61/101. Strengthening of security and cooperation in the Mediterranean region

The General Assembly,

Recalling its previous resolutions on the subject, including resolution 60/94 of 8 December 2005,

Reaffirming the primary role of the Mediterranean countries in strengthening and promoting peace, security and cooperation in the Mediterranean region,

Welcoming the efforts deployed by the Euro-Mediterranean countries to strengthen their cooperation in combating terrorism, in particular by the adoption of the Euro-Mediterranean Code of Conduct on Countering Terrorism by the Euro-Mediterranean Summit, held in Barcelona, Spain, on 27 and 28 November 2005,

Bearing in mind all the previous declarations and commitments, as well as all the initiatives taken by the riparian countries at the recent summits, ministerial meetings and various forums concerning the question of the Mediterranean region,

Recognizing the indivisible character of security in the Mediterranean and that the enhancement of cooperation among Mediterranean countries with a view to promoting the economic and social development of all peoples of the region will contribute significantly to stability, peace and security in the region,

Recognizing also the efforts made so far and the determination of the Mediterranean countries to intensify the process of dialogue and consultations with a view to resolving the problems existing in the Mediterranean region and to eliminating the causes of tension and the consequent threat to peace and security, and their growing awareness of the need for further joint efforts to strengthen economic, social, cultural and environmental cooperation in the region,

Recognizing further that prospects for closer Euro-Mediterranean cooperation in all spheres can be enhanced by positive developments worldwide, in particular in Europe, in the Maghreb and in the Middle East,

Reaffirming the responsibility of all States to contribute to the stability and prosperity of the Mediterranean region and their commitment to respecting the purposes and principles of the Charter of the United Nations as well as the provisions of the Declaration on Principles of International Law concerning Friendly Relations and Cooperation among States in accordance with the Charter of the United Nations,[1]

Noting the peace negotiations in the Middle East, which should be of a comprehensive nature and represent an appropriate framework for the peaceful settlement of contentious issues in the region,

Expressing its concern at the persistent tension and continuing military activities in parts of the Mediterranean that hinder efforts to strengthen security and cooperation in the region,

Taking note of the report of the Secretary-General,[2]

1. *Reaffirms* that security in the Mediterranean is closely linked to European security as well as to international peace and security;

2. *Expresses its satisfaction* at the continuing efforts by Mediterranean countries to contribute actively to the elimination of all causes of tension in the region and to the promotion of just and lasting solutions to the persistent problems of the region through peaceful means, thus ensuring the withdrawal of foreign forces of occupation and respecting the sovereignty, independence and territorial integrity of all countries of the Mediterranean and the right of peoples to self-determination, and therefore calls for full adherence to the principles of non-interference, non-intervention, non-use of force or threat of use of force and the inadmissibility of the acquisition of territory by force, in accordance with the Charter and the relevant resolutions of the United Nations;

3. *Commends* the Mediterranean countries for their efforts in meeting common challenges through coordinated overall responses, based on a spirit of multilateral partnership, towards the general objective of turning the Mediterranean basin into an area of dialogue, exchanges and cooperation, guaranteeing peace, stability and prosperity, encourages them to strengthen such efforts through, inter alia, a lasting multilateral and action-oriented cooperative dialogue among States of the region, and recognizes the role of the United Nations in promoting regional and international peace and security;

4. *Recognizes* that the elimination of the economic and social disparities in levels of development and other obstacles as well as respect and greater understanding among cultures in the Mediterranean area will contribute to enhancing peace, security and cooperation among Mediterranean countries through the existing forums;

5. *Calls upon* all States of the Mediterranean region that have not yet done so to adhere to all the multilaterally negotiated legal instruments related to the field of disarmament and non-proliferation, thus creating the necessary conditions for strengthening peace and cooperation in the region;

6. *Encourages* all States of the region to favour the necessary conditions for strengthening the confidence-building measures among them by promoting genuine openness and transparency on all military matters, by participating, inter alia, in the United Nations system for the standardized reporting of military expenditures and by providing accurate data and information to the United Nations Register of Conventional Arms;[3]

7. *Encourages* the Mediterranean countries to strengthen further their cooperation in combating terrorism in all its forms and manifestations, including the possible resort by terrorists to weapons of mass destruction, taking into account the relevant resolutions of the United Nations, and in combating international crime and illicit arms transfers and illicit drug production, consumption and trafficking, which pose a serious threat to peace, security and stability in the region and therefore to the improvement of the current political, economic and social situation and which jeopardize friendly relations among States, hinder the development of international cooperation and result in the destruction of human rights, fundamental freedoms and the democratic basis of pluralistic society;

8. *Requests* the Secretary-General to submit a report on means to strengthen security and cooperation in the Mediterranean region;

9. *Decides* to include in the provisional agenda of its sixty-second session the item entitled "Strengthening of security and cooperation in the Mediterranean region".

67th plenary meeting
6 December 2006

---

[1] Resolution 2625 (XXV), annex.

[2] A/61/123.

[3] See resolution 46/36 L.

Resolution 61/102

[on the report of the First Committee (A/61/401)]

61/102. Convention on the Prohibition of the Development, Production and Stockpiling of Bacteriological (Biological) and Toxin Weapons and on Their Destruction

The General Assembly,

Recalling its previous resolutions relating to the complete and effective prohibition of bacteriological (biological) and toxin weapons and to their destruction,

Noting with satisfaction that there are one hundred and fifty-five States parties to the Convention on the Prohibition of the Development, Production and Stockpiling of Bacteriological (Biological) and Toxin Weapons and on Their Destruction,[1] including all of the permanent members of the Security Council,

Bearing in mind its call upon all States parties to the Convention to participate in the implementation of the recommendations of the Review Conferences, including the exchange of information and data agreed to in the Final Declaration of the Third Review Conference of the Parties to the Convention,[2] and to provide such information and data in conformity with standardized procedure to the Secretary-General on an annual basis and no later than 15 April,

Welcoming the reaffirmation made in the Final Declaration of the Fourth Review Conference[3] that under all circumstances the use of bacteriological (biological) and toxin weapons and their development, production and stockpiling are effectively prohibited under article I of the Convention,

1. *Reaffirms* the call upon all signatory States that have not yet ratified the Convention on the Prohibition of the Development, Production and Stockpiling of Bacteriological (Biological) and Toxin Weapons and on Their Destruction[1] to do so without delay, and calls upon those States that have not signed the Convention to become parties thereto at an early date, thus contributing to the achievement of universal adherence to the Convention;

2. *Welcomes* the information and data provided to date, and reiterates its call upon all States parties to the Convention to participate in the exchange of information and data agreed to in the Final Declaration of the Third Review Conference of the Parties to the Convention;[2]

3. *Appreciates* the significant participation of the States parties at the meetings of States parties and meetings of experts to date and the constructive and useful exchange of information achieved;

4. *Welcomes* the discussion and the promotion of common understanding and effective action on topics agreed upon at the Fifth Review Conference:[4] the adoption of necessary national measures to implement the prohibitions set forth in the Convention, including the enactment of penal legislation, and national mechanisms to establish and maintain the security and oversight of pathogenic micro-organisms and toxins in 2003; enhancing international capabilities for responding to, investigating and mitigating the effects of cases of alleged use of biological or toxin weapons or suspicious outbreaks of disease and strengthening and broadening national and international institutional efforts and existing mechanisms for the surveillance, detection, diagnosis and combating of infectious diseases affecting humans, animals and plants in 2004; and the content, promulgation and adoption of codes of conduct for scientists in 2005;

5. *Recalls* that the Sixth Review Conference was mandated to consider issues identified in the review of the operation of the Convention as provided for in article XII thereof and any possible consensus follow-up action;

6. *Welcomes* the convening of the Sixth Review Conference in Geneva from 20 November to 8 December 2006, pursuant to the decision reached by the Preparatory Committee of the States Parties to the Convention;[5]

7. *Requests* the Secretary-General to continue to render the necessary assistance to the depositary Governments of the Convention and to provide such services as may be required for the implementation of the decisions and recommendations of the Review Conferences;

8. *Decides* to include in the provisional agenda of its sixty-second session, also in view of the outcome of the Sixth Review Conference, the item entitled "Convention on the Prohibition of the Development, Production and Stockpiling of Bacteriological (Biological) and Toxin Weapons and on Their Destruction".

67th plenary meeting
6 December 2006

---

[1] Resolution 2826 (XXVI), annex.

[2] BWC/CONF.III/23, part II.

[3] BWC/CONF.IV/9, part II.

[4] See BWC/CONF.V/17.

[5] See BWC/CONF.VI/PC/2, para. 17.

Resolution 61/103

[on the report of the First Committee (A/61/397)]

61/103. The risk of nuclear proliferation in the Middle East

The General Assembly,

Bearing in mind its relevant resolutions,

Taking note of the relevant resolutions adopted by the General Conference of the International Atomic Energy Agency, the latest of which is resolution GC(50)/RES/16, adopted on 22 September 2006,[1]

Cognizant that the proliferation of nuclear weapons in the region of the Middle East would pose a serious threat to international peace and security,

Mindful of the immediate need for placing all nuclear facilities in the region of the Middle East under full-scope safeguards of the Agency,

Recalling the decision on principles and objectives for nuclear non-proliferation and disarmament adopted by the 1995 Review and Extension Conference of the Parties to the Treaty on the Non-Proliferation of Nuclear Weapons on 11 May 1995,[2] in which the Conference urged universal adherence to the Treaty[3] as an urgent priority and called upon all States not yet parties to the Treaty to accede to it at the earliest date, particularly those States that operate unsafeguarded nuclear facilities,

Recognizing with satisfaction that, in the Final Document of the 2000 Review Conference of the Parties to the Treaty on the Non-Proliferation of Nuclear Weapons, the Conference undertook to make determined efforts towards the achievement of the goal of universality of the Treaty, called upon those remaining States not parties to the Treaty to accede to it, thereby accepting an international legally binding commitment not to acquire nuclear weapons or nuclear explosive devices and to accept Agency safeguards on all their nuclear activities, and underlined the necessity of universal adherence to the Treaty and of strict compliance by all parties with their obligations under the Treaty,[4]

Recalling the resolution on the Middle East adopted by the 1995 Review and Extension Conference on 11 May 1995,[2] in which the Conference noted with concern the continued existence in the Middle East of unsafeguarded nuclear facilities, reaffirmed the importance of the early realization of universal adherence to the Treaty and called upon all States in the Middle East that had not yet done so, without exception, to accede to the Treaty as soon as possible and to place all their nuclear facilities under full-scope Agency safeguards,

Noting that Israel remains the only State in the Middle East that has not yet become party to the Treaty,

Concerned about the threats posed by the proliferation of nuclear weapons to the security and stability of the Middle East region,

Stressing the importance of taking confidence-building measures, in particular the establishment of a nuclear-weapon-free zone in the Middle East, in order to enhance peace and security in the region and to consolidate the global non-proliferation regime,

Emphasizing the need for all parties directly concerned to consider seriously taking the practical and urgent steps required for the implementation of the proposal to establish a nuclear-weapon-free zone in the region of the Middle East in accordance with the relevant resolutions of the General Assembly and, as a means of promoting this objective, inviting the countries concerned to adhere to the Treaty and, pending the establishment of the zone, to agree to place all their nuclear activities under Agency safeguards,

Noting that one hundred and seventy-six States have signed the Comprehensive Nuclear-Test-Ban Treaty,[5] including a number of States in the region,

1. *Welcomes* the conclusions on the Middle East of the 2000 Review Conference of the Parties to the Treaty on the Non-Proliferation of Nuclear Weapons;[6]

2. *Reaffirms* the importance of Israel's accession to the Treaty on the Non-Proliferation of Nuclear Weapons[3] and placement of all its nuclear facilities under comprehensive International Atomic Energy Agency safeguards, in realizing the goal of universal adherence to the Treaty in the Middle East;

3. *Calls upon* that State to accede to the Treaty without further delay and not to develop, produce, test or otherwise acquire nuclear weapons, and to renounce possession of nuclear weapons, and to place all its unsafeguarded nuclear facilities under full-scope Agency safeguards as an important confidence-building measure among all States of the region and as a step towards enhancing peace and security;

4. *Requests* the Secretary-General to report to the General Assembly at its sixty-second session on the implementation of the present resolution;

5. *Decides* to include in the provisional agenda of its sixty-second session the item entitled "The risk of nuclear proliferation in the Middle East".

67th plenary meeting
6 December 2006

---

1 See International Atomic Energy Agency, *Resolutions and Other Decisions of the General Conference, Fiftieth Regular Session, 18–22 September 2006* (GC(50)/RES/DEC(2006)).

2 See *1995 Review and Extension Conference of the Parties to the Treaty on the Non-Proliferation of Nuclear Weapons, Final Document, Part I* (NPT/CONF.1995/32 (Part I) and Corr.2), annex.

3 United Nations, *Treaty Series*, vol. 729, No. 10485.

4 See *2000 Review Conference of the Parties to the Treaty on the Non-Proliferation of Nuclear Weapons, Final Document*, vol. I (NPT/CONF.2000/28 (Parts I and II)), part I, section entitled "Article IX".

5 See resolution 50/245.

6 See *2000 Review Conference of the Parties to the Treaty on the Non-Proliferation of Nuclear Weapons, Final Document*, vol. I (NPT/CONF.2000/28 (Parts I and II)), part I, section entitled "Article VII and the security of non-nuclear-weapon States", para. 16.

Resolution 61/104

[on the report of the First Committee (A/61/400)]

61/104. Comprehensive Nuclear-Test-Ban Treaty

The General Assembly,

Reiterating that the cessation of nuclear-weapon test explosions or any other nuclear explosions constitutes an effective nuclear disarmament and non-proliferation measure, and convinced that this is a meaningful step in the realization of a systematic process to achieve nuclear disarmament,

Recalling that the Comprehensive Nuclear-Test-Ban Treaty, adopted by its resolution 50/245 of 10 September 1996, was opened for signature on 24 September 1996,

Stressing that a universal and effectively verifiable Treaty constitutes a fundamental instrument in the field of nuclear disarmament and non-proliferation and that after ten years, its entry into force is more urgent than ever before,

Encouraged by the signing of the Treaty by one hundred and seventy-six States, including forty-one of the forty-four needed for its entry into force, and welcoming the ratification of one hundred and twenty-five States, including thirty-four of the forty-four needed for its entry into force, among which there are three nuclear-weapon States,

Recalling its resolution 60/95 of 8 December 2005,

Welcoming the Final Declaration of the fourth Conference on Facilitating the Entry into Force of the Comprehensive Nuclear-Test-Ban Treaty, held in New York from 21 to 23 September 2005,[1] pursuant to article XIV of the Treaty, and the Ministerial Meeting of States Parties, held in New York on 20 September 2006,

1. *Stresses* the vital importance and urgency of signature and ratification, without delay and without conditions, to achieve the earliest entry into force of the Comprehensive Nuclear-Test-Ban Treaty;

2. *Welcomes* the contributions by the States signatories to the work of the Preparatory Commission for the Comprehensive Nuclear-Test-Ban Treaty Organization, in particular its efforts to ensure that the Treaty's verification regime will be capable of meeting the verification requirements of the Treaty upon its entry into force, in accordance with article IV of the Treaty;

3. *Underlines* the need to maintain momentum towards completion of the verification regime;

4. *Urges* all States to maintain their moratoriums on nuclear-weapon test explosions or any other nuclear explosions and to refrain from acts that would defeat the object and purpose of the Treaty, while stressing that these measures do not have the same permanent and legally binding effect as the entry into force of the Treaty;

5. *Condemns* the nuclear test proclaimed by the Democratic People's Republic of Korea on 9 October 2006, and demands that the Democratic People's Republic of Korea not conduct any further nuclear tests;

6. *Urges* all States that have not yet signed the Treaty to sign and ratify it as soon as possible;

7. *Urges* all States that have signed but not yet ratified the Treaty, in particular those whose ratification is needed for its entry into force, to accelerate their ratification processes with a view to ensuring their earliest successful conclusion;

8. *Urges* all States to remain seized of the issue at the highest political level and, where in a position to do so, to promote adherence to the Treaty through bilateral and joint outreach, seminars and other means;

9. *Requests* the Secretary-General, in consultation with the Preparatory Commission for the Comprehensive Nuclear-Test-Ban Treaty Organization, to prepare a report on the efforts of States that have ratified the Treaty towards its universalization and possibilities for providing assistance on ratification procedures to States that so request it, and to submit such a report to the General Assembly at its sixty-second session;

10. *Decides* to include in the provisional agenda of its sixty-second session the item entitled "Comprehensive Nuclear-Test-Ban Treaty".

67th plenary meeting
6 December 2006

[1] CTBT-Art.XIV/2005/6, annex.

Resolution 61/105

[without reference to a Main Committee (A/61/L.38 and Add.1)]

61/105. Sustainable fisheries, including through the 1995 Agreement for the Implementation of the Provisions of the United Nations Convention on the Law of the Sea of 10 December 1982 relating to the Conservation and Management of Straddling Fish Stocks and Highly Migratory Fish Stocks, and related instruments

The General Assembly,

Reaffirming its resolutions 46/215 of 20 December 1991, 49/116 and 49/118 of 19 December 1994, 50/25 of 5 December 1995 and 57/142 of 12 December 2002, as well as other resolutions on large-scale pelagic drift-net fishing, unauthorized fishing in zones of national jurisdiction and on the high seas, fisheries by-catch and discards, and other developments, its resolutions 56/13 of 28 November 2001 and 57/143 of 12 December 2002 on the Agreement for the Implementation of the Provisions of the United Nations Convention on the Law of the Sea of 10 December 1982 relating to the Conservation and Management of Straddling Fish Stocks and Highly Migratory Fish Stocks ("the Agreement"),[1] and its resolutions 58/14 of 24 November 2003, 59/25 of 17 November 2004 and 60/31 of 29 November 2005 on sustainable fisheries, including through the Agreement and related instruments,

Recalling the relevant provisions of the United Nations Convention on the Law of the Sea ("the Convention"),[2] and bearing in mind the relationship between the Convention and the Agreement,

Recognizing that, in accordance with the Convention, the Agreement sets forth provisions concerning the conservation and management of straddling fish stocks and highly migratory fish stocks, including provisions on compliance and enforcement by the flag State and subregional and regional cooperation in enforcement, binding dispute settlement and the rights and obligations of States in authorizing the use of vessels flying their flags for fishing on the high seas, and specific provisions to address the requirements of developing States in relation to the conservation and management of straddling fish stocks and highly migratory fish stocks and the development of fisheries for such stocks,

Welcoming the fact that a growing number of States, and entities referred to in the Convention and in article 1, paragraph 2 (*b*), of the Agreement, as well as regional and subregional fisheries management organizations and arrangements, have taken measures, as appropriate, towards the implementation of the provisions of the Agreement,

Welcoming also the work of the Food and Agriculture Organization of the United Nations and its Committee on Fisheries and the 2005 Rome Declaration on Illegal, Unreported and Unregulated Fishing, adopted by the Ministerial Meeting on Fisheries of the Food and Agriculture Organization of the United Nations on 12 March 2005,[3] which calls for effective implementation of the various instruments already developed to ensure responsible fisheries, and recognizing that the Code of Conduct for Responsible Fisheries of the Food and Agriculture Organization of the United Nations ("the Code")[4] and its associated international plans of action set out principles and global standards of behaviour for responsible practices for conservation of fisheries resources and the management and development of fisheries,

Noting with concern that effective management of marine capture fisheries has been made difficult in some areas by unreliable information and data caused by unreported and misreported fish catch and fishing effort and this lack of accurate data contributes to overfishing in some areas, and therefore welcoming the adoption of the Strategy for Improving Information on Status and Trends of Capture Fisheries[5] and the development of the Fishery Resources Monitoring System (FIRMS) initiative by the Food and Agriculture Organization of the United Nations to improve knowledge and understanding of fishery status and trends,

Recognizing the significant contribution of sustainable fisheries to food security, income and wealth for present and future generations,

Recognizing also the urgent need for action at all levels to ensure the long-term sustainable use and management of fisheries resources through the wide application of the precautionary approach,

Deploring the fact that fish stocks, including straddling fish stocks and highly migratory fish stocks, in many parts of the world are overfished or subject to sparsely regulated and heavy fishing efforts, as a result of, inter alia, illegal, unreported and unregulated fishing, inadequate flag State control and enforcement, including monitoring, control and surveillance measures, inadequate regulatory measures, harmful fisheries subsidies and overcapacity,

Particularly concerned that illegal, unreported and unregulated fishing constitutes a serious threat to fish stocks and marine habitats and ecosystems, to the detriment of sustainable fisheries as well as the food security and the economies of many States, particularly developing States,

Recognizing the duty provided in the Convention, the Agreement to Promote Compliance with International Conservation and Management Measures by Fishing Vessels on the High

Seas ("the Compliance Agreement"),[6] the Agreement and the Code for flag States to exercise effective control over fishing vessels flying their flag, and vessels flying their flag which provide support to fishing vessels, to ensure that the activities of such fishing and support vessels do not undermine the effectiveness of conservation and management measures taken in accordance with international law and adopted at the national, subregional, regional or global levels,

Noting the obligation of all States, pursuant to the provisions of the Convention, to cooperate in the conservation and management of living marine resources, and recognizing the importance of coordination and cooperation at the global, regional, subregional as well as national levels in the areas, inter alia, of data collection, information-sharing, capacity-building and training for the conservation, management and sustainable development of marine living resources,

Noting with appreciation the report of the Review Conference on the Agreement ("the Review Conference"), held in New York from 22 to 26 May 2006,[7] and welcoming the adoption of the recommendations therein, which assessed the effectiveness of the Agreement in securing the conservation and management of straddling and highly migratory fish stocks by reviewing and assessing the adequacy of its provisions and proposed means of strengthening the substance and methods of implementation of those provisions in order better to address any continuing problems in the conservation and management of those stocks, and also noting that the Conference agreed that there is a compelling need for all States and subregional and regional fisheries management organizations and arrangements to ensure the conservation and sustainable use of straddling and highly migratory fish stocks,

Noting with satisfaction that the Review Conference agreed to continue the informal consultations of States parties to the Agreement and to keep the Agreement under review through the resumption of the Conference at a date not later than 2011, to be agreed at a future informal consultation of States parties to the Agreement,

Calling attention to the need for more work to develop port State measures and schemes, and the critical need for cooperation with developing States to build their capacity in this regard,

Concerned that marine pollution from all sources, including vessels and, in particular, land-based sources, constitutes a serious threat to human health and safety, endangers fish stocks, marine biodiversity and marine habitats and has significant costs to local and national economies,

Recognizing that marine debris is a global transboundary pollution problem and that, due to the many different types and sources of marine debris, different approaches to their prevention and removal are necessary,

Noting that the contribution of sustainable aquaculture to global fish supplies continues to respond to opportunities in developing countries to enhance local food security and poverty alleviation and, together with efforts of other aquaculture producing countries, will make a significant contribution to meeting future demands in fish consumption, bearing in mind article 9 of the Code,

Calling attention to the circumstances affecting fisheries in many developing States, in particular African States and small island developing States, and recognizing the urgent need for capacity-building, including the transfer of marine technology and in particular fisheries-related technology, to enhance the ability of such States to meet their obligations and exercise their rights under international instruments, in order to realize the benefits from fisheries resources,

Recognizing the need for appropriate measures to minimize waste, discards, loss of fishing gear and other factors, which adversely affect fish stocks,

Recognizing also the importance of applying ecosystem approaches to oceans management and the need to integrate such approaches into fisheries conservation and management, and in this regard welcoming the report of the seventh meeting of the United Nations Open-ended Informal Consultative Process on Oceans and the Law of the Sea,[8] held in New York from 12 to 16 June 2006,

Recognizing further the economic and cultural importance of sharks in many countries, the biological importance of sharks in the marine ecosystem, the vulnerability of certain shark species to overexploitation, some of which are threatened with extinction, and the need for measures to promote the long-term sustainability of shark populations and fisheries, and the relevance of the International Plan of Action for the Conservation and Management of Sharks, adopted by the Food and Agriculture Organization of the United Nations in 1999, in providing development guidance of such measures,

Reaffirming its support for the initiative of the Food and Agriculture Organization of the United Nations and relevant regional and subregional fisheries management organizations and arrangements on the conservation and management of sharks, while noting with concern that only a small number of countries have implemented the International Plan of Action for the Conservation and Management of Sharks,

Taking note with appreciation of the report of the Secretary-General on the impacts of fishing on vulnerable marine ecosystems: actions taken by States and regional fisheries management organizations and arrangements to give effect to paragraphs 66 to 69 of General Assembly resolution 59/25 on sustainable fisheries, regarding the impacts of fishing on vulnerable marine ecosystems,[9] in particular its useful role in gathering and disseminating information on this issue,

Expressing concern that the practice of large-scale pelagic drift-net fishing remains a threat to marine living resources, although the incidence of this practice has continued to be low in most regions of the world's oceans and seas,

Emphasizing that efforts should be made to ensure that the implementation of resolution 46/215 in some parts of the world does not result in the transfer to other parts of the world of drift nets that contravene the resolution,

Expressing concern over reports of continued losses of seabirds, particularly albatrosses and petrels, as well as other marine species, including sharks, fin-fish species and marine turtles, as a result of incidental mortality in fishing operations, particularly longline fishing, and other activities, while recognizing considerable efforts to reduce by-catch in longline fishing by States and through various regional fisheries management organizations and arrangements,

I
Achieving sustainable fisheries

1. *Reaffirms* the importance it attaches to the long-term conservation, management and sustainable use of the marine living resources of the world's oceans and seas and the obligations of States to cooperate to this end, in accordance with international law, as reflected in the relevant provisions of the Convention,[2] in particular the provisions on cooperation set out in Part V and Part VII, section 2, of the Convention, and where applicable, the Agreement;[1]

2. *Encourages* States to give due priority to the implementation of the Plan of Implementation of the World Summit on Sustainable Development ("Johannesburg Plan of Implementation"),[10] in relation to achieving sustainable fisheries;

3. *Emphasizes* the obligations of flag States to discharge their responsibilities, in accordance with the Convention and the Agreement, to ensure compliance by vessels flying their flag with the conservation and management measures adopted and in force with respect to fisheries resources on the high seas;

4. *Calls upon* all States that have not done so, in order to achieve the goal of universal participation, to become parties to the Convention, which sets out the legal framework within which all activities in the oceans and seas must be carried out, taking into account the relationship between the Convention and the Agreement;

5. *Calls upon* all States, directly or through regional fisheries management organizations and arrangements, to apply widely, in accordance with international law and the Code,[4] the precautionary approach and an ecosystem approach to the conservation, management and exploitation of fish stocks, including straddling fish stocks, highly migratory fish stocks and discrete high seas fish stocks, and also calls upon States parties to the Agreement to implement fully the provisions of article 6 of the Agreement as a matter of priority;

6. *Encourages* States to increase their reliance on scientific advice in developing, adopting and implementing conservation and management measures, and to increase their efforts to promote science for conservation and management measures that apply, in accordance with international law, the precautionary approach and an ecosystem approach to fisheries management, enhancing understanding of ecosystem approaches, in order to ensure the long-term conservation and sustainable use of marine living resources, and in this regard encourages the implementation of the international Strategy for Improving Information on Status and Trends of Capture Fisheries of the Food and Agriculture Organization of the United Nations[5] as a framework for the improvement and understanding of fishery status and trends;

7. *Also encourages* States to apply the precautionary approach and an ecosystem approach in adopting and implementing conservation and management measures addressing, inter alia, by-catch, pollution, overfishing, and protecting habitats of specific concern, taking into account existing guidelines developed by the Food and Agriculture Organization of the United Nations;

8. *Calls upon* States and regional fisheries management organizations and arrangements to collect and, where appropriate, report to the Food and Agriculture Organization of the United Nations required catch and effort data, and fishery-related information, in a complete, accurate and timely way, including for straddling fish stocks and highly migratory fish stocks within and beyond areas under national jurisdiction, discrete high seas fish stocks, and by-catch and discards; and where they do not exist, to establish processes to

strengthen data collection and reporting by members of regional fisheries management organizations and arrangements, including through regular reviews of member compliance with such obligations, and when such obligations are not met, require the member concerned to rectify the problem, including through the preparation of plans of action with timelines;

9. *Invites* States and regional fisheries management organizations and arrangements to cooperate with the Food and Agriculture Organization of the United Nations in the implementation and further development of the Fishery Resources Monitoring System (FIRMS) initiative;

10. *Urges* States, including those working through subregional or regional fisheries management organizations and arrangements, to implement fully the International Plan of Action for the Conservation and Management of Sharks, notably through the collection of scientific data regarding shark catches and the adoption of conservation and management measures, particularly where shark catches from directed and non-directed fisheries have a significant impact on vulnerable or threatened shark stocks, in order to ensure the conservation and management of sharks and their long-term sustainable use, including by banning directed shark fisheries conducted solely for the purpose of harvesting shark fins and by taking measures for other fisheries to minimize waste and discards from shark catches, and to encourage the full use of dead sharks;

11. *Urges* States to eliminate barriers to trade in fish and fisheries products which are not consistent with their rights and obligations under the World Trade Organization agreements, taking into account the importance of the trade in fish and fisheries products, particularly for developing countries;

12. *Urges* States and relevant international and national organizations to provide for participation of small-scale fishery stakeholders in related policy development and fisheries management strategies in order to achieve long-term sustainability for such fisheries, consistent with the duty to ensure the proper conservation and management of fisheries resources;

II

Implementation of the 1995 Agreement for the Implementation of the Provisions of the United Nations Convention on the Law of the Sea of 10 December 1982 relating to the Conservation and Management of Straddling Fish Stocks and Highly Migratory Fish Stocks

13. *Calls upon* all States, and entities referred to in the Convention and in article 1, paragraph 2 (*b*), of the Agreement, that have not done so to ratify or accede to the Agreement and in the interim to consider applying it provisionally;

14. *Calls upon* States parties to the Agreement to harmonize, as a matter of priority, their national legislation with the provisions of the Agreement, and to ensure that the provisions of the Agreement are effectively implemented into regional fisheries management organizations and arrangements of which they are a member;

15. *Emphasizes* the importance of those provisions of the Agreement relating to bilateral, regional and subregional cooperation in enforcement, and urges continued efforts in this regard;

16. *Calls upon* all States to ensure that their vessels comply with the conservation and management measures that have been adopted by regional and subregional fisheries management organizations and arrangements in accordance with relevant provisions of the Convention and of the Agreement;

17. *Urges* States parties to the Agreement, in accordance with article 21, paragraph 4, thereof to inform, either directly or through the relevant regional or subregional fisheries management organization or arrangement, all States whose vessels fish on the high seas in the same region or subregion of the form of identification issued by those States parties to officials duly authorized to carry out boarding and inspection functions in accordance with articles 21 and 22 of the Agreement;

18. *Also urges* States parties to the Agreement, in accordance with article 21, paragraph 4, to designate an appropriate authority to receive notifications pursuant to article 21 and to give due publicity to such designation through the relevant subregional or regional fisheries management organization or arrangement;

19. *Calls upon* States individually and, as appropriate, through regional and subregional fisheries management organizations and arrangements with competence over discrete high seas fish stocks, to adopt the necessary measures to ensure the long-term conservation, management and sustainable use of such stocks in accordance with the Convention and consistent with the general principles set forth in the Agreement;

20. *Invites* States and international financial institutions and organizations of the United Nations system to provide assistance according to Part VII of the Agreement, including, if appropriate, the development of special financial mechanisms or instruments to assist developing States, in particular the least developed among them and small island developing States, to enable them to develop their national capacity to exploit fishery resources, including developing their domestically flagged fishing fleet, value-added processing and the expansion of their economic base in the fishing industry, consistent with the duty to ensure the proper conservation and management of fisheries resources;

21. *Invites* States to assist developing States in enhancing their participation in regional fisheries management organizations or arrangements, including through facilitating access to fisheries for straddling fish stocks and highly migratory fish stocks, in accordance with article 25, paragraph 1 (*b*), of the Agreement, taking into account the need to ensure that such access benefits the developing States concerned and their nationals;

22. *Notes with satisfaction* that the Assistance Fund under Part VII of the Agreement has begun to operate and consider applications for assistance by developing States parties to the Agreement, and encourages States, intergovernmental organizations, international financial institutions, national institutions and non-governmental organizations, as well as natural and juridical persons, to make voluntary financial contributions to the Assistance Fund;

23. *Requests* that the Food and Agriculture Organization of the United Nations and the Division for Ocean Affairs and the Law of the Sea of the Office of Legal Affairs of the Secretariat further publicize the availability of assistance through the Assistance Fund, and solicit views from developing States parties to the Agreement regarding the application and award procedures of the Fund, and consider changes where necessary to improve the process;

24. *Encourages* States, individually and, as appropriate, through regional and subregional fisheries management organizations and arrangements, to implement the recommendations of the Review Conference;[7]

25. *Recalls* paragraph 6 of resolution 56/13, and requests the Secretary-General to convene in 2007, in accordance with past practice, a sixth round of informal consultations of States parties to the Agreement, for the purposes and objectives of considering the national, regional, subregional and global implementation of the Agreement, as well as considering initial preparatory steps for the resumption of the Review Conference convened by the Secretary-General pursuant to article 36 of the Agreement, and making any appropriate recommendation to the General Assembly;

26. *Requests* the Secretary-General to invite States, and entities referred to in the Convention and in article 1, paragraph 2 (*b*), of the Agreement, not party to the Agreement, as well as the United Nations Development Programme, the Food and Agriculture Organization of the United Nations and other specialized agencies, the Commission on Sustainable Development, the World Bank, the Global Environment Facility and other relevant international financial institutions, subregional and regional fisheries management organizations and arrangements, other fisheries bodies, other relevant intergovernmental bodies and relevant non-governmental organizations, in accordance with past practice, to attend the sixth round of informal consultations of States parties to the Agreement as observers;

27. *Requests* the Food and Agriculture Organization of the United Nations to initiate arrangements with States for the collection and dissemination of data on fishing in the high seas by vessels flying their flag at the subregional and regional levels where none exist;

28. *Also requests* the Food and Agriculture Organization of the United Nations to revise its global fisheries statistics database to provide information on straddling fish stocks, highly migratory fish stocks and discrete high seas fish stocks on the basis of where the catch is taken;

III
Related fisheries instruments

29. *Emphasizes* the importance of the effective implementation of the provisions of the Compliance Agreement,[6] and urges continued efforts in this regard;

30. *Calls upon* all States and other entities referred to in article X, paragraph 1, of the Compliance Agreement that have not yet become parties to that Agreement to do so as a matter of priority and, in the interim, to consider applying it provisionally;

31. *Urges* States and subregional and regional fisheries management organizations and arrangements to implement and promote the application of the Code within their areas of competence;

32. *Urges* States to develop and implement, as a matter of priority, national and, as appropriate, regional plans of action to put into effect the international plans of action of the Food and Agriculture Organization of the United Nations;

IV
Illegal, unreported and unregulated fishing

33. *Emphasizes once again its serious concern* that illegal, unreported and unregulated fishing remains one of the greatest threats to marine ecosystems and continues to have serious and major implications for the conservation and management of ocean resources, and renews its call upon States to comply fully with all existing obligations and to combat such fishing and urgently to take all necessary steps to implement the International Plan of Action to Prevent, Deter and Eliminate Illegal, Unreported and Unregulated Fishing of the Food and Agriculture Organization of the United Nations;

34. *Urges* States to exercise effective control over their nationals, including beneficial owners, and vessels flying their flag in order to prevent and deter them from engaging in or supporting illegal, unreported and unregulated fishing activities, and to facilitate mutual assistance to ensure that such actions can be investigated and proper sanctions imposed;

35. *Also urges* States to take effective measures, at the national, regional and global levels, to deter the activities, including illegal, unreported and unregulated fishing, of any vessel which undermines conservation and management measures that have been adopted by regional and subregional fisheries management organizations and arrangements in accordance with international law;

36. *Calls upon* States not to permit vessels flying their flag to engage in fishing on the high seas or in areas under the national jurisdiction of other States, unless duly authorized by the authorities of the States concerned and in accordance with the conditions set out in the authorization, and to take specific measures, including deterring the reflagging of vessels by their nationals, in accordance with the relevant provisions of the Convention, the Agreement and the Compliance Agreement, to control fishing operations by vessels flying their flag;

37. *Reaffirms* the need to strengthen, where necessary, the international legal framework for intergovernmental cooperation, in particular at the subregional and regional levels, in the management of fish stocks and in combating illegal, unreported and unregulated fishing, in a manner consistent with international law, and for States and entities referred to in the Convention and in article 1, paragraph 2 (*b*), of the Agreement to collaborate in efforts to address these types of fishing activities, including, inter alia, the development and implementation of vessel monitoring systems and the listing of vessels in order to prevent illegal, unreported and unregulated fishing activities and, where appropriate and consistent with international law, trade monitoring schemes, including to collect global catch data, through subregional and regional fisheries management organizations and arrangements;

38. *Calls upon* States to take all measures consistent with international law necessary to prevent, deter and eliminate illegal, unreported and unregulated fishing activities, such as developing measures consistent with national law to prohibit vessels flying their flag from supporting vessels engaging in illegal, unreported and unregulated fishing activities, including those listed by regional fisheries management organizations or arrangements;

39. *Also calls upon* States to take all necessary measures consistent with international law, without prejudice to reasons of force majeure or distress, including the prohibition of vessels from accessing their ports followed by a report to the flag State concerned, when there

is clear evidence that they are or have been engaged in or have supported illegal, unreported and unregulated fishing, or when they refuse to give information either on the origin of the catch or on the authorization under which the catch has been made;

40. *Urges* further international action to eliminate illegal, unreported and unregulated fishing by vessels flying "flags of convenience" as well as to require that a "genuine link" be established between States and fishing vessels flying their flags, and calls upon States to implement the 2005 Rome Declaration on Illegal, Unreported and Unregulated Fishing[3] as a matter of priority;

41. *Urges* States individually and collectively through regional fisheries management organizations and arrangements to cooperate to clarify the role of the "genuine link" in relation to the duty of States to exercise effective control over fishing vessels flying their flag and to develop appropriate processes to assess performance of States with respect to implementing the obligations regarding fishing vessels flying their flag set out in relevant international instruments;

42. *Recognizes* the need for enhanced port State controls to combat illegal, unreported and unregulated fishing, and urges States to cooperate, in particular at the regional level and through subregional and regional fisheries management organizations and arrangements, to adopt all necessary port measures, consistent with international law taking into account article 23 of the Agreement, particularly those identified in the Model Scheme on Port State Measures to Combat Illegal, Unreported, and Unregulated Fishing, adopted by the Food and Agriculture Organization of the United Nations in 2005, and to promote the development and application of minimum standards at the regional level;

43. *Encourages* States to initiate, as soon as possible, a process within the Food and Agriculture Organization of the United Nations to develop, as appropriate, a legally binding instrument on minimum standards for port State measures, building on the Model Scheme on Port State Measures to Combat Illegal, Unreported, and Unregulated Fishing and the International Plan of Action to Prevent, Deter and Eliminate Illegal, Unreported and Unregulated Fishing;

44. *Encourages* States, with respect to vessels flying their flag, and port States, to make every effort to share data on landings and catch quotas, and in this regard encourages regional fisheries management organizations or arrangements to consider developing open databases containing such data for the purpose of enhancing the effectiveness of fisheries management;

45. *Calls upon* States to take all necessary measures to ensure that vessels flying their flag do not engage in trans-shipment of fish caught by fishing vessels engaged in illegal, unreported and unregulated fishing;

46. *Urges* States, individually and through regional fisheries management organizations and arrangements, to adopt and implement internationally agreed market-related measures in accordance with international law, including principles, rights and obligations established in World Trade Organization agreements, as called for in the International Plan of Action to Prevent, Deter and Eliminate Illegal, Unreported and Unregulated Fishing;

V

Monitoring, control and surveillance and compliance enforcement

47. *Calls upon* States in accordance with international law to strengthen implementation of or, where they do not exist, adopt comprehensive monitoring, control and surveillance measures and compliance and enforcement schemes individually and within those regional fisheries management organizations or arrangements in which they participate in order to provide an appropriate framework for promoting compliance with agreed conservation and management measures, and further urges enhanced coordination among all relevant States and regional fisheries management organizations and arrangements in these efforts;

48. *Encourages* further work by competent international organizations, including the Food and Agriculture Organization of the United Nations and subregional and regional fisheries management organizations and arrangements, to develop guidelines on flag State control of fishing vessels;

49. *Urges* States, individually and through relevant regional fisheries management organizations and arrangements, to establish mandatory vessel monitoring, control and surveillance systems, in particular to require that vessel monitoring systems be carried by all vessels fishing on the high seas as soon as practicable, and in the case of large-scale fishing vessels no later than December 2008, and share information on fisheries enforcement matters;

50. *Calls upon* States, individually and through regional fisheries management organizations or arrangements, to strengthen or establish, consistent with national and international law, positive or negative lists of vessels fishing within the areas covered by relevant regional fisheries management organizations and arrangements in order to verify compliance with conservation and management measures and identify products from illegal, unreported and unregulated catches, and encourages improved coordination among all parties and regional fisheries management organizations and arrangements in sharing and using this information, taking into account the forms of cooperation with developing States as set out in article 25 of the Agreement;

51. *Requests* States and relevant international bodies to develop, in accordance with international law, more effective measures to trace fish and fishery products to enable importing States to identify fish or fishery products caught in a manner that undermines international conservation and management measures agreed in accordance with international law, taking into account the special requirements of developing States and the forms of cooperation with developing States as set out in article 25 of the Agreement, and at the same time to recognize the importance of market access, in accordance with provisions 11.2.4, 11.2.5 and 11.2.6 of the Code, for fish and fishery products caught in a manner that is in conformity with such international measures;

52. *Encourages* States to establish and undertake cooperative surveillance and enforcement activities in accordance with international law to strengthen and enhance efforts to ensure compliance with conservation and management measures, and prevent and deter illegal, unreported and unregulated fishing;

53. *Urges* States, individually and through regional fisheries management organizations or arrangements, to develop and adopt effective measures to regulate trans-shipment, in particular at-sea transshipment, in order to, inter alia, monitor compliance, collect and verify fisheries data, and to prevent and suppress illegal, unregulated and unreported fishing activities in accordance with international law; and, in parallel, encourage and support the Food and Agriculture Organization of the United Nations in studying the current practices of trans-shipment as it relates to fishing operations for straddling fish stocks and highly migratory fish stocks and produce a set of guidelines for this purpose;

54. *Encourages* States to join and actively participate in the existing voluntary International Monitoring, Control and Surveillance Network for Fisheries-Related Activities and to consider supporting, when appropriate, transformation of the Monitoring, Control and Surveillance Network in accordance with international law into an international unit with dedicated resources to further assist Network members, taking into account the forms of cooperation with developing States as set out in article 25 of the Agreement;

55. *Notes with satisfaction* the completion of the first Global Fisheries Enforcement Training Conference, held in Kuala Lumpur from 18 to 22 July 2005 and hosted by the Government of Malaysia in cooperation with the Monitoring, Control and Surveillance Network and the FishCode programme of the Food and Agriculture Organization of the United Nations, and encourages widespread participation in the upcoming Second Global Fisheries Enforcement Training Conference, to be held in Trondheim, Norway, in August 2008 and sponsored by the Norwegian Directorate of Fisheries in conjunction with the Network;

56. *Encourages* States to cooperate in the development of a comprehensive global record within the Food and Agriculture Organization of the United Nations of fishing vessels, including refrigerated transport vessels and supply vessels, that incorporates available information on beneficial ownership, subject to confidentiality requirements in accordance with national law, as called for in the 2005 Rome Declaration on Illegal, Unreported and Unregulated Fishing;

VI
Fishing overcapacity

57. *Calls upon* States to commit to urgently reducing the capacity of the world's fishing fleets to levels commensurate with the sustainability of fish stocks, through the establishment of target levels and plans or other appropriate mechanisms for ongoing capacity assessment, while avoiding the transfer of fishing capacity to other fisheries or areas in a manner that undermines the sustainable management of fish stocks, including, inter alia, those areas where fish stocks are overexploited or in a depleted condition, and recognizing in this context the legitimate rights of developing States to develop their fisheries for straddling fish stocks and highly migratory fish stocks consistent with article 25 of the Agreement, article 5 of the Code, and paragraph 10 of the International Plan of Action for the Management of Fishing Capacity;

58. *Urges* States to eliminate subsidies that contribute to illegal, unreported and unregulated fishing and to fishing overcapacity, while completing the efforts undertaken at the World Trade Organization in accordance with the Doha Declaration[11] to clarify and improve its disciplines on fisheries subsidies, taking into account the importance of this sector, including small-scale and artisanal fisheries and aquaculture, to developing countries;

VII
Large-scale pelagic drift-net fishing

59. *Reaffirms* the importance it attaches to continued compliance with its resolution 46/215 and other subsequent resolutions on large-scale pelagic drift-net fishing, and urges States and entities referred to in the Convention and in article 1, paragraph 2 (*b*), of the Agreement to enforce fully the measures recommended in those resolutions;

VIII
Fisheries by-catch and discards

60. *Urges* States, regional and subregional fisheries management organizations and arrangements and other relevant international organizations that have not done so to take action to reduce or eliminate by-catch, catch by lost or abandoned gear, fish discards and post-harvest losses, including juvenile fish, consistent with international law and relevant international instruments, including the Code, and in particular to consider measures including, as appropriate, technical measures related to fish size, mesh size or gear, discards, closed seasons and areas and zones reserved for selected fisheries, particularly artisanal fisheries, the establishment of mechanisms for communicating information on areas of high concentration of juvenile fish, taking into account the importance of ensuring confidentiality of such information, and support for studies and research that will reduce or eliminate by-catch of juvenile fish;

61. *Encourages* States and entities referred to in the Convention and in article 1, paragraph 2 (*b*), of the Agreement to give due consideration to participation, as appropriate, in regional and subregional instruments and organizations with mandates to conserve non-target species taken incidentally in fishing operations;

62. *Requests* States and regional fisheries management organizations and arrangements to urgently implement, as appropriate, the measures recommended in the Guidelines to Reduce Sea Turtle Mortality in Fishing Operations [12] and the International Plan of Action for Reducing Incidental Catch of Seabirds in Longline Fisheries of the Food and Agriculture Organization of the United Nations in order to prevent the decline of sea turtles and seabird populations by reducing by-catch and increasing post-release survival in their fisheries, including through research and development of gear and bait alternatives, promoting the use of available by-catch mitigation technology, and promotion and strengthening of data-collection programmes to obtain standardized information to develop reliable estimates of the by-catch of these species;

IX
Subregional and regional cooperation

63. *Urges* coastal States and States fishing on the high seas, in accordance with the Convention and the Agreement, to pursue cooperation in relation to straddling fish stocks and highly migratory fish stocks, either directly or through appropriate subregional or regional fisheries management organizations or arrangements, to ensure the effective conservation and management of such stocks;

64. *Urges* States fishing for straddling fish stocks and highly migratory fish stocks on the high seas, and relevant coastal States, where a subregional or regional fisheries management organization or arrangement has the competence to establish conservation and management measures for such stocks, to give effect to their duty to cooperate by becoming members of such an organization or participants in such an arrangement, or by agreeing to apply the conservation and management measures established by such an organization or arrangement, or to otherwise ensure that no vessel flying their flag be authorized to access the fisheries resources to which regional fisheries management organizations and arrangements or conservation and management measures established by such organizations or arrangements apply;

65. *Invites*, in this regard, subregional and regional fisheries management organizations and arrangements to ensure that all States having a real interest in the fisheries concerned may become members of such organizations or participants in such arrangements, in accordance with the Convention and the Agreement;

66. *Encourages* relevant coastal States and States fishing on the high seas for a straddling fish stock or a highly migratory fish stock, where there is no subregional or regional fisheries management organization or arrangement to establish conservation and management measures for such stocks, to cooperate to establish such an organization or enter into another appropriate arrangement to ensure the conservation and management of such stocks, and to participate in the work of the organization or arrangement;

67. *Welcomes* the adoption of conservation measures by the South-East Atlantic Fisheries Organization at its third annual meeting, held in Windhoek on 4 October 2006, including an interim prohibition of fishing activities in ten marine areas with prominent seamounts, and urges all signatory States and other States whose vessels fish within the area of the Convention on the Conservation and Management of Fishery Resources in the South-East Atlantic Ocean for fishery resources covered by that Convention to become parties to that Convention as a matter of priority and, in the interim, to ensure that vessels flying their flags fully comply with the measures adopted;

68. *Also welcomes* the adoption of the South Indian Ocean Fisheries Agreement in Rome on 7 July 2006, encourages signatory States and States having a real interest to become parties to that Agreement, and urges those States to agree on and implement interim measures to ensure the conservation and management of the fisheries resources and their marine ecosystems and habitats in the area to which that Agreement applies until such time as that Agreement enters into force;

69. *Further welcomes* the initiation and progress of negotiations to establish regional and subregional fisheries management organizations or arrangements in several fisheries, in particular in the South Pacific and North-West Pacific, encourages States having a real interest to participate in such negotiations, urges participants to expedite those negotiations and to apply provisions of the Convention and the Agreement to their work, and further urges participants to agree on and implement interim conservation and management measures until such regional and subregional fisheries management organizations or arrangements are established;

70. *Urges* further efforts by regional fisheries management organizations and arrangements, as a matter of priority, in accordance with international law, to strengthen and modernize their mandates and the measures adopted by such organizations or arrangements, to implement modern approaches to fisheries management as reflected in the Agreement and other relevant international instruments relying on the best scientific information available and application of the precautionary approach, and incorporating an ecosystem approach to fisheries management and biodiversity considerations, where these aspects are lacking, to ensure that they effectively contribute to long-term conservation and management and sustainable use of marine living resources;

71. *Urges* States to strengthen and enhance cooperation among existing and developing regional fisheries management organizations and arrangements in which they participate, including increased communication and further coordination of measures, and in this regard encourages wide participation in the joint tuna regional fisheries management organization and arrangement meeting that will be hosted by the Government of Japan in 2007, and encourages members of other existing regional fisheries management organizations or

arrangements and participants in establishing new regional fisheries management organizations or arrangements to hold similar consultations;

72. *Urges* regional fisheries management organizations and arrangements to improve transparency and to ensure that their decision-making processes are fair and transparent, rely on best scientific information available, incorporate the precautionary approach and ecosystem approaches, address participatory rights, including through, inter alia, the development of transparent criteria for allocating fishing opportunities which reflects, where appropriate, the relevant provisions of the Agreement, taking due account, inter alia, of the status of the relevant stocks and the respective interests in the fishery, and strengthen integration, coordination and cooperation with other relevant fisheries organizations, regional seas arrangements and other relevant international organizations;

73. *Urges* States, through their participation in regional fisheries management organizations and arrangements, to undertake, on an urgent basis, performance reviews of those regional fisheries management organizations and arrangements, initiated either by the organization or arrangement itself or with external partners, including in cooperation with the Food and Agriculture Organization of the United Nations, using transparent criteria based on the provisions of the Agreement and other relevant instruments, including the best practices of regional fisheries management organizations or arrangements; and further encourages that such performance reviews include some element of independent evaluation and that the results be made publicly available, noting that the North East Atlantic Fisheries Commission has completed a performance review;

74. *Also urges* States to cooperate to develop best practice guidelines for regional fisheries management organizations and arrangements and to apply, to the extent possible, those guidelines to organizations and arrangements in which they participate;

75. *Encourages* the development of regional guidelines for States to use in establishing sanctions, for non-compliance by vessels flying their flag and by their nationals, to be applied in accordance with national law, that are adequate in severity for effectively securing compliance, deterring further violations and depriving offenders of the benefits deriving from their illegal activities, as well as in evaluating their systems of sanctions to ensure that they are effective in securing compliance and deterring violations;

X
Responsible fisheries in the marine ecosystem

76. *Encourages* States to apply by 2010 the ecosystem approach, notes the Reykjavik Declaration on Responsible Fisheries in the Marine Ecosystem[13] and decision VII/11[14] and other relevant decisions of the Conference of the Parties to the Convention on Biological Diversity, notes the work of the Food and Agriculture Organization of the United Nations related to guidelines for the implementation of the ecosystem approach to fisheries management, and also notes the importance to this approach of relevant provisions of the Agreement and the Code;

77. *Also encourages* States, individually or through regional fisheries management organizations and arrangements and other relevant international organizations, to work to ensure that fisheries and other ecosystem data collection is performed in a coordinated and integrated manner, facilitating incorporation into global observation initiatives, where appropriate;

78. *Further encourages* States to increase scientific research in accordance with international law on the marine ecosystem;

79. *Calls upon* States, the Food and Agriculture Organization of the United Nations and other specialized agencies of the United Nations, subregional and regional fisheries management organizations and arrangements, where appropriate, and other appropriate intergovernmental bodies, to cooperate in achieving sustainable aquaculture, including through information exchange, developing equivalent standards on such issues as aquatic animal health and human health and safety concerns, assessing the potential positive and negative impacts of aquaculture, including socio-economics, on the marine and coastal environment, including biodiversity, and adopting relevant methods and techniques to minimize and mitigate adverse effects;

80. *Calls upon* States to take action immediately, individually and through regional fisheries management organizations and arrangements, and consistent with the precautionary approach and ecosystem approaches, to sustainably manage fish stocks and protect vulnerable marine ecosystems, including seamounts, hydrothermal vents and cold water corals, from destructive fishing practices, recognizing the immense importance and value of deep sea ecosystems and the biodiversity they contain;

81. *Reaffirms* the importance it attaches to paragraphs 66 to 69 of its resolution 59/25 concerning the impacts of fishing on vulnerable marine ecosystems;

82. *Welcomes* the important progress made by States and regional fisheries management organizations or arrangements with the competence to regulate bottom fisheries to give effect to paragraphs 66 to 69 of its resolution 59/25 to address the impacts of fishing on vulnerable marine ecosystems, including through initiating negotiations to establish new regional fisheries management organizations or arrangements, but on the basis of the review called for in paragraph 71 of that resolution, recognizes that additional actions are urgently needed;

83. *Calls upon* regional fisheries management organizations or arrangements with the competence to regulate bottom fisheries to adopt and implement measures, in accordance with the precautionary approach, ecosystem approaches and international law, for their respective regulatory areas as a matter of priority, but not later than 31 December 2008:

(*a*) To assess, on the basis of the best available scientific information, whether individual bottom fishing activities would have significant adverse impacts on vulnerable marine ecosystems, and to ensure that if it is assessed that these activities would have significant adverse impacts, they are managed to prevent such impacts, or not authorized to proceed;

(*b*) To identify vulnerable marine ecosystems and determine whether bottom fishing activities would cause significant adverse impacts to such ecosystems and the long-term sustainability of deep sea fish stocks, inter alia, by improving scientific research and data collection and sharing, and through new and exploratory fisheries;

(*c*) In respect of areas where vulnerable marine ecosystems, including seamounts, hydrothermal vents and cold water corals, are known to occur or are likely to occur based on the best available scientific information, to close such areas to bottom fishing and ensure that such activities do not proceed unless conservation and management measures have been established to prevent significant adverse impacts on vulnerable marine ecosystems;

(*d*) To require members of the regional fisheries management organizations or arrangements to require vessels flying their flag to cease bottom fishing activities in areas where, in the course of fishing operations, vulnerable marine ecosystems are encountered, and to report the encounter so that appropriate measures can be adopted in respect of the relevant site;

84. *Also calls upon* regional fisheries management organizations or arrangements with the competence to regulate bottom fisheries to make the measures adopted pursuant to paragraph 83 of the present resolution publicly available;

85. *Calls upon* those States participating in negotiations to establish a regional fisheries management organization or arrangement competent to regulate bottom fisheries to expedite such negotiations and, by no later than 31 December 2007, to adopt and implement interim measures consistent with paragraph 83 of the present resolution and make these measures publicly available;

86. *Calls upon* flag States to either adopt and implement measures in accordance with paragraph 83 of the present resolution, mutatis mutandis, or cease to authorize fishing vessels flying their flag to conduct bottom fisheries in areas beyond national jurisdiction where there is no regional fisheries management organization or arrangement with the competence to regulate such fisheries or interim measures in accordance with paragraph 85 of the present resolution, until measures are taken in accordance with paragraph 83 or 85 of the present resolution;

87. *Further calls upon* States to make publicly available through the Food and Agriculture Organization of the United Nations a list of those vessels flying their flag authorized to conduct bottom fisheries in areas beyond national jurisdiction, and the measures they have adopted pursuant to paragraph 86 of the present resolution;

88. *Emphasizes* the critical role played by the Food and Agriculture Organization of the United Nations in providing expert technical advice, in assisting with international fisheries policy development and management standards, and in collection and dissemination of information on fisheries-related issues, including the protection of vulnerable marine ecosystems from the impacts of fishing;

89. *Commends* the Food and Agriculture Organization of the United Nations for its work on the management of deep sea fisheries in the high seas, including the expert consultation held from 21 to 23 November 2006 in Bangkok, and further invites the Food and Agriculture Organization of the United Nations to establish at its next Committee on Fisheries meeting a time frame of relevant work with respect to the management of deep sea fisheries in the high seas, including enhancing data collection and dissemination, promoting information exchange and increased knowledge on deep sea fishing activities, such as through convening a meeting of States engaged in such fisheries, developing standards and criteria for use by States and regional fisheries management organizations or arrangements in identifying vulnerable marine ecosystems and the impacts of fishing on such ecosystems, and establishing standards for the management of deep sea fisheries, such as through the development of an international plan of action;

90. *Invites* the Food and Agriculture Organization of the United Nations to consider creating a global database of information on vulnerable marine ecosystems in areas beyond national jurisdiction to assist States in assessing any impacts of bottom fisheries on vulnerable marine ecosystems, and invites States and regional fisheries management organizations or arrangements

to submit information to any such database on all vulnerable marine ecosystems identified in accordance with paragraph 83 of the present resolution;

91. *Requests* the Secretary-General, in cooperation with the Food and Agriculture Organization of the United Nations, to include in his report concerning fisheries to the General Assembly at its sixty-fourth session a section on the actions taken by States and regional fisheries management organizations and arrangements in response to paragraphs 83 to 90 of the present resolution, and decides to conduct a further review of such actions at that session in 2009, with a view to further recommendations, where necessary;

92. *Encourages* accelerated progress to establish criteria on the objectives and management of marine protected areas for fisheries purposes, and in this regard welcomes the proposed work of the Food and Agriculture Organization of the United Nations to develop technical guidelines in accordance with the Convention on the design, implementation and testing of marine protected areas for such purposes, and urges coordination and cooperation among all relevant international organizations and bodies;

93. *Notes* that the Second Intergovernmental Review Meeting of the Global Programme of Action for the Protection of the Marine Environment from Land-based Activities was held from 16 to 20 October 2006 in Beijing, and urges all States to implement the Global Programme of Action and to accelerate activity to safeguard the marine ecosystem, including fish stocks, against pollution and physical degradation;

94. *Reaffirms* the importance it attaches to paragraphs 77 to 81 of its resolution 60/31 concerning the issue of lost, abandoned, or discarded fishing gear and related marine debris and the adverse impacts such debris and derelict fishing gear have on, inter alia, fish stocks, habitats and other marine species, and urges accelerated progress by States and regional fisheries management organizations and arrangements in implementing those paragraphs of the resolution;

95. *Further encourages* the Committee on Fisheries of the Food and Agriculture Organization of the United Nations to consider the issue of derelict fishing gear and related marine debris at its next meeting in 2007, and in particular the implementation of relevant provisions of the Code;

XI
Capacity-building

96. *Reiterates* the crucial importance of cooperation by States directly or, as appropriate, through the relevant regional and subregional organizations, and by other international organizations, including the Food and Agriculture Organization of the United Nations through its FishCode programme, including through financial and/or technical assistance, in accordance with the Agreement, the Compliance Agreement, the Code, the International Plan of Action to Prevent, Deter and Eliminate Illegal, Unreported and Unregulated Fishing, the International Plan of Action for the Conservation and Management of Sharks, the International Plan of Action for the Management of Fishing Capacity, the International Plan of Action for Reducing Incidental Catch of Seabirds in Longline Fisheries, and the Guidelines to Reduce Sea Turtle Mortality in Fishing Operations of the Food and Agriculture Organization of the United Nations, to increase the capacity of developing States to achieve the goals and implement the actions called for in the present resolution;

97. *Welcomes* the work of the Food and Agriculture Organization of the United Nations in developing guidance on the strategies and measures required for the creation of an enabling environment for small-scale fisheries, including the development of a code of conduct and guidelines for enhancing the contribution of small-scale fisheries to poverty alleviation and food security that include adequate provisions with regard to financial measures and capacity-building, including transfer of technology, and encourages studies for creating possible alternative livelihoods for coastal communities;

98. *Encourages* increased capacity-building and technical assistance by States, international financial institutions and relevant intergovernmental organizations and bodies for fishers, in particular small-scale fishers, in developing countries, and in particular small island developing States, consistent with environmental sustainability;

99. *Encourages* the international community to enhance the opportunities for sustainable development in developing countries, in particular the least developed countries, small island developing States and coastal African States, by encouraging greater participation of those States in authorized fisheries activities being undertaken within areas under their national jurisdiction, in accordance with the Convention, by distant-water fishing nations in order to achieve better economic returns for developing countries from their fisheries resources within areas under their national jurisdiction and an enhanced role in regional fisheries management, as well as by enhancing the ability of developing countries to develop their own fisheries, as well as to participate in high seas fisheries, including access to such fisheries, in conformity with international law, in particular the Convention and the Agreement;

100. *Requests* distant-water fishing nations, when negotiating access agreements and arrangements with developing coastal States, to do so on an equitable and sustainable basis, including by giving greater attention to fish processing, including fish processing facilities, within the national jurisdiction of the developing coastal State to assist the realization of the benefits from the development of fisheries resources, and also including, inter alia, the transfer of technology and assistance for monitoring, control and surveillance and compliance and enforcement within areas under the national jurisdiction of the developing coastal State providing fisheries access, taking into account the forms of cooperation set out in article 25 of the Agreement;

101. *Encourages* States individually and through regional fisheries management organizations and arrangements to provide greater assistance and to promote coherence in such assistance for developing States in designing, establishing and implementing relevant agreements, instruments and tools for the conservation and sustainable management of fish stocks, including in designing and strengthening their domestic regulatory fisheries policies and those of regional fisheries management organizations or arrangements in their regions, and the enhancement of research and scientific capabilities through existing funds, such as the Assistance Fund under Part VII of the Agreement, bilateral assistance, regional fisheries management organizations and arrangements assistance funds, the FishCode programme, the World Bank's global programme on fisheries and the Global Environment Facility;

102. *Calls upon* States to promote, through continuing dialogue and the assistance and cooperation provided in accordance with articles 24 to 26 of the Agreement, further ratification of or accession to the Agreement by seeking to address, inter alia, the issue of lack

of capacity and resources that might stand in the way of developing States becoming parties;

XII
Cooperation within the United Nations system

103. *Requests* the relevant parts of the United Nations system, international financial institutions and donor agencies to support increased enforcement and compliance capabilities for regional fisheries management organizations and their member States;

104. *Invites* the Food and Agriculture Organization of the United Nations to continue its cooperative arrangements with United Nations agencies on the implementation of the international plans of action and to report to the Secretary-General, for inclusion in his annual report on sustainable fisheries, on priorities for cooperation and coordination in this work;

105. *Invites* the Division for Ocean Affairs and the Law of the Sea, the Food and Agriculture Organization of the United Nations and other relevant bodies of the United Nations system to consult and cooperate in the preparation of questionnaires designed to collect information on sustainable fisheries, in order to avoid duplication;

XIII
Sixty-second session of the General Assembly

106. *Requests* the Secretary-General to bring the present resolution to the attention of all members of the international community, relevant intergovernmental organizations, the organizations and bodies of the United Nations system, regional and subregional fisheries management organizations and relevant non-governmental organizations, and to invite them to provide the Secretary-General with information relevant to the implementation of the present resolution;

107. *Also requests* the Secretary-General to submit to the General Assembly at its sixty-second session a report on "Sustainable fisheries, including through the 1995 Agreement for the Implementation of the Provisions of the United Nations Convention on the Law of the Sea of 10 December 1982 relating to the Conservation and Management of Straddling Fish Stocks and Highly Migratory Fish Stocks, and related instruments", taking into account information provided by States, relevant specialized agencies, in particular the Food and Agriculture Organization of the United Nations, and other appropriate organs, organizations and programmes of the United Nations system, regional and subregional organizations and arrangements for the conservation and management of straddling fish stocks and highly migratory fish stocks, as well as other relevant intergovernmental bodies and non-governmental organizations, and consisting, inter alia, of elements provided in relevant paragraphs in the present resolution;

108. *Decides* to include in the provisional agenda of its sixty-second session, under the item entitled "Oceans and the law of the sea", the sub-item entitled "Sustainable fisheries, including through the 1995 Agreement for the Implementation of the Provisions of the United Nations Convention on the Law of the Sea of 10 December 1982 relating to the

Conservation and Management of Straddling Fish Stocks and Highly Migratory Fish Stocks, and related instruments".

71st plenary meeting
8 December 2006

---

[1] United Nations, *Treaty Series*, vol. 2167, No. 37924.

[2] Ibid., vol. 1833, No. 31363.

[3] Food and Agriculture Organization of the United Nations, *Outcome of the Ministerial Meeting on Fisheries, Rome, 12 March 2005* (CL 128/INF/11), appendix B.

[4] *International Fisheries Instruments with Index* (United Nations publication, Sales No. E.98.V.11), sect. III.

[5] Food and Agriculture Organization of the United Nations, *Report of the twenty-fifth session of the Committee on Fisheries, Rome, 24–28 February 2003*, FAO Fisheries Report No. 702 (FIPL/R702(En)), appendix H.

[6] *International Fisheries Instruments with Index* (United Nations publication, Sales No. E.98.V.11), sect. II.

[7] A/CONF.210/2006/15.

[8] See A/61/156.

[9] A/61/154.

[10] *Report of the World Summit on Sustainable Development, Johannesburg, South Africa, 26 August–4 September 2002* (United Nations publication, Sales No. E.03.II.A.1 and corrigendum), chap. I, resolution 2, annex.

[11] World Trade Organization, document WT/MIN(01)/DEC/1. Available from http://docsonline.wto.org.

[12] Food and Agriculture Organization of the United Nations, *Report of the Technical Consultation on Sea Turtles Conservation and Fisheries, Bangkok, Thailand, 29 November–2 December 2004*, FAO Fisheries Report No. 765 (FIRM/R765(En)), appendix E.

[13] E/CN.17/2002/PC.2/3, annex.

[14] See UNEP/CBD/COP/7/21, annex.

Resolution 61/106

[without reference to a Main Committee (A/61/611)]

61/106. Convention on the Rights of Persons with Disabilities

The General Assembly,

Recalling its resolution 56/168 of 19 December 2001, by which it decided to establish an Ad Hoc Committee, open to the participation of all Member States and observers to the United Nations, to consider proposals for a comprehensive and integral international convention to promote and protect the rights and dignity of persons with disabilities, based on a holistic approach in the work done in the fields of social development, human rights and non-discrimination and taking into account the recommendations of the Commission on Human Rights and the Commission for Social Development,

Recalling also its previous relevant resolutions, the most recent of which was resolution 60/232 of 23 December 2005, as well as relevant resolutions of the Commission for Social Development and the Commission on Human Rights,

Welcoming the valuable contributions made by intergovernmental and non-governmental organizations and national human rights institutions to the work of the Ad Hoc Committee,

1. *Expresses its appreciation* to the Ad Hoc Committee for having concluded the elaboration of the draft Convention on the Rights of Persons with Disabilities and the draft Optional Protocol to the Convention;

2. *Adopts* the Convention on the Rights of Persons with Disabilities and the Optional Protocol to the Convention annexed to the present resolution, which shall be open for signature at United Nations Headquarters in New York as of 30 March 2007;

3. *Calls upon* States to consider signing and ratifying the Convention and the Optional Protocol as a matter of priority, and expresses the hope that they will enter into force at an early date;

4. *Requests* the Secretary-General to provide the staff and facilities necessary for the effective performance of the functions of the Conference of States Parties and the Committee under the Convention and the Optional Protocol after the entry into force of the Convention, as well as for the dissemination of information on the Convention and the Optional Protocol;

5. *Also requests* the Secretary-General to implement progressively standards and guidelines for the accessibility of facilities and services of the United Nations system, taking into account relevant provisions of the Convention, in particular when undertaking renovations;

6. *Requests* United Nations agencies and organizations, and invites intergovernmental and non-governmental organizations, to undertake efforts to disseminate information on the Convention and the Optional Protocol and to promote their understanding;

7. *Requests* the Secretary-General to submit to the General Assembly at its sixty-second session a report on the status of the Convention and the Optional Protocol and the implementation of the present resolution, under a sub-item entitled "Convention on the Rights of Persons with Disabilities".

76th plenary meeting
13 December 2006

Annex I
Convention on the Rights of Persons with Disabilities

Preamble

The States Parties to the present Convention,

(*a*) *Recalling* the principles proclaimed in the Charter of the United Nations which recognize the inherent dignity and worth and the equal and inalienable rights of all members of the human family as the foundation of freedom, justice and peace in the world,

(*b*) *Recognizing* that the United Nations, in the Universal Declaration of Human Rights and in the International Covenants on Human Rights, has proclaimed and agreed that everyone is entitled to all the rights and freedoms set forth therein, without distinction of any kind,

(*c*) *Reaffirming* the universality, indivisibility, interdependence and interrelatedness of all human rights and fundamental freedoms and the need for persons with disabilities to be guaranteed their full enjoyment without discrimination,

(*d*) *Recalling* the International Covenant on Economic, Social and Cultural Rights, the International Covenant on Civil and Political Rights, the International Convention on the Elimination of All Forms of Racial Discrimination, the Convention on the Elimination of All Forms of Discrimination against Women, the Convention against Torture and Other Cruel, Inhuman or Degrading Treatment or Punishment, the Convention on the Rights of the Child, and the International Convention on the Protection of the Rights of All Migrant Workers and Members of Their Families,

(*e*) *Recognizing* that disability is an evolving concept and that disability results from the interaction between persons with impairments and attitudinal and environmental barriers that hinders their full and effective participation in society on an equal basis with others,

(*f*) *Recognizing* the importance of the principles and policy guidelines contained in the World Programme of Action concerning Disabled Persons and in the Standard Rules on the Equalization of Opportunities for Persons with Disabilities in influencing the promotion, formulation and evaluation of the policies, plans, programmes and actions at the national, regional and international levels to further equalize opportunities for persons with disabilities,

(*g*) *Emphasizing* the importance of mainstreaming disability issues as an integral part of relevant strategies of sustainable development,

(*h*) *Recognizing also* that discrimination against any person on the basis of disability is a violation of the inherent dignity and worth of the human person,

(*i*) *Recognizing further* the diversity of persons with disabilities,

(*j*) *Recognizing* the need to promote and protect the human rights of all persons with disabilities, including those who require more intensive support,

(*k*) *Concerned* that, despite these various instruments and undertakings, persons with disabilities continue to face barriers in their participation as equal members of society and violations of their human rights in all parts of the world,

(*l*) *Recognizing* the importance of international cooperation for improving the living conditions of persons with disabilities in every country, particularly in developing countries,

(*m*) *Recognizing* the valued existing and potential contributions made by persons with disabilities to the overall well-being and diversity of their communities, and that the promotion of the full enjoyment by persons with disabilities of their human rights and fundamental freedoms and of full participation by persons with disabilities will result in their enhanced sense of belonging and in significant advances in the human, social and economic development of society and the eradication of poverty,

(*n*) *Recognizing* the importance for persons with disabilities of their individual autonomy and independence, including the freedom to make their own choices,

(*o*) *Considering* that persons with disabilities should have the opportunity to be actively involved in decision-making processes about policies and programmes, including those directly concerning them,

(*p*) *Concerned* about the difficult conditions faced by persons with disabilities who are subject to multiple or aggravated forms of discrimination on the basis of race, colour, sex, language, religion, political or other opinion, national, ethnic, indigenous or social origin, property, birth, age or other status,

(*q*) *Recognizing* that women and girls with disabilities are often at greater risk, both within and outside the home, of violence, injury or abuse, neglect or negligent treatment, maltreatment or exploitation,

(*r*) *Recognizing* that children with disabilities should have full enjoyment of all human rights and fundamental freedoms on an equal basis with other children, and recalling obligations to that end undertaken by States Parties to the Convention on the Rights of the Child,

(*s*) *Emphasizing* the need to incorporate a gender perspective in all efforts to promote the full enjoyment of human rights and fundamental freedoms by persons with disabilities,

(*t*) *Highlighting* the fact that the majority of persons with disabilities live in conditions of poverty, and in this regard recognizing the critical need to address the negative impact of poverty on persons with disabilities,

(*u*) *Bearing in mind* that conditions of peace and security based on full respect for the purposes and principles contained in the Charter of the United Nations and observance of applicable human rights instruments are indispensable for the full protection of persons with disabilities, in particular during armed conflicts and foreign occupation,

(*v*) *Recognizing* the importance of accessibility to the physical, social, economic and cultural environment, to health and education and to information and communication, in enabling persons with disabilities to fully enjoy all human rights and fundamental freedoms,

(*w*) *Realizing* that the individual, having duties to other individuals and to the community to which he or she belongs, is under a responsibility to strive for the promotion and observance of the rights recognized in the International Bill of Human Rights,

(*x*) *Convinced* that the family is the natural and fundamental group unit of society and is entitled to protection by society and the State, and that persons with disabilities and their family members should receive the necessary protection and assistance to enable families to contribute towards the full and equal enjoyment of the rights of persons with disabilities,

(*y*) *Convinced* that a comprehensive and integral international convention to promote and protect the rights and dignity of persons with disabilities will make a significant contribution to redressing the profound social disadvantage of persons with disabilities and promote their participation in the civil, political, economic, social and cultural spheres with equal opportunities, in both developing and developed countries,

Have agreed as follows:

Article 1
Purpose

The purpose of the present Convention is to promote, protect and ensure the full and equal enjoyment of all human rights and fundamental freedoms by all persons with disabilities, and to promote respect for their inherent dignity.

Persons with disabilities include those who have long-term physical, mental, intellectual or sensory impairments which in interaction with various barriers may hinder their full and effective participation in society on an equal basis with others.

Article 2
Definitions

For the purposes of the present Convention:

"Communication" includes languages, display of text, Braille, tactile communication, large print, accessible multimedia as well as written, audio, plain-language, human-reader and augmentative and alternative modes, means and formats of communication, including accessible information and communication technology;

"Language" includes spoken and signed languages and other forms of non-spoken languages;

"Discrimination on the basis of disability" means any distinction, exclusion or restriction on the basis of disability which has the purpose or effect of impairing or nullifying the recognition, enjoyment or exercise, on an equal basis with others, of all human rights and fundamental freedoms in the political, economic, social, cultural, civil or any other field. It includes all forms of discrimination, including denial of reasonable accommodation;

"Reasonable accommodation" means necessary and appropriate modification and adjustments not imposing a disproportionate or undue burden, where needed in a particular case, to ensure to persons with disabilities the enjoyment or exercise on an equal basis with others of all human rights and fundamental freedoms;

"Universal design" means the design of products, environments, programmes and services to be usable by all people, to the greatest extent possible, without the need for adaptation or specialized design. "Universal design" shall not exclude assistive devices for particular groups of persons with disabilities where this is needed.

Article 3
General principles

The principles of the present Convention shall be:

(*a*) Respect for inherent dignity, individual autonomy including the freedom to make one's own choices, and independence of persons;

(*b*) Non-discrimination;

(*c*) Full and effective participation and inclusion in society;

(*d*) Respect for difference and acceptance of persons with disabilities as part of human diversity and humanity;

(*e*) Equality of opportunity;

(*f*) Accessibility;

(*g*) Equality between men and women;

(*h*) Respect for the evolving capacities of children with disabilities and respect for the right of children with disabilities to preserve their identities.

Article 4
General obligations

1. States Parties undertake to ensure and promote the full realization of all human rights and fundamental freedoms for all persons with disabilities without discrimination of any kind on the basis of disability. To this end, States Parties undertake:

(*a*) To adopt all appropriate legislative, administrative and other measures for the implementation of the rights recognized in the present Convention;

(*b*) To take all appropriate measures, including legislation, to modify or abolish existing laws, regulations, customs and practices that constitute discrimination against persons with disabilities;

(*c*) To take into account the protection and promotion of the human rights of persons with disabilities in all policies and programmes;

(*d*) To refrain from engaging in any act or practice that is inconsistent with the present Convention and to ensure that public authorities and institutions act in conformity with the present Convention;

(*e*) To take all appropriate measures to eliminate discrimination on the basis of disability by any person, organization or private enterprise;

(*f*) To undertake or promote research and development of universally designed goods, services, equipment and facilities, as defined in article 2 of the present Convention, which should require the minimum possible adaptation and the least cost to meet the specific needs of a person with disabilities, to promote their availability and use, and to promote universal design in the development of standards and guidelines;

(*g*) To undertake or promote research and development of, and to promote the availability and use of new technologies, including information and communications technologies, mobility aids, devices and assistive technologies, suitable for persons with disabilities, giving priority to technologies at an affordable cost;

(*h*) To provide accessible information to persons with disabilities about mobility aids, devices and assistive technologies, including new technologies, as well as other forms of assistance, support services and facilities;

(*i*) To promote the training of professionals and staff working with persons with disabilities in the rights recognized in the present Convention so as to better provide the assistance and services guaranteed by those rights.

2. With regard to economic, social and cultural rights, each State Party undertakes to take measures to the maximum of its available resources and, where needed, within the framework of international cooperation, with a view to achieving progressively the full realization of these rights, without prejudice to those obligations contained in the present Convention that are immediately applicable according to international law.

3. In the development and implementation of legislation and policies to implement the present Convention, and in other decision-making processes concerning issues relating to persons with disabilities, States Parties shall closely consult with and actively involve

persons with disabilities, including children with disabilities, through their representative organizations.

4. Nothing in the present Convention shall affect any provisions which are more conducive to the realization of the rights of persons with disabilities and which may be contained in the law of a State Party or international law in force for that State. There shall be no restriction upon or derogation from any of the human rights and fundamental freedoms recognized or existing in any State Party to the present Convention pursuant to law, conventions, regulation or custom on the pretext that the present Convention does not recognize such rights or freedoms or that it recognizes them to a lesser extent.

5. The provisions of the present Convention shall extend to all parts of federal States without any limitations or exceptions.

Article 5
Equality and non-discrimination

1. States Parties recognize that all persons are equal before and under the law and are entitled without any discrimination to the equal protection and equal benefit of the law.

2. States Parties shall prohibit all discrimination on the basis of disability and guarantee to persons with disabilities equal and effective legal protection against discrimination on all grounds.

3. In order to promote equality and eliminate discrimination, States Parties shall take all appropriate steps to ensure that reasonable accommodation is provided.

4. Specific measures which are necessary to accelerate or achieve de facto equality of persons with disabilities shall not be considered discrimination under the terms of the present Convention.

Article 6
Women with disabilities

1. States Parties recognize that women and girls with disabilities are subject to multiple discrimination, and in this regard shall take measures to ensure the full and equal enjoyment by them of all human rights and fundamental freedoms.

2. States Parties shall take all appropriate measures to ensure the full development, advancement and empowerment of women, for the purpose of guaranteeing them the exercise and enjoyment of the human rights and fundamental freedoms set out in the present Convention.

Article 7
Children with disabilities

1. States Parties shall take all necessary measures to ensure the full enjoyment by children with disabilities of all human rights and fundamental freedoms on an equal basis with other children.

2. In all actions concerning children with disabilities, the best interests of the child shall be a primary consideration.

3. States Parties shall ensure that children with disabilities have the right to express their views freely on all matters affecting them, their views being given due weight in accordance with their age and maturity, on an equal basis with other children, and to be provided with disability and age-appropriate assistance to realize that right.

Article 8
Awareness-raising

1. States Parties undertake to adopt immediate, effective and appropriate measures:

(*a*) To raise awareness throughout society, including at the family level, regarding persons with disabilities, and to foster respect for the rights and dignity of persons with disabilities;

(*b*) To combat stereotypes, prejudices and harmful practices relating to persons with disabilities, including those based on sex and age, in all areas of life;

(*c*) To promote awareness of the capabilities and contributions of persons with disabilities.

2. Measures to this end include:

(*a*) Initiating and maintaining effective public awareness campaigns designed:

(i) To nurture receptiveness to the rights of persons with disabilities;

(ii) To promote positive perceptions and greater social awareness towards persons with disabilities;

(iii) To promote recognition of the skills, merits and abilities of persons with disabilities, and of their contributions to the workplace and the labour market;

(*b*) Fostering at all levels of the education system, including in all children from an early age, an attitude of respect for the rights of persons with disabilities;

(*c*) Encouraging all organs of the media to portray persons with disabilities in a manner consistent with the purpose of the present Convention;

(*d*) Promoting awareness-training programmes regarding persons with disabilities and the rights of persons with disabilities.

Article 9
Accessibility

1. To enable persons with disabilities to live independently and participate fully in all aspects of life, States Parties shall take appropriate measures to ensure to persons with disabilities access, on an equal basis with others, to the physical environment, to transportation, to information and communications, including information and communications technologies and systems, and to other facilities and services open or provided to the public, both in urban and in rural areas. These measures, which shall include the identification and elimination of obstacles and barriers to accessibility, shall apply to, inter alia:

(*a*) Buildings, roads, transportation and other indoor and outdoor facilities, including schools, housing, medical facilities and workplaces;

(*b*) Information, communications and other services, including electronic services and emergency services.

2. States Parties shall also take appropriate measures:

(*a*) To develop, promulgate and monitor the implementation of minimum standards and guidelines for the accessibility of facilities and services open or provided to the public;

(*b*) To ensure that private entities that offer facilities and services which are open or provided to the public take into account all aspects of accessibility for persons with disabilities;

(*c*) To provide training for stakeholders on accessibility issues facing persons with disabilities;

(*d*) To provide in buildings and other facilities open to the public signage in Braille and in easy to read and understand forms;

(*e*) To provide forms of live assistance and intermediaries, including guides, readers and professional sign language interpreters, to facilitate accessibility to buildings and other facilities open to the public;

(*f*) To promote other appropriate forms of assistance and support to persons with disabilities to ensure their access to information;

(*g*) To promote access for persons with disabilities to new information and communications technologies and systems, including the Internet;

(*h*) To promote the design, development, production and distribution of accessible information and communications technologies and systems at an early stage, so that these technologies and systems become accessible at minimum cost.

Article 10
Right to life

States Parties reaffirm that every human being has the inherent right to life and shall take all necessary measures to ensure its effective enjoyment by persons with disabilities on an equal basis with others.

Article 11
Situations of risk and humanitarian emergencies

States Parties shall take, in accordance with their obligations under international law, including international humanitarian law and international human rights law, all necessary measures to ensure the protection and safety of persons with disabilities in situations of risk, including situations of armed conflict, humanitarian emergencies and the occurrence of natural disasters.

Article 12
Equal recognition before the law

1. States Parties reaffirm that persons with disabilities have the right to recognition everywhere as persons before the law.

2. States Parties shall recognize that persons with disabilities enjoy legal capacity on an equal basis with others in all aspects of life.

3. States Parties shall take appropriate measures to provide access by persons with disabilities to the support they may require in exercising their legal capacity.

4. States Parties shall ensure that all measures that relate to the exercise of legal capacity provide for appropriate and effective safeguards to prevent abuse in accordance with international human rights law. Such safeguards shall ensure that measures relating to the exercise of legal capacity respect the rights, will and preferences of the person, are free of conflict of interest and undue influence, are proportional and tailored to the person's circumstances, apply for the shortest time possible and are subject to regular review by a competent, independent and impartial authority or judicial body. The safeguards shall be proportional to the degree to which such measures affect the person's rights and interests.

5. Subject to the provisions of this article, States Parties shall take all appropriate and effective measures to ensure the equal right of persons with disabilities to own or inherit property, to control their own financial affairs and to have equal access to bank loans, mortgages and other forms of financial credit, and shall ensure that persons with disabilities are not arbitrarily deprived of their property.

Article 13
Access to justice

1. States Parties shall ensure effective access to justice for persons with disabilities on an equal basis with others, including through the provision of procedural and age-appropriate accommodations, in order to facilitate their effective role as direct and indirect participants, including as witnesses, in all legal proceedings, including at investigative and other preliminary stages.

2. In order to help to ensure effective access to justice for persons with disabilities, States Parties shall promote appropriate training for those working in the field of administration of justice, including police and prison staff.

Article 14
Liberty and security of person

1. States Parties shall ensure that persons with disabilities, on an equal basis with others:

(*a*) Enjoy the right to liberty and security of person;

(*b*) Are not deprived of their liberty unlawfully or arbitrarily, and that any deprivation of liberty is in conformity with the law, and that the existence of a disability shall in no case justify a deprivation of liberty.

2. States Parties shall ensure that if persons with disabilities are deprived of their liberty through any process, they are, on an equal basis with others, entitled to guarantees in accordance with international human rights law and shall be treated in compliance with the objectives and principles of the present Convention, including by provision of reasonable accommodation.

Article 15
Freedom from torture or cruel, inhuman or degrading treatment or punishment

1. No one shall be subjected to torture or to cruel, inhuman or degrading treatment or punishment. In particular, no one shall be subjected without his or her free consent to medical or scientific experimentation.

2. States Parties shall take all effective legislative, administrative, judicial or other measures to prevent persons with disabilities, on an equal basis with others, from being subjected to torture or cruel, inhuman or degrading treatment or punishment.

Article 16
Freedom from exploitation, violence and abuse

1. States Parties shall take all appropriate legislative, administrative, social, educational and other measures to protect persons with disabilities, both within and outside the home, from all forms of exploitation, violence and abuse, including their gender-based aspects.

2. States Parties shall also take all appropriate measures to prevent all forms of exploitation, violence and abuse by ensuring, inter alia, appropriate forms of gender-and age-sensitive assistance and support for persons with disabilities and their families and caregivers, including through the provision of information and education on how to avoid, recognize and report instances of exploitation, violence and abuse. States Parties shall ensure that protection services are age-, gender- and disability-sensitive.

3. In order to prevent the occurrence of all forms of exploitation, violence and abuse, States Parties shall ensure that all facilities and programmes designed to serve persons with disabilities are effectively monitored by independent authorities.

4. States Parties shall take all appropriate measures to promote the physical, cognitive and psychological recovery, rehabilitation and social reintegration of persons with disabilities who become victims of any form of exploitation, violence or abuse, including through the provision of protection services. Such recovery and reintegration shall take place in an environment that fosters the health, welfare, self-respect, dignity and autonomy of the person and takes into account gender- and age-specific needs.

5. States Parties shall put in place effective legislation and policies, including women- and child-focused legislation and policies, to ensure that instances of exploitation, violence and abuse against persons with disabilities are identified, investigated and, where appropriate, prosecuted.

Article 17
Protecting the integrity of the person

Every person with disabilities has a right to respect for his or her physical and mental integrity on an equal basis with others.

Article 18
Liberty of movement and nationality

1. States Parties shall recognize the rights of persons with disabilities to liberty of movement, to freedom to choose their residence and to a nationality, on an equal basis with others, including by ensuring that persons with disabilities:

(*a*) Have the right to acquire and change a nationality and are not deprived of their nationality arbitrarily or on the basis of disability;

(*b*) Are not deprived, on the basis of disability, of their ability to obtain, possess and utilize documentation of their nationality or other documentation of identification, or to utilize relevant processes such as immigration proceedings, that may be needed to facilitate exercise of the right to liberty of movement;

(*c*) Are free to leave any country, including their own;

(*d*) Are not deprived, arbitrarily or on the basis of disability, of the right to enter their own country.

2. Children with disabilities shall be registered immediately after birth and shall have the right from birth to a name, the right to acquire a nationality and, as far as possible, the right to know and be cared for by their parents.

Article 19
Living independently and being included in the community

States Parties to the present Convention recognize the equal right of all persons with disabilities to live in the community, with choices equal to others, and shall take effective and appropriate measures to facilitate full enjoyment by persons with disabilities of this right and their full inclusion and participation in the community, including by ensuring that:

(*a*) Persons with disabilities have the opportunity to choose their place of residence and where and with whom they live on an equal basis with others and are not obliged to live in a particular living arrangement;

(*b*) Persons with disabilities have access to a range of in-home, residential and other community support services, including personal assistance necessary to support living and inclusion in the community, and to prevent isolation or segregation from the community;

(*c*) Community services and facilities for the general population are available on an equal basis to persons with disabilities and are responsive to their needs.

Article 20
Personal mobility

States Parties shall take effective measures to ensure personal mobility with the greatest possible independence for persons with disabilities, including by:

(*a*) Facilitating the personal mobility of persons with disabilities in the manner and at the time of their choice, and at affordable cost;

(*b*) Facilitating access by persons with disabilities to quality mobility aids, devices, assistive technologies and forms of live assistance and intermediaries, including by making them available at affordable cost;

(*c*) Providing training in mobility skills to persons with disabilities and to specialist staff working with persons with disabilities;

(*d*) Encouraging entities that produce mobility aids, devices and assistive technologies to take into account all aspects of mobility for persons with disabilities.

Article 21
Freedom of expression and opinion, and access to information

States Parties shall take all appropriate measures to ensure that persons with disabilities can exercise the right to freedom of expression and opinion, including the freedom to seek, receive and impart information and ideas on an equal basis with others and through all forms of communication of their choice, as defined in article 2 of the present Convention, including by:

(*a*) Providing information intended for the general public to persons with disabilities in accessible formats and technologies appropriate to different kinds of disabilities in a timely manner and without additional cost;

(*b*) Accepting and facilitating the use of sign languages, Braille, augmentative and alternative communication, and all other accessible means, modes and formats of communication of their choice by persons with disabilities in official interactions;

(*c*) Urging private entities that provide services to the general public, including through the Internet, to provide information and services in accessible and usable formats for persons with disabilities;

(*d*) Encouraging the mass media, including providers of information through the Internet, to make their services accessible to persons with disabilities;

(*e*) Recognizing and promoting the use of sign languages.

Article 22
Respect for Privacy

1. No person with disabilities, regardless of place of residence or living arrangements, shall be subjected to arbitrary or unlawful interference with his or her privacy, family, home or correspondence or other types of communication or to unlawful attacks on his or her honour and reputation. Persons with disabilities have the right to the protection of the law against such interference or attacks.

2. States Parties shall protect the privacy of personal, health and rehabilitation information of persons with disabilities on an equal basis with others.

Article 23
Respect for home and the family

1. States Parties shall take effective and appropriate measures to eliminate discrimination against persons with disabilities in all matters relating to marriage, family, parenthood and relationships, on an equal basis with others, so as to ensure that:

(*a*) The right of all persons with disabilities who are of marriageable age to marry and to found a family on the basis of free and full consent of the intending spouses is recognized;

(*b*) The rights of persons with disabilities to decide freely and responsibly on the number and spacing of their children and to have access to age-appropriate information, reproductive and family planning education are recognized, and the means necessary to enable them to exercise these rights are provided;

(*c*) Persons with disabilities, including children, retain their fertility on an equal basis with others.

2. States Parties shall ensure the rights and responsibilities of persons with disabilities, with regard to guardianship, wardship, trusteeship, adoption of children or similar institutions, where these concepts exist in national legislation; in all cases the best interests of the child shall be paramount. States Parties shall render appropriate assistance to persons with disabilities in the performance of their child-rearing responsibilities.

3. States Parties shall ensure that children with disabilities have equal rights with respect to family life. With a view to realizing these rights, and to prevent concealment, abandonment, neglect and segregation of children with disabilities, States Parties shall undertake to provide early and comprehensive information, services and support to children with disabilities and their families.

4. States Parties shall ensure that a child shall not be separated from his or her parents against their will, except when competent authorities subject to judicial review determine, in accordance with applicable law and procedures, that such separation is necessary for the best interests of the child. In no case shall a child be separated from parents on the basis of a disability of either the child or one or both of the parents.

5. States Parties shall, where the immediate family is unable to care for a child with disabilities, undertake every effort to provide alternative care within the wider family, and failing that, within the community in a family setting.

Article 24
Education

1. States Parties recognize the right of persons with disabilities to education. With a view to realizing this right without discrimination and on the basis of equal opportunity, States Parties shall ensure an inclusive education system at all levels and lifelong learning directed to:

(*a*) The full development of human potential and sense of dignity and self-worth, and the strengthening of respect for human rights, fundamental freedoms and human diversity;

(*b*) The development by persons with disabilities of their personality, talents and creativity, as well as their mental and physical abilities, to their fullest potential;

(*c*) Enabling persons with disabilities to participate effectively in a free society.

2. In realizing this right, States Parties shall ensure that:

(*a*) Persons with disabilities are not excluded from the general education system on the basis of disability, and that children with disabilities are not excluded from free and compulsory primary education, or from secondary education, on the basis of disability;

(*b*) Persons with disabilities can access an inclusive, quality and free primary education and secondary education on an equal basis with others in the communities in which they live;

(*c*) Reasonable accommodation of the individual's requirements is provided;

(*d*) Persons with disabilities receive the support required, within the general education system, to facilitate their effective education;

(*e*) Effective individualized support measures are provided in environments that maximize academic and social development, consistent with the goal of full inclusion.

3. States Parties shall enable persons with disabilities to learn life and social development skills to facilitate their full and equal participation in education and as members of the community. To this end, States Parties shall take appropriate measures, including:

(*a*) Facilitating the learning of Braille, alternative script, augmentative and alternative modes, means and formats of communication and orientation and mobility skills, and facilitating peer support and mentoring;

(*b*) Facilitating the learning of sign language and the promotion of the linguistic identity of the deaf community;

(*c*) Ensuring that the education of persons, and in particular children, who are blind, deaf or deafblind, is delivered in the most appropriate languages and modes and means of communication for the individual, and in environments which maximize academic and social development.

4. In order to help ensure the realization of this right, States Parties shall take appropriate measures to employ teachers, including teachers with disabilities, who are qualified in sign language and/or Braille, and to train professionals and staff who work at all levels of education. Such training shall incorporate disability awareness and the use of appropriate augmentative and alternative modes, means and formats of communication, educational techniques and materials to support persons with disabilities.

5. States Parties shall ensure that persons with disabilities are able to access general tertiary education, vocational training, adult education and lifelong learning without discrimination and on an equal basis with others. To this end, States Parties shall ensure that reasonable accommodation is provided to persons with disabilities.

Article 25
Health

States Parties recognize that persons with disabilities have the right to the enjoyment of the highest attainable standard of health without discrimination on the basis of disability. States Parties shall take all appropriate measures to ensure access for persons with disabilities to health services that are gender-sensitive, including health-related rehabilitation. In particular, States Parties shall:

(*a*) Provide persons with disabilities with the same range, quality and standard of free or affordable health care and programmes as provided to other persons, including in the area of sexual and reproductive health and population-based public health programmes;

(*b*) Provide those health services needed by persons with disabilities specifically because of their disabilities, including early identification and intervention as appropriate, and services designed to minimize and prevent further disabilities, including among children and older persons;

(*c*) Provide these health services as close as possible to people's own communities, including in rural areas;

(*d*) Require health professionals to provide care of the same quality to persons with disabilities as to others, including on the basis of free and informed consent by, inter alia, raising awareness of the human rights, dignity, autonomy and needs of persons with disabilities through training and the promulgation of ethical standards for public and private health care;

(*e*) Prohibit discrimination against persons with disabilities in the provision of health insurance, and life insurance where such insurance is permitted by national law, which shall be provided in a fair and reasonable manner;

(*f*) Prevent discriminatory denial of health care or health services or food and fluids on the basis of disability.

Article 26
Habilitation and rehabilitation

1. States Parties shall take effective and appropriate measures, including through peer support, to enable persons with disabilities to attain and maintain maximum independence, full physical, mental, social and vocational ability, and full inclusion and participation in all aspects of life. To that end, States Parties shall organize, strengthen and extend comprehensive habilitation and rehabilitation services and programmes, particularly in the areas of health, employment, education and social services, in such a way that these services and programmes:

(*a*) Begin at the earliest possible stage, and are based on the multidisciplinary assessment of individual needs and strengths;

(*b*) Support participation and inclusion in the community and all aspects of society, are voluntary, and are available to persons with disabilities as close as possible to their own communities, including in rural areas.

2. States Parties shall promote the development of initial and continuing training for professionals and staff working in habilitation and rehabilitation services.

3. States Parties shall promote the availability, knowledge and use of assistive devices and technologies, designed for persons with disabilities, as they relate to habilitation and rehabilitation.

Article 27
Work and employment

1. States Parties recognize the right of persons with disabilities to work, on an equal basis with others; this includes the right to the opportunity to gain a living by work freely chosen or accepted in a labour market and work environment that is open, inclusive and accessible

to persons with disabilities. States Parties shall safeguard and promote the realization of the right to work, including for those who acquire a disability during the course of employment, by taking appropriate steps, including through legislation, to, inter alia:

(*a*) Prohibit discrimination on the basis of disability with regard to all matters concerning all forms of employment, including conditions of recruitment, hiring and employment, continuance of employment, career advancement and safe and healthy working conditions;

(*b*) Protect the rights of persons with disabilities, on an equal basis with others, to just and favourable conditions of work, including equal opportunities and equal remuneration for work of equal value, safe and healthy working conditions, including protection from harassment, and the redress of grievances;

(*c*) Ensure that persons with disabilities are able to exercise their labour and trade union rights on an equal basis with others;

(*d*) Enable persons with disabilities to have effective access to general technical and vocational guidance programmes, placement services and vocational and continuing training;

(*e*) Promote employment opportunities and career advancement for persons with disabilities in the labour market, as well as assistance in finding, obtaining, maintaining and returning to employment;

(*f*) Promote opportunities for self-employment, entrepreneurship, the development of cooperatives and starting one's own business;

(*g*) Employ persons with disabilities in the public sector;

(*h*) Promote the employment of persons with disabilities in the private sector through appropriate policies and measures, which may include affirmative action programmes, incentives and other measures;

(*i*) Ensure that reasonable accommodation is provided to persons with disabilities in the workplace;

(*j*) Promote the acquisition by persons with disabilities of work experience in the open labour market;

(*k*) Promote vocational and professional rehabilitation, job retention and return-to-work programmes for persons with disabilities.

2. States Parties shall ensure that persons with disabilities are not held in slavery or in servitude, and are protected, on an equal basis with others, from forced or compulsory labour.

Article 28
Adequate standard of living and social protection

1. States Parties recognize the right of persons with disabilities to an adequate standard of living for themselves and their families, including adequate food, clothing and housing, and to the continuous improvement of living conditions, and shall take appropriate steps to

safeguard and promote the realization of this right without discrimination on the basis of disability.

2. States Parties recognize the right of persons with disabilities to social protection and to the enjoyment of that right without discrimination on the basis of disability, and shall take appropriate steps to safeguard and promote the realization of this right, including measures:

(*a*) To ensure equal access by persons with disabilities to clean water services, and to ensure access to appropriate and affordable services, devices and other assistance for disability-related needs;

(*b*) To ensure access by persons with disabilities, in particular women and girls with disabilities and older persons with disabilities, to social protection programmes and poverty reduction programmes;

(*c*) To ensure access by persons with disabilities and their families living in situations of poverty to assistance from the State with disability-related expenses, including adequate training, counselling, financial assistance and respite care;

(*d*) To ensure access by persons with disabilities to public housing programmes;

(*e*) To ensure equal access by persons with disabilities to retirement benefits and programmes.

Article 29
Participation in political and public life

States Parties shall guarantee to persons with disabilities political rights and the opportunity to enjoy them on an equal basis with others, and shall undertake:

(*a*) To ensure that persons with disabilities can effectively and fully participate in political and public life on an equal basis with others, directly or through freely chosen representatives, including the right and opportunity for persons with disabilities to vote and be elected, inter alia, by:

(i) Ensuring that voting procedures, facilities and materials are appropriate, accessible and easy to understand and use;

(ii) Protecting the right of persons with disabilities to vote by secret ballot in elections and public referendums without intimidation, and to stand for elections, to effectively hold office and perform all public functions at all levels of government, facilitating the use of assistive and new technologies where appropriate;

(iii) Guaranteeing the free expression of the will of persons with disabilities as electors and to this end, where necessary, at their request, allowing assistance in voting by a person of their own choice;

(*b*) To promote actively an environment in which persons with disabilities can effectively and fully participate in the conduct of public affairs, without discrimination and on an equal basis with others, and encourage their participation in public affairs, including:

(i) Participation in non-governmental organizations and associations concerned with the public and political life of the country, and in the activities and administration of political parties;

(ii) Forming and joining organizations of persons with disabilities to represent persons with disabilities at international, national, regional and local levels.

Article 30
Participation in cultural life, recreation, leisure and sport

1. States Parties recognize the right of persons with disabilities to take part on an equal basis with others in cultural life, and shall take all appropriate measures to ensure that persons with disabilities:

(*a*) Enjoy access to cultural materials in accessible formats;

(*b*) Enjoy access to television programmes, films, theatre and other cultural activities, in accessible formats;

(*c*) Enjoy access to places for cultural performances or services, such as theatres, museums, cinemas, libraries and tourism services, and, as far as possible, enjoy access to monuments and sites of national cultural importance.

2. States Parties shall take appropriate measures to enable persons with disabilities to have the opportunity to develop and utilize their creative, artistic and intellectual potential, not only for their own benefit, but also for the enrichment of society.

3. States Parties shall take all appropriate steps, in accordance with international law, to ensure that laws protecting intellectual property rights do not constitute an unreasonable or discriminatory barrier to access by persons with disabilities to cultural materials.

4. Persons with disabilities shall be entitled, on an equal basis with others, to recognition and support of their specific cultural and linguistic identity, including sign languages and deaf culture.

5. With a view to enabling persons with disabilities to participate on an equal basis with others in recreational, leisure and sporting activities, States Parties shall take appropriate measures:

(*a*) To encourage and promote the participation, to the fullest extent possible, of persons with disabilities in mainstream sporting activities at all levels;

(*b*) To ensure that persons with disabilities have an opportunity to organize, develop and participate in disability-specific sporting and recreational activities and, to this end, encourage the provision, on an equal basis with others, of appropriate instruction, training and resources;

(*c*) To ensure that persons with disabilities have access to sporting, recreational and tourism venues;

(*d*) To ensure that children with disabilities have equal access with other children to participation in play, recreation and leisure and sporting activities, including those activities in the school system;

(*e*) To ensure that persons with disabilities have access to services from those involved in the organization of recreational, tourism, leisure and sporting activities.

Article 31
Statistics and data collection

1. States Parties undertake to collect appropriate information, including statistical and research data, to enable them to formulate and implement policies to give effect to the present Convention. The process of collecting and maintaining this information shall:

(*a*) Comply with legally established safeguards, including legislation on data protection, to ensure confidentiality and respect for the privacy of persons with disabilities;

(*b*) Comply with internationally accepted norms to protect human rights and fundamental freedoms and ethical principles in the collection and use of statistics.

2. The information collected in accordance with this article shall be disaggregated, as appropriate, and used to help assess the implementation of States Parties' obligations under the present Convention and to identify and address the barriers faced by persons with disabilities in exercising their rights.

3. States Parties shall assume responsibility for the dissemination of these statistics and ensure their accessibility to persons with disabilities and others.

Article 32
International cooperation

1. States Parties recognize the importance of international cooperation and its promotion, in support of national efforts for the realization of the purpose and objectives of the present Convention, and will undertake appropriate and effective measures in this regard, between and among States and, as appropriate, in partnership with relevant international and regional organizations and civil society, in particular organizations of persons with disabilities. Such measures could include, inter alia:

(*a*) Ensuring that international cooperation, including international development programmes, is inclusive of and accessible to persons with disabilities;

(*b*) Facilitating and supporting capacity-building, including through the exchange and sharing of information, experiences, training programmes and best practices;

(*c*) Facilitating cooperation in research and access to scientific and technical knowledge;

(*d*) Providing, as appropriate, technical and economic assistance, including by facilitating access to and sharing of accessible and assistive technologies, and through the transfer of technologies.

2. The provisions of this article are without prejudice to the obligations of each State Party to fulfil its obligations under the present Convention.

Article 33
National implementation and monitoring

1. States Parties, in accordance with their system of organization, shall designate one or more focal points within government for matters relating to the implementation of the present Convention, and shall give due consideration to the establishment or designation of a

coordination mechanism within government to facilitate related action in different sectors and at different levels.

2. States Parties shall, in accordance with their legal and administrative systems, maintain, strengthen, designate or establish within the State Party, a framework, including one or more independent mechanisms, as appropriate, to promote, protect and monitor implementation of the present Convention. When designating or establishing such a mechanism, States Parties shall take into account the principles relating to the status and functioning of national institutions for protection and promotion of human rights.

3. Civil society, in particular persons with disabilities and their representative organizations, shall be involved and participate fully in the monitoring process.

Article 34
Committee on the Rights of Persons with Disabilities

1. There shall be established a Committee on the Rights of Persons with Disabilities (hereafter referred to as "the Committee"), which shall carry out the functions hereinafter provided.

2. The Committee shall consist, at the time of entry into force of the present Convention, of twelve experts. After an additional sixty ratifications or accessions to the Convention, the membership of the Committee shall increase by six members, attaining a maximum number of eighteen members.

3. The members of the Committee shall serve in their personal capacity and shall be of high moral standing and recognized competence and experience in the field covered by the present Convention. When nominating their candidates, States Parties are invited to give due consideration to the provision set out in article 4, paragraph 3, of the present Convention.

4. The members of the Committee shall be elected by States Parties, consideration being given to equitable geographical distribution, representation of the different forms of civilization and of the principal legal systems, balanced gender representation and participation of experts with disabilities.

5. The members of the Committee shall be elected by secret ballot from a list of persons nominated by the States Parties from among their nationals at meetings of the Conference of States Parties. At those meetings, for which two thirds of States Parties shall constitute a quorum, the persons elected to the Committee shall be those who obtain the largest number of votes and an absolute majority of the votes of the representatives of States Parties present and voting.

6. The initial election shall be held no later than six months after the date of entry into force of the present Convention. At least four months before the date of each election, the Secretary-General of the United Nations shall address a letter to the States Parties inviting them to submit the nominations within two months. The Secretary-General shall subsequently prepare a list in alphabetical order of all persons thus nominated, indicating the State Parties which have nominated them, and shall submit it to the States Parties to the present Convention.

7. The members of the Committee shall be elected for a term of four years. They shall be eligible for re-election once. However, the term of six of the members elected at the first

election shall expire at the end of two years; immediately after the first election, the names of these six members shall be chosen by lot by the chairperson of the meeting referred to in paragraph 5 of this article.

8. The election of the six additional members of the Committee shall be held on the occasion of regular elections, in accordance with the relevant provisions of this article.

9. If a member of the Committee dies or resigns or declares that for any other cause she or he can no longer perform her or his duties, the State Party which nominated the member shall appoint another expert possessing the qualifications and meeting the requirements set out in the relevant provisions of this article, to serve for the remainder of the term.

10. The Committee shall establish its own rules of procedure.

11. The Secretary-General of the United Nations shall provide the necessary staff and facilities for the effective performance of the functions of the Committee under the present Convention, and shall convene its initial meeting.

12. With the approval of the General Assembly of the United Nations, the members of the Committee established under the present Convention shall receive emoluments from United Nations resources on such terms and conditions as the Assembly may decide, having regard to the importance of the Committee's responsibilities.

13. The members of the Committee shall be entitled to the facilities, privileges and immunities of experts on mission for the United Nations as laid down in the relevant sections of the Convention on the Privileges and Immunities of the United Nations.

Article 35
Reports by States Parties

1. Each State Party shall submit to the Committee, through the Secretary-General of the United Nations, a comprehensive report on measures taken to give effect to its obligations under the present Convention and on the progress made in that regard, within two years after the entry into force of the present Convention for the State Party concerned.

2. Thereafter, States Parties shall submit subsequent reports at least every four years and further whenever the Committee so requests.

3. The Committee shall decide any guidelines applicable to the content of the reports.

4. A State Party which has submitted a comprehensive initial report to the Committee need not, in its subsequent reports, repeat information previously provided. When preparing reports to the Committee, States Parties are invited to consider doing so in an open and transparent process and to give due consideration to the provision set out in article 4, paragraph 3, of the present Convention.

5. Reports may indicate factors and difficulties affecting the degree of fulfilment of obligations under the present Convention.

Article 36
Consideration of reports

1. Each report shall be considered by the Committee, which shall make such suggestions and general recommendations on the report as it may consider appropriate and shall forward these to the State Party concerned. The State Party may respond with any information it chooses to the Committee. The Committee may request further information from States Parties relevant to the implementation of the present Convention.

2. If a State Party is significantly overdue in the submission of a report, the Committee may notify the State Party concerned of the need to examine the implementation of the present Convention in that State Party, on the basis of reliable information available to the Committee, if the relevant report is not submitted within three months following the notification. The Committee shall invite the State Party concerned to participate in such examination. Should the State Party respond by submitting the relevant report, the provisions of paragraph 1 of this article will apply.

3. The Secretary-General of the United Nations shall make available the reports to all States Parties.

4. States Parties shall make their reports widely available to the public in their own countries and facilitate access to the suggestions and general recommendations relating to these reports.

5. The Committee shall transmit, as it may consider appropriate, to the specialized agencies, funds and programmes of the United Nations, and other competent bodies, reports from States Parties in order to address a request or indication of a need for technical advice or assistance contained therein, along with the Committee's observations and recommendations, if any, on these requests or indications.

Article 37
Cooperation between States Parties and the Committee

1. Each State Party shall cooperate with the Committee and assist its members in the fulfilment of their mandate.

2. In its relationship with States Parties, the Committee shall give due consideration to ways and means of enhancing national capacities for the implementation of the present Convention, including through international cooperation.

Article 38
Relationship of the Committee with other bodies

In order to foster the effective implementation of the present Convention and to encourage international cooperation in the field covered by the present Convention:

(*a*) The specialized agencies and other United Nations organs shall be entitled to be represented at the consideration of the implementation of such provisions of the present Convention as fall within the scope of their mandate. The Committee may invite the specialized agencies and other competent bodies as it may consider appropriate to provide expert advice on the implementation of the Convention in areas falling within the scope of their respective mandates. The Committee may invite specialized agencies and other United Nations organs to submit reports on the implementation of the Convention in areas falling within the scope of their activities;

(*b*) The Committee, as it discharges its mandate, shall consult, as appropriate, other relevant bodies instituted by international human rights treaties, with a view to ensuring the consistency of their respective reporting guidelines, suggestions and general recommendations, and avoiding duplication and overlap in the performance of their functions.

Article 39
Report of the Committee

The Committee shall report every two years to the General Assembly and to the Economic and Social Council on its activities, and may make suggestions and general recommendations based on the examination of reports and information received from the States Parties. Such suggestions and general recommendations shall be included in the report of the Committee together with comments, if any, from States Parties.

Article 40
Conference of States Parties

1. The States Parties shall meet regularly in a Conference of States Parties in order to consider any matter with regard to the implementation of the present Convention.

2. No later than six months after the entry into force of the present Convention, the Conference of States Parties shall be convened by the Secretary-General of the United Nations. The subsequent meetings shall be convened by the Secretary-General biennially or upon the decision of the Conference of States Parties.

Article 41
Depositary

The Secretary-General of the United Nations shall be the depositary of the present Convention.

Article 42
Signature

The present Convention shall be open for signature by all States and by regional integration organizations at United Nations Headquarters in New York as of 30 March 2007.

Article 43
Consent to be bound

The present Convention shall be subject to ratification by signatory States and to formal confirmation by signatory regional integration organizations. It shall be open for accession by any State or regional integration organization which has not signed the Convention.

Article 44
Regional integration organizations

1. "Regional integration organization" shall mean an organization constituted by sovereign States of a given region, to which its member States have transferred competence in respect of matters governed by the present Convention. Such organizations shall declare, in their instruments of formal confirmation or accession, the extent of their competence with

respect to matters governed by the present Convention. Subsequently, they shall inform the depositary of any substantial modification in the extent of their competence.

2. References to "States Parties" in the present Convention shall apply to such organizations within the limits of their competence.

3. For the purposes of article 45, paragraph 1, and article 47, paragraphs 2 and 3, of the present Convention, any instrument deposited by a regional integration organization shall not be counted.

4. Regional integration organizations, in matters within their competence, may exercise their right to vote in the Conference of States Parties, with a number of votes equal to the number of their member States that are Parties to the present Convention. Such an organization shall not exercise its right to vote if any of its member States exercises its right, and vice versa.

Article 45
Entry into force

1. The present Convention shall enter into force on the thirtieth day after the deposit of the twentieth instrument of ratification or accession.

2. For each State or regional integration organization ratifying, formally confirming or acceding to the present Convention after the deposit of the twentieth such instrument, the Convention shall enter into force on the thirtieth day after the deposit of its own such instrument.

Article 46
Reservations

1. Reservations incompatible with the object and purpose of the present Convention shall not be permitted.

2. Reservations may be withdrawn at any time.

Article 47
Amendments

1. Any State Party may propose an amendment to the present Convention and submit it to the Secretary-General of the United Nations. The Secretary-General shall communicate any proposed amendments to States Parties, with a request to be notified whether they favour a conference of States Parties for the purpose of considering and deciding upon the proposals. In the event that, within four months from the date of such communication, at least one third of the States Parties favour such a conference, the Secretary-General shall convene the conference under the auspices of the United Nations. Any amendment adopted by a majority of two thirds of the States Parties present and voting shall be submitted by the Secretary-General to the General Assembly of the United Nations for approval and thereafter to all States Parties for acceptance.

2. An amendment adopted and approved in accordance with paragraph 1 of this article shall enter into force on the thirtieth day after the number of instruments of acceptance deposited

reaches two thirds of the number of States Parties at the date of adoption of the amendment. Thereafter, the amendment shall enter into force for any State Party on the thirtieth day following the deposit of its own instrument of acceptance. An amendment shall be binding only on those States Parties which have accepted it.

3. If so decided by the Conference of States Parties by consensus, an amendment adopted and approved in accordance with paragraph 1 of this article which relates exclusively to articles 34, 38, 39 and 40 shall enter into force for all States Parties on the thirtieth day after the number of instruments of acceptance deposited reaches two thirds of the number of States Parties at the date of adoption of the amendment.

Article 48
Denunciation

A State Party may denounce the present Convention by written notification to the Secretary-General of the United Nations. The denunciation shall become effective one year after the date of receipt of the notification by the Secretary-General.

Article 49
Accessible format

The text of the present Convention shall be made available in accessible formats.

Article 50
Authentic texts

The Arabic, Chinese, English, French, Russian and Spanish texts of the present Convention shall be equally authentic.

IN WITNESS THEREOF the undersigned plenipotentiaries, being duly authorized thereto by their respective Governments, have signed the present Convention.

Annex II
Optional Protocol to the Convention on the Rights of Persons with Disabilities

The States Parties to the present Protocol have agreed as follows:

Article 1

1. A State Party to the present Protocol ("State Party") recognizes the competence of the Committee on the Rights of Persons with Disabilities ("the Committee") to receive and consider communications from or on behalf of individuals or groups of individuals subject to its jurisdiction who claim to be victims of a violation by that State Party of the provisions of the Convention.

2. No communication shall be received by the Committee if it concerns a State Party to the Convention that is not a party to the present Protocol.

Article 2

The Committee shall consider a communication inadmissible when:

(a) The communication is anonymous;

(*b*) The communication constitutes an abuse of the right of submission of such communications or is incompatible with the provisions of the Convention;

(*c*) The same matter has already been examined by the Committee or has been or is being examined under another procedure of international investigation or settlement;

(*d*) All available domestic remedies have not been exhausted. This shall not be the rule where the application of the remedies is unreasonably prolonged or unlikely to bring effective relief;

(*e*) It is manifestly ill-founded or not sufficiently substantiated; or when

(*f*) The facts that are the subject of the communication occurred prior to the entry into force of the present Protocol for the State Party concerned unless those facts continued after that date.

Article 3

Subject to the provisions of article 2 of the present Protocol, the Committee shall bring any communications submitted to it confidentially to the attention of the State Party. Within six months, the receiving State shall submit to the Committee written explanations or statements clarifying the matter and the remedy, if any, that may have been taken by that State.

Article 4

1. At any time after the receipt of a communication and before a determination on the merits has been reached, the Committee may transmit to the State Party concerned for its urgent consideration a request that the State Party take such interim measures as may be necessary to avoid possible irreparable damage to the victim or victims of the alleged violation.

2. Where the Committee exercises its discretion under paragraph 1 of this article, this does not imply a determination on admissibility or on the merits of the communication.

Article 5

The Committee shall hold closed meetings when examining communications under the present Protocol. After examining a communication, the Committee shall forward its suggestions and recommendations, if any, to the State Party concerned and to the petitioner.

Article 6

1. If the Committee receives reliable information indicating grave or systematic violations by a State Party of rights set forth in the Convention, the Committee shall invite that State Party to cooperate in the examination of the information and to this end submit observations with regard to the information concerned.

2. Taking into account any observations that may have been submitted by the State Party concerned as well as any other reliable information available to it, the Committee may designate one or more of its members to conduct an inquiry and to report urgently to the Committee. Where warranted and with the consent of the State Party, the inquiry may include a visit to its territory.

3. After examining the findings of such an inquiry, the Committee shall transmit these findings to the State Party concerned together with any comments and recommendations.

4. The State Party concerned shall, within six months of receiving the findings, comments and recommendations transmitted by the Committee, submit its observations to the Committee.

5. Such an inquiry shall be conducted confidentially and the cooperation of the State Party shall be sought at all stages of the proceedings.

Article 7

1. The Committee may invite the State Party concerned to include in its report under article 35 of the Convention details of any measures taken in response to an inquiry conducted under article 6 of the present Protocol.

2. The Committee may, if necessary, after the end of the period of six months referred to in article 6, paragraph 4, invite the State Party concerned to inform it of the measures taken in response to such an inquiry.

Article 8

Each State Party may, at the time of signature or ratification of the present Protocol or accession thereto, declare that it does not recognize the competence of the Committee provided for in articles 6 and 7.

Article 9

The Secretary-General of the United Nations shall be the depositary of the present Protocol.

Article 10

The present Protocol shall be open for signature by signatory States and regional integration organizations of the Convention at United Nations Headquarters in New York as of 30 March 2007.

Article 11

The present Protocol shall be subject to ratification by signatory States of the present Protocol which have ratified or acceded to the Convention. It shall be subject to formal confirmation by signatory regional integration organizations of the present Protocol which have formally confirmed or acceded to the Convention. It shall be open for accession by any State or regional integration organization which has ratified, formally confirmed or acceded to the Convention and which has not signed the Protocol.

Article 12

1. "Regional integration organization" shall mean an organization constituted by sovereign States of a given region, to which its member States have transferred competence in respect of matters governed by the Convention and the present Protocol. Such organizations shall declare, in their instruments of formal confirmation or accession, the extent of their competence with respect to matters governed by the Convention and the present Protocol. Subsequently, they shall inform the depositary of any substantial modification in the extent of their competence.

2. References to "States Parties" in the present Protocol shall apply to such organizations within the limits of their competence.

3. For the purposes of article 13, paragraph 1, and article 15, paragraph 2, of the present Protocol, any instrument deposited by a regional integration organization shall not be counted.

4. Regional integration organizations, in matters within their competence, may exercise their right to vote in the meeting of States Parties, with a number of votes equal to the number of their member States that are Parties to the present Protocol. Such an organization shall not exercise its right to vote if any of its member States exercises its right, and vice versa.

Article 13

1. Subject to the entry into force of the Convention, the present Protocol shall enter into force on the thirtieth day after the deposit of the tenth instrument of ratification or accession.

2. For each State or regional integration organization ratifying, formally confirming or acceding to the present Protocol after the deposit of the tenth such instrument, the Protocol shall enter into force on the thirtieth day after the deposit of its own such instrument.

Article 14

1. Reservations incompatible with the object and purpose of the present Protocol shall not be permitted.

2. Reservations may be withdrawn at any time.

Article 15

1. Any State Party may propose an amendment to the present Protocol and submit it to the Secretary-General of the United Nations. The Secretary-General shall communicate any proposed amendments to States Parties, with a request to be notified whether they favour a meeting of States Parties for the purpose of considering and deciding upon the proposals. In the event that, within four months from the date of such communication, at least one third of the States Parties favour such a meeting, the Secretary-General shall convene the meeting under the auspices of the United Nations. Any amendment adopted by a majority of two thirds of the States Parties present and voting shall be submitted by the Secretary-General to the General Assembly of the United Nations for approval and thereafter to all States Parties for acceptance.

2. An amendment adopted and approved in accordance with paragraph 1 of this article shall enter into force on the thirtieth day after the number of instruments of acceptance deposited

reaches two thirds of the number of States Parties at the date of adoption of the amendment. Thereafter, the amendment shall enter into force for any State Party on the thirtieth day following the deposit of its own instrument of acceptance. An amendment shall be binding only on those States Parties which have accepted it.

Article 16

A State Party may denounce the present Protocol by written notification to the Secretary-General of the United Nations. The denunciation shall become effective one year after the date of receipt of the notification by the Secretary-General.

Article 17

The text of the present Protocol shall be made available in accessible formats.

Article 18

The Arabic, Chinese, English, French, Russian and Spanish texts of the present Protocol shall be equally authentic.

IN WITNESS THEREOF the undersigned plenipotentiaries, being duly authorized thereto by their respective Governments, have signed the present Protocol.

Resolution 61/107

[without reference to a main Committee (A/61/L.48/Rev.1)]

61/107. Tribute to Mr. Kofi Annan, Secretary-General of the United Nations

The General Assembly

Welcoming Security Council resolution 1715 (2006) of 9 October 2006,

Recalling its resolution 61/3 of 13 October 2006 by which it appointed the Secretary-General,

Acknowledging with deep gratitude the indefatigable efforts and dedicated service provided to the Organization during the past ten years by Secretary-General Kofi Annan,

Recognizing the high professional and personal qualities he brought to the performance of his duties and responsibilities,

Placing on special record his many bold initiatives – political, diplomatic and organizational – and his important achievements, in particular with respect to the Millennium Development Goals, peace and security issues, environmental issues and United Nations reform,

1. *Pays warm tribute* to Securitary-General Kofi Annan for his exceptional contribution to international peace and security, as well as his outstanding efforts to strengthen the Unites Nations systems and to promote and protect human rights and fundamental freedoms for all, in the interest of a better world;

2. Expressess its deep gratitude to Secretary-General Kofi Annan for having undertaken reforms and advanced numerous proposals with a view to enhancing the Organization's capacity to meet the major challenges of our time.

78th plenary meeting
14 December 2006

Resolution 61/108

[on the report of the Special Political and Decolonization Committee (Fourth Committee) (A/61/404)]

61/108. University for Peace

The General Assembly,

Recalling its resolution 58/12 of 10 November 2003, in which it recalled that, in its resolution 34/111 of 14 December 1979, it had approved the idea of establishing the University for Peace as a specialized international centre for higher education, research and the dissemination of knowledge relative to peace and its universal promotion within the United Nations system, and in which it also recalled its resolution 35/55 of 5 December 1980, in which it had approved the establishment of the University, as well as all preceding resolutions on this item,

Noting with appreciation the vigorous actions taken by the Secretary-General, in consultation with the Director-General of the United Nations Educational, Scientific and Cultural Organization and with the encouragement and support of the Government of Costa Rica, to revitalize the University,[1]

Recognizing the significant progress made in the implementation of the five-year revitalization programme, leading to the achievement of the targets established by the Council of the University for Peace, by building high-quality programmes on subjects related to peace and security and extending them to different regions of the world through networks of partner academic and research institutions,

Noting with appreciation that the future development strategy of the University focuses on consolidating the progress already made in developing and conducting innovative academic and training programmes and at the same time strengthening its collaborative arrangement in different regions of the world and promoting the sharing knowledge for peace programme, including distance learning and dissemination of toolkits for teaching, with a view to strengthening education for peace,

Noting with satisfaction the activities directed towards expanding the University's educational and research programmes to Africa, Asia and the Pacific, Central Asia and Latin America and the Caribbean,

Also noting with satisfaction the progress made in the development of teaching programmes at the master's level, short courses, programmes to disseminate course materials and distance education and the establishment of a digital library on peace-related issues,

Noting that the University has placed special emphasis on the areas of conflict prevention, peacekeeping, peacebuilding and the peaceful settlement of disputes, and that it has launched academic and training programmes in the areas of democratic consensus-building and the techniques of peaceful settlement of conflicts,

Noting also that the University has launched a broad programme for building a culture of peace worldwide in the context of the efforts being made by the United Nations and the United Nations Educational, Scientific and Cultural Organization for the development and promotion of a culture of peace,

Noting with appreciation the intensifying collaboration between the University and organizations and agencies of the United Nations system, particularly the United Nations University, the United Nations Educational, Scientific and Cultural Organization, the Department of Political Affairs and the Department for Disarmament Affairs of the Secretariat, the United Nations Development Programme, the United Nations Institute for Training and Research and others,

Considering the importance of promoting education that fosters peaceful coexistence among people, including respect for the life, dignity and integrity of human beings, irrespective of their nationality, race, sex, religion or culture, as well as friendship and solidarity among peoples,

1. *Welcomes* the report of the Secretary-General outlining the progress made in revitalizing the University for Peace, especially in regard to implementation of the five-year programme of expansion and revitalization;[2]

2. *Requests* the Secretary-General, in view of the important work of the University and its potential role in developing new concepts and approaches to security through research, training and dialogue in order to respond effectively to emerging threats to peace, to consider ways to further strengthen cooperation between the United Nations and the University, and invites the University to consider ways to further strengthen its programmes and activities for cooperation with and capacity-building for Member States in the areas of conflict prevention, conflict resolution and peacebuilding;

3. *Also requests* the Secretary-General to continue using the services of the University as part of his conflict-resolution and peacebuilding efforts, in providing training to staff in building their capacities in this area and in the promotion of the Declaration and the Programme of Action on a Culture of Peace;[3]

4. *Encourages* Member States, intergovernmental bodies, non-governmental organizations and interested individuals to contribute to the programmes and core budget of the University to enable it to continue to perform its valuable work;

5. *Invites* Member States to accede to the International Agreement for the Establishment of the University for Peace,[4] thereby demonstrating their support for an educational institution devoted to the promotion of a universal culture of peace;

6. *Decides* to include in the provisional agenda of its sixty-fourth session the item entitled "University for Peace", and requests the Secretary-General to submit to the General Assembly at that session a report on the work of the University.

79th plenary meeting
14 December 2006

---

[1] See A/54/312, para. 2.

[2] A/61/285.

[3] Resolutions 53/243 A and B.

[4] See resolution 35/55, annex.

Resolution 61/109

[on the report of the Special Political and Decolonization Committee (Fourth Committee) (A/61/405)]

61/109. Effects of atomic radiation

The General Assembly,

Recalling its resolution 913 (X) of 3 December 1955, by which it established the United Nations Scientific Committee on the Effects of Atomic Radiation, and its subsequent resolutions on the subject, including resolution 60/98 of 8 December 2005, in which, inter alia, it requested the Scientific Committee to continue its work,

Taking note with appreciation of the work of the Scientific Committee, and of the release of its report on its fifty-fourth session,[1]

Reaffirming the desirability of the Scientific Committee continuing its work,

Concerned about the potentially harmful effects on present and future generations resulting from the levels of radiation to which mankind and the environment are exposed,

Noting the views expressed by Member States at its sixty-first session with regard to the work of the Scientific Committee,

Noting that some Member States have expressed particular interest in becoming members of the Scientific Committee, and expressing its intention to consider the issue further at its next session,

Conscious of the continuing need to examine and compile information about atomic and ionizing radiation and to analyse its effects on mankind and the environment,

1. *Commends* the United Nations Scientific Committee on the Effects of Atomic Radiation for the valuable contribution it has been making in the course of the past fifty-one years, since its inception, to wider knowledge and understanding of the levels, effects and risks of ionizing radiation, and for fulfilling its original mandate with scientific authority and independence of judgement;

2. *Reaffirms* the decision to maintain the present functions and independent role of the Scientific Committee;

3. *Takes note with appreciation* of the work of the Scientific Committee and of the release of its extensive report to the General Assembly, with scientific annexes, which provides the scientific and world community with the Committee's latest evaluations of the effects of ionizing radiation on human beings;

4. *Requests* the Scientific Committee to continue its work, including its important activities to increase knowledge of the levels, effects and risks of ionizing radiation from all sources;

5. *Endorses* the intentions and plans of the Scientific Committee for completing its present programme of work of scientific review and assessment on behalf of the General Assembly, and requests the Scientific Committee to submit plans for its future programme of work to the General Assembly at its sixty-second session;

6. *Requests* the Scientific Committee to continue at its next session the review of the important problems in the field of ionizing radiation and to report thereon to the General Assembly at its sixty-second session;

7. *Emphasizes* the need for the Scientific Committee to hold regular sessions on an annual basis so that its report can reflect the latest developments and findings in the field of ionizing radiation and thereby provide updated information for dissemination among all States;

8. *Expresses its appreciation* for the assistance rendered to the Scientific Committee by Member States, the specialized agencies, the International Atomic Energy Agency and non-governmental organizations, and invites them to increase their cooperation in this field;

9. *Invites* the Scientific Committee to continue its consultations with scientists and experts from interested Member States in the process of preparing its future scientific reports, and requests the Secretariat to facilitate such consultations;

10. *Welcomes*, in this context, the readiness of Member States to provide the Scientific Committee with relevant information on the effects of ionizing radiation in affected areas, and invites the Scientific Committee to analyse and give due consideration to such information, particularly in the light of its own findings;

11. *Invites* Member States, the organizations of the United Nations system and non-governmental organizations concerned to provide further relevant data about doses, effects and risks from various sources of radiation, which would greatly help in the preparation of future reports of the Scientific Committee to the General Assembly;

12. *Requests* the United Nations Environment Programme to continue providing support for the effective conduct of the work of the Scientific Committee and for the dissemination of its findings to the General Assembly, the scientific community and the public;

13. *Urges* the United Nations Environment Programme to review and strengthen the present funding of the Scientific Committee, pursuant to paragraph 11 of resolution 60/98, and to continue to seek out and consider alternative funding mechanisms to complement existing ones, so that the Committee can discharge the responsibilities and mandate entrusted to it by the General Assembly;

14. *Invites* those Member States that desire to join the Scientific Committee to inform the President of the General Assembly, before 28 February 2007, of their interest, and decides to further consider the question of membership of the Scientific Committee in all its aspects, including financial implications, at the next session.

79th plenary meeting
14 December 2006

---

[1] *Official Records of the General Assembly, Sixty-first Session, Supplement No. 46* and corrigendum (A/61/46 and Corr.1).

Resolution 61/110

[on the report of the Special Political and Decolonization Committee (Fourth Committee) (A/61/406)]

61/110. United Nations Platform for Space-based Information for Disaster Management and Emergency Response

The General Assembly,

Recalling its resolutions 54/68 of 6 December 1999, 59/2 of 20 October 2004 and 59/116 of 10 December 2004,

Seriously concerned about the devastating impact of disasters,[1] causing the loss of lives and property, displacing people from their homes and destroying their livelihoods, and causing tremendous damage to societies around the world,

Equally concerned that disasters reverse, as well as affect and hinder, current and future development efforts in all parts of the world, in particular in developing countries,

Deeply convinced of the urgent need for enhanced coordination efforts at the global level to reduce the impact of disasters,

Recognizing, in that regard, that unnecessary loss of life and property could be avoided if better information were available regarding the risk and onset of disasters, through improved risk assessment, early warning and monitoring of disasters,

Convinced that the use of existing space technology, such as Earth observation and meteorological satellites, communications satellites and satellite navigation and positioning systems, and their applications, can play a vital role in supporting disaster management by providing accurate and timely information for decision-making and re-establishing communication in case of disasters,

Desirous of enhancing international coordination at the global level in disaster management and emergency response through greater access to and use of space-based services for all countries and facilitating capacity-building and institutional strengthening for disaster management, in particular in developing countries,

Having considered the report of the Committee on the Peaceful Uses of Outer Space on the work of its forty-ninth session,[2]

1. *Recognizes* that disasters affect many areas of the Earth and that coordinated international efforts are required to reduce their impacts, and that space technology and its application can play a vital role in supporting disaster relief operations by providing accurate and timely information and communication support;

2. *Also recognizes* the important role that coordinated applications of space technology can play in the implementation of the Hyogo Declaration and the Hyogo Framework for Action 2005–2015: Building the Resilience of Nations and Communities to Disasters, adopted by the World Conference on Disaster Reduction, held at Kobe, Hyogo, Japan, from 18 to 22 January 2005;[3]

3. *Further recognizes* that different international initiatives aimed at utilizing space-based disaster information and services exist, such as the Integrated Global Observing Strategy Partnership, the Global Earth Observation System of Systems, the Charter on Cooperation to Achieve the Coordinated Use of Space Facilities in the Event of Natural or Technological

Disasters and the International Strategy for Disaster Reduction, and that the availability of such services should be promoted among developing countries;

4. *Notes with concern* that unless a global, integrated and coordinated approach is undertaken, building upon the experiences of existing international initiatives, the utilization of space assets in support of disaster management will continue to lag significantly in most parts of the world and that a considerable gap will exist and is likely to remain in all areas of space technology applications to disaster management;

5. *Takes note with appreciation* of the study of the ad hoc expert group established by the Committee on the Peaceful Uses of Outer Space on the possibility of creating an international entity to provide for coordination and the means of realistically optimizing the effectiveness of space-based services for use in disaster management;[4]

6. *Decides* to establish a programme within the United Nations to provide universal access to all countries and all relevant international and regional organizations to all types of space-based information and services relevant to disaster management to support the full disaster management cycle by being a gateway to space information for disaster management support, serving as a bridge to connect the disaster management and space communities and being a facilitator of capacity-building and institutional strengthening, in particular for developing countries;

7. *Agrees* that the programme would be supported through voluntary contributions and through a rearrangement of priorities within the framework of the United Nations reform process and, if necessary, a rearrangement of priorities of the Office for Outer Space Affairs of the Secretariat and that the additional activities would not, as far as possible, have a negative impact on the current programme activities of the Office and should not result in an increase in the total regular budget of the United Nations;

8. *Endorses* the recommendation of the Committee on the Peaceful Uses of Outer Space that the programme have an office in Beijing and an office in Bonn, Germany, and that the activities of the programme be carried out within the proposed implementation framework presented to the Committee;

9. *Notes* that due consideration would be given to the possibility that the programme could have a liaison office in Geneva that would contribute to disseminating and integrating the work of the programme within the disaster reduction and humanitarian response communities;

10. *Takes note with appreciation* of the commitments of support for the establishment of the programme made by Austria, China, Germany and India and the offers of support once it is established made by Algeria, Argentina, Italy, Morocco, Nigeria, Romania, the Russian Federation, Switzerland and Turkey;

11. *Agrees* that the programme should work closely with regional and national centres of expertise in the use of space technology in disaster management to form a network of regional support offices for implementing the activities of the programme in their respective regions in a coordinated manner and to take advantage of the important experience and capabilities being offered, and to be offered, by Member States, particularly by developing countries;

12. *Requests* that the programme also work closely with the international initiatives noted in paragraph 3 above in order to avoid duplication of efforts;

13. *Requests* the Office for Outer Space Affairs to develop a detailed workplan for the programme for 2007 and for the biennium 2008–2009 to be considered during the forty-fourth session of the Scientific and Technical Subcommittee of the Committee on the Peaceful Uses of Outer Space, taking into consideration the commitments received, and in consultation with the representatives of countries that have provided or would be providing commitments, as well as with the representatives of other countries that have indicated their interest in contributing to the development of the workplan;

14. *Agrees* that the partners implementing the programme should endeavour to initiate activities in January 2007 or as soon as it is practicable, in order to enable the programme to begin providing support for disaster management at the earliest possible time;

15. *Also agrees* that the programme should be named the United Nations Platform for Space-based Information for Disaster Management and Emergency Response (SPIDER), and that it should be implemented as a programme of the Office for Outer Space Affairs under the Director of the Office, as an open network of providers of disaster management support, and that the Director of the Office would be responsible for the overall supervision of the programme;

16. *Further agrees* that the programme should report to and receive guidance from the Committee on the Peaceful Uses of Outer Space through the Office for Outer Space Affairs.

79th plenary meeting
14 December 2006

---

[1] The term "disasters" refers to natural or technological disasters.

[2] *Official Records of the General Assembly, Sixty-first Session, Supplement No. 20* (A/61/20).

[3] A/CONF.206/6 and Corr.1, chap. I, resolutions 1 and 2.

[4] A/AC.105/873.

Resolution 61/111

[on the report of the Special Political and Decolonization Committee (Fourth Committee) (A/61/406)]

61/111. International cooperation in the peaceful uses of outer space

The General Assembly,

Recalling its resolutions 51/122 of 13 December 1996, 54/68 of 6 December 1999, 59/2 of 20 October 2004 and 60/99 of 8 December 2005,

Deeply convinced of the common interest of mankind in promoting and expanding the exploration and use of outer space, as the province of all mankind, for peaceful purposes and in continuing efforts to extend to all States the benefits derived therefrom, and also of the importance of international cooperation in this field, for which the United Nations should continue to provide a focal point,

Reaffirming the importance of international cooperation in developing the rule of law, including the relevant norms of space law and their important role in international cooperation for the exploration and use of outer space for peaceful purposes, and of the widest possible adherence to international treaties that promote the peaceful uses of outer space in order to meet emerging new challenges, especially for developing countries,

Seriously concerned about the possibility of an arms race in outer space, and bearing in mind the importance of article IV of the Treaty on Principles Governing the Activities of States in the Exploration and Use of Outer Space, including the Moon and Other Celestial Bodies,[1]

Recognizing that all States, in particular those with major space capabilities, should contribute actively to the goal of preventing an arms race in outer space as an essential condition for the promotion and strengthening of international cooperation in the exploration and use of outer space for peaceful purposes,

Considering that space debris is an issue of concern to all nations,

Noting the progress achieved in the further development of peaceful space exploration and applications as well as in various national and cooperative space projects, which contributes to international cooperation, and the importance of further developing the legal framework to strengthen international cooperation in this field,

Convinced of the importance of the recommendations in the resolution entitled "The Space Millennium: Vienna Declaration on Space and Human Development", adopted by the Third United Nations Conference on the Exploration and Peaceful Uses of Outer Space (UNISPACE III), held at Vienna from 19 to 30 July 1999,[2] and the need to promote the use of space technology towards implementing the United Nations Millennium Declaration,[3]

Taking note of the actions already taken as well as those to be embarked upon to further implement the recommendations of UNISPACE III, as reflected in resolution 59/2 and the Plan of Action of the Committee on the Peaceful Uses of Outer Space,[4]

Convinced that the use of space science and technology and their applications in such areas as telemedicine, tele-education, disaster management and environmental protection as well as other Earth observation applications contribute to achieving the objectives of the global conferences of the United Nations that address various aspects of economic, social and cultural development, inter alia, poverty eradication,

Taking note, in that regard, that the 2005 World Summit recognized the important role that science and technology play in promoting sustainable development,[5]

Having considered the report of the Committee on the Peaceful Uses of Outer Space on the work of its forty-ninth session,[6]

1. *Endorses* the report of the Committee on the Peaceful Uses of Outer Space on the work of its forty-ninth session;[6]

2. *Urges* States that have not yet become parties to the international treaties governing the uses of outer space[7] to give consideration to ratifying or acceding to those treaties as well as incorporating them in their national legislation;

3. *Notes* that, at its forty-fifth session, the Legal Subcommittee of the Committee on the Peaceful Uses of Outer Space continued its work, as mandated by the General Assembly in its resolution 60/99;[8]

4. *Endorses* the recommendation of the Committee that the Legal Subcommittee, at its forty-sixth session, taking into account the concerns of all countries, in particular those of developing countries:

(*a*) Consider the following as regular agenda items:

(i) General exchange of views;

(ii) Status and application of the five United Nations treaties on outer space;

(iii) Information on the activities of international intergovernmental and nongovernmental organizations relating to space law;

(iv) Matters relating to:

a. The definition and delimitation of outer space;

b. The character and utilization of the geostationary orbit, including consideration of ways and means to ensure the rational and equitable use of the geostationary orbit without prejudice to the role of the International Telecommunication Union;

(*b*) Consider the following single issues/items for discussion:

(i) Review and possible revision of the Principles Relevant to the Use of Nuclear Power Sources in Outer Space;[9]

(ii) Examination and review of the developments concerning the draft protocol on matters specific to space assets to the Convention on International Interests in Mobile Equipment;

(*c*) Consider the practice of States and international organizations in registering space objects in accordance with the workplan adopted by the Committee;[10]

5. *Notes* that the Legal Subcommittee, at its forty-sixth session, will submit its proposals to the Committee for new items to be considered by the Subcommittee at its forty-seventh session, in 2008;

6. *Also notes* that, in the context of paragraph 4 (*a*) (ii) above, the Legal Subcommittee, at its forty-sixth session, will reconvene its Working Group and review the need to extend the mandate of the Working Group beyond that session of the Subcommittee;

7. *Further notes* that, in the context of paragraph 4 (*a*) (iv) *a*. above, the Legal Subcommittee will reconvene its Working Group on the item only to consider matters relating to the definition and delimitation of outer space;

8. *Notes* that, in the context of paragraph 4 (*c*) above, the Legal Subcommittee will reconvene its Working Group;

9. *Also notes* that the Scientific and Technical Subcommittee, at its forty-third session, continued its work as mandated by the General Assembly in its resolution 60/99;[11]

10. *Endorses* the recommendation of the Committee that the Scientific and Technical Subcommittee, at its forty-fourth session, taking into account the concerns of all countries, in particular those of developing countries:

(a) Consider the following items:

(i) General exchange of views and introduction to reports submitted on national activities;

(ii) United Nations Programme on Space Applications;

(iii) Implementation of the recommendations of the Third United Nations Conference on the Exploration and Peaceful Uses of Outer Space (UNISPACE III);

(iv) Matters relating to remote sensing of the Earth by satellite, including applications for developing countries and monitoring of the Earth's environment;

(*b*) Consider the following items in accordance with the workplans adopted by the Committee:[12]

(i) Space debris;

(ii) Use of nuclear power sources in outer space;

(iii) Near-Earth objects;

(iv) Space-system-based disaster management support;

(v) International Heliophysical Year 2007;

(*c*) Consider the following single issue/item for discussion: examination of the physical nature and technical attributes of the geostationary orbit and its utilization and applications, including in the field of space communications, as well as other questions relating to developments in space communications, taking particular account of the needs and interests of developing countries;

11. *Notes* that the Scientific and Technical Subcommittee, at its forty-fourth session, will submit its proposal to the Committee for a draft provisional agenda for the forty-fifth session of the Subcommittee, in 2008;

12. *Endorses* the recommendation of the Committee that the Committee on Space Research and the International Astronautical Federation, in liaison with member States, be invited to arrange a symposium to address the theme "The use of the equatorial orbit for space applications: challenges and opportunities", with as wide participation as possible, to be held during the first week of the forty-fourth session of the Scientific and Technical Subcommittee;

13. *Agrees* that, in the context of paragraphs 10 (*a*) (ii) and (iii) and 11 above, the Scientific and Technical Subcommittee, at its forty-fourth session, should reconvene the Working Group of the Whole;

14. *Also agrees* that, in the context of paragraph 10 (*b*) (i) above, the Scientific and Technical Subcommittee could, at any time during its forty-fourth session, reconvene its Working Group on Space Debris to consider comments resulting from the referral of the guidelines to the national level and any further developments, particularly the relationship between the revised draft of the space debris mitigation guidelines and nuclear power sources in outer space;[13]

15. *Further agrees* that, in the context of paragraph 10 (*b*) (ii) above, the Scientific and Technical Subcommittee, at its forty-fourth session, should reconvene its Working Group on the Use of Nuclear Power Sources in Outer Space and that the Working Group should continue its intersessional work on the topics described in the multi-year workplan as amended by the Subcommittee at its forty-second session and as agreed by the Subcommittee at its forty-third session and the Committee at its forty-ninth session;[14]

16. *Agrees* that, in the context of paragraph 10 (*b*) (iii) above, the Scientific and Technical Subcommittee, at its forty-fourth session, should establish, for one year, a working group on near-Earth objects, in accordance with the workplan under this item;[15]

17. *Endorses* the United Nations Programme on Space Applications for 2007, as proposed to the Committee by the Expert on Space Applications and endorsed by the Committee;[16]

18. *Notes with satisfaction* that, in accordance with paragraph 30 of General Assembly resolution 50/27 of 6 December 1995, the African regional centres for space science and technology education, in the French language and in the English language, located in Morocco and Nigeria, respectively, as well as the Centre for Space Science and Technology Education in Asia and the Pacific and the Regional Centre for Space Science and Technology Education for Latin America and the Caribbean, entered into an affiliation agreement with the Office for Outer Space Affairs and have continued their education programmes in 2006;

19. *Agrees* that the regional centres referred to in paragraph 18 above should continue to report to the Committee on their activities on an annual basis;

20. *Notes with satisfaction* the contribution being made by the Scientific and Technical Subcommittee and the efforts of Member States and the Office for Outer Space Affairs to promote and support the activities being organized within the framework of the International Heliophysical Year 2007;

21. *Also notes with satisfaction* that the African Leadership Conference on Space Science and Technology for Sustainable Development, the first of which was hosted by the Government of Nigeria in collaboration with the Governments of Algeria and South Africa from 23 to 25 November 2005, will be held on a biennial basis;

22. *Notes with appreciation* that the Fifth Space Conference of the Americas was held in Quito from 24 to 28 July 2006 under the auspices of the Office for Outer Space Affairs, the European Space Agency and the United Nations Educational, Scientific and Cultural Organization, and that the Government of Chile held a preparatory meeting for that Conference on 28 and 29 March 2006, with support from the Government of Colombia; notes that the theme of the Fifth Conference was "Regional space cooperation for security and human development" and that its results were set out in the Declaration of San Francisco de Quito and in the Plan of Action of the Conference; notes also that Ecuador will serve as secretariat pro tempore of the Conference for a period of three years, during which it will be responsible for the implementation of the recommended activities and programmes, for which purpose it will work in cooperation with the international group of experts; and notes further that the Sixth Space Conference of the Americas will be held in Guatemala in 2009;

23. *Notes with satisfaction* that the Convention on the Establishment of the Asia-Pacific Space Cooperation Organization was opened for signature in Beijing on 28 October 2005,

that as at 1 June 2006 the Convention had been signed by nine States and that once the Convention has been ratified by five States, it will enter into force, thereby establishing the organization, with its headquarters in Beijing;

24. *Considers* that it is essential that Member States pay more attention to the problem of collisions of space objects, including those with nuclear power sources, with space debris, and other aspects of space debris, calls for the continuation of national research on this question, for the development of improved technology for the monitoring of space debris and for the compilation and dissemination of data on space debris, also considers that, to the extent possible, information thereon should be provided to the Scientific and Technical Subcommittee, and agrees that international cooperation is needed to expand appropriate and affordable strategies to minimize the impact of space debris on future space missions;

25. *Urges* all States, in particular those with major space capabilities, to contribute actively to the goal of preventing an arms race in outer space as an essential condition for the promotion of international cooperation in the exploration and use of outer space for peaceful purposes;

26. *Emphasizes* the need to increase the benefits of space technology and its applications and to contribute to an orderly growth of space activities favourable to sustained economic growth and sustainable development in all countries, including mitigation of the consequences of disasters, in particular in the developing countries;

27. *Notes* that space science and technology and their applications could make important contributions to economic, social and cultural development and welfare, as indicated in the resolution entitled "The Space Millennium: Vienna Declaration on Space and Human Development";[2]

28. *Reiterates* that the benefits of space technology and its applications should be prominently brought to the attention, in particular, of the major United Nations conferences and summits for economic, social and cultural development and related fields and that the use of space technology should be promoted towards achieving the objectives of those conferences and summits and for implementing the United Nations Millennium Declaration;[3]

29. *Takes note* of the report of the Secretary-General on the inclusion of the issue of the use of space technology in the reports submitted by the Secretary-General to major United Nations conferences and summits for economic, social and cultural development, and its inclusion in the outcomes and commitments of those conferences and summits;[17]

30. *Notes with satisfaction* the increased efforts of the Committee and its Scientific and Technical Subcommittee as well as the Office for Outer Space Affairs and the Inter-Agency Meeting on Outer Space Activities to promote the use of space science and technology and their applications in carrying out actions recommended in the Plan of Implementation of the World Summit on Sustainable Development ("Johannesburg Plan of Implementation");[18]

31. *Urges* entities of the United Nations system, particularly those participating in the Inter-Agency Meeting on Outer Space Activities, to examine, in cooperation with the Committee, how space science and technology and their applications could contribute to implementing the United Nations Millennium Declaration, particularly in the areas relating to, inter alia, food security and increasing opportunities for education;

32. *Invites* the Inter-Agency Meeting on Outer Space Activities to continue to contribute to the work of the Committee and to report to the Committee and its Scientific and Technical Subcommittee on the work conducted at its annual sessions;

33. *Notes with satisfaction* that the open informal meetings, held in conjunction with the annual sessions of the Inter-Agency Meeting on Outer Space Activities and in which representatives of member States and observers in the Committee participate, provide a constructive mechanism for an active dialogue between the entities of the United Nations system and member States and observers in the Committee;

34. *Encourages* entities of the United Nations system to participate fully in the work of the Inter-Agency Meeting on Outer Space Activities;

35. *Notes* that space technology could play a central role in disaster reduction;

36. *Requests* the Committee to continue to consider, as a matter of priority, ways and means of maintaining outer space for peaceful purposes and to report thereon to the General Assembly at its sixty-second session, and agrees that during its consideration of the matter, the Committee could continue to consider ways to promote regional and interregional cooperation based on experiences stemming from the Space Conference of the Americas, the African Leadership Conference on Space Science and Technology for Sustainable Development and the role space technology could play in the implementation of recommendations of the World Summit on Sustainable Development;

37. *Notes with satisfaction* that the Committee established a closer link between its work to implement the recommendations of UNISPACE III and the work of the Commission on Sustainable Development by contributing to the thematic areas that are addressed by the Commission;

38. *Agrees* that the Director of the Division for Sustainable Development of the Department of Economic and Social Affairs of the Secretariat should be invited to participate in the sessions of the Committee to inform it how it could best contribute to the work of the Commission on Sustainable Development and that the Director of the Office for Outer Space Affairs should participate in the sessions of the Commission to raise awareness and promote the benefits of space science and technology for sustainable development;

39. *Notes with appreciation* that the International Committee on Global Navigation Satellite Systems was established on a voluntary basis as an informal body to promote cooperation, as appropriate, on matters of mutual interest related to civil satellite-based positioning, navigation, timing and value-added services, as well as the compatibility and interoperability of global navigation satellite systems, while increasing their use to support sustainable development, particularly in developing countries;

40. *Notes* the fact that the Office for Outer Space Affairs could integrate into its programme of work a number of actions identified for implementation by the Office in the Plan of Action of the Committee on the Peaceful Uses of Outer Space for the further implementation of the recommendations of UNISPACE III[19] and that some of those actions could be integrated into its programme of work only if additional staff and financial resources were provided;[20]

41. *Urges* all Member States to contribute to the Trust Fund for the United Nations Programme on Space Applications to enhance the capacity of the Office for Outer Space

Affairs to provide technical and legal advisory services and initiate pilot projects in accordance with the Plan of Action of the Committee, while maintaining the priority thematic areas agreed by the Committee;

42. *Agrees* that the Committee should continue to consider a report on the activities of the International Satellite System for Search and Rescue as a part of its consideration of the United Nations Programme on Space Applications under the agenda item entitled "Report of the Scientific and Technical Subcommittee" and invites Member States to report on their activities regarding the System;

43. *Requests* the Committee to continue to consider, at its fiftieth session, its agenda item entitled "Spin-off benefits of space technology: review of current status";

44. *Also requests* the Committee, in view of the importance of space and education, to continue to consider, at its fiftieth session, under its agenda item entitled "Space and society", the special theme for the focus of discussions for the period 2004–2006 "Space and education", in accordance with the workplan adopted by the Committee;[21]

45. *Agrees* that the Committee should continue to consider, at its fiftieth session, its agenda item entitled "Space and water";

46. *Also agrees* that a symposium on space and water should be held during the fiftieth session of the Committee;

47. *Notes with satisfaction* that the Committee agreed to consider, at its fiftieth session, under its agenda item entitled "Other matters", the issue of the future role and activities of the Committee and noted that the Chairman of the Committee could conduct intersessional, open-ended informal consultations with a view to presenting to the Committee a list of elements that could be taken into consideration at its next session;

48. *Agrees* to include in the agenda of the fiftieth session of the Committee a new item, entitled "International cooperation in promoting the use of space-derived geospatial data for sustainable development", under a multi-year workplan;[22]

49. *Also agrees* that a panel on space exploration activities, including the participation of the private sector, should be convened during the fiftieth session of the Committee;

50. *Notes with satisfaction* that in accordance with the agreement reached by the Committee at its forty-sixth session on the measures relating to the future composition of the bureaux of the Committee and its subsidiary bodies,[23] on the basis of the measures relating to the working methods of the Committee and its subsidiary bodies,[24] the Group of African States, the Group of Asian States, the Group of Eastern European States, the Group of Latin American and Caribbean States and the Group of Western European and Other States have nominated their candidates for the offices of Chair of the Scientific and Technical Subcommittee, First Vice-Chair of the Committee, Chair of the Legal Subcommittee, Chair of the Committee and Second Vice-Chairman/Rapporteur of the Committee, respectively, for the period 2008–2009;

51. *Endorses* the composition of the bureaux of the Committee and its subsidiary bodies for the period 2008–2009, as reflected in paragraph 50 above, and agrees that the Committee and its Subcommittees should elect their officers at their respective sessions in 2008 in accordance with that composition;

52. *Notes* that each of the regional groups has the responsibility to actively promote the participation in the work of the Committee and its subsidiary bodies of the member States of the Committee that are also members of the respective regional groups, and agrees that the regional groups should consider this Committee-related matter among their members;

53. *Requests* entities of the United Nations system and other international organizations to continue and, where appropriate, to enhance their cooperation with the Committee and to provide it with reports on the issues dealt with in the work of the Committee and its subsidiary bodies.

79th plenary meeting
14 December 2006

---

[1] Resolution 2222 (XXI), annex.

[2] See *Report of the Third United Nations Conference on the Exploration and Peaceful Uses of Outer Space, Vienna, 19-30 July 1999* (United Nations publication, Sales No. E.00.I.3), chap. I, resolution 1.

[3] See resolution 55/2.

[4] A/59/174, chap. VI.B.

[5] See resolution 60/1, para. 60.

[6] *Official Records of the General Assembly, Sixty-first Session, Supplement No. 20* (A/61/20).

[7] Treaty on Principles Governing the Activities of States in the Exploration and Use of Outer Space, including the Moon and Other Celestial Bodies (resolution 2222 (XXI), annex); Agreement on the Rescue of Astronauts, the Return of Astronauts and the Return of Objects Launched into Outer Space (resolution 2345 (XXII), annex); Convention on International Liability for Damage Caused by Space Objects (resolution 2777 (XXVI), annex); Convention on Registration of Objects Launched into Outer Space (resolution 3235 (XXIX), annex); and Agreement Governing the Activities of States on the Moon and Other Celestial Bodies (resolution 34/68, annex).

[8] See *Official Records of the General Assembly, Sixty-first Session, Supplement No. 20* (A/61/20), chap. II.D.

[9] See resolution 47/68.

[10] See *Official Records of the General Assembly, Fifty-eighth Session, Supplement No. 20* (A/58/20), para. 199.

[11] Ibid., *Sixty-first Session, Supplement No. 20* (A/61/20), chap. II.C.

[12] See A/AC.105/848, annex II, para. 6, for item (i); ibid., annex III, para. 8, for item (ii); ibid., annex I, para. 20, and A/AC.105/869, annex I, para. 22, for item (iii); A/AC.105/823, annex II, para. 15, and A/AC.105/848, annex I, para. 21, for item (iv); and A/AC.105/848, annex I, para. 22, for item (v).

[13] See A/AC.105/869, para. 101, and annex II, para. 8.

[14] See A/AC.105/848, annex III, para. 8; A/AC.105/869, annex III; and *Official Records of the General Assembly, Sixty-first Session, Supplement No. 20* (A/61/20), paras. 139–141.

[15] See *Official Records of the General Assembly, Sixty-first Session, Supplement No. 20* (A/61/20), para. 178.

[16] Ibid., paras. 81 and 87; see also A/AC.105/861, sects. II and III and annex III.

[17] A/61/495.

[18] *Report of the World Summit on Sustainable Development, Johannesburg, South Africa, 26 August–4 September 2002* (United Nations publication, Sales No. E.03.II.A.1 and corrigendum), chap. I, resolution 2, annex.

[19] See A/AC.105/L.262.

[20] Ibid., annex, para. 6.

[21] *Official Records of the General Assembly, Fifty-eighth Session, Supplement No. 20* (A/58/20), para. 239; and ibid., *Sixty-first Session, Supplement No. 20* (A/61/20), paras. 245 and 260.

[22] Ibid., *Sixty-first Session, Supplement No. 20* (A/61/20), paras. 301–303.

[23] Ibid., *Fifty-eighth Session, Supplement No. 20* (A/58/20), annex II, paras. 4–9.

[24] Ibid., *Fifty-second Session, Supplement No. 20* (A/52/20), annex I; see also *Official Records of the General Assembly, Fifty-eighth Session, Supplement No. 20* (A/58/20), annex II, appendix III.

Resolution 61/112

[on the report of the Special Political and Decolonization Committee (Fourth Committee) (A/61/407)]

61/112. Assistance to Palestine refugees

The General Assembly,

Recalling its resolution 194 (III) of 11 December 1948 and all its subsequent resolutions on the question, including resolution 60/100 of 8 December 2005,

Recalling also its resolution 302 (IV) of 8 December 1949, by which, inter alia, it established the United Nations Relief and Works Agency for Palestine Refugees in the Near East,

Recalling further relevant Security Council resolutions,

Aware of the fact that, for more than five decades, the Palestine refugees have suffered from the loss of their homes, lands and means of livelihood,

Affirming the imperative of resolving the problem of the Palestine refugees for the achievement of justice and for the achievement of lasting peace in the region,

Acknowledging the essential role that the United Nations Relief and Works Agency for Palestine Refugees in the Near East has played for more than fifty-six years since its establishment in ameliorating the plight of the Palestine refugees in the fields of education, health and relief and social services,

Taking note of the report of the Commissioner-General of the United Nations Relief and Works Agency for Palestine Refugees in the Near East covering the period from 1 January to 31 December 2005,[1]

Aware of the continuing needs of the Palestine refugees throughout all the fields of operation, namely, Jordan, Lebanon, the Syrian Arab Republic and the Occupied Palestinian Territory,

Expressing grave concern at the especially difficult situation of the Palestine refugees under occupation, including with regard to their safety, well-being and living conditions,

Noting the signing of the Declaration of Principles on Interim Self-Government Arrangements on 13 September 1993 by the Government of Israel and the Palestine Liberation Organization[2] and the subsequent implementation agreements,

Aware of the important role to be played in the peace process by the Multilateral Working Group on Refugees of the Middle East peace process,

1. *Notes with regret* that repatriation or compensation of the refugees, as provided for in paragraph 11 of General Assembly resolution 194 (III), has not yet been effected, that, therefore, the situation of the Palestine refugees continues to be a matter of grave concern

and that the Palestine refugees continue to require assistance to meet basic health, education and living needs;

2. *Also notes with regret* that the United Nations Conciliation Commission for Palestine has been unable to find a means of achieving progress in the implementation of paragraph 11 of General Assembly resolution 194 (III), and reiterates its request to the Conciliation Commission to exert continued efforts towards the implementation of that paragraph and to report to the Assembly as appropriate, but no later than 1 September 2007;

3. *Affirms* the necessity for the continuation of the work of the United Nations Relief and Works Agency for Palestine Refugees in the Near East and the importance of its unimpeded operation and its provision of services for the wellbeing of the Palestine refugees and for the stability of the region, pending the just resolution of the question of the Palestine refugees;

4. *Calls upon* all donors to continue to make the most generous efforts possible to meet the anticipated needs of the Agency, including with regard to increased expenditures arising from the deteriorating socio-economic and humanitarian situation in the region, particularly in the Occupied Palestinian Territory, and those mentioned in recent emergency appeals.

79th plenary meeting
14 December 2006

[1] *Official Records of the General Assembly, Sixty-first Session, Supplement No. 13* (A/61/13).

[2] A/48/486-S/26560, annex.

Resolution 61/113

[on the report of the Special Political and Decolonization Committee (Fourth Committee) (A/61/407)]

61/113. Persons displaced as a result of the June 1967 and subsequent hostilities

The General Assembly,

Recalling its resolutions 2252 (ES-V) of 4 July 1967, 2341 B (XXII) of 19 December 1967 and all subsequent related resolutions,

Recalling also Security Council resolutions 237 (1967) of 14 June 1967 and 259 (1968) of 27 September 1968,

Taking note of the report of the Secretary-General submitted in pursuance of its resolution 60/101 of 8 December 2005,[1]

Taking note also of the report of the Commissioner-General of the United Nations Relief and Works Agency for Palestine Refugees in the Near East covering the period from 1 January to 31 December 2005,[2]

Concerned about the continuing human suffering resulting from the June 1967 and subsequent hostilities,

Taking note of the relevant provisions of the Declaration of Principles on Interim Self-Government Arrangements of 13 September 1993[3] with regard to the modalities for the admission of persons displaced in 1967, and concerned that the process agreed upon has not yet been effected,

1. *Reaffirms* the right of all persons displaced as a result of the June 1967 and subsequent hostilities to return to their homes or former places of residence in the territories occupied by Israel since 1967;

2. *Expresses deep concern* that the mechanism agreed upon by the parties in article XII of the Declaration of Principles on Interim Self-Government Arrangements of 13 September 1993[3] on the return of displaced persons has not been complied with, and stresses the necessity for an accelerated return of displaced persons;

3. *Endorses*, in the meanwhile, the efforts of the Commissioner-General of the United Nations Relief and Works Agency for Palestine Refugees in the Near East to continue to provide humanitarian assistance, as far as practicable, on an emergency basis, and as a temporary measure, to persons in the area who are currently displaced and in serious need of continued assistance as a result of the June 1967 and subsequent hostilities;

4. *Strongly appeals* to all Governments and to organizations and individuals to contribute generously to the Agency and to the other intergovernmental and non-governmental organizations concerned for the above-mentioned purposes;

5. *Requests* the Secretary-General, after consulting with the Commissioner-General, to report to the General Assembly before its sixty-second session on the progress made with regard to the implementation of the present resolution.

79th plenary meeting
14 December 2006

---

[1] A/61/358.

[2] *Official Records of the General Assembly, Sixty-first Session, Supplement No. 13* (A/61/13).

[3] A/48/486-S/26560, annex.

Resolution 61/114

[on the report of the Special Political and Decolonization Committee (Fourth Committee) (A/61/407)]

61/114. Operations of the United Nations Relief and Works Agency for Palestine Refugees in the Near East

The General Assembly,

Recalling its resolutions 194 (III) of 11 December 1948, 212 (III) of 19 November 1948, 302 (IV) of 8 December 1949 and all subsequent related resolutions, including its resolution 60/102 of 8 December 2005,

Recalling also the relevant Security Council resolutions,

Having considered the report of the Commissioner-General of the United Nations Relief and Works Agency for Palestine Refugees in the Near East covering the period from 1 January to 31 December 2005,[1]

Taking note of the letter dated 28 September 2006 from the Chairperson of the Advisory Commission of the United Nations Relief and Works Agency for Palestine Refugees in the Near East addressed to the Commissioner-General,[2]

Deeply concerned about the critical financial situation of the Agency, as well as about the rising expenditures of the Agency resulting from the deterioration of the socio-economic and humanitarian conditions in the region and their significant negative impact on the provision of necessary Agency services to the Palestine refugees, including its emergency-related and development programmes,

Recalling Articles 100, 104 and 105 of the Charter of the United Nations and the Convention on the Privileges and Immunities of the United Nations,[3]

Recalling also the Convention on the Safety of United Nations and Associated Personnel,[4]

Affirming the applicability of the Geneva Convention relative to the Protection of Civilian Persons in Time of War, of 12 August 1949,[5] to the Palestinian territory occupied since 1967, including East Jerusalem,

Aware of the continuing needs of the Palestine refugees throughout the Occupied Palestinian Territory and in the other fields of operation, namely Jordan, Lebanon and the Syrian Arab Republic,

Gravely concerned about the extremely difficult living conditions being faced by the Palestine refugees in the Occupied Palestinian Territory, including East Jerusalem, particularly in the refugee camps in the Gaza Strip, resulting, inter alia, from the loss of life and injury, the extensive destruction of their shelters, properties and vital infrastructure and the displacement of the Palestine refugees,

Aware of the extraordinary efforts being undertaken by the Agency for the repair or rebuilding of thousands of damaged or destroyed refugee shelters and for the provision of shelter for those refugee families internally displaced as a result of recent Israeli military actions,

Aware also of the valuable work done by the refugee affairs officers of the Agency in providing protection to the Palestinian people, in particular Palestine refugees,

Gravely concerned about the endangerment of the safety of the Agency's staff and about the damage caused to the facilities of the Agency as a result of Israeli military operations during the reporting period,

Deploring the killing of fourteen Agency staff members by the Israeli occupying forces in the Occupied Palestinian Territory since September 2000 and of one Agency staff member by the Israeli air force in Lebanon in August 2006,

Deploring also the killing and wounding of refugee children, including in the Agency's schools, by the Israeli occupying forces,

Expressing deep concern about the policies of closure and severe restrictions that continue to be imposed on the movement of persons and goods throughout the Occupied Palestinian Territory, including East Jerusalem, as well as the continued construction of the wall, contrary to international law, in the Occupied Palestinian Territory, including in and around East Jerusalem, which have had a grave impact on the socio-economic situation of the

Palestine refugees and have greatly contributed to the dire humanitarian crisis facing the Palestinian people,

Deeply concerned about the continuing imposition of restrictions on the freedom of movement of the Agency's staff, vehicles and goods, and the harassment and intimidation of the Agency's staff, which undermine and obstruct the work of the Agency, including its ability to provide its essential basic and emergency services,

Recalling the signing, on 13 September 1993, of the Declaration of Principles on Interim Self-Government Arrangements by the Government of Israel and the Palestine Liberation Organization[6] and the subsequent implementation agreements,

Aware of the agreement between the Agency and the Government of Israel,

Taking note of the agreement reached on 24 June 1994, embodied in an exchange of letters between the Agency and the Palestine Liberation Organization,[7]

Recalling the Geneva Conference convened by the United Nations Relief and Works Agency for Palestine Refugees in the Near East and the Swiss Agency for Development and Cooperation on 7 and 8 June 2004 to increase support for the United Nations Relief and Works Agency,

1. *Expresses its appreciation* to the Commissioner-General of the United Nations Relief and Works Agency for Palestine Refugees in the Near East, as well as to all of the staff of the Agency, for their tireless efforts and valuable work, particularly in the light of the difficult conditions during the past year;

2. *Also expresses its appreciation* to the Advisory Commission of the Agency, and requests it to continue its efforts and to keep the General Assembly informed of its activities;

3. *Takes note with appreciation* of the report of the Working Group on the Financing of the United Nations Relief and Works Agency for Palestine Refugees in the Near East[8] and the efforts of the Working Group to assist in ensuring the financial security of the Agency, and requests the Secretary-General to provide the necessary services and assistance to the Working Group for the conduct of its work;

4. *Commends* the continuing efforts of the Commissioner-General to increase the budgetary transparency and efficiency of the Agency, as reflected in the Agency's programme budget for the biennium 2006–2007;[9]

5. *Also commends* the organizational reform measures taken by the Agency to modernize and strengthen its management aimed at enhancing its ability to address the needs of the Palestine refugees;

6. *Endorses*, meanwhile, the efforts of the Commissioner-General to continue to provide humanitarian assistance, as far as practicable, on an emergency basis, and as a temporary measure, to persons in the area who are internally displaced and in serious need of continued assistance as a result of recent incursions in the Occupied Palestinian Territory and hostilities in Lebanon;

7. *Acknowledges* the important support provided by the host Governments to the Agency in the discharge of its duties;

8. *Encourages* the Agency's further consideration of the needs and rights of children in its operations in accordance with the Convention on the Rights of the Child;[10]

9. *Expresses concern* about the temporary relocation of the international staff of the Agency from its headquarters in Gaza City and the disruption of operations at the headquarters;

10. *Calls upon* Israel, the occupying Power, to comply fully with the provisions of the Geneva Convention relative to the Protection of Civilian Persons in Time of War, of 12 August 1949;[5]

11. *Also calls upon* Israel to abide by Articles 100, 104 and 105 of the Charter of the United Nations and the Convention on the Privileges and Immunities of the United Nations[3] in order to ensure the safety of the personnel of the Agency, the protection of its institutions and the safeguarding of the security of its facilities in the Occupied Palestinian Territory, including East Jerusalem;

12. *Urges* the Government of Israel to speedily compensate the Agency for damage to its property and facilities resulting from actions by the Israeli side and to expeditiously reimburse the Agency for port and related charges, including storage, demurrage and transit charges, incurred by the Agency and other financial losses sustained by the Agency as a result of delays and restrictions on movement and access imposed by Israel;

13. *Calls upon* Israel particularly to cease obstructing the movement of the staff, vehicles and supplies of the Agency and to cease the levying of extra fees and charges, which affect the Agency's operations detrimentally;

14. *Requests* the Commissioner-General to proceed with the issuance of identification cards for Palestine refugees and their descendants in the Occupied Palestinian Territory;

15. *Affirms* that the functioning of the Agency remains essential in all the fields of operation;

16. *Notes* the success of the Agency's microfinance and microenterprise programmes, and calls upon the Agency, in close cooperation with the relevant agencies, to continue to contribute to the development of the economic and social stability of the Palestine refugees in all the fields of operation;

17. *Reiterates its request* to the Commissioner-General to proceed with the modernization of the archives of the Agency through the Palestine Refugee Records Project, and to indicate progress in her report to the General Assembly at its sixty-second session;

18. *Reiterates its previous appeals* to all States, specialized agencies and non-governmental organizations to continue and to augment the special allocations for grants and scholarships for higher education to Palestine refugees in addition to their contributions to the regular budget of the Agency and to contribute to the establishment of vocational training centres for Palestine refugees, and requests the Agency to act as the recipient and trustee for the special allocations for grants and scholarships;

19. *Urges* all States, specialized agencies and non-governmental organizations to continue and to increase their contributions to the Agency so as to ease the ongoing financial constraints, exacerbated by the current humanitarian situation on the ground that has resulted in rising expenditures, in particular with regard to emergency services, and to support the

Agency's valuable and necessary work in assisting the Palestine refugees in all fields of operation.

79th plenary meeting
14 December 2006

[1] *Official Records of the General Assembly, Sixty-first Session, Supplement No. 13* (A/61/13).

[2] Ibid., p. viii.

[3] Resolution 22 A (I).

[4] United Nations, *Treaty Series*, vol. 2051, No. 35457.

[5] Ibid., vol. 75, No. 973.

[6] A/48/486-S/26560, annex.

[7] *Official Records of the General Assembly, Forty-ninth Session, Supplement No. 13* (A/49/13), annex I.

[8] A/61/347.

[9] *Official Records of the General Assembly, Sixtieth Session, Supplement No. 13 A* (A/60/13/Add.1).

[10] United Nations, *Treaty Series*, vol. 1577, No. 27531.

Resolution 61/115

[on the report of the Special Political and Decolonization Committee (Fourth Committee) (A/61/407)]

61/115. Palestine refugees' properties and their revenues

The General Assembly,

Recalling its resolutions 194 (III) of 11 December 1948 and 36/146 C of 16 December 1981 and all its subsequent resolutions on the question,

Taking note of the report of the Secretary-General submitted in pursuance of resolution 60/103 of 8 December 2005,[1]

Taking note also of the report of the United Nations Conciliation Commission for Palestine for the period from 1 September 2005 to 31 August 2006,[2]

Recalling that the Universal Declaration of Human Rights[3] and the principles of international law uphold the principle that no one shall be arbitrarily deprived of his or her property,

Recalling in particular its resolution 394 (V) of 14 December 1950, in which it directed the Conciliation Commission, in consultation with the parties concerned, to prescribe measures for the protection of the rights, property and interests of the Palestine refugees,

Noting the completion of the programme of identification and evaluation of Arab property, as announced by the Conciliation Commission in its twenty-second progress report,[4] and the fact that the Land Office had a schedule of Arab owners and a file of documents defining the location, area and other particulars of Arab property,

Expressing its appreciation for the work done to preserve and modernize the existing records, including the land records, of the Conciliation Commission and the importance of such records for a just resolution of the plight of the Palestine refugees in conformity with resolution 194 (III),

Recalling that, in the framework of the Middle East peace process, the Palestine Liberation Organization and the Government of Israel agreed, in the Declaraion of Principles on Interim Self-Government Arrangements of 13 September 1993,[5] to commence negotiations on permanent status issues, including the important issue of the refugees,

1. *Reaffirms* that the Palestine refugees are entitled to their property and to the income derived therefrom, in conformity with the principles of equity and justice;

2. *Requests* the Secretary-General to take all appropriate steps, in consultation with the United Nations Conciliation Commission for Palestine, for the protection of Arab property, assets and property rights in Israel;

3. *Calls once again upon* Israel to render all facilities and assistance to the Secretary-General in the implementation of the present resolution;

4. *Calls upon* all the parties concerned to provide the Secretary-General with any pertinent information in their possession concerning Arab property, assets and property rights in Israel that would assist him in the implementation of the present resolution;

5. *Urges* the Palestinian and Israeli sides, as agreed between them, to deal with the important issue of Palestine refugees' properties and their revenues within the framework of the final status negotiations of the Middle East peace process;

6. *Requests* the Secretary-General to report to the General Assembly at its sixty-second session on the implementation of the present resolution.

79th plenary meeting
14 December 2006

---

1 A/61/278.

2 See A/61/172.

3 Resolution 217 A (III).

4 *Official Records of the General Assembly, Nineteenth Session, Annexes*, Annex No. 11, document A/5700.

5 A/48/486-S/26560, annex.

Resolution 61/116

[on the report of the Special Political and Decolonization Committee (Fourth Committee) (A/61/408)]

61/116. Work of the Special Committee to Investigate Israeli Practices Affecting the Human Rights of the Palestinian People and Other Arabs of the Occupied Territories

The General Assembly,

Guided by the purposes and principles of the Charter of the United Nations,

Guided also by international humanitarian law, in particular the Geneva Convention relative to the Protection of Civilian Persons in Time of War, of 12 August 1949,[1] as well as international standards of human rights, in particular the Universal Declaration of Human Rights[2] and the International Covenants on Human Rights,[3]

Recalling its relevant resolutions, including resolutions 2443 (XXIII) of 19 December 1968 and 60/104 of 8 December 2005, and the relevant resolutions of the Commission on Human Rights and the Human Rights Council,

Recalling also the relevant resolutions of the Security Council,

Taking into account the advisory opinion rendered on 9 July 2004 by the International Court of Justice on the *Legal Consequences of the Construction of a Wall in the Occupied Palestinian Territory*,[4] and recalling in this regard General Assembly resolution ES-10/15 of 20 July 2004,

Convinced that occupation itself represents a gross and grave violation of human rights,

Gravely concerned about the continuing detrimental impact of the events that have taken place since 28 September 2000, including the excessive use of force by the Israeli occupying forces against Palestinian civilians, resulting in thousands of deaths and injuries, the widespread destruction of property and vital infrastructure and the internal displacement of civilians,

Having considered the report of the Special Committee to Investigate Israeli Practices Affecting the Human Rights of the Palestinian People and Other Arabs of the Occupied Territories[5] and the relevant reports of the Secretary-General,[6]

Recalling the Declaration of Principles on Interim Self-Government Arrangements of 13 September 1993[7] and the subsequent implementation agreements between the Palestinian and Israeli sides,

Welcoming the free and democratic Palestinian Legislative Council elections that took place on 25 January 2006 and welcoming also the efforts to form a national unity government working towards a peaceful resolution of the Israeli-Palestinian conflict, based on relevant United Nations resolutions and the agreements concluded between the two sides,

Expressing the hope that the Israeli occupation will be brought to an early and complete end and that therefore the violation of the human rights of the Palestinian people will cease, and recalling in this regard its resolution 58/292 of 6 May 2004,

1. *Commends* the Special Committee to Investigate Israeli Practices Affecting the Human Rights of the Palestinian People and Other Arabs of the Occupied Territories for its efforts in performing the tasks assigned to it by the General Assembly and for its impartiality;

2. *Reiterates its demand* that Israel, the occupying Power, cooperate, in line with its obligations as a State Member of the United Nations, with the Special Committee in implementing its mandate;

3. *Deplores* those policies and practices of Israel that violate the human rights of the Palestinian people and other Arabs of the occupied territories, as reflected in the report of the Special Committee covering the reporting period;[5]

4. *Expresses grave concern* about the critical situation in the Occupied Palestinian Territory, including East Jerusalem, since 28 September 2000, as a result of unlawful Israeli practices and measures, and especially condemns all Israeli settlement activities and the construction of the wall, as well as the excessive and indiscriminate use of force against the civilian population, including extrajudicial executions;

5. *Welcomes* the free and democratic Palestinian Legislative Council elections that took place on 25 January 2006 and welcomes also the efforts to form a national unity government

working towards a peaceful resolution of the Israeli-Palestinian conflict, based on relevant United Nations resolutions and the agreements concluded between the two sides;

6. *Requests* the Special Committee, pending complete termination of the Israeli occupation, to continue to investigate Israeli policies and practices in the Occupied Palestinian Territory, including East Jerusalem, and other Arab territories occupied by Israel since 1967, especially Israeli violations of the Geneva Convention relative to the Protection of Civilian Persons in Time of War, of 12 August 1949,[1] and to consult, as appropriate, with the International Committee of the Red Cross according to its regulations in order to ensure that the welfare and human rights of the peoples of the occupied territories are safeguarded and to report to the Secretary-General as soon as possible and whenever the need arises thereafter;

7. *Also requests* the Special Committee to submit regularly to the Secretary-General periodic reports on the current situation in the Occupied Palestinian Territory, including East Jerusalem;

8. *Further requests* the Special Committee to continue to investigate the treatment of the thousands of prisoners and detainees in the Occupied Palestinian Territory, including East Jerusalem, and other Arab territories occupied by Israel since 1967;

9. *Requests* the Secretary-General:

(*a*) To provide the Special Committee with all necessary facilities, including those required for its visits to the occupied territories, so that it may investigate Israeli policies and practices referred to in the present resolution;

(*b*) To continue to make available such staff as may be necessary to assist the Special Committee in the performance of its tasks;

(*c*) To circulate regularly to Member States the periodic reports mentioned in paragraph 7 above;

(*d*) To ensure the widest circulation of the reports of the Special Committee and of information regarding its activities and findings, by all means available, through the Department of Public Information of the Secretariat and, where necessary, to reprint those reports of the Special Committee that are no longer available;

(*e*) To report to the General Assembly at its sixty-second session on the tasks entrusted to him in the present resolution;

10. *Decides* to include in the provisional agenda of its sixty-second session the item entitled "Report of the Special Committee to Investigate Israeli Practices Affecting the Human Rights of the Palestinian People and Other Arabs of the Occupied Territories".

79th plenary meeting
14 December 2006

---

[1] United Nations, *Treaty Series*, vol. 75, No. 973.

[2] Resolution 217 A (III).

[3] See resolution 2200 A (XXI), annex.

[4] See A/ES-10/273 and Corr.1.

[5] See A/61/500.

[6] A/61/327-331.

[7] A/48/486-S/26560, annex.

Resolution 61/117

[on the report of the Special Political and Decolonization Committee (Fourth Committee) (A/61/408)]

61/117. Applicability of the Geneva Convention relative to the Protection of Civilian Persons in Time of War, of 12 August 1949, to the Occupied Palestinian Territory, including East Jerusalem, and the other occupied Arab territories

The General Assembly,

Recalling its relevant resolutions, including its resolution 60/105 of 8 December 2005,

Recalling also its resolution ES-10/15 of 20 July 2004,

Bearing in mind the relevant resolutions of the Security Council,

Recalling the Regulations annexed to the Hague Convention IV of 1907,[1] the Geneva Convention relative to the Protection of Civilian Persons in Time of War, of 12 August 1949,[2] and relevant provisions of customary law, including those codified in Additional Protocol I,[3] to the four Geneva Conventions,[4]

Having considered the report of the Special Committee to Investigate Israeli Practices Affecting the Human Rights of the Palestinian People and Other Arabs of the Occupied Territories[5] and the relevant reports of the Secretary-General,[6]

Considering that the promotion of respect for the obligations arising from the Charter of the United Nations and other instruments and rules of international law is among the basic purposes and principles of the United Nations,

Recalling the advisory opinion rendered on 9 July 2004 by the International Court of Justice,[7] and also recalling General Assebly resolution ES-10/15,

Noting in particular the Court's reply, including that the Fourth Geneva Convention[2] is applicable in the Occupied Palestinian Territory, including East Jerusalem, and that Israel is in breach of several of the provisions of the Convention,

Noting the convening, on 15 July 1999, of a Conference of High Contracting Parties to the Fourth Geneva Convention on measures to enforce the Convention in the Occupied Palestinian Territory, including East Jerusalem, and to ensure respect thereof in accordance with article 1 common to the four Geneva Conventions, and stressing the importance of the Declaration adopted by the reconvened Conference on 5 December 2001 and the need for the parties to follow up the implementation of the Declaration,

Welcoming and encouraging the initiatives by States parties to the Convention, both individually and collectively, according to article 1 common to the four Geneva Conventions, aimed at ensuring respect for the Convention,

Stressing that Israel, the occupying Power, should comply strictly with its obligations under international law, including international humanitarian law,

1. *Reaffirms* that the Geneva Convention relative to the Protection of Civilian Persons in Time of War, of 12 August 1949,[2] is applicable to the Occupied Palestinian Territory, including East Jerusalem, and other Arab territories occupied by Israel since 1967;

2. *Demands* that Israel accept the de jure applicability of the Convention in the Occupied Palestinian Territory, including East Jerusalem, and other Arab territories occupied by Israel since 1967, and that it comply scrupulously with the provisions of the Convention;

3. *Calls upon* all High Contracting Parties to the Convention, in accordance with article 1 common to the four Geneva Conventions[4] and as mentioned in the advisory opinion of the International Court of Justice of 9 July 2004,[7] to continue to exert all efforts to ensure respect for its provisions by Israel, the occupying Power, in the Occupied Palestinian Territory, including East Jerusalem, and other Arab territories occupied by Israel since 1967;

4. *Reiterates* the need for speedy implementation of the relevant recommendations contained in the resolutions adopted by the General Assembly at its tenth emergency special session, including resolution ES-10/15, with regard to ensuring respect by Israel, the occupying Power, for the provisions of the Convention;

5. *Requests* the Secretary-General to report to the General Assembly at its sixty-second session on the implementation of the present resolution.

79th plenary meeting
14 December 2006

---

[1] See Carnegie Endowment for International Peace, *The Hague Conventions and Declarations of 1899 and 1907* (New York, Oxford University Press, 1915).

[2] United Nations, *Treaty Series*, vol. 75, No. 973.

[3] Ibid., vol. 1125, No. 17512.

[4] Ibid., vol. 75, Nos. 970-973.

[5] See A/61/500.

[6] A/61/327-331.

[7] See A/ES-10/273 and Corr.1.

Resolution 61/118

[on the report of the Special Political and Decolonization Committee (Fourth Committee) (A/61/408)]

61/118. Israeli settlements in the Occupied Palestinian Territory, including East Jerusalem, and the occupied Syrian Golan

The General Assembly,

Guided by the principles of the Charter of the United Nations, and affirming the inadmissibility of the acquisition of territory by force,

Recalling its relevant resolutions, including resolution 60/106 of 8 December 2005, as well as those resolutions adopted at its tenth emergency special session,

Recalling also relevant Security Council resolutions, including resolutions 242 (1967) of 22 November 1967, 446 (1979) of 22 March 1979, 465 (1980) of 1 March 1980, 476 (1980) of 30 June 1980, 478 (1980) of 20 August 1980, 497 (1981) of 17 December 1981 and 904 (1994) of 18 March 1994,

Reaffirming the applicability of the Geneva Convention relative to the Protection of Civilian Persons in Time of War, of 12 August 1949,[1] to the Occupied Palestinian Territory, including East Jerusalem, and to the occupied Syrian Golan,

Considering that the transfer by the occupying Power of parts of its own civilian population into the territory it occupies constitutes a breach of the Fourth Geneva Convention[1] and relevant provisions of customary law, including those codified in Additional Protocol I[2] to the Geneva Conventions,[3]

Recalling the advisory opinion rendered on 9 July 2004 by the International Court of Justice on the *Legal Consequences of the Construction of a Wall in the Occupied Palestinian Territory*,[4] and recalling also General Assembly resolution ES-10/15 of 20 July 2004,

Noting that the International Court of Justice concluded that "the Israeli settlements in the Occupied Palestinian Territory (including East Jerusalem) have been established in breach of international law",[5]

Taking note of the recent report of the Special Rapporteur of the Human Rights Council on the situation of human rights in the Palestinian territories occupied by Israel since 1967,[6]

Recalling the Declaration of Principles on Interim Self-Government Arrangements of 13 September 1993[7] and the subsequent implementation agreements between the Palestinian and Israeli sides,

Recalling also the Quartet road map to a permanent two-State solution to the Israeli-Palestinian conflict,[8] and noting specifically its call for a freeze on all settlement activity,

Aware that Israeli settlement activities involve, inter alia, the transfer of nationals of the occupying Power into the occupied territories, the confiscation of land, the exploitation of natural resources and other illegal actions against the Palestinian civilian population,

Bearing in mind the detrimental impact of Israeli settlement policies, decisions and activities on efforts to achieve peace in the Middle East,

Expressing grave concern about the continuation by Israel, the occupying Power, of settlement activities, including in and around East Jerusalem, in violation of international humanitarian law, relevant United Nations resolutions and the agreements reached between the parties, and concerned in particular about the construction and expansion of the settlements in Jabal Abu-Ghneim and Ras Al-Amud in and around Occupied East Jerusalem and Israel's intentions to proceed with the so-called E-1 plan, aimed at connecting its illegal settlements around and further isolating Occupied East Jerusalem,

Expressing grave concern also about the continuing unlawful construction by Israel of the wall inside the Occupied Palestinian Territory, including in and around East Jerusalem, and expressing its concern in particular about the route of the wall in departure from the Armistice Line of 1949, which could prejudge future negotiations and make the two-State solution physically impossible to implement and which is causing serious humanitarian hardship and a serious decline of socioeconomic conditions for the Palestinian people,

Deeply concerned that the wall's route has been traced in such a way as to include the great majority of the Israeli settlements in the Occupied Palestinian Territory, including East Jerusalem,

Reiterating its opposition to settlement activities in the Occupied Palestinian Territory, including East Jerusalem, and in the occupied Syrian Golan and to any activities involving the confiscation of land, the disruption of the livelihood of protected persons and the de facto annexation of land,

Recalling the need to end all acts of violence, including acts of terror, provocation, incitement and destruction,

Gravely concerned about the dangerous situation resulting from actions taken by the illegal armed Israeli settlers in the occupied territory,

Noting the Israeli withdrawal from within the Gaza Strip and parts of the northern West Bank and the importance of the dismantlement of the settlements therein as a step towards the implementation of the road map,

Taking note of the relevant reports of the Secretary-General,[9]

1. *Reaffirms* that Israeli settlements in the Palestinian territory, including East Jerusalem, and in the occupied Syrian Golan are illegal and an obstacle to peace and economic and social development;

2. *Calls upon* Israel to accept the de jure applicability of the Geneva Convention relative to the Protection of Civilian Persons in Time of War, of 12 August 1949,[1] to the Occupied Palestinian Territory, including East Jerusalem, and to the occupied Syrian Golan and to abide scrupulously by the provisions of the Convention, in particular article 49;

3. *Notes* the Israeli withdrawal from within the Gaza Strip and parts of the northern West Bank and the importance of the dismantlement of the settlements therein as a step towards the implementation of the road map;[8]

4. *Calls upon* Israel, the occupying Power, in this regard, to comply strictly with its obligations under international law, including international humanitarian law, with respect to the alteration of the character and status of the Occupied Palestinian Territory, including East Jerusalem;

5. *Emphasizes* the need for the parties to speedily resolve all remaining issues in the Gaza Strip, including the removal of rubble;

6. *Reiterates its demand* for the immediate and complete cessation of all Israeli settlement activities in all of the Occupied Palestinian Territory, including East Jerusalem, and in the occupied Syrian Golan, and calls for the full implementation of the relevant resolutions of the Security Council;

7. *Demands* that Israel, the occupying Power, comply with its legal obligations, as mentioned in the advisory opinion rendered on 9 July 2004 by the International Court of Justice;[4]

8. *Stresses* the need for full implementation of the relevant Security Council resolutions regarding the Israeli settlements, including Security Council resolution 904 (1994), in which, among other things, the Council called upon Israel, the occupying Power, to continue to take and implement measures, including confiscation of arms, with the aim of preventing illegal acts of violence by Israeli settlers, and called for measures to be taken to guarantee the safety and protection of the Palestinian civilians in the occupied territory;

9. *Reiterates its calls* for the prevention of all acts of violence by Israeli settlers, especially against Palestinian civilians and properties, particularly in the light of recent developments;

10. *Requests* the Secretary-General to report to the General Assembly at its sixty-second session on the implementation of the present resolution.

79th plenary meeting
14 December 2006

---

[1] United Nations, *Treaty Series*, vol. 75, No. 973.

[2] Ibid., vol. 1125, No. 17512.

[3] Ibid., vol. 75, Nos. 970-973.

[4] See A/ES-10/273 and Corr.1.

[5] Ibid., advisory opinion, para. 120.

[6] See A/61/470.

[7] A/48/486-S/26560, annex.

[8] S/2003/529, annex.

[9] A/61/327-331 and A/61/500.

Resolution 61/119

[on the report of the Special Political and Decolonization Committee (Fourth Committee) (A/61/408)]

61/119. Israeli practices affecting the human rights of the Palestinian people in the Occupied Palestinian Territory, including East Jerusalem

The General Assembly,

Recalling its relevant resolutions, including resolution 60/107 of 8 December 2005, as well as those adopted at its tenth emergency special session,

Recalling also the relevant resolutions of the Commission on Human Rights and the Human Rights Council,

Bearing in mind the relevant resolutions of the Security Council,

Having considered the report of the Special Committee to Investigate Israeli Practices Affecting the Human Rights of the Palestinian People and Other Arabs of the Occupied Territories[1] and the report of the Secretary-General,[2]

Taking note of the recent reports of the Special Rapporteur of the Human Rights Council on the situation of human rights in the Palestinian territories occupied since 1967,[3]

Recalling the advisory opinion rendered on 9 July 2004 by the International Court of Justice,[4] and recalling also General Assembly resolution ES-10/15 of 20 July 2004,

Noting in particular the Court's reply, including that the construction of the wall being built by Israel, the occupying Power, in the Occupied Palestinian Territory, including in and around East Jerusalem, and its associated regime are contrary to international law,

Recalling the International Covenant on Civil and Political Rights,[5] the International Covenant on Economic, Social and Cultural Rights[5] and the Convention on the Rights of the Child,[6] and affirming that these human rights instruments must be respected in the Occupied Palestinian Territory, including East Jerusalem,

Aware of the responsibility of the international community to promote human rights and ensure respect for international law, and recalling in this regard its resolution 2625 (XXV) of 24 October 1970,

Reaffirming the principle of the inadmissibility of the acquisition of territory by force,

Reaffirming also the applicability of the Geneva Convention relative to the Protection of Civilian Persons in Time of War, of 12 August 1949,[7] to the Occupied Palestinian Territory, including East Jerusalem, and other Arab territories occupied by Israel since 1967,

Reaffirming further the obligation of the States parties to the Fourth Geneva Convention[7] under articles 146, 147 and 148 with regard to penal sanctions, grave breaches and responsibilities of the High Contracting Parties,

Reaffirming that all States have the right and the duty to take actions in conformity with international law and international humanitarian law to counter deadly acts of violence against their civilian population in order to protect the lives of their citizens,

Stressing the need for full compliance with the Israeli-Palestinian agreements reached within the context of the Middle East peace process, including the Sharm El-Sheikh understandings, and the implementation of the Quartet road map to a permanent two-State solution to the Israeli-Palestinian conflict,[8]

Stressing also the need for the full implementation of the Agreement on Movement and Access and the Agreed Principles for the Rafah Crossing, both of 15 November 2005, to allow for the freedom of movement of the Palestinian civilian population within and into and out of the Gaza Strip,

Noting the Israeli withdrawal from within the Gaza Strip and parts of the northern West Bank and the importance of the dismantlement of settlements therein as a step towards the implementation of the road map,

Expressing grave concern about the continuing systematic violation of the human rights of the Palestinian people by Israel, the occupying Power, including that arising from the excessive use of force, the use of collective punishment, the reoccupation and closure of areas, the confiscation of land, the establishment and expansion of settlements, the construction of the wall inside the Occupied Palestinian Territory in departure from the Armistice Line of 1949, the destruction of property and infrastructure, and all other actions by it designed to change the legal status, geographical nature and demographic composition of the Occupied Palestinian Territory, including East Jerusalem,

Gravely concerned about the military actions that have been carried out since 28 September 2000 and that have led to thousands of deaths among Palestinian civilians, including hundreds of children, and tens of thousands of injuries,

Expressing deep concern about the recent deterioration in the humanitarian and security situation in the Gaza Strip, including that resulting from the bombardment against civilian areas, air raids and sonic booms, and the firing of rockets into Israel, and in particular from the military actions carried out by Israel, the occupying Power, that endanger the Palesinian civilian population, and especially deploring the killing of Palestinian civilians, including women and children, that took place in Beit Hanoun on 8 November 2006,

Expressing deep concern also about the vast destruction caused by the Israeli occupying forces, including of religious, cultural and historical sites, of vital infrastructure and institutions of the Palestinian Authority, and of agricultural land throughout Palestinian cities, towns, villages and refugee camps, and expressing deep concern about the short- and long-term detrimental impact of such destruction on the socio-economic and humanitarian conditions of the Palestinian civilian population,

Expressing deep concern further about the Israeli policy of closure and the severe restrictions, including curfews and the permit regime, that continue to be imposed on the movement of persons and goods, including medical and humanitarian personnel and goods, throughout the Occupied Palestinian Territory, including East Jerusalem, and the consequent negative impact on the socio-economic situation of the Palestinian people, which remains that of a dire humanitarian crisis,

Concerned about the continued establishment of Israeli checkpoints in the Occupied Palestinian Territory, including East Jerusalem, and the transformation of several of these checkpoints into structures akin to permanent border crossings inside the Occupied Palestinian Territory, which are severely impairing the territorial contiguity of the Territory and severely undermining efforts to rehabilitate and develop the Palestinian economy,

Expressing deep concern that thousands of Palestinians, including children and women, continue to be held in Israeli prisons or detention centres under harsh conditions that impair their well-being, and expressing concern about the ill treatment and harassment of any of the Palestinian prisoners and all reports of torture,

Convinced of the need for an international presence to monitor the situation, to contribute to ending the violence and protecting the Palestinian civilian population and to help the parties implement the agreements reached and, in this regard, recalling the positive contribution of the Temporary International Presence in Hebron,

Welcoming the Palestinian truce initiative and its acceptance by Israel that came into effect on 26 November 2006, and urging both parties to maintain this truce, which could pave the way for genuine negotiations towards a just resolution of the conflict,

Stressing the necessity for the full implementation of all relevant Security Council resolutions,

1. *Reiterates* that all measures and actions taken by Israel, the occupying Power, in the Occupied Palestinian Territory, including East Jerusalem, in violation of the relevant provisions of the Geneva Convention relative to the Protection of Civilian Persons in Time of War, of 12 August 1949,[7] and contrary to the relevant resolutions of the Security Council, are illegal and have no validity;

2. *Demands* that Israel, the occupying Power, comply fully with the provisions of the Fourth Geneva Convention of 1949[7] and cease immediately all measures and actions taken in violation and in breach of the Convention, including all of its settlement activities and the construction of the wall in the Occupied Palestinian Territory, including in and around East Jerusalem, as well as the extrajudicial executions;

3. *Condemns* all acts of violence, including all acts of terror, provocation, incitement and destruction, especially the excessive use of force by the Israeli occupying forces against Palestinian civilians, resulting in extensive loss of life and vast numbers of injuries, including among children, massive destruction of homes, properties, agricultural lands and vital infrastructure, and the internal displacement of civilians;

4. *Expresses grave concern* at the use of suicide bombing attacks against Israeli civilians resulting in extensive loss of life and injury;

5. *Notes* the Israeli withdrawal from within the Gaza Strip and parts of the northern West Bank and the dismantlement of the settlements therein as a step towards the implementation of the road map;[8]

6. *Calls upon* Israel, the occupying Power, in this regard, to comply strictly with its obligations under international law, including international humanitarian law, with respect to the alteration of the character and status of the Occupied Palestinian Territory, including East Jerusalem;

7. *Demands* that Israel, the occupying Power, cease all practices and actions that violate the human rights of the Palestinian people, and that it respect human rights law and comply with its legal obligations in this regard;

8. *Urges* Member States to continue to provide emergency assistance to the Palestinian people to alleviate the financial crisis and the dire socio-economic and humanitarian situation being faced by the Palestinian people;

9. *Calls upon* Israel, the occupying Power, to release the tax revenues due to the Palestinian Authority, in accordance with the Paris Economic Protocol of 1994, and to ease the severe closures and restrictions on movement;

10. *Acknowledges* the role the temporary international mechanism plays in assisting directly the Palestinian people, and encourages interested donors to make use of the mechanism;

11. *Emphasizes* the need to preserve the Palestinian institutions and infrastructure for the provision of vital public services to the Palestinian civilian population and the promotion of Palestinian civil, political, economic, social and cultural rights;

12. *Demands* that Israel, the occupying Power, comply with its legal obligations under international law, as mentioned in the advisory opinion rendered on 9 July 2004 by the International Court of Justice[4] and as demanded in resolutions ES-10/15 of 20 July 2004 and ES-10/13 of 21 October 2003, and that it immediately cease the construction of the wall in the Occupied Palestinian Territory, including in and around East Jerusalem, dismantle forthwith the structure situated therein, repeal or render ineffective all legislative and regulatory acts relating thereto, and make reparation for all damage caused by the construction of the wall, which has gravely impacted the human rights and the socio-economic living conditions of the Palestinian people;

13. *Stresses* the need for respect for the unity and territorial integrity of all of the Occupied Palestinian Territory and for guarantees of the freedom of movement of persons and goods within the Palestinian territory, including the removal of restrictions on movement into and from East Jerusalem, and the freedom of movement to and from the outside world;

14. *Also stresses* the need for the full implementation by both parties of the Sharm El-Sheikh understandings and the Agreement on Movement and Access and the Agreed Principles for the Rafah Crossing;

15. *Requests* the Secretary-General to report to the General Assembly at its sixty-second session on the implementation of the present resolution.

79th plenary meeting
14 December 2006

---

[1] See A/61/500.

[2] A/61/329.

[3] See E/CN.4/2006/29 and A/61/470.

[4] See A/ES-10/273 and Corr.1.

[5] See resolution 2200 A (XXI), annex.

[6] United Nations, *Treaty Series*, vol. 1577, No. 27531.

[7] Ibid., vol. 75, No. 973.

[8] S/2003/529, annex.

Resolution 61/120

[on the report of the Special Political and Decolonization Committee (Fourth Committee) (A/61/408)]

61/120. The occupied Syrian Golan

The General Assembly,

Having considered the report of the Special Committee to Investigate Israeli Practices Affecting the Human Rights of the Palestinian People and Other Arabs of the Occupied Territories,[1]

Deeply concerned that the Syrian Golan, occupied since 1967, has been under continued Israeli military occupation,

Recalling Security Council resolution 497 (1981) of 17 December 1981,

Recalling also its previous relevant resolutions, the most recent of which was resolution 60/108 of 8 December 2005,

Having considered the report of the Secretary-General submitted in pursuance of resolution 60/108,[2]

Recalling its previous relevant resolutions in which, inter alia, it called upon Israel to put an end to its occupation of the Arab territories,

Reaffirming once more the illegality of the decision of 14 December 1981 taken by Israel to impose its laws, jurisdiction and administration on the occupied Syrian Golan, which has resulted in the effective annexation of that territory,

Reaffirming that the acquisition of territory by force is inadmissible under international law, including the Charter of the United Nations,

Reaffirming also the applicability of the Geneva Convention relative to the Protection of Civilian Persons in Time of War, of 12 August 1949,[3] to the occupied Syrian Golan,

Bearing in mind Security Council resolution 237 (1967) of 14 June 1967,

Welcoming the convening at Madrid of the Peace Conference on the Middle East on the basis of Security Council resolutions 242 (1967) of 22 November 1967 and 338 (1973) of

22 October 1973 aimed at the realization of a just, comprehensive and lasting peace, and expressing grave concern about the stalling of the peace process on all tracks,

1. *Calls upon* Israel, the occupying Power, to comply with the relevant resolutions on the occupied Syrian Golan, in particular Security Council resolution 497 (1981), in which the Council, inter alia, decided that the Israeli decision to impose its laws, jurisdiction and administration on the occupied Syrian Golan was null and void and without international legal effect and demanded that Israel, the occupying Power, rescind forthwith its decision;

2. *Also calls upon* Israel to desist from changing the physical character, demographic composition, institutional structure and legal status of the occupied Syrian Golan and in particular to desist from the establishment of settlements;

3. *Determines* that all legislative and administrative measures and actions taken or to be taken by Israel, the occupying Power, that purport to alter the character and legal status of the occupied Syrian Golan are null and void, constitute a flagrant violation of international law and of the Geneva Convention relative to the Protection of Civilian Persons in Time of War, of 12 August 1949,[3] and have no legal effect;

4. *Calls upon* Israel to desist from imposing Israeli citizenship and Israeli identity cards on the Syrian citizens in the occupied Syrian Golan, and from its repressive measures against the population of the occupied Syrian Golan;

5. *Deplores* the violations by Israel of the Geneva Convention relative to the Protection of Civilian Persons in Time of War, of 12 August 1949;

6. *Calls once again upon* Member States not to recognize any of the legislative or administrative measures and actions referred to above;

7. *Requests* the Secretary-General to report to the General Assembly at its sixty-second session on the implementation of the present resolution.

79th plenary meeting
14 December 2006

---

[1] See A/61/500.

[2] A/61/327.

[3] United Nations, *Treaty Series*, vol. 75, No. 973.

Resolution 61/121

[on the report of the Special Political and Decolonization Committee (Fourth Committee) (A/61/410)]

61/121. Questions relating to information

A

INFORMATION IN THE SERVICE OF HUMANITY

The General Assembly,

Taking note of the comprehensive and important report of the Committee on Information,[1]

Also taking note of the report of the Secretary-General on questions relating to information,[2]

Urges all countries, organizations of the United Nations system as a whole and all others concerned, reaffirming their commitment to the principles of the Charter of the United Nations and to the principles of freedom of the press and freedom of information, as well as to those of the independence, pluralism and diversity of the media, deeply concerned by the disparities existing between developed and developing countries and the consequences of every kind arising from those disparities that affect the capability of the public, private or other media and individuals in developing countries to disseminate information and communicate their views and their cultural and ethical values through endogenous cultural production, as well as to ensure the diversity of sources and their free access to information, and recognizing the call in this context for what in the United Nations and at various international forums has been termed "a new world information and communication order, seen as an evolving and continuous process":

(*a*) To cooperate and interact with a view to reducing existing disparities in information flows at all levels by increasing assistance for the development of communication infrastructures and capabilities in developing countries, with due regard for their needs and the priorities attached to such areas by those countries, and in order to enable them and the public, private or other media in developing countries to develop their own information and communication policies freely and independently and increase the participation of media and individuals in the communication process, and to ensure a free flow of information at all levels;

(*b*) To ensure for journalists the free and effective performance of their professional tasks and condemn resolutely all attacks against them;

(*c*) To provide support for the continuation and strengthening of practical training programmes for broadcasters and journalists from public, private and other media in developing countries;

(*d*) To enhance regional efforts and cooperation among developing countries, as well as cooperation between developed and developing countries, to strengthen communication capacities and to improve the media infrastructure and communication technology in the developing countries, especially in the areas of training and dissemination of information;

(*e*) To aim at, in addition to bilateral cooperation, providing all possible support and assistance to the developing countries and their media, public, private or other, with due regard to their interests and needs in the field of information and to action already adopted within the United Nations system, including:

(i) The development of the human and technical resources that are indispensable for the improvement of information and communication systems in developing countries and support for the continuation and strengthening of practical training programmes, such as those already operating under both public and private auspices throughout the developing world;

(ii) The creation of conditions that will enable developing countries and their media, public, private or other, to have, by using their national and regional resources, the communication technology suited to their national needs, as well as the necessary programme material, especially for radio and television broadcasting;

(iii) Assistance in establishing and promoting telecommunication links at the subregional, regional and interregional levels, especially among developing countries;

(iv) The facilitation, as appropriate, of access by the developing countries to advanced communication technology available on the open market;

(*f*) To provide full support for the International Programme for the Development of Communication of the United Nations Educational, Scientific and Cultural Organization,[3] which should support both public and private media.

79th plenary meeting
14 December 2006

B

UNITED NATIONS PUBLIC INFORMATION POLICIES AND ACTIVITIES

The General Assembly,

Emphasizing the role of the Committee on Information as its main subsidiary body mandated to make recommendations to it relating to the work of the Department of Public Information of the Secretariat,

Reaffirming its resolution 13 (I) of 13 February 1946, establishing the Department, which states in paragraph 2 of annex I that "the activities of the Department should be so organized and directed as to promote to the greatest possible extent an informed understanding of the work and purposes of the United Nations among the peoples of the world",

Emphasizing that the contents of public information and communications should be placed at the heart of the strategic management of the United Nations and that a culture of communications and transparency should permeate all levels of the Organization, as a means of fully informing the peoples of the world of the aims and activities of the United Nations, in accordance with the purposes and principles enshrined in the Charter of the United Nations, in order to create broad-based global support for the United Nations,

Stressing that the primary mission of the Department of Public Information is to provide, through its outreach activities, accurate, impartial, comprehensive, timely and relevant information to the public on the tasks and responsibilities of the United Nations in order to strengthen international support for the activities of the Organization with the greatest transparency,

Recalling the comprehensive review of the work of the Department of Public Information, requested by the General Assembly in its resolution 56/253 of 24 December 2001, as well as the report of the Secretary-General entitled "Strengthening of the United Nations: an agenda for further change",[4] and Assembly resolutions 57/300 of 20 December 2002 and 60/109 B of 8 December 2005, which provided an opportunity to take due steps to enhance the efficiency and effectiveness of the Department and to maximize the use of its resources,

Expressing its concern that the gap in information and communication technologies between the developed and the developing countries has continued to widen and that vast segments of the population in developing countries are not benefiting from the present information and communication technologies and, in this regard, underlining the necessity of rectifying the imbalances in the present development of information and communication technologies in order to make it more just, equitable and effective,

Recognizing that developments in the information and communication technologies open vast new opportunities for economic growth and social development and can play an important role in the eradication of poverty in developing countries, and, at the same time, emphasizing that the development of these technologies poses challenges and risks and could lead to the further widening of disparities between and within countries,

Recalling its resolution 59/309 of 22 June 2005 on multilingualism, and emphasizing the importance of making appropriate use of the official languages of the United Nations in the activities of the Department of Public information, with the aim of eliminating the disparity between the use of English and the five other official languages,

Welcoming Austria to membership in the Committee on Information,

I
Introduction

1. *Reaffirms* its resolution 13 (I), in which it established the Department of Public Information, and all other relevant resolutions of the General Assembly related to the activities of the Department, and requests the Secretary-General, in respect of the public information policies and activities of the United Nations, to continue to implement fully the recommendations contained in paragraph 2 of its resolution 48/44 B of 10 December 1993 and other mandates as established by the General Assembly;

2. *Also reaffirms* that the United Nations remains the indispensable foundation of a peaceful and just world and that its voice must be heard in a clear and effective manner, and emphasizes the essential role of the Department of Public Information in this context, the activities of which should be so organized and directed as to promote to the greatest possible extent an informed understanding of the work and purposes of the United Nations among the peoples of the world;

3. *Stresses* the importance of the clear and timely provision of information by the Secretariat to Member States, upon their request, within the framework of existing mandates and procedures;

4. *Reaffirms* the central role of the Committee on Information in United Nations public information policies and activities, including the prioritization of those activities, and decides that recommendations relating to the programme of the Department of Public Information shall originate, to the extent possible, in the Committee and shall be considered by the Committee;

5. *Requests* the Department of Public Information, following the priorities laid down by the General Assembly in its resolution 59/275 of 23 December 2004, and guided by the United Nations Millennium Declaration[5] to pay particular attention to such major issues as the eradication of poverty, conflict prevention, sustainable development, human rights, the HIV/AIDS epidemic, combating terrorism in all its forms and manifestations and the needs of the African continent;

6. *Also requests* the Department of Public Information to pay particular attention to progress in implementing the internationally agreed development goals, including those contained in the Millennium Declaration, and the outcomes of the major related United Nations summits and conferences in carrying out its activities;

7. *Reaffirms* the need to enhance the technological infrastructure of the Department of Public Information on a continuous basis in order to widen its outreach and improve the United Nations website;

8. *Recognizes* the important work carried out by the United Nations Educational, Scientific and Cultural Organization and its collaboration with news agencies and broadcasting organizations in developing countries in disseminating information on priority issues, and

encourages continued collaboration between the Department of Public Information and the United Nations Educational, Scientific and Cultural Organization in the promotion of culture and in the fields of education and communication, bridging the existing gap between the developed and the developing countries;

II
General activities of the Department of Public Information

9. *Notes* the report of the Secretary-General on the activities of the Department of Public Information[6] and requests the Secretary-General to continue reporting to the Committee on Information on the activities of the Department at successive sessions;

10. *Acknowledges* that the Department of Public Information has concluded its collaborative project with the Office of Internal Oversight Services on the systematic evaluation of public information products and activities, and notes with appreciation the report of the Secretary-General on the final outcome of this three-year project;[7]

11. *Requests* the Department of Public Information, while acknowledging its commitment to a culture of evaluation, to continue to evaluate its products and activities with the objective of improving their effectiveness, including through interdepartmental consultations;

12. *Reaffirms* that the Department of Public Information is the focal point for information policies of the United Nations and the primary news centre for information about the United Nations, its activities and those of the Secretary-General;

13. *Also reaffirms* the importance of more effective coordination between the Department of Public Information and the Office of the Spokesman for the Secretary-General, and requests the Secretary-General to ensure consistency in the messages of the Organization;

14. *Further reaffirms* that the Department of Public Information must prioritize its work programme while respecting existing mandates and in line with regulation 5.6 of the Regulations and Rules Governing Programme Planning, the Programme Aspects of the Budget, the Monitoring of Implementation and the Methods of Evaluation,[8] to focus its message and better concentrate its efforts and, as a function of performance management, to match its programmes with the needs of its target audiences, on the basis of improved feedback and evaluation mechanisms;

15. *Notes with appreciation* the efforts of the Department of Public Information to continue to publicize the work and decisions of the General Assembly, requests the Department to continue to enhance its working relationship with the Office of the President of the General Assembly and request the Secretary-General to report thereon to the Committee on Information at its twenty-ninth session;

16. *Requests* the Secretary-General to continue to exert all efforts to ensure that publications and other information services of the Secretariat, including the United Nations website and the United Nations News Service, contain comprehensive, objective and equitable information about the issues before the Organization and that they maintain editorial independence, impartiality, accuracy and full consistency with resolutions and decisions of the General Assembly;

17. *Requests* the Department of Public Information to ensure that United Nations publications are produced in a cost-effective manner and to continue to coordinate closely with all other entities, including all other departments of the Secretariat and funds and programmes

of the United Nations system, in order to avoid duplication, within their respective mandates, in the issuance of United Nations publications;

18. *Emphasizes* that the Department of Public Information should maintain and improve its activities in the areas of special interest to developing countries and, where appropriate, other countries with special needs, and that the activities of the Department should contribute to bridging the existing gap between the developing and the developed countries in the crucial field of public information and communications;

19. *Also emphasizes* that the Secretary-General should continue to strengthen the coordination between the Department of Public Information and all other entities, including all other departments of the Secretariat and funds and programmes of the United Nations system, in the context of the client-oriented approach of the Department, which should identify target audiences and develop information programmes and media strategies for priority issues, and emphasizes that public information capacities and activities in other departments should function under the guidance of the Department;

20. *Notes with appreciation* the continued efforts of the Department of Public Information in issuing daily press releases, and requests the Department to continue providing this service to both Member States and representatives of the media, while considering possible means of improving their production process and streamlining their format, structure and length, keeping in mind the views of Member States;

21. *Also notes with appreciation* the efforts of the Department of Public Information to work at the local level with other organizations and bodies of the United Nations system to enhance the coordination of their communication activities, and requests the Secretary-General to report to the Committee on Information at its twenty-ninth session on progress achieved in this regard and on the activities of the United Nations Communications Group;

22. *Calls upon* the Department of Public Information to continue to examine its policies and activities regarding the durable preservation of its radio, television and photographic archives, to take action, within existing resources, to ensure that such archives are preserved and are accessible and to report to the Committee on Information at its twenty-ninth session;

Multilingualism and public information

23. *Emphasizes* the importance of making appropriate use of all the official languages of the United Nations in all the activities of the Department of Public Information, including in presentations to the Committee on Information, with the aim of eliminating the disparity between the use of English and the five other official languages;

24. *Also emphasizes* the importance of ensuring the full, equitable treatment of all the official languages of the United Nations in all the activities of the Department of Public Information and, in this regard, reaffirms its request to the Secretary-General to ensure that the Department has appropriate staffing capacity in all the official languages of the United Nations to undertake all its activities;

25. *Stresses* the importance of fully implementing its resolution 52/214 of 22 December 1997, in section C of which it requested the Secretary-General to ensure that the texts of all

new public documents in all six official languages and information materials of the United Nations are made available daily through the United Nations website and are accessible to Member States without delay;

26. *Welcomes* the ongoing efforts of the Department of Public Information to enhance multilingualism in its activities, and requests the Department to continue its endeavours in this regard;

27. *Reiterates* paragraph 4 of section C of its resolution 52/214, and requests the Secretary-General to continue towards completion of the task of uploading all important older United Nations documents on the United Nations website in all six official languages on a priority basis, so that these archives are also available to Member States through that medium;

28. *Reaffirms* that it is important that the Secretary-General include in future programme budget proposals for the Department of Public Information the importance of using all six official languages in its activities;

29. *Welcomes* the work done by the network of United Nations information centres in favour of the publication of United Nations information materials and the translation of important documents in languages other than the United Nations official languages, with a view to reaching the widest possible spectrum of audiences and extending the United Nations message to all the corners of the world in order to strengthen international support for the activities of the Organization;

Bridging the digital divide

30. *Recalls with satisfaction* General Assembly resolution 60/252 of 27 March 2006, in which it endorsed the Tunis Commitment and the Tunis Agenda for the Information Society[9] and proclaimed 17 May annual World Information Society Day, and also recalls the adoption of the Declaration of Principles and the Plan of Action[10] at the first phase of the World Summit on the Information Society, held in Geneva from 10 to 12 December 2003, and in this regard requests the Department of Public Information to contribute to the celebration of this event and to play a role in raising awareness of the possibilities that the use of the Internet and other information and communication technologies can bring to societies and economies, as well as of ways to bridge the digital divide;

31. *Calls upon* the Department of Public Information to contribute to raising the awareness of the international community of the importance of the implementation of the outcome documents of the World Summit on the Information Society;

Network of United Nations information centres

32. *Emphasizes* the importance of the network of United Nations information centres in enhancing the public image of the United Nations and in disseminating messages on the United Nations to local populations, especially in developing countries;

33. *Takes note* of the report of the Secretary-General on the further rationalization of the network of United Nations information centres,[11] and, in this regard, recognizes the constraints of further regionalization as described in paragraph 25 of the report;

34. *Stresses* the importance of rationalizing the network of United Nations information centres, and, in this regard, requests the Secretary-General to continue to make proposals in this direction, including through the redeployment of resources where necessary, and to report to the Committee on Information at its twenty-ninth session;

35. *Reaffirms* that rationalization of United Nations information centres must be carried out on a case-by-case basis in consultation with all concerned Member States in which existing information centres are located, the countries served by those information centres and other interested countries in the region, taking into consideration the distinctive characteristics of each region;

36. *Recognizes* that the network of United Nations information centres, especially in developing countries, should continue to enhance its impact and activities, including through strategic communications support, and calls upon the Secretary-General to submit a report on the implementation of this approach to the Committee on Information at its twenty-ninth session;

37. *Stresses* the importance of taking into account the special needs and requirements of developing countries in the field of information and communications technology for the effective flow of information in those countries;

38. *Also stresses* that the Department of Public Information, through the network of United Nations information centres, should continue to promote public awareness of and mobilize support for the work of the United Nations at the local level, bearing in mind that information in local languages has the strongest impact on local populations;

39. *Further stresses* the importance of efforts to strengthen the outreach activities of the United Nations to those Member States remaining outside the network of United Nations information centres, and encourages the Secretary-General, within the context of rationalization, to extend the services of the network of United Nations information centres to those Member States;

40. *Stresses* that the Department of Public Information should continue to review the allocation of both staff and financial resources to the United Nations information centres in developing countries, emphasizing the needs of the least developed countries;

41. *Encourages* the network of United Nations information centres to continue to develop web pages in local languages, also encourages the Department of Public Information to provide resources and technical facilities, in particular to those information centres whose web pages are not yet operational, and further encourages host countries to respond to the needs of the information centres;

42. *Takes note* of the proposal by the Secretary-General to work closely with the Governments concerned to explore the possibility of identifying rent-free premises, while taking into account the economic condition of the host countries and bearing in mind that such support should not be a substitute for the full allocation of financial resources for the information centres in the context of the programme budget of the United Nations;

43. *Also takes note* of the report of the Secretary-General containing the discussion regarding the creation of a United Nations information centre in Luanda[12] to address the special needs of Portuguese-speaking African countries, welcomes the offer made by the Government of Angola to host the centre as part of the network of United Nations information centres by providing rent-free premises, and encourages the Secretary-General, within the context of rationalization, to take all necessary measures to accommodate those needs;

III
Strategic communications services

44. *Takes note* of the report of the Secretary-General on the activities of the Department of Public Information[6] and, in this context, reaffirms that the Department of Public Information is the principal department responsible for the implementation of information strategies, as mandated;

45. *Reaffirms* the role of the strategic communications services in devising and disseminating United Nations messages by developing communications strategies, in close collaboration with the substantive departments, United Nations funds and programmes and the specialized agencies, in full compliance with the legislative mandates;

Promotional campaigns

46. *Recognizes* that promotional campaigns aimed at supporting special sessions and international conferences of the United Nations are part of the core responsibility of the Department of Public Information, welcomes the efforts of the Department to examine creative ways in which it can organize and implement these campaigns in partnership with the substantive departments concerned, using the United Nations Millennium Declaration[5] as its guide, and requests the Department to pay particular attention to progress in implementing the internationally agreed development goals, including those contained in the Millennium Declaration, and the outcomes of the major related United Nations summits and conferences in carrying out its activities;

47. *Appreciates* the work of the Department of Public Information in promoting, through its campaigns, issues of importance to the international community, such as United Nations reform, the eradication of poverty, conflict prevention, sustainable development, disarmament, decolonization, human rights, including the rights of women and children and of persons with disabilities, strategic coordination in humanitarian relief, especially in natural disasters and other crises, HIV/AIDS, malaria, tuberculosis and other diseases, the needs of the African continent, combating terrorism in all its forms and manifestations, as well as dialogue among civilizations, the culture of peace and tolerance and the consequences of the Chernobyl disaster, and requests the Department, in cooperation with the countries concerned and with the relevant organizations and bodies of the United Nations system, to continue to take appropriate measures to enhance world public awareness of these and other important global issues;

48. *Invites* the Department of Public Information to continue to work within the United Nations Communications Group to coordinate the preparation and implementation of communication strategies with the heads of information of the agencies, funds and programmes of the United Nations system, and requests the Secretary-General to report to the Committee on Information at its twenty-ninth session on the activities of the Group;

49. *Stresses* the need to continue the renewed emphasis in support of Africa's development, in particular by the Department of Public Information, in order to promote awareness in the international community of the nature of the critical economic and social situation in Africa and of the priorities of the New Partnership for Africa's Development;[13]

Role of the Department of Public Information in United Nations peacekeeping

50. *Requests* the Secretariat to continue to ensure the involvement of the Department of Public Information from the planning stage of future peacekeeping operations through interdepartmental consultations and coordination with other departments of the Secretariat, in particular with the Department of Peacekeeping Operations;

51. *Stresses* the importance of enhancing the public information capacity of the Department of Public Information in the field of peacekeeping operations and its role, in close cooperation with the Department of Peacekeeping Operations, in the selection process of public information staff for United Nations peacekeeping operations or missions, and, in this regard, invites the Department of Public Information to second public information staff who have the necessary skills to fulfil the tasks of the operations or missions, taking into account the principle of equitable geographical distribution in accordance with Chapter XV, Article 101, paragraph 3, of the Charter of the United Nations, and to consider views expressed, especially by host countries, when appropriate, in this regard;

52. *Emphasizes* the importance of the peacekeeping gateway on the United Nations website, and requests the Department of Public Information to continue its efforts in supporting the peacekeeping missions to further develop their websites;

53. *Requests* the Department of Public Information and the Department of Peacekeeping Operations to continue their cooperation in raising awareness of the new realities, successes and challenges faced by peacekeeping operations, especially multidimensional and complex ones, and of the recent surge in United Nations peacekeeping activities, and welcomes efforts by the two Departments to develop and implement a comprehensive communications strategy on current challenges facing United Nations peacekeeping;

54. *Also requests* the Department of Public Information and the Department of Peacekeeping Operations to continue to cooperate in implementing an effective outreach programme to explain the policy of the Organization against sexual exploitation and abuse;

55. *Requests* the Secretary-General to continue to report to the Committee on Information at its successive sessions on the role of the Department of Public Information in United Nations peacekeeping operations;

Role of the Department of Public Information in strengthening dialogue among civilizations and the culture of peace as means of enhancing understanding among nations

56. *Recalls* its resolutions[14] on dialogue among civilizations and the culture of peace and requests the Department of Public Information, while ensuring the pertinence and relevance of subjects for promotional campaigns under this issue, to continue to provide the necessary support for the dissemination of information pertaining to dialogue among civilizations and the culture of peace, as well as the initiative on the Alliance of Civilizations and to take due steps in fostering the culture of dialogue among civilizations and promoting religious and cultural understanding via all mass media, such as the Internet, print, radio and television, and requests the Secretary-General to submit a report in this regard to the Committee on Information at its successive sessions;

IV
News services

57. *Stresses* that the central objective of the news services implemented by the Department of Public Information is the timely delivery of accurate, objective and balanced news and

information emanating from the United Nations system in all four mass media—print, radio, television and Internet—to the media and other audiences worldwide, with the overall emphasis on multilingualism, and reiterates its request to the Department to ensure that all news-breaking stories and news alerts are accurate, impartial and free of bias;

58. *Emphasizes* the importance of the Department of Public Information continuing to draw the attention of world media to stories that do not obtain prominent coverage, through the initiative entitled "Ten Stories the World Should Hear More About";

Traditional means of communication

59. *Stresses* that radio remains one of the most cost-effective and far-reaching traditional media available to the Department of Public Information and an important instrument in United Nations activities, including development and peacekeeping, with a view to achieving a broad client base around the world;

60. *Notes* that the international radio broadcasting capacity for the United Nations is an integral part of the activities of the Department of Public Information, and requests the Secretary-General to make every effort to ensure its success and to report on its activities to the Committee on Information at its twenty-ninth session;

61. *Requests* the Secretary-General to continue to make every effort to achieve parity in the six official languages in United Nations radio production;

62. *Notes* the efforts being made by the Department of Public Information to disseminate programmes directly to broadcasting stations all over the world in the six official languages, with the addition of Portuguese, as well as in other languages where possible;

63. *Welcomes* the efforts being made by the Department of Public Information to produce and disseminate television news video and feature material to broadcasters around the world through satellite distribution and web delivery;

64. *Requests* the Department of Public Information to continue building partnerships with local, national and regional broadcasters to extend the United Nations message to all the corners of the world in an accurate and impartial way, and also requests the Radio and Television Service of the Department to continue to take full advantage of the technological infrastructure made available in recent years;

United Nations website

65. *Reaffirms* that the United Nations website is an essential tool for the media, non-governmental organizations, educational institutions, Member States and the general public, and, in this regard, reiterates the continued need for efforts by the Department of Public Information to maintain and improve it;

66. *Recognizes* the efforts made by the Department of Public Information to implement the basic accessibility requirements for persons with disabilities to the United Nations website, calls upon the Department to continue to work towards compliance with all levels of accessibility requirements on all pages of the website with the aim of ensuring its accessibility by persons with different kinds of disabilities, and requests the Secretary-General to report to the Committee on Information at its twenty-ninth session on progress made in this regard;

67. *Reaffirms* the need to achieve full parity among the six official languages on United Nations websites while noting with satisfaction that progress is being made to narrow the gap among different official languages on United Nations websites;

68. *Takes note* of the fact that the multilingual development and enrichment of the United Nations website has improved, although at a slower rate than expected owing to several constraints that need to be addressed, and, in this regard, requests the Department of Public Information, in coordination with content-providing offices, to improve the actions taken to achieve parity among the six official languages on the United Nations website;

69. *Welcomes* the cooperative arrangements undertaken by the Department of Public Information with academic institutions to increase the number of web pages available in some official languages, and requests the Secretary-General to explore additional cost-neutral ways to further extend these cooperative arrangements to include all the official languages of the United Nations;

70. *Reaffirms* section IX, paragraph 2, of its resolution 59/276 of 23 December 2004 on proposals to strengthen the United Nations website;

71. *Reaffirms* its request to the Secretary-General to ensure, while maintaining an up-to-date and accurate website, the adequate distribution of financial and human resources within the Department of Public Information allocated to the United Nations website among all official languages, taking into consideration the specificity of each official language on a continuous basis;

72. *Recalls* paragraph 74 of its resolution 60/109 B and, in this regard, reiterates that all content-providing offices in the Secretariat should continue their efforts to translate into all official languages all English language materials and databases posted on the United Nations website in the most practical, efficient and cost-effective manner;

73. *Requests* the Secretary-General to continue to take full advantage of recent developments in information technology in order to improve, in a cost-effective manner, the expeditious dissemination of information on the United Nations, in accordance with the priorities established by the General Assembly in its resolutions and taking into account the linguistic diversity of the Organization;

74. *Recognizes* that some official languages use non-Latin and bidirectional scripts and that technological infrastructures and supportive applications in the United Nations are based on Latin script, which leads to difficulties in processing non-Latin and bidirectional scripts, and requests the Department of Public Information, in cooperation with the Information Technology Services Division of the Department of Management, to continue its efforts to ensure that technological infrastructures and supportive applications in the United Nations fully support Latin, non-Latin and bidirectional scripts in order to enhance the equality of all official languages on the United Nations website;

75. *Notes with satisfaction* that United Nations webcast services provide live video of United Nations meetings and events, which is also available in the original language in which it is delivered;

76. *Welcomes* the electronic mail-based United Nations News Service, distributed worldwide in the English and French languages through e-mail by the Department of Public Information, and requests the Department as a matter of priority to continue to examine ways to provide this service in all official languages;

77. *Requests* the Secretary-General to continue to work within the United Nations System Chief Executives Board for Coordination and other appropriate inter-agency bodies to

establish a United Nations gateway, an inter-agency search facility in which all entities of the United Nations system should be encouraged to participate, and requests the Secretary-General to report to the Committee on Information at its successive sessions on the activities of the High-level Committee on Management in this regard;

V
Library services

78. *Welcomes* the report of the Secretary-General entitled "Modernization and integrated management of United Nations libraries: update on new strategic directions";[15]

79. *Calls upon* the Department of Public Information to continue to lead the Steering Committee for the Modernization and Integrated Management of United Nations Libraries, and requests the member libraries of the Steering Committee to continue to coordinate closely in the implementation of its programme of work;

80. *Takes note* of the steps taken by the Dag Hammarskjöld Library and the other member libraries of the Steering Committee to align their activities, services and outputs more closely with the goals, objectives and operational priorities of the Organization;

81. *Reiterates* the need to enable the provision of hard copies of library materials to Member States, and notes the efforts of the Secretary-General to enrich, on a multilingual basis, the stock of books and journals in the Dag Hammarskjöld Library, including publications on peace and security and development-related issues, in order to ensure that the Library is enriched and continues to be a broadly accessible resource for information about the United Nations and its activities;

82. *Recognizes* the importance of the depository libraries in disseminating information and knowledge about United Nations activities, and, in this connection, urges the Dag Hammarskjöld Library, in its capacity as the focal point, to continue to take the initiatives necessary to strengthen such libraries by providing regional training and other assistance and by improving their role with the aim of strengthening their support to users in developing countries;

83. *Requests* the Secretary-General to report to the Committee on Information at its twenty-ninth session on the activities of the Steering Committee and the work of the Dag Hammarskjöld Library, including on the application of measures to enhance the effectiveness of the libraries within existing legislative mandates;

84. *Acknowledges* the role of the Dag Hammarskjöld Library, as part of the Outreach Division of the Department of Public Information, in enhancing knowledge-sharing and networking activities to ensure access to the vast store of United Nations knowledge by delegates, permanent missions of Member States, the Secretariat, researchers and depository libraries worldwide, and takes note of the proposal to rename the library the Dag Hammarskjöld Library and Knowledge-Sharing Centre, reflecting its new direction;

85. *Notes* the new approaches taken by the Dag Hammarskjöld Library, in particular the Personal Knowledge Management initiative, to assist representatives of Member States and Secretariat staff in the use of information products and tools as a complement to the traditional training programmes;

86. *Recalls* paragraph 44 of its resolution 56/64 B of 24 December 2001, in which it welcomed the role of the Department of Public Information in fostering increased collaboration among libraries of the United Nations system;

VI
Outreach services

87. *Acknowledges* that the outreach services provided by the Department of Public Information continue to work towards promoting awareness of the role and work of the United Nations on priority issues;

88. *Notes* the importance of the continued implementation by the Department of Public Information of the ongoing programme for broadcasters and journalists from developing countries and countries with economies in transition, as mandated by the General Assembly, and requests the Department to consider how best to maximize the benefits derived from the programme by reviewing, inter alia, its duration and the number of its participants;

89. *Welcomes* the movement towards educational outreach and the orientation of the *UN Chronicle*, both print and online editions, and, to this end, encourages the *UN Chronicle* to continue to develop co-publishing partnerships, collaborative educational activities and events, including the "Unlearning Intolerance" seminar series, with civil society organizations and institutions of higher learning;

90. *Reaffirms* the important role that guided tours play as a means of reaching out to the general public, including children and students at all levels;

91. *Welcomes* the efforts undertaken by the Department of Public Information in organizing exhibitions on important United Nations-related issues within existing mandates at United Nations Headquarters and at other United Nations offices as a useful tool for reaching out to the general public;

92. *Requests* the Department of Public Information to strengthen its role as a focal point for two-way interaction with civil society relating to the priorities and concerns of the Organization;

93. *Commends* the United Nations Correspondents Association for its ongoing activities and for its Dag Hammarskjöld Memorial Scholarship Fund, which sponsors journalists from developing countries to come to the United Nations Headquarters and report on the activities during the General Assembly, and urges donors to extend financial support to the Fund so that it may increase the number of such scholarships to journalists in this context;

94. *Expresses its appreciation* for the efforts and contribution of United Nations Messengers of Peace, Goodwill Ambassadors and other advocates to promote the work of the United Nations and to enhance international public awareness of its priorities and concerns, and calls upon the Department of Public Information to continue to involve them in its communications and media strategies and outreach activities;

95. *Requests* the Secretary-General to report to the Committee on Information at its next session on the activities being carried out by the Department of Public Information to enhance the public image of the Organization, especially where there is a component of the network of United Nations information centres;

VII
Final remarks

96. *Requests* the Secretary-General to ensure that all reports requested by the Committee on Information are submitted and issued in accordance with the legislative mandate;

97. *Also requests* the Secretary-General to report to the Committee on Information at its twenty-ninth session and to the General Assembly at its sixty-second session on the activities of the Department of Public Information and on the implementation of the recommendations contained in the present resolution;

98. *Requests* the Committee on Information to report to the General Assembly at its sixty-second session;

99. *Decides* to include in the provisional agenda of its sixty-second session the item entitled "Questions relating to information".

79th plenary meeting
14 December 2006

---

[1] *Official Records of the General Assembly, Sixty-first Session, Supplement No. 21* and addendum (A/61/21 and Add.1).

[2] A/61/216 and Corr.1.

[3] See United Nations Educational, Scientific and Cultural Organization, *Records of the General Conference, Twenty-first Session, Belgrade, 23 September–28 October 1980*, vol. 1, *Resolutions*, sect. III.4, resolution 4/21.

[4] A/57/387 and Corr.1.

[5] See resolution 55/2.

[6] A/AC.198/2006/5.

[7] A/AC.198/2006/4 and Corr.1.

[8] ST/SGB/2000/8.

[9] See A/60/687.

[10] See A/C.2/59/3.

[11] A/AC.198/2005/3.

[12] Ibid., para. 40.

[13] A/57/304, annex.

[14] Resolutions 53/22 of 4 November 1998 and 55/23 of 13 November 2000 on the United Nations Year of Dialogue among Civilizations, 52/15 of 20 November 1997, by which it proclaimed 2000 the International Year for the Culture of Peace, 53/25 of 10 November 1998, by which it proclaimed the period 2001–2010 the International Decade for a Culture of Peace and Non-Violence for the Children of the World, 56/6 of 9 November 2001 on the Global Agenda for Dialogue among Civilizations, and 59/142 of 15 December 2004 on the promotion of religious and cultural understanding, harmony and cooperation.

[15] A/AC.198/2006/2.

Resolution 61/122

[on the report of the Special Political and Decolonization Committee (Fourth Committee) (A/61/411)]

61/122. Information from Non-Self-Governing Territories transmitted under Article 73 *e* of the Charter of the United Nations

The General Assembly,

Recalling its resolution 1970 (XVIII) of 16 December 1963, in which it requested the Special Committee on the Situation with regard to the Implementation of the Declaration on the Granting of Independence to Colonial Countries and Peoples to study the information transmitted to the Secretary-General in accordance with Article 73 *e* of the Charter of the United Nations and to take such information fully into account in examining the situation with regard to the implementation of the Declaration, contained in General Assembly resolution 1514 (XV) of 14 December 1960,

Recalling also its resolution 60/110 of 8 December 2005, in which it requested the Special Committee to continue to discharge the functions entrusted to it under resolution 1970 (XVIII),

Stressing the importance of timely transmission by the administering Powers of adequate information under Article 73 *e* of the Charter, in particular in relation to the preparation by the Secretariat of the working papers on the Territories concerned,

Having examined the report of the Secretary-General,[1]

1. *Reaffirms* that, in the absence of a decision by the General Assembly itself that a Non-Self-Governing Territory has attained a full measure of self-government in terms of Chapter XI of the Charter of the United Nations, the administering Power concerned should continue to transmit information under Article 73 *e* of the Charter with respect to that Territory;

2. *Requests* the administering Powers concerned in accordance with their Charter obligations to transmit or continue to transmit regularly to the Secretary-General for information purposes, subject to such limitation as security and constitutional considerations may require, statistical and other information of a technical nature relating to economic, social and educational conditions in the Territories for which they are respectively responsible, as well as the fullest possible information on political and constitutional developments in the Territories concerned, including the constitution, legislative act or executive order providing for the government of the Territory and the constitutional relationship of the Territory to the administering Power, within a maximum period of six months following the expiration of the administrative year in those Territories;

3. *Requests* the Secretary-General to continue to ensure that adequate information is drawn from all available published sources in connection with the preparation of the working papers relating to the Territories concerned;

4. *Requests* the Special Committee on the Situation with regard to the Implementation of the Declaration on the Granting of Independence to Colonial Countries and Peoples to continue to discharge the functions entrusted to it under General Assembly resolution 1970 (XVIII), in accordance with established procedures.

79th plenary meeting
14 December 2006

[1] A/61/70.

Resolution 61/123

[on the report of the Special Political and Decolonization Committee (Fourth Committee) (A/61/412)]

61/123. Economic and other activities which affect the interests of the peoples of the Non-Self-Governing Territories

The General Assembly,

Having considered the item entitled "Economic and other activities which affect the interests of the peoples of the Non-Self-Governing Territories",

Having examined the chapter of the report of the Special Committee on the Situation with regard to the Implementation of the Declaration on the Granting of Independence to Colonial Countries and Peoples relating to the item,[1]

Recalling General Assembly resolution 1514 (XV) of 14 December 1960, as well as all other relevant resolutions of the Assembly, including, in particular, resolutions 46/181 of 19 December 1991 and 55/146 of 8 December 2000,

Reaffirming the solemn obligation of the administering Powers under the Charter of the United Nations to promote the political, economic, social and educational advancement of the inhabitants of the Territories under their administration and to protect the human and natural resources of those Territories against abuses,

Reaffirming also that any economic or other activity that has a negative impact on the interests of the peoples of the Non-Self-Governing Territories and on the exercise of their right to self-determination in conformity with the Charter and General Assembly resolution 1514 (XV) is contrary to the purposes and principles of the Charter,

Reaffirming further that the natural resources are the heritage of the peoples of the Non-Self-Governing Territories, including the indigenous populations,

Aware of the special circumstances of the geographical location, size and economic conditions of each Territory, and bearing in mind the need to promote the economic stability, diversification and strengthening of the economy of each Territory,

Conscious of the particular vulnerability of the small Territories to natural disasters and environmental degradation,

Conscious also that foreign economic investment, when undertaken in collaboration with the peoples of the Non-Self-Governing Territories and in accordance with their wishes, could make a valid contribution to the socio-economic development of the Territories and also to the exercise of their right to self-determination,

Concerned about any activities aimed at exploiting the natural and human resources of the Non-Self-Governing Territories to the detriment of the interests of the inhabitants of those Territories,

Bearing in mind the relevant provisions of the final documents of the successive Conferences of Heads of State or Government of Non-Aligned Countries and of the resolutions adopted by the Assembly of Heads of State and Government of the African Union, the Pacific Islands Forum and the Caribbean Community,

1. *Reaffirms* the right of peoples of Non-Self-Governing Territories to self-determination in conformity with the Charter of the United Nations and with General Assembly resolution

1514 (XV), containing the Declaration on the Granting of Independence to Colonial Countries and Peoples, as well as their right to the enjoyment of their natural resources and their right to dispose of those resources in their best interest;

2. *Affirms* the value of foreign economic investment undertaken in collaboration with the peoples of the Non-Self-Governing Territories and in accordance with their wishes in order to make a valid contribution to the socioeconomic development of the Territories;

3. *Reaffirms* the responsibility of the administering Powers under the Charter to promote the political, economic, social and educational advancement of the Non-Self-Governing Territories, and reaffirms the legitimate rights of their peoples over their natural resources;

4. *Reaffirms its concern* about any activities aimed at the exploitation of the natural resources that are the heritage of the peoples of the Non-Self-Governing Territories, including the indigenous populations, in the Caribbean, the Pacific and other regions, and of their human resources, to the detriment of their interests, and in such a way as to deprive them of their right to dispose of those resources;

5. *Reaffirms* the need to avoid any economic and other activities that adversely affect the interests of the peoples of the Non-Self-Governing Territories;

6. *Calls once again upon* all Governments that have not yet done so to take, in accordance with the relevant provisions of General Assembly resolution 2621 (XXV) of 12 October 1970, legislative, administrative or other measures in respect of their nationals and the bodies corporate under their jurisdiction that own and operate enterprises in the Non-Self-Governing Territories that are detrimental to the interests of the inhabitants of those Territories, in order to put an end to such enterprises;

7. *Reiterates* that the damaging exploitation and plundering of the marine and other natural resources of the Non-Self-Governing Territories, in violation of the relevant resolutions of the United Nations, are a threat to the integrity and prosperity of those Territories;

8. *Invites* all Governments and organizations of the United Nations system to take all possible measures to ensure that the permanent sovereignty of the peoples of the Non-Self-Governing Territories over their natural resources is fully respected and safeguarded in accordance with the relevant resolutions of the United Nations on decolonization;

9. *Urges* the administering Powers concerned to take effective measures to safeguard and guarantee the inalienable right of the peoples of the Non-Self-Governing Territories to their natural resources and to establish and maintain control over the future development of those resources, and requests the administering Powers to take all necessary steps to protect the property rights of the peoples of those Territories in accordance with the relevant resolutions of the United Nations on decolonization;

10. *Calls upon* the administering Powers concerned to ensure that no discriminatory working conditions prevail in the Territories under their administration and to promote in each Territory a fair system of wages applicable to all the inhabitants without any discrimination;

11. *Requests* the Secretary-General to continue, through all means at his disposal, to inform world public opinion of any activity that affects the exercise of the right of the peoples of

the Non-Self-Governing Territories to self-determination in conformity with the Charter and General Assembly resolution 1514 (XV);

12. *Appeals* to trade unions and non-governmental organizations, as well as individuals, to continue their efforts to promote the economic well-being of the peoples of the Non-Self-Governing Territories, and also appeals to the media to disseminate information about the developments in this regard;

13. *Decides* to follow the situation in the Non-Self-Governing Territories so as to ensure that all economic activities in those Territories are aimed at strengthening and diversifying their economies in the interest of their peoples, including the indigenous populations, and at promoting the economic and financial viability of those Territories;

14. *Requests* the Special Committee on the Situation with regard to the Implementation of the Declaration on the Granting of Independence to Colonial Countries and Peoples to continue to examine this question and to report thereon to the General Assembly at its sixty-second session.

79th plenary meeting
14 December 2006

[1] Official Records of the General Assembly, Sixty-first Session, Supplement No. 23 (A/61/23), chap. V.

Resolution 61/124

[on the report of the Special Political and Decolonization Committee (Fourth Committee) (A/61/414)]

61/124. Offers by Member States of study and training facilities for inhabitants of Non-Self-Governing Territories

The General Assembly,

Recalling its resolution 60/113 of 8 December 2005,

Having examined the report of the Secretary-General on offers by Member States of study and training facilities for inhabitants of Non-Self-Governing Territories,[1] prepared pursuant to its resolution 845 (IX) of 22 November 1954,

Conscious of the importance of promoting the educational advancement of the inhabitants of Non-Self-Governing Territories,

Strongly convinced that the continuation and expansion of offers of scholarships is essential in order to meet the increasing need of students from Non-Self-Governing Territories for educational and training assistance, and considering that students in those Territories should be encouraged to avail themselves of such offers,

1. *Takes note* of the report of the Secretary-General;[1]

2. *Expresses its appreciation* to those Member States that have made scholarships available to the inhabitants of Non-Self-Governing Territories;

3. *Invites* all States to make or continue to make generous offers of study and training facilities to the inhabitants of those Territories that have not yet attained self-government or independence and, wherever possible, to provide travel funds to prospective students;

4. *Urges* the administering Powers to take effective measures to ensure the widespread and continuous dissemination in the Territories under their administration of information relating to offers of study and training facilities made by States and to provide all the necessary facilities to enable students to avail themselves of such offers;

5. *Requests* the Secretary-General to report to the General Assembly at its sixty-second session on the implementation of the present resolution;

6. *Draws the attention* of the Special Committee on the Situation with regard to the Implementation of the Declaration on the Granting of Independence to Colonial Countries and Peoples to the present resolution.

79th plenary meeting
14 December 2006

[1] A/61/66.

Resolution 61/125

[on the report of the Special Political and Decolonization Committee (Fourth Committee) (A/61/415)]

61/125. Question of Western Sahara

The General Assembly,

Having considered in depth the question of Western Sahara,

Reaffirming the inalienable right of all peoples to self-determination and independence, in accordance with the principles set forth in the Charter of the United Nations and General Assembly resolution 1514 (XV) of 14 December 1960 containing the Declaration on the Granting of Independence to Colonial Countries and Peoples,

Recalling its resolution 60/114 of 8 December 2005,

Recalling also all resolutions of the General Assembly and the Security Council on the question of Western Sahara,

Recalling further Security Council resolutions 658 (1990) of 27 June 1990 and 690 (1991) of 29 April 1991, by which the Council approved the settlement plan for Western Sahara,[1]

Recalling Security Council resolutions 1359 (2001) of 29 June 2001 and 1429 (2002) of 30 July 2002, as well as 1495 (2003) of 31 July 2003, in which the Council expressed its support of the peace plan for self-determination of the people of Western Sahara[2] as an optimum political solution on the basis of agreement between the two parties, and resolutions 1541 (2004) of 29 April 2004, 1570 (2004) of 28 October 2004, 1598 (2005) of 28 April 2005, 1634 (2005) of 28 October 2005 and 1675 (2006) of 28 April 2006,

Taking note of the responses of the parties and neighbouring States to the Personal Envoy of the Secretary-General concerning the peace plan contained in the report of the Secretary-General of 23 May 2003,[3]

Reaffirming the responsibility of the United Nations towards the people of Western Sahara,

Noting with satisfaction the entry into force of the ceasefire in accordance with the proposal made by the Secretary-General, and stressing the importance it attaches to the maintenance of the ceasefire as an integral part of the settlement plan,

Underlining, in this regard, the validity of the settlement plan, while noting the fundamental differences between the parties in its implementation,

Stressing that the lack of progress in the settlement of the dispute on Western Sahara continues to cause suffering to the people of Western Sahara, remains a source of potential instability in the region and obstructs the economic development of the Maghreb region and that, in view of this, the search for a political solution is critically needed,

Welcoming the efforts of the Secretary-General and his Personal Envoy in search of a mutually acceptable political solution, which will provide for self-determination of the people of Western Sahara,

Having examined the relevant chapter of the report of the Special Committee on the Situation with regard to the Implementation of the Declaration on the Granting of Independence to Colonial Countries and Peoples,[4]

Having also examined the report of the Secretary-General,[5]

1. *Takes note* of the report of the Secretary-General;[5]

2. *Underlines* Security Council resolution 1495 (2003), in which the Council expressed its support of the peace plan for self-determination of the people of Western Sahara as an optimum political solution on the basis of agreement between the two parties;

3. *Underlines also* that the parties reacted differently to this plan;

4. *Continues to support strongly* the efforts of the Secretary-General and his Personal Envoy to achieve a mutually acceptable political solution to the dispute over Western Sahara;

5. *Commends* the Secretary-General and his Personal Envoy for their outstanding efforts and the two parties for the spirit of cooperation they have shown in the support they provide for those efforts;

6. *Calls upon* all the parties and the States of the region to cooperate fully with the Secretary-General and his Personal Envoy;

7. *Reaffirms* the responsibility of the United Nations towards the people of Western Sahara;

8. *Calls upon* the parties to cooperate with the International Committee of the Red Cross in its efforts to solve the problem of the fate of the people unaccounted for, and calls upon the parties to abide by their obligations under international humanitarian law to release without further delay all those held since the start of the conflict;

9. *Requests* the Special Committee on the Situation with regard to the Implementation of the Declaration on the Granting of Independence to Colonial Countries and Peoples to continue to consider the situation in Western Sahara and to report thereon to the General Assembly at its sixty-second session;

10. *Invites* the Secretary-General to submit to the General Assembly at its sixty-second session a report on the implementation of the present resolution.

79th plenary meeting
14 December 2006

---

[1] See S/21360 and S/22464 and Corr.1.

[2] S/2003/565 and Corr.1, annex II.

[3] S/2003/565 and Corr.1.

[4] See *Official Records of the General Assembly, Sixty-first Session, Supplement No. 23* (A/61/23), chap. VIII.

[5] A/61/121.

Resolution 61/126

[on the report of the Special Political and Decolonization Committee (Fourth Committee) (A/61/415)]

61/126. Question of New Caledonia

The General Assembly,

Having considered the question of New Caledonia,

Having examined the chapter of the report of the Special Committee on the Situation with regard to the Implementation of the Declaration on the Granting of Independence to Colonial Countries and Peoples relating to New Caledonia,[1]

Reaffirming the right of peoples to self-determination as enshrined in the Charter of the United Nations,

Recalling General Assembly resolutions 1514 (XV) of 14 December 1960 and 1541 (XV) of 15 December 1960,

Noting the importance of the positive measures being pursued in New Caledonia by the French authorities, in cooperation with all sectors of the population, to promote political, economic and social development in the Territory, including measures in the area of environmental protection and action with respect to drug abuse and trafficking, in order to provide a framework for its peaceful progress to self-determination,

Noting also, in this context, the importance of equitable economic and social development, as well as continued dialogue among the parties involved in New Caledonia in the preparation of the act of self-determination of New Caledonia,

Noting with satisfaction the intensification of contacts between New Caledonia and neighbouring countries of the South Pacific region,

1. *Welcomes* the significant developments that have taken place in New Caledonia since the signing of the Nouméa Accord of 5 May 1998 by the representatives of New Caledonia and the Government of France;[2]

2. *Urges* all the parties involved, in the interest of all the people of New Caledonia, to maintain, in the framework of the Nouméa Accord, their dialogue in a spirit of harmony;

3. *Notes* the relevant provisions of the Nouméa Accord aimed at taking more broadly into account the Kanak identity in the political and social organization of New Caledonia, and also those provisions of the Accord relating to control of immigration and protection of local employment;

4. *Takes note* of the concerns expressed by a group of indigenous people in New Caledonia regarding their underrepresentation in the Territory's governmental and social structures;

5. *Notes* the relevant provisions of the Nouméa Accord to the effect that New Caledonia may become a member or associate member of certain international organizations, such as international organizations in the Pacific region, the United Nations, the United Nations Educational, Scientific and Cultural Organization and the International Labour Organization, according to their regulations;

6. *Also notes* the agreement between the signatories of the Nouméa Accord that the progress made in the emancipation process shall be brought to the attention of the United Nations;

7. *Welcomes* the fact that the administering Power invited to New Caledonia, at the time the new institutions were established, a mission of information which comprised representatives of countries of the Pacific region;

8. *Calls upon* the administering Power to continue to transmit to the Secretary-General information as required under Article 73 *e* of the Charter of the United Nations;

9. *Invites* all the parties involved to continue promoting a framework for the peaceful progress of the Territory towards an act of self-determination in which all options are open and which would safeguard the rights of all sectors of the population, according to the letter and the spirit of the Nouméa Accord, which is based on the principle that it is for the populations of New Caledonia to choose how to control their destiny;

10. *Welcomes* the intention expressed by the French authorities to resolve in the coming years the question of voter registration;

11. *Also welcomes* the measures that have been taken to strengthen and diversify the New Caledonian economy in all fields, and encourages further such measures in accordance with the spirit of the Matignon and Nouméa Accords;

12. *Further welcomes* the importance attached by the parties to the Matignon and Nouméa Accords to greater progress in housing, employment, training, education and health care in New Caledonia;

13. *Notes* the increase by the Government of France in financial assistance to the Territory, amounting to 910 million euros in 2005 for health, education, payment of public-service salaries and funding development schemes;

14. *Acknowledges* the contribution of the Melanesian Cultural Centre to the protection of the indigenous Kanak culture of New Caledonia;

15. *Notes* the positive initiatives aimed at protecting the natural environment of New Caledonia, notably the "Zonéco" operation designed to map and evaluate marine resources within the economic zone of New Caledonia;

16. *Welcomes* the establishment of a new form of cooperation among Australia, France and New Zealand in terms of surveillance of fishing zones, in accordance with the wishes expressed by France during the France-Oceania Summit in July 2003;

17. *Acknowledges* the close links between New Caledonia and the peoples of the South Pacific and the positive actions being taken by the French and territorial authorities to facilitate the further development of those links, including the development of closer relations with the countries members of the Pacific Islands Forum;

18. *Welcomes*, in this regard, the accession by New Caledonia to the status of observer in the Pacific Islands Forum, continuing high-level visits to New Caledonia by delegations from countries of the Pacific region and high-level visits by delegations from New Caledonia to countries members of the Pacific Islands Forum, and notes with satisfaction the request by New Caledonia, with the approval and support of the French authorities, to obtain associate member status in the Pacific Islands Forum;

19. *Welcomes also* the cooperative attitude of other States and Territories in the region towards New Caledonia, its economic and political aspirations and its increasing participation in regional and international affairs;

20. *Welcomes further* the endorsement of the report of the Forum Ministerial Committee on New Caledonia by leaders of the Pacific Islands Forum at its 36th Summit, in October 2005 in Papua New Guinea, and the continuing role of the Forum Ministerial Committee in monitoring developments in the Territory and encouraging closer regional engagements;

21. *Decides* to keep under continuous review the process unfolding in New Caledonia as a result of the signing of the Nouméa Accord;

22. *Requests* the Special Committee on the Situation with regard to the Implementation of the Declaration on the Granting of Independence to Colonial Countries and Peoples to continue the examination of the question of the Non-Self-Governing Territory of New Caledonia and to report thereon to the General Assembly at its sixty-second session.

79th plenary meeting
14 December 2006

---

[1] See *Official Records of the General Assembly, Sixty-first Session, Supplement No. 23* (A/61/23), chap. VIII.

[2] A/AC.109/2114, annex.

Resolution 61/127

[on the report of the Special Political and Decolonization Committee (Fourth Committee) (A/61/415)]

61/127. Question of Tokelau

The General Assembly,

Having considered the question of Tokelau,

Having examined the chapter of the report of the Special Committee on the Situation with regard to the Implementation of the Declaration on the Granting of Independence to Colonial Countries and Peoples relating to Tokelau,[1]

Recalling its resolution 1514 (XV) of 14 December 1960, containing the Declaration on the Granting of Independence to Colonial Countries and Peoples, and all resolutions and decisions of the United Nations relating to Non-Self-Governing Territories, in particular General Assembly resolution 60/116 of 8 December 2005,

Noting with appreciation the continuing exemplary cooperation of New Zealand as the administering Power with regard to the work of the Special Committee relating to Tokelau and its readiness to permit access by United Nations visiting missions to the Territory,

Also noting with appreciation the collaborative contribution to the development of Tokelau by New Zealand and the specialized agencies and other organizations of the United Nations system, in particular the United Nations Development Programme,

Recalling the inauguration in 1999 of a national legislative body, the General Fono, based on village elections by universal adult suffrage and the assumption by that body in June 2003 of full responsibility for the Tokelau budget,

Recalling also the report of the United Nations mission dispatched in August 2002 to Tokelau at the invitation of the Government of New Zealand and the representatives of Tokelau,[2]

Noting that, as a small island Territory, Tokelau exemplifies the situation of most remaining Non-Self-Governing Territories and that, as a case study pointing to successful cooperation for decolonization, Tokelau has wider significance for the United Nations as it seeks to complete its work in decolonization,

Recalling that New Zealand and Tokelau signed in November 2003 a document entitled "Joint statement of the principles of partnership", which sets out in writing, for the first time, the rights and obligations of the two partner countries,

Bearing in mind the decision of the General Fono at its meeting in November 2003, following extensive consultations undertaken in all three villages, to explore formally with New Zealand the option of self-government in free association and its decision in August 2005 to hold a referendum on self-government on the basis of a draft constitution for Tokelau and a treaty of free association with New Zealand,

1. *Notes* that Tokelau remains firmly committed to the development of its capacity for self-government and to an act of self-determination that would result in Tokelau assuming a status in accordance with the options on future status for Non-Self-Governing Territories contained in principle VI of the annex to General Assembly resolution 1541 (XV) of 15 December 1960;

2. *Welcomes* the substantial progress made towards the devolution of power to the three taupulega (village councils), in particular the delegation of the Administrator's powers to the three taupulega with effect from 1 July 2004 and the assumption by each taupulega from that date of full responsibility for the management of all its public services;

3. *Recalls* the decision of the General Fono in November 2003, following extensive consultations in all three villages and a meeting of the Special Committee on the Constitution of Tokelau, to explore formally with New Zealand the option of self-government in free association,

and the discussions subsequently held between Tokelau and New Zealand pursuant to the General Fono decision;

4. *Recalls also* the decision of the General Fono in August 2005 to hold a referendum on self-government on the basis of a draft constitution for Tokelau and a treaty of free association with New Zealand, and notes the enactment by the General Fono of rules for the referendum;

5. *Welcomes* the invitation extended to the United Nations by Tokelau and New Zealand to monitor Tokelau's act of self-determination;

6. *Acknowledges* Tokelau's initiative in devising a strategic economic development plan for the period 2002–2005, and notes that a strategic plan for the period 2006–2009 is now being developed in consultation with New Zealand;

7. *Also acknowledges* the continuing assistance that New Zealand has committed to promoting Tokelau's welfare, as well as the cooperation of the United Nations Development Programme, including the relief and recovery assistance provided in the aftermath of Cyclone Percy in 2005;

8. *Further acknowledges* Tokelau's need for continued support, given the adjustments that are taking place with the strengthening of its capacity for self-government, and the ongoing responsibility of Tokelau's external partners to assist Tokelau in balancing its desire to be self-reliant to the greatest extent possible with its need for external assistance;

9. *Welcomes* the establishment of the Tokelau International Trust Fund to support the future development needs of Tokelau and the offer of a donor round table by the United Nations Development Programme, and calls upon Member States and international and regional agencies to announce contributions to the Fund and thereby lend practical support to assist this emerging country in overcoming the problems of smallness, isolation and lack of resources;

10. *Also welcomes* the assurance of the Government of New Zealand that it will meet its obligations to the United Nations with respect to Tokelau and abide by the freely expressed wishes of the people of Tokelau with regard to their future status;

11. *Further welcomes* the cooperative attitude of the other States and territories in the region towards Tokelau, and their support for its economic and political aspirations and increasing participation in regional and international affairs;

12. *Welcomes* the associate membership of Tokelau in the United Nations Educational, Scientific and Cultural Organization, and its recent accession to membership in the Forum Fisheries Agency, observer status at the Pacific Islands Forum and associate membership in the South Pacific Applied Geoscience Commission;

13. *Calls upon* the administering Power and United Nations agencies to continue to provide assistance to Tokelau as it further develops its economy and governance structures;

14. *Welcomes* the actions taken by the administering Power to transmit information regarding the political, economic and social situation of Tokelau to the Secretary-General;

15. *Notes with satisfaction* the successful visit to Tokelau in October 2004 by the Chairman of the Special Committee on the Situation with regard to the Implementation of the Declaration on the Granting of Independence to Colonial Countries and Peoples;

16. *Notes* the considerable progress made towards the adoption of a Constitution and of national symbols by Tokelau, the steps taken by Tokelau and New Zealand to agree to a draft treaty of free association as a basis for an act of self-determination and the support expressed by Tokelauan communities in New Zealand for the move by Tokelau towards self-determination;

17. *Commends* the professional and transparent conduct of the referendum to determine the future status of Tokelau, which was held from 11 to 15 February 2006 and monitored by the United Nations;

18. *Notes* that the referendum failed by a narrow margin to produce the two-thirds majority of the valid votes cast required by the General Fono to change Tokelau's status as a Non-Self-Governing Territory under the administration of New Zealand;

19. *Welcomes* the agreement of New Zealand to the request by the Tokelau Council of Ongoing Government to maintain the referendum package of a draft Constitution and draft Treaty of Free Association as a possible basis for a future act of self-determination by Tokelau;

20. *Requests* the Special Committee to continue to examine the question of the Non-Self-Governing Territory of Tokelau and to report thereon to the General Assembly at its sixty-second session.

79th plenary meeting
14 December 2006

---

[1] *Official Records of the General Assembly, Sixty-first Session, Supplement No. 23* (A/61/23), chap. X.

[2] A/AC.109/2002/31.

Resolution 61/128

[on the report of the Special Political and Decolonization Committee (Fourth Committee) (A/61/415)]

61/128. Questions of American Samoa, Anguilla, Bermuda, the British Virgin Islands, the Cayman Islands, Guam, Montserrat, Pitcairn, Saint Helena, the Turks and Caicos Islands and the United States Virgin Islands

A

GENERAL

The General Assembly,

Having considered the questions of the Non-Self-Governing Territories of American Samoa, Anguilla, Bermuda, the British Virgin Islands, the Cayman Islands, Guam, Montserrat, Pitcairn, Saint Helena, the Turks and Caicos Islands and the United States Virgin Islands, hereinafter referred to as "the Territories",

Having examined the relevant chapter of the report of the Special Committee on the Situation with regard to the Implementation of the Declaration on the Granting of Independence to Colonial Countries and Peoples,[1]

Recalling all resolutions and decisions of the United Nations relating to those Territories, including, in particular, the resolutions adopted by the General Assembly at its sixtieth session on the individual Territories covered by the present resolution,

Recognizing that all available options for self-determination of the Territories are valid as long as they are in accordance with the freely expressed wishes of the peoples concerned and in conformity with the clearly defined principles contained in General Assembly resolutions 1514 (XV) of 14 December 1960, 1541 (XV) of 15 December 1960 and other resolutions of the Assembly,

Recalling its resolution 1541 (XV), containing the principles that should guide Member States in determining whether or not an obligation exists to transmit the information called for under Article 73 *e* of the Charter of the United Nations,

Expressing concern that more than forty-five years after the adoption of the Declaration on the Granting of Independence to Colonial Countries and Peoples,[2] there still remain a number of Non-Self-Governing Territories,

Conscious of the importance of continuing effective implementation of the Declaration, taking into account the target set by the United Nations to eradicate colonialism by 2010 and the plan of action for the Second International Decade for the Eradication of Colonialism,[3]

Recognizing that the specific characteristics and the sentiments of the peoples of the Territories require flexible, practical and innovative approaches to the options of self-determination, without any prejudice to territorial size, geographical location, size of population or natural resources,

Taking note of the stated positions of the Government of the United Kingdom of Great Britain and Northern Ireland and the stated position of the Government of the United States of America on the Non-Self-Governing Territories under their administration,

Taking note also of the stated positions of the representatives of the Non-Self-Governing Territories before the Special Committee and in its regional seminars,

Noting the constitutional developments in some Non-Self-Governing Territories affecting the internal structure of governance about which the Special Committee has received information,

Aware of the importance both to the Territories and to the Special Committee of the participation of elected and appointed representatives of the Territories in the work of the Special Committee,

Convinced that the wishes and aspirations of the peoples of the Territories should continue to guide the development of their future political status and that referendums, free and fair elections and other forms of popular consultation play an important role in ascertaining the wishes and aspirations of the people,

Convinced also that any negotiations to determine the status of a Territory must take place with the active involvement and participation of the people of that Territory, under the supervision of the United Nations, on a case-by-case basis, and that the views of the peoples of the Non-Self-Governing Territories in respect of their right to self-determination should be ascertained,

Aware of the importance of the international financial services for the economies of some of the Non-Self-Governing Territories,

Noting the continued cooperation of the Non-Self-Governing Territories at the local and regional levels, including participation in the work of regional organizations,

Mindful that United Nations visiting and special missions provide an effective means of ascertaining the situation in the Territories, that some Territories have not received a United Nations visiting mission for a long time and that no visiting missions have been sent to some of the Territories, and considering the possibility of sending further visiting missions to the Territories at an appropriate time and in consultation with the administering Powers,

Mindful also that, in order for the Special Committee to enhance its understanding of the political status of the peoples of the Territories and to fulfil its mandate effectively, it is important for it to be apprised by the administering Powers and to receive information from other appropriate sources, including the representatives of the Territories, concerning the wishes and aspirations of the peoples of the Territories,

Recognizing the need for the Special Committee to ensure that the appropriate bodies of the United Nations embark actively on a public awareness campaign aimed at assisting the peoples of the Territories in gaining an understanding of the options of self-determination,

Mindful, in this connection, that the holding of regional seminars in the Caribbean and Pacific regions and at Headquarters and other venues, with the active participation of representatives of the Non-Self-Governing Territories, provides a helpful means for the Special Committee to fulfil its mandate, and that the regional nature of the seminars, which alternate between the Caribbean and the Pacific, is a crucial element in the context of a United Nations programme for ascertaining the political status of the Territories,

Mindful also that the 2006 Pacific regional seminar, originally scheduled to be held in Timor-Leste from 23 to 25 May 2006, is to be rescheduled to a later date in 2006,

Conscious of the particular vulnerability of the Territories to natural disasters and environmental degradation, and, in this connection, bearing in mind the applicability to the Territories of the programmes of action of all United Nations world conferences[4] and special sessions of the General Assembly in the economic and social sphere,

Noting with appreciation the contribution to the development of some Territories by the specialized agencies and other organizations of the United Nations system, in particular the United Nations Development Programme, the Economic Commission for Latin America and the Caribbean and the Economic and Social Commission for Asia and the Pacific, as well as regional institutions such as the Caribbean Development Bank, the Caribbean Community, the Organization of Eastern Caribbean States, the Pacific Islands Forum and the agencies of the Council of Regional Organizations in the Pacific,

Aware that the Human Rights Committee, as part of its mandate under the International Covenant on Civil and Political Rights,[5] reviews the status of the self-determination process of small island Territories under examination by the Special Committee,

Recalling the ongoing efforts of the Special Committee in carrying out a critical review of its work with the aim of making appropriate and constructive recommendations and decisions to attain its objectives in accordance with its mandate,

Recognizing that the annual background working papers prepared by the Secretariat on developments in each of the small Territories,[6] as well as the substantive documentation and information furnished by independent experts, scholars, non-governmental organizations and other independent sources, have provided important inputs in updating the present resolution,

1. *Reaffirms* the inalienable right of the peoples of the Territories to self-determination, in conformity with the Charter of the United Nations and with General Assembly resolution 1514 (XV), containing the Declaration on the Granting of Independence to Colonial Countries and Peoples;

2. *Also reaffirms* that, in the process of decolonization, there is no alternative to the principle of self-determination, which is also a fundamental human right, as recognized under the relevant human rights conventions;

3. *Further reaffirms* that it is ultimately for the peoples of the Territories themselves to determine freely their future political status in accordance with the relevant provisions of the Charter, the Declaration and the relevant resolutions of the General Assembly, and in that connection reiterates its long-standing call for the administering Powers, in cooperation with the territorial Governments and appropriate bodies of the United Nations system, to develop political education programmes for the Territories in order to foster an awareness among the people of their right to self-determination in conformity with the legitimate political status options, based on the principles clearly defined in General Assembly resolution 1541 (XV);

4. *Requests* the administering Powers to transmit regularly to the Secretary-General information called for under Article 73 *e* of the Charter;

5. *Stresses* the importance of the Special Committee being apprised of the views and wishes of the peoples of the Territories and enhancing its understanding of their conditions, including the nature and scope of the existing political and constitutional arrangements between the Non-Self-Governing Territories and their respective administering Powers;

6. *Reaffirms* the responsibility of the administering Powers under the Charter to promote the economic and social development and to preserve the cultural identity of the Territories, and recommends that priority continue to be given, in consultation with the territorial Governments concerned, to the strengthening and diversification of their respective economies;

7. *Requests* the Special Committee to continue to follow closely the developments in legislation in the area of international financial services and their impact on the economy in some of the Territories;

8. *Requests* the Territories and the administering Powers to take all necessary measures to protect and conserve the environment of the Territories against any degradation, and once again requests the specialized agencies concerned to continue to monitor environmental conditions in the Territories;

9. *Welcomes* the participation of the Non-Self-Governing Territories in regional activities, including the work of regional organizations;

10. *Stresses* the importance of implementing the plan of action for the Second International Decade for the Eradication of Colonialism,[3] in particular by expediting the application of the work programme for the decolonization of each Non-Self-Governing Territory, on a

case-by-case basis, and by completing the periodic analyses of the progress and extent of the implementation of the Declaration in each Territory;

11. *Calls upon* the administering Powers to participate in and cooperate fully with the work of the Special Committee in order to implement the provisions of Article 73 *e* of the Charter and the Declaration, and in order to advise the Special Committee on the implementation of provisions under Article 73 *b* of the Charter on efforts to promote self-government in the Territories;

12. *Urges* Member States to contribute to the efforts of the United Nations to usher in a world free of colonialism within the Second International Decade for the Eradication of Colonialism, and calls upon them to continue to give their full support to the Special Committee in its endeavours towards that noble goal;

13. *Notes* that a number of Non-Self-Governing Territories have expressed concern at the procedure followed by some administering Powers, contrary to the wishes of the Territories themselves, of amending or enacting legislation for application to the Territories, either through Orders in Council, in order to apply to the Territories the international treaty obligations of the administering Power, or through unilateral application of laws and regulations;

14. *Takes note* of the constitutional reviews in the Territories administered by the United Kingdom of Great Britain and Northern Ireland, and led by the territorial Governments, designed to address the internal constitutional structure within the present territorial arrangement;

15. *Also takes note* of the report of the Secretary-General on the midterm review of the Second International Decade for the Eradication of Colonialism,[7] and reiterates its long-standing request that the Secretary-General report to the General Assembly at its next session on the implementation of decolonization resolutions adopted since the declaration of the First and Second International Decades;

16. *Reiterates its request* that the Human Rights Committee collaborate with the Special Committee, within the framework of its mandate on the right to self-determination as contained in the International Covenant on Civil and Political Rights[5] with the aim of exchanging information, given that the Committee reviews political and constitutional developments in many of the Non-Self-Governing Territories that are under review by the Special Committee;

17. *Requests* the Special Committee to collaborate with the Permanent Forum on Indigenous Issues and the Committee on the Elimination of Racial Discrimination, within the framework of their respective mandates, with the aim of exchanging information on developments in those Non-Self-Governing Territories which are reviewed by these bodies;

18. *Also requests* the Special Committee to continue to examine the question of the Non-Self-Governing Territories and to report thereon to the General Assembly at its sixty-second session and on the implementation of the present resolution.

79th plenary meeting
14 December 2006

B

INDIVIDUAL TERRITORIES

The General Assembly,

Referring to resolution A above,

I
American Samoa

Taking note of the working paper prepared by the Secretariat on American Samoa[8] and other relevant information,

Taking note also of the position of the administering Power and the statements made by representatives of American Samoa in the regional seminars expressing satisfaction with the Territory's present relationship with the United States of America,

Noting that the Territory's non-voting delegate to the Congress of the United States of America has formally requested that the administering Power declare its official position on the status of American Samoa before the Special Committee on the Situation with regard to the Implementation of the Declaration on the Granting of Independence to Colonial Countries and Peoples,

Noting with satisfaction the establishment of the Future Political Status Study Commission, which began its work in June 2006, to study alternative forms of future political status open to American Samoa and to assess the advantages and disadvantages of each,

Recalling the negative economic impacts of Cyclone Heta in 2004 and Cyclone Olaf in 2005 on the agricultural sector, noting the importance to the economy of remittances and tourism, and bearing in mind the request of the territorial Government to the administering Power to continue to extend favourable tax benefits with regard to its exports,

1. *Notes* that the Department of the Interior of the United States of America provides that the Secretary of the Interior has administrative jurisdiction over American Samoa;[9]

2. *Also notes* that American Samoa continues to be the only United States Territory to receive financial assistance from the administering Power for the operations of the territorial Government, and calls upon the administering Power to continue to assist the territorial Government in the diversification of its economy;

3. *Welcomes* the invitation extended to the Special Committee by the Governor of American Samoa and reiterated, most recently at the Caribbean regional seminar held in Canouan, Saint Vincent and the Grenadines, from 17 to 19 May 2005, to send a visiting mission to the Territory, calls upon the administering Power to facilitate such a mission, and requests the Chairman of the Special Committee to take all the necessary steps to that end;

4. *Takes note* of the statement of the representative of the Governor of the Territory at the Caribbean regional seminar in 2005 requesting the Special Committee to provide information on the process of self-governance, which could be provided within the context of a visiting mission, or by other acceptable means;

5. *Requests* the administering Power to assist the Territory in facilitating the work of the newly established Future Political Status Study Commission, consistent with Article 73 *b* of the Charter of the United Nations, and calls upon the relevant United Nations organizations to provide assistance to the Territory, if requested, in the context of its public education programme;

II
Anguilla

Taking note of the working paper prepared by the Secretariat on Anguilla[10] and other relevant information,

Taking note also of the constitutional review process resumed by the territorial Government in 2006,

Recalling the holding of the 2003 Caribbean regional seminar in Anguilla, the first time that the seminar had been held in a Non-Self-Governing Territory, and the desire of the territorial Government and the people of Anguilla for a visiting mission by the Special Committee,

Noting the appointment by the administering Power of a new Governor who maintains reserved powers in the Territory,

Aware that the Government has placed a halt on all new and major foreign investment tourism-related projects in order to carefully manage the development of the island's economy to achieve long-term sustainability,

1. *Welcomes* the establishment of a new Constitutional and Electoral Reform Commission in 2006, with the aim of making recommendations to the administering Power on proposed changes to the Constitution in place in the Territory;

2. *Notes* that changes in the visa requirements for Anguillan passport holders entering nearby French Saint Martin could make it more difficult for them to enter the French overseas department, the closest neighbour to the Territory;

3. *Welcomes* the participation of the Territory as an associate member in the Caribbean Community, the Organization of Eastern Caribbean States and the Economic Commission for Latin America and the Caribbean;

III
Bermuda

Taking note of the working paper prepared by the Secretariat on Bermuda[11] and other relevant information,

Conscious of the different viewpoints of the political parties on the future status of the Territory,

Noting the statement of the Premier of Bermuda in his Founder's Day address that there could never be a true democracy as long as the country remains a colony or an overseas dependent Territory, and that only with independence can national unity be forged and pride in being Bermudian fully developed,

Bearing in mind the conclusions in the report of the United Nations special mission to Bermuda, which visited the Territory in March and May 2005,[12]

1. *Welcomes* the dispatch of the United Nations special mission to Bermuda at the request of the territorial Government and with the concurrence of the administering Power, which provided information to the people of the Territory on the role of the United Nations in the process of self-determination, on the legitimate political status options as clearly defined in General Assembly resolution 1541 (XV) of 15 December 1960 and on the experiences of other small States that have achieved a full measure of self-government;

2. *Also welcomes* the 2005 report of the Bermuda Independence Commission, which provides a thorough and meticulous examination of the facts surrounding independence, and takes note of the plans for public meetings and the presentation of a Green Paper to the House of Assembly followed by a White Paper outlining the policy proposals for an independent Bermuda;

3. *Decides* to follow closely the public consultations on the future political status of Bermuda under way in the Territory, and requests the relevant United Nations organizations to provide assistance to the Territory, if requested, in the context of its public education programme;

IV
British Virgin Islands

Taking note of the working paper prepared by the Secretariat on the British Virgin Islands[13] and other relevant information,

Recalling the 1993 report of the Constitutional Commissioners, appointed by the administering Power to review the existing Constitution, and its recommendation to assess the costs, obligations and liabilities of independence, and the 1996 debate on the report in the Legislative Council,

Welcoming the establishment of the Constitutional Commission in 2004 and the completion of its report in 2005 providing recommendations on constitutional modernization, and noting that the Legislative Council of the Territory debated the report in 2005,

Noting the appointment by the administering Power of a new Governer who maintains reserved powers in the Territory,

Also noting that the Territory continues to emerge as one of the world's leading offshore financial centres,

1. *Takes note* of the statement made by the representative of the Legislative Council of the Territory at the Caribbean regional seminar held in Canouan, Saint Vincent and the Grenadines, from 17 to 19 May 2005, who presented an analysis of the internal constitutional review process;

2. *Welcomes* the 2005 report of the Constitutional Commission, which contains a series of recommendations on constitutional advancement, including the scaling back of the powers of the appointed Governor, and also welcomes the discussions which commenced in 2006 between the elected Government and the administering Power on constitutional advancement and devolution of power;

3. *Further welcomes* the ongoing work of the Inter-Virgin Islands Council between the elected Governments of the British Virgin Islands and the United States Virgin Islands as a mechanism for functional cooperation between the two neighbouring Territories;

V
Cayman Islands

Taking note of the working paper prepared by the Secretariat on the Cayman Islands[14] and other relevant information,

Noting the 2002 report of the Constitutional Modernization Review Commission, which contained a draft constitution for the consideration of the people of the Territory, the 2003

draft constitution offered by the administering Power and the subsequent discussions between the Territory and the administering Power in 2003,

Also noting the 2003 visit to the Territory by the Chairman of the Special Committee at the invitation of the Cayman Islands Chamber of Commerce,

1. *Takes note* of the decision by the new territorial Government to reopen discussions with the administering Power in 2006 on constitutional modernization with the aim of ascertaining the views of the people by way of referendum;

2. *Also takes note* of the statement made by the representative of the Non-Governmental Organizations Constitutional Working Group of the Cayman Islands Chamber of Commerce at the Caribbean regional seminar held in Canouan, Saint Vincent and the Grenadines, from 17 to 19 May 2005, which called for a comprehensive educational programme, to be defined by the Special Committee, on the issue of self-determination, as well as a visiting mission to the Territory;

VI
Guam

Taking note of the working paper prepared by the Secretariat on Guam[15] and other relevant information,

Recalling that, in a referendum held in 1987, the registered and eligible voters of Guam endorsed a draft Guam Commonwealth Act that would establish a new framework for relations between the Territory and the administering Power, providing for a greater measure of internal self-government for Guam and recognition of the right of the Chamorro people of Guam to self-determination for the Territory,

Recalling also the requests by the elected representatives and nongovernmental organizations of the Territory that Guam not be removed from the list of the Non-Self-Governing Territories with which the Special Committee is concerned, pending the self-determination of the Chamorro people and taking into account their legitimate rights and interests,

Aware that negotiations between the administering Power and the territorial Government on the draft Guam Commonwealth Act are no longer continuing and that Guam has established the process for a self-determination vote by the eligible Chamorro voters,

Cognizant that the administering Power continues to implement its programme of transferring surplus federal land to the Government of Guam,

Noting that the people of the Territory have called for reform in the programme of the administering Power with respect to the thorough, unconditional and expeditious transfer of land property to the people of Guam,

Aware of concerns expressed by many residents regarding the potential social and other impacts of the impending transfer of additional military personnel of the administering Power to the Territory,

Conscious that immigration into Guam has resulted in the indigenous Chamorros becoming a minority in their homeland,

Recalling the dispatch in 1979 of a United Nations visiting mission to the Territory, and noting the recommendation of the 1996 Pacific regional seminar for sending a visiting mission to Guam,

Also recalling the invitation made in 2000 by the Governor and legislature of the Territory to hold the Pacific regional seminar in the Territory and the opposition to the invitation expressed by the administering Power,

1. *Calls once again upon* the administering Power to take into consideration the expressed will of the Chamorro people as supported by Guam voters in the plebiscite of 1987 and as provided for in Guam law, encourages the administering Power and the territorial Government of Guam to enter into negotiations on the matter, and requests the administering Power to inform the Secretary-General of progress to that end;

2. *Requests* the administering Power to continue to assist the elected territorial Government in achieving its political, economic and social goals;

3. *Also requests* the administering Power, in cooperation with the territorial Government, to continue to transfer land to the original landowners of the Territory, to continue to recognize and respect the political rights and the cultural and ethnic identity of the Chamorro people of Guam and to take all necessary measures to respond to the concerns of the territorial Government with regard to the question of immigration;

4. *Further requests* the administering Power to cooperate in establishing programmes specifically intended to promote the sustainable development of economic activities and enterprises, noting the special role of the Chamorro people in the development of Guam;

5. *Takes note* of the request by the elected Governor to the administering Power to lift restrictions to allow for foreign airlines to transport passengers between Guam and the United States of America to provide for a more competitive market and increased visitor arrivals;

VII
Montserrat

Taking note of the working paper prepared by the Secretariat on Montserrat[16] and other relevant information,

Taking note with interest of the statements made and the information on the political and economic situation in Montserrat provided by the Chief Minister of the Territory to the Caribbean regional seminar, held at The Valley, Anguilla, from 20 to 22 May 2003,

Noting with concern the continued consequences of the volcanic eruption, which led to the evacuation of three quarters of the Territory's population to safe areas of the island and to areas outside the Territory, which continues to have enduring consequences for the economy of the island,

Welcoming the continued assistance provided to the Territory by States members of the Caribbean Community, in particular Antigua and Barbuda, which has offered safe refuge and access to educational and health facilities, as well as employment for thousands who have left the Territory,

Noting the continuing efforts of the administering Power and the territorial Government to deal with the consequences of the volcanic eruption,

1. *Calls upon* the administering Power, the specialized agencies and other organizations of the United Nations system, as well as regional and other organizations, to continue to provide assistance to the Territory in alleviating the consequences of the volcanic eruption;

2. *Recalls* the 2002 report of the Constitutional Review Commission, which contains a series of recommendations on constitutional advancement, including the devolution of

power from the appointed Governor to the elected Government, and the call in favour of a free-association arrangement;

3. *Welcomes* the convening of a committee of the House of Assembly in 2005 to review the report, and the subsequent discussions between the elected Government and the administering Power on constitutional advancement and devolution of power;

VIII
Pitcairn

Taking note of the working paper prepared by the Secretariat on Pitcairn[17] and other relevant information,

Taking into account the unique nature of Pitcairn in terms of population and area,

Noting the position of the representative of the elected Government, as expressed at the 2004 Pacific regional seminar, that the people of the Territory did not fully understand all the possibilities or the significance of the various self-determination options that might be available to them, and that the review of the Constitution was deferred to after 2006,

1. *Requests* the administering Power to continue its assistance for the improvement of the economic, social, educational and other conditions of the population of the Territory and to continue its discussions with the representatives of Pitcairn on how best to support their economic security;

2. *Takes note* of the position of the representative of the elected Government of the Territory favouring discussions on self-determination in advance of a constitutional review, and notes that a United Nations visiting mission to the Territory would heighten the awareness of the people of their political future;

IX
Saint Helena

Taking note of the working paper prepared by the Secretariat on Saint Helena[18] and other relevant information,

Taking into account the unique character of Saint Helena, its population and its natural resources,

Taking note of the constitutional review process led by the territorial Government and the consultative poll with regard to a new Constitution held in Saint Helena on 25 May 2005,

Aware of the efforts of the administering Power and the territorial authorities to improve the socio-economic conditions of the population of Saint Helena, in particular in the sphere of food production, continuing high unemployment and limited transport and communications,

Noting the importance of improving the infrastructure and accessibility of Saint Helena,

Noting also the importance of the right to nationality for Saint Helenians and their request that it, in principle, be included in the new Constitution,

Noting with concern the problem of unemployment on the island and the joint action of the administering Power and the territorial Government to deal with it,

1. *Welcomes* the continuing constitutional review process and the recent consultative poll led by the Government of Saint Helena in cooperation with the administering Power;

2. *Also welcomes* the decision by the administering Power to provide funding for the construction of an international airport on Saint Helena to become operational in 2010, including all required infrastructure;

3. *Requests* the administering Power and relevant international organizations to continue to support the efforts of the territorial Government to address the socioeconomic development challenges, including the high unemployment and the limited transport and communications problems, as well as to support the additional infrastructure required for the airport project;

4. *Calls upon* the administering Power to take into account the concerns of Saint Helenians with regard to the right to nationality;

X
Turks and Caicos Islands

Taking note of the working paper prepared by the Secretariat on the Turks and Caicos Islands[19] and other relevant information,

Recalling the 2002 report of the Constitutional Modernization Review Body, which examined the existing Constitution and made recommendations on the internal structure of government and devolution of power from the appointed Governor to the elected Government,

Welcoming the dispatch of the United Nations special mission to the Turks and Caicos Islands in 2006, at the request of the territorial Government and with the concurrence of the administering Power, which provided information to the people of the Territory on the role of the United Nations in the process of self-determination, on the legitimate political status options as clearly defined in General Assembly resolution 1541 (XV) and on the experiences of other small States that have achieved a full measure of self-government,

Taking note of the conclusions of the report of the United Nations special mission to the Turks and Caicos Islands,[20]

1. *Recalls* the statement made by the Chief Minister of the Territory at the Caribbean regional seminar held in Canouan, Saint Vincent and the Grenadines, from 17 to 19 May 2005, that his Government was in favour of a reasonable period of full internal self-government before moving to independence;

2. *Takes note* of the announcement made by the Chief Minister in 2006 of the conclusion of discussions between the territorial Government and the administering Power resulting in an agreement for an advance constitution, which would be circulated to the Government and the opposition for comment and to the general public for information, with the consultative process concluding with a debate in the Legislative Council;

3. *Also takes note* of the significant and steady period of economic expansion, in particular over the last decade, fuelled by the emergence of high-end tourism, and the need for attention to be paid to the enhancement of social cohesion in the Territory;

XI
United States Virgin Islands

Taking note of the working paper prepared by the Secretariat on the United States Virgin Islands[21] and other relevant information,

Taking note with interest of the statements made and the information provided by the representative of the Governor of the Territory at the Caribbean regional seminar held in Canouan, Saint Vincent and the Grenadines, from 17 to 19 May 2005,

Noting the continuing interest of the territorial Government in seeking associate membership in the Organization of Eastern Caribbean States and observer status in the Caribbean Community and the pending request by the Territory to the administering Power for the delegation of authority to proceed, as well as the 2003 resolution of the territorial legislature in support of that request,

Noting also the expressed interest of the territorial Government in being included in regional programmes of the United Nations Development Programme and in the records and archives management programme of the United Nations Educational, Scientific and Cultural Organization,

Recalling that the Territory has not received a United Nations visiting mission since 1977, and bearing in mind the formal request of the Territory for such a mission in 1993 to assist the Territory in its political education process and to observe the Territory's only referendum on political status options in its history,

Noting the ongoing cooperation between the territorial Government and Denmark on the repatriation of artefacts and archives,

Also noting that the convening of a fifth Constitutional Convention to review the existing Revised Organic Act, which organizes the internal governance arrangement, has been postponed to 2007,

1. *Requests* the administering Power to continue to assist the territorial Government in achieving its political, economic and social goals;

2. *Once again requests* the administering Power to facilitate the participation of the Territory, as appropriate, in various organizations, in particular the Organization of Eastern Caribbean States, the Caribbean Community and the Association of Caribbean States;

3. *Calls for* the inclusion of the Territory in regional programmes of the United Nations Development Programme, consistent with the participation of other Non-Self-Governing Territories;

4. *Welcomes* the establishment of the Inter-Virgin Islands Council between the elected Governments of the United States Virgin Islands and the British Virgin Islands as a mechanism of functional cooperation between the two neighbouring Terrirtories;

5. *Notes* the position of the territorial Government supporting the ownership and control of the natural resources of the Territory, including marine resources, and its calls for the return of those marine resources to its jurisdiction;

6. *Welcomes* the cooperation agreements existing between the Territory and Denmark, the former colonial Power of the Territory, on the exchange of artefacts and the repatriation of archival material.

79th plenary meeting
14 December 2006

---

[1] *Official Records of the General Assembly, Sixty-first Session, Supplement No. 23* (A/61/23), chap. IX.

[2] Resolution 1514 (XV).

[3] A/56/61, annex.

[4] See *Report of the United Nations Conference on Environment and Development, Rio de Janeiro, 3–14 June 1992*, vol. I, *Resolutions Adopted by the Conference* (United Nations publication, Sales No. E.93.I.8 and corrigendum); *Report of the World Conference on Natural Disaster Reduction, Yokohama, Japan, 23–27 May 1994* (A/CONF.172/9), chap. I; *Report of the Global Conference on the Sustainable Development of Small Island Developing States, Bridgetown, Barbados, 25 April–6 May 1994* (United Nations publication, Sales No. E.94.I.18 and corrigenda), chap. I; *Report of the International Conference on Population and Development, Cairo, 5–13 September 1994* (United Nations publication, Sales No. E.95.XIII.18), chap. I, resolution 1, annex; *Report of the United Nations Conference on Human Settlements (Habitat II), Istanbul, 3–14 June 1996* (United Nations publication, Sales No. E.97.IV.6), chap. I, resolution 1, annex II; *Report of the World Summit on Sustainable Development, Johannesburg, South Africa, 26 August–4 September 2002* (United Nations publication, Sales No. E.03.II.A.1 and corrigendum), chap. I, resolution 2, annex; *Report of the World Conference against Racism, Racial Discrimination, Xenophobia and Related Intolerance, Durban, 31 August–8 September 2001* (A/CONF.189/12 and Corr.1), chap. I.

[5] See resolution 2200 A (XXI), annex.

[6] See A/AC.109/2006/3-8, 11 and 12, 13 and 13/Corr.1, 15 and 16.

[7] A/60/71 and Add.1.

[8] A/AC.109/2006/7.

[9] Pursuant to Secretary's Order 2657, Department of the Interior, United States of America.

[10] A/AC.109/2006/4.

[11] A/AC.109/2006/6.

[12] A/AC.109/2005/19.

[13] A/AC.109/2006/12.

[14] A/AC.109/2006/16.

[15] A/AC.109/2006/8.

[16] A/AC.109/2006/13 and Corr.1.

[17] A/AC.109/2006/5.

[18] A/AC.109/2006/3.

[19] A/AC.109/2006/15.

[20] A/AC.109/2006/19.

[21] A/AC.109/2006/11.

Resolution 61/129

[on the report of the Special Political and Decolonization Committee (Fourth Committee) (A/61/415)]

61/129. Dissemination of information on decolonization

The General Assembly,

Having examined the chapter of the report of the Special Committee on the Situation with regard to the Implementation of the Declaration on the Granting of Independence to Colonial Countries and Peoples relating to the dissemination of information on decolonization and publicity for the work of the United Nations in the field of decolonization,[1]

Recalling General Assembly resolution 1514 (XV) of 14 December 1960, containing the Declaration on the Granting of Independence to Colonial Countries and Peoples, and other resolutions and decisions of the United Nations concerning the dissemination of information on decolonization, in particular Assembly resolution 60/118 of 8 December 2005,

Recognizing the need for flexible, practical and innovative approaches towards reviewing the options of self-determination for the peoples of Non-Self-Governing Territories with a view to implementing the plan of action for the Second International Decade for the Eradication of Colonialism,[2]

Reiterating the importance of dissemination of information as an instrument for furthering the aims of the Declaration, and mindful of the role of world public opinion in effectively assisting the peoples of Non-Self-Governing Territories to achieve self-determination,

Recognizing the role played by the administering Powers in transmitting information to the Secretary-General in accordance with the terms of Article 73 *e* of the Charter of the United Nations,

Also recognizing the role of the Department of Public Information of the Secretariat, through its United Nations information centres, in the dissemination of information at the regional level on the activities of the United Nations,

Recalling its resolution 60/112 of 8 December 2005, in which it requested the Department, in consultation with the United Nations Development Programme, the specialized agencies and the Speical Committee, to prepare an information leaflet on assistance programmes available to the Non-Self-Governing Territories and to disseminate it widely in them,

Aware of the role of non-governmental organizations in the dissemination of information on decolonization,

1. *Approves* the activities in the field of dissemination of information on decolonization undertaken by the Department of Public Information and the Department of Political Affairs of the Secretariat, in accordance with the relevant resolutions of the United Nations on decolonization;

2. *Considers it important* to continue and expand its efforts to ensure the widest possible dissemination of information on decolonization, with particular emphasis on the options of self-determination available for the peoples of the Non-Self-Governing Territories, and to this end, requests the Department of Public Information, including through the United Nations information centres in the relevant regions, to disseminate material to the Non-Self-Governing Territories;

3. *Requests* the Secretary-General to further enhance the information provided on the United Nations decolonization website by including the statements and scholarly papers presented at the regional seminars, as well as the full series of reports of the Special Committee on the Situation with regard to the Implementation of the Declaration on the Granting of Independence to Colonial Countries and Peoples;

4. *Requests* the Department of Public Information to implement the relevant provisions of General Assembly resolution 60/112 on the preparation of an information leaflet on the assistance programmes available to the Non-Self-Governing Territories;

5. *Requests* the Department of Political Affairs and the Department of Public Information to implement the recommendations of the Special Committee to continue their efforts to take measures through all the media available, including publications, radio and television, as well as the Internet, to give publicity to the work of the United Nations in the field of decolonization and, inter alia:

(*a*) To develop procedures to collect, prepare and disseminate, particularly to the Territories, basic material on the issue of self-determination of the peoples of the Non-Self-Governing Territories;

(*b*) To seek the full cooperation of the administering Powers in the discharge of the tasks referred to above;

(*c*) To develop a programme of collaboration with the appropriate regional and intergovernmental organizations, particularly in the Pacific and Caribbean regions, by holding periodic expert briefings and exchanging information;

(*d*) To encourage the involvement of non-governmental organizations in the dissemination of information on decolonization;

(*e*) To encourage the involvement of the Non-Self-Governing Territories in the dissemination of information on decolonization;

(*f*) To report to the Special Committee on measures taken in the implementation of the present resolution;

6. *Requests* all States, including the administering Powers, to accelerate the dissemination of information referred to in paragraph 2 above;

7. *Requests* the Special Committee to continue to examine this question and to report to the General Assembly at its sixty-second session on the implementation of the present resolution.

79th plenary meeting
14 December 2006

[1] *Official Records of the General Assembly, Sixty-first Session, Supplement No. 23* (A/61/23), chap. III.

[2] A/56/61, annex.

Resolution 61/130

[on the report of the Special Political and Decolonization Committee (Fourth Committee) (A/61/415)]

61/130. Implementation of the Declaration on the Granting of Independence to Colonial Countries and Peoples

The General Assembly,

Having examined the report of the Special Committee on the Situation with regard to the Implementation of the Declaration on the Granting of Independence to Colonial Countries and Peoples,[1]

Recalling its resolution 1514 (XV) of 14 December 1960, containing the Declaration on the Granting of Independence to Colonial Countries and Peoples, and all its subsequent resolutions concerning the implementation of the Declaration, the most recent of which was resolution 60/119 of 8 December 2005, as well as the relevant resolutions of the Security Council,

Bearing in mind its resolution 55/146 of 8 December 2000, by which it declared the period 2001–2010 the Second International Decade for the Eradication of Colonialism, and the need to examine ways to ascertain the wishes of the peoples of the Non-Self-Governing Territories on the basis of resolution 1514 (XV) and other relevant resolutions on decolonization,

Welcoming the Plan of Implementation of the Decolonization Mandate 2006– 2007,[2] which organizes the actions of the decolonization mandate to be carried out by the wider United Nations system,

Recognizing that the eradication of colonialism has been one of the priorities of the United Nations and continues to be one of its priorities for the decade that began in 2001,

Reconfirming the need to take measures to eliminate colonialism by 2010, as called for in its resolution 55/146,

Reiterating its conviction of the need for the eradication of colonialism, as well as racial discrimination and violations of basic human rights,

Stressing the importance of the formal participation of the administering Powers in the work of the Special Committee,

Noting with interest the cooperation and active participation of some administering Powers in the work of the Special Committee, and encouraging the others also to do so,

Taking note that the Pacific regional seminar, originally scheduled to convene from 23 to 25 May 2006 in Timor-Leste, is to be rescheduled to a later date in 2006,

1. *Reaffirms* its resolution 1514 (XV) and all other resolutions and decisions on decolonization, including its resolution 55/146, by which it declared the period 2001–2010 the Second International Decade for the Eradication of Colonialism, and calls upon the administering Powers, in accordance with those resolutions, to take all necessary steps to enable the peoples of the Non-Self-Governing Territories concerned to exercise fully as soon as possible their right to self-determination, including independence;

2. *Reaffirms once again* that the existence of colonialism in any form or manifestation, including economic exploitation, is incompatible with the Charter of the United Nations, the Declaration on the Granting of Independence to Colonial Countries and Peoples and the Universal Declaration of Human Rights;[3]

3. *Reaffirms its determination* to continue to take all steps necessary to bring about the complete and speedy eradication of colonialism and the faithful observance by all States of the relevant provisions of the Charter, the Declaration on the Granting of Independence to Colonial Countries and Peoples and the Universal Declaration of Human Rights;

4. *Affirms once again its support* for the aspirations of the peoples under colonial rule to exercise their right to self-determination, including independence, in accordance with relevant resolutions of the United Nations on decolonization;

5. *Calls upon* the administering Powers to cooperate fully with the Special Committee on the Situation with regard to the Declaration on the Granting of Independence to Colonial Countries and Peoples to finalize before the end of 2007 a constructive programme of work on a case-by-case basis for the Non-Self-Governing Territories to facilitate the implementation of the mandate of the Special Committee and the relevant resolutions on decolonization, including resolutions on specific Territories;

6. *Commends* the professional, open and transparent referendum to determine the future status of Tokelau, held under United Nations supervision from 11 to 15 February 2006;

7. *Notes* that the referendum did not produce the two-thirds majority of the valid votes cast required by the General Fono to change the status of Tokelau as a Non-Self-Governing Territory under the administration of New Zealand;

8. *Welcomes* the agreement of New Zealand and the Tokelau Council of Ongoing Government to maintain the referendum package of a draft constitution and draft treaty of free association as a possible future basis for an act of self-determination by Tokelau;

9. *Also welcomes* the dispatch of the United Nations special mission to the Turks and Caicos Islands, at the request of the territorial Government and with the concurrence of the administering Power, which provided information to the people of the Territory on the role of the United Nations in the process of self-determination, on the legitimate political status options, as clearly defined in General Assembly resolution 1541 (XV) of 15 December 1960, and on the experiences of other small States which have achieved a full measure of self-government;

10. *Requests* the Special Committee to continue to seek suitable means for the immediate and full implementation of the Declaration and to carry out the actions approved by the General Assembly regarding the International Decade for the Eradication of Colonialism and the Second International Decade for the Eradication of Colonialism in all Territories that have not yet exercised their right to self-determination, including independence, and in particular:

(*a*) To formulate specific proposals to bring about an end to colonialism and to report thereon to the General Assembly at its sixty-second session;

(*b*) To continue to examine the implementation by Member States of resolution 1514 (XV) and other relevant resolutions on decolonization;

(*c*) To continue to examine the political, economic and social situation in the Non-Self-Governing Territories, and to recommend, as appropriate, to the General Assembly the most suitable steps to be taken to enable the populations of those Territories to exercise their right to self-determination, including independence, in accordance with relevant resolutions on decolonization, including resolutions on specific Territories;

(*d*) To finalize before the end of 2007 a constructive programme of work on a case-by-case basis for the Non-Self-Governing Territories to facilitate the implementation of the mandate of the Special Committee and the relevant resolutions on decolonization, including resolutions on specific Territories;

(*e*) To continue to dispatch visiting missions to the Non-Self-Governing Territories in accordance with relevant resolutions on decolonization, including resolutions on specific Territories;

(*f*) To conduct seminars, as appropriate, for the purpose of receiving and disseminating information on the work of the Special Committee, and to facilitate participation by the peoples of the Non-Self-Governing Territories in those seminars;

(*g*) To take all necessary steps to enlist worldwide support among Governments, as well as national and international organizations, for the achievement of the objectives of the Declaration and the implementation of the relevant resolutions of the United Nations;

(*h*) To observe annually the Week of Solidarity with the Peoples of Non-Self-Governing Territories;[4]

11. *Recognizes* that the plan of action for the Second International Decade for the Eradication of Colonialism,[5] the case-by-case process of assessment of the attainment of self-government in each Territory, and the Plan of Implementation of the Decolonization Mandate 2006–2007[2] represent an important legislative authority for the attainment of self-government by the end of 2010;

12. *Calls upon* all States, in particular the administering Powers, as well as the specialized agencies and other organizations of the United Nations system, to give effect within their respective spheres of competence to the recommendations of the Special Committee for the implementation of the Declaration and other relevant resolutions of the United Nations;

13. *Calls upon* the administering Powers to ensure that the economic activities in the Non-Self-Governing Territories under their administration do not adversely affect the interests of the peoples but instead promote development, and to assist them in the exercise of their right to self-determination;

14. *Urges* the administering Powers concerned to take effective measures to safeguard and guarantee the inalienable rights of the peoples of the Non-Self-Governing Territories to their natural resources, including land, and to establish and maintain control over the future development of those resources, and requests the administering Powers to take all necessary steps to protect the property rights of the peoples of those Territories;

15. *Urges* all States, directly and through their action in the specialized agencies and other organizations of the United Nations system, to provide moral and material assistance to the peoples of the Non-Self-Governing Territories, and requests the administering Powers to take steps to enlist and make effective use of all possible assistance, on both a bilateral and a multilateral basis, in the strengthening of the economies of those Territories;

16. *Reaffirms* that the United Nations visiting missions to the Territories are an effective means of ascertaining the situation in the Territories, as well as the wishes and aspirations of their inhabitants, and calls upon the administering Powers to continue to cooperate with the Special Committee in the discharge of its mandate and to facilitate visiting missions to the Territories;

17. *Calls upon* the administering Powers that have not participated formally in the work of the Special Committee to do so at its session in 2007;

18. *Requests* the Secretary-General, the specialized agencies and other organizations of the United Nations system to provide economic, social and other assistance to the Non-Self-Governing Territories and to continue to do so, as appropriate, after they exercise their right to self-determination, including independence;

19. *Approves* the report of the Special Committee on the Situation with regard to the Implementation of the Declaration on the Granting of Independence to Colonial Countries and Peoples covering its work during 2006, including the programme of work envisaged for 2007;[1]

20. *Requests* the Secretary-General to provide the Special Committee with the facilities and services required for the implementation of the present resolution, as well as the other resolutions and decisions on decolonization adopted by the General Assembly and the Special Committee.

79th plenary meeting
14 December 2006

---

[1] *Official Records of the General Assembly, Sixty-first Session, Supplement No. 23* (A/61/23).

[2] A/60/853-E/2006/75, annex.

[3] Resolution 217 A (III).

[4] See resolution 54/91.

[5] A/56/61, annex.

Resolution 61/131

[without reference to a Main Committee (A/61/L.42 and Add.1)]

61/131. International cooperation on humanitarian assistance in the field of natural disasters, from relief to development

The General Assembly,

Reaffirming its resolution 46/182 of 19 December 1991, the annex to which contains the guiding principles for the strengthening of the coordination of emergency humanitarian assistance of the United Nations system, as well as all its resolutions on international cooperation on humanitarian assistance in the field of natural disasters, from relief to development, and recalling the resolutions of the humanitarian segments of the substantive sessions of the Economic and Social Council,

Recognizing the importance of the principles of neutrality, humanity, impartiality and independence for the provision of humanitarian assistance,

Reiterating that independence means the autonomy of humanitarian objectives as distinct from the political, economic, military or other objectives that may be pursued by any actor with regard to areas where humanitarian action is being implemented,

Welcoming the Hyogo Declaration,[1] the Hyogo Framework for Action 2005–2015: Building the Resilience of Nations and Communities to Disasters[2] and the common statement of the special session on the Indian Ocean disaster: risk reduction for a safer future,[3] as adopted by the World Conference on Disaster Reduction, held in Kobe, Hyogo, Japan, from 18 to 22 January 2005,

Emphasizing that the affected State has the primary responsibility in the initiation, organization, coordination and implementation of humanitarian assistance within its territory and in the facilitation of the work of humanitarian organizations in mitigating the consequences of natural disasters,

Emphasizing also the responsibility of all States to undertake disaster preparedness, response and mitigation efforts in order to minimize the impact of natural disasters, while recognizing the importance of international cooperation in support of the efforts of affected countries which may have limited capacities in this regards,

Noting the critical role played by local resources, and by existing in-country capacities, in natural disaster management and risk reduction, disaster response, rehabilitation and development,

Recognizing the importance of international cooperation in support of the efforts of the affected States in dealing with natural disasters in all their phases, and of strengthening the response capacity of countries affected by disaster,

Noting with appreciation the important role played by Member States, including developing countries, that have granted necessary and continued generous assistance to countries and peoples stricken by natural disasters,

Recognizing the significant role played by national Red Cross and Red Crescent societies, as part of the International Red Cross and Red Crescent Movement, in disaster preparedness and risk reduction, disaster response, rehabilitation and development,

Emphasizing the importance of addressing vulnerability and integrating risk reduction into all phases of natural disaster management, post-natural disaster recovery and development planning,

Welcoming the work carried out by the Intergovernmental Oceanographic Commission of the United Nations Educational, Scientific and Cultural Organization in the setting up of regional tsunami early warning systems, in the Indian Ocean, the Mediterranean and the north-east Atlantic, and noting with appreciation the convening of the Third International Conference on Early Warning, held in Bonn, Germany, from 27 to 29 March 2006,

Recognizing that efforts to achieve economic growth, sustainable development and internationally agreed development goals, including the Millennium Development Goals, can be adversely affected by natural disasters, and noting the positive contribution that those efforts can make in strengthening the resilience of populations to such disasters,

Emphasizing, in this context, the important role of development organizations in supporting national efforts to mitigate the consequences of natural disasters,

1. *Takes note* of the reports of the Secretary-General entitled "International cooperation on humanitarian assistance in the field of natural disasters, from relief to development";[4] "Strengthening of the coordination of emergency humanitarian assistance of the United Nations";[5] "Strengthening emergency relief, rehabilitation, reconstruction, recovery and prevention in the aftermath of the Indian Ocean tsunami disaster";[6] and "Central Emergency Response Fund";[7]

2. *Expresses its deep concern* at the number and scale of natural disasters and their increasing impact, resulting in massive losses of life and property worldwide, in particular in vulnerable societies lacking adequate capacity to mitigate effectively the long-term negative social, economic and environmental consequences of natural disasters;

3. *Calls upon* States to fully implement the Hyogo Declaration[1] and the Hyogo Framework for Action 2005–2015: Building the Resilience of Nations and Communities to Disasters,[2] in particular those commitments related to assistance for developing countries that are prone to natural disasters and for disaster-stricken States in the transition phase towards sustainable physical, social and economic recovery, for risk-reduction activities in post-disaster recovery and for rehabilitation processes;

4. *Calls upon* all States to adopt, where required, and to continue to implement effectively, necessary legislative and other appropriate measures to mitigate the effects of natural disasters and integrate disaster risk reduction strategies into development planning, and in this regard requests the international community to continue to assist developing countries as well as countries with economies in transition;

5. *Welcomes* the effective cooperation among the affected States, relevant bodies of the United Nations system, donor countries, regional and international financial institutions and other relevant organizations, such as the International Red Cross and Red Crescent Movement, and civil society, in the coordination and delivery of emergency relief, and stresses the need to continue such cooperation and delivery throughout relief operations and medium- and long-term rehabilitation and reconstruction efforts, in a manner that reduces vulnerability to future natural hazards;

6. *Reiterates* the commitment to support the efforts of countries, in particular developing countries, to strengthen their capacities at all levels in order to prepare for and respond rapidly to natural disasters and mitigate their impact;

7. *Stresses* that, to increase further the effectiveness of humanitarian assistance, particular international cooperation efforts should be undertaken to enhance and broaden further the utilization of national and local capacities and, where appropriate, of regional and subregional capacities of developing countries for disaster preparedness and response, which may be made available in closer proximity to the site of a disaster, and more efficiently and at lower cost;

8. *Also stresses*, in this context, the importance of strengthening international cooperation, particularly through the effective use of multilateral mechanisms, in the timely provision of humanitarian assistance through all phases of a disaster, from relief and mitigation to development, including the provision of adequate resources;

9. *Welcomes* the role of the Office for the Coordination of Humanitarian Affairs of the Secretariat as the focal point within the overall United Nations system for the promotion

and coordination of disaster response among United Nations humanitarian organizations and other humanitarian partners;

10. *Also welcomes*, so as to increase further the effectiveness of humanitarian assistance, the incorporation of experts from developing countries that are prone to natural disasters into the United Nations Disaster Assessment and Coordination system, and the work of the International Search and Rescue Advisory Group in assisting such countries in strengthening urban search and rescue capacities and establishing mechanisms for improving their coordination of national and international response in the field, and recalls in this regard its resolution 57/150 of 16 December 2002 entitled "Strengthening the effectiveness and coordination of international urban search and rescue assistance";

11. *Requests* the Secretary-General, in consultation with States and relevant organizations, to continue to explore ways to strengthen the rapid response capacities of the international community to provide immediate humanitarian relief, building on existing arrangements and ongoing initiatives;

12. *Requests* the Secretary-General to develop more systematic links with Member States offering military assets for natural disaster response in order to identify the availability of such assets;

13. *Notes* that the Central Register of Disaster Management Capacities, including the Directory of Advanced Technologies for Disaster Response, has the potential to support planning preparedness and response activities, and requests the Secretary-General to propose options to enhance its relevance;

14. *Encourages* donors to consider the importance of ensuring that assistance in the case of higher-profile natural disasters does not come at the expense of those natural disasters that may be relatively lower-profile, bearing in mind that the allocation of resources should be driven by needs;

15. *Recognizes* that information and telecommunication technology can play an important role in disaster response, encourages Member States to develop emergency response telecommunication capacities, and encourages the international community to assist the efforts of developing countries in this area, where needed;

16. *Encourages* States that have not acceded to or ratified the Tampere Convention on the Provision of Telecommunication Resources for Disaster Mitigation and Relief Operations, which entered into force on 8 January 2005,[8] to consider doing so;

17. *Encourages* the further use of space-based and ground-based remote-sensing technologies, as well as the sharing of geographical data, for the prevention, mitigation and management of natural disasters, where appropriate;

18. *Encourages* Member States, relevant United Nations organizations and international financial institutions to enhance the global capacity for sustainable post-disaster recovery in areas such as coordination with traditional and non-traditional partners, identification and dissemination of lessons learned, development of common tools and mechanisms for recovery needs assessment, strategy development and programming, and incorporation of risk reduction into all recovery processes, and welcomes the ongoing efforts to this end;

19. *Requests* the United Nations system to improve its coordination of disaster recovery efforts, from relief to development, inter alia, by strengthening institutional, coordination and strategic planning efforts in disaster recovery, in support of national authorities;

20. *Stresses* the importance of rapid access to funds to ensure a more predictable and timely United Nations response to humanitarian emergencies, and welcomes in this regard the establishment of the Central Emergency Response Fund in its resolution 60/124 of 15 December 2005;

21. *Requests* the Secretary-General to continue to improve the international response to natural disasters, and to report thereon to the General Assembly at its sixty-second session.

79th plenary meeting
14 December 2006

---

[1] A/CONF.206/6 and Corr.1, chap. I, resolution 1.

[2] Ibid., resolution 2.

[3] A/CONF.206/6 and Corr.1, annex II.

[4] A/61/314.

[5] A/61/85-E/2006/81.

[6] A/61/87-E/2006/77.

[7] A/61/85/Add.1-E/2006/81/Add.1.

[8] United Nations, *Treaty Series*, vol. 2296, No. 40906.

Resolution 61/132

[without reference to a Main Committee (A/61/L.44 and Add.1)]

61/132. Strengthening emergency relief, rehabilitation, reconstruction and prevention in the aftermath of the Indian Ocean tsunami disaster

The General Assembly,

Recalling its resolutions 46/182 of 19 December 1991, 57/152 of 16 December 2002, 57/256 of 20 December 2002, 58/25 of 5 December 2003, 58/214 and 58/215 of 23 December 2003, 59/212 of 20 December 2004, 59/231 and 59/233 of 22 December 2004, 59/279 of 19 January 2005 and 60/15 of 14 November 2005,

Noting the Declaration on Action to Strengthen Emergency Relief, Rehabilitation, Reconstruction and Prevention in the Aftermath of the Earthquake and Tsunami Disaster of 26 December 2004, adopted at the special meeting of leaders of the Association of Southeast Asian Nations, held in Jakarta on 6 January 2005,[1]

Recalling the Hyogo Declaration[2] and the Hyogo Framework for Action 2005–2015,[3] as well as the common statement of the special session on the Indian Ocean disaster,[4] adopted at the World Conference on Disaster Reduction, held in Kobe, Hyogo, Japan, from 18 to 22 January 2005,

Taking note of the report of the Secretary-General,[5]

Taking note with appreciation of the convening of the Global Consortium for Tsunami-Affected Countries by the Office of the United Nations Special Envoy for Tsunami Recovery in April 2006, which brought together national Governments, United Nations agencies, other intergovernmental organizations, the international financial institutions, consortia of non-governmental organizations and donor Governments with the aim of identifying common priorities and implementing actions towards achieving community-driven development, meeting funding gaps, fostering accountability and transparency, intergrating disaster disk reduction, disaster resilience and an effective early warning system that is, inter alia, people-centerd into national development plans, building social and physical infrastructure and supporting microfinance activites,

Welcoming the convening of the final meeting of the Global Consortium for Tsunami-Affected Countries in New York on 15 November 2006, chaired by Mr. William Jefferson Clinton, former President of the United States of America, in his capacity as Special Envoy for Tsunami Recovery, which aimed to review the progress made and to identify key recovery and reconstruction goals,

Noting with appreciation the convening of the Third International Conference on Early Warning, in Bonn, Germany, from 27 to 29 March 2006,

Stressing the need to develop and implement risk reduction strategies and to integrate them, where appropriate, into national development plans, in particular through the implementation of the International Strategy for Disaster Reduction, so as to enhance the resilience of populations in disasters and reduce the risks to them, their livelihoods, the social and economic infrastructure and environmental resources, and stressing also the need for Governments to develop and implement effective national plans for hazard warning systems with a disaster risk reduction approach,

Emphasizing that disaster reduction, including reducing vulnerability to natural disasters, is an important element that contributes to the achievement of sustainable development,

Welcoming the role of the Intergovernmental Oceanographic Commission of the United Nations Educational, Scientific and Cultural Organization in the establishment and implementation of the Indian Ocean Tsunami Warning and Mitigation System, given the importance of strengthening regional and subregional cooperation and coordination, which is essential for effective early warning system arrangements for tsunamis,

Noting the communiqué relating to support for tsunami and multi-hazard warning systems within the context of the Global Earth Observation System of Systems, which supports the interoperability of systems and free and open real-time data exchange, adopted at the third Earth Observation Summit, in Brussels, on 16 February 2005,

Welcoming the establishment of the Multi-Donor Voluntary Trust Fund on Tsunami Early Warning Arrangements in the Indian Ocean and Southeast Asia, and inviting Governments, donor countries, relevant international organizations, international and regional financial institutions, the private sector and civil society to consider contributing to the Trust Fund through financial contributions and technical cooperation to support the establishment of the tsunami early warning system in accordance with the needs of the countries of the Indian Ocean and Southeast Asia so that the Trust Fund contributes to the development of an integrated early warning system based on adequate resources and comprising a network of collaborative centres connected to the global system,

Stressing the need for continued commitment to assist the affected countries and their peoples, particularly the most vulnerable groups, to fully recover from the catastrophic and traumatic effects of the disaster, including in their medium- and long-term rehabilitation and reconstruction efforts, and welcoming Government and international assistance measures in this regard,

1. *Notes with appreciation* the efforts by the Governments of affected countries to undertake the rehabilitation and reconstruction phase, as well as in enhancing financial transparency and accountability, with respect to the channelling and utilization of resources, including, as appropriate, through the involvement of international public auditors;

2. *Commends* the prompt response, continued support, generous assistance and contributions of the international community, donor Governments, civil society, the private sector and individuals, in the relief, rehabilitation and reconstruction efforts, which reflect the spirit of international solidarity and cooperation to address the disaster;

3. *Takes note with appreciation* of the continued work of Mr. William Jefferson Clinton, former President of the United States of America, the United Nations Special Envoy for Tsunami Recovery, and his various initiatives, and encourages his efforts to continue sustaining the political will and to promote the identification of priorities and integration of efforts of the international community, particularly regional and international financial institutions, civil society and the private sector, to support medium- and long-term rehabilitation, reconstruction and risk reduction efforts led by the Governments of affected countries;

4. *Encourages* donor communities and international and regional financial institutions, as well as the private sector and civil society, to strengthen partnerships and to continue to support the medium- and long-term rehabilitation and reconstruction needs of the affected countries;

5. *Encourages* the continued effective coordination among the Governments of affected countries, relevant bodies of the United Nations system, international organizations, donor countries, regional and international financial institutions, civil society, the International Red Cross and Red Crescent Movement and private sectors involved in rehabilitation and reconstruction efforts, in order to ensure the effective implementation of existing joint programmes and to prevent unnecessary duplication and reduce vulnerability to future natural hazards, as well as to adequately respond to the remaining humanitarian needs, where needed;

6. *Stresses* the need for the development of stronger institutions, mechanisms and capacities at the regional, national and local levels, as affirmed in the Hyogo Declaration[2] and the Hyogo Framework for Action 2005–2015,[3] and the promotion of public education, awareness and community participation, in order to systematically build resilience to hazards and disasters, as well as reduce the risks and the vulnerability of populations to disasters, including an effective and sustained tsunami warning system, particularly in tsunami-prone countries;

7. *Calls upon* States to fully implement the Hyogo Declaration and the Hyogo Framework for Action 2005–2015, in particular those commitments related to assistance for developing countries that are prone to natural disasters and for disaster-stricken States in the

transition phase towards sustainable, physical, social and economic recovery, for risk-reduction activities in post-disaster recovery and for rehabilitation processes;

8. *Stresses* the importance of and the need for regular updating of recovery assessment by the Governments of affected countries, the United Nations system and international and regional financial institutions, based on the affected countries' national data and utilizing a consistent methodology, in order to reassess progress and identify gaps and priorities, with the participation of the local community during the recovery and reconstruction phase in order to build back better;

9. *Emphasizes* the need to promote transparency and accountability among donors and recipient countries by means of, inter alia, a unified financial and sectoral information online tracking system, and highlights the importance of timely and accurate information on assessed needs and the sources and uses of funds, and the continued support of donors, where needed, for further development of online tracking systems in the affected countries;

10. *Stresses* the need for relevant bodies of the United Nations system, international organizations, regional and international financial institutions, civil society and the private sector to implement programmes according to assessed needs and agreed priorities of the Governments of tsunami-affected countries and to ensure full transparency and accountability for their programme activities;

11. *Notes with appreciation* the efforts of international agencies, donor countries and relevant civil society organizations in supporting the Governments of affected countries to develop national capacity for tsunami warning and response so as to increase public awareness and provide community-based support for disaster risk reduction;

12. *Encourages* international agencies and Governments to enhance and accelerate their support for the development, implementation and maintenance of the Indian Ocean Tsunami Warning and Mitigation System, under the Intergovernmental Oceanographic Commission, as the appropriate vehicle for the rapid and timely exchange of alerts and related information required to deliver effective tsunami warnings at the national level;

13. *Requests* the Secretary-General to continue to explore ways to strengthen the rapid response capacities of the international community to provide immediate humanitarian relief, building on existing arrangements and ongoing initiatives;

14. *Encourages* the Emergency Relief Coordinator to continue his efforts to strengthen the coordination of humanitarian assistance, and calls upon relevant United Nations organizations and other humanitarian and relevant development actors to work with the Office for the Coordination of Humanitarian Affairs of the Secretariat to enhance the coordination, effectiveness and efficiency of humanitarian assistance;

15. *Urges* Governments and the United Nations system, in planning for disaster preparedness and responding to natural disasters, and in implementing recovery, rehabilitation and reconstruction efforts, to integrate a gender perspective and to ensure that women take an active and equal role in all phases of disaster management;

16. *Stresses* the importance of a coordinated process of assessing lessons learned in the international response to a given humanitarian emergency, and notes the efforts of Governments of the affected countries, donor Governments and international organizations

in providing reports on evaluations of and lessons learned from the Indian Ocean tsunami disaster;[6]

17. *Requests* the Secretary-General to report to the General Assembly at its sixty-second session on the implementation of the present resolution under the item entitled "Strengthening of the coordination of humanitarian and disaster relief assistance of the United Nations, including special economic assistance", through the Economic and Social Council at its substantive session of 2007.

79th plenary meeting
14 December 2006

---

[1] A/59/669, annex.

[2] A/CONF.206/6 and Corr.1, chap. I, resolution 1.

[3] Hyogo Framework for Action 2005–2015: Building the Resilience of Nations and Communities to Disasters (A/CONF.206/6 and Corr.1, chap. I, resolution 2).

[4] Common statement of the special session on the Indian Ocean disaster: risk reduction for a safer future (A/CONF.206/6 and Corr.1, annex II).

[5] A/61/87-E/2006/77.

[6] Reports include: "The 2004 Indian Ocean Tsunami Disaster: Evaluation of UNICEF's Response (Emergency and Initial Recovery Phase)"; "Survivors of the Tsunami: One Year Later – UNDP Assisting Communities to Build Back Better"; "Towards a United Nations humanitarian assistance programme for disaster response and reduction: Lessons learned from the Indian Ocean tsunami disaster"; "Building a land of hope: one year report"; "Joint evaluation of the international response to the Indian Ocean tsunami: synthesis report".

Resolution 61/133

[without reference to a Main Committee (A/61/L.45 and Add.1)]

61/133. Safety and security of humanitarian personnel and protection of United Nations personnel

The General Assembly,

Reaffirming its resolution 46/182 of 19 December 1991 on strengthening of the coordination of humanitarian emergency assistance of the United Nations,

Recalling all relevant resolutions on safety and security of humanitarian personnel and protection of United Nations personnel, including its resolution 60/123 of 15 December 2005, as well as Security Council resolution 1502 (2003) of 26 August 2003 and relevant statements by the President of the Council,

Recalling also all Security Council resolutions and presidential statements and reports of the Secretary-General to the Council on the protection of civilians in armed conflict,

Recalling further all relevant provisions of international law, including international humanitarian law and human rights law, as well as all relevant treaties,[1]

Reaffirming the need to promote and ensure respect for the principles and rules of international law, including international humanitarian law,

Recalling that primary responsibility under international law for the security and protection of humanitarian personnel and United Nations and associated personnel lies with the Government hosting a United Nations operation conducted under the Charter of the United Nations or its agreements with relevant organizations,

Urging all parties involved in armed conflicts, in compliance with international humanitarian law, in particular their obligations under the Geneva Conventions of 12 August 1949[2] and the obligations applicable to them under the Additional Protocols thereto, of 8 June 1977,[3] to ensure the security and protection of all humanitarian personnel and United Nations and associated personnel,

Welcoming the fact that the number of States parties to the Convention on the Safety of United Nations and Associated Personnel,[4] which entered into force on 15 January 1999, has continued to rise, the number now having reached eighty-one, and mindful of the need to promote universality of the Convention,

Deeply concerned by the dangers and security risks faced by humanitarian personnel and United Nations and associated personnel at the field level, as they operate in increasingly complex contexts, as well as the continuous erosion, in many cases, of respect for the principles and rules of international law, in particular international humanitarian law,

Commending the courage and commitment of those who take part in humanitarian operations, often at great personal risk, especially locally recruited staff,

Expressing profound regret at the deaths of and violent acts against international and national humanitarian personnel and United Nations and associated personnel involved in the provision of humanitarian assistance, and strongly deploring the rising toll of casualties among such personnel in complex humanitarian emergencies, in particular in armed conflicts and in post-conflict situations,

Strongly condemning acts of murder and other forms of violence, rape and sexual assault and all forms of violence committed in particular against women and children, and intimidation, armed robbery, abduction, hostage-taking, kidnapping, harassment and illegal arrest and detention to which those participating in humanitarian operations are increasingly exposed, as well as attacks on humanitarian convoys and acts of destruction and looting of property,

Expressing deep concern that the occurrence of attacks and threats against humanitarian personnel and United Nations and associated personnel is a factor that increasingly restricts the provision of assistance and protection to populations in need,

Affirming the need for States to ensure that perpetrators of attacks committed on their territory against humanitarian personnel and United Nations and associated personnel do not operate with impunity, and that the perpetrators of such acts are brought to justice as provided for by national law and obligations under international law,

Recalling the inclusion of attacks intentionally directed against personnel involved in a humanitarian assistance or peacekeeping mission in accordance with the Charter as a war crime in the Rome Statute of the International Criminal Court,[5] and noting the role that the Court could play in appropriate cases in bringing to justice those responsible for serious violations of international humanitarian law,

Reaffirming the need to ensure adequate levels of safety and security for United Nations personnel and associated humanitarian personnel, which constitutes an underlying duty of the Organization, and mindful of the need to promote and enhance the security consciousness within the organizational culture of the United Nations and a culture of accountability at all levels,

1. *Welcomes* the report of the Secretary-General;[6]

2. *Urges* all States to take the necessary measures to ensure the full and effective implementation of the relevant principles and rules of international law, including international humanitarian law, human rights law and refugee law related to the safety and security of humanitarian personnel and United Nations personnel;

3. *Strongly urges* all States to take the necessary measures to ensure the safety and security of humanitarian personnel and United Nations and associated personnel and to respect and ensure respect for the inviolability of United Nations premises, which are essential to the continuation and successful implementation of United Nations operations;

4. *Calls upon* all Governments and parties in complex humanitarian emergencies, in particular in armed conflicts and in post-conflict situations, in countries in which humanitarian personnel are operating, in conformity with the relevant provisions of international law and national laws, to cooperate fully with the United Nations and other humanitarian agencies and organizations and to ensure the safe and unhindered access of humanitarian personnel and delivery of supplies and equipment in order to allow those personnel to perform efficiently their task of assisting the affected civilian population, including refugees and internally displaced persons;

5. *Calls upon* all States to consider becoming parties to and to respect fully their obligations under the relevant international instruments;

6. *Also calls upon* all States to consider becoming parties to the Rome Statute of the International Criminal Court;[5]

7. *Takes note with appreciation* of the adoption of the Optional Protocol[7] to the Convention on the Safety of United Nations and Associated Personnel,[4] which expands the scope of legal protection under the Convention, and calls upon all States to consider signing and ratifying the Optional Protocol as soon as possible so as to ensure its rapid entry into force, and urges States parties to put in place appropriate national legislation, as necessary, to enable its effective implementation;

8. *Expresses deep concern* that, over the past decade, threats and attacks against the safety and security of humanitarian personnel and United Nations and associated personnel have escalated dramatically and that perpetrators of acts of violence seemingly operate with impunity;

9. *Strongly condemns* all threats and acts of violence against humanitarian personnel and United Nations and associated personnel, reaffirms the need to hold accountable those responsible for such acts, strongly urges all States to take stronger action to ensure that any such acts committed on their territory are investigated fully and to ensure that the perpetrators of such acts are brought to justice in accordance with international law and national law, and urges States to end impunity for such acts;

10. *Calls upon* all States to provide adequate and prompt information in the event of the arrest or detention of humanitarian personnel or United Nations and associated personnel, so as to afford them the necessary medical assistance and to allow independent medical teams to visit and examine the health of those detained, and urges them to take the necessary measures to ensure the speedy release of those who have been arrested or detained

in violation of the relevant conventions referred to in the present resolution and applicable international humanitarian law;

11. *Calls upon* all other parties involved in armed conflicts to refrain from abducting humanitarian personnel or United Nations and associated personnel or detaining them in violation of the relevant conventions referred to in the present resolution and applicable international humanitarian law, and speedily to release, without harm or requirement of concession, any abductee or detainee;

12. *Requests* the Secretary-General to take the necessary measures to ensure full respect for the human rights, privileges and immunities of United Nations and other personnel carrying out activities in fulfilment of the mandate of a United Nations operation, and also requests the Secretary-General to seek the inclusion, in negotiations of headquarters and other mission agreements concerning United Nations and associated personnel, of the applicable conditions contained in the Convention on the Privileges and Immunities of the United Nations, [8] the Convention on the Privileges and Immunities of the Specialized Agencies[9] and the Convention on the Safety of United Nations and Associated Personnel;

13. *Recommends* that the Secretary-General continue to seek the inclusion of, and that host countries include, key provisions of the Convention on the Safety of United Nations and Associated Personnel, among others, those regarding the prevention of attacks against members of the operation, the establishment of such attacks as crimes punishable by law and the prosecution or extradition of offenders, in future as well as, if necessary, in existing status-of-forces, status-of-mission, host country agreements and other related agreements negotiated between the United Nations and those countries, mindful of the importance of the timely conclusion of such agreements, and encourages further efforts in this regard;

14. *Reaffirms* the obligation of all humanitarian personnel and United Nations and associated personnel to observe and respect the national laws of the country in which they are operating, in accordance with international law and the Charter of the United Nations;

15. *Stresses* the importance of ensuring that humanitarian personnel and United Nations and associated personnel remain sensitive to national and local customs and traditions in their countries of assignment and communicate clearly their purpose and objectives to local populations;

16. *Welcomes* ongoing efforts to promote and enhance the security consciousness within the organizational culture of the United Nations system, and requests the Secretary-General to continue to take the necessary measures in this regard, including by further developing and implementing a unified security management system, as well as by disseminating and ensuring the implementation of the security procedures and regulations and by ensuring accountability at all levels, and also welcomes the creation and the work of the Department of Safety and Security of the Secretariat;

17. *Emphasizes* the importance of paying special attention to the safety and security of United Nations and associated personnel engaged in United Nations peacekeeping and peacebuilding operations;

18. *Also emphasizes* the need to pay particular attention to the safety and security of locally recruited humanitarian personnel, who are particularly vulnerable to attacks and who account for the majority of casualties, and calls upon humanitarian organizations to ensure that their staff are adequately informed about and trained in their respective organization's relevant security measures, plans and initiatives, which should be in line with applicable national law and international law;

19. *Requests* the Secretary-General to continue to take the necessary measures to ensure that United Nations and other personnel carrying out activities in fulfilment of the mandate of a United Nations operation are properly informed about and operate in conformity with the minimum operating security standards and relevant codes of conduct and are properly informed about the conditions under which they are called upon to operate and the standards that they are required to meet, including those contained in relevant national and international law, and that adequate training in security, human rights law and international humanitarian law is provided so as to enhance their security and effectiveness in accomplishing their functions, and reaffirms the necessity for all other humanitarian organizations to provide their personnel with similar support;

20. *Welcomes* the ongoing efforts of the Secretary-General and stresses the need to ensure that all United Nations staff members receive adequate security training, including training to enhance cultural awareness, prior to their deployment to the field, as well as the need to attach a high priority to stress management training and related counselling services for United Nations staff throughout the system;

21. *Takes note* of the report of the Secretary-General on a strengthened and unified security management system for the United Nations;[10]

22. *Emphasizes* the importance of information on the range and scope of security incidents involving humanitarian personnel and United Nations and associated personnel, including attacks against them, to clarify their operating environment;

23. *Welcomes* the ongoing efforts of the Secretary-General to further enhance the security management system of the United Nations, and in this regard invites the United Nations and, as appropriate, other humanitarian organizations, working closely with host States, to further strengthen the analysis of threats to their safety and security in order to manage security risks by facilitating informed decisions on the maintenance of an effective presence in the field, inter alia, to fulfil their humanitarian mandate;

24. *Stresses* that the effective functioning at the country level of security operations requires a unified capacity for policy, standards, coordination, communication, compliance and threat and risk assessment, and notes the benefits thereof to United Nations and associated personnel, including those achieved by the Department of Safety and Security since its establishment;

25. *Recognizes* the need to continue efforts to achieve a strengthened and unified security management system for the United Nations, both at the headquarters and the field levels, and requests the United Nations system, as well as Member States, to take all appropriate measures to that end;

26. *Requests* the Secretary-General, inter alia, through the Inter-Agency Security Management Network, to continue to promote increased cooperation and collaboration among United Nations departments, organizations, funds and programmes and affiliated international organizations, including between their headquarters and field offices, in the planning and implementation of measures aimed at improving staff security, training and awareness, and calls upon all relevant United Nations departments, organizations, funds and programmes and affiliated international organizations to support those efforts;

27. *Recognizes* the steps taken by the Secretary-General thus far, as well as the need for continued efforts to enhance coordination and cooperation, both at the headquarters and the field levels, between the United Nations and other humanitarian and non-governmental

organizations on matters relating to the safety and security of humanitarian personnel and United Nations and associated personnel, with a view to addressing mutual security concerns in the field, and encourages collaborative initiatives to address security training needs;

28. *Underlines* the need to allocate adequate and predictable resources to the safety and security of United Nations personnel, including through the consolidated appeals process, and encourages all States to contribute to the Trust Fund for Security of Staff Members of the United Nations System, inter alia, with a view to reinforcing the efforts of the United Nations Department of Safety and Security for the safety and security of personnel working in emergency and humanitarian operations;

29. *Recalls* the essential role of telecommunication resources in facilitating the safety of humanitarian personnel and United Nations and associated personnel, calls upon States to consider acceding to or ratifying the Tampere Convention on the Provision of Telecommunication Resources for Disaster Mitigation and Relief Operations of 18 June 1998, which entered into force on 8 January 2005,[11] and urges them to facilitate and expedite, consistent with their national laws and international obligations applicable to them, the use of communications equipment in such operations, inter alia, through limiting and, whenever possible, expeditiously lifting the restrictions placed on the use of communications equipment by United Nations and associated personnel;

30. *Requests* the Secretary-General to submit to the General Assembly at its sixty-second session a comprehensive and updated report on the safety and security of humanitarian personnel and protection of United Nations personnel and on the implementation of the present resolution.

79th plenary meeting
14 December 2006

---

[1] They include, notably, the Convention on the Privileges and Immunities of the United Nations of 13 February 1946, the Convention on the Privileges and Immunities of the Specialized Agencies of 21 November 1947, the Convention on the Safety of United Nations and Associated Personnel of 9 December 1994, the Geneva Convention relative to the Protection of Civilian Persons in Time of War of 12 August 1949 and the Additional Protocols to the Geneva Conventions of 8 June 1977, and Amended Protocol II of 3 May 1996 to the Convention on Prohibitions or Restrictions on the Use of Certain Conventional Weapons Which May Be Deemed to Be Excessively Injurious or to Have Indiscriminate Effects of 10 October 1980.

[2] United Nations, *Treaty Series*, vol. 75, Nos. 970–973.

[3] Ibid., vol. 1125, Nos. 17512 and 17513.

[4] Ibid., vol. 2051, No. 35457.

[5] Ibid., vol. 2187, No. 38544.

[6] A/61/463.

[7] Resolution 60/42, annex.

[8] Resolution 22 A (I).

[9] Resolution 179 (II).

[10] A/61/531.

[11] United Nations, *Treaty Series*, vol. 2296, No. 40906.

Resolution 61/134

[without reference to a Main Committee (A/61/L.46 and Add.1)]

61/134. Strengthening of the coordination of emergency humanitarian assistance of the United Nations

The General Assembly,

Reaffirming its resolution 46/182 of 19 December 1991 and the guiding principles contained in the annex thereto, other relevant General Assembly and Economic and Social Council resolutions and agreed conclusions of the Council,

Taking note of the report of the Secretary-General on the strengthening of the coordination of emergency humanitarian assistance of the United Nations,[1]

Taking note also of the report of the Secretary-General on the Central Emergency Response Fund,[2]

Reaffirming the principles of neutrality, humanity, impartiality and independence for the provision of humanitarian assistance,

Noting with grave concern the number and scale of natural disasters and their increasing impact within recent years, and reaffirming the need for sustainable measures at all levels to reduce the vulnerability of societies to natural hazards using an integrated, multi-hazard approach, and the importance of including disaster risk reduction as part of long-term and sustainable development strategies, taking into account the Hyogo Declaration[3] and the Hyogo Framework for Action 2005–2015: Building the Resilience of Nations and Communities to Disasters,[4]

Noting also with grave concern that violence, including gender-based violence and violence against children, continues to be deliberately directed against civilian populations in many emergency situations,

Emphasizing the need to mobilize adequate resources for humanitarian assistance and with a view to ensuring more equitable distribution across humanitarian emergencies as well as fuller coverage of the needs in all sectors,

Noting with appreciation the efforts made by the United Nations to improve humanitarian response, including by strengthening humanitarian response capacities, by improving humanitarian coordination, and by enhancing predictable and adequate funding,

1. *Takes note with appreciation* of the outcome of the ninth humanitarian affairs segment of the Economic and Social Council, held during its substantive session of 2006;

2. *Requests* the Emergency Relief Coordinator to continue his efforts to strengthen the coordination of humanitarian assistance, and calls upon relevant United Nations and other relevant intergovernmental organizations, as well as other humanitarian and relevant development actors, to continue to work with the Office for the Coordination of Humanitarian Affairs of the Secretariat to enhance the coordination, effectiveness and efficiency of humanitarian assistance;

3. *Calls upon* the relevant organizations of the United Nations system and, as appropriate, other relevant humanitarian actors, to pursue efforts to improve the humanitarian response to natural and man-made disasters and complex emergencies by further strengthening the

humanitarian response capacities at all levels, by continuing to strengthen the coordination of humanitarian assistance at the field level, including with national authorities of the affected State, as appropriate, and by further enhancing transparency, performance and accountability;

4. *Encourages* States to create an enabling environment for the capacity-building of local authorities and local and national non-governmental and community-based organizations in providing humanitarian assistance;

5. *Emphasizes* the fundamentally civilian character of humanitarian assistance, reaffirms the leading role of civilian organizations in implementing humanitarian assistance, particularly in areas affected by conflicts, and affirms the need, in situations where military capacity and assets are used to support the implementation of humanitarian assistance, for their use to be in conformity with international humanitarian law and humanitarian principles;

6. *Requests* the Secretary-General to continue to develop more systematic links with Member States offering military assets for natural disaster response in order to identify the availability of such assets;

7. *Also requests* the Secretary-General, in consultation with States and relevant organizations, to further develop and improve, as required, mechanisms for the use of emergency standby capacities, including, where appropriate, regional humanitarian capacities, under the auspices of the United Nations, inter alia, through formal agreements with appropriate regional organizations;

8. *Recognizes* the benefits of engagement of and coordination with relevant humanitarian actors to the effectiveness of humanitarian response, and encourages the United Nations to pursue recent efforts to strengthen partnerships at the global level with the International Red Cross and Red Crescent Movement, relevant humanitarian non-governmental organizations and other participants of the Inter-Agency Standing Committee;

9. *Reiterates* the need for a more effective, efficient, coherent, coordinated and better-performing United Nations country presence, with a strengthened role for the senior United Nations resident official responsible for the coordination of United Nations humanitarian assistance, including appropriate authority, resources and accountability;

10. *Requests* the Secretary-General to strengthen the support provided to United Nations resident/humanitarian coordinators and to United Nations country teams, including through the provision of necessary training, the identification of resources, and improving the identification and selection of United Nations resident/humanitarian coordinators;

11. *Calls upon* relevant United Nations organizations to support the improvements of the consolidated appeals process, inter alia, by engaging in the preparation of needs analysis and common action plans, in order to further development of the process as an instrument for United Nations strategic planning and prioritization, and by involving other relevant humanitarian organizations in the process, while reiterating that consolidated appeals are prepared in consultation with affected States;

12. *Calls upon* United Nations humanitarian organizations to further develop common mechanisms to improve their transparency and the reliability of their humanitarian needs assessments, to assess their performance in assistance, and to ensure the most effective use of humanitarian resources by these organizations;

13. *Calls upon* donors to provide adequate, predictable and flexible resources based on and in proportion to assessed needs, and to encourage efforts to implement the principles of Good Humanitarian Donorship;

14. *Welcomes* the establishment of the Central Emergency Response Fund as set out in resolution 60/124 of 15 December 2005 and the fact that fifty-four donors have pledged 297.9 million United States dollars in the first year of operations, notes the assessment of the Secretary-General on its initial functioning, as reflected in his report on the Fund,[2] and looks forward to the independent review in 2008;

15. *Also welcomes* the Secretary-General's efforts to set up appropriate reporting and accountability mechanisms for the Fund, and stresses the importance of ensuring that the resources are allocated and used in the most efficient, effective and transparent manner possible;

16. *Urges* all Member States and invites the private sector and all concerned individuals and institutions to consider making voluntary contributions to the Fund, reaffirms the target of 500 million dollars by 2008, and emphasizes that contributions should be additional to current commitments to humanitarian programming and not to the detriment of resources made available for international cooperation for development;

17. *Reiterates* that the Office for the Coordination of Humanitarian Affairs should benefit from adequate and more predictable funding;

18. *Urges* all Member States to take effective measures to address gender-based violence in humanitarian emergencies, and to make all possible efforts to ensure that their laws and institutions are adequate to prevent, promptly investigate and prosecute acts of gender-based violence;

19. *Calls upon* all Member States and encourages the relevant organizations of the United Nations to strengthen support services, including psychosocial support, to victims of gender-based violence in humanitarian emergencies;

20. *Calls upon* all States and parties in complex humanitarian emergencies, in particular in armed conflicts and in post-conflict situations, in countries in which humanitarian personnel are operating, in conformity with the relevant provisions of international law and national laws, to cooperate fully with the United Nations and other humanitarian agencies and organizations and to ensure the safe and unhindered access of humanitarian personnel as well as delivery of supplies and equipment in order to allow them to perform efficiently their task of assisting the affected civilian population, including refugees and internally displaced persons;

21. *Reaffirms* the obligation of all States and parties to an armed conflict to protect civilians in armed conflicts in accordance with international humanitarian law, and invites States to promote a culture of protection, taking into account the particular needs of women, children, older persons and persons with disabilities;

22. *Calls upon* States to adopt preventive measures and effective responses to acts of violence committed against civilian populations in armed conflicts as well as to ensure that those responsible are promptly brought to justice, as provided for by national law and obligations under international law;

23. *Recognizes* the Guiding Principles on Internal Displacement[5] as an important international framework for the protection of internally displaced persons, and encourages Member States and humanitarian agencies to continue to work together in endeavours to provide a

more predictable response to the needs of internally displaced persons, and in this regard calls for international support, upon request, to capacity-building efforts of States;

24. *Re-emphasizes* the importance of the discussion of humanitarian policies and activities in the General Assembly and the Economic and Social Council and that these discussions should be continuously revitalized by Member States with a view to enhancing their relevance, efficiency and impact;

25. *Encourages* Member States to continue to strengthen cooperation and coordination between the General Assembly and the Economic and Social Council on humanitarian issues, based on their respective mandates and taking into account comparative advantages and existing complementarities of the two bodies;

26. *Decides*, in order to have a more focused and consolidated discussion on humanitarian issues, that the sub-items of its agenda related to the strengthening of the coordination of humanitarian and disaster relief assistance of the United Nations currently considered by the Second Committee shall be reallocated to its plenary as of its sixty-second session;

27. *Recalls* the request to the Secretary-General, in the ninth humanitarian affairs segment of the Economic and Social Council, to include in his report lessons learned and best practices in the implementation of the pilot projects using the cluster approach, in consultation with affected countries and with the active involvement of relevant United Nations humanitarian entities;[6]

28. *Requests* the Secretary-General to report to the General Assembly at its sixty-second session, through the Economic and Social Council at its substantive session of 2007, on progress made in strengthening the coordination of emergency humanitarian assistance of the United Nations and to submit a report to the Assembly through the Council on the detailed use of the Central Emergency Response Fund.

79th plenary meeting
14 December 2006

---

[1] A/61/85-E/2006/81.

[2] A/61/85/Add.1-E/2006/81/Add.1.

[3] A/CONF.206/6 and Corr.1, chap. I, resolution 1.

[4] Ibid., resolution 2.

[5] E/CN.4/1998/53/Add.2, annex.

[6] See Economic and Social Council resolution 2006/5, para. 26.

Resolution 61/135

[without reference to a Main Committee (A/61/L.47 and Add.1)]

61/135. Assistance to the Palestinian people

The General Assembly,

Recalling its resolution 60/126 of 15 December 2005, as well as previous resolutions on the question,

Recalling also the signing of the Declaration of Principles on Interim Self-Government Arrangements in Washington, D.C., on 13 September 1993, by the Government of the State of Israel and the Palestine Liberation Organization, the representative of the Palestinian people,[1] and the subsequent implementation agreements concluded by the two sides,

Recalling further the International Covenant on Civil and Political Rights,[2] the International Covenant on Economic, Social and Cultural Rights[2] and the Convention on the Rights of the Child,[3]

Gravely concerned at the deterioration in the living conditions of the Palestinian people, in particular children, throughout the occupied territory, which constitutes a mounting humanitarian crisis,

Conscious of the urgent need for improvement in the economic and social infrastructure of the occupied territory,

Aware that development is difficult under occupation and is best promoted in circumstances of peace and stability,

Noting the great economic and social challenges facing the Palestinian people and their leadership,

Emphasizing the importance of the safety and well-being of all children in the whole Middle East region,

Deeply concerned about the negative impact, including the health and psychological consequences, of violence on the present and future well-being of children in the region,

Conscious of the urgent necessity for international assistance to the Palestinian people, taking into account the Palestinian priorities,

Welcoming the results of the Conference to Support Middle East Peace, convened in Washington, D.C., on 1 October 1993, the establishment of the Ad Hoc Liaison Committee and the work being done by the World Bank as its secretariat and the establishment of the Consultative Group, as well as all follow-up meetings and international mechanisms established to provide assistance to the Palestinian people,

Welcoming also the results of the "Stockholm International Donor Conference on the Humanitarian Situation in the Occupied Palestinian Territories" of 1 September 2006,

Welcoming further the work of the Joint Liaison Committee, which provides a forum in which economic policy and practical matters related to donor assistance are discussed with the Palestinian Authority,

Stressing the continued importance of the Ad Hoc Liaison Committee in the coordination of assistance to the Palestinian people,

Stressing also the need for the full engagement of the United Nations in the process of building Palestinian institutions and in providing broad assistance to the Palestinian people, and welcoming in this regard the support provided to the Palestinian Authority by the Task Force on Palestinian Reform, established by the Quartet in 2002,

Noting, in this regard, the active participation of the United Nations Special Coordinator for the Middle East Peace Process and Personal Representative of the Secretary-General to the Palestine Liberation Organization and the Palestinian Authority in the activities of the Special Envoys of the Quartet,

Welcoming the endorsement by the Security Council, in its resolution 1515 (2003) of 19 November 2003, of the performance-based road map to a permanent two-State solution to the Israeli-Palestinian conflict,[4] and stressing the need for its implementation and compliance with its provisions,

Noting the Israeli withdrawal from the Gaza Strip and parts of the northern West Bank as a step towards implementation of the road map,

Having considered the report of the Secretary-General,[5]

Expressing grave concern at the continuation of the recent tragic and violent events that have led to many deaths and injuries, including among children,

1. *Takes note* of the report of the Secretary-General;[5]

2. *Also takes note* of the report of the Personal Humanitarian Envoy of the Secretary-General on the humanitarian conditions and needs of the Palestinian people;[6]

3. *Expresses its appreciation* to the Secretary-General for his rapid response and efforts regarding assistance to the Palestinian people;

4. *Also expresses its appreciation* to the Member States, United Nations bodies and intergovernmental, regional and non-governmental organizations that have provided and continue to provide assistance to the Palestinian people;

5. *Stresses* the importance of the work of the United Nations Special Coordinator for the Middle East Peace Process and Personal Representative of the Secretary-General to the Palestine Liberation Organization and the Palestinian Authority and of the steps taken under the auspices of the Secretary-General to ensure the achievement of a coordinated mechanism for United Nations activities throughout the occupied territories;

6. *Urges* Member States, international financial institutions of the United Nations system, intergovernmental and non-governmental organizations and regional and interregional organizations to extend, as rapidly and as generously as possible, economic and social assistance to the Palestinian people, in close cooperation with the Palestine Liberation Organization and through official Palestinian institutions;

7. *Calls upon* relevant organizations and agencies of the United Nations system to intensify their assistance in response to the urgent needs of the Palestinian people in accordance with priorities set forth by the Palestinian side;

8. *Calls upon* the international community to provide urgently needed assistance and services in an effort to alleviate the dire humanitarian crisis being faced by Palestinian children and their families and to help in the reconstruction of relevant Palestinian institutions;

9. *Welcomes* the role that the temporary international mechanism plays in assisting directly the Palestinian people under the current circumstances, and encourages interested donors to make use of the mechanism;

10. *Urges* Member States to open their markets to exports of Palestinian products on the most favourable terms, consistent with appropriate trading rules, and to implement fully existing trade and cooperation agreements;

11. *Calls upon* the international donor community to expedite the delivery of pledged assistance to the Palestinian people to meet their urgent needs;

12. *Stresses*, in this context, the importance of ensuring the free passage of aid to the Palestinian people and the free movement of persons and goods;

13. *Also stresses* the need for the full implementation by both parties of the Agreement on Movement and Access and of the Agreed Principles for the Rafah Crossing, of 15 November 2005, to allow for the freedom of movement of the Palestinian civilian population within and into and out of the Gaza Strip;

14. *Urges* the international donor community, United Nations agencies and organizations and non-governmental organizations to extend as rapidly as possible emergency economic and humanitarian assistance to the Palestinian people to counter the impact of the current crisis;

15. *Stresses* the need to implement the Paris Protocol on Economic Relations of 29 April 1994, fifth annex to the Israeli-Palestinian Interim Agreement on the West Bank and the Gaza Strip, signed in Washington, D.C., on 28 September 1995,[7] in particular with regard to the full and prompt of Palestinian indirect tax revenues;

16. *Requests* the Secretary-General to submit a report to the General Assembly at its sixty-second session, through the Economic and Social Council, on the implementation of the present resolution, containing:

(*a*) An assessment of the assistance actually received by the Palestinian people;

(*b*) An assessment of the needs still unmet and specific proposals for responding effectively to them;

17. *Decides* to include in the provisional agenda of its sixty-second session the sub-item entitled "Assistance to the Palestinian people".

79th plenary meeting
14 December 2006

---

[1] A/48/486-S/26560, annex.

[2] See resolution 2200 A (XXI), annex.

[3] United Nations, *Treaty Series*, vol. 1577, No. 27531.

[4] S/2003/529, annex.

[5] A/60/90-E/2005/80.

[6] Available from http://domino.un.org/bertini_rpt.htm.

[7] A/51/889-S/1997/357, annex.

Resolution 61/136

[on the report of the Third Committee (A/61/436)]

61/136. Enlargement of the Executive Committee of the Programme of the United Nations High Commissioner for Refugees

The General Assembly,

Taking note of Economic and Social Council decision 2006/237 of 26 July 2006 concerning the enlargement of the Executive Committee of the Programme of the United Nations High Commissioner for Refugees,

Taking note also of the requests regarding the enlargement of the Executive Committee contained in the letter dated 8 March 2006 from the Deputy Permanent Representative of Costa Rica to the United Nations addressed to the SecretaryGeneral[1] and the letter dated 30 May 2006 from the Permanent Representative of Estonia to the United Nations addressed to the Secretary-General,[2]

1. *Decides* to increase the number of members of the Executive Committee of the Programme of the United Nations High Commissioner for Refugees from seventy to seventy-two States;

2. *Requests* the Economic and Social Council to elect the additional members at its resumed organizational session for 2007.

81st plenary meeting
19 December 2006

[1] E/2006/3.

[2] E/2006/82.

Resolution 61/137

[on the report of the Third Committee (A/61/436)]

61/137. Office of the United Nations High Commissioner for Refugees

The General Assembly,

Having considered the report of the United Nations High Commissioner for Refugees on the activities of his Office[1] and the report of the Executive Committee of the Programme of the United Nations High Commissioner for Refugees on the work of its fifty-seventh session [2] and the conclusions and decisions contained therein,

Recalling its previous annual resolutions on the work of the Office of the High Commissioner since its establishment by the General Assembly,

Expressing its appreciation for the leadership shown by the High Commissioner, commending the staff and implementing partners of the Office of the High Commissioner for the competent, courageous and dedicated manner in which they discharge their responsibilities, and underlining its strong condemnation of all forms of violence to which humanitarian personnel and United Nations and associated personnel are increasingly exposed,

1. *Endorses* the report of the Executive Committee of the Programme of the United Nations High Commissioner for Refugees on the work of its fifty-seventh session;[2]

2. *Welcomes* the important work undertaken by the Office of the United Nations High Commissioner for Refugees and its Executive Committee in the course of the year, and notes in this context the adoption of the conclusion on women and girls at risk and the conclusion on identification, prevention and reduction of statelessness and protection of stateless persons,[3] which are aimed at strengthening the international protection regime,

consistent with the Agenda for Protection,[4] and at assisting Governments in meeting their protection responsibilities in today's changing international environment, including by promoting the progressive implementation of mechanisms and standards through relevant national public policies supported by the international community;

3. *Reaffirms* the 1951 Convention relating to the Status of Refugees[5] and the 1967 Protocol thereto[6] as the foundation of the international refugee protection regime, recognizes the importance of their full and effective application by States parties and the values they embody, notes with satisfaction that one hundred and forty-six States are now parties to one instrument or to both, encourages States not parties to consider acceding to those instruments, underlines in particular the importance of full respect for the principle of non-refoulement, and recognizes that a number of States not parties to the international refugee instruments have shown a generous approach to hosting refugees;

4. *Notes* that sixty-two States are now parties to the 1954 Convention relating to the Status of Stateless Persons[7] and that thirty-three States are parties to the 1961 Convention on the Reduction of Statelessness,[8] encourages States that have not done so to give consideration to acceding to these instruments, notes the work of the High Commissioner in regard to identifying stateless persons, preventing and reducing statelessness, and protecting stateless persons, and urges the Office of the High Commissioner to continue to work in this area in accordance with relevant General Assembly resolutions and Executive Committee conclusions;

5. *Takes note* of the current activities of the Office of the High Commissioner related to protection of and assistance to internally displaced persons, including in the context of inter-agency arrangements in this field, emphasizes that such activities should be consistent with relevant General Assembly resolutions and should not undermine the mandate of the Office for refugees and the institution of asylum, and encourages the High Commissioner to continue his dialogue with States on the role of his Office in this regard;

6. *Re-emphasizes* that the protection of refugees is primarily the responsibility of States, whose full and effective cooperation, action and resolve are required to enable the Office of the High Commissioner to fulfil its mandated functions, and strongly emphasizes, in this context, the importance of active international solidarity and burden- and responsibility-sharing;

7. *Emphasizes* that prevention and reduction of statelessness are primarily the responsibility of States, in appropriate cooperation with the international community;

8. *Also emphasizes* that protection of and assistance to internally displaced persons are primarily the responsibility of States, in appropriate cooperation with the international community;

9. *Urges* all States and relevant non-governmental and other organizations, in conjunction with the Office of the High Commissioner, in a spirit of international solidarity and burden- and responsibility-sharing, to cooperate and to mobilize resources with a view to enhancing the capacity of and reducing the heavy burden borne by host countries, in particular those that have received large numbers of refugees and asylum-seekers, and calls upon the Office to continue to play its catalytic role in mobilizing assistance from the internationa community to address the root causes as well as the economic, environmental and social

impact of large scale refugee populations in developing countries, in particular the least developed counties, and countries with economies in transition;

10. *Strongly condemns* attacks on refugees, asylum-seekers and internally displaced persons as well as acts that pose a threat to their personal security and well-being, and calls upon all concerned States and, where applicable, parties involved in an armed conflict to take all necessary measures to ensure respect for human rights and international humanitarian law;

11. *Deplores* the refoulement and unlawful expulsion of refugees and asylum-seekers, and calls upon all concerned States to ensure respect for the principles of refugee protection and human rights;

12. *Emphasizes* that international protection of refugees is a dynamic and action-oriented function that is at the core of the mandate of the Office of the High Commissioner and that it includes, in cooperation with States and other partners, the promotion and facilitation of, inter alia, the admission, reception and treatment of refugees in accordance with internationally agreed standards and the ensuring of durable, protection-oriented solutions, bearing in mind the particular needs of vulnerable groups and paying special attention to those with specific needs, and notes in this context that the delivery of international protection is a staff-intensive service that requires adequate staff with the appropriate expertise, especially at the field level;

13. *Affirms* the importance of mainstreaming the protection needs of women and children to ensure their participation in the planning and implementation of programmes of the Office of the High Commissioner and State policies and the importance of according priority to addressing the problem of sexual and gender-based violence;

14. *Acknowledges* that forcibly displaced women and girls can be exposed to particular protection problems related to their gender, their cultural and socioeconomic position, and their legal status, that they may be less likely than men and boys to be able to exercise their rights, and that, therefore, specific action in favour of women and girls may be necessary to ensure that they can enjoy protection and assistance on an equal basis with men and boys, and notes the important guidance provided in the Executive Committee conclusion on women and girls at risk to address issues of identification of those individuals and action to be taken in prevention and response;

15. *Strongly reaffirms* the fundamental importance and the purely humanitarian and non-political character of the function of the Office of the High Commissioner of providing international protection to refugees and seeking permanent solutions to refugee problems, and recalls that those solutions include voluntary repatriation and, where appropriate and feasible, local integration and resettlement in a third country, while reaffirming that voluntary repatriation, supported by necessary rehabilitation and development assistance to facilitate sustainable reintegration, remains the preferred solution;

16. *Expresses concern* about the particular difficulties faced by the millions of refugees in protracted situations, and emphasizes the need to redouble international efforts and cooperation to find practical and comprehensive approaches to resolving their plight and to realize durable solutions for them, consistent with relevant General Assembly resolutions and international law;

17. *Recalls* the important role of effective partnerships and coordination in meeting the needs of refugees and in finding durable solutions to their situations, welcomes the efforts under way, in cooperation with countries hosting refugees and countries of origin, including their respective local communities, United Nations agencies and other development actors, to promote a framework for durable solutions, particularly in protracted refugee situations, which includes the "4Rs" approach (repatriation, reintegration, rehabilitation and reconstruction) to sustainable return, and encourages States, in cooperation with United Nations agencies and other development actors, to support, inter alia, through the allocation of funds, the development and implementation of the 4Rs and other programming tools to facilitate the transition from relief to development;

18. *Welcomes* the progress that has been achieved in increasing the number of refugees resettled and the number of States offering opportunities for resettlement, notes that the Multilateral Framework of Understandings on Resettlement[9] sets out the strategic use of resettlement as part of a comprehensive approach to refugee situations aimed at improving access to durable solutions for a greater number of refugees, and invites interested States, the Office of the High Commissioner and other relevant partners to make use of the Multilateral Framework, where appropriate and feasible;

19. *Notes* the progress that is being made by interested States and the Office of the High Commissioner to take forward elements outlined in the Mexico Plan of Action to Strengthen International Protection of Refugees in Latin America, adopted on 16 November 2004,[9] and expresses its support for the efforts to promote its implementation with the cooperation and assistance of the international community, as appropriate, including in the area of resettlement, as well as in supporting host communities that receive large numbers of persons who require international protection;

20. *Also notes* that some progress is being made by interested States and the Office of the High Commissioner within the context of the European-Asian Programme on Forced Displacement and Migration on issues related to asylum and forced displacement, consistent with the mandate of the Office;

21. *Further notes* the importance of States and the Office of the High Commissioner discussing and clarifying the role of the Office in mixed migratory flows, in order to better address protection needs in the context of mixed migratory flows, including by safeguarding access to asylum for those in need of international protection, and notes the readiness of the High Commissioner, consistent with his mandate, to assist States in fulfilling their protection responsibilities in this regard;

22. *Emphasizes* the obligation of all States to accept the return of their nationals, calls upon States to facilitate the return of their nationals who have been determined not to be in need of international protection, and affirms the need for the return of persons to be undertaken in a safe and humane manner and with full respect for their human rights and dignity, irrespective of the status of the persons concerned;

23. *Encourages* the Office of the High Commissioner to continue to improve its management systems and to ensure effective and transparent use of its resources, recognizes that adequate and timely resources are essential for the Office to continue to fulfil the mandate conferred upon it through its statute[10] and by subsequent General Assembly resolutions on refugees and other persons of concern, recalls its resolutions 58/153 of 22 December 2003,

58/270 of 23 December 2003, 59/170 of 20 December 2004 and 60/129 of 16 December 2005 concerning, inter alia, the implementation of paragraph 20 of the statute of the Office, and urges Governments and other donors to respond promptly to annual and supplementary appeals issued by the Office for requirements under its programmes;

24. *Calls upon* the Office of the High Commissioner to widen its donor base, so as to achieve greater burden-sharing by reinforcing cooperation with traditional governmental donors, non-traditional donors and the private sector;

25. *Requests* the High Commissioner to report on his activities to the General Assembly at its sixty-second session.

81st plenary meeting
19 December 2006

[1] *Official Records of the General Assembly, Sixty-first Session, Supplement No. 12* (A/61/12).

[2] Ibid., *Supplement No. 12A* (A/61/12/Add.1).

[3] Ibid., chap. III, sects. A and B.

[4] Ibid., *Fifty-seventh Session, Supplement No. 12A* (A/57/12/Add.1), annex IV.

[5] United Nations, *Treaty Series*, vol. 189, No. 2545.

[6] Ibid., vol. 606, No. 8791.

[7] Ibid., vol. 360, No. 5158.

[8] Ibid., vol. 989, No. 14458.

[9] Available from www.unhcr.org.

[10] Resolution 428 (V), annex.

Resolution 61/138

[on the report of the Third Committee (A/61/436)]

61/138. New international humanitarian order

The General Assembly,

Recalling its resolution 59/171 of 20 December 2004, all previous resolutions concerning the promotion of a new international humanitarian order[1] and all relevant resolutions, in particular resolution 46/182 of 19 December 1991, on the strengthening of the coordination of humanitarian emergency assistance of the United Nations, and the annex thereto,

Noting with appreciation the continuing efforts of the United Nations system to increase its capacity and that of its Member States to provide assistance to victims of humanitarian emergencies,

Taking note of the report of the Secretary-General,[2]

1. *Recognizes* the need for the further strengthening of national, regional and international efforts to address humanitarian emergencies;

2. *Invites* Member States, the Office for the Coordination of Humanitarian Affairs of the Secretariat, relevant entities of the United Nations system, and intergovernmental and non-governmental organizations, including the Independent Bureau for Humanitarian Issues, to reinforce activities and cooperation so as to continue to develop an agenda for humanitarian action;

3. *Requests* the Secretary-General to continue to strengthen efforts in the humanitarian field and to report thereon to the General Assembly at its sixty-third session.

81st plenary meeting
19 December 2006

[1] Resolutions 36/136, 37/201, 38/125, 40/126, 42/120, 42/121, 43/129, 43/130, 45/101, 45/102, 47/106, 49/170, 51/74, 53/124, 55/73 and 57/184.

[2] A/61/224.

Resolution 61/139

[on the report of the Third Committee (A/61/436)]

61/139. Assistance to refugees, returnees and displaced persons in Africa

The General Assembly,

Recalling the Organization of African Unity Convention governing the specific aspects of refugee problems in Africa of 1969[1] and the African Charter on Human and Peoples' Rights,[2]

Reaffirming that the 1951 Convention relating to the Status of Refugees,[3] together with the 1967 Protocol thereto,[4] as complemented by the Organization of African Unity Convention of 1969, remains the foundation of the international refugee protection regime in Africa,

1. *Takes note* of the reports of the Secretary-General[5] and the United Nations High Commissioner for Refugees;[6]

2. *Notes* the need for African States to address resolutely the root causes of all forms of forced displacement in Africa and to foster peace, stability and prosperity throughout the African continent so as to forestall refugee flows;

3. *Notes with great concern* that, despite all of the efforts made so far by the United Nations, the African Union and others, the situation of refugees and displaced persons in Africa remains precarious, and calls upon States and other parties to armed conflict to observe scrupulously the letter and spirit of international humanitarian law, bearing in mind that armed conflict is one of the principal causes of forced displacement in Africa;

4. *Welcomes* decision EX.CL/Dec.284 (IX) on the situation of refugees, returnees and displaced persons in Africa, adopted by the Executive Council of the African Union at its ninth ordinary session, held at Banjul on 28 and 29 June 2006;[7]

5. *Expresses its appreciation* for the leadership shown by the Office of the United Nations High Commissioner for Refugees, and commends the Office for its ongoing efforts, with the support of the international community, to assist African countries of asylum and to respond to the protection and assistance needs of refugees, returnees and displaced persons in Africa;

6. *Recognizes* that, among refugees, returnees and internally displaced persons, women and children are the majority of the population affected by conflict, and in this context notes the conclusion on women and girls at risk adopted by the Executive Committee of the

Programme of the United Nations High Commissioner for Refugees at its fifty-seventh session;[8]

7. *Notes* the conclusion on identification, prevention and reduction of statelessness and protection of stateless persons adopted by the Executive Committee at its fifty-seventh session,[9] which is aimed at enhancing the protection of stateless persons as well as the prevention and reduction of statelessness;

8. *Reiterates* the importance of the full and effective implementation of standards and procedures, including the monitoring and reporting mechanism outlined in Security Council resolution 1612 (2005) of 26 July 2005, to better address the specific protection needs of refugee children and adolescents and to safeguard rights and, in particular, to ensure adequate attention to unaccompanied and separated children and children affected by armed conflict, including former child soldiers in refugee settings, as well as in the context of voluntary repatriation and reintegration measures;

9. *Recognizes* the importance of early registration and effective registration systems and censuses as a tool of protection and as a means to the quantification and assessment of needs for the provision and distribution of humanitarian assistance and to implement appropriate durable solutions;

10. *Recalls* the conclusion on registration of refugees and asylum-seekers adopted by the Executive Committee at its fifty-second session,[10] notes the many forms of harassment faced by refugees and asylum-seekers who remain without any form of documentation attesting to their status, recalls the responsibility of States to register refugees on their territories, and, as appropriate, the responsibility of the Office of the High Commissioner or mandated international bodies to do so, reiterates in this context the central role which early and effective registration and documentation can play, guided by protection considerations, in enhancing protection and supporting efforts to find durable solutions, and calls upon the Office, as appropriate, to help States to conduct this procedure should they be unable to register refugees on their territory;

11. *Calls upon* the international community, including States and the Office of the High Commissioner and other relevant United Nations organizations, within their respective mandates, to take concrete action to meet the protection and assistance needs of refugees, returnees and displaced persons and to contribute generously to projects and programmes aimed at alleviating their plight and facilitating durable solutions for refugees and displaced persons;

12. *Reaffirms* the importance of timely and adequate assistance and protection for refugees, also reaffirms that assistance and protection are mutually reinforcing and that inadequate material assistance and food shortages undermine protection, notes the importance of a rights- and community-based approach in engaging constructively with individual refugees and their communities to achieve fair and equitable access to food and other forms of material assistance, and expresses concern in regard to situations in which minimum standards of assistance are not met, including those in which adequate needs assessments have yet to be undertaken;

13. *Also reaffirms* that respect by States for their protection responsibilities towards refugees is strengthened by international solidarity involving all members of the international community and that the refugee protection regime is enhanced through

committed international cooperation in a spirit of solidarity and burden- and responsibility-sharing among all States;

14. *Further reaffirms* that host States have the primary responsibility to ensure the civilian and humanitarian character of asylum, and calls upon States, in cooperation with international organizations, within their mandates, to take all necessary measures to ensure respect for the principles of refugee protection and, in particular, to ensure that the civilian and humanitarian nature of refugee camps is not compromised by the presence or the activities of armed elements or used for purposes that are incompatible with their civilian character, and encourages the High Commissioner to continue efforts, in consultation with States and other relevant actors, to ensure the civilian and humanitarian character of camps;

15. *Condemns* all acts that pose a threat to the personal security and wellbeing of refugees and asylum-seekers, such as refoulement, unlawful expulsion and physical attacks, and calls upon States of refuge, in cooperation with international organizations, where appropriate, to take all necessary measures to ensure respect for the principles of refugee protection, including the humane treatment of asylum-seekers;

16. *Deplores* the continuing violence and insecurity which constitute an ongoing threat to the safety and security of staff members of the Office of the High Commissioner and other humanitarian organizations and an obstacle to the effective fulfilment of the mandate of the Office and the ability of its implementing partners and other humanitarian personnel to discharge their respective humanitarian functions, urges States, parties to conflict and all other relevant actors to take all necessary measures to protect activities related to humanitarian assistance, prevent attacks on and kidnapping of national and international humanitarian workers and ensure the safety and security of the personnel and property of the Office and that of all humanitarian organizations discharging functions mandated by the Office, and calls upon States to investigate fully any crime committed against humanitarian personnel and bring to justice the persons responsible for such crimes;

17. *Calls upon* the Office of the High Commissioner, the African Union, subregional organizations and all African States, in conjunction with agencies of the United Nations system, intergovernmental and non-governmental organizations and the international community, to strengthen and revitalize existing partnerships and forge new ones in support of the international refugee protection system;

18. *Calls upon* the Office of the High Commissioner, the international community and other concerned entities to intensify their support to African Governments through appropriate capacity-building activities, including training of relevant officers, disseminating information about refugee instruments and principles, providing financial, technical and advisory services to accelerate the enactment or amendment and implementation of legislation relating to refugees, strengthening emergency response and enhancing capacities for the coordination of humanitarian activities;

19. *Reaffirms* the right of return and the principle of voluntary repatriation, appeals to countries of origin and countries of asylum to create conditions that are conducive to voluntary repatriation, recognizes that, while voluntary repatriation remains the pre-eminent solution, local integration and third-country resettlement, where appropriate and feasible, are also viable options for dealing with the situation of African refugees who, owing to prevailing circumstances in their respective countries of origin, are unable to return home;

20. *Also reaffirms* that voluntary repatriation should not necessarily be conditioned on the accomplishment of political solutions in the country of origin in order not to impede the exercise of the refugees' right to return, recognizes that the voluntary repatriation and

reintegration process is normally guided by the conditions in the country of origin, in particular that voluntary repatriation can be accomplished in conditions of safety and dignity, and urges the High Commissioner to promote sustainable return through the development of durable and lasting solutions, particularly in protracted refugee situations;

21. *Calls upon* the international donor community to provide financial and material assistance that allows for the implementation of community-based development programmes that benefit both refugees and host communities, as appropriate, in agreement with host countries and consistent with humanitarian objectives;

22. *Appeals* to the international community to respond positively, in the spirit of solidarity and burden- and responsibility-sharing, to the third-country resettlement needs of African refugees, notes in this regard the importance of using resettlement strategically, as part of situation-specific comprehensive responses to refugee situations, and to this end encourages interested States, the Office of the High Commissioner and other relevant partners to make full use of the Multilateral Framework of Understandings on Resettlement,[11] where appropriate;

23. *Calls upon* the international donor community to provide material and financial assistance for the implementation of programmes intended for the rehabilitation of the environment and infrastructure affected by refugees in countries of asylum;

24. *Urges* the international community, in the spirit of international solidarity and burden-sharing, to continue to fund generously the refugee programmes of the Office of the High Commissioner and, taking into account the substantially increased needs of programmes in Africa, inter alia, as a result of repatriation possibilities, to ensure that Africa receives a fair and equitable share of the resources designated for refugees;

25. *Encourages* the Office of the High Commissioner and interested States to identify protracted refugee situations which might lend themselves to resolution through the development of specific, multilateral, comprehensive and practical approaches to resolving such refugee situations, including improvement of international burden- and responsibility-sharing and realization of durable solutions, within a multilateral context;

26. *Expresses grave concern* at the increasing numbers of internally displaced persons in Africa, calls upon States to take concrete action to pre-empt internal displacement and to meet the protection and assistance needs of internally displaced persons, recalls in this regard the Guiding Principles on Internal Displacement,[12] takes note of the current activities of the Office of the High Commissioner related to protection of and assistance to internally displaced persons, including in the context of inter-agency arrangements in this field, emphasizes that such activities should be consistent with relevant General Assembly resolutions and should not undermine the mandate of the Office and the institution of asylum, and encourages the High Commissioner to continue his dialogue with States on the role of his Office in this regard;

27. *Invites* the Representative of the Secretary-General on the human rights of internally displaced persons to continue his ongoing dialogue with Member States and the intergovernmental and non-governmental organizations concerned, in accordance with his mandate, and to include information thereon in his reports to the Human Rights Council and the General Assembly;

28. *Requests* the Secretary-General to submit a comprehensive report on assistance to refugees, returnees and displaced persons in Africa to the General Assembly at its sixty-second session, taking fully into account the efforts expended by countries of asylum, under the item entitled "Report of the United Nations High Commissioner for Refugees, questions relating to refugees, returnees and displaced persons and humanitarian questions".

81st plenary meeting
19 December 2006

---

[1] United Nations, *Treaty Series*, vol. 1001, No. 14691.

[2] Ibid., vol. 1520, No. 26363.

[3] Ibid., vol. 189, No. 2545.

[4] Ibid., vol. 606, No. 8791.

[5] A/61/301.

[6] *Official Records of the General Assembly, Sixty-first Session, Supplement No. 12* (A/61/12).

[7] See African Union, document EX.CL/Dec.278–314 (IX).

[8] *Official Records of the General Assembly, Sixty-first Session, Supplement No. 12A* (A/61/12/Add.1), chap. III, sect. A.

[9] Ibid., sect. B.

[10] Ibid., *Fifty-sixth Session, Supplement No. 12A* (A/56/12/Add.1), chap. III, sect. B.

[11] Available from www.unhcr.org.

[12] E/CN.4/1998/53/Add.2, annex.

Resolution 61/140

[on the report of the Third Committee (A/61/437 and Corr.1)]

61/140. United Nations Literacy Decade: education for all

The General Assembly,

Recalling its resolution 56/116 of 19 December 2001, by which it proclaimed the ten-year period beginning on 1 January 2003 the United Nations Literacy Decade, its resolution 57/166 of 18 December 2002, in which it welcomed the International Plan of Action for the United Nations Literacy Decade, and its resolution 59/149 of 20 December 2004,

Recalling also the United Nations Millennium Declaration,[1] in which Member States resolved to ensure that, by 2015, children everywhere, boys and girls alike, will be able to complete a full course of primary schooling and that girls and boys will have equal access to all levels of education, which requires a renewed commitment to promote literacy for all,

Reaffirming the emphasis placed by the 2005 World Summit on the critical role of both formal and informal education in the achievement of poverty eradication and other development goals as envisaged in the Millennium Declaration, in particular basic education and training for eradicating illiteracy, and the need to strive for expanded secondary and higher education as well as vocational education and technical training, especially for girls and women, the creation of human resources and infrastructure capabilities and the empowerment of those living in poverty,

Reaffirming also that a basic education is crucial to nation-building, that literacy for all is at the heart of basic education for all and that creating literate environments and societies is essential for achieving the goals of eradicating poverty, reducing child mortality, curbing population growth, achieving gender equality and ensuring sustainable development, peace and democracy,

Convinced that literacy is crucial to the acquisition by every child, youth and adult of the essential life skills that will enable them to address the challenges that they can face in life and represents an essential step in basic education, which is an indispensable means for effective participation in the societies and economies of the twenty-first century,

Affirming that the realization of the right to education, especially for girls, Contributes to the promotion of gender equality and the eradication of poverty,

Welcoming the considerable efforts that have been made to address the objectives of the Decade at various levels,

Noting with deep concern that 771 million adults over the age of 15 lack basic literacy skills worldwide and about 100 million children of primary school age are still not enrolled in primary schools, that the issue of illiteracy may not be sufficiently high on national agendas to generate the kind of political and economic support required to address global illiteracy challenges and that the world is unlikely to meet those challenges if the present trends continue,

Deeply concerned about the persistence of the gender gap in education, which is reflected by the fact that nearly two thirds of the world's adult illiterates are women,

1. *Takes note* of the report of the Director-General of the United Nations Educational, Scientific and Cultural Organization on the implementation of the International Plan of Action for the United Nations Literacy Decade;[2]

2. *Welcomes* the efforts made so far by Member States and the international community in implementing the International Plan of Action;

3. *Appeals* to all Governments to develop reliable literacy data and information and to further reinforce political will, mobilize adequate national resources, develop more inclusive policymaking environments and devise innovative strategies for reaching the poorest and most marginalized groups and for seeking alternative formal and non-formal approaches to learning with a view to achieving the goals of the Decade;

4. *Urges* all Governments to take the lead in coordinating the activities of the Decade at the national level, bringing all relevant national actors together in a sustained dialogue and collaborative action on policy formulation, implementation and evaluation of literacy efforts;

5. *Appeals* to all Governments and professional organizations to strengthen national and professional educational institutions in their countries with a view to expanding their capacity and promoting the quality of education, with particular focus on literacy;

6. *Appeals* to all Governments and to economic and financial organizations and institutions, both national and international, to lend greater financial and material support to the efforts to increase literacy and achieve the goals of Education for All and those of the Decade, through, inter alia, the 20/20 initiative,[3] as appropriate;

7. *Invites* Member States, the specialized agencies and other organizations of the United Nations system, as well as relevant intergovernmental and non-governmental organizations, to intensify their efforts to implement effectively the International Plan of Action and

to integrate substantially those efforts in the Education for All process and other initiatives and activities of the United Nations Educational, Scientific and Cultural Organization and within the framework of the internationally agreed development goals, including those contained in the United Nations Millennium Declaration;[1]

8. *Requests* the United Nations Educational, Scientific and Cultural Organization to reinforce its lead role in coordinating and catalysing the activities of the Decade at the regional and international levels, prepare and conduct the mid-Decade review in collaboration with all Decade partners during 2007 and 2008 and submit its results to the General Assembly;

9. *Invites* Member States and the relevant intergovernmental and non-governmental organizations to take an active part in the preparation and organization of high-level regional conferences, scheduled to be held in 2007–2008 in Qatar, Azerbaijan, Mali, Costa Rica and in Asia and the Pacific, aimed at marshalling high political commitment, building an effective partnership among all the stakeholders and mobilizing resources needed for achieving the goals of the Decade and the International Plan of Action;

10. *Requests* all relevant entities of the United Nations system, particularly the United Nations Educational, Scientific and Cultural Organization, in cooperation with national Governments, to take immediate, concrete steps to address the needs of countries with high illiteracy rates and/or with large populations of illiterate adults, with particular regard to women, including through programmes that promote low-cost and effective literacy provisions;

11. *Requests* the Secretary-General, in cooperation with the Director-General of the United Nations Educational, Scientific and Cultural Organization, to seek the views of Member States on the progress achieved in implementing their national programmes and plans of action for the Decade and to submit the next progress report on the implementation of the International Plan of Action to the General Assembly in 2008;

12. *Decides* to include in the provisional agenda of its sixty-third session, under the item entitled "Social development", the sub-item entitled "United Nations Literacy Decade: education for all".

81st plenary meeting
19 December 2006

---

[1] See resolution 55/2.

[2] See A/61/151.

[3] See *Report of the World Summit for Social Development, Copenhagen, 6–12 March 1995* (United Nations publication, Sales No. E.96.IV.8), chap. I, resolution 1, annex II, para. 88 (*c*).

Resolution 61/141

[on the report of the Third Committee (A/61/437 and Corr.1)]

61/141. Implementation of the outcome of the World Summit for Social Development and of the twenty-fourth special session of the General Assembly

The General Assembly,

Recalling the World Summit for Social Development, held at Copenhagen from 6 to 12 March 1995, and the twenty-fourth special session of the General Assembly entitled "World Summit for Social Development and beyond: achieving social development for all in a globalizing world", held at Geneva from 26 June to 1 July 2000,

Reaffirming that the Copenhagen Declaration on Social Development and the Programme of Action[1] and the further initiatives for social development adopted by the General Assembly at its twenty-fourth special session,[2] as well as a continued global dialogue on social development issues, constitute the basic framework for the promotion of social development for all at the national and international levels,

Recalling the United Nations Millennium Declaration[3] and the development goals contained therein, as well as the commitments made at major United Nations summits, conferences and special sessions, including the commitments made at the 2005 World Summit,[4]

Recalling also its resolution 60/209 of 22 December 2005 on the implementation of the first United Nations Decade for the Eradication of Poverty (1997–2006),

Recalling further its resolution 57/270 B of 23 June 2003 on the integrated and coordinated implementation of and follow-up to the outcomes of the major United Nations conferences and summits in the economic and social fields,

Emphasizing the need to enhance the role of the Commission for Social Development in the follow-up and review of the World Summit for Social Development and the outcome of the twenty-fourth special session of the General Assembly,

1. *Takes note* of the report of the Secretary-General;[5]

2. *Welcomes* the reaffirmation by Governments of their will and commitment to continue implementing the Copenhagen Declaration on Social Development and the Programme of Action,[1] in particular to eradicate poverty, promote full and productive employment and foster social integration to achieve stable, safe and just societies for all;

3. *Recognizes* that the implementation of the Copenhagen commitments and the attainment of the internationally agreed development goals, including the Millennium Development Goals, are mutually reinforcing and that the Copenhagen commitments are crucial to a coherent people-centred approach to development;

4. *Reaffirms* that the Commission for Social Development continues to have the primary responsibility for the follow-up and review of the World Summit for Social Development and the outcome of the twenty-fourth special session of the General Assembly and that it serves as the main United Nations forum for an intensified global dialogue on social development issues, and calls upon Member States, the relevant specialized agencies, funds and programmes of the United Nations system and civil society to enhance their support for its work;

5. *Recognizes* that the broad concept of social development affirmed by the World Summit for Social Development and the twenty-fourth special session of the General Assembly has been weakened in national and international policymaking and that, while poverty eradication is a central part of development policy and discourse, further attention should be given to the other commitments agreed to at the Summit, in particular those concerning employment and social integration, which have also suffered from a general disconnect between economic and social policymaking;

6. *Acknowledges* that the first United Nations Decade for the Eradication of Poverty (1997–2006), launched after the World Summit for Social Development, has provided the long-term vision for sustained and concerted efforts at the national and international levels to eradicate poverty, and recognizes that the implementation of the commitments made by Governments during the Decade has fallen short of expectations;

7. *Emphasizes* that the major United Nations conferences and summits, including the Millennium Summit and the 2005 World Summit, have reinforced the priority and urgency of poverty eradication within the United Nations development agenda;

8. *Also emphasizes* that poverty eradication policies should attack poverty by addressing its root and structural causes and manifestations, and that equity and the reduction of inequalities need to be incorporated in those policies;

9. *Stresses* that an enabling environment is a critical precondition for achieving equity and social development and that, while economic growth is essential, entrenched inequality and marginalization are an obstacle to the broad-based and sustained growth required for sustainable, inclusive people-centred development, and recognizes the need to balance and ensure complementarity between measures to achieve growth and measure to achieve economic and social equity in order for there to be an impact on overall poverty levels;

10. *Also stresses* that policies and programmes designed to achieve poverty eradication should include specific measures to foster social integration, including by providing marginalized socio-economic sectors and groups with equal access to opportunities and social protection;

11. *Reaffirms* that social integration policies should seek to reduce inequalities, promote access to basic social services, education for all and health care, increase the participation and integration of social groups, particularly youth, older persons and persons with disabilities, and address the challenges posed by globalization and market-driven reforms to social development in order for all people in all countries to benefit from globalization;

12. *Recognizes* the need to promote respect for all human rights and fundamental freedoms in order to address the most pressing social needs of people living in poverty, including through the design and development of appropriate mechanisms to strengthen and consolidate democratic institutions and governance;

13. *Reaffirms* the commitment to the empowerment of women and gender equality and to strengthening policies and programmes that improve, ensure and broaden the full participation of women in all spheres of political, economic, social and cultural life, as equal partners, and to improving their access to all resources needed for the full exercise of all their human rights and fundamental freedoms by removing persistent barriers;

14. *Welcomes* the ministerial declaration, adopted at the high-level segment of the substantive session of 2006 of the Economic and Social Council, on "Creating an environment at

the national and international levels conducive to generating full and productive employment and decent work for all, and its impact on sustainable development";[6]

15. *Reaffirms* that there is an urgent need to create an environment at the national and international levels that is conducive to the attainment of full and productive employment and decent work for all as a foundation for sustainable development and that an environment that supports investment, growth and entrepreneurship is essential to the creation of new job opportunities, and also reaffirms that opportunities for men and women to obtain productive work in conditions of freedom, equity, security and human dignity are essential to ensuring the eradication of hunger and poverty, the improvement of economic and social well-being for all, the achievement of sustained economic growth and sustainable development of all nations and a fully inclusive and equitable globalization;

16. *Also reaffirms* the commitment to employment policies that promote full and productive employment and decent work for all under conditions of equity, equality, security and dignity, and further reaffirms that employment creation should be incorporated into macroeconomic policies;

17. *Further reaffirms* the commitments made in respect of "Meeting the special needs of Africa" at the 2005 World Summit,[7] underlines the call of the Economic and Social Council for enhanced coordination within the United Nations systems and the ongoing efforts to harmonize the current initiatives on Africa, and request the Commission for Social Development to continue to give due prominence in its work to the social dimensions of the New Partnership for Africa's Development;[8]

18. *Reaffirms* that each country has the primary responsibility for its own economic and social development and that the role of national policies and development strategies cannot be overemphasized, and underlines the importance of adopting effective measures, including new financial mechanisms, as appropriate, to support the efforts of developing countries to achieve sustained economic growth, sustainable development, poverty eradication and the strengthening of their democratic systems;

19. *Also reaffirms*, in this context, that international cooperation has an essential role in assisting developing countries, including the least developed countries, in strengthening their human, institutional and technological capacity;

20. *Stresses* that the international community shall enhance its efforts to create an enabling environment for social development and poverty eradication through increasing market access for developing countries, technology transfer on mutually agreed terms, financial aid and a comprehensive solution to the external debt problem;

21. *Acknowledges* that good governance and the rule of law at the national and international levels are essential for sustained economic growth, sustainable development and the eradication of poverty and hunger;

22. *Urges* developed countries that have not yet done so in accordance with their commitments, to make concrete efforts towards meeting the targets of 0.7 per cent of their gross national product for official development assistance to developing countries and 0.15 to 0.2 per cent of their gross national product to least developed countries, and encourages developing countries to build on the progress achieved in ensuring that official development assistance is used effectively to help meet development goals and targets;

23. *Welcomes* the contribution to the mobilization of resources for social development by the initiatives on a voluntary basis taken by groups of Member States based on innovative

financing mechanisms, including those that aim to provide further drug access at affordable prices to developing countries on a sustainable and predictable basis, such as the International Drug Purchase Facility, UNITAID, as well as other initiatives, such as the International Finance Facility for Immunisation, and notes the New York Declaration of 20 September 2004, which launched the Action against Hunger and Poverty initiative and called for further attention to raise funds urgently needed to help meet the Millennium Development Goals and to complement and ensure long-term stability and predictability to foreign aid;

24. *Reaffirms* that social development requires the active involvement of all actors in the development process, including civil society organizations, corporations and small businesses, and that partnerships among all relevant actors are increasingly becoming part of national and international cooperation for social development, and also reaffirms that, within countries, partnerships among the Government, civil society and the private sector can contribute effectively to the achievement of social development goals;

25. *Underlines* the responsibility of the private sector, at both the national and the international levels, including small and large companies and transnational corporations, regarding not only the economic and financial but also the development, social, gender and environmental implications of their activities, their obligations towards their workers and their contributions to achieving sustainable development, including social development, and emphasizes the need to take concrete actions on corporate responsibility and accountability, including through the participation of all relevant stakeholders, inter alia, for the prevention or prosecution of corruption;

26. *Invites* the Secretary-General, the Economic and Social Council, the regional commissions, the relevant specialized agencies, funds and programmes of the United Nations system and other intergovernmental forums, within their respective mandates, to continue to integrate into their work programmes and give priority attention to the Copenhagen commitments and the Declaration on the tenth anniversary of the World Summit for Social Development,[9] to continue to be actively involved in their follow-up and to monitor the achievement of those commitments and undertakings;

27. *Decides* to include in the provisional agenda of its sixty-second session the sub-item entitled "Implementation of the outcome of the World Summit for Social Development and of the twenty-fourth special session of the General Assembly", and requests the Secretary-General to submit a report on the question to the Assembly at that session.

81st plenary meeting
19 December 2006

---

[1] *Report of the World Summit for Social Development, Copenhagen, 6–12 March 1995* (United Nations publication, Sales No. E.96.IV.8), chap. I, resolution 1, annexes I and II.

[2] Resolution S-24/2, annex.

[3] See resolution 55/2.

[4] See resolution 60/1.

[5] A/61/99.

[6] See A/61/3, chap. III, para. 50. For the final text, see *Official Records of the General Assembly, Sixty-first Session, Supplement No. 3*.

[7] See resolution 60/1, para. 68.

[8] A/57/304, annex.

[9] See *Official Records of the Economic and Social Council, 2005, Supplement No. 6* (E/2005/26), chap. I, sect. A; see also Economic and Social Council decision 2005/234.

Resolution 61/142

[on the report of the Third Committee (A/61/437 and Corr.1)]

61/142. Follow-up to the Second World Assembly on Ageing

The General Assembly,

Recalling its resolution 57/167 of 18 December 2002, in which it endorsed the Political Declaration and the Madrid International Plan of Action on Ageing, 2002,[1] as well as its resolution 58/134 of 22 December 2003, in which it took note, inter alia, of the road map for the implementation of the Madrid Plan of Action, and its resolutions 59/150 of 20 December 2004 and 60/135 of 16 December 2005,

Recalling also Economic and Social Council resolution 2003/14 of 21 July 2003, in which the Council invited Governments, the United Nations system and civil society to participate in a "bottom-up" approach to the review and appraisal of the Madrid Plan of Action,

Recalling further Commission for Social Development resolution 42/1 of 13 February 2004,[2] in which the Commission decided to undertake the review and appraisal of the Madrid Plan of Action every five years,

Mindful that, in its resolution 44/1 of 17 February 2006,[3] the Commission for Social Development endorsed the calendar and the global theme for the first review and appraisal of the implementation of the Madrid Plan of Action, "Addressing the challenges and opportunities of ageing", and decided to start the first global cycle of review and appraisal in 2007 at its forty-fifth session and to conclude it in 2008 at its forty-sixth session,

Taking note of the report of the Secretary-General,[4]

1. *Encourages* Governments to pay greater attention to building capacity to eradicate poverty among older persons, particularly older women, by mainstreaming ageing issues into poverty eradication strategies and national development plans, and by encouraging greater consultation with older persons in the course of developing, implementing and monitoring poverty eradication plans;

2. *Invites* Governments to conduct their ageing-related policies through inclusive consultations with relevant stakeholders and social development partners, in the interest of creating national policy ownership and consensus-building;

3. *Encourages* the international community to support national efforts to forge stronger partnerships with civil society, including organizations of older persons, academia, research foundations, community-based organizations, including caregivers, and the private sector, in an effort to help to build capacity on ageing issues;

4. *Invites* Governments that have not done so to designate focal points for handling follow-up of national plans of action on ageing;

5. *Calls upon* Governments to promote a bottom-up participatory approach throughout the entire implementation process;

6. *Encourages* the international community to support national efforts to provide funding for research and data-collection initiatives on ageing in order to better understand the challenges

and opportunities presented by population ageing and provide policymakers with more accurate and more specific information on gender and ageing;

7. *Stresses* the need for additional capacity-building at the national level in order to promote and facilitate implementation of the Madrid International Plan of Action on Ageing, 2002,[5] and in this connection encourages Governments to support the United Nations Trust Fund for Ageing to enable the Department of Economic and Social Affairs of the Secretariat to provide expanded assistance to countries, upon their request;

8. *Recommends* that ongoing efforts to achieve the internationally agreed development goals, including those contained in the United Nations Millennium Declaration,[6] take into account the situation of older persons;

9. *Takes note* of Commission for Social Development resolution 44/1,[3] in this context invites Member States to undertake an initial identification of actions they have taken since the Second World Assembly on Ageing in 2002 as well as policy recommendations for the further implementation of the Madrid Plan of Action, and encourages regional commissions to identify modalities for conducting the regional review and appraisal, including best practices, with the aim of presenting this information to the Commission at its forty-fifth session in 2007;

10. *Recommends* to the Economic and Social Council the integration of ageing into the monitoring, review and appraisal exercises of other major international development initiatives and policy frameworks, including the United Nations Millennium Declaration, the Programme of Action of the International Conference on Population and Development,[7] the Copenhagen Declaration on Social Development,[8] the Programme of Action of the World Summit for Social Development[9] and the Beijing Platform for Actoin[10] and their follow-up processess;

11. *Requests* the Secretary-General to report to the General Assembly at its sixty-second session on the implementation of the present resolution, including information on the commemoration of the five-year review and appraisal of the implementation of the Madrid Plan of Action in 2007.

81st plenary meeting
19 December 2006

---

[1] *Report of the Second World Assembly on Ageing, Madrid, 8–12 April 2002* (United Nations publication, Sales No. E.02.IV.4), chap. I, resolution 1, annexes I and II.

[2] See *Official Records of the Economic and Social Council, 2004, Supplement No. 6* (E/2004/26), chap. I, sect. E.

[3] Ibid., *2006, Supplement No. 6* (E/2006/26), chap. I, sect. C.

[4] A/61/167.

[5] *Report of the Second World Assembly on Ageing, Madrid, 8–12 April 2002* (United Nations publication, Sales No. E.02.IV.4), chap. I, resolution 1, annex II.

[6] See resolution 55/2.

[7] *Report of the International Conference on Population and Development, Cairo, 5–13 September 1994* (United Nations publication, Sales No. E.95.XIII.18), chap. I, resolution 1, annex.

[8] *Report of the World Summit for Social Development, Copenhagen, 6–12 March 1995* (United Nations publication, Sales No. E.96.IV.8), chap. I, resolution 1, annex I.

[9] Ibid., annex II.

[10] *Report of the Fourth World Conference on Women, Beijing, 4–15 September 1995* (United Nations publication, Sales No. E.96.IV.13), chap. I, resolution 1, annex II.

Resolution 61/143

[on the report of the Third Committee (A/61/438)]

61/143. Intensification of efforts to eliminate all forms of violence against women

The General Assembly,

Reaffirming the obligation of all States to promote and protect all human rights and fundamental freedoms, and reaffirming also that discrimination on the basis of sex is contrary to the Charter of the United Nations, the Convention on the Elimination of All Forms of Discrimination against Women[1] and other international human rights instruments, and that its elimination is an integral part of efforts towards the elimination of all forms of violence against women,

Reaffirming also the Declaration on the Elimination of Violence against Women,[2] the Beijing Declaration and Platform for Action,[3] the outcome of the twenty-third special session of the General Assembly entitled "Women 2000: gender equality, development and peace for the twenty-first century",[4] and the declaration adopted at the forty-ninth session of the Commission on the Status of Women,[5]

Reaffirming further the international commitments in the field of social development and to gender equality and the advancement of women made at the World Conference on Human Rights, the International Conference on Population and Development, the World Summit for Social Development and the World Conference against Racism, Racial Discrimination, Xenophobia and Related Intolerance, as well as those made in the United Nations Millennium Declaration[6] and at the 2005 World Summit,

Recalling all its previous resolutions on the elimination of violence against women and on the in-depth study on all forms of violence against women, and Security Council resolution 1325 (2000) of 31 October 2000 on women and peace and security,

Recalling also Commission on Human Rights resolution 2005/41 of 19 April 2005 on the elimination of violence against women,[7]

Recalling further the inclusion of gender-related crimes and crimes of sexual violence in the Rome Statute of the International Criminal Court,[8]

Recognizing that violence against women is rooted in historically unequal power relations between men and women and that all forms of violence against women seriously violate and impair or nullify the enjoyment by women of all human rights and fundamental freedoms and constitute a major impediment to the ability of women to make use of their capabilities,

Recognizing also that women's poverty and lack of empowerment, as well as their marginalization resulting from their exclusion from social policies and from the benefits of sustainable development, can place them at increased risk of violence,

Recognizing further that violence against women impedes the social and economic development of communities and States, as well as the achievement of the internationally agreed development goals, including the Millennium Development Goals,

Recognizing the serious immediate and long-term implications for health, including sexual and reproductive health, as well as an increased vulnerability to HIV/AIDS, and the negative impact on psychological, social and economic development that violence against women represents for individuals, families, communities and States,

Deeply concerned about the pervasiveness of violence against women and girls in all its forms and manifestations worldwide, and reiterating the need to intensify efforts to prevent and eliminate all forms of violence against women and girls throughout the world,

Taking note of the report of the Secretary-General on the in-depth study on all forms of violence against women,[9] and having considered with interest the recommendations contained therein,

1. *Recognizes* that violence against women and girls persists in every country in the world as a pervasive violation of the enjoyment of human rights and a major impediment to achieving gender equality, development and peace;

2. *Welcomes* the efforts and important contributions at the local, national, regional and international levels to eliminate all forms of violence against women, and takes note with appreciation of the work done by the Committee on the Elimination of Discrimination against Women and the Special Rapporteur on violence against women, its causes and consequences;

3. *Stresses* that "violence against women" means any act of gender-based violence that results in, or is likely to result in, physical, sexual or psychological harm or suffering to women, including threats of such acts, coercion or arbitrary deprivation of liberty, whether occurring in public or in private life;

4. *Strongly condemns* all acts of violence against women and girls, whether these acts are perpetrated by the State, by private persons or by non-State actors, calls for the elimination of all forms of gender-based violence in the family, within the general community and where perpetrated or condoned by the State, and stresses the need to treat all forms of violence against women and girls as a criminal offence, punishable by law;

5. *Stresses* that it is important that States strongly condemn violence against women and refrain from invoking any custom, tradition or religious consideration to avoid their obligations with respect to its elimination as set out in the Declaration on the Elimination of Violence against Women;[2]

6. *Stresses also* that challenges and obstacles remain in the implementation of international standards and norms to address the inequality between men and women and violence against women in particular, and pledges to intensify action to ensure their full and accelerated implementation;

7. *Stresses further* that States have the obligation to promote and protect all human rights and fundamental freedoms of women and girls and must exercise due diligence to prevent, investigate and punish the perpetrators of violence against women and girls and to provide protection to the victims, and that failure to do so violates and impairs or nullifies the enjoyment of their human rights and fundamental freedoms;

8. *Urges* States to take action to eliminate all forms of violence against women by means of a more systematic, comprehensive, multisectoral and sustained approach, adequately

supported and facilitated by strong institutional mechanisms and financing, through national action plans, including those supported by international cooperation and, where appropriate, national development plans, including poverty eradication strategies and programme-based and sector-wide approaches, and to this end:

(*a*) To ensure that all human rights and fundamental freedoms are respected and protected;

(*b*) To consider ratifying or acceding to all human rights treaties, including, as a particular matter of priority, the Convention on the Elimination of All Forms of Discrimination against Women[1] and the Optional Protocol thereto,[10] limit the extent of any reservations that they lodge and regularly review such reservations with a view to withdrawing them so as to ensure that no reservation is incompatible with the object and purpose of the relevant treaty;

(*c*) To review and, where appropriate, revise, amend or abolish all laws, regulations, policies, practices and customs that discriminate against women or have a discriminatory impact on women, and ensure that provisions of multiple legal systems, where they exist, comply with international human rights obligations, commitments and principles, including the principle of non-discrimination;

(*d*) To exercise leadership to end all forms of violence against women and support advocacy in this regard at all levels, including at the local, national, regional and international levels, and by all sectors, especially by political and community leaders, as well as the public and private sectors, the media and civil society;

(*e*) To empower women, particularly poor women, through, inter alia, social and economic policies that guarantee them full and equal access to all levels of quality education and training and to affordable and adequate public and social services, as well as full and equal rights to own land and other property, and to take further appropriate measures to address the increasing rate of homelessness or inadequate housing for women in order to reduce their vulnerability to violence;

(*f*) To take positive measures to address structural causes of violence against women and to strengthen prevention efforts that address discriminatory practices and social norms, including with regard to women who need special attention in the development of policies to address violence, such as women belonging to minority groups, including those based on nationality, ethnicity, religion or language, indigenous women, migrant women, stateless women, women living in underdeveloped, rural or remote communities, homeless women, women in institutions or in detention, women with disabilities, elderly women, widows and women who are otherwise discriminated against;

(*g*) To ensure that diverse strategies that take into account the intersection of gender with other factors are developed in order to eradicate all forms of violence against women;

(*h*) To exercise due diligence to prevent all acts of violence against women, including by improving the safety of public environments;

(*i*) To end impunity for violence against women, by prosecuting and punishing all perpetrators, by ensuring that women have equal protection of the law and equal access to justice and by holding up to public scrutiny and eliminating those attitudes that foster, justify or tolerate violence;

(*j*) To strengthen national health and social infrastructure to reinforce measures to promote women's equal access to public health and address the health consequences of violence against women, including by providing support to victims;

(*k*) To recognize that gender inequalities and all forms of violence against women and girls increase their vulnerability to HIV/AIDS and ensure that women can exercise their right to have control over, and decide freely and responsibly on, matters related to their sexuality in order to increase their ability to protect themselves from HIV infection, including their sexual and reproductive health, free of coercion, discrimination and violence;

(*l*) To ensure that men and women and boys and girls have access to education and literacy programmes and are educated on gender equality and human rights, particularly women's rights and their responsibility to respect the rights of others, inter alia, by integrating women's rights into all appropriate curricula and by developing gender-sensitive teaching materials and classroom practices, especially for early childhood education;

(*m*) To provide training and capacity-building on gender equality and women's rights for, inter alia, health workers, teachers, law enforcement personnel, military personnel, social workers, the judiciary, community leaders and the media;

(*n*) To promote awareness and information campaigns on women's rights and the responsibility to respect them, including in rural areas, and encourage men and boys to speak out strongly against violence against women;

(*o*) To protect women and girls in situations of armed conflict, post-conflict settings and refugee and internally displaced persons settings, where women are at greater risk of being targeted for violence and where their ability to seek and receive redress is often restricted, bearing in mind that peace is inextricably linked with equality between women and men and development, that armed and other types of conflicts and terrorism and hostage-taking still persist in many parts of the world and that aggression, foreign occupation and ethnic and other types of conflicts are an ongoing reality affecting women and men in nearly every region, undertake efforts to eliminate impunity for all gender-based violence in situations of armed conflict, bearing in mind relevant General Assembly resolutions and Security Council resolution 1325 (2000) on women and peace and security, and adopt, consistent with their obligations under the 1951 Convention relating to the Status of Refugees[11] and the 1967 Protocol thereto,[12] international human rights norms and relevant conclusions of the Executive Committee of the Programme of the United Nations High Commissioner for Refugees and General Assembly resolutions, a gender-sensitive approach to the consideration of claims for the granting of asylum and refugee status;

(*p*) To integrate a gender perspective into national plans of action and establish or strengthen specific national plans of action on the elimination of violence against women, supported by the necessary human, financial and technical resources, including, where appropriate, time-bound measurable targets, to promote the protection of women against any form of violence, and accelerate the implementation of existing national action plans that are regularly monitored and updated by Governments, taking into account inputs by civil society, in particular women's organizations, networks and other stakeholders;

(*q*) To allocate adequate resources to promote the empowerment of women and gender equality and to prevent and redress all forms and manifestations of violence against women;

9. *Calls upon* the international community, including the United Nations system and, as appropriate, regional and subregional organizations, to support national efforts to promote the empowerment of women and gender equality in order to enhance national efforts to eliminate violence against women and girls, including, upon request, in the development and implementation of national action plans on the elimination of violence against women and girls, through, inter alia, and taking into account national priorities, official development assistance and other appropriate assistance, such as facilitating the sharing of guidelines, methodologies and best practices;

10. *Urges* States to integrate gender perspectives into the comprehensive national development plans and poverty eradication strategies that address social, structural and macroeconomic issues, and to ensure that such strategies address violence against women and girls, and urges the United Nations funds and programmes and the specialized agencies and invites the Bretton Woods institutions to support national efforts in this regard;

11. *Also urges* States to ensure the systematic collection and analysis of data on violence against women, including with the involvement of national statistical offices and, where appropriate, in partnership with other actors, taking note of the World Health Organization multi-country study on women's health and domestic violence against women and its recommendation to enhance capacity and establish systems for data collection to monitor violence against women;

12. *Urges* the United Nations bodies, entities, funds and programmes and the specialized agencies, and invites the Bretton Woods institutions, in accordance with their mandates, to support, upon request and within existing resources, the strengthening of national capacities and efforts on the collection, processing and dissemination of data, including data disaggregated by sex, age and other relevant information, for their possible use for legislative, policy and programme development and in the national plans of action against all forms of violence against women;

13. *Notes* the work carried out for the elimination of all forms of violence against women by relevant United Nations bodies, entities, funds and programmes and relevant specialized agencies, including those responsible for the promotion of gender equality and women's rights, and urges them and invites the Bretton Woods institutions:

(*a*) To enhance the coordination of and intensify their efforts to eliminate all forms of violence against women and girls in a more systematic, comprehensive and sustained way, inter alia, through the Inter-Agency Network on Women and Gender Equality supported by the newly established Task Force on Violence against Women, in close collaboration with relevant civil society, including non-governmental organizations;

(*b*) To enhance coordination in a more systematic, comprehensive and sustained way of their assistance to States in their efforts to eliminate all forms of violence against women, including in the development or implementation of national action plans and, where appropriate, national development plans, including poverty reduction strategies where they exist, and programme-based and sector-wide approaches and in close collaboration with relevant civil society, including non-governmental organizations;

14. *Calls upon* the Inter-Agency Network on Women and Gender Equality to consider ways and means to enhance the effectiveness of the United Nations Trust Fund in Support of Actions to Eliminate Violence against Women as a system-wide funding mechanism for preventing and redressing all forms of violence against women and girls;

15. *Strongly encourages* States to increase significantly their voluntary financial support for activities related to preventing and eliminating all forms of violence against women, the empowerment of women and gender equality carried out by the specialized agencies and the United Nations funds and programmes, including the United Nations Trust Fund in Support of Actions to Eliminate Violence against Women;

16. *Stresses* that within the United Nations system adequate resources should be assigned to those bodies, specialized agencies, funds and programmes responsible for the promotion of gender equality and women's rights and to efforts throughout the United Nations system to eliminate violence against women and girls;

17. *Invites* the Economic and Social Council and its functional commissions, the Peacebuilding Commission, the Human Rights Council and other relevant United Nations bodies to discuss, by 2008, within their respective mandates, the question of violence against women in all its forms and manifestations, bearing in mind the recommendations contained in the report of the Secretary-General on the in-depth study on all forms of violence against women,[9] and to set priorities for addressing this issue in their future efforts and work programmes and to transmit the outcome of those discussions to the Secretary-General for his annual report to the General Assembly;

18. *Requests* the Statistical Commission to develop and propose, in consultation with the Commission on the Status of Women, and building on the work of the Special Rapporteur on violence against women, its causes and consequences, a set of possible indicators on violence against women in order to assist States in assessing the scope, prevalence and incidence of violence against women;

19. *Requests* the Secretary-General to establish a coordinated database, containing data provided by States, in particular national statistical offices, including, where appropriate, through relevant United Nations entities and other relevant regional intergovernmental organizations, disaggregated by sex, age and other relevant information, on the extent, nature and consequences of all forms of violence against women, and on the impact and effectiveness of policies and programmes for, including best practices in, combating such violence;

20. *Also requests* the Secretary-General to submit an annual report to the General Assembly on the implementation of the present resolution, addressing the question of violence against women, and requests that the report include:

(*a*) At the sixty-second session of the General Assembly, information provided by the United Nations bodies, funds and programmes and the specialized agencies on their follow-up activities to implement the resolution;

(*b*) At the sixty-third session of the General Assembly, information provided by States on their follow-up activities to implement the resolution;

21. *Decides* to continue its consideration of the question at its sixty-second session under the item entitled "Advancement of women".

81st plenary meeting
19 December 2006

[1] United Nations, *Treaty Series*, vol. 1249, No. 20378.

[2] See resolution 48/104.

[3] *Report of the Fourth World Conference on Women, Beijing, 4–15 September 1995* (United Nations publication, Sales No. E.96.IV.13), chap. I, resolution 1, annexes I and II.

[4] Resolution S-23/2, annex, and resolution S-23/3, annex.

[5] See *Official Records of the Economic and Social Council, 2005, Supplement No. 7* and corrigendum (E/2005/27 and Corr.1), chap. I, sect. A; see also Economic and Social Council decision 2005/232.

[6] See resolution 55/2.

[7] See *Official Records of the Economic and Social Council, 2005, Supplement No. 3* and corrigendum (E/2005/23 and Corr.1), chap. II, sect. A.

[8] United Nations, *Treaty Series*, vol. 2187, No. 38544.

[9] A/61/122 and Add.1 and Add.1/Corr.1.

[10] United Nations, *Treaty Series*, vol. 2131, No. 20378.

[11] Ibid., vol. 189, No. 2545.

[12] Ibid., vol. 606, No. 8791.

Resolution 61/144

[on the report of the Third Committee (A/61/438)]

61/144. Trafficking in women and girls

The General Assembly,

Recalling all international conventions that deal specifically with the problem of trafficking in women and girls, such as the Convention on the Elimination of All Forms of Discrimination against Women[1] and the Optional Protocol thereto,[2] the Convention on the Rights of the Child[3] and the Optional Protocol thereto on the sale of children, child prostitution and child pornography,[4] the Convention for the Suppression of the Traffic in Persons and of the Exploitation of the Prostitution of Others,[5] the United Nations Convention against Transnational Organized Crime[6] and the Protocols thereto, in particular the Protocol to Prevent, Suppress and Punish Trafficking in Persons, Especially Women and Children, supplementing the United Nations Convention against Transnational Organized Crime [7] and the Protocol against the Smuggling of Migrants by Land, Sea and Air, supplementing the United Nations Convention against Transnational Organized Crime,[8] as well as previous resolutions of the General Assembly, the Economic and Social Council and the Commission on Human Rights on the issue,

Reaffirming the provisions pertaining to trafficking in women and girls contained in the outcome documents of relevant international conferences and summits, in particular the strategic objective on the issue of trafficking contained in the Beijing Declaration and Platform for Action adopted by the Fourth World Conference on Women,[9]

Reaffirming also the commitment made by world leaders at the Millennium Summit and the 2005 World Summit to devise, enforce and strengthen effective measures to combat and eliminate all forms of trafficking in persons to counter the demand for trafficked victims and to protect the victims,

Recalling the reports of the Special Rapporteur on the sale of children, child prostitution and child pornography, the Special Rapporteur on trafficking in persons, especially women and children, and the Special Rapporteur on violence against women, its causes and consequences, as well as the information that deals with trafficking in women and girls contained in the report of the Secretary-General on the in-depth study on all forms of violence against women,[10]

Recalling also the report of the United Nations Office on Drugs and Crime entitled "Trafficking in Persons: Global Patterns", and the attention paid in it to the situation of trafficked women and girls,

Acknowledging the inclusion of gender-related crimes in the Rome Statute of the International Criminal Court,[11] which entered into force on 1 July 2002,

Bearing in mind that all States have an obligation to exercise due diligence to prevent, investigate and punish perpetrators of trafficking in persons, to rescue victims as well as provide for their protection and that not doing so violates and impairs or nullifies the enjoyment of the human rights and fundamental freedoms of the victims,

Recognizing the need for a stronger gender- and age-sensitive approach in all efforts to fight trafficking and protect its victims, taking into account that women and girls are particularly vulnerable to trafficking for the purposes of sexual exploitation, as well as for forced labour or services,

Recognizing also the need to address the impact of globalization on the particular problem of trafficking in women and children, in particular girls,

Recognizing further the challenges to combating trafficking in women and girls owing to the lack of adequate legislation and implementation of existing legislation, the lack of availability of reliable sex-disaggregated data and statistics, as well as the lack of resources,

Seriously concerned that an increasing number of women and girls from developing countries and from some countries with economies in transition are being trafficked to developed countries, as well as within and between regions and States, and that men and boys are also victims of trafficking, including for sexual exploitation,

Concerned about the use of new information technologies, including the Internet, for purposes of exploitation of the prostitution of others, for trafficking in women as brides, for sex tourism exploiting women and children and for child pornography, paedophilia and any other forms of sexual exploitation of children,

Concerned also about the increasing activities of transnational criminal organizations and others that profit from international trafficking in persons, especially women and children, without regard to dangerous and inhuman conditions and in flagrant violation of domestic laws and international standards,

Recognizing that victims of trafficking are particularly exposed to racism, racial discrimination, xenophobia and related intolerance and that women and girl victims are often subject to multiple forms of discrimination and violence, including on the grounds of their gender, age, ethnicity, culture and religion, as well as their origins, and that these forms of discrimination themselves may fuel trafficking in persons,

Noting that some of the demand for prostitution and forced labour is met by trafficking in persons in some parts of the world,

Acknowledging that women and girl victims of trafficking, on account of their gender, are further disadvantaged and marginalized by a general lack of information or awareness and recognition of their human rights and by the stigmatization often associated with trafficking, as well as by the obstacles they meet in gaining access to information and recourse mechanisms in cases of violation of their rights, and that special measures are required for their protection and to increase their awareness,

Recognizing the importance of bilateral, subregional, regional and international cooperation mechanisms and initiatives, including information exchanges on best practices, of Governments and intergovernmental and non-governmental organizations to address the problem of trafficking in persons, especially women and children,

Recognizing also that global efforts, including international cooperation and technical assistance programmes, to eradicate trafficking in persons, especially women and children, demand the strong political commitment, shared responsibility and active cooperation of all Governments of countries of origin, transit and destination,

Recognizing further that policies and programmes for prevention, rehabilitation, repatriation and reintegration should be developed through a gender-and age-sensitive, comprehensive and multidisciplinary approach, with concern for the security of the victims and respect for the full enjoyment of their human rights and with the involvement of all actors in countries of origin, transit and destination,

Convinced of the need to protect and assist all victims of trafficking, with full respect for the victims' human rights,

1. *Welcomes* the efforts of Governments, United Nations bodies and agencies and intergovernmental and non-governmental organizations to address the particular problem of trafficking in women and girls, and encourages them to continue doing so and to share their knowledge and best practices as widely as possible;

2. *Calls upon* Governments to eliminate the demand for trafficked women and girls for all forms of exploitation;

3. *Also calls upon* Governments to take appropriate measures to address the factors that increase vulnerability to being trafficked, including poverty and gender inequality, as well as other factors that encourage the particular problem of trafficking in women and girls for prostitution and other forms of commercialized sex, forced marriage and forced labour, in order to eliminate such trafficking, including by strengthening existing legislation with a view to providing better protection of the rights of women and girls and to punishing perpetrators, through both criminal and civil measures;

4. *Urges* Governments to devise, enforce and strengthen effective gender-and age-sensitive measures to combat and eliminate all forms of trafficking in women and girls, including for sexual and economic exploitation, as part of a comprehensive anti-trafficking strategy that integrates a human rights perspective and takes into account the situation of trafficked victims, and to draw up, as appropriate, national action plans in this regard;

5. *Also urges* Governments to consider signing and ratifying and States parties to implement relevant United Nations legal instruments, such as the United Nations Convention against Transnational Organized Crime[6] and the Protocols thereto, in particular the Protocol to Prevent, Suppress and Punish Trafficking in Persons, Especially Women and Children, supplementing the United Nations Convention against Transnational Organized Crime,[7] the Convention on the Elimination of All Forms of Discrimination against Women,[1] the Convention on the Rights of the Child,[3] the Optional Protocol to the Convention on the Elimination of All Forms of Discrimination against Women[2] and the Optional Protocol to the Convention on the Rights of the Child on the sale of children, child prostitution and child pornography,[4] as well as the Convention concerning Forced or Compulsory Labour, 1930 (Convention No. 29), the Convention concerning Discrimination in respect of Employment and Occupation, 1958 (Convention No. 111) and the Convention concerning the Prohibition and Immediate Action for the Elimination of the Worst Forms of Child Labour, 1999 (Convention No. 182), of the International Labour Organization;

6. *Encourages* Member States to conclude bilateral, subregional, regional and international agreements, as well as to undertake initiatives, including regional initiatives,[12] to address the problem of trafficking in persons, and to ensure that such agreements and initiatives pay particular attention to the problem of trafficking in women and girls;

7. *Calls upon* all Governments to criminalize all forms of trafficking in persons, recognizing its increasing occurrence for purposes of sexual exploitation and sex tourism, and to condemn and penalize all those offenders involved, including intermediaries, whether local or foreign, through the competent national authorities, either in the country of origin of the offender or in the country in which the abuse occurs, in accordance with due process of law, as well as to penalize persons in authority found guilty of sexually assaulting victims of trafficking in their custody;

8. *Urges* Governments to take all appropriate measures to ensure that victims of trafficking are not penalized for being trafficked and that they do not suffer from revictimization as a result of actions taken by government authorities, and encourages Governments to prevent, within their legal framework and in accordance with national policies, victims of trafficking in persons from being prosecuted for their illegal entry or residence;

9. *Recognizes* the urgent need for broad and concerted cooperation among all relevant actors, including States, intergovernmental organizations and civil society, to counter effectively the threat of trafficking in persons, particularly women and girls;

10. *Invites* Governments to strengthen bilateral, regional and international cooperation aimed at preventing and combating corruption and the laundering of proceeds derived from trafficking, including for purposes of commercialized sexual exploitation;

11. *Also invites* Governments to consider setting up or strengthening a national coordinating mechanism, for example, a national rapporteur or an interagency body, with the participation of civil society, including non-governmental organizations, to encourage the exchange of information and to report on data, root causes, factors and trends in violence against women, in particular trafficking;

12. *Encourages* Governments and relevant United Nations bodies, within existing resources, to take appropriate measures to raise public awareness of the issue of trafficking in persons, particularly in women and girls; to discourage, with a view to eliminating, the demand that

fosters all forms of exploitation, including sexual exploitation and forced labour; to publicize the laws, regulations and penalties relating to this issue; and to emphasize that trafficking is a serious crime;

13. *Encourages* Governments to take appropriate measures to eliminate sex tourism demand, especially of children, through all possible preventive actions;

14. *Urges* concerned Governments, in cooperation with intergovernmental and non-governmental organizations, to support and allocate resources for programmes to strengthen preventive action, in particular education for women and men, as well as for boys and girls, on gender equality, self-respect and mutual respect, and campaigns to increase public awareness of the issue at the national and grass-roots levels;

15. *Calls upon* concerned Governments to allocate resources, as appropriate, to provide comprehensive programmes for the physical, psychological and social recovery of victims of trafficking, including through job training, legal assistance, including in a language that they can understand, and health care, including for HIV/AIDS, and by taking measures to cooperate with intergovernmental and non-governmental organizations to provide for the social, medical and psychological care of the victims;

16. *Encourages* Governments, in cooperation with intergovernmental and non-governmental organizations, to undertake or strengthen campaigns aimed at clarifying opportunities, limitations and rights in the event of migration, as well as information on the risks of irregular migration and the ways and means used by traffickers so as to enable women to make informed decisions and to prevent them from becoming victims of trafficking;

17. *Also encourages* Governments to intensify collaboration with non-governmental organizations to develop and implement gender-and age-sensitive programmes for effective counselling, training and reintegration into society of victims of trafficking and programmes that provide shelter and helplines to victims or potential victims;

18. *Calls upon* Governments to take steps to ensure that the treatment of victims of trafficking, as well as all measures taken against trafficking in persons, in particular those that affect the victims of such trafficking, pay particular attention to the needs of women and girls, are applied with full respect for the human rights of those victims and are consistent with internationally recognized principles of nondiscrimination, including the prohibition of racial discrimination and the availability of appropriate legal redress, which may include measures that offer victims the possibility of obtaining compensation for damage suffered;

19. *Invites* Governments to take steps to ensure that criminal justice procedures and witness protection programmes are sensitive to the particular situation of trafficked women and girls and that they are supported and assisted, as appropriate, in making complaints to the police or other authorities, without fear, and being available when required by the criminal justice system, and to ensure that during this time they have access to protection and social, medical, financial and legal assistance, as appropriate;

20. *Also invites* Governments to encourage media providers, including Internet service providers, to adopt or strengthen self-regulatory measures to promote the responsible use of media, particularly the Internet, with a view to eliminating the exploitation of women and children, in particular girls, which could foster trafficking;

21. *Invites* the business sector, in particular the tourism and telecommunications industries, including mass media organizations, to cooperate with Governments in eliminating trafficking in women and children, in particular girls, including through the dissemination by the media of information regarding the dangers of trafficking, the rights of trafficked persons and the services available to victims of trafficking;

22. *Stresses* the need for the systematic collection of sex- and age-disaggregated data and comprehensive studies at both the national and the international levels and the development of common methodologies and internationally defined indicators to make it possible to develop relevant and comparable figures, and encourages Governments to enhance information-sharing and data-collection capacity as a way of promoting cooperation to combat the trafficking problem;

23. *Urges* Governments to strengthen national programmes to combat trafficking in persons, especially women and girls, through increased bilateral, regional and international cooperation, taking into account innovative approaches and best practices, and invites Governments, United Nations bodies and organizations, intergovernmental and non-governmental organizations and the private sector to undertake collaborative and joint research and studies on trafficking in women and girls that can serve as a basis for policy formulation or change;

24. *Invites* Governments, with the support of the United Nations, when necessary, and other intergovernmental organizations, taking into account best practices, to formulate training manuals and other informational materials and provide training for law enforcement, judicial and other relevant officers, and medical and support personnel, with a view to sensitizing them to the special needs of women and girl victims;

25. *Urges* Governments to provide or strengthen training for law enforcement, judicial, immigration and other relevant officials in the prevention and combating of trafficking in persons, including the sexual exploitation of women and girls, which should focus on methods used in preventing such trafficking, prosecuting the traffickers and protecting the rights of victims, including protecting the victims from traffickers, to ensure that the training includes human rights and gender-and age-sensitive perspectives, and to encourage cooperation with non-governmental organizations, other relevant organizations and other elements of civil society;

26. *Encourages* Governments, relevant intergovernmental bodies and international organizations to ensure that military, peacekeeping and humanitarian personnel deployed in conflict, post-conflict and other emergency situations are provided training on conduct that does not promote, facilitate or exploit trafficking in women and girls, including for sexual exploitation, and to raise the awareness of such personnel of the potential risks to victims of conflict and other emergency situations, including natural disasters, of being trafficked;

27. *Invites* States parties to the Convention on the Elimination of All Forms of Discrimination against Women, the Convention on the Rights of the Child and the International Covenants on Human Rights[13] to include information and statistics on trafficking in women and girls as part of their national reports to their respective committees and to work towards developing a common methodology and statistics to obtain comparable data;

28. *Requests* the Secretary-General to submit to the General Assembly at its sixty-third session a report that compiles successful interventions and strategies, as well as challenges, in addressing the gender dimensions of the problem of trafficking in persons, that identifies gender-related aspects of anti-trafficking efforts that remain unaddressed or inadequately addressed, and that evaluates the measures taken through appropriate indicators; and invites the Secretary-General to take into account in his report the work of Governments, relevant United Nations agencies and mechanisms and other international organizations.

81st plenary meeting
19 December 2006

---

[1] United Nations, *Treaty Series*, vol. 1249, No. 20378.

[2] Ibid., vol. 2131, No. 20378.

[3] Ibid., vol. 1577, No. 27531.

[4] Ibid., vol. 2171, No. 27531.

[5] Ibid., vol. 96, No. 1342.

[6] Resolution 55/25, annex I.

[7] Ibid., annex II.

[8] Ibid., annex III.

[9] *Report of the Fourth World Conference on Women, Beijing, 4–15 September 1995* (United Nations publication, Sales No. E.96.IV.13), chap. I, resolution 1, annexes I and II.

[10] A/61/122 and Add.1 and Add.1/Corr.1.

[11] United Nations, *Treaty Series*, vol. 2187, No. 38544.

[12] Such as the Bali Process on People Smuggling, Trafficking in Persons and Related Transnational Crime, the Coordinated Mekong Ministerial Initiative against Trafficking, the Action Plan for the Asia-Pacific region of the Asian Regional Initiative against Trafficking in Persons, Especially Women and Children (see A/C.3/55/3, annex), the initiatives of the European Union on a comprehensive European policy and programmes on trafficking in human beings, as expressed most recently in the European Union plan on best practices, standards and procedures for combating and preventing trafficking in human beings, adopted in December 2005, the activities of the Council of Europe and the Organization for Security and Cooperation in Europe, the South Asian Association for Regional Cooperation Convention on Preventing and Combating Trafficking in Women and Children for Prostitution, the Organization of American States Meeting of National Authorities on Trafficking in Persons, and the activities of the International Labour Organization and the International Organization for Migration in this field.

[13] Resolution 2200 A (XXI), annex.

Resolution 61/145

[on the report of the Third Committee (A/61/438)]

61/145. Follow-up to the Fourth World Conference on Women and full implementation of the Beijing Declaration and Platform for Action and the outcome of the twenty-third special session of the General Assembly

The General Assembly,

Recalling its previous resolutions on the question, including resolution 60/140 of 16 December 2005,

Deeply convinced that the Beijing Declaration and Platform for Action[1] and the outcome of the twenty-third special session of the General Assembly entitled "Women 2000: gender equality, development and peace for the twenty-first century"[2] are important contributions to the achievement of gender equality and the empowerment of women, and must be translated into effective action by all States, the United Nations system and other organizations concerned,

Reaffirming the commitments to gender equality and the advancement of women made at the Millennium Summit,[3] the 2005 World Summit[4] and other major United Nations summits, conferences and special sessions, and reaffirming also that their full, effective and accelerated implementation are integral to achieving the internationally agreed development goals, including the Millennium Development Goals,

Welcoming progress made towards achieving gender equality, but stressing that challenges and obstacles remain in the implementation of the Beijing Declaration and Platform for Action and the outcome of the twenty-third special session,

Recognizing that the responsibility for the implementation of the Beijing Declaration and Platform for Action and the outcome of the twenty-third special session rests primarily at the national level and that strengthened efforts are necessary in this respect, and reiterating that enhanced international cooperation is essential for full, effective and accelerated implementation,

Reaffirming that gender mainstreaming is a globally accepted strategy for promoting the empowerment of women and achieving gender equality by transforming structures of inequality, and reaffirming also the commitment to actively promote the mainstreaming of a gender perspective in the design, implementation, monitoring and evaluation of policies and programmes in all political, economic and social spheres, as well as the commitment to strengthen the capabilities of the United Nations system in the area of gender equality,

Bearing in mind the challenges and obstacles to changing discriminatory attitudes and gender stereotypes, and stressing that challenges and obstacles remain in the implementation of international standards and norms to address the inequality between men and women,

Expressing serious concern that the urgent goal of 50/50 gender balance in the United Nations system, especially at senior and policymaking levels, with full respect for the principle of equitable geographical distribution, in conformity with Article 101, paragraph 3, of the Charter of the United Nations, remains unmet, and that the representation of women in the United Nations system has remained almost static, with negligible improvement in some parts of the system, and in some cases has even decreased, as reflected in the report of the Secretary-General on the improvement of the status of women in the United Nations system,[5]

Reaffirming the important role of women in the prevention and resolution of conflicts and in peacebuilding,

Reaffirming also the Declaration of Commitment on HIV/AIDS[6] and the Political Declaration on HIV/AIDS adopted at the High-level Meeting on AIDS, held from 31 May to 2 June 2006,[7] which, inter alia, acknowledged the feminization of the pandemic,

Noting with appreciation the report of the Secretary-General on the United Nations system-wide policy and strategy on gender mainstreaming,[8]

1. *Takes note with appreciation* of the report of the Secretary-General on the measures taken and progress achieved in follow-up to the implementation of the Beijing Declaration and Platform for Action and the outcome of the twenty-third special session of the General Assembly;[9]

2. *Reaffirms* the Beijing Declaration and Platform for Action adopted at the Fourth World Conference on Women,[1] the outcome of the twenty-third special session of the General Assembly,[2] and the declaration adopted on the occasion of the ten-year review and appraisal of the Beijing Declaration and Platform for Action at the forty-ninth session of the Commission on the Status of Women,[10] and also reaffirms its commitment to their full, effective and accelerated implementation;

3. *Recognizes* that the implementation of the Beijing Declaration and Platform for Action and the fulfilment of the obligations under the Convention on the Elimination of All Forms of Discrimination against Women[11] are mutually reinforcing in achieving gender equality and the empowerment of women, and in this regard welcomes the contributions of the Committee on the Elimination of Discrimination against Women to promoting the implementation of the Platform for Action and the outcome of the twenty-third special session, and invites States parties to the Convention to include information on measures taken to enhance implementation at the national level in their reports to the Committee under article 18 of the Convention;

4. *Calls upon* Governments, the United Nations system and other international and regional organizations, and all sectors of civil society, including non-governmental organizations, as well as all women and men, to fully commit themselves and to intensify their contributions to the implementation of the Beijing Declaration and Platform for Action and the outcome of the twenty-third special session;

5. *Calls upon* States parties to comply fully with their obligations under the Convention on the Elimination of All Forms of Discrimination against Women and the Optional Protocol thereto[12] and to take into consideration the concluding comments as well as the general recommendations of the Committee, urges States parties to consider limiting the extent of any reservations that they lodge to the Convention, to formulate any reservations as precisely and narrowly as possible, and to regularly review such reservations with a view to withdrawing them so as to ensure that no reservation is incompatible with the object and purpose of the Convention, also urges all Member States that have not yet ratified or acceded to the Convention to consider doing so, and calls upon those Member States that have not yet done so to consider signing, ratifying or acceding to the Optional Protocol;

6. *Encourages* all actors, inter alia, Governments, the United Nations system, other international organizations and civil society, to continue to support the work of the Commission on the Status of Women in fulfilling its central role in the follow-up to and review of the implementation of the Beijing Declaration and Platform for Action and the outcome of the twenty-third special session, and, as applicable, to carry out its recommendations, and welcomes, in this regard, the revised programme and methods of work of the Commission adopted at its fiftieth session,[13] which give particular attention to the sharing of experiences, lessons learned and good practices in overcoming challenges to full implementation

at the national and international levels as well as to the evaluation of progress in the implementation of priority themes;

7. *Calls upon* Governments, and the relevant funds and programmes, organs and specialized agencies of the United Nations system, within their respective mandates, and invites the international financial institutions and all relevant actors of civil society, including non-governmental organizations, to intensify action to achieve the full and effective implementation of the Beijing Declaration and Platform for Action and the outcome of the twenty-third special session, through, inter alia:

(*a*) Sustained political will and commitment at the national, regional and international levels to take further action, inter alia, through the mainstreaming of gender perspectives, including through the development and use of gender equality indicators, as applicable, in all polices and programmes and the promotion of full and equal participation and empowerment of women, and enhanced international cooperation;

(*b*) Promotion and protection of, and respect for, the full enjoyment of all human rights and fundamental freedoms by women and girls, including through the full implementation by States of their obligations under all human rights instruments, especially the Convention on the Elimination of All Forms of Discrimination against Women;

(*c*) Ensuring full representation and full and equal participation of women in political, social and economic decision-making as an essential condition for gender equality, and the empowerment of women and girls as a critical factor in the eradication of poverty;

(*d*) Respect for the rule of law, including legislation, and continued efforts to repeal laws and eradicate policies and practices that discriminate against women and girls, and to adopt laws and promote practices that protect their rights;

(*e*) Strengthening the role of national institutional mechanisms for gender equality and the advancement of women, including through financial and other appropriate assistance, to increase their direct impact on women;

(*f*) Undertaking socio-economic policies that promote sustainable development and ensure poverty eradication programmes, especially for women and girls, and strengthening the provision of and ensuring equal access to adequate, affordable and accessible public and social services, including education and training at all levels, as well as to all types of permanent and sustainable social protection/social security systems for women throughout their life cycle, and supporting national efforts in this regard;

(*g*) Taking further steps to ensure that the educational system and the media, to the extent consistent with freedom of expression, support the use of non-stereotypic, balanced and diverse images of women presenting them as key actors of the process of development as well as promoting non-discriminatory roles of women and men in their private and public life;

(*h*) Incorporating gender perspectives and human rights in health-sector policies and programmes, paying attention to women's specific needs and priorities, ensuring women's right to the highest attainable standards of physical and mental health and their access to affordable and adequate health-care services, including sexual, reproductive and maternal health care and lifesaving obstetric care, in accordance with the Programme of Action of the International Conference on Population and Development,[14] and recognizing that the lack of economic empowerment and independence has increased women's vulnerability to a range of negative consequences, involving the risk of contracting HIV/AIDS, malaria, tuberculosis and other poverty-related diseases;

(*i*) Eliminating gender inequalities, gender-based abuse and violence; increasing the capacity of women and adolescent girls to protect themselves from the risk of HIV infection, principally through the provision of health care and services, including, inter alia, sexual and reproductive health, and the provision of full access to comprehensive information and education; ensuring that women can exercise their right to have control over, and decide freely and responsibly on, matters related to their sexuality in order to increase their ability to protect themselves from HIV infection, including their sexual and reproductive health, free of coercion, discrimination and violence; and taking all necessary measures to create an enabling environment for the empowerment of women and to strengthen their economic independence, while, in this context, reiterating the importance of the role of men and boys in achieving gender equality;

(*j*) Strengthening national health and social infrastructures to reinforce measures to promote women's access to public health and taking action at the national level to address shortages of human resources for health, by, inter alia, developing, financing and implementing policies, within national development strategies, to improve training and management and effectively govern the recruitment, retention and deployment of health workers, including through international cooperation in this area;

(*k*) Adequate mobilization of resources at the national and international levels, as well as new and additional resources for the developing countries, including the least developed countries and countries with economies in transition, from all available funding mechanisms, including multilateral, bilateral and private sources;

(*l*) Increased partnerships among Governments, civil society and the private sector;

(*m*) Encouraging joint responsibility of men and boys with women and girls in the promotion of gender equality, based on the conviction that this is essential to the achievement of the goals of gender equality, development and peace;

(*n*) Removing structural and legal barriers, as well as eliminating stereotypic attitudes, to gender equality at work, promoting equal pay for equal work, and promoting the recognition of the value of women's unremunerated work, as well as developing and promoting policies that facilitate the reconciliation of employment and family responsibilities;

8. *Reaffirms* that States have an obligation to exercise due diligence to prevent violence against women and girls, provide protection to the victims and investigate, prosecute and punish the perpetrators of violence against women and girls, and that failure to do so violates and impairs or nullifies the enjoyment of their human rights and fundamental freedoms, and calls upon Governments to eliminate violence against women and girls and to elaborate and implement strategies in this regard;

9. *Strongly encourages* Governments to continue to support the role and contribution of civil society, in particular non-governmental organizations and women's organizations, in the implementation of the Beijing Declaration and Platform for Action and the outcome of the twenty-third special session;

10. *Resolves* to intensify the efforts of its Main Committees and subsidiary bodies to fully mainstream a gender perspective in their work, as well as in all United Nations summits, conferences and special sessions and in their follow-up processes;

11. *Requests* that reports of the Secretary-General submitted to the General Assembly and its subsidiary bodies systematically address gender perspectives through qualitative gender analysis and, where available, quantitative data, in particular through concrete conclusions and recommendations for further action on gender equality and the advancement of women, in order to facilitate gender-sensitive policy development;

12. *Urges* Governments and all entities of the United Nations system, including United Nations agencies, funds and programmes, and all relevant actors of civil society, to ensure the integration of gender perspectives in the implementation of and follow-up to all United Nations summits, conferences and special sessions and to give attention to gender perspectives in preparation for such events, including the upcoming special session on children;

13. *Reaffirms its call* to recently established subsidiary bodies, namely, the Peacebuilding Commission and the Human Rights Council, to integrate attention to gender perspectives into their consideration of all issues in their respective agendas, including the development of their methods of work;

14. *Encourages* the Economic and Social Council to continue its efforts to ensure that gender mainstreaming is an integral part of its work and that of its subsidiary bodies, through, inter alia, implementation of its agreed conclusions 1997/2 of 18 July 1997[15] and its resolution 2004/4 of 7 July 2004;

15. *Welcomes* the ministerial declaration of the high-level segment of the substantive session of 2006 of the Economic and Social Council,[16] which, inter alia, underlined the need for the consistent use of a gender mainstreaming strategy for the creation of an enabling environment for women's participation in development, and calls upon all stakeholders to work to ensure the full incorporation of gender perspectives in the implementation of the declaration;

16. *Requests* all bodies that deal with programme and budgetary matters, including the Committee for Programme and Coordination, to ensure that programmes, plans and budgets visibly mainstream gender perspectives;

17. *Reaffirms* the primary and essential role of the General Assembly and the Economic and Social Council, as well as the central role of the Commission on the Status of Women, in promoting the advancement of women and gender equality;

18. *Also reaffirms* the commitment made at the 2005 World Summit to the full and effective implementation of Security Council resolution 1325 (2000) of 31 October 2000, while noting the sixth anniversary of its adoption and the open debates in the Council on women and peace and security;

19. *Urges* Governments and the United Nations system to take further steps to ensure the integration of a gender perspective and the full and equal participation of women in all efforts to promote peace and security, as well as to increase their role in decision-making at all levels, including through the development of national action plans and strategies;

20. *Calls upon* all parts of the United Nations system to continue to play an active role in ensuring the full, effective and accelerated implementation of the Beijing Platform for Action and the outcome of the twenty-third special session, through, inter alia, the work of

the Office of the Special Adviser on Gender Issues and Advancement of Women and the Division for the Advancement of Women and the maintenance of gender specialists in all entities of the United Nations system, as well as by ensuring that all personnel, especially in the field, receive training and appropriate follow-up, including tools, guidance and support, for accelerated gender mainstreaming, and reaffirms the need to strengthen the capabilities of the United Nations system in the area of gender;

21. *Requests* the Secretary-General to review and redouble his efforts to make progress towards achieving the goal of 50/50 gender balance at all levels in the Secretariat and throughout the United Nations system, with full respect for the principle of equitable geographical distribution, in conformity with Article 101, paragraph 3, of the Charter of the United Nations, considering in particular women from developing and least developed countries, from countries with economies in transition and from unrepresented or largely underrepresented Member States, and to ensure managerial and departmental accountability with respect to gender balance targets, and strongly encourages Member States to identify and regularly submit more women candidates for appointment to positions in the United Nations system, especially at more senior and policymaking levels;

22. *Also requests* the Secretary-General to continue to report annually to the General Assembly, under the item entitled "Advancement of women", as well as to the Commission on the Status of Women and the Economic and Social Council, on the follow-up to and progress made in the implementation of the Beijing Declaration and Platform for Action and the outcome of the twenty-third special session, with an assessment of progress in gender mainstreaming, including information on key achievements, lessons learned and good practices, and recommendations on further measures to enhance implementation.

81st plenary meeting
19 December 2006

---

[1] *Report of the Fourth World Conference on Women, Beijing, 4–15 September 1995* (United Nations publication, Sales No. E.96.IV.13), chap. I, resolution 1, annexes I and II.

[2] Resolution S-23/2, annex, and resolution S-23/3, annex.

[3] See resolution 55/2.

[4] See resolution 60/1.

[5] A/61/318.

[6] Resolution S-26/2, annex.

[7] Resolution 60/262, annex.

[8] E/2006/83.

[9] A/61/174.

[10] See *Official Records of the Economic and Social Council, 2005, Supplement No. 7* and corrigendum (E/2005/27 and Corr.1), chap. I, sect. A; see also Economic and Social Council decision 2005/232.

[11] United Nations, *Treaty Series*, vol. 1249, No. 20378.

[12] Ibid., vol. 2131, No. 20378.

[13] See Economic and Social Council resolution 2006/9.

[14] *Report of the International Conference on Population and Development, Cairo, 5–13 September 1994* (United Nations publication, Sales No. E.95.XIII.18), chap. I, resolution 1, annex.

[15] See *Official Records of the General Assembly, Fifty-second Session, Supplement No. 3* (A/52/3/Rev.1), chap. IV, para. 4.

[16] See A/61/3, chap. III, para. 50. For the final text, see *Official Records of the General Assembly, Sixty-first Session, Supplement No. 3.*

Resolution 61/146

[on the report of the Third Committee (A/61/439 and Corr.1)]

61/146. Rights of the child

The General Assembly,

Recalling its previous resolutions on the rights of the child, the most recent of which is resolution 60/231 of 23 December 2005, and its resolution 60/141 of 16 December 2005, as well as Commission on Human Rights resolution 2005/44 of 19 April 2005,[1]

Emphasizing that the Convention on the Rights of the Child[2] must constitute the standard in the promotion and protection of the rights of the child, and bearing in mind the importance of the Optional Protocols to the Convention,[3] as well as other human rights instruments,

Reaffirming the Vienna Declaration and Programme of Action,[4] the United Nations Millennium Declaration[5] and the outcome document of the twenty-seventh special session of the General Assembly on children, entitled "A world fit for children",[6] and recalling the Copenhagen Declaration on Social Development and the Programme of Action,[7] the Dakar Framework for Action adopted at the World Education Forum,[8] the Declaration on Social Progress and Development,[9] the Universal Declaration on the Eradication of Hunger and Malnutrition[10] and the Declaration on the Right to Development,[11]

Recognizing the importance of the integration of child rights issues into the follow-up the outcome documents of all major United Nations conferences, special sessions and summits,

Taking note with appreciation of the reports of the Secretary-General on progress made towards achieving the commitments set out in the outcome document of the twenty-seventh special session of the General Assembly[12] and on the status of the Convention on the Rights of the Child and the issues raised in Assembly resolution 60/231,[13] as well as the report of the Chairman of the Committee on the Rights of the Child,[14]

Reaffirming that the best interests of the child shall be a primary consideration in all actions concerning children,

Recognizing the importance of incorporating a child-protection perspective across the human rights agenda, as highlighted in the outcome of the 2005 World Summit,

Taking note with appreciation of the attention paid to children in the Convention on the Rights of Persons with Disabilities[15] and in the International Convention for the Protection of All Persons from Enforced Disappearance,[16]

Profoundly concerned that the situation of children in many parts of the world remains critical, in an increasingly globalized environment, as a result of the persistence of poverty, social inequality, inadequate social and economic conditions, pandemics, in particular HIV/AIDS, malaria and tuberculosis, environmental damage, natural disasters, armed conflict, foreign occupation, displacement, violence, terrorism, abuse, exploitation, trafficking in children and their organs, child prostitution, child pornography and child sex tourism, neglect, illiteracy, hunger, intolerance, discrimination, racism, xenophobia, gender inequality, disability and inadequate legal protection, and convinced that urgent and effective national and international action is called for,

Reaffirming the need for mainstreaming a gender perspective in all policies and programmes relating to children, and recognizing the child as a rights holder in all policies and programmes relating to children,

I
Implementation of the Convention on the Rights of the Child and the Optional Protocols thereto

1. *Reaffirms* that the general principles of, inter alia, the best interests of the child, non-discrimination, participation and survival and development provide the framework for all actions concerning children, including adolescents;

2. *Urges* States that have not yet done so to become parties to the Convention on the Rights of the Child[2] and the Optional Protocols thereto[3] as a matter of priority and to implement them fully by, inter alia, putting in place effective national legislation, policies and action plans, strengthening relevant governmental structures for children and ensuring adequate and systematic training in the rights of the child for professional groups working with and for children;

3. *Urges* States parties to withdraw reservations that are incompatible with the object and purpose of the Convention or the Optional Protocols thereto and to consider reviewing other reservations with a view to withdrawing them;

4. *Welcomes* the work of the Committee on the Rights of the Child, and calls upon all States to strengthen their cooperation with the Committee, to comply in a timely manner with their reporting obligations under the Convention and the Optional Protocols thereto, in accordance with the guidelines elaborated by the Committee, and to take into account its recommendations on implementation of the Convention;

5. *Requests* all relevant organs and mechanisms of the United Nations system regularly and systematically to incorporate a strong child rights perspective throughout all activities in the fulfilment of their mandates, as well as to ensure that their staff are trained in child rights matters, and calls upon States to continue to cooperate closely with all those organs and mechanisms, in particular the special rapporteurs and special representatives of the United Nations system;

6. *Encourages* States to strengthen their national statistical capacities and to use statistics disaggregated, inter alia, by age, gender and other relevant factors that may lead to disparities and other statistical indicators at the national, subregional, regional and international levels to develop and assess social policies and programmes so that economic and social resources are used efficiently and effectively for the full realization of the rights of the child;

II
Promotion and protection of the rights of the child

Registration, family relations and adoption or other forms of alternative care

7. *Once again urges* all States parties to intensify their efforts to comply with their obligations under the Convention on the Rights of the Child[2] to preserve the child's identity, including nationality, name and family relations, as recognized by law, to allow for the registration of the child immediately after birth, to ensure that registration procedures are simple, expeditious and effective and provided at minimal or no cost and to raise awareness of the importance of birth registration at the national, regional and local levels;

8. *Encourages* States to adopt and enforce laws and improve the implementation of policies and programmes to protect children growing up without parents or caregivers, recognizing that, where alternative care is necessary, family-and community-based care should be promoted over placement in institutions;

9. *Calls upon* States to guarantee, to the extent consistent with the obligations of each State, the right of a child whose parents reside in different States to maintain, on a regular basis, save in exceptional circumstances, personal relations and direct contact with both parents by providing enforceable means of access and visitation in both States and by respecting the principle that both parents have common responsibilities for the upbringing and development of their children;

10. *Also calls upon* States to address and pay particular attention to cases of international parental or familial child abduction, and encourages States to engage in multilateral and bilateral cooperation to resolve these cases, preferably by accession to or ratification of the Hague Convention on the Civil Aspects of International Child Abduction,[17] and therefore to be in full compliance with the Convention, and to facilitate, inter alia, the return of the child to the country in which he or she resided immediately before the removal or retention;

11. *Further calls upon* States to take all necessary measures to prevent and combat illegal adoptions and all adoptions that are not in the best interests of the child;

Economic and social well-being of children

12. *Calls upon* States and the international community to create an environment in which the well-being of the child is ensured, inter alia, by:

(*a*) Cooperating, supporting and participating in the global efforts for poverty eradication at the global, regional and country levels, recognizing that strengthened availability and effective allocation of resources are required at all these levels, in order to ensure that all the internationally agreed development and poverty eradication goals, including those set out in the United Nations Millennium Declaration,[5] are realized within their time framework, and reaffirming that investments in children and the realization of their rights are among the most effective ways to eradicate poverty;

(*b*) Recognizing the right to education on the basis of equal opportunity and non-discrimination by making primary education compulsory and available free to all children, ensuring that all children have access to education of good quality, as well as making secondary education generally available and accessible to all, in particular through the progressive introduction of free education, bearing in mind that special measures to ensure equal access, including affirmative action, contribute to achieving equal opportunity and combating exclusion, and ensuring school attendance, in particular for girls and children from low-income families;

(*c*) Taking all necessary measures to ensure the right of the child to the enjoyment of the highest attainable standard of health and developing sustainable health systems and social services, ensuring access to such systems and services without discrimination, paying special attention to adequate food and nutrition, to the special needs of adolescents and to reproductive and sexual health, and securing appropriate prenatal and post-natal care for mothers, including measures to prevent mother-to-child transmission of HIV;

(*d*) Assigning priority to developing and implementing activities and programmes aimed at treating and preventing addictions, in particular addiction to alcohol and tobacco, and the abuse of narcotic drugs, psychotropic substances and inhalants;

(*e*) Supporting adolescents to be able to deal positively and responsibly with their sexuality in order to protect themselves from HIV/AIDS infection and implementing measures to increase their capacity to protect themselves from HIV/AIDS through, inter alia, the provision of health care, including for sexual and reproductive health, and through preventive education that promotes gender equality;

(*f*) Putting in place strategies, policies and programmes that identify and address those factors that make individuals particularly vulnerable to HIV infection in order to complement prevention programmes that address activities that place individuals at risk for HIV infection, such as risky and unsafe behaviour and injecting drug use;

(*g*) Designing and implementing programmes to provide social services and support to pregnant adolescents and adolescent mothers, in particular by enabling them to continue and complete their education;

Violence against children

13. *Welcomes* the United Nations study on violence against children, led by the independent expert for the study,[18] takes fully into account its recommendations, and encourages Member States and requests United Nations entities, regional organizations and civil society, including non-governmental organizations, to widely disseminate and follow up on the study;

14. *Commends* the independent expert for the participatory process through which the report was prepared in close collaboration with Member States, United Nations bodies and organizations, other relevant intergovernmental organizations and civil society, including non-governmental organizations, and in particular for the unprecedented level and quality of participation by children;

15. *Condemns* all forms of violence against children, and urges States to take effective legislative and other measures to prevent and eliminate all such violence, including physical, mental, psychological and sexual violence, torture, child abuse and exploitation, hostage-taking, domestic violence, trafficking in or sale of children and their organs, paedophilia, child prostitution, child pornography, child sex tourism, gang-related violence and harmful traditional practices in all settings;

16. *Also condemns* the abduction of children, in particular extortive abduction and abduction of children in situations of armed conflict, including for the recruitment and use of children in armed conflicts, and urges States to take all appropriate measures to secure their unconditional release, rehabilitation, reintegration and reunification with their families;

17. *Urges* States:

(*a*) To strengthen efforts to prevent and protect children from all forms of violence through a comprehensive approach and to develop a multifaceted and systematic framework to respond to violence against children, including by giving priority attention to prevention and addressing its underlying causes, which is integrated into national planning processes;

(*b*) To strive to change attitudes that condone or normalize any form of violence against children;

(*c*) To end impunity for perpetrators of crimes against children, investigate and prosecute such acts of violence and impose appropriate penalties;

(*d*) To protect children from all forms of violence or abuse by government officials, such as the police, law enforcement authorities and employees and officials in detention centres or welfare institutions;

(*e*) To take measures to protect children from all forms of physical and mental violence and abuse in schools, including by using non-violent teaching and learning strategies and adopting classroom management and disciplinary measures that are not based on any form of cruel or degrading punishment, and to establish complaint mechanisms that are age- and gender-appropriate and accessible to children, taking into account children's evolving capacities and the importance of respecting their views;

(*f*) To take measures to promote constructive and positive forms of discipline and child development approaches in all settings, including the home, schools and other educational settings and throughout care and justice systems;

(*g*) To take measures to ensure that all those who work with and for children protect children from bullying and implement preventive and anti-bullying policies;

(*h*) To address the gender dimension of all forms of violence against children and incorporate a gender perspective in all policies adopted and actions taken to protect children against all forms of violence;

(*i*) To ensure national research and documentation to identify vulnerable groups of children, inform policy and programmes at all levels and track progress and best practices towards preventing all forms of violence against children;

(*j*) To strengthen international cooperation and mutual assistance to prevent and protect children from all forms of violence and to end impunity for crimes against children;

18. *Recognizes* the contribution of the International Criminal Court in ending impunity for the most serious crimes against children, including genocide, crimes against humanity and war crimes, and calls upon States not to grant amnesties for such crimes;

19. *Calls upon* the relevant organizations of the United Nations system, in particular the Office of the United Nations High Commissioner for Human Rights, the United Nations Children's Fund, the World Health Organization, the International Labour Organization, the Office of the United Nations High Commissioner for Refugees, the United Nations Educational, Scientific and Cultural Organization, the United Nations Office on Drugs and Crime and the Division for the Advancement of Women of the Secretariat, to explore ways

and means, within their respective mandates, by which they can contribute more effectively to addressing the need to prevent and to respond to all forms of violence against children;

Non-discrimination

20. *Calls upon* all States to ensure the enjoyment by children of all their civil, political, economic, social and cultural rights without discrimination of any kind;

21. *Notes with concern* the large number of children who are victims of racism, racial discrimination, xenophobia and related intolerance, stresses the need to incorporate special measures, in accordance with the principle of the best interests of the child and respect for his or her views, in programmes to combat racism, racial discrimination, xenophobia and related intolerance, and calls upon States to provide special support and ensure equal access to services for all children;

22. *Calls upon* States to take all necessary measures, including legal reforms where appropriate, to eliminate all forms of discrimination against girls and all forms of violence, including female infanticide and prenatal sex selection, rape, sexual abuse and harmful traditional or customary practices, including female genital mutilation, marriage without the free and full consent of the intending spouses, early marriage and forced sterilization, by enacting and enforcing legislation and by formulating, where appropriate, comprehensive, multidisciplinary and coordinated national plans, programmes or strategies to protect girls;

23. *Also calls upon* States to take the necessary measures to ensure the full and equal enjoyment of all human rights and fundamental freedoms by children with disabilities in both the public and the private spheres, including access to good quality education and health care and protection from violence, abuse and neglect, and to develop and, where it already exists, to enforce legislation to prohibit discrimination against them in order to ensure their inherent dignity, promote their self-reliance and facilitate their active participation and integration in the community, taking into account the particularly difficult situation of children with disabilities living in poverty;

Promoting and protecting the rights of children, including children in particularly difficult situations

24. *Calls upon* all States to prevent violations of the rights of children working and/or living on the street, including discrimination, arbitrary detention and extrajudicial, arbitrary or summary executions, torture and all kinds of violence and exploitation, and to bring the perpetrators to justice, to adopt and implement policies for the protection, social and psychosocial rehabilitation and reintegration of those children and to adopt economic, social and educational strategies to address the problems of children working and/or living on the street;

25. *Also calls upon* all States to protect refugee, asylum-seeking and internally displaced children, in particular those who are unaccompanied, who are particularly exposed to violence and risks in connection with armed conflict, such as recruitment, sexual violence and exploitation, stressing the need for States as well as the international community to continue to pay more systematic and in-depth attention to the special assistance, protection and development needs of those children through, inter alia, programmes aimed at rehabilitation and physical and psychological recovery, and to programmes for voluntary repatriation and, wherever possible, local integration and resettlement, to give priority to family tracing

and family reunification and, where appropriate, to cooperate with international humanitarian and refugee organizations, including by facilitating their work;

26. *Further calls upon* all States to ensure, for children belonging to minorities and vulnerable groups, including migrant children and indigenous children, the enjoyment of all human rights as well as access to health care, social services and education on an equal basis with others and to ensure that all such children, in particular victims of violence and exploitation, receive special protection and assistance;

27. *Calls upon* all States to address, as a matter of priority, the vulnerabilities faced by children affected by and living with HIV, by providing support and rehabilitation to those children and their families, women and the elderly, particularly in their role as caregivers, promoting child-oriented HIV/AIDS policies and programmes and increased protection for children orphaned and affected by HIV/AIDS, ensuring access to treatment and intensifying efforts to develop new treatments for children, and building, where needed, and supporting the social security systems that protect them;

28. *Also calls upon* all States to protect, in law and in practice, the inheritance and property rights of orphans, with particular attention to underlying gender-based discrimination, which may interfere with the fulfilment of these rights;

29. *Further calls upon* all States to translate into concrete action their commitment to the progressive and effective elimination of child labour that is likely to be hazardous or to interfere with the child's education or to be harmful to the child's health or physical, mental, spiritual, moral or social development, to eliminate immediately the worst forms of child labour, to promote education as a key strategy in this regard, including the creation of vocational training and apprenticeship programmes and the integration of working children into the formal education system, and to examine and devise economic policies, where necessary, in cooperation with the international community, that address factors contributing to these forms of child labour;

30. *Urges* all States that have not yet signed and ratified or acceded to the Convention concerning Minimum Age for Admission to Employment, 1973 (Convention No. 138) and the Convention concerning the Prohibition and Immediate Action for the Elimination of the Worst Forms of Child Labour, 1999 (Convention No. 182) of the International Labour Organization to consider doing so;

31. *Calls upon* all States, in particular those States in which the death penalty has not been abolished:

(*a*) To abolish by law, as soon as possible, the death penalty and life imprisonment without possibility of release for those under the age of 18 years at the time of the commission of the offence;

(*b*) To comply with their obligations as assumed under relevant provisions of international human rights instruments, including the Convention on the Rights of the Child and the International Covenant on Civil and Political Rights;[19]

(*c*) To keep in mind the safeguards guaranteeing protection of the rights of those facing the death penalty and the guarantees set out in United Nations safeguards adopted by the Economic and Social Council;

32. *Also calls upon* all States to ensure that no child in detention is sentenced to forced labour or any form of cruel or degrading punishment, or deprived of access to and provision

of health-care services, hygiene and environmental sanitation, education, basic instruction and vocational training;

33. *Encourages* States to promote actions, including through bilateral and multilateral technical cooperation and financial assistance, for the social reintegration of children in difficult situations, considering, inter alia, views, skills and capacities that those children have developed in the conditions in which they lived and, where appropriate, with their meaningful participation;

Prevention and eradication of the sale of children, child prostitution and child pornography

34. *Calls upon* all States:

(*a*) To criminalize and penalize effectively all forms of sexual exploitation and sexual abuse of children, including all acts of paedophilia, including within the family or for commercial purposes, child pornography and child prostitution, child sex tourism, trafficking in children, the sale of children and the use of the Internet for these purposes, and to take effective measures against the criminalization of children who are victims of exploitation;

(*b*) To ensure the prosecution of offenders, whether local or foreign, by the competent national authorities, either in the country in which the crime was committed, in the country of which the offender is a national or resident, in the country of which the victim is a national, or on any other basis permitted under domestic law, and for these purposes to afford one another the greatest measure of assistance in connection with investigations or criminal or extradition proceedings;

(*c*) To criminalize and penalize effectively the sale of children, including for the purposes of transfer of organs of the child for profit, to increase cooperation at all levels to prevent and dismantle networks trafficking or selling children and their organs and, for those States that have not yet done so, to consider signing and ratifying or acceding to the Protocol to Prevent, Suppress and Punish Trafficking in Persons, Especially Women and Children, supplementing the United Nations Convention against Transnational Organized Crime;[20]

(*d*) In cases of trafficking in children, the sale of children, child prostitution and child pornography, to address effectively the needs of victims, including their safety and protection, physical and psychological recovery and full reintegration into society, including through bilateral and multilateral technical cooperation and financial assistance;

(*e*) To combat the existence of a market that encourages such criminal practices against children, including through the adoption, effective application and enforcement of preventive, rehabilitative and punitive measures targeting customers or individuals who sexually exploit or sexually abuse children, as well as by ensuring public awareness;

(*f*) To contribute to the elimination of the sale of children, child prostitution and child pornography by adopting a holistic approach, addressing the contributing factors, including underdevelopment, poverty, economic disparities, inequitable socio-economic structures, dysfunctional families, lack of education, urban-rural migration, gender discrimination, criminal or irresponsible adult sexual behaviour, child sex tourism, organized crime, harmful traditional practices, armed conflicts and trafficking in children;

Children affected by armed conflict

35. *Strongly condemns* any recruitment or use of children in armed conflict contrary to international law, as well as other violations and abuses committed against children affected by armed conflict, and urges all States and other parties to armed conflict that are engaged in such practices to end them;

36. *Calls upon* States:

(*a*) When ratifying the Optional Protocol to the Convention on the Rights of the Child on the involvement of children in armed conflict,[21] to raise the minimum age for voluntary recruitment of persons into the national armed forces from that set out in article 38, paragraph 3, of the Convention, bearing in mind that under the Convention persons under 18 years of age are entitled to special protection, and to adopt safeguards to ensure that such recruitment is not forced or coerced;

(*b*) To take all feasible measures to ensure the demobilization and effective disarmament of children used in armed conflicts and to implement effective measures for their rehabilitation, physical and psychological recovery and reintegration into society, in particular through educational measures, taking into account the rights and the specific needs and capacities of girls;

(*c*) To ensure timely and adequate funding for rehabilitation and reintegration efforts for all children associated with armed forces and groups, particularly in support of national initiatives, to secure the long-term sustainability of such efforts;

(*d*) To encourage the involvement of young people in activities concerning the protection of children affected by armed conflict, including programmes for reconciliation, peace consolidation, peacebuilding and children-to-children networks;

(*e*) To protect children affected by armed conflict, in particular from violations of international humanitarian law and human rights law and to ensure that they receive timely, effective humanitarian assistance, in accordance with international humanitarian law, including the Geneva Conventions of 12 August 1949,[22] and calls upon the international community to hold those responsible for violations accountable, inter alia, through the International Criminal Court;

(*f*) To take all necessary measures, in accordance with international humanitarian law and human rights law, as a matter of priority, to prevent the recruitment and use of children by armed groups, as distinct from the armed forces of a State, including the adoption of policies that do not tolerate the recruitment and use of children in armed conflict, and legal measures necessary to prohibit and criminalize such practices;

37. *Welcomes* the valuable work of the United Nations Children's Fund, and looks forward to the results of updating the Cape Town principles on child soldiers;

38. *Reaffirms* the essential roles of the General Assembly, the Economic and Social Council and the Human Rights Council for the promotion and protection of the rights and welfare of children, including children affected by armed conflict, and notes the increasing role played by the Security Council in ensuring protection for children affected by armed conflict;

39. *Notes with appreciation* the steps taken regarding Security Council resolution 1612 (2005) of 26 July 2005 and the efforts of the Secretary-General to implement the monitoring and reporting mechanism on children and armed conflict in accordance with that resolution, with the participation of and in cooperation with national Governments and relevant United Nations and civil society actors, including at the country level, as well as the work carried out by United Nations child protection advisers in peacekeeping operations;

40. *Welcomes* the appointment of Ms. Radhika Coomaraswamy as the Special Representative of the Secretary-General for Children and Armed Conflict, pursuant to General Assembly resolutions 51/77 of 12 December 1996 and 60/231, and recognizes the progress achieved since the establishment of the mandate of the Special Representative, as extended by resolution 60/231;

41. *Takes note with appreciation* of the report of the Special Representative;[23]

III
Children and poverty

42. *Reiterates* that eradicating poverty is the greatest global challenge facing the world today and an indispensable requirement for sustainable development, in particular for developing countries, and recognizes that chronic poverty remains the single biggest obstacle to meeting the needs and protecting and promoting the rights of children, and that urgent national and international action is therefore required to eliminate it;

43. *Recognizes* that the number of people living in extreme poverty in many countries continues to increase, with women and children constituting the majority and the most affected groups, in particular in the least developed countries and in sub-Saharan Africa;

44. *Also recognizes* that growing inequality within countries is a major challenge to poverty eradication, particularly affecting those living in middle-income countries, and stresses the need to support the development efforts of those countries;

45. *Reaffirms* that democracy, development, peace and security, and the full and effective enjoyment of human rights and fundamental freedoms are interdependent and mutually reinforcing and contribute to the eradication of extreme poverty;

46. *Recognizes* that children living in poverty are deprived of nutrition, water and sanitation facilities, access to basic health-care services, shelter, education, participation and protection, and that while a severe lack of goods and services hurts every human being, it is most threatening and harmful to children, leaving them unable to enjoy their rights, to reach their full potential and to participate as full members of society;

47. *Emphasizes* the critical role of education, both formal and non-formal, in particular basic education and training, especially for girls, in empowering those living in poverty, and in this regard reaffirms the importance of Education for All programmes and the need to bridge the divide between formal and non-formal education, taking into account the need to ensure the good quality of educational services;

48. *Recognizes* the devastating effect of HIV/AIDS, malaria, tuberculosis and other infectious and contagious diseases on human development, economic growth, food security and poverty eradication efforts in all regions, in particular in the least developed countries and

in sub-Saharan Africa, and urges Governments and the international community to give urgent priority to preventing and combating those diseases;

49. *Also recognizes* that countries struggle to develop when their children grow up malnourished, poorly educated or ravaged by disease, as these factors can perpetuate the generational cycle of poverty;

50. *Reaffirms* that the primary responsibility for ensuring an enabling environment for securing the well-being of children, in which the rights of each and every child are promoted and respected, rests with each individual State;

51. *Calls upon* all States and the international community to mobilize all necessary resources, support and efforts to eradicate poverty, according to national plans and strategies and in consultation with national Governments, including through an integrated and multifaceted approach based on the rights and well-being of children;

52. *Also calls upon* all States, and the international community, where appropriate:

(*a*) To integrate the international obligations related to the rights and wellbeing of the child and the internationally agreed development goals, including the Millennium Development Goals, in national development strategies and plans, including poverty reduction strategy papers where they exist, and calls upon the international community to continue to support developing countries in the implementation of those development strategies and plans;

(*b*) To ensure a continuum of care from pregnancy through childhood, recognizing that maternal, newborn and child health are inseparable and interdependent, and that the achievement of the Millennium Development Goals must be based on a strong commitment to the rights of women, children and adolescents;

(*c*) To work for a solid effort of national and international action to enhance children's health, to promote prenatal care and to lower infant and child mortality in all countries and among all peoples;

(*d*) To develop a national strategy of prevention and treatment to effectively address the condition of obstetric fistula and to further develop a multisectoral, comprehensive and integrated approach to bring about lasting solutions and a meaningful response to the problem of obstetric fistula and related morbidities;

(*e*) To promote the provision of clean water in all communities for all their children, as well as universal access to sanitation;

(*f*) To take all necessary measures to eradicate hunger, malnutrition and famine;

(*g*) To mobilize the necessary additional resources from all sources of financing for development, including domestic resources, international investment flows, official development assistance and external debt relief, and to commit themselves to a universal, open, equitable, rule-based, predictable and nondiscriminatory global trading system in order to stimulate development worldwide to ensure the well-being of the most vulnerable sectors of populations, in particular children;

53. *Decides:*

(*a*) To request the Secretary-General to submit to the General Assembly at its sixty-second session a report on the rights of the child, containing information on the status of the Convention on the Rights of the Child[2] and the issues contained in the present resolution;

(*b*) To request the Special Representative of the Secretary-General for Children and Armed Conflict to continue to submit reports to the General Assembly and the Human Rights Council on the progress achieved and the remaining challenges on the children and armed conflict agenda;

(*c*) To invite the independent expert for the United Nations study on violence against children, in cooperation with Member States, relevant organizations and bodies of the United Nations system, in particular the Office of the United Nations High Commissioner for Human Rights, the United Nations Children's Fund, the World Health Organization, the Committee on the Rights of the Child and the Human Rights Council, and regional organizations, national institutions and civil society, including non-governmental organizations, to promote the wide dissemination of the United Nations study on violence against children,[18] to give support to the first year of effective follow-up to its recommendations with an integrated approach that bridges the dimensions of public health, education, child protection and human rights, to submit to the General Assembly at its sixty-second session a report on progress made in the initial phase of the follow-up and to anticipate the necessary strategy for follow-up to the implementation of the study;

(*d*) To reiterate its invitation to the Chairman of the Committee on the Rights of the Child to present an oral report on the work of the Committee to the General Assembly at its sixty-second session as a way to enhance communication between the Assembly and the Committee;

(*e*) To pay particular attention to the protection of and the rights of children living in poverty at the commemorative plenary meeting to be held in 2007 devoted to the follow-up to the outcome of the twenty-seventh special session of the General Assembly;

(*f*) To continue its consideration of the question at its sixty-second session under the item entitled "Promotion and protection of the rights of children", focusing section III of the resolution on the rights of the child on "Violence against children".

81st plenary meeting
19 December 2006

---

[1] See *Official Records of the Economic and Social Council, 2005, Supplement No. 3* and corrigendum (E/2005/23 and Corr.1), chap. II, sect. A.

[2] United Nations, *Treaty Series*, vol. 1577, No. 27531.

[3] Ibid., vol. 2171, No. 27531; and ibid., vol. 2173, No. 27531.

[4] A/CONF.157/24 (Part I), chap. III.

[5] See resolution 55/2.

[6] Resolution S-27/2, annex.

[7] *Report of the World Summit for Social Development, Copenhagen, 6–12 March 1995* (United Nations publication, Sales No. E.96.IV.8), chap. I, resolution 1, annexes I and II.

[8] See United Nations Educational, Scientific and Cultural Organization, *Final Report of the World Education Forum, Dakar, Senegal, 26–28 April 2000* (Paris, 2000).

[9] See resolution 2542 (XXIV).

[10] *Report of the World Food Conference, Rome, 5–16 November 1974* (United Nations publication, Sales No. E.75.II.A.3), chap. I.

[11] Resolution 41/128, annex.

[12] A/61/270.

[13] A/61/207.

[14] See *Official Records of the General Assembly, Sixty-first Session, Third Committee*, 15th meeting (A/C.3/61/SR.15), and corrigendum.

[15] Resolution 61/106, annex I.

[16] Resolution 61/177, annex.

[17] United Nations, *Treaty Series*, vol. 1343, No. 22514.

[18] See A/61/299.

[19] See resolution 2200 A (XXI), annex.

[20] Resolution 55/25, annex II.

[21] United Nations, *Treaty Series*, vol. 2173, No. 27531.

[22] Ibid., vol. 75, Nos. 970–973.

[23] A/61/275 and Corr.1.

Resolution 61/147

[on the report of the Third Committee (A/61/441)]

61/147. Inadmissibility of certain practices that contribute to fuelling contemporary forms of racism, racial discrimination, xenophobia and related intolerance

The General Assembly,

Guided by the Charter of the United Nations, the Universal Declaration of Human Rights,[1] the International Covenant on Civil and Political Rights,[2] the International Convention on the Elimination of All Forms of Racial Discrimination[3] and other relevant human rights instruments,

Recalling the provisions of Commission on Human Rights resolutions 2004/16 of 16 April 2004[4] and 2005/5 of 14 April 2005,[5] as well as General Assembly resolution 60/143 of 16 December 2005 on this issue and Assembly resolution 60/144 of 16 December 2005 entitled "Global efforts for the total elimination of racism, racial discrimination, xenophobia and related intolerance and the comprehensive implementation of and follow-up to the Durban Declaration and Programme of Action",

Recalling also the Charter of the Nuremberg Tribunal and the Judgement of the Tribunal, which recognized the Waffen SS organization and all its integral parts as criminal and declared it responsible for many war crimes and crimes against humanity,

Recalling further the relevant provisions of the Durban Declaration and Programme of Action adopted by the World Conference against Racism, Racial Discrimination, Xenophobia and Related Intolerance on 8 September 2001,[6] in particular paragraph 2 of the Declaration and paragraph 86 of the Programme of Action,

Recalling equally the study undertaken by the Speical Rapporteur on contemporary forms of racism, racial discrimination, xenophobia and related intolerance,[7] and taking note of his report,[8]

Alarmed, in this regard, at the spread in many parts of the world of various extremist political parties, movements and groups, including neo-Nazis and skinhead groups,

1. *Reaffirms* the provision of the Durban Declaration[6] in which States condemned the persistence and resurgence of neo-Nazism, neo-Fascism and violent nationalist ideologies based on racial and national prejudice and stated that those phenomena could never be justified in any instance or in any circumstances;

2. *Expresses deep concern* over the glorification of the Nazi movement and former members of the Waffen SS organization, including by erecting monuments and memorials as well as holding public demonstrations in the name of the glorification of the Nazi past, the Nazi movement and neo-Nazism;

3. *Notes with concern* the increase in the number of racist incidents in several countries and the rise of skinhead groups, which have been responsible for many of these incidents, as observed by the Special Rapporteur on contemporary forms of racism, racial discrimination, xenophobia and related intolerance;

4. *Reaffirms* that such acts may be qualified to fall within the scope of activities described in article 4 of the International Convention on the Elimination of All Forms of Racial Discrimination,[3] and that they represent a clear and manifest abuse of the rights to freedom of peaceful assembly and of association as well as the rights to freedom of opinion and expression within the meaning of those rights as guaranteed by the Universal Declaration of Human Rights,[1] the International Covenant on Civil and Political Rights[2] and the International Convention on the Elimination of All Forms of Racial Discrimination;

5. *Stresses* that the practices described above do injustice to the memory of the countless victims of crimes against humanity committed in the Second World War, in particular those committed by the SS organization, and poison the minds of young people, and that those practices are incompatible with the obligations of States Members of the United Nations under its Charter and are incompatible with the goals and principles of the Organization;

6. *Also stresses* that such practices fuel contemporary forms of racism, racial discrimination, xenophobia and related intolerance and contribute to the spread and multiplication of various extremist political parties, movements and groups, including neo-Nazis and skinhead groups;

7. *Emphasizes* the need to take the necessary measures to put an end to the practices described above, and calls upon States to take more effective measures to combat those phenomena and the extremist movements, which pose a real threat to democratic values;

8. *Reaffirms* that, according to article 4 of the International Convention on the Elimination of All Forms of Racial Discrimination, States parties to that instrument are, inter alia, under the obligation:

(*a*) To condemn all propaganda and all organizations that are based on ideas of racial superiority or that attempt to justify or promote racial hatred and discrimination in any form;

(*b*) To undertake to adopt immediate and positive measures designed to eradicate all incitement to, or acts of, such discrimination with due regard to the principles embodied in the Universal Declaration of Human Rights and the rights expressly set forth in article 5 of the Convention;

(*c*) To declare as an offence punishable by law all dissemination of ideas based on racial superiority or hatred, incitement to racial discrimination, as well as all acts of violence or incitement to such acts against any race or group of persons of another colour or ethnic origin, and also the provision of any assistance to racist activities, including the financing thereof;

(*d*) To declare illegal and prohibit organizations and organized and all other propaganda activities that promote and incite racial discrimination and to recognize participation in such organizations or activities as an offence punishable by law;

(*e*) To prohibit public authorities or public institutions, national or local, from promoting or inciting racial discrimination;

9. *Calls upon* those States that have made reservations to article 4 of the International Convention on the Elimination of All Forms of Racial Discrimination to give serious consideration to withdrawing such reservations as a matter of priority;

10. *Recalls* the request of the Commission on Human Rights in its resolution 2005/5[5] that the Special Rapporteur continue to reflect on this issue, make relevant recommendations in his future reports and seek and take into account in this regard the views of Governments and non-governmental organizations;

11. *Invites* Governments and non-governmental organizations to cooperate fully with the Special Rapporteur in the exercise of the aforementioned task;

12. *Decides* to remain seized of the issue.

81st plenary meeting
19 December 2006

---

[1] Resolution 217 A (III).

[2] See resolution 2200 A (XXI), annex.

[3] United Nations, *Treaty Series*, vol. 660, No. 9464.

[4] See *Official Records of the Economic and Social Council, 2004, Supplement No. 3* (E/2004/23), chap. II, sect. A.

[5] Ibid., *2005, Supplement No. 3* and corrigendum (E/2005/23 and Corr.1), chap. II, sect. A.

[6] See A/CONF.189/12 and Corr.1, chap. I.

[7] E/CN.4/2005/18 and Add.1 and Add.1/Corr.1 and Add.2–6.

[8] See A/61/335.

Resolution 61/148

[on the report of the Third Committee (A/61/441)]

61/148. International Convention on the Elimination of All Forms of Racial Discrimination

The General Assembly,

Recalling its previous resolutions on the International Convention on the Elimination of All Forms of Racial Discrimination,[1] most recently resolution 59/176 of 20 December 2004,

Bearing in mind the Vienna Declaration and Programme of Action adopted by the World Conference on Human Rights on 25 June 1993,[2] in particular section II.B of the Declaration, relating to equality, dignity and tolerance,

Reiterating the need to intensify the struggle to eliminate all forms of racism, racial discrimination, xenophobia and related intolerance throughout the world,

Reiterating also the importance of the Convention, which is one of the most widely accepted human rights instruments adopted under the auspices of the United Nations,

Reaffirming that universal adherence to and full implementation of the Convention are of paramount importance for promoting equality and non-discrimination in the world, as stated in the Durban Declaration and Programme of Action adopted by the World Conference against Racism, Racial Discrimination, Xenophobia and Related Intolerance on 8 September 2001,[3]

Mindful of the importance of the contributions of the Committee on the Elimination of Racial Discrimination to the effective implementation of the Convention and to the efforts of the United Nations to combat racism, racial discrimination, xenophobia and related intolerance,

Emphasizing the obligation of all States parties to the Convention to take legislative, judicial and other measures in order to secure full implementation of the provisions of the Convention,

Recalling its resolution 47/111 of 16 December 1992, in which it welcomed the decision, taken on 15 January 1992 by the Fourteenth Meeting of States Parties to the International Convention on the Elimination of All Forms of Racial Discrimination, to amend paragraph 6 of article 8 of the Convention and to add a new paragraph, as paragraph 7 of article 8, with a view to providing for the financing of the Committee from the regular budget of the United Nations,[4] and reiterating its deep concern that the amendment to the Convention has not yet entered into force,

Stressing the importance of enabling the Committee to function smoothly and to have all necessary facilities for the effective performance of its functions under the Convention,

I
Reports of the Committee on the Elimination of Racial Discrimination

1. *Takes note* of the reports of the Committee on the Elimination of Racial Discrimination on its sixty-sixth and sixty-seventh[5] and its sixty-eighth and sixtyninth[6] sessions;

2. *Commends* the Committee for its contributions to the effective implementation of the International Convention on the Elimination of All Forms of Racial Discrimination,[1] especially through the examination of reports under article 9 of the Convention, action on communications under article 14 of the Convention and thematic discussions, which contribute to the prevention and elimination of racism, racial discrimination, xenophobia and related intolerance;

3. *Calls upon* States parties to fulfil their obligation, under article 9, paragraph 1, of the Convention, to submit their periodic reports on measures taken to implement the Convention in due time;

4. *Expresses its concern* at the fact that a great number of reports are overdue and continue to be overdue, in particular initial reports, which constitutes an obstacle to the full implementation of the Convention;

5. *Encourages* States parties to the Convention whose reports are seriously overdue to avail themselves of the advisory services and technical assistance that the Office of the United Nations High Commissioner for Human Rights can provide, upon their request, for the preparation of the reports;

6. *Encourages* the Committee to continue to cooperate and exchange information with United Nations bodies and mechanisms, in particular with the Human Rights Council, the Subcommission on the Promotion and Protection of Human Rights and the Special Rapporteur on contemporary forms of racism, racial discrimination, xenophobia and related intolerance, and with intergovernmental organizations, as well as with non-governmental organizations;

7. *Encourages* States parties to the Convention to continue to include a gender perspective in their reports to the Committee, and invites the Committee to take into account a gender perspective in the implementation of its mandate;

8. *Notes with appreciation* the engagement of the Committee in the follow-up to the Durban Declaration and Programme of Action;[3]

9. *Expresses its appreciation* for the efforts made so far by the Committee to improve the efficiency of its working methods, and encourages the Committee to continue its activities in this regard;

10. *Welcomes*, in this regard, measures taken by the Committee to follow up on its concluding observations and recommendations, such as the decision to appoint a follow-up coordinator[7] and to adopt guidelines on the follow-up;[8]

11. *Encourages* the continued participation of members of the Committee in the annual inter-committee meetings and meetings of chairpersons of the human rights treaty bodies, especially with a view to a more coordinated approach to the activities of the treaty body system and standardized reporting;

II
Financial situation of the Committee on the Elimination of Racial Discrimination

12. *Takes note* of the report of the Secretary-General on the financial situation of the Committee on the Elimination of Racial Discrimination;[9]

13. *Expresses its profound concern* at the fact that a number of States parties to the International Convention on the Elimination of All Forms of Racial Discrimination[1] have still not fulfilled their financial obligations, as shown in the report of the Secretary-General, and strongly appeals to all States parties that are in arrears to fulfil their outstanding financial obligations under article 8, paragraph 6, of the Convention;

14. *Strongly urges* States parties to the Convention to accelerate their domestic ratification procedures with regard to the amendment to the Convention concerning the financing of the Committee and to notify the Secretary-General expeditiously in writing of their agreement to the amendment, as decided upon at the Fourteenth Meeting of States Parties to the International Convention on the Elimination of All Forms of Racial Discrimination on 15 January 1992,[4] endorsed by the General Assembly in its resolution 47/111 and further reiterated at the Sixteenth Meeting of States Parties on 16 January 1996;

15. *Requests* the Secretary-General to continue to ensure adequate financial arrangements and to provide the necessary support, including an adequate level of Secretariat assistance, in order to ensure the functioning of the Committee and to enable it to cope with its increasing amount of work;

16. *Also requests* the Secretary-General to invite those States parties to the Convention that are in arrears to pay the amounts in arrears, and to report thereon to the General Assembly at its sixty-third session;

III
Status of the International Convention on the Elimination of All Forms of Racial Discrimination

17. *Takes note* of the report of the Secretary-General on the status of the International Convention on the Elimination of All Forms of Racial Discrimination;[10]

18. *Expresses its satisfaction* at the number of States that have ratified or acceded to the Convention, which now stands at one hundred and seventy-three;

19. *Urges* States parties to comply fully with their obligations under the Convention and to take into consideration the concluding observations and general recommendations of the Committee on the Elimination of Racial Discrimination;

20. *Reaffirms its conviction* that ratification of or accession to the Convention on a universal basis and the implementation of its provisions are necessary for the effectiveness of the fight against racism, racial discrimination, xenophobia and related intolerance and for the implementation of the commitments undertaken under the Durban Declaration and Programme of Action,[3] and expresses its disappointment that universal ratification of the Convention was not achieved by the targeted date of 2005;

21. *Urges* all States that have not yet become parties to the Convention to ratify or accede to it as a matter of urgency;

22. *Urges* States to limit the extent of any reservation they lodge to the Convention and to formulate any reservation as precisely and as narrowly as possible in order to ensure that no reservation is incompatible with the object and purpose of the Convention, to review their reservations on a regular basis with a view to withdrawing them, and to withdraw reservations that are contrary to the object and purpose of the Convention;

23. *Notes* that the number of States parties to the Convention that have made the declaration provided for in article 14 of the Convention now stands at forty-nine, and requests the States parties that have not yet done so to consider making that declaration;

24. *Invites* the Chairman of the Committee on the Elimination of Racial Discrimination to present an oral report on the work of the Committee to the General Assembly at its sixty-third session under the item entitled "Elimination of racism and racial discrimination";

25. *Decides* to consider, at its sixty-third session, under the item entitled "Elimination of racism and racial discrimination", the reports of the Committee on its seventieth and seventy-first and its seventy-second and seventy-third sessions, the report of the Secretary-General on the financial situation of the Committee and the report of the Secretary-General on the status of the Convention.

81st plenary meeting
19 December 2006

---

[1] United Nations, *Treaty Series*, vol. 660, No. 9464.

[2] A/CONF.157/24 (Part I), chap. III.

[3] See A/CONF.189/12 and Corr.1, chap. I.

[4] See CERD/SP/45, annex.

[5] *Official Records of the General Assembly, Sixtieth Session, Supplement No. 18* (A/60/18).

[6] Ibid., *Sixty-first Session, Supplement No. 18* (A/61/18).

[7] Ibid., *Sixtieth Session, Supplement No. 18* (A/60/18), annex IV.

[8] Ibid., *Sixty-first Session, Supplement No. 18* (A/61/18), annex VI.

[9] A/61/186.

[10] A/61/260.

Resolution 61/149

[on the report of the Third Committee (A/61/441)]

61/149. Global efforts for the total elimination of racism, racial discrimination, xenophobia and related intolerance and the comprehensive implementation of and follow-up to the Durban Declaration and Programme of Action

The General Assembly,

Recalling its resolution 60/144 of 16 December 2005, in which it reiterated its firm commitment to continue its global efforts towards the total elimination of the scourges of racism, racial discrimination, xenophobia and related intolerance, and towards the effective and comprehensive implementation of and follow-up to the Durban Declaration and Programme of Action adopted by the World Conference against Racism, Racial Discrimination, Xenophobia and Related Intolerance, held in Durban, South Africa, from 31 August to 8 September 2001,[1]

Recalling also its resolution 59/177 of 20 December 2004, in which it firmly consolidated the global drive for the total elimination of racism, racial discrimination, xenophobia and related intolerance and recognized the absolute necessity and the imperative nature of the political will for the achievement of the commitments undertaken in the Durban Declaration and Programme of Action,

Recalling further its resolution 58/160 of 22 December 2003, in which it decided to place emphasis on the concrete implementation of the Durban Declaration and Programme of Action as a solid foundation for a broad-based consensus for further action and initiatives towards the total elimination of the scourge of racism,

Recalling its resolution 57/195 of 18 December 2002, in which it outlined the important roles and responsibilities of the various organs of the United Nations and other stakeholders at the international, regional and national levels, including, in particular, the Commission on Human Rights, and its resolution 56/266 of 27 March 2002, in which it endorsed the Durban Declaration and Programme of Action as constituting a solid foundation for further action and initiatives towards the total elimination of the scourge of racism,

Reiterating that all human beings are born free and equal in dignity and rights and have the potential to contribute constructively to the development and wellbeing of their societies, and that any doctrine of racial superiority is scientifically false, morally condemnable, socially unjust and dangerous and must be rejected, together with theories that attempt to determine the existence of separate human races,

Convinced that racism, racial discrimination, xenophobia and related intolerance manifest themselves in a differentiated manner for women and girls and may be among the factors leading to a deterioration in their living conditions, poverty, violence, multiple forms of discrimination and the limitation or denial of their human rights, and recognizing the need to integrate a gender perspective into relevant policies, strategies and programmes of action against racism, racial discrimination, xenophobia and related intolerance in order to address multiple forms of discrimination,

Taking note of Human Rights Council resolution 1/5 of 30 June 2006,[2]

Taking note also of Commission on Human Rights resolutions 2002/68 of 25 April 2002,[3] 2003/30 of 23 April 2003,[4] 2004/88 of 22 April 2004[5] and 2005/64 of 20 April 2005,[6] by which the international community put into effect mechanisms for the effective implementation of the Durban Declaration and Programme of Action,

Underlining the primacy of political will, international cooperation and adequate funding at the national, regional and international levels for the successful implementation of the Durban Programme of Action,

Alarmed at the increase in racist violence and xenophobic ideas in many parts of the world, in political circles, in the sphere of public opinion and in society at large, inter alia, as a result of the resurgent activities of associations established on the basis of racist and xenophobic platforms and charters, and the persistent use of those platforms and charters to promote or incite racist ideologies,

Underlining the importance of urgently eliminating continuing and violent trends involving racism and racial discrimination, and conscious that any form of impunity for crimes motivated by racist and xenophobic attitudes plays a role in weakening the rule of law and democracy, tends to encourage the recurrence of such crimes and requires resolute action and cooperation for its eradication,

Welcoming the determination of the United Nations High Commissioner for Human Rights to profile and increase the visibility of the struggle against racism, racial discrimination, xenophobia and related intolerance and her intention to make this a cross-cutting issue in the activities and programmes of her Office,

Taking note of the report of the Secretary-General,[7] the interim report of the Special Rapporteur on contemporary forms of racism, racial discrimination, xenophobia and related intolerance[8] and Human Rights Council decision 1/102 of 30 June 2006,[9]

I
Basic general principles

1. *Acknowledges* that no derogation from the prohibition of racial discrimination, genocide, the crime of apartheid or slavery is permitted, as defined in the obligations under the relevant human rights instruments;

2. *Expresses its profound concern about and its unequivocal condemnation* of all forms of racism and racial discrimination, including related acts of racially motivated violence, xenophobia and intolerance, as well as propaganda activities and organizations that attempt to justify or promote racism, racial discrimination, xenophobia and related intolerance in any form;

3. *Expresses deep concern* at recent attempts to establish hierarchies among emerging and resurgent forms of racism, racial discrimination, xenophobia and related intolerance, and urges States to adopt measures to address these scourges with the same emphasis and vigour with a view to preventing this practice and protecting victims;

4. *Stresses* that States and international organizations have a responsibility to ensure that measures taken in the struggle against terrorism do not discriminate in purpose or effect on grounds of race, colour, descent or national or ethnic origin, and urges all States to rescind or refrain from all forms of racial profiling;

5. *Recognizes* that States should implement and enforce appropriate and effective legislative, judicial, regulatory and administrative measures to prevent and protect against acts of racism, racial discrimination, xenophobia and related intolerance, thereby contributing to the prevention of human rights violations;

6. *Also recognizes* that racism, racial discrimination, xenophobia and related intolerance occur on the grounds of race, colour, descent or national or ethnic origin and that victims can suffer multiple or aggravated forms of discrimination based on other related grounds, such as sex, language, religion, political or other opinion, social origin, property, birth or other status;

7. *Reaffirms* that any advocacy of national, racial or religious hatred that constitutes incitement to discrimination, hostility or violence shall be prohibited by law;

8. *Emphasizes* that it is the responsibility of States to adopt effective measures to combat criminal acts motivated by racism, racial discrimination, xenophobia and related intolerance, including measures to ensure that such motivations are considered an aggravating factor for the purposes of sentencing, to prevent those crimes from going unpunished and to ensure the rule of law;

9. *Urges* all States to review and, where necessary, revise their immigration laws, policies and practices so that they are free of racial discrimination and compatible with their obligations under international human rights instruments;

10. *Condemns* the misuse of print, audio-visual and electronic media and new communication technologies, including the Internet, to incite violence motivated by racial hatred, and calls upon States to take all necessary measures to combat this form of racism in accordance with the commitments that they have undertaken under the Durban Declaration and Programme of Action,[1] in particular paragraph 147 of the Programme of Action, in accordance with existing international and regional standards of freedom of expression and taking all necessary measures to guarantee the right to freedom of opinion and expression;

11. *Encourages* all States to include in their educational curricula and social programmes at all levels, as appropriate, knowledge of and tolerance and respect for all cultures, civilizations, religions, peoples and countries;

12. *Stresses* the responsibility of States to mainstream a gender perspective in the design and development of prevention, education and protection measures aimed at the eradication of racism, racial discrimination, xenophobia and related intolerance at all levels, to ensure that they effectively target the distinct situations of women and men;

II
International Convention on the Elimination of All Forms of Racial Discrimination

13. *Reaffirms* that universal adherence to and full implementation of the International Convention on the Elimination of All Forms of Racial Discrimination[10] are of paramount importance for the fight against racism, racial discrimination, xenophobia and related intolerance, including contemporary forms of racism and racial discrimination, and for the promotion of equality and non-discrimination in the world;

14. *Reiterates* the call made by the World Conference against Racism, Racial Discrimination, Xenophobia and Related Intolerance, in paragraph 75 of the Durban Programme of Action,[1] to achieve universal ratification of the Convention by 2005 and for all States to consider making the declaration envisaged under article 14 of the Convention, and endorses the grave concern expressed by the Commission on Human Rights in its resolution 2005/64[6] to the effect that, with one hundred and seventy-three ratifications and only forty-nine declarations, the deadline for universal ratification decided by the World Conference has, regrettably, not been realized;

15. *Urges*, in the above context, the Office of the United Nations High Commissioner for Human Rights to maintain and issue regular updates on its website of a list of countries that have not yet ratified the Convention and to encourage such countries to ratify it at the earliest;

16. *Expresses its concern* at the serious delays in the submission of overdue reports to the Committee on the Elimination of Racial Discrimination, which impedes the effectiveness of the Committee, makes a strong appeal to all States parties to the Convention to comply with their treaty obligations, and reaffirms the importance of the provision of technical assistance to the requesting countries in the preparation of their reports to the Committee;

17. *Invites* States parties to the Convention to ratify the amendment to article 8 of the Convention on the financing of the Committee, and calls for adequate additional resources from the regular budget of the United Nations to enable the Committee to discharge its mandate fully;

18. *Urges* all States parties to the Convention to intensify their efforts to implement the obligations that they have accepted under article 4 of the Convention, with due regard to the principles of the Universal Declaration of Human Rights[11] and article 5 of the Convention;

19. *Welcomes* the work of the Committee in applying the Convention to the new and contemporary forms of racism and racial discrimination;

20. *Recalls* that the Committee holds that the prohibition of the dissemination of ideas based on racial superiority or racial hatred is compatible with the right to freedom of opinion and expression as outlined in article 19 of the Universal Declaration of Human Rights and in article 5 of the Convention;

21. *Welcomes* the emphasis placed by the Committee on the importance of follow-up to the World Conference and the measures recommended to strengthen the implementation of the Convention as well as the functioning of the Committee;[12]

III
Comprehensive implementation of and follow-up to the Durban Declaration and Programme of Action

22. *Acknowledges* that the outcome of the World Conference against Racism, Racial Discrimination, Xenophobia and Related Intolerance is on an equal footing with the outcomes of all the major United Nations conferences, summits and special sessions in the human rights and social fields;

23. *Also acknowledges* that the World Conference, which was the third world conference against racism, was significantly different from the previous two conferences, as evidenced by the inclusion in its title of two important components relating to contemporary forms of racism, namely, xenophobia and related intolerance;

24. *Emphasizes* that the basic responsibility for effectively combating racism, racial discrimination, xenophobia and related intolerance lies with States, and to this end stresses that States have the primary responsibility to ensure full and effective implementation of all commitments and recommendations contained in the Durban Declaration and Programme of Action;[1]

25. *Also emphasizes* the fundamental and complementary role of national human rights institutions, regional bodies or centres and civil society, working jointly with States towards the achievement of the objectives of the Durban Declaration and Programme of Action;

26. *Welcomes* the steps taken by numerous Governments, in particular the elaboration and implementation of national action plans to combat racism, racial discrimination, xenophobia and related intolerance, and steps taken by national human rights institutions and non-governmental organizations, towards the full implementation of the Durban Declaration and Programme of Action, and affirms this trend as a demonstration of commitment for the elimination of all scourges of racism at the national level;

27. *Calls upon* all States that have not yet elaborated their national action plans on combating racism, racial discrimination, xenophobia and related intolerance to comply with their commitments undertaken at the World Conference;

28. *Calls upon* all States to formulate and implement without delay, at the national, regional and international levels, policies and plans of action to combat racism, racial discrimination, xenophobia and related intolerance, including their gender-based manifestations;

29. *Urges* States to support the activities of existing regional bodies or centres that combat racism, racial discrimination, xenophobia and related intolerance in their respective regions, and recommends the establishment of such bodies in all regions where they do not exist;

30. *Recognizes* the fundamental role of civil society in the fight against racism, racial discrimination, xenophobia and related intolerance, in particular in assisting States to develop regulations and strategies, in taking measures and action against such forms of discrimination and through follow-up implementation;

31. *Decides* that the General Assembly, through its role in policy formulation, the Economic and Social Council, through its role in overall guidance and coordination, in accordance with their respective roles under the Charter of the United Nations and Assembly resolution 50/227 of 24 May 1996, and the Human Rights Council shall constitute a three-tiered intergovernmental process for the comprehensive implementation of and follow-up to the Durban Declaration and Programme of Action;

32. *Stresses and reaffirms* its role as the highest intergovernmental mechanism for the formulation and appraisal of policy on matters related to the economic, social and related fields, in accordance with Chapter IX of the Charter, including in the comprehensive implementation of and follow-up to the goals and targets set at all the major United Nations conferences, summits and special sessions;

33. *Decides* to convene in 2009 a review conference on the implementation of the Durban Declaration and Programme of Action to be conducted within the framework of the General Assembly, and, to this end, requests the Human Rights Council to undertake preparations for this event, making use of the three existing and ongoing follow-up mechanisms, and to formulate a concrete plan and provide updates and reports on this issue on an annual basis starting in 2007;

34. *Reaffirms* that the Human Rights Council shall have a central role in the monitoring of the implementation of the Durban Declaration and Programme of Action within the United Nations system and in advising the General Assembly thereon;

35. *Expresses its appreciation* for the continuing work in follow-up to the World Conference undertaken by the Intergovernmental Working Group on the Effective Implementation of the Durban Declaration and Programme of Action, the group of independent eminent experts on the implementation of the Durban Declaration and Programme of Action and the Working Group of Experts on People of African Descent;

36. *Welcomes* the conclusions and recommendations agreed upon by the Intergovernmental Working Group on the Effective Implementation of the Durban Declaration and Programme of Action at its fourth session,[13] and welcomes in particular the identification and/or consideration of substantive and procedural gaps, as well as the request for the nomination of five highly qualified experts to further study the content and scope of those gaps, including but not limited to the areas identified in the conclusions of the Chair of the high-level seminar, and, in consultation with human rights treaty bodies, the Special Rapporteur on contemporary forms of racism, racial discrimination, xenophobia and related intolerance and other relevant mandate-holders, to produce a base document that contains concrete recommendations on the means or avenues to bridge those gaps, including but not limited

to the drafting of a new protocol to the International Convention on the Elimination of All Forms of Racial Discrimination or the adoption of new instruments, and for the Committee on the Elimination of Racial Discrimination to conduct further study on possible measures to strengthen the implementation of the Convention and its proposals regarding the assessment and evaluation of the implementation of existing international human rights instruments by States parties, and to this end encourages the Intergovernmental Working Group to continue its work related to the preparation of complementary international standards in accordance with the Durban Declaration and Programme of Action;

37. *Acknowledges* the centrality of resource mobilization, effective global partnership and international cooperation in the context of paragraphs 157 and 158 of the Durban Programme of Action for the successful realization of commitments undertaken at the World Conference, and to this end emphasizes the importance of the mandate of the group of independent eminent experts on the implementation of the Durban Declaration and Programme of Action, especially in mobilizing the necessary political will required for the successful implementation of the Declaration and Programme of Action;

38. *Requests* the Secretary-General to provide the necessary resources for the effective fulfilment of the mandates of the Intergovernmental Working Group on the Effective Implementation of the Durban Declaration and Programme of Action, the Working Group of Experts on People of African Descent and the group of independent eminent experts on the implementation of the Durban Declaration and Programme of Action;

39. *Expresses its concern* at the increasing incidence of racism in various sporting events, while noting with appreciation the efforts made by some governing bodies of the various sporting codes to combat racism, and in this regard invites all international sporting bodies to promote, through their national, regional and international federations, a world of sport free from racism and racial discrimination;

40. *Invites*, in this context, the Fédération internationale de football association, in connection with the 2010 soccer World Cup tournament to be held in South Africa, to consider introducing a visible theme on non-racism in football, requests the Secretary-General to bring this invitation to the attention of the Fédération and to bring the issue of racism in sport to the attention of other relevant international sporting bodies, and, in this regard, appreciates the joint efforts of the Government of Germany, the Secretary-General and the Special Rapporteur on contemporary forms of racism, racial discrimination, xenophobia and related intolerance during the 2006 World Cup;

IV
Special Rapporteur on contemporary forms of racism, racial discrimination, xenophobia and related intolerance and follow-up to his visits

41. *Expresses its full support and appreciation* for the work of the Special Rapporteur on contemporary forms of racism, racial discrimination, xenophobia and related intolerance, and encourages its continuation;

42. *Reiterates its call* to all Member States, intergovernmental organizations, relevant organizations of the United Nations system and non-governmental organizations to cooperate fully with the Special Rapporteur, and calls upon States to consider responding favourably to his requests for visits so as to enable him to fulfil his mandate fully and effectively;

43. *Recognizes with deep concern* the increase in anti-Semitism, Christianophobia and Islamophobia in various parts of the world, as well as the emergence of racial and violent movements based on racism and discriminatory ideas directed against Arab, Christian, Jewish and Muslim communities, as well as all religious communities, communities of people of African descent, communities of people of Asian descent, communities of indigenous people and other communities;

44. *Encourages* closer collaboration between the Special Rapporteur and the Office of the United Nations High Commissioner for Human Rights, in particular the Anti-Discrimination Unit;

45. *Urges* the United Nations High Commissioner for Human Rights to provide States, at their request, with advisory services and technical assistance to enable them to implement fully the recommendations of the Special Rapporteur;

46. *Requests* the Secretary-General to provide the Special Rapporteur with all the necessary human and financial assistance to carry out his mandate efficiently, effectively and expeditiously and to enable him to submit an interim report to the General Assembly at its sixty-second session;

47. *Takes note* of the recommendations contained in the interim report of the Special Rapporteur,[8] and urges Member States and other relevant stakeholders to consider implementing those recommendations;

48. *Requests* the Special Rapporteur to continue giving particular attention to the negative impact of racism, racial discrimination, xenophobia and related intolerance on the full enjoyment of civil, cultural, economic, political and social rights by national or ethnic, religious and linguistic minorities, immigrant populations, asylum-seekers and refugees;

49. *Invites* Member States to demonstrate greater commitment to fighting racism in sport by conducting educational and awareness-raising activities and by strongly condemning the perpetrators of racist incidents, in cooperation with national and international sports organizations;

V
General

50. *Requests* the Secretary-General to submit a report on the implementation of the present resolution to the General Assembly at its sixty-second session;

51. *Decides* to remain seized of this important matter at its sixty-second session under the item entitled "Elimination of racism and racial discrimination".

81st plenary meeting
19 December 2006

---

[1] See A/CONF.189/12 and Corr.1, chap. I.

[2] See *Official Records of the General Assembly, Sixty-first Session, Supplement No. 53* (A/61/53), part one, chap. II, sect. A.

[3] See *Official Records of the Economic and Social Council, 2002, Supplement No. 3* (E/2002/23), chap. II, sect. A.

[4] Ibid., *2003, Supplement No. 3* (E/2003/23), chap. II, sect. A. [5] Ibid., *2004, Supplement No. 3* (E/2004/23), chap. II, sect. A.

[6] Ibid., *2005, Supplement No. 3* and corrigendum (E/2005/23 and Corr.1), chap. II, sect. A.

[7] A/61/337.

[8] See A/61/335.

[9] See *Official Records of the General Assembly, Sixty-first Session, Supplement No. 53* (A/61/53), part one, chap. II, sect. B.

[10] United Nations, *Treaty Series*, vol. 660, No. 9464.

[11] Resolution 217 A (III).

[12] See *Official Records of the General Assembly, Fifty-seventh Session, Supplement No. 18* (A/57/18), chap. XI, sect. E.

[13] E/CN.4/2006/18, sect. VI.

Resolution 61/150

[on the report of the Third Committee (A/61/442)]

61/150. Universal realization of the right of peoples to self-determination

The General Assembly,

Reaffirming the importance, for the effective guarantee and observance of human rights, of the universal realization of the right of peoples to self-determination enshrined in the Charter of the United Nations and embodied in the International Covenants on Human Rights,[1] as well as in the Declaration on the Granting of Independence to Colonial Countries and Peoples contained in General Assembly resolution 1514 (XV) of 14 December 1960,

Welcoming the progressive exercise of the right to self-determination by peoples under colonial, foreign or alien occupation and their emergence into sovereign statehood and independence,

Deeply concerned at the continuation of acts or threats of foreign military intervention and occupation that are threatening to suppress, or have already suppressed, the right to self-determination of peoples and nations,

Expressing grave concern that, as a consequence of the persistence of such actions, millions of people have been and are being uprooted from their homes as refugees and displaced persons, and emphasizing the urgent need for concerted international action to alleviate their condition,

Recalling the relevant resolutions regarding the violation of the right of peoples to self-determination and other human rights as a result of foreign military intervention, aggression and occupation, adopted by the Commission on Human Rights at its sixty-first[2] and previous sessions,

Reaffirming its previous resolutions on the universal realization of the right of peoples to self-determination, including resolution 60/145 of 16 December 2005,

Reaffirming also its resolution 55/2 of 8 September 2000, containing the United Nations Millennium Declarion, and recalling its resolution 60/1 of 16 September 2005, containing the 2005 World Summit Outcome, which, inter alia, upheld the right to self-determination of peoples under colonial domination and foreign occupation,

Taking note of the report of the Secretary-General,[3]

1. *Reaffirms* that the universal realization of the right of all peoples, including those under colonial, foreign and alien domination, to self-determination is a fundamental condition for the effective guarantee and observance of human rights and for the preservation and promotion of such rights;

2. *Declares its firm opposition* to acts of foreign military intervention, aggression and occupation, since these have resulted in the suppression of the right of peoples to self-determination and other human rights in certain parts of the world;

3. *Calls upon* those States responsible to cease immediately their military intervention in and occupation of foreign countries and territories and all acts of repression, discrimination, exploitation and maltreatment, in particular the brutal and inhumane methods reportedly employed for the execution of those acts against the peoples concerned;

4. *Deplores* the plight of millions of refugees and displaced persons who have been uprooted as a result of the aforementioned acts, and reaffirms their right to return to their homes voluntarily in safety and honour;

5. *Requests* the Human Rights Council to continue to give special attention to the violation of human rights, especially the right to self-determination, resulting from foreign military intervention, aggression or occupation;

6. *Requests* the Secretary-General to report on the question to the General Assembly at its sixty-second session under the item entitled "Right of peoples to self-determination".

81st plenary meeting
19 December 2006

---

[1] Resolution 2200 A (XXI), annex.

[2] See *Official Records of the Economic and Social Council, 2005, Supplement No. 3* and corrigendum (E/2005/23 and Corr.1), chap. II, sect. A.

[3] A/61/333.

Resolution 61/151

[on the report of the Third Committee (A/61/442)]

61/151. Use of mercenaries as a means of violating human rights and impeding the exercise of the right of peoples to self-determination

The General Assembly,

Recalling all of its previous resolutions on the subject, including resolution 59/178 of 20 December 2004, and taking note of Commission on Human Rights resolution 2005/2 of 7 April 2005,[1]

Recalling also all of its relevant resolutions, in which, inter alia, it condemned any State that permitted or tolerated the recruitment, financing, training, assembly, transit and use of mercenaries with the objective of overthrowing the Governments of States Members of the United Nations, especially those of developing countries, or of fighting against national liberation movements, and recalling further the relevant resolutions and international instruments adopted by the General Assembly, the Security Council, the Economic and Social Council and the Organization of African Unity, inter alia, the Organization of African Unity Convention for the elimination of mercenarism in Africa,[2] as well as the African Union,[3]

Reaffirming the purposes and principles enshrined in the Charter of the United Nations concerning the strict observance of the principles of sovereign equality, political independence, the territorial integrity of States, the self-determination of peoples, the non-use of force or of the threat of use of force in international relations and non-interference in affairs within the domestic jurisdiction of States,

Reaffirming also that, by virtue of the principle of self-determination, all peoples have the right freely to determine their political status and to pursue their economic, social and cultural development, and that every State has the duty to respect this right in accordance with the provisions of the Charter,

Reaffirming further the Declaration on Principles of International Law concerning Friendly Relations and Cooperation among States in accordance with the Charter of the United Nations,[4]

Alarmed and concerned at the danger that the activities of mercenaries constitute to peace and security in developing countries, in particular in Africa and in small States,

Deeply concerned at the loss of life, the substantial damage to property and the negative effects on the policy and economies of affected countries resulting from criminal mercenary activities,

Extremely alarmed and concerned about recent mercenary activities in Africa and the threat they pose to the integrity of and respect for the constitutional order of those countries,

Convinced that, notwithstanding the way in which they are used or the form that they take to acquire some semblance of legitimacy, mercenaries or mercenary-related activities are a threat to peace, security and the self-determination of peoples and an obstacle to the enjoyment of all human rights by peoples,

1. *Takes note* of the report of the Working Group on the use of mercenaries as a means of violating human rights and impeding the exercise of the right of peoples to self-determination;[5]

2. *Reaffirms* that the use of mercenaries and their recruitment, financing and training are causes for grave concern to all States and violate the purposes and principles enshrined in the Charter of the United Nations;

3. *Recognizes* that armed conflict, terrorism, arms trafficking and covert operations by third Powers, inter alia, encourage the demand for mercenaries on the global market;

4. *Urges once again* all States to take the necessary steps and to exercise the utmost vigilance against the menace posed by the activities of mercenaries and to take legislative measures to ensure that their territories and other territories under their control, as well as their nationals, are not used for the recruitment, assembly, financing, training and transit of mercenaries for the planning of activities designed to impede the right of peoples to self-determination, to destabilize or overthrow the Government of any State or to dismember or impair, totally or in part, the territorial integrity or political unity of sovereign and independent States conducting themselves in compliance with the right of peoples to self-determination;

5. *Requests* all States to exercise the utmost vigilance against any kind of recruitment, training, hiring or financing of mercenaries by private companies offering international military consultancy and security services, as well as to impose a specific ban on such companies intervening in armed conflicts or actions to destabilize constitutional regimes;

6. *Calls upon* all States that have not yet done so to consider taking the necessary action to accede to or ratify the International Convention against the Recruitment, Use, Financing and Training of Mercenaries;[6]

7. *Welcomes* the adoption by some States of national legislation that restricts the recruitment, assembly, financing, training and transit of mercenaries;

8. *Condemns* recent mercenary activities in Africa, and commends the African Governments on their collaboration in thwarting those illegal actions, which posed a threat to the integrity of and respect for the constitutional order of those countries and the exercise of the right of their peoples to self-determination;

9. *Calls upon* States to investigate the possibility of mercenary involvement whenever and wherever criminal acts of a terrorist nature occur and to bring to trial those found responsible or to consider their extradition, if so requested, in accordance with domestic law and applicable bilateral or international treaties;

10. *Condemns* any form of impunity granted to perpetrators of mercenary activities and to those responsible for the use, recruitment, financing and training of mercenaries, and urges all States, in accordance with their obligations under international law, to bring them, without distinction, to justice;

11. *Calls upon* Member States, in accordance with their obligations under international law, to cooperate with and assist the judicial prosecution of those accused of mercenary activities in transparent, open and fair trials;

12. *Requests* the Working Group to continue the work already done by the previous Special Rapporteurs on the strengthening of the international legal framework for the prevention and sanction of the recruitment, use, financing and training of mercenaries, taking into account the proposal for a new legal definition of a mercenary drafted by the Special Rapporteur in his report to the Commission on Human Rights at its sixtieth session;[7]

13. *Requests* the Office of the United Nations High Commissioner for Human Rights, as a matter of priority, to publicize the adverse effects of the activities of mercenaries on the right of peoples to self-determination and, when requested and where necessary, to render advisory services to States that are affected by those activities;

14. *Expresses its appreciation* to the Office of the High Commissioner for convening the third meeting of experts on traditional and new forms of mercenary activities as a means of violating human rights and impeding the exercise of the right of peoples to self-determination, and takes note of the report of the meeting;[8]

15. *Requests* the Working Group to continue to take into account, in the discharge of its mandate, the fact that mercenary activities continue to occur in many parts of the world and are taking on new forms, manifestations and modalities, and, in this regard, requests its members to continue to pay particular attention to the impact of the activities of private companies offering military assistance, consultancy and security services on the international market on the exercise of the right of peoples to self-determination;

16. *Urges* all States to cooperate fully with the Working Group in the fulfilment of its mandate;

17. *Requests* the Secretary-General and the United Nations High Commissioner for Human Rights to provide the Working Group with all the necessary assistance and support for the fulfilment of its mandate, both professional and financial, including through the promotion of cooperation between the Working Group and other components of the United Nations system that deal with countering mercenary-related activities, in order to meet the demands of its current and future activities;

18. *Requests* the Working Group to consult States and intergovernmental and non-governmental organizations in the implementation of the present resolution and to report, with specific recommendations, to the General Assembly at its sixty-second session its findings on the use of mercenaries to undermine the enjoyment of all human rights and to impede the exercise of the right of peoples to self-determination;

19. *Decides* to consider at its sixty-second session the question of the use of mercenaries as a means of violating human rights and impeding the exercise of the right of peoples to self-determination under the item entitled "Right of peoples to self-determination".

81st plenary meeting
19 December 2006

[1] See *Official Records of the Economic and Social Council, 2005, Supplement No. 3* and corrigendum (E/2005/23 and Corr.1), chap. II, sect. A.

[2] United Nations, *Treaty Series*, vol. 1490, No. 25573.

[3] On 8 July 2002, the Organization of African Unity ceased to exist and, in its place, the African Union came into force on 9 July 2002.

[4] Resolution 2625 (XXV), annex.

[5] See A/61/341.

[6] United Nations, *Treaty Series*, vol. 2163, No. 37789.

[7] See E/CN.4/2004/15, para. 47.

[8] See E/CN.4/2005/23.

Resolution 61/152

[on the report of the Third Committee (A/61/442)]

61/152. The right of the Palestinian people to self-determination

The General Assembly,

Aware that the development of friendly relations among nations, based on respect for the principle of equal rights and self-determination of peoples, is among the purposes and principles of the United Nations, as defined in the Charter,

Recalling, in this regard, its resolution 2625 (XXV) of 24 October 1970 entitled "Declaration on Principles of International Law concerning Friendly Relations and Cooperation among States in accordance with the Charter of the United Nations",

Bearing in mind the International Covenants on Human Rights,[1] the Universal Declaration of Human Rights,[2] the Declaration on the Granting of Independence to Colonial Countries and Peoples [3] and the Vienna Declaration and Programme of Action adopted at the World Conference on Human Rights on 25 June 1993,[4]

Recalling the Declaration on the Occasion of the Fiftieth Anniversary of the United Nations,[5]

Recalling also the United Nations Millennium Declaration,[6]

Recalling further the advisory opinion rendered on 9 July 2004 by the International Court of Justice on the *Legal Consequences of the Construction of a Wall in the Occupied Palestinian Territory*,[7] and noting in particular the reply of the Court, including on the right of peoples to self-determination, which is a right *erga omnes*,[8]

Recalling the conclusion of the Court, in its advisory opinion of 9 July 2004, that the construction of the wall by Israel, the occupying Power, in the Occupied Palestinian Territory, including East Jerusalem, along with measures previously taken, severly impedes the right of the Palestinian people to self-determination,[9]

Expressing the urgent need for the resumption of negotiations within the Middle East peace process on its agreed basis and for the speedy achievement of a just, lasting and comprehensive peace settlement between the Palestinian and Israeli sides,

Recalling its resolution 60/146 of 16 December 2005,

Affirming the right of all States in the region to live in peace within secure and internationally recognized borders,

1. *Reaffirms* the right of the Palestinian people to self-determination, including the right to their independent State of Palestine;

2. *Urges* all States and the specialized agencies and organizations of the United Nations system to continue to support and assist the Palestinian people in the early realization of their right to self-determination.

81st plenary meeting
19 December 2006

---

[1] Resolution 2200 A (XXI), annex.

[2] Resolution 217 A (III).

[3] Resolution 1514 (XV).

[4] A/CONF.157/24 (Part I), chap. III.

[5] See resolution 50/6.

[6] See resolution 55/2.

[7] See A/ES-10/273 and Corr.1.

[8] Ibid., advisory opinion, para. 88.

[9] Ibid., para. 122.

Resolution 61/153

[on the report of the Third Committee (A/61/443/Add.1 and Corr.1)]

61/153. Torture and other cruel, inhuman or degrading treatment or punishment

The General Assembly,

Reaffirming that no one shall be subjected to torture or to other cruel, inhuman or degrading treatment or punishment,

Recalling that freedom from torture and other cruel, inhuman or degrading treatment or punishment is a non-derogable right that must be protected under all circumstances, including in times of international or internal armed conflict or disturbance, and that the absolute prohibition of torture and other cruel, inhuman or degrading treatment or punishment is affirmed in relevant international instruments,

Recalling also that a number of international, regional and domestic courts, including the International Tribunal for the Prosecution of Persons Responsible for Serious Violations of International Humanitarian Law Committed in the Territory of the Former Yugoslavia since 1991, have recognized that the prohibition of torture is a peremptory norm of international law and have held that the prohibition of cruel, inhuman or degrading treatment or punishment is customary international law,

Recalling further the definition of torture contained in article 1 of the Convention against Torture and Other Cruel, Inhuman or Degrading Treatment or Punishment,[1]

Noting that under the Geneva Conventions of 1949 [2] torture and inhuman treatment are a grave breach and that under the statutes of the International Tribunal for the Former Yugoslavia and the International Criminal Tribunal for the Prosecution of Persons Responsible for Genocide and Other Serious Violations of International Humanitarian Law Committed in the Territory of Rwanda and Rwandan Citizens Responsible for Genocide and Other Such Violations Committed in the Territory of Neighbouring States between 1 January and 31 December 1994 and the Rome Statute of the International Criminal Court[3] acts of torture constitute war crimes and can constitute crimes against humanity,

Commending the persistent efforts by non-governmental organizations, including the considerable network of centres for the rehabilitation of victims of torture, to combat torture and to alleviate the suffering of victims of torture,

1. *Condemns* all forms of torture and other cruel, inhuman or degrading treatment or punishment, including through intimidation, which are and shall remain prohibited at any time and in any place whatsoever and can thus never be justified, and calls upon all States to implement fully the absolute prohibition of torture and other cruel, inhuman or degrading treatment or punishment;

2. *Emphasizes* that States must take persistent, determined and effective measures to prevent and combat torture and other cruel, inhuman or degrading treatment or punishment, including their gender-based manifestations, and stresses that all acts of torture must be made offences under domestic criminal law;

3. *Also emphasizes* the importance of States ensuring proper follow-up to the recommendations and conclusions of the relevant treaty bodies and mechanisms, including the Committee against Torture and the Special Rapporteur of the Human Rights Council on torture and other cruel, inhuman or degrading treatment or punishment;

4. *Condemns* any action or attempt by States or public officials to legalize, authorize or acquiesce in torture and other cruel, inhuman or degrading treatment or punishment under any circumstances, including on grounds of national security or through judicial decisions;

5. *Stresses* that all allegations of torture or other cruel, inhuman or degrading treatment or punishment must be promptly and impartially examined by the competent national authority, that those who encourage, order, tolerate or perpetrate acts of torture must be held responsible and severely punished, including the officials in charge of the place of detention where the prohibited act is found to have been committed, and takes note in this respect of the Principles on the Effective Investigation and Documentation of Torture and Other Cruel, Inhuman or Degrading Treatment or Punishment (the Istanbul Principles)[4] as a useful

tool in efforts to combat torture and of the updated set of principles for the protection of human rights through action to combat impunity;[5]

6. *Emphasizes* that acts of torture are serious violations of international humanitarian law and in this regard constitute war crimes and can constitute crimes against humanity, and that the perpetrators of all acts of torture must be prosecuted and punished;

7. *Urges* States to ensure that any statement that is established to have been made as a result of torture shall not be invoked as evidence in any proceedings, except against a person accused of torture as evidence that the statement was made;

8. *Stresses* that States must not punish personnel who are involved in the custody, interrogation or treatment of any individual subjected to any form of arrest, detention or imprisonment or any other form of deprivation of liberty for not obeying orders to commit or conceal acts amounting to torture or other cruel, inhuman or degrading treatment or punishment;

9. *Urges* States not to expel, return ("refouler"), extradite or in any other way transfer a person to another State where there are substantial grounds for believing that the person would be in danger of being subjected to torture, and recognizes that diplomatic assurances, where used, do not release States from their obligations under international human rights, humanitarian and refugee law, in particular the principle of non-refoulement;

10. *Stresses* that national legal systems must ensure that victims of torture and other cruel, inhuman or degrading treatment or punishment obtain redress, are awarded fair and adequate compensation and receive appropriate social and medical rehabilitation, urges States to take effective measures to this end, and in this regard encourages the development of rehabilitation centres;

11. *Recalls* its resolution 43/173 of 9 December 1988 on the Body of Principles for the Protection of All Persons under Any Form of Detention or Imprisonment, and in this context stresses that ensuring that any individual arrested or detained is promptly brought before a judge or other independent judicial officer in person and permitting prompt and regular medical care and legal counsel as well as visits by family members and independent monitoring mechanisms are effective measures for the prevention of torture and other cruel, inhuman or degrading treatment and punishment;

12. *Reminds* all States that prolonged incommunicado detention or detention in secret places may facilitate the perpetration of torture and other cruel, inhuman or degrading treatment or punishment and can in itself constitute a form of such treatment, and urges all States to respect the safeguards concerning the liberty, security and dignity of the person;

13. *Calls upon* all States to take appropriate effective legislative, administrative, judicial and other measures to prevent and prohibit the production, trade, export and use of equipment that is specifically designed to inflict torture or other cruel, inhuman or degrading treatment;

14. *Urges* all States that have not yet done so to become parties to the Convention against Torture and Other Cruel, Inhuman or Degrading Treatment or Punishment[1] as a matter of priority;

15. *Invites* all States parties to the Convention that have not yet done so to make the declarations provided for in articles 21 and 22 of the Convention concerning inter-State and

individual communications, to consider the possibility of withdrawing their reservations to article 20 of the Convention and to notify the Secretary-General of their acceptance of the amendments to articles 17 and 18 of the Convention as soon as possible;

16. *Urges* States parties to comply strictly with their obligations under the Convention, including, in view of the high number of reports not submitted in time, their obligation to submit reports in accordance with article 19 of the Convention, and invites States parties to incorporate a gender perspective and information concerning children and juveniles and persons with disabilities when submitting reports to the Committee against Torture;

17. *Acknowledges with appreciation* the entry into force of the Optional Protocol to the Convention against Torture and Other Cruel, Inhuman or Degrading Treatment or Punishment,[6] and calls upon States parties to give early consideration to signing and ratifying the Optional Protocol, which provides further measures for use in the fight against and prevention of torture and other cruel, inhuman or degrading treatment or punishment;

18. *Welcomes* the work of the Committee against Torture and its report submitted in accordance with article 24 of the Convention,[7] and recommends that the Committee continue to include information on the follow-up by States to its recommendations;

19. *Calls upon* the United Nations High Commissioner for Human Rights, in conformity with her mandate established by the General Assembly in its resolution 48/141 of 20 December 1993, to continue to provide, at the request of States, advisory services for the prevention of torture and other cruel, inhuman or degrading treatment or punishment, including for the preparation of national reports to the Committee against Torture and for the establishment and operation of national preventive mechanisms, as well as technical assistance for the development, production and distribution of teaching material for this purpose;

20. *Notes with appreciation* the interim report of the Special Rapporteur on torture and other cruel, inhuman or degrading treatment or punishment,[8] and encourages the Special Rapporteur to continue to include in his recommendations proposals on the prevention and investigation of torture and other cruel, inhuman or degrading treatment or punishment, including its gender-based manifestations;

21. *Requests* the Special Rapporteur to continue to consider including in his report information on the follow-up by States to his recommendations, visits and communications, including progress made and problems encountered, and on other official contacts;

22. *Calls upon* all States to cooperate with and assist the Special Rapporteur in the performance of his task, to supply all necessary information requested by the Special Rapporteur, to fully and expeditiously respond to and follow up his urgent appeals, to give serious consideration to responding favourably to requests by the Special Rapporteur to visit their countries and to enter into a constructive dialogue with the Special Rapporteur on requested visits to their countries as well as with respect to the follow-up to his recommendations;

23. *Stresses* the need for the continued regular exchange of views among the Committee against Torture, the Subcommittee on Prevention of Torture and Other Cruel, Inhuman or Degrading Treatment or Punishment, the Special Rapporteur and other relevant United Nations mechanisms and bodies, as well as for the pursuance of cooperation with relevant United Nations programmes, notably the United Nations Crime Prevention and Criminal Justice Programme, with a view to enhancing further their effectiveness and cooperation on issues relating to torture, inter alia, by improving their coordination;

24. *Recognizes* the global need for international assistance to victims of torture, stresses the importance of the work of the Board of Trustees of the United Nations Voluntary Fund for Victims of Torture, and appeals to all States and organizations to contribute annually to the Fund, preferably with a substantial increase in the level of contributions;

25. *Requests* the Secretary-General to continue to transmit to all States the appeals of the General Assembly for contributions to the Fund and to include the Fund on an annual basis among the programmes for which funds are pledged at the United Nations Pledging Conference for Development Activities;

26. *Also requests* the Secretary-General to ensure, within the overall budgetary framework of the United Nations, the provision of adequate staff and facilities for the bodies and mechanisms involved in preventing and combating torture and assisting victims of torture commensurate with the strong support expressed by Member States for preventing and combating torture and assisting victims of torture;

27. *Further requests* the Secretary-General to submit to the Human Rights Council and to the General Assembly at its sixty-second session a report on the status of the Convention and a report on the operations of the Fund;

28. *Calls upon* all States, the Office of the United Nations High Commissioner for Human Rights and other United Nations bodies and agencies, as well as relevant intergovernmental and non-governmental organizations, to commemorate, on 26 June, the United Nations International Day in Support of Victims of Torture;

29. *Decides* to consider at its sixty-second session the reports of the Secretary-General, including the report on the United Nations Voluntary Fund for Victims of Torture, the report of the Committee against Torture and the interim report of the Special Rapporteur on torture and other cruel, inhuman or degrading treatment or punishment.

81st plenary meeting
19 December 2006

---

1 United Nations, *Treaty Series*, vol. 1465, No. 24841.

2 Ibid., vol. 75, Nos. 970–973.

3 Ibid., vol. 2187, No. 38544.

4 Resolution 55/89, annex.

5 See E/CN.4/2005/102/Add.1.

6 Resolution 57/199, annex.

7 *Official Records of the General Assembly, Sixty-first Session, Supplement No. 44* (A/61/44).

8 See A/61/259.

Resolution 61/154

[on the report of the Third Committee (A/61/443/Add.2 and Corr.1)]

61/154. The human rights situation arising from the recent Israeli military operations in Lebanon

The General Assembly,

Reaffirming the Universal Declaration of Human Rights[1] and the Vienna Declaration and Programme of Action of 1993,[2] and recalling the International Covenant on Civil and Political Rights,[3] the International Covenant on Economic, Social and Cultural Rights,[3] the Convention on the Rights of the Child[4] and other human rights instruments,

Guided by relevant human rights instruments and international humanitarian law, in particular the Hague Conventions of 1899 and 1907 respecting the Laws and Customs of War on Land,[5] which prohibit attacks on and bombardment of civilian populations and objects and lay down obligations for general protection against dangers arising from military operations against civilian objects, hospitals, relief materials and means of transportation,

Recalling the commitments of the High Contracting Parties to the Geneva Conventions of 12 August 1949[6] and the Additional Protocols thereto of 1977,[7]

Recalling also the World Declaration on the Survival, Protection and Development of Children and the Plan of Action for Implementing the World Declaration on the Survival, Protection and Development of Children in the 1990s adopted by the World Summit for Children, held in New York on 29 and 30 September 1990,[8]

Stressing that the right to life constitutes the most fundamental of all human rights,

Emphasizing that human rights law and international humanitarian law are complementary and mutually reinforcing,

Bearing in mind Security Council resolution 1701 (2006) of 11 August 2006 and the statement by the President of the Council of 30 July 2006,[9]

Bearing in mind also Human Rights Council resolution S-2/1 entitled "The grave situation of human rights in Lebanon caused by Israeli military operations", adopted by the Council at its second special session on 11 August 2006,[10]

1. *Condemns* all acts of violence against civilians, including the bombardment by Israeli military forces of Lebanese civilians causing extensive loss of life and injuries, including among children, immense destruction of homes, properties, agricultural lands and vital civilian infrastructure, and the displacement of up to one million Lebanese civilians and outflows of refugees fleeing heavy shelling and bombardment directed against the civilian population, thus exacerbating the magnitude of human suffering in Lebanon;

2. *Emphasizes* the importance of the safety and well-being of all children;

3. *Expresses deep concern* about the negative consequences, including the mental and psychological impact, of the Israeli military operations for the wellbeing of Lebanese children;

4. *Emphasizes* that attacks against civilians, wherever they may occur, are contrary to international humanitarian law and constitute flagrant violations of human rights, condemns the killing of children, women, the elderly and other civilians in Lebanon, underlines that there should be no impunity for such acts, and calls particularly upon Israel to abide scrupulously

by its obligations under human rights law, in particular the Convention on the Rights of the Child,[4] and international humanitarian law;

5. *Deplores* the death of more than 1,100 civilians, one third being children, as a result of the Israeli military operations in Lebanon;

6. *Strongly condemns* the deliberate use by Israel of cluster munitions in Lebanon, most of which had been used in the seventy-two hours directly preceding the cessation of hostilities and after the adoption of Security Council resolution 1701 (2006), which left over one million unexploded cluster bomblets, threatening the lives of children and civilians and adversely affecting recovery and rebuilding efforts;

7. *Deplores* the environmental degradation caused by Israeli air strikes against power plants in Lebanon and their adverse impact on the health and wellbeing of children and other civilians;

8. *Calls upon* the international community to urgently provide the Government of Lebanon with financial assistance in support of the national early recovery, reconstruction and enhancing the national economy, including the rehabilitation of victims, return of displaced persons and restoration of the essential infrastructure, and expresses its appreciation to the Member States, United Nations bodies and intergovernmental, regional and non-governmental organizations that have provided and continue to provide assistance to the people and Government of Lebanon.

81st plenary meeting
19 December 2006

---

[1] Resolution 217 A (III).

[2] A/CONF.157/24 (Part I), chap. III.

[3] See resolution 2200 A (XXI), annex.

[4] United Nations, *Treaty Series*, vol. 1577, No. 27531.

[5] See Carnegie Endowment for International Peace, *The Hague Conventions and Declarations of 1899 and 1907* (New York, Oxford University Press, 1915)

[6] United Nations, *Treaty Series*, vol. 75, Nos. 970–973.

[7] Ibid., vol. 1125, Nos. 17512 and 17513.

[8] A/45/625, annex.

[9] S/PRST/2006/35; see *Resolutions and Decisions of the Security Council, 1 August 2005–31 July 2006.*

[10] See *Official Records of the General Assembly, Sixty-first Session, Supplement No. 53* (A/61/53), part three, chap. I.

Resolution 61/155

[on the report of the Third Committee (A/61/443/Add.2 and Corr.1)]

61/155. Missing persons

The General Assembly,

Guided by the purposes, principles and provisions of the Charter of the United Nations,

Guided also by the principles and norms of international humanitarian law, in particular the Geneva Conventions of 12 August 1949[1] and the Additional Protocols thereto of 1977,[2] as well as international standards of human rights, in particular the Universal Declaration of Human Rights,[3] the International Covenant on Economic, Social and Cultural Rights,[4] the International Covenant on Civil and Political Rights,[4] the Convention on the Elimination of All Forms of Discrimination against Women,[5] the Convention on the Rights of the Child[6] and the Vienna Declaration and Programme of Action adopted by the World Conference on Human Rights on 25 June 1993,[7]

Recalling all previous relevant resolutions on missing persons adopted by the General Assembly, as well as the resolutions adopted by the Commission on Human Rights,

Noting with deep concern that armed conflicts are continuing in various parts of the world, often resulting in serious violations of international humanitarian law and human rights law,

Bearing in mind the effective search for and identification of missing persons through traditional forensic methods, and recognizing that great technological progress has been achieved in the field of DNA forensic sciences, which could significantly assist efforts to identify missing persons,

Noting that the issue of persons reported missing in connection with international armed conflicts, in particular those who are victims of serious violations of international humanitarian law and human rights law, continues to have a negative impact on efforts to put an end to those conflicts and causes suffering to the families of missing persons, and stressing in this regard the need to address the issue from a humanitarian perspective, among others,

Recalling the observations and recommendations to address the problems of missing persons and of their families that were adopted at the International Conference of Governmental and Non-Governmental Experts on "The missing: action to resolve the problem of people unaccounted for as a result of armed conflict or internal violence and to assist their families", held in Geneva from 19 to 21 February 2003,

Recalling also the Agenda for Humanitarian Action, in particular its general objective 1, to "respect and restore the dignity of persons missing as a result of armed conflicts or other situations of armed violence and of their families", adopted at the Twenty-eighth International Conference of the Red Cross and Red Crescent, held in Geneva from 2 to 6 December 2003,

Taking note with appreciation of the ongoing regional efforts to address the question of missing persons,

1. *Urges* States strictly to observe and respect and ensure respect for the rules of international humanitarian law, as set out in the Geneva Conventions of 12 August 1949[1] and, where applicable, in the Additional Protocols thereto of 1977;[2]

2. *Calls upon* States that are parties to an armed conflict to take all appropriate measures to prevent persons from going missing in connection with armed conflict and account for persons reported missing as a result of such a situation;

3. *Reaffirms* the right of families to know the fate of their relatives reported missing in connection with armed conflicts;

4. *Also reaffirms* that each party to an armed conflict, as soon as circumstances permit and, at the latest, from the end of active hostilities, shall search for the persons who have been reported missing by an adverse party;

5. *Calls upon* States that are parties to an armed conflict to take all necessary measures, in a timely manner, to determine the identity and fate of persons reported missing in connection with the armed conflict and, to the greatest possible extent, to provide their family members, through appropriate channels, with all relevant information they have on their fate;

6. *Recognizes*, in this regard, the need for the collection, protection and management of data on missing persons according to international and national legal norms and standards, and urges States to cooperate with each other and with other concerned actors working in this area, inter alia, by providing all relevant and appropriate information related to missing persons;

7. *Requests* States to pay the utmost attention to cases of children reported missing in connection with armed conflicts and to take appropriate measures to search for and identify those children;

8. *Invites* States that are parties to an armed conflict to cooperate fully with the International Committee of the Red Cross in establishing the fate of missing persons and to adopt a comprehensive approach to this issue, including all practical and coordination mechanisms as may be necessary, based on humanitarian considerations only;

9. *Urges* States and encourages intergovernmental and non-governmental organizations to take all necessary measures at the national, regional and international levels to address the problem of persons reported missing in connection with armed conflicts and to provide appropriate assistance as requested by the concerned States, and welcomes, in this regard, the establishment and efforts of commissions and working groups on missing persons;

10. *Calls upon* States, without prejudice to their efforts to determine the fate of persons missing in connection with armed conflicts, to take appropriate steps with regard to the legal situation of the missing persons and that of their family members, in fields such as social welfare, financial matters, family law and property rights;

11. *Invites* relevant human rights mechanisms and procedures, as appropriate, to address the problem of persons reported missing in connection with armed conflicts in their forthcoming reports to the General Assembly;

12. *Requests* the Secretary-General to bring the present resolution to the attention of all Governments, the competent United Nations bodies, the specialized agencies, regional intergovernmental organizations and international humanitarian organizations;

13. *Also requests* the Secretary-General to submit a comprehensive report on the implementation of the present resolution, including relevant recommendations, to the Human Rights Council at its relevant session and to the General Assembly at its sixty-third session;

14. *Decides* to consider the question at its sixty-third session.

81st plenary meeting
19 December 2006

---

[1] United Nations, *Treaty Series*, vol. 75, Nos. 970–973.

[2] Ibid., vol. 1125, Nos. 17512 and 17513.

[3] Resolution 217 A (III).

[4] See resolution 2200 A (XXI), annex.

[5] United Nations, *Treaty Series*, vol. 1249, No. 20378.

[6] Ibid., vol. 1577, No. 27531.

[7] A/CONF.157/24 (Part I), chap. III.

Resolution 61/156

[on the report of the Third Committee (A/61/443/Add.2 and Corr.1)]

61/156. Globalization and its impact on the full enjoyment of all human rights

The General Assembly,

Guided by the purposes and principles of the Charter of the United Nations, and expressing, in particular, the need to achieve international cooperation in promoting and encouraging respect for human rights and fundamental freedoms for all without distinction,

Recalling the Universal Declaration of Human Rights,[1] as well as the Vienna Declaration and Programme of Action adopted by the World Conference on Human Rights on 25 June 1993,[2]

Recalling also the International Covenant on Civil and Political Rights[3] and the International Covenant on Economic, Social and Cultural Rights,[3]

Recalling further the Declaration on the Right to Development adopted by the General Assembly in its resolution 41/128 of 4 December 1986,

Recalling the United Nations Millennium Declaration[4] and the outcome documents of the twenty-third[5] and twenty-fourth[6] special sessions of the General Assembly, held in New York from 5 to 10 June 2000 and in Geneva from 26 June to 1 July 2000, respectively,

Recalling also its resolution 60/152 of 16 December 2005,

Recalling further Commission on Human Rights resolution 2005/17 of 14 April 2005 on globalization and its impact on the full enjoyment of all human rights,[7]

Realizing that globalization affects all countries differently and makes them more exposed to external developments, positive as well as negative, inter alia, in the field of human rights,

Realizing also that globalization is not merely an economic process, but that it also has social, political, environmental, cultural and legal dimensions, which have an impact on the full enjoyment of all human rights,

Reaffirming the commitment contained in paragraphs 19 and 47 of the 2005 World Summit Outcome[8] to promote fair globalization and the development of the productive sectors in developing countries to enable them to participate more effectively in and benefit from the process of globalization,

Realizing the need to undertake a thorough, independent and comprehensive assessment of the social, environmental and cultural impact of globalization on societies,

Recognizing in each culture a dignity and value that deserve recognition, respect and preservation, convinced that, in their rich variety and diversity and in the reciprocal influences that they exert on one another, all cultures form part of the common heritage belonging to all humankind, and aware that the risk of a global monoculture poses more of a threat if the developing world remains poor and marginalized,

Recognizing also that multilateral mechanisms have a unique role to play in meeting the challenges and opportunities presented by globalization,

Emphasizing the global character of the migratory phenomenon, the importance of international, regional and bilateral cooperation and the need to protect the human rights of migrants, particularly at a time in which migration flows have increased in the globalized economy,

Expressing concern at the negative impact of international financial turbulence on social and economic development and on the full enjoyment of all human rights,

Recognizing that globalization should be guided by the fundamental principles that underpin the corpus of human rights, such as equity, participation, accountability, non-discrimination at both the national and the international levels, respect for diversity, tolerance and international cooperation and solidarity,

Emphasizing that the existence of widespread extreme poverty inhibits the full and effective enjoyment of human rights; its immediate alleviation and eventual elimination must remain a high priority for the international community,

Strongly reiterating the determination to ensure the timely and full realization of the development goals and objectives agreed at the major United Nations conferences and summits, including those agreed at the Millennium Summit that are described as the Millennium Development Goals, which have helped to galvanize efforts towards poverty eradication,

Deeply concerned at the inadequacy of measures to narrow the widening gap between the developed and the developing countries, and within countries, which has contributed, inter alia, to deepening poverty and has adversely affected the full enjoyment of all human rights, in particular in developing countries,

Noting that human beings strive for a world that is respectful of human rights and cultural diversity and that, in this regard, they work to ensure that all activities, including those affected by globalization, are consistent with those aims,

1. *Recognizes* that, while globalization, by its impact on, inter alia, the role of the State, may affect human rights, the promotion and protection of all human rights is first and foremost the responsibility of the State;

2. *Emphasizes* that development should be at the centre of the international economic agenda and that coherence between national development strategies and international obligations and commitments is imperative for an enabling environment for development and an inclusive and equitable globalization;

3. *Reaffirms* that narrowing the gap between rich and poor, both within and between countries, is an explicit goal at the national and international levels, as part of the effort to create an enabling environment for the full enjoyment of all human rights;

4. *Reaffirms also* the commitment to create an environment at both the national and the global levels that is conducive to development and to the elimination of poverty through, inter alia, good governance within each country and at the international level, transparency in the financial, monetary and trading systems and commitment to an open, equitable, rule-based, predictable and non-discriminatory multilateral trading and financial system;

5. *Recognizes* that, while globalization offers great opportunities, the fact that its benefits are very unevenly shared and its costs unevenly distributed represents an aspect of the process that affects the full enjoyment of all human rights, in particular in developing countries;

6. *Welcomes* the report of the United Nations High Commissioner for Human Rights on globalization and its impact on the full enjoyment of human rights,[9] which focuses on the liberalization of agricultural trade and its impact on the realization of the right to development,

including the right to food, and takes note of the conclusions and recommendations contained therein;

7. *Calls upon* Member States, relevant agencies of the United Nations system, intergovernmental organizations and civil society to promote equitable and environmentally sustainable economic growth for managing globalization so that poverty is systematically reduced and the international development targets are achieved;

8. *Recognizes* that only through broad and sustained efforts, including policies and measures at the global level to create a shared future based upon our common humanity in all its diversity, can globalization be made fully inclusive and equitable and have a human face, thus contributing to the full enjoyment of all human rights;

9. *Underlines* the urgent need to establish an equitable, transparent and democratic international system to strengthen and broaden the participation of developing countries in international economic decision-making and norm-setting;

10. *Affirms* that globalization is a complex process of structural transformation, with numerous interdisciplinary aspects, which has an impact on the enjoyment of civil, political, economic, social and cultural rights, including the right to development;

11. *Affirms also* that the international community should strive to respond to the challenges and opportunities posed by globalization in a manner that ensures respect for the cultural diversity of all;

12. *Underlines*, therefore, the need to continue to analyse the consequences of globalization for the full enjoyment of all human rights;

13. *Takes note* of the report of the Secretary-General,[10] and requests him to seek further the views of Member States and relevant agencies of the United Nations system and to submit a substantive report on the subject to the General Assembly at its sixty-second session.

81st plenary meeting
19 December 2006

[1] Resolution 217 A (III).

[2] A/CONF.157/24 (Part I), chap. III.

[3] See resolution 2200 A (XXI), annex.

[4] See resolution 55/2.

[5] Resolution S-23/2, annex, and resolution S-23/3, annex.

[6] Resolution S-24/2, annex.

[7] See *Official Records of the Economic and Social Council, 2005, Supplement No. 3* and corrigendum (E/2005/23 and Corr.1), chap. II, sect. A.

[8] See resolution 60/1.

[9] E/CN.4/2002/54.

[10] A/61/281.

Resolution 61/157

[on the report of the Third Committee (A/61/443/Add.2 and Corr.1)]

61/157. Human rights and extreme poverty

The General Assembly,

Reaffirming the Universal Declaration of Human Rights,[1] the International Covenant on Civil and Political Rights,[2] the International Covenant on Economic, Social and Cultural Rights,[2] the Convention on the Elimination of All Forms of Discrimination against Women,[3] the Convention on the Rights of the Child,[4] the International Convention on the Elimination of All Forms of Racial Discrimination[5] and other human rights instruments adopted by the United Nations,

Recalling its resolution 47/196 of 22 December 1992, by which it declared 17 October the International Day for the Eradication of Poverty, and its resolution 50/107 of 20 December 1995, by which it proclaimed the first United Nations Decade for the Eradication of Poverty (1997–2006), as well as its resolution 59/186 of 20 December 2004 and its previous resolutions on human rights and extreme poverty, in which it reaffirmed that extreme poverty and exclusion from society constitute a violation of human dignity and that urgent national and international action is therefore required to eliminate them,

Recalling also its resolution 52/134 of 12 December 1997, in which it recognized that the enhancement of international cooperation in the field of human rights was essential for the understanding, promotion and protection of all human rights,

Reaffirming the internationally agreed development goals, including the Millennium Development Goals,

Deeply concerned that extreme poverty persists in all countries of the world, regardless of their economic, social and cultural situation, and that its extent and manifestations, such as hunger, trafficking in human beings, disease, lack of adequte shelter, illiteracy and hopelessness, are particularly severe in developing countries, while acknowledging the significant progress made in parts of the world combating extreme poverty,

Deeply concerned also that gender inequality, violence and discrimination exacerbate extreme poverty, disproportionally impacting women and girls,

Recalling Commission on Human Rights resolution 2005/16 of 14 April 2005,[6] as well as resolution 2005/9 of 8 August 2005 of the Subcommission on the Promotion and Protection of Human Rights,[7]

Welcoming the Summit of World Leaders for Action against Hunger and Poverty of 20 September 2004, convened in New York by the Presidents of Brazil, Chile and France and the Prime Minister of Spain with the support of the Secretary-General,

Recognizing that the eradication of extreme poverty is a major challenge within the process of globalization and requires coordinated and continued policies through decisive national action and international cooperation,

Stressing the necessity of better understanding the causes and consequences of extreme poverty,

Reaffirming that, since the existence of widespread extreme poverty inhibits the full and effective enjoyment of human rights and might, in some situations, constitute a threat to the right to life, its immediate alleviation and eventual eradication must remain a high priority for the international community,

Reaffirming also that democracy, development and the full and effective enjoyment of human rights and fundamental freedoms are interdependent and mutually reinforcing and contribute to the eradication of extreme poverty,

Recalling Human Rights Council decision 1/102 of 30 June 2006,[8]

1. *Reaffirms* that extreme poverty and exclusion from society constitute a violation of human dignity and that urgent national and international action is therefore required to eliminate them;

2. *Reaffirms also* that it is essential for States to foster participation by the poorest people in the decision-making process in the societies in which they live, in the promotion of human rights and in efforts to combat extreme poverty, and that it is essential for people living in poverty and vulnerable groups to be empowered to organize themselves and to participate in all aspects of political, economic and social life, in particular the planning and implementation of policies that affect them, thus enabling them to become genuine partners in development;

3. *Emphasizes* that extreme poverty is a major issue to be addressed by Governments, civil society and the United Nations system, including international financial institutions, and in this context reaffirms that political commitment is a prerequisite for the eradication of poverty;

4. *Reaffirms* that the existence of widespread absolute poverty inhibits the full and effective enjoyment of human rights and renders democracy and popular participation fragile;

5. *Recognizes* the need to promote respect for human rights and fundamental freedoms in order to address the most pressing social needs of people living in poverty, including through the design and development of appropriate mechanisms to strengthen and consolidate democratic institutions and governance;

6. *Reaffirms* the commitments contained in the United Nations Millennium Declaration,[9] in particular the commitments to spare no effort to fight against extreme poverty and to achieve development and poverty eradication, including the commitment to halve, by 2015, the proportion of the world's people whose income is less than one United States dollar a day and the proportion of people who suffer from hunger;

7. *Reaffirms also* the commitment made at the 2005 World Summit to eradicate poverty and promote sustained economic growth, sustainable development and global prosperity for all, including women and girls;[10]

8. *Reaffirms further* the critical role of both formal and informal education in the achievement of poverty eradication and other development goals as envisaged in the Millennium Declaration, in particular basic education and training for eradicating illiteracy, and efforts towards expanded secondary and higher education as well as vocational education and technical training, especially for girls and women, the creation of human resources and infrastructure capabilities and the empowerment of those living in poverty, and in this context

reaffirms the Dakar Framework for Action adopted at the World Education Forum in 2000[11] and recognizes the importance of the United Nations Educational, Scientific and Cultural Organization strategy for the eradication of poverty, especially extreme poverty, in supporting the Education for All programmes as a tool to achieve the millennium development goal of universal primary education by 2015;

9. *Invites* the United Nations High Commissioner for Human Rights to continue to give high priority to the question of the relationship between extreme poverty and human rights, and also invites her to further pursue the work in this area;

10. *Calls upon* States, United Nations bodies, in particular the Office of the United Nations High Commissioner for Human Rights and the United Nations Development Programme, intergovernmental organizations and non-governmental organizations to continue to give appropriate attention to the links between human rights and extreme poverty, and encourages the private sector and the international financial institutions to proceed likewise;

11. *Welcomes* the efforts of entities throughout the United Nations system to incorporate the Millennium Declaration and the internationally agreed development goals set out therein into their work;

12. *Takes note* of the reports of the independent expert on the question of human rights and extreme poverty[12] submitted to the Commission on Human Rights at its sixty-first and sixty-second sessions and presented to the Human Rights Council at its second session;

13. *Decides* to consider the question further at its sixty-third session under the sub-item entitled "Human rights questions, including alternative approaches for improving the effective enjoyment of human rights and fundamental freedoms".

81st plenary meeting
19 December 2006

---

[1] Resolution 217 A (III).

[2] See resolution 2200 A (XXI), annex.

[3] United Nations, *Treaty Series*, vol. 1249, No. 20378.

[4] Ibid., vol. 1577, No. 27531.

[5] Ibid., vol. 660, No. 9464.

[6] See *Official Records of the Economic and Social Council, 2005, Supplement No. 3* and corrigendum (E/2005/23 and Corr.1), chap. II, sect. A.

[7] See E/CN.4/2006/2-E/CN.4/Sub.2/2005/44, chap. II, sect. A.

[8] See *Official Records of the General Assembly, Sixty-first Session, Supplement No. 53* (A/61/53), part one, chap. II, sect. B.

[9] See resolution 55/2.

[10] See resolution 60/1.

[11] See United Nations Educational, Scientific and Cultural Organization, *Final Report of the World Education Forum, Dakar, Senegal, 26–28 April 2000* (Paris, 2000).

[12] E/CN.4/2005/49 and E/CN.4/2006/43 and Add.1.

Resolution 61/158

[on the report of the Third Committee (A/61/443/Add.2 and Corr.1)]

61/158. Subregional Centre for Human Rights and Democracy in Central Africa

The General Assembly,

Recalling its resolution 55/105 of 4 December 2000 concerning regional arrangements for the promotion and protection of human rights,

Recalling also its resolutions 55/34 B of 20 November 2000 and 55/233 of 23 December 2000, section III of its resolution 55/234 of 23 December 2000, and its resolutions 58/176 of 22 December 2003, 59/183 of 20 December 2004 and 60/151 of 16 December 2005 on the Subregional Centre for Human Rights and Democracy in Central Africa,

Recalling further that the World Conference on Human Rights recommended that more resources be made available for the strengthening of regional arrangements for the promotion and protection of human rights under the programme of technical cooperation in the field of human rights of the Office of the United Nations High Commissioner for Human Rights,[1]

Recalling the report of the High Commissioner,[2]

Taking note of the holding of the twenty-third and twenty-fourth ministerial meetings of the United Nations Standing Advisory Committee on Security Questions in Central Africa in Brazzaville from 29 August to 2 September 2006 and in Kigali from 25 to 29 September 2006,

Taking note also of the report of the Secretary-General,[3]

Welcoming the 2005 World Summit Outcome,[4] in particular the decision confirmed therein to double the regular budget of the Office of the High Commissioner over the next five years,

1. *Welcomes* the activities of the Subregional Centre for Human Rights and Democracy in Central Africa at Yaoundé;

2. *Notes with satisfaction* the support provided for the establishment of the Centre by the host country;

3. *Requests* the Secretary-General and the United Nations High Commissioner for Human Rights to provide additional funds and human resources within the existing Office of the United Nations High Commissioner for Human Rights to enable the Centre to respond positively and effectively to the growing needs in the promotion and protection of human rights and in developing a culture of democracy and the rule of law in the Central African subregion;

4. *Requests* the Secretary-General to submit to the General Assembly at its sixty-second session a report on the implementation of the present resolution.

81st plenary meeting
19 December 2006

---

[1] See A/CONF.157/24 (Part I), chap. III.

[2] *Official Records of the General Assembly, Fifty-sixth Session, Supplement No. 36*, addendum (A/56/36/Add.1).

[3] A/61/352.

[4] See resolution 60/1.

Resolution 61/159

[on the report of the Third Committee (A/61/443/Add.2 and Corr.1)]

61/159. Composition of the staff of the Office of the United Nations High Commissioner for Human Rights

The General Assembly,

Recalling paragraph 5 (*g*) of its resolution 60/251 of 15 March 2006, in which it decided that the Human Rights Council should assume the role and responsibilities of the Commission on Human Rights relating to the work of the Office of the United Nations High Commissioner for Human Rights, as decided by the General Assembly in its resolution 48/141 of 20 December 1993,

Taking note of all relevant resolutions on this issue adopted by the General Assembly and the Commission on Human Rights,

Taking note also of the relevant reports of the United Nations High Commissioner for Human Rights[1] and the Joint Inspection Unit,[2]

Bearing in mind that the imbalance in the actual composition of the staff could result in diminishing the effectiveness of the work of the Office of the High Commissioner if it is perceived to be culturally biased and unrepresentative of the United Nations as a whole,

Regretting that efforts to address the imbalance regarding the regional geographical diversity of the staff have not resulted in a significant improvement, and noting the low representation from the United Nations regional groups of African, Asian, Eastern European, and Latin American and Caribbean States in the staff of the Office of the High Commissioner,

Reaffirming that the Fifth Committee is the appropriate Main Committee of the General Assembly entrusted with responsibilities for administrative and budgetary matters,

1. *Decides*, while considering the report of the Joint Inspection Unit:[2]

(*a*) To provide concrete support and guidance to the United Nations High Commissioner for Human Rights in her ongoing efforts to overcome the status quo;

(*b*) To allow, in the effort to redress the specific geographical imbalance of the Office of the United Nations High Commissioner for Human Rights, the establishment of a temporary mechanism whereby recruitment of staff in the Office at the P-2 level would not be restricted to successful candidates from the national competitive examination;

(*c*) To re-evaluate the financing of human rights activities, as noted in the report of the Joint Inspection Unit, with a view to increasing the support from core resources;

2. *Encourages* participation from a broader range of Member States in the associate experts programme, and, in this respect, urges participants to increase sponsorship of associate experts from developing countries;

3. *Requests* the Joint Inspection Unit to assist the Human Rights Council to monitor systematically the implementation of the present resolution, inter alia, by submitting to the Human Rights Council in May 2009 a follow-up comprehensive report on the implementation of

the recommendations contained in the report of the Joint Inspection Unit pending their fulfilment;

4. *Requests* the High Commissioner:

(*a*) To take further measures for the full and effective implementation of the recommendations contained in the report of the Joint Inspection Unit;

(*b*) To submit a comprehensive and updated report on the basis of paragraph 26 (*e*) of Commission on Human Rights resolution 2005/72 of 20 April 2005[3] to the Human Rights Council at its fourth session and to the General Assembly at its sixty-third session;

5. *Requests* the President of the General Assembly at its sixty-first session to bring those recommendations to the attention of the Fifth Committee, as soon as possible, for its consideration.

81st plenary meeting
19 December 2006

[1] E/CN.4/2006/103.

[2] JIU/REP/2006/3.

[3] See *Official Records of the Economic and Social Council, 2005, Supplement No. 3* and corrigendum (E/2005/23 and Corr.1), chap. II, sect. A.

Resolution 61/160

[on the report of the Third Committee (A/61/443/Add.2 and Corr.1)]

61/160. Promotion of a democratic and equitable international order

The General Assembly,

Recalling its previous resolutions on the promotion of a democratic and equitable international order, including resolution 59/193 of 20 December 2004, and taking note of Commission on Human Rights resolution 2005/57 of 20 April 2005,[1]

Reaffirming the commitment of all States to fulfil their obligations to promote universal respect for, and observance and protection of, all human rights and fundamental freedoms for all, in accordance with the Charter of the United Nations, other instruments relating to human rights and international law,

Affirming that the enhancement of international cooperation for the promotion and protection of all human rights should continue to be carried out in full conformity with the purposes and principles of the Charter and international law as set forth in Articles 1 and 2 of the Charter and, inter alia, with full respect for sovereignty, territorial integrity, political independence, the non-use of force or the threat of force in international relations and non-intervention in matters that are essentially within the domestic jurisdiction of any State,

Recalling the Preamble to the Charter, in particular the determination to reaffirm faith in fundamental human rights, in the dignity and worth of the human person and in the equal rights of men and women and of nations large and small,

Reaffirming that everyone is entitled to a social and international order in which the rights and freedoms set forth in the Universal Declaration of Human Rights[2] can be fully realized,

Reaffirming also the determination expressed in the Preamble to the Charter to save succeeding generations from the scourge of war, to establish conditions under which justice and respect for the obligations arising from treaties and other sources of international law can be maintained, to promote social progress and better standards of life in larger freedom, to practice tolerance and good-neighbourliness, and to employ international machinary for the promotion of the economic and social advancement of all peoples,

Considering the major changes taking place on the international scene and the aspirations of all peoples for an international order based on the principles enshrined in the Charter, including promoting and encouraging respect for human rights and fundamental freedoms for all and respect for the principle of equal rights and self-determination of peoples, peace, democracy, justice, equality, the rule of law, pluralism, development, better standards of living and solidarity,

Considering also that the Universal Declaration of Human Rights proclaims that all human beings are born free and equal in dignity and rights and that everyone is entitled to all the rights and freedoms set out therein, without distinction of any kind, such as race, colour, sex, language, religion, political or other opinion, national or social origin, property, birth or other status,

Reaffirming that democracy, development and respect for human rights and fundamental freedoms are interdependent and mutually reinforcing, and that democracy is based on the freely expressed will of the people to determine their own political, economic, social and cultural systems and their full participation in all aspects of their lives,

Emphasizing that democracy is not only a political concept but that it also has economic and social dimensions,

Recognizing that democracy, respect for all human rights, including the right to development, transparent and accountable governance and administration in all sectors of society, and effective participation by civil society are an essential part of the necessary foundations for the realization of social and people-centred sustainable development,

Noting with concern that racism, racial discrimination, xenophobia and related intolerance may be aggravated by, inter alia, inequitable distribution of wealth, marginalization and social exclusion,

Underlining the fact that it is imperative for the international community to ensure that globalization becomes a positive force for all the world's people, and that only through broad and sustained efforts, based on common humanity in all its diversity, can globalization be made fully inclusive and equitable,

Stressing that efforts to make globalization fully inclusive and equitable must include policies and measures, at the global level, that correspond to the needs of developing countries and countries with economies in transition and are formulated and implemented with their effective participation,

Having listened to the peoples of the world, and recognizing their aspirations to justice, to equality of opportunity for all, to the enjoyment of their human rights, including the right to development, to live in peace and freedom and to equal participation without discrimination in economic, social, cultural, civil and political life,

Resolved to take all measures within its power to secure a democratic and equitable international order,

1. *Affirms* that everyone is entitled to a democratic and equitable international order;

2. *Also affirms* that a democratic and equitable international order fosters the full realization of all human rights for all;

3. *Calls upon* all Member States to fulfil their commitment expressed in Durban, South Africa, during the World Conference against Racism, Racial Discrimination, Xenophobia and Related Intolerance to maximize the benefits of globalization through, inter alia, the strengthening and enhancement of international cooperation to increase equality of opportunities for trade, economic growth and sustainable development, global communications through the use of new technologies, and increased intercultural exchange through the preservation and promotion of cultural diversity,[3] and reiterates that only through broad and sustained efforts to create a shared future based upon our common humanity and all its diversity can globalization be made fully inclusive and equitable;

4. *Affirms* that a democratic and equitable international order requires, inter alia, the realization of the following:

(*a*) The right of all peoples to self-determination, by virtue of which they can freely determine their political status and freely pursue their economic, social and cultural development;

(*b*) The right of peoples and nations to permanent sovereignty over their natural wealth and resources;

(*c*) The right of every human person and all peoples to development;

(*d*) The right of all peoples to peace;

(*e*) The right to an international economic order based on equal participation in the decision-making process, interdependence, mutual interest, solidarity and cooperation among all States;

(*f*) Solidarity, as a fundamental value, by virtue of which global challenges must be managed in a way that distributes costs and burdens fairly, in accordance with basic principles of equity and social justice, and ensures that those who suffer or benefit the least receive help from those who benefit the most;

(*g*) The promotion and consolidation of transparent, democratic, just and accountable international institutions in all areas of cooperation, in particular through the implementation of the principles of full and equal participation in their respective decision-making mechanisms;

(*h*) The right to equitable participation of all, without any discrimination, in domestic and global decision-making;

(*i*) The principle of equitable regional and gender-balanced representation in the composition of the staff of the United Nations system;

(*j*) The promotion of a free, just, effective and balanced international information and communications order, based on international cooperation for the establishment of a new equilibrium and greater reciprocity in the international flow of information, in particular correcting the inequalities in the flow of information to and from developing countries;

(*k*) Respect for cultural diversity and the cultural rights of all, since this enhances cultural pluralism, contributes to a wider exchange of knowledge and understanding of cultural backgrounds, advances the application and enjoyment of universally accepted human rights across the world and fosters stable, friendly relations among peoples and nations worldwide;

(*l*) The right of every person and all peoples to a healthy environment;

(*m*) The promotion of equitable access to benefits from the international distribution of wealth through enhanced international cooperation, in particular in economic, commercial and financial international relations;

(*n*) The enjoyment by everyone of ownership of the common heritage of mankind;

(*o*) The shared responsibility of the nations of the world for managing worldwide economic and social development as well as threats to international peace and security that should be exercised multilaterally;

5. *Stresses* the importance of preserving the rich and diverse nature of the international community of nations and peoples, as well as respect for national and regional particularities and various historical, cultural and religious backgrounds in the enhancement of international cooperation in the field of human rights;

6. *Also stresses* that all human rights are universal, indivisible, interdependent and interrelated and that the international community must treat human rights globally in a fair and equal manner, on the same footing and with the same emphasis, and reaffirms that, while the significance of national and regional particularities and various historical, cultural and religious backgrounds must be borne in mind, it is the duty of States, regardless of their political, economic and cultural systems, to promote and protect all human rights and fundamental freedoms;

7. *Urges* all actors on the international scene to build an international order based on inclusion, justice, equality and equity, human dignity, mutual understanding and promotion of and respect for cultural diversity and universal human rights, and to reject all doctrines of exclusion based on racism, racial discrimination, xenophobia and related intolerance;

8. *Reaffirms* that all States should promote the establishment, maintenance and strengthening of international peace and security and, to that end, should do their utmost to achieve general and complete disarmament under effective international control, as well as to ensure that the resources released by effective disarmament measures are used for comprehensive development, in particular that of the developing countries;

9. *Recalls* the proclamation by the General Assembly of its determination to work urgently for the establishment of an international economic order based on equity, sovereign equality,

interdependence, common interest and cooperation among all States, irrespective of their economic and social systems, which shall correct inequalities and redress existing injustices, make it possible to eliminate the widening gap between the developed and the developing countries, and ensure steadily accelerating economic and social development and peace and justice for present and future generations;[4]

10. *Reaffirms* that the international community should devise ways and means to remove the current obstacles and meet the challenges to the full realization of all human rights and to prevent the continuation of human rights violations resulting therefrom throughout the world;

11. *Urges* States to continue their efforts, through enhanced international cooperation, towards the promotion of a democratic and equitable international order;

12. *Requests* the Human Rights Council, the human rights treaty bodies, the Office of the United Nations High Commissioner for Human Rights and the special mechanisms extended by the Human Rights Council and the Subcommission on the Promotion and Protection of Human Rights or its successor expert advice mechanism to pay due attention, within their respective mandates, to the present resolution and to make contributions towards its implementation;

13. *Calls upon* the Office of the High Commissioner to build upon the issue of the promotion of a democratic and equitable international order;

14. *Requests* the Secretary-General to bring the present resolution to the attention of Member States, United Nations organs, bodies and components, intergovernmental organizations, in particular the Bretton Woods institutions, and non-governmental organizations, and to disseminate it on the widest possible basis;

15. *Decides* to continue consideration of the matter at its sixty-third session under the item entitled "Promotion and protection of human rights".

81st plenary meeting
19 December 2006

---

[1] See *Official Records of the Economic and Social Council, 2005, Supplement No. 3* and corrigendum (E/2005/23 and Corr.1), chap. II, sect. A.

[2] Resolution 217 A (III).

[3] See A/CONF.189/12 and Corr.1, chap. I.

[4] See resolution 3201 (S-VI).

Resolution 61/161

[on the report of the Third Committee (A/61/443/Add.2 and Corr.1)]

61/161. Elimination of all forms of intolerance and of discrimination based on religion or belief

The General Assembly,

Recalling its resolution 36/55 of 25 November 1981, by which it proclaimed the Declaration on the Elimination of All Forms of Intolerance and of Discrimination Based on Religion or Belief,

Recalling also article 18 of the International Covenant on Civil and Political Rights,[1] article 18 of the Universal Declaration of Human Rights[2] and other relevant human rights provisions,

Reaffirming the call of the World Conference on Human Rights upon all Governments to take all appropriate measures in compliance with their international obligations and with due regard to their respective legal systems to counter intolerance and related violence based on religion or belief, including practices of discrimination against women and the desecration of religious sites, recognizing that every individual has the right to freedom of thought, conscience, expression and religion,[3]

Reaffirming also the recognition by the World Conference on Human Rights that all human rights are universal, indivisible, interdependent and interrelated,

Recalling General Assembly resolution 56/6 of 9 November 2001 on the Global Agenda for Dialogue among Civilizations, in which the Assembly recognized the valuable contribution that dialogue among civilizations could make to an improved awareness and understanding of the common values shared by all humankind,

Acknowledging that in order to be effective, such a dialogue should be based on respect for the dignity of adherents of religions and beliefs, as well as respect for diversity and the universal promotion and protection of human rights,

Considering that religion or belief, for those who profess either, is one of the fundamental elements in their conception of life and that freedom of religion or belief should be fully respected and guaranteed,

Considering also that the disregard for and infringement of human rights and fundamental freedoms, in particular the right to freedom of thought, conscience, religion or belief, have brought, directly or indirectly, wars and great suffering to humankind,

Recognizing the importance of promoting dialogue among civilizations in order to enhance mutual understanding and knowledge among different social groups, cultures and civilizations in various areas, including culture, religion, education, information, science and technology, and in order to contribute to the promotion and protection of human rights and fundamental freedoms,

Recalling Commission on Human Rights resolution 2005/40 of 19 April 2005 on the elimination of all forms of intolerance and of discrimination based on religion or belief,[4]

Seriously concerned at all attacks upon religious places, sites and shrines, including any deliberate destruction of relics and monuments,

Seriously concerned also at the misuse of registration procedures as a means to limit the right to freedom of religion or belief of members of certain religious communities and at the limitations placed on religious publications,

Recognizing the important work carried out by the Human Rights Committee in providing guidance with respect to the scope of the freedom of religion or belief,

Convinced of the need to address, for instance, in the context of the Global Agenda for Dialogue among Civilizations[5] and the Alliance of Civilizations the rise in all parts of the world of religious extremism affecting the rights of individuals and groups based on religion or belief, the situations of violence and discrimination that affect many women as a result of religion or belief and the abuse of religion or belief for ends inconsistent with the Charter of the United Nations and other relevant instruments of the United Nations,

Resolved to adopt all necessary and appropriate measures for the speedy elimination of such intolerance based on religion or belief in all its forms and manifestations and prevent and combat discrimination based on religion or belief,

Noting that a formal or legal distinction at the national level between different kinds of religions or faith-based communities may, in some cases, constitute discrimination and may impinge on the enjoyment of the freedom of religion or belief,

Underlining the importance of education in the promotion of tolerance, which involves the acceptance by the public of, and its respect for, diversity, including with regard to religious expressions, and underlining also the fact that education, in particular at school, should contribute in a meaningful way to promoting tolerance and the elimination of discrimination based on religion or belief,

Recalling the importance of the International Consultative Conference on School Education in relation to Freedom of Religion or Belief, Tolerance and Non-Discrimination, held in Madrid from 23 to 25 November 2001, and continuing to invite Governments to give consideration to the Final Document adopted at the Conference,[6]

Emphasizing that States, regional organizations, non-governmental organizations, and religious bodies and the media have an important role to play in promoting tolerance, respect and freedom of religion or belief,

Recognizing the importance of interreligious and intrareligious dialogue and the role of religious and other non-governmental organizations in promoting tolerance in matters relating to religion or belief,

Believing that further intensified efforts are therefore required to promote and protect the right to freedom of thought, conscience, religion or belief and to eliminate all forms of hatred, intolerance and discrimination based on religion or belief, as also noted at the World Conference against Racism, Racial Discrimination, Xenophobia and Related Intolerance,

1. *Welcomes* the work and the report of the Special Rapporteur of the Human Rights Council on freedom of religion or belief;[7]

2. *Condemns* all forms of intolerance and of discrimination based on religion or belief;

3. *Encourages* the efforts made by the United Nations High Commissioner for Human Rights to coordinate in the field of human rights the activities of relevant United Nations organs, bodies and mechanisms dealing with all forms of intolerance and of discrimination based on religion or belief;

4. *Urges* States:

(*a*) To ensure that their constitutional and legislative systems provide adequate and effective guarantees of freedom of thought, conscience, religion and belief to all without distinction, inter alia, by the provision of effective remedies in cases where the right to freedom of thought, conscience, religion or belief, or the right to practise freely one's religion, including the right to change one's religion or belief, is violated;

(*b*) To exert the utmost efforts, in accordance with their national legislation and in conformity with international human rights law, to ensure that religious places, sites, shrines and symbols are fully respected and protected and to take additional measures in cases where they are vulnerable to desecration or destruction;

(*c*) To review, whenever relevant, existing registration practices in order to ensure the right of all persons to manifest their religion or belief, alone or in community with others and in public or in private;

(*d*) To ensure, in particular, the right of all persons to worship or assemble in connection with a religion or belief and to establish and maintain places for these purposes and the right of all persons to write, issue and disseminate relevant publications in these areas;

(*e*) To ensure that, in accordance with appropriate national legislation and in conformity with international human rights law, the freedom of all persons and members of groups to establish and maintain religious, charitable or humanitarian institutions is fully respected and protected;

(*f*) To ensure that no one within their jurisdiction is deprived of the right to life, liberty or security of person because of religion or belief and that no one is subjected to torture or arbitrary arrest or detention on that account and to bring to justice all perpetrators of violations of these rights;

(*g*) To ensure that all public officials and civil servants, including members of law enforcement bodies, the military and educators, in the course of their official duties, respect different religions and beliefs and do not discriminate on the grounds of religion or belief, and that all necessary and appropriate education or training is provided;

5. *Recognizes with deep concern* the overall rise in instances of intolerance and violence directed against members of many religious and other communities in various parts of the world, including cases motivated by Islamophobia, anti-Semitism and Christianophobia;

6. *Expresses concern* over the persistence of institutionalized social intolerance and discrimination practised against many in the name of religion or belief;

7. *Condemns* any advocacy of religious hatred that constitutes incitement to discrimination, hostility or violence, whether it involves the use of print, audio-visual and electronic media or any other means;

8. *Stresses* the need to strengthen dialogue, inter alia, through the Global Agenda for Dialogue among Civilizations[5] and the Alliance of Civilizations;

9. *Invites* States, the Special Rapporteur, the Office of the United Nations High Commissioner for Human Rights and other relevant entities of the United Nations system, such as the United Nations Educational, Scientific and Cultural Organization, and other international and regional organizations and civil society to consider promoting dialogue among civilizations in order to contribute to the elimination of intolerance and discrimination based on religion or belief, inter alia, by addressing the following issues within the framework of international standards of human rights:

(*a*) The rise of religious extremism affecting religions in all parts of the world;

(*b*) The situations of violence and discrimination that affect many women as a result of religion or belief;

(*c*) The use of religion or belief for ends inconsistent with the Charter of the United Nations and other relevant instruments of the United Nations;

10. *Urges* States to step up their efforts to eliminate intolerance and discrimination based on religion or belief, notably by:

(*a*) Taking all necessary and appropriate action, in conformity with international standards of human rights, to combat hatred, intolerance and acts of violence, intimidation and coercion motivated by intolerance based on religion or belief, as well as incitement to hostility and violence, with particular regard to religious minorities, and devoting particular attention to practices that violate the human rights of women and discriminate against women, including in the exercise of their right to freedom of thought, conscience, religion or belief;

(b) Promoting and encouraging, through education and other means, understanding, tolerance and respect in all matters relating to freedom of religion or belief;

(c) Undertaking all appropriate efforts to encourage those engaged in teaching to cultivate respect for all religions or beliefs, thereby promoting mutual understanding and tolerance;

11. *Invites* Governments, religious bodies and civil society to continue to undertake dialogue at all levels to promote greater tolerance, respect and understanding;

12. *Emphasizes* the importance of a continued and strengthened dialogue among and within religions or beliefs, including as encompassed in the dialogue among civilizations, to promote greater tolerance, respect and mutual understanding;

13. *Also emphasizes* that equating any religion with terrorism should be avoided, as this may have adverse consequences on the enjoyment of the right to freedom of religion or belief of all members of the religious communities concerned;

14. *Further emphasizes* that, as underlined by the Human Rights Committee, restrictions on the freedom to manifest religion or belief are permitted only if limitations are prescribed by law, are necessary to protect public safety, order, health or morals, or the fundamental rights and freedoms of others, and are applied in a manner that does not vitiate the right to freedom of thought, conscience and religion;

15. *Encourages* the continuing efforts in all parts of the world of the Special Rapporteur to examine incidents and governmental actions that are incompatible with the provisions of the Declaration on the Elimination of All Forms of Intolerance and of Discrimination Based on Religion or Belief[8] and to recommend remedial measures, as appropriate;

16. *Stresses* the need for the Special Rapporteur to continue to apply a gender perspective, inter alia, through the identification of gender-specific abuses, in the reporting process, including in information collection and in recommendations;

17. *Welcomes and encourages* the continuing efforts of all actors in society, including non-governmental organizations and bodies and groups based on religion or belief, to promote the implementation of the Declaration, and further encourages their work in promoting freedom of religion or belief and in highlighting cases of religious intolerance, discrimination and persecution;

18. *Recommends* that the United Nations and other actors, in their efforts to promote freedom of religion or belief, ensure the widest possible dissemination of the text of the Declaration in as many different languages as possible by United Nations information centres and by other interested bodies;

19. *Decides* to continue its consideration of measures to implement the Declaration;

20. *Welcomes* the work of the Special Rapporteur, and urges all Governments to cooperate fully with the Special Rapporteur and to respond favourably to her requests to visit their countries and to provide her with all necessary information so as to enable her to fulfil her mandate even more effectively;

21. *Requests* the Secretary-General to ensure that the Special Rapporteur receives the necessary resources to enable her to discharge her mandate fully;

22. *Requests* the Special Rapporteur to submit an interim report to the General Assembly at its sixty-second session;

23. *Decides* to consider the question of the elimination of all forms of religious intolerance at its sixty-second session under the item entitled "Promotion and protection of human rights".

81st plenary meeting
19 December 2006

---

[1] See resolution 2200 A (XXI), annex.

[2] Resolution 217 A (III).

[3] See A/CONF.157/24 (Part I), chap. III, sect. II, para. 22.

[4] See *Official Records of the Economic and Social Council, 2005, Supplement No. 3* and corrigendum (E/2005/23 and Corr.1), chap. II, sect. A.

[5] See resolution 56/6.

[6] E/CN.4/2002/73, appendix.

[7] See A/61/340.

[8] See resolution 36/55.

Resolution 61/162

[on the report of the Third Committee (A/61/443/Add.2 and Corr.1)]

61/162. Respect for the right to universal freedom of travel and the vital importance of family reunification

The General Assembly,

Recalling its resolution 59/203 of 20 December 2004,

Reaffirming that all human rights and fundamental freedoms are universal, indivisible, interdependent and interrelated,

Recalling the provisions of the Universal Declaration of Human Rights,[1] as well as article 12 of the International Covenant on Civil and Political Rights,[2]

Stressing that, as stated in the Programme of Action of the International Conference on Population and Development,[3] family reunification of documented migrants is an important factor in international migration and that remittances by documented migrants to their countries of origin often constitute a very important source of foreign exchange and are instrumental in improving the well-being of relatives left behind,

Noting with great concern that, while some positive developments have occurred during the past few years in the accomplishment of the objectives highlighted in resolutions 57/227 of 18 December 2002 and 59/203, in particular relating to facilitating the flow of remittances across international borders to help families, in certain cases it has been reported that measures have been adopted that increased the restrictions imposed on documented migrants in relation to family reunification and the possibility of sending remittances to their relatives in the country of origin,

Recalling that the family is the basic unit of society and, as such, should be strengthened, and that it is entitled to receive comprehensive protection and support,

1. *Once again calls upon* all States to guarantee the universally recognized freedom of travel to all foreign nationals legally residing in their territory;

2. *Reaffirms* that all Governments, in particular those of receiving countries, must recognize the vital importance of family reunification and promote its incorporation into national legislation in order to ensure protection of the unity of families of documented migrants;

3. *Calls upon* all States to allow, in conformity with international legislation, the free flow of financial remittances by foreign nationals residing in their territory to relatives in the country of origin;

4. *Also calls upon* all States to refrain from enacting, and to repeal if it already exists, legislation intended as a coercive measure that discriminates against individuals or groups of legal migrants by adversely affecting family reunification and the right to send financial remittances to relatives in the country of origin;

5. *Decides* to continue its consideration of the question at its sixty-third session under the item entitled "Promotion and protection of human rights".

81st plenary meeting
19 December 2006

---

[1] Resolution 217 A (III).

[2] See resolution 2200 A (XXI), annex.

[3] *Report of the International Conference on Population and Development, Cairo, 5–13 September 1994* (United Nations publication, Sales No. E.95.XIII.18), chap. I, resolution 1, annex.

Resolution 61/163

[on the report of the Third Committee (A/61/443/Add.2 and Corr.1)]

61/163. The right to food

The General Assembly,

Recalling all its previous resolutions on the issue of the right to food, in particular resolution 60/165 of 16 December 2005, as well as all resolutions of the Commission on Human Rights in this regard,

Recalling also the Universal Declaration of Human Rights,[1] which provides that everyone has the right to a standard of living adequate for her or his health and well-being, including food, the Universal Declaration on the Eradication of Hunger and Malnutrition[2] and the United Nations Millennium Declaration,[3]

Recalling further the provisions of the International Covenant on Economic, Social and Cultural Rights,[4] in which the fundamental right of every person to be free from hunger is recognized,

Bearing in mind the Rome Declaration on World Food Security and the World Food Summit Plan of Action[5] and the Declaration of the World Food Summit: five years later, adopted in Rome on 13 June 2002,[6]

Reaffirming the concrete recommendations contained in the Voluntary Guidelines to Support the Progressive Realization of the Right to Adequate Food in the Context of National Food Security, adopted by the Council of the Food and Agriculture Organization of the United Nations in November 2004,[7]

Reaffirming also that all human rights are universal, indivisible, interdependent and interrelaed,

Reaffirming further that a peaceful, stable and enabling political, social and economic environment, at both the national and the international levels, is the essential foundation that will enable States to give adequate priority to food security and poverty eradication,

Reiterating, as in the Rome Declaration on World Food Security and the Declaration of the World Food Summit: five years later, that food should not be used as an instrument of political or economic pressure, and reaffirming in this regard the importance of international cooperation and solidarity, as well as the necessity of refraining from unilateral measures that are not in accordance with international law and the Charter of the United Nations and that endanger food security,

Convinced that each State must adopt a strategy consistent with its resources and capacities to achieve its individual goals in implementing the recommendations contained in the Rome Declaration on World Food Security and the World Food Summit Plan of Action and, at the same time, cooperate regionally and internationally in order to organize collective solutions to global issues of food security in a world of increasingly interlinked institutions, societies and economies where coordinated efforts and shared responsibilities are essential,

Recognizing that the problems of hunger and food insecurity have global dimensions and that they are likely to persist and even to increase dramatically in some regions unless urgent, determined and concerted action is taken, given the anticipated increase in the world's population and the stress on natural resources,

Noting that the global environment continues to suffer degradation, causing a negative impact on the realization of the right to food, in particular in developing countries,

Expressing its deep concern at the number and scale of natural disasters, diseases and pests and their increasing impact in recent years, which have resulted in massive loss of life and livelihood and threatened agricultural production and food security, in particular in developing countries,

Stressing the importance of reversing the continuing decline of official development assistance devoted to agriculture, both in real terms and as a share of total official development assistance,

1. *Reaffirms* that hunger constitutes an outrage and a violation of human dignity and therefore requires the adoption of urgent measures at the national, regional and international levels for its elimination;

2. *Also reaffirms* the right of everyone to have access to safe and nutritious food, consistent with the right to adequate food and the fundamental right of everyone to be free from hunger, so as to be able to fully develop and maintain their physical and mental capacities;

3. *Considers it intolerable* that every five seconds a child under the age of 5 dies from hunger or hunger-related diseases somewhere in the world, that there are about 854 million undernourished people in the world and that, while the prevalence of hunger has diminished, the absolute number of undernourished people has been increasing in recent years when, according to the Food and Agriculture Organization of the United Nations, the planet could produce enough food to feed 12 billion people, twice the world's present population;

4. *Expresses its concern* that women and girls are disproportionately affected by hunger, food insecurity and poverty, in part as a result of gender inequality and discrimination, that in many countries, girls are twice as likely as boys to die from malnutrition and preventable childhood diseases, and that it is estimated that almost twice as many women as men suffer from malnutrition;

5. *Encourages* all States to take action to address gender inequality and discrimination against women, in particular where it contributes to the malnutrition of women and girls, including measures to ensure the full and equal realization of the right to food and ensuring that women have equal access to resources, including income, land and water, to enable them to feed themselves and their families;

6. *Encourages* the Special Rapporteur of the Human Rights Council on the right to food to continue mainstreaming a gender perspective in the fulfilment of his mandate, and encourages the Food and Agriculture Organization of the United Nations and all other United Nations bodies and mechanisms addressing the right to food and food insecurity to integrate a gender perspective into their relevant policies, programmes and activities;

7. *Encourages* all States to take steps with a view to achieving progressively the full realization of the right to food, including steps to promote the conditions for everyone to be free from hunger and, as soon as possible, to enjoy fully the right to food, and to create and adopt national plans to combat hunger;

8. *Stresses* that improving access to productive resources and public investment in rural development is essential for eradicating hunger and poverty, in particular in developing countries, including through the promotion of investments in appropriate, small-scale irrigation and water management technologies in order to reduce vulnerability to droughts;

9. *Stresses also* the importance of fighting hunger in rural areas, including through national efforts supported by international partnerships to stop desertification and land degradation and through investments and public policies that are specifically appropriate to the risk of drylands, and, in this regard, calls for the full implementation of the United Nations Convention to Combat Desertification in Those Countries Experiencing Serious Drought and/or Desertification, Particularly in Africa;[8]

10. *Acknowledges* that many indigenous organizations and representatives of indigenous communities have expressed in different forums their deep concerns over the obstacles and challenges they face for the full enjoyment of the right to food, and calls upon States to take special actions to combat the root causes of the disproportionately high level of hunger and malnutrition among indigenous peoples and the continuous discrimination against them;

11. *Requests* all States and private actors, as well as international organizations within their respective mandates, to take fully into account the need to promote the effective realization of the right to food for all, including in the ongoing negotiations in different fields;

12. *Stresses* the need to make efforts to mobilize and optimize the allocation and utilization of technical and financial resources from all sources, including external debt relief for developing countries, and to reinforce national actions to implement sustainable food security policies;

13. *Recognizes* the need for a successful conclusion of the Doha Development Round negotiations of the World Trade Organization as a contribution for creating international conditions that permit the realization of the right to food;

14. *Recalls* the importance of the New York Declaration on Action against Hunger and Poverty, and recommends the continuation of efforts aimed at identifying additional sources of financing for the fight against hunger and poverty;

15. *Recognizes* that the promises made at the World Food Summit in 1996 to halve the number of persons who are undernourished are not being fulfilled, and invites once again all international financial and development institutions, as well as the relevant United Nations agencies and funds, to give priority to and provide the necessary funding to realize the aim of halving by 2015 the proportion of people who suffer from hunger, as well as the right to food as set out in the Rome Declaration on World Food Security[5] and the United Nations Millennium Declaration;[3]

16. *Reaffirms* that integrating food and nutritional support, with the goal that all people at all times will have access to sufficient, safe and nutritious food to meet their dietary needs and food preferences for an active and healthy life, is part of a comprehensive response to the spread of HIV/AIDS, tuberculosis, malaria and other communicable diseases;

17. *Urges* States to give adequate priority in their development strategies and expenditures to the realization of the right to food;

18. *Stresses* the importance of international development cooperation and assistance, in particular in activities related to disaster risk reduction and in emergency situations such as natural and man-made disasters, diseases and pests, for the realization of the right to food and the achievement of sustainable food security, while recognizing that each country has the primary responsibility for ensuring the implementation of national programmes and strategies in this regard;

19. *Calls upon* Member States, the United Nations system and other relevant stakeholders to support national efforts aimed at responding rapidly to the food crises currently occurring across Africa;

20. *Invites* all relevant international organizations, including the World Bank and the International Monetary Fund, to promote policies and projects that have a positive impact

on the right to food, to ensure that partners respect the right to food in the implementation of common projects, to support strategies of Member States aimed at the fulfilment of the right to food and to avoid any actions that could have a negative impact on the realization of the right to food;

21. *Takes note* of the interim report of the Special Rapporteur on the right to food,[9] and also takes note of his valuable work in the promotion of the right to food;

22. *Supports* the realization of the mandate of the Special Rapporteur as extended by the Human Rights Council in its decision 1/102 of 30 June 2006;[10]

23. *Requests* the Secretary-General and the United Nations High Commissioner for Human Rights to provide all the necessary human and financial resources for the effective fulfilment of the mandate of the Special Rapporteur;

24. *Welcomes* the work already done by the Committee on Economic, Social and Cultural Rights in promoting the right to adequate food, in particular its General Comment No. 12 (1999) on the right to adequate food (article 11 of the International Covenant on Economic, Social and Cultural Rights),[11] in which the Committee affirmed, inter alia, that the right to adequate food is indivisibly linked to the inherent dignity of the human person and is indispensable for the fulfilment of other human rights enshrined in the International Bill of Human Rights, and is also inseparable from social justice, requiring the adoption of appropriate economic, environmental and social policies, at both the national and the international levels, oriented to the eradication of poverty and the fulfilment of all human rights for all;

25. *Recalls* General Comment No. 15 (2002) of the Committee on the right to water (articles 11 and 12 of the Covenant),[12] in which the Committee noted, inter alia, the importance of ensuring sustainable water resources for human consumption and agriculture in realization of the right to adequate food;

26. *Reaffirms* that the Voluntary Guidelines to Support the Progressive Realization of the Right to Adequate Food in the Context of National Food Security, adopted by the Council of the Food and Agriculture Organization of the United Nations in November 2004,[7] represent a practical tool to promote the realization of the right to food for all, contribute to the achievement of food security and thus provide an additional instrument in the attainment of internationally agreed development goals, including those contained in the Millennium Declaration;

27. *Welcomes* the continued cooperation of the High Commissioner, the Committee and the Special Rapporteur, and encourages them to continue their cooperation in this regard;

28. *Calls upon* all Governments to cooperate with and assist the Special Rapporteur in his task, to supply all necessary information requested by him and to give serious consideration to responding favourably to the requests of the Special Rapporteur to visit their countries to enable him to fulfil his mandate more effectively;

29. *Requests* the Special Rapporteur to submit an interim report to the General Assembly at its sixty-second session on the implementation of the present resolution;

30. *Invites* Governments, relevant United Nations agencies, funds and programmes, treaty bodies and civil society actors, including non-governmental organizations, as well as the private sector, to cooperate fully with the Special Rapporteur in the fulfilment of his mandate, inter alia, through the submission of comments and suggestions on ways and means of realizing the right to food;

31. *Decides* to continue the consideration of the question at its sixty-second session under the item entitled "Promotion and protection of human rights".

81st plenary meeting
19 December 2006

[1] Resolution 217 A (III).

[2] *Report of the World Food Conference, Rome, 5–16 November 1974* (United Nations publication, Sales No. E.75.II.A.3), chap. I.

[3] See resolution 55/2.

[4] See resolution 2200 A (XXI), annex.

[5] Food and Agriculture Organization of the United Nations, *Report of the World Food Summit, 13–17 November 1996* (WFS 96/REP), part one, appendix.

[6] Food and Agriculture Organization of the United Nations, *Report of the World Food Summit: five years later, 10–13 June 2002*, part one, appendix; see also A/57/499, annex.

[7] Food and Agriculture Organization of the United Nations, *Report of the Council of the Food and Agriculture Organization of the United Nations, One Hundred and Twenty-seventh Session, Rome, 22–27 November 2004* (CL 127/REP), appendix D; see also E/CN.4/2005/131, annex.

[8] United Nations, *Treaty Series*, vol. 1954, No. 33480.

[9] See A/61/306.

[10] See *Official Records of the General Assembly, Sixty-first Session, Supplement No. 53* (A/61/53), part one, chap. II, sect. B.

[11] See *Official Records of the Economic and Social Council, 2000, Supplement No. 2* and corrigendum (E/2000/22 and Corr.1), annex V.

[12] Ibid., *2003, Supplement No. 2* (E/2003/22), annex IV.

Resolution 61/164

[on the report of the Third Committee (A/61/443/Add.2 and Corr.1)]

61/164. Combating defamation of religions

The General Assembly,

Recalling that all States have pledged themselves, under the Charter of the United Nations, to promote and encourage universal respect for and observance of all human rights and fundamental freedoms without distinction as to race, sex, language or religion,

Recalling also the relevant resolutions of the Commission on Human Rights in this regard,

Recalling further the United Nations Millennium Declaration adopted by the General Assembly on 8 September 2000,[1] welcoming the resolve expressed in the Millennium Declaration to take measures to eliminate the increasing acts of racism and xenophobia in many societies and to promote greater harmony and tolerance in all societies, and looking forward to its effective implementation at all levels, including in the context of the Durban Declaration and Programme of Action adopted by the World Conference against Racism, Racial Discrimination, Xenophobia and Related Intolerance, held in Durban, South Africa, from 31 August to 8 September 2001,[2]

Recalling the proclamation of the Global Agenda for Dialogue among Civilizations,[3] and inviting States, the organizations and bodies of the United Nations system, within existing resources, other international and regional organizations and civil societies to contribute to the implementation of the Programme of Action contained in the Global Agenda,

Welcoming the launch of the Alliance of Civilizations initiative, intended to respond to the need for a committed effort by the international community, in order to promote mutual respect and understanding among different cultures and societies,

Welcoming also the progress achieved in the follow-up to the Durban Declaration and Programme of Action,

Underlining the importance of increasing contacts at all levels in order to deepen dialogue and reinforce understanding among different cultures, religions and civilizations, and noting with regret, in this regard, the cancellation of the meeting on "Civilization and harmony: values and mechanisms of the global order", which was to be held in Turkey in 2004 as a follow-up to the Organization of the Islamic Conference-European Union Joint Forum on the theme "Civilization and harmony: the political dimension", held in Turkey in 2002,

Reaffirming that discrimination against human beings on the grounds of religion or belief constitutes an affront to human dignity and a disavowal of the principles of the Charter,

Convinced that respect for cultural, ethnic, religious and linguistic diversity, as well as dialogue among and within civilizations, is essential for peace, understanding and friendship among individuals and people of the different cultures and nations of the world, while manifestations of cultural prejudice, intolerance and xenophobia towards different cultures and religions generate hatred and violence among peoples and nations throughout the world,

Recognizing the valuable contributions of all religions to modern civilization and the contribution that dialogue among civilizations can make to an improved awareness and understanding of the common values shared by all humankind,

Reaffirming the need for all States to continue international efforts to enhance dialogue and broaden understanding among civilizations, cultures and religions, and emphasizing that States, regional organizations, non-governmental organizations, religious bodies and the media have an important role to play in promoting tolerance, respect for and freedom of religion and belief,

Underlining the important role of education in the promotion of cultural and religious tolerance and the elimination of discrimination based on religion or belief,

Alarmed at the continuing negative impact of the events of 11 September 2001 on Muslim minorities and communities in some non-Muslim countries, the negative projection of Islam in the media and the introduction and enforcement of laws that specifically discriminate against and target Muslims,

Alarmed also at the serious instances of intolerance, discrimination and acts of violence based on religion or belief, intimidation and coercion motivated by extremism, religious or otherwise, occurring in many parts of the world and threatening the enjoyment of human rights and fundamental freedoms,

Noting with concern that defamation of religions is among the causes of social disharmony and leads to violations of human rights,

Deeply alarmed at the rising trends towards discrimination based on religion and faith, including in some national policies and laws that stigmatize groups of people belonging to certain religions and faiths under a variety of pretexts relating to security and illegal immigration, and noting that the increased intellectual and media discourse is among the factors exacerbating such discrimination,

Noting with deep concern the increasing trend in recent years of statements attacking religions, Islam and Muslims in particular, especially in human rights forums,

1. *Expresses its deep concern* about the negative stereotyping of religions and manifestations of intolerance and discrimination in matters of religion or belief still in evidence in some regions of the world;

2. *Strongly deplores* physical attacks and assaults on businesses, cultural centres and places of worship of all religions as well as targeting of religious symbols;

3. *Notes with deep concern* the intensification of the campaign of defamation of religions and the ethnic and religious profiling of Muslim minorities in the aftermath of the tragic events of 11 September 2001;

4. *Expresses its deep concern* that Islam is frequently and wrongly associated with human rights violations and terrorism;

5. *Also expresses its deep concern* about programmes and agendas pursued by extremist organizations and groups aimed at the defamation of religions, in particular when supported by Governments;

6. *Deplores* the use of the print, audio-visual and electronic media, including the Internet, and any other means to incite acts of violence, xenophobia or related intolerance and discrimination against Islam or any other religion;

7. *Recognizes* that, in the context of the fight against terrorism and the reaction to counter-terrorism measures, defamation of religions becomes an aggravating factor that contributes to the denial of fundamental rights and freedoms of target groups, as well as their economic and social exclusion;

8. *Stresses* the need to effectively combat defamation of all religions, Islam and Muslims in particular, especially in human rights forums;

9. *Emphasizes* that everyone has the right to freedom of expression, which should be exercised with responsibility and may therefore be subject to limitations as provided by law and necessary for respect of the rights or reputations of others, protection of national security or of public order, public health or morals and respect for religions and beliefs;

10. *Urges* States to take resolute action to prohibit the dissemination of racist and xenophobic ideas and material aimed at any religion or its followers that constitute incitement to discrimination, hostility or violence;

11. *Also urges* States to provide, within their respective legal and constitutional systems, adequate protection against acts of hatred, discrimination, intimidation and coercion resulting from defamation of religions, to take all possible measures to promote tolerance and respect for all religions and their value systems and to complement legal systems with intellectual and moral strategies to combat religious hatred and intolerance;

12. *Urges* all States to ensure that all public officials, including members of law enforcement bodies, the military, civil servants and educators, in the course of their official duties, respect different religions and beliefs and do not discriminate against persons on the grounds of their religion or belief, and that any necessary and appropriate education or training is provided;

13. *Underscores* the need to combat defamation of religions by strategizing and harmonizing actions at the local, national, regional and international levels through education and awareness-raising;

14. *Urges* States to ensure equal access to education for all, in law and in practice, including access to free primary education for all children, both girls and boys, and access for adults to lifelong learning and education based on respect for human rights, diversity and tolerance, without discrimination of any kind, and to refrain from any legal or other measures leading to racial segregation in access to schooling;

15. *Calls upon* the international community to initiate a global dialogue to promote a culture of tolerance and peace based on respect for human rights and religious diversity, and urges States, non-governmental organizations, religious bodies and the print and electronic media to support and promote such a dialogue;

16. *Affirms* that the Human Rights Council shall promote universal respect for all religious and cultural values and address instances of intolerance, discrimination and incitement of hatred against any community or adherents of any religion;

17. *Calls upon* the United Nations High Commissioner for Human Rights to promote and include human rights aspects in the dialogue among civilizations, inter alia, through:

(*a*) Integrating them into topical seminars and special debates on the positive contributions of cultures, as well as religious and cultural diversity, including through educational programmes, particularly the World Programme for Human Rights Education proclaimed on 10 December 2004;[4]

(*b*) Collaboration by the Office of the United Nations High Commissioner for Human Rights with other relevant international organizations in holding joint conferences designed to encourage this dialogue and promote understanding of the universality of human rights and their implementation at various levels;

18. *Requests* the Secretary-General to submit a report on the implementation of the present resolution, including on the possible correlation between defamation of religions and the upsurge in incitement, intolerance and hatred in many parts of the world, to the General Assembly at its sixty-second session.

81st plenary meeting
19 December 2006

---

[1] See resolution 55/2.

[2] See A/CONF.189/12 and Corr.1, chap. I.

[3] See resolution 56/6.

[4] See resolutions 59/113 A and B.

Resolution 61/165

[on the report of the Third Committee (A/61/443/Add.2 and Corr.1)]

61/165. Protection of migrants

The General Assembly,

Recalling all its previous resolutions on the protection of migrants, the most recent of which is resolution 60/169 of 16 December 2005, and recalling also Commission on Human Rights resolution 2005/47 of 19 April 2005,[1]

Reaffirming the Universal Declaration of Human Rights,[2] which proclaims that all human beings are born free and equal in dignity and rights and that everyone is entitled to all the rights and freedoms set out therein, without distinction of any kind, in particular as to race, colour or national origin,

Reaffirming also that everyone has the right to freedom of movement and residence within the borders of each State, and to leave any country, including his own, and return to his country,

Recalling the International Covenant on Civil and Political Rights[3] and the International Covenant on Economic, Social and Cultural Rights,[3] the Convention against Torture and Other Cruel, Inhuman or Degrading Treatment or Punishment,[4] the Convention on the Elimination of All Forms of Discrimination against Women,[5] the Convention on the Rights of the Child,[6] the International Convention on the Elimination of All Forms of Racial Discrimination [7] and the International Convention on the Protection of the Rights of All Migrant Workers and Members of Their Families,[8]

Recalling also the provisions concerning migrants contained in the outcomes of all major United Nations conferences and summits,

Welcoming the establishment of the Human Rights Council, which is responsible for promoting universal respect for the protection of all human rights and fundamental freedoms for all, without distinction of any kind and in a fair and equal manner,

Welcoming also the convening of the High-level Dialogue on International Migration and Development, held in New York on 14 and 15 September 2006 for the purpose of discussing the multidimensional aspects of international migration and development, which recognized the relationship between international migration, development and human rights,

Bearing in mind that policies and initiatives on the issue of migration, including those that refer to the orderly management of migration, should promote holistic approaches that take into account the causes and consequences of the phenomenon, as well as the full respect for the human rights and fundamental freedoms of migrants,

Noting that many migrant women are employed in the informal economy and in less skilled work compared with that of men, which puts those women at greater risk of abuse and exploitation,

Concerned about the large and growing number of migrants, especially women and children, who place themselves in a vulnerable situation by attempting to cross international borders without the required travel documents, and underlining the obligation of States to respect the human rights of those migrants,

Underlining the importance for States, in cooperation with non-governmental organizations, to undertake information campaigns aimed at clarifying opportunities, limitations and rights in the event of migration, so as to enable everyone to make informed decisions and to prevent them from utilizing dangerous means to cross international borders,

Emphasizing the global character of the migratory phenomenon, the importance of international, regional and bilateral cooperation and dialogue in this regard, as appropriate, and the need to protect the human rights of migrants, particularly at a time in which migration flows have increased in the globalized economy and take place in a context of new security concerns,

1. *Requests* States effectively to promote and protect the human rights and fundamental freedoms of all migrants, regardless of their immigration status, especially those of women and children;

2. *Takes note with interest* of the interim report of the Special Rapporteur of the Human Rights Council on the human rights of migrants;[9]

3. *Calls upon* States that have not done so to consider signing and ratifying or acceding to the International Convention on the Protection of the Rights of All Migrant Workers and Members of Their Families[8] as a matter of priority, and requests the Secretary-General to continue his efforts to raise awareness and promote the Convention;

4. *Urges* States parties to the United Nations Convention against Transnational Organized Crime[10] and supplementing protocols thereto, namely, the Protocol against the Smuggling of Migrants by Land, Sea and Air[11] and the Protocol to Prevent, Suppress and Punish Trafficking in Persons, Especially Women and Children,[12] to implement them fully, and calls upon States that have not done so to consider ratifying them as a matter of priority;

5. *Takes note* of the report of the Committee on the Protection of the Rights of All Migrant Workers and Members of Their Families on its third and fourth sessions;[13]

6. *Requests* all States, international organizations and relevant stakeholders to take into account in their policies and initiatives on migration issues the global character of the migratory phenomenon and to give due consideration to international, regional and bilateral cooperation in this field, including by undertaking dialogues on migration that include countries of origin, destination and transit, as well as civil society, including migrants, with a view to addressing, in a comprehensive manner, inter alia, its causes and consequences and the challenge of undocumented or irregular migration, granting priority to the protection of the human rights of migrants;

7. *Expresses concern* about legislation and measures adopted by some States that may restrict the human rights and fundamental freedoms of migrants, and reaffirms that, when exercising their sovereign right to enact and implement migratory and border security measures, States have the duty to comply with their obligations under international law, including international human rights law, in order to ensure full respect for the human rights of migrants;

8. *Requests* States to adopt concrete measures to prevent the violation of the human rights of migrants while in transit, including in ports and airports and at borders and migration checkpoints, to train public officials who work in those facilities and in border areas to treat migrants respectfully and in accordance with the law, and to prosecute, in conformity with applicable law, any act of violation of the human rights of migrants, inter alia, arbitrary detention, torture and violations of the right to life, including extrajudicial executions,

during their transit from their country of origin to the country of destination and vice versa, including their transit through national borders;

9. *Calls upon* States to address international migration through international, regional or bilateral cooperation and dialogue and through a comprehensive and balanced approach, recognizing the roles and responsibilities of countries of origin, transit and destination in promoting and protecting the human rights of migrants and avoiding approaches that may aggravate their vulnerability;

10. *Strongly condemns* the manifestations and acts of racism, racial discrimination, xenophobia and related intolerance against migrants and the stereotypes often applied to them, including on the basis of religion or belief, and urges States to apply the existing laws when xenophobic or intolerant acts, manifestations or expressions against migrants occur, in order to eradicate impunity for those who commit xenophobic and racist acts;

11. *Requests* all States, in conformity with national legislation and applicable international legal instruments to which they are party, to enforce labour law effectively, including by addressing violations of such law, with regard to migrant workers' labour relations and working conditions, *inter alia*, those related to their remuneration and conditions of health, safety at work and the right to freedom of association;

12. *Encourages* all States to remove obstacles that may prevent the safe, unrestricted and expeditious transfer of remittances of migrants to their country of origin or to any other countries, in conformity with applicable legislation, and to consider, as appropriate, measures to solve other problems that may impede such transfers;

13. *Welcomes* immigration programmes, adopted by some countries, that allow migrants to integrate fully into the host countries, facilitate family reunification and promote a harmonious, tolerant and respectful environment, and encourages States to consider the possibility of adopting these types of programmes;

14. *Requests* Member States, the United Nations system, international organizations, civil society and all relevant stakeholders, especially the United Nations High Commissioner for Human Rights and the Special Rapporteur on the human rights of migrants, to ensure that the perspective of the human rights of migrants is included among the priority issues in the ongoing discussions on international migration and development within the United Nations system, bearing in mind the discussions of the High-level Dialogue on International Migration and Development held pursuant to General Assembly resolution 58/208 of 23 December 2003;

15. *Requests* the Secretary-General to report on the implementation of the present resolution at its sixty-second session and decides to examine the question further under the item entitled "Promotion and protection of human rights".

81st plenary meeting
19 December 2006

---

[1] See *Official Records of the Economic and Social Council, 2005, Supplement No. 3* and corrigendum (E/2005/23 and Corr.1), chap. II, sect. A.

[2] Resolution 217 A (III).

[3] See resolution 2200 A (XXI), annex.

[4] United Nations, *Treaty Series*, vol. 1465, No. 24841.

[5] Ibid., vol. 1249, No. 20378.

[6] Ibid., vol. 1577, No. 27531.

[7] Ibid., vol. 660, No. 9464.

[8] Ibid., vol. 2220, No. 39481.

[9] See A/61/324.

[10] Resolution 55/25, annex I.

[11] Ibid., annex III.

[12] Ibid., annex II.

[13] *Official Records of the General Assembly, Sixty-first Session, Supplement No. 48* (A/61/48).

Resolution 61/166

[on the report of the Third Committee (A/61/443/Add.2 and Corr.1)]

61/166. Promotion of equitable and mutually respectful dialogue on human rights

The General Assembly,

Guided by the purposes and principles of the Charter of the United Nations, the Universal Declaration of Human Rights,[1] the Vienna Declaration and Programme of Action,[2] the International Covenants on Human Rights[3] and other relevant human rights instruments,

Reaffirming that all human rights are universal, indivisible, interdependent and interrelated and that the international community must treat human rights globally in a fair and equal manner, on the same footing and with the same emphasis, and that the significance of national and regional particularities and various historical, cultural and religious backgrounds must be borne in mind,

Stressing the importance of developing friendly relations among nations based on respect for the principle of equal rights and self-determination of peoples and achieving international cooperation in promoting and encouraging respect for human rights and fundamental freedoms for all,

Emphasizing the responsibilities of all States, in conformity with the Charter, to respect human rights and fundamental freedoms for all, without distinction of any kind as to race, colour, sex, language or religion, political or other opinion, national or social origin, property, birth or other status,

Bearing in mind General Assembly resolution 60/251 of 15 March 2006 entitled "Human Rights Council", in particular the decision of the Assembly that the Council should undertake a universal periodic review, in a manner that ensures universality of coverage and equal treatment with respect to all States, and the decision of the Council on the establishment of an intersessional open-ended intergovernmental working group to develop the modalities of the universal periodic review mechanism, based on an interactive dialogue as well as on objective and reliable information,[4]

Recalling that the General Assembly shall make recommendations for the purpose of promoting international cooperation in the economic, social, cultural, education and health fields, and of assisting in the realization of human rights and fundamental freedoms for all without distinction as to race, sex, language or religion,

Recognizing that politically motivated and biased country-specific resolutions on the situation of human rights severely undermine the principles of objectivity and non-selectivity in the consideration of human rights issues and are counterproductive to the cause of promoting human rights,

1. *Urges* Member States to further strengthen international cooperation in promoting and encouraging respect for human rights in order to enhance dialogue and broaden understanding among civilizations, cultures and religions;

2. *Calls upon* Member States to base their approaches towards development of international dialogue on human rights on the Charter of the United Nations, the Universal Declaration of Human Rights,[1] the Vienna Declaration and Programme of Action[2] and other relevant international human rights instruments and to refrain from approaches that are inconsistent with that international framework;

3. *Reaffirms* that the promotion and protection of human rights and fundamental freedoms, as a legitimate concern of the world community, and the development of international dialogue on human rights should be guided by the principles of universality, non selectivity, impartiality and objectivity and should not be used for political purposes;

4. *Stresses* the need to avoid politically motivated and biased country-specific resolutions on the situation of human rights, confrontational approaches, exploitation of human rights for political purposes, selective targeting of individual countries for extraneous considerations and double standards in the work of the United Nations on human rights issues;

5. *Affirms* that respect for political, economic and cultural diversity for all contributes to the development of stable and friendly relations among countries and equitable and mutually respectful international dialogue on human rights;

6. *Stresses* the continuing need for unbiased and objective information on the situation of human rights in all countries and the need to present this information in an impartial manner, including through the reports of the special rapporteurs and representatives, independent experts and working groups;

7. *Decides* to consider the matter at its sixty-second session under the item entitled "Promotion and protection of human rights".

81st plenary meeting
19 December 2006

---

[1] Resolution 217 A (III).

[2] A/CONF.157/24 (Part I), chap. III.

[3] Resolution 2200 A (XXI), annex.

[4] See *Official Records of the General Assembly, Sixty-first Session, Supplement No. 53* (A/61/53), part one, chap. II, sect. B, decision 1/103.

Resolution 61/167

[on the report of the Third Committee (A/61/443/Add.2 and Corr.1)]

61/167. Regional arrangements for the promotion and protection of human rights

The General Assembly,

Recalling its resolution 32/127 of 16 December 1977 and its subsequent resolutions concerning regional arrangements for the promotion and protection of human rights,

Recalling also Commission on Human Rights resolution 1993/51 of 9 March 1993[1] and its subsequent resolutions in this regard,

Bearing in mind the relevant resolutions of the Commission concerning advisory services and technical cooperation in the field of human rights, including its most recent on that subject, resolution 2004/81 of 21 April 2004,[2]

Bearing in mind also the Vienna Declaration and Programme of Action adopted by the World Conference on Human Rights on 25 June 1993,[3] which reiterates, inter alia, the need to consider the possibility of establishing regional and subregional arrangements for the promotion and protection of human rights where they do not already exist,

Recalling that the World Conference recommended that more resources should be made available for the strengthening of regional arrangements for the promotion and protection of human rights under the programme of technical cooperation in the field of human rights of the Office of the United Nations High Commissioner for Human Rights,

Reaffirming that regional arrangements play an important role in promoting and protecting human rights and should reinforce universal human rights standards, as contained in international human rights instruments,

Welcoming the fact that the Office of the High Commissioner has been systematically pursuing a regional and subregional approach through a variety of complementary means and methods, in order to maximize the impact of the activities of the United Nations at the national level, and that the Office intends to establish new regional offices,

1. *Takes note with satisfaction* of the report of the Secretary-General;[4]

2. *Welcomes* the continuing cooperation and assistance of the Office of the United Nations High Commissioner for Human Rights in the further strengthening of the existing regional arrangements and regional machinery for the promotion and protection of human rights, in particular through technical cooperation aimed at national capacity-building, public information and education, with a view to exchanging information and experience in the field of human rights;

3. *Also welcomes*, in that respect, the close cooperation of the Office of the High Commissioner in the organization of regional and subregional training courses and workshops in the field of human rights, high-level governmental expert meetings and regional conferences of national human rights institutions, aimed at creating greater understanding in the regions of issues concerning the promotion and protection of human rights, improving procedures and examining the various systems for the promotion and protection of universally accepted human rights standards and identifying obstacles to ratification of the principal international human rights treaties and strategies to overcome them;

4. *Recognizes*, therefore, that progress in promoting and protecting all human rights depends primarily on efforts made at the national and local levels, and that the regional approach

should imply intensive cooperation and coordination with all partners involved, while bearing in mind the importance of international cooperation;

5. *Stresses* the importance of the programme of technical cooperation in the field of human rights, renews its appeal to all Governments to consider making use of the possibilities offered by the United Nations under the programme of organizing information or training courses at the national level for government personnel on the application of international human rights standards and the experience of relevant international bodies, and notes with satisfaction, in that respect, the establishment of technical cooperation projects with Governments of all regions;

6. *Welcomes* the growing exchanges between the United Nations and the United Nations human rights treaty bodies, on the one hand, and regional organizations and institutions, such as the African Commission on Human and Peoples' Rights, the Community of Portuguese-speaking Countries, the Council of Europe, the Inter-American Commission on Human Rights, the International Organization of la Francophonie, the League of Arab States, the Organization for Security and Cooperation in Europe and other regional institutions, on the other;

7. *Also welcomes* the placement by the Office of the High Commissioner of regional representatives in subregions and in regional commissions, in particular the deployment to Bishkek of a regional representative for Central Asia;

8. *Further welcomes* the progress achieved in the establishment of regional and subregional arrangements for the promotion and protection of human rights, and, in this regard, notes with interest:

(*a*) The increasing cooperation between the Office of the High Commissioner and African organizations and suborganizations, in particular the African Union, the Economic Community of Central African States, the Economic Community of West African States and the Southern African Development Community;

(*b*) The support provided by the Office of the High Commissioner to the African Union for the strengthening of the promotion and protection of human rights in Africa, and welcomes in this regard the establishment of the African Court on Human and Peoples' Rights;

(*c*) The increased, valuable sharing of concrete national experiences at the thirteenth Workshop on Regional Cooperation for the Promotion and Protection of Human Rights in the Asia-Pacific Region, held in Beijing from 30 August to 2 September 2005, regarding the implementation of the Regional Framework for the Promotion and Protection of Human Rights in the Asia-Pacific Region, which contributes to the enhancement of the promotion and protection of human rights in the region, and welcomes in this regard the establishment in Suva of an office of the High Commissioner for the Pacific region and the steps undertaken by the Office of the High Commissioner to set up a United Nations human rights training and documentation centre for South-West Asia and the Arab region, pursuant to General Assembly resolution 60/153 of 16 December 2005;

(*d*) The ongoing consultations among Governments aimed at the possible establishment of regional human rights arrangements held in the context of the Regional Framework, with the support and advice of national human rights institutions and civil society organizations of the Asia-Pacific region;

(*e*) Activities undertaken within the framework of the regional project of the Office of the High Commissioner for the promotion and protection of human rights in the Latin American and Caribbean region and the strengthening of the cooperation between the Office of the High Commissioner, the Inter-American Commission on Human Rights and the Organization of American States;

(*f*) Activities undertaken within the framework of cooperation between the Office of the High Commissioner and the League of Arab States;

(*g*) The continued cooperation towards the realization of universal standards between the Office of the High Commissioner and regional organizations in Europe and Central Asia, namely, the Council of Europe, the European Union and the Organization for Security and Cooperation in Europe, in particular for activities at the country level;

9. *Invites* States in areas in which regional arrangements in the field of human rights do not yet exist to consider, with the support and advice of national human rights institutions and civil society organizations, concluding agreements with a view to establishing, within their respective regions, suitable regional machinery for the promotion and protection of human rights;

10. *Requests* the Secretary-General to continue to strengthen exchanges between the United Nations and regional intergovernmental organizations dealing with human rights and to make available adequate resources from within the regular budget of technical cooperation to the activities of the Office of the High Commissioner to promote regional arrangements;

11. *Requests* the Office of the High Commissioner to continue to pay special attention to the most appropriate ways of assisting countries of the various regions, at their request, under the programme of technical cooperation and to make, where necessary, relevant recommendations, and in this regard welcomes the decision of the Office to strengthen national protection systems in accordance with action 2 of the reform programme of the Secretary-General;[5]

12. *Invites* the Secretary-General to provide, in the report that he will submit to the Human Rights Council at its fourth session, information on progress made since the adoption of the Vienna Declaration and Programme of Action[3] on reinforcing the exchange of information and extending collaboration between the organs of the United Nations dealing with human rights and regional organizations in the field of the promotion and protection of human rights;

13. *Requests* the Secretary-General to submit to the General Assembly at its sixty-third session a report on the state of regional arrangements for the promotion and protection of human rights, formulating concrete proposals and recommendations on ways and means to strengthen cooperation between the United Nations and regional arrangements in the field of human rights, and to include therein the results of action taken in pursuance of the present resolution;

14. *Decides* to consider the question further at its sixty-third session.

81st plenary meeting
19 December 2006

---

[1] See *Official Records of the Economic and Social Council, 1993, Supplement No. 3* and corrigenda (E/1993/23 and Corr.2, 4 and 5), chap. II, sect. A.

[2] Ibid., *2004, Supplement No. 3* (E/2004/23), chap. II, sect. A.

[3] A/CONF.157/24 (Part I), chap. III.

[4] A/61/513.

[5] See A/57/387 and Corr.1.

Resolution 61/168

[on the report of the Third Committee (A/61/443/Add.2 and Corr.1)]

61/168. Enhancement of international cooperation in the field of human rights

The General Assembly,

Reaffirming its commitment to promoting international cooperation, as set forth in the Charter of the United Nations, in particular Article 1, paragraph 3, as well as relevant provisions of the Vienna Declaration and Programme of Action adopted by the World Conference on Human Rights on 25 June 1993,[1] for enhancing genuine cooperation among Member States in the field of human rights,

Recalling its adoption of the United Nations Millennium Declaration on 8 September 2000[2] and its resolution 60/156 of 16 December 2005, and taking note of Commission on Human Rights resolution 2005/54 of 20 April 2005 on the enhancement of international cooperation in the field of human rights,[3]

Recalling also the World Conference against Racism, Racial Discrimination, Xenophobia and Related Intolerance, held at Durban, South Africa, from 31 August to 8 September 2001, and its role in the enhancement of international cooperation in the field of human rights,

Recognizing that the enhancement of international cooperation in the field of human rights is essential for the full achievement of the purposes of the United Nations, including the effective promotion and protection of all human rights,

Recognizing also that the promotion and protection of human rights should be based on the principle of cooperation and genuine dialogue and aimed at strengthening the capacity of Member States to comply with their human rights obligations for the benefit of all human beings,

Reaffirming that dialogue among religions, cultures and civilizations in the field of human rights could contribute greatly to the enhancement of international cooperation in this field,

Emphasizing the need for further progress in the promotion and encouragement of respect for human rights and fundamental freedoms through, inter alia, international cooperation,

Underlining the fact that mutual understanding, dialogue, cooperation, transparency and confidence-building are important elements in all the activities for the promotion and protection of human rights,

Recalling the adoption of resolution 2000/22 of 18 August 2000, on the promotion of dialogue on human rights issues, by the Subcommission on the Promotion and Protection of Human Rights at its fifty-second session,[4]

1. *Reaffirms* that it is one of the purposes of the United Nations and the responsibility of all Member States to promote, protect and encourage respect for human rights and fundamental freedoms through, inter alia, international cooperation;

2. *Recognizes* that, in addition to their separate responsibilities to their individual societies, States have a collective responsibility to uphold the principles of human dignity, equality and equity at the global level;

3. *Reaffirms* that dialogue among cultures and civilizations facilitates the promotion of a culture of tolerance and respect for diversity, and welcomes in this regard the holding of conferences and meetings at the national, regional and international levels on dialogue among civilizations;

4. *Urges* all actors on the international scene to build an international order based on inclusion, justice, equality and equity, human dignity, mutual understanding and promotion of and respect for cultural diversity and universal human rights, and to reject all doctrines of exclusion based on racism, racial discrimination, xenophobia and related intolerance;

5. *Reaffirms* the importance of the enhancement of international cooperation for the promotion and protection of human rights and for the achievement of the objectives of the fight against racism, racial discrimination, xenophobia and related intolerance;

6. *Considers* that international cooperation in the field of human rights, in conformity with the purposes and principles set out in the Charter of the United Nations and international law, should make an effective and practical contribution to the urgent task of preventing violations of human rights and fundamental freedoms;

7. *Reaffirms* that the promotion, protection and full realization of all human rights and fundamental freedoms should be guided by the principles of universality, non-selectivity, objectivity and transparency, in a manner consistent with the purposes and principles set out in the Charter;

8. *Calls upon* Member States, specialized agencies and intergovernmental organizations to continue to carry out a constructive dialogue and consultations for the enhancement of understanding and the promotion and protection of all human rights and fundamental freedoms, and encourages non-governmental organizations to contribute actively to this endeavour;

9. *Invites* States and relevant United Nations human rights mechanisms and procedures to continue to pay attention to the importance of mutual cooperation, understanding and dialogue in ensuring the promotion and protection of all human rights;

10. *Requests* the Secretary-General, in collaboration with the United Nations High Commissioner for Human Rights, to consult States and intergovernmental and

non-governmental organizations on ways and means to enhance international cooperation and dialogue in the United Nations human rights machinery;

11. *Decides* to continue its consideration of the question at its sixty-second session.

81st plenary meeting
19 December 2006

---

[1] A/CONF.157/24 (Part I), chap. III.

[2] See resolution 55/2.

[3] See *Official Records of the Economic and Social Council, 2005, Supplement No. 3* and corrigendum (E/2005/23 and Corr.1), chap. II, sect. A.

[4] See E/CN.4/2001/2-E/CN.4/Sub.2/2000/46, chap. II, sect. A.

Resolution 61/169

[on the report of the Third Committee (A/61/443/Add.2 and Corr.1)]

61/169. The right to development

The General Assembly,

Guided by the Charter of the United Nations, which expresses, in particular, the determination to promote social progress and better standards of life in larger freedom, as well as to employ international mechanisms for the promotion of the economic and social advancement of all peoples,

Recalling the Universal Declaration of Human Rights,[1] as well as the International Covenant on Civil and Political Rights[2] and the International Covenant on Economic, Social and Cultural Rights,[2]

Recalling also the outcomes of all the major United Nations conferences and summits in the economic and social fields,

Recalling further that the Declaration on the Right to Development, adopted by the General Assembly in its resolution 41/128 of 4 December 1986, confirmed that the right to development is an inalienable human right and that equality of opportunity for development is a prerogative both of nations and of individuals who make up nations, and that the individual is the central subject and beneficiary of development,

Stressing that the Vienna Declaration and Programme of Action[3] reaffirmed the right to development as a universal and inalienable right and an integral part of fundamental human rights, and the individual as the central subject and beneficiary of development,

Reaffirming the objective of making the right to development a reality for everyone, as set out in the United Nations Millennium Declaration, adopted by the General Assembly on 8 September 2000,[4]

Reaffirming also the universality, indivisibility, interrelatedness, interdependence and mutually reinforcing nature of all civil, cultural, economic, political and social rights, including the right to development,

Expressing concern over the suspension of the trade negotiations of the World Trade Organization, and stressing the need for a successful outcome of the Doha Development Round in key areas such as agriculture, market access for nonagricultural products, trade facilitation, development and services,

Recalling the outcome of the eleventh session of the United Nations Conference on Trade and Development, held in São Paulo, Brazil, from 13 to 18 J une 2004, on the theme "Enhancing the coherence between national development strategies and global economic processes towards economic growth and development, particularly of developing countries",[5]

Recalling also all its previous resolutions, Human Rights Council resolution 1/4 of 30 June 2006[6] and those of the Commission on Human Rights on the right to development, in particular Commission resolution 1998/72 of 22 April 1998,[7] on the urgent need to make further progress towards the realization of the right to development as set out in the Declaration on the Right to Development,

Welcoming the outcome of the seventh session of the Working Group on the Right to Development of the Commission on Human Rights, held in Geneva from 9 to 13 January 2006, as contained in the report of the Working Group,[8]

Recalling the Fourteenth Conference of Heads of State or Government of Non-Aligned Countries, held in Havana on 15 and 16 September 2006, the Ministerial Meeting of the Coordinating Bureau of the Movement of Non-Aligned Countries, held in Putrajaya, Malaysia, on 29 and 30 May 2006, and the Fourteenth Ministerial Conference of the Movement of Non-Aligned Countries, held in Durban, South Africa, from 17 to 19 August 2004,

Reiterating its continuing support for the New Partnership for Africa's Development[9] as a development framework for Africa,

Recognizing that poverty is an affront to human dignity,

Recognizing also that extreme poverty and hunger are a global threat that requires the collective commitment of the international community for its eradication, pursuant to millennium development goal 1, and therefore calling upon the international community, including the Human Rights Council, to contribute towards achieving that goal,

Recognizing further that historical injustices have undeniably contributed to the poverty, underdevelopment, marginalization, social exclusion, economic disparity, instability and insecurity that affect many people in different parts of the world, in particular in developing countries,

Stressing that poverty eradication is one of the critical elements in the promotion and realization of the right to development and that poverty is a multifaceted problem that requires a multifaceted and integrated approach in addressing economic, political, social, environmental and institutional dimensions at all levels, especially in the context of the millennium development goal of halving, by 2015, the proportion of the world's people whose income is less than one dollar a day and the proportion of people who suffer from hunger,

1. *Endorses* the conclusions and recommendations adopted by consensus by the Working Group on the Right to Development of the Commission on Human Rights at its seventh session,[8] and calls for their immediate, full and effective implementation by the Office of the United Nations High Commissioner for Human Rights and other relevant actors;

2. *Recognizes* the relevance of the decisions contained in Human Rights Council resolution 1/4[6] to renew the mandate of the Working Group and to request the Working Group to meet in the first three months of 2007;

3. *Also recognizes* the relevance of the request of the Human Rights Council to the high-level task force on the right to development to meet before the end of 2006 with a view to implementing the relevant recommendations contained in the report on the seventh session of the Working Group;

4. *Emphasizes* the relevant provisions of General Assembly resolution 60/251 of 15 March 2006 establishing the Human Rights Council, and, in this regard, calls upon the Council:

(*a*) To promote and advance sustainable development and the achievement of the Millennium Development Goals;

(*b*) To agree on a programme that will lead to the elevation of the right to development to the same level, in order that it may be on a par with them, as all other human rights and fundamental freedoms elaborated in the human rights instruments;

5. *Notes with appreciation* that the high-level task force, at its second meeting, examined millennium development goal 8, on developing a global partnership for development, and suggested criteria for its periodic evaluation with the aim of improving the effectiveness of global partnership with regard to the realization of the right to development;[10]

6. *Stresses* the importance of the core principles contained in the conclusions of the Working Group at its third session,[11] congruent with the purpose of international human rights instruments, such as equality, non-discrimination, accountability, participation and international cooperation, as critical to mainstreaming the right to development at the national and international levels, and underlines the importance of the principles of equity and transparency;

7. *Also stresses* that it is important that the high-level task force and the Working Group, in the discharge of their mandates, take into account the need:

(*a*) To promote the democratization of the system of international governance in order to increase the effective participation of developing countries in international decision-making;

(*b*) To also promote effective partnerships such as the New Partnership for Africa's Development[9] and other similar initiatives with the developing countries, particularly the least developed countries, for the purpose of the realization of their right to development, including the achievement of the Millennium Development Goals;

(*c*) To strive for greater acceptance, operationalization and realization of the right to development at the international level, while urging all States to undertake at the national level the necessary policy formulation and to institute the measures required for the implementation of the right to development as a fundamental human right, and also urging all States to expand and deepen mutually beneficial cooperation in ensuring development and eliminating obstacles to development in the context of promoting effective international cooperation for the realization of the right to development, bearing in mind that lasting progress towards the implementation of the right to development requires effective development policies at the national level as well as equitable economic relations and a favourable economic environment at the international level;

(*d*) To consider ways and means to ensure the operationalization of the right to development as a priority, including through further consideration of the elaboration of a convention on the right to development;

(*e*) To mainstream the right to development in the policies and operational activities of the United Nations and the specialized agencies, programmes and funds, as well as in policies and strategies of the international financial and multilateral trading system, taking into account in this regard that the core principles of the international economic, commercial and financial spheres, such as equity, non-discrimination, transparency, accountability, participation and international cooperation, including effective partnerships for development, are indispensable in achieving the right to development and preventing discriminatory treatment arising out of political or other non-economic considerations, in addressing the issues of concern to the developing countries;

8. *Recognizes* the relevance of the request to the Subcommission on the Promotion and Protection of Human Rights or its successor expert advice mechanism to pursue its ongoing work on the right to development, in accordance with the relevant provisions of General Assembly and Commission on Human Rights resolutions, and in compliance with decisions to be taken by the Human Rights Council, and requests the Secretary-General to report on progress in this regard to the Assembly at its sixty-second session;

9. *Invites* Member States and all other stakeholders to participate actively in future sessions of the Social Forum, while recognizing the strong support extended to the Forum at its previous three sessions by the Subcommission on the Promotion and Protection of Human Rights;

10. *Reaffirms* the commitment to implement the goals and targets set out in all the outcome documents of the major United Nations conferences and summits and their review processes, in particular those relating to the realization of the right to development, recognizing that the realization of the right to development is critical to achieving the objectives, goals and targets set in those outcome documents;

11. *Also reaffirms* that the realization of the right to development is essential to the implementation of the Vienna Declaration and Programme of Action,[3] which regards all human rights as universal, indivisible, interdependent and interrelated, places the human person at the centre of development and recognizes that, while development facilitates the enjoyment of all human rights, the lack of development may not be invoked to justify the abridgement of internationally recognized human rights;

12. *Stresses* that the primary responsibility for the promotion and protection of all human rights lies with the State, and reaffirms that States have the primary responsibility for their own economic and social development and that the role of national policies and development strategies cannot be overemphasized;

13. *Reaffirms* the primary responsibility of States to create national and international conditions favourable to the realization of the right to development, as well as their commitment to cooperate with each other to that end;

14. *Also reaffirms* the need for an international environment that is conducive to the realization of the right to development;

15. *Stresses* the need to strive for greater acceptance, operationalization and realization of the right to development at the international and national levels, and calls upon States to institute the measures required for the implementation of the right to development as a fundamental human right;

16. *Emphasizes* the critical importance of identifying and analysing obstacles impeding the full realization of the right to development at both the national and the international levels;

17. *Affirms* that, while globalization offers both opportunities and challenges, the process of globalization remains deficient in achieving the objectives of integrating all countries into a globalized world, and stresses the need for policies and measures at the national and global levels to respond to the challenges and opportunities of globalization if this process is to be made fully inclusive and equitable;

18. *Recognizes* that, despite continuous efforts on the part of the international community, the gap between developed and developing countries remains unacceptably wide, that developing countries continue to face difficulties in participating in the globalization process and that many risk being marginalized and effectively excluded from its benefits;

19. *Underlines* the fact that the international community is far from meeting the target set in the United Nations Millennium Declaration[4] of halving the number of people living in poverty by 2015, reaffirms the commitment made to meet that target, and emphasizes the principle of international cooperation, including partnership and commitment, between developed and developing countries towards achieving the goal;

20. *Urges* developed countries that have not yet done so to make concrete efforts towards meeting the targets of 0.7 per cent of their gross national product for official development assistance to developing countries and 0.15 to 0.2 per cent of their gross national product to least developed countries, and encourages developing countries to build on the progress achieved in ensuring that official development assistance is used effectively to help to meet development goals and targets;

21. *Recognizes* the need to address market access for developing countries, including in agriculture, services and non-agricultural products, in particular those of interest to developing countries;

22. *Calls for* the implementation of a desirable pace of meaningful trade liberalization, including in areas under negotiation; implementation of commitments on implementation-related issues and concerns; review of special and differential-treatment provisions, with a view to strengthening them and making them more precise, effective and operational; avoidance of new forms of protectionism; and capacity-building and technical assistance for developing countries as important issues in making progress towards the effective implementation of the right to development;

23. *Recognizes* the important link between the international economic, commercial and financial spheres and the realization of the right to development, stresses, in this regard, the need for good governance and broadening the base of decision-making at the international level on issues of development concern and the need to fill organizational gaps, as well as strengthen the United Nations system and other multilateral institutions, and also stresses the need to broaden and strengthen the participation of developing countries and countries with economies in transition in international economic decision-making and norm-setting;

24. *Also recognizes* that good governance and the rule of law at the national level assist all States in the promotion and protection of human rights, including the right to development, and agrees on the value of the ongoing efforts being made by States to identify and strengthen good governance practices, including transparent, responsible, accountable and participatory government, that are responsive and appropriate to their needs and aspirations,

including in the context of agreed partnership approaches to development, capacity-building and technical assistance;

25. *Further recognizes* the important role and the rights of women and the application of a gender perspective as a cross-cutting issue in the process of realizing the right to development, and notes in particular the positive relationship between women's education and their equal participation in the civil, cultural, economic, political and social activities of the community and the promotion of the right to development;

26. *Stresses* the need for the integration of the rights of children, girls and boys alike, in all policies and programmes, and for ensuring the promotion and protection of those rights, especially in areas relating to health, education and the full development of their capacities;

27. *Welcomes* the Political Declaration on HIV/AIDS adopted at the High-level Meeting of the General Assembly on 2 June 2006,[12] stresses that further and additional measures must be taken at the national and international levels to fight HIV/AIDS and other communicable diseases, taking into account ongoing efforts and programmes, and reiterates the need for international assistance in this regard;

28. *Recognizes* the need for strong partnerships with civil society organizations and the private sector in pursuit of poverty eradication and development, as well as for corporate social responsibility;

29. *Emphasizes* the urgent need for taking concrete and effective measures to prevent, combat and criminalize all forms of corruption at all levels, to prevent, detect and deter in a more effective manner international transfers of illicitly acquired assets and to strengthen international cooperation in asset recovery consistent with the principles of the United Nationtion against Corruption,[13] particularly chapter V thereof, stresses the importance of a genuine political commitment on the part of all Governments through a firm legal framework, and in this context urges States to sign and ratify as soon as possible, and States parties to implement effectively, the Convention;

30. *Also emphasizes* the need to strengthen further the activities of the Office of the United Nations High Commissioner for Human Rights in the promotion and realization of the right to development, including ensuring effective use of the financial and human resources necessary to fulfil its mandate, and calls upon the Secretary-General to provide the Office of the High Commissioner with the necessary resources;

31. *Reaffirms* the request to the High Commissioner, in mainstreaming the right to development, to undertake effectively activities aimed at strengthening the global partnership for development between Member States, development agencies and the international development, financial and trade institutions, and to reflect those activities in detail in her next report to the Human Rights Council;

32. *Calls upon* the United Nations agencies, funds and programmes, as well as the specialized agencies, to mainstream the right to development in their operational programmes and objectives, and stresses the need for the international financial and multilateral trading systems to mainstream the right to development in their policies and objectives;

33. *Requests* the Secretary-General to bring the present resolution to the attention of Member States, United Nations organs and bodies, specialized agencies, funds and programmes, international development and financial institutions, in particular the Bretton Woods institutions, and non-governmental organizations;

34. *Also requests* the Secretary-General to submit a report to the General Assembly at its sixty-second session and an interim report to the Human Rights Council on the implementation of the present resolution, including efforts undertaken at the national, regional and international levels in the promotion and realization of the right to development, and invites the Chairperson of the Working Group on the Right to Development to present a verbal update to the Assembly at its sixty-second session.

81st plenary meeting
19 December 2006

---

[1] Resolution 217 A (III).

[2] See resolution 2200 A (XXI), annex.

[3] A/CONF.157/24 (Part I), chap. III.

[4] See resolution 55/2.

[5] See TD/412.

[6] See *Official Records of the General Assembly, Sixty-first Session, Supplement No. 53* (A/61/53), part one, chap. II, sect. A.

[7] See *Official Records of the Economic and Social Council, 1998, Supplement No. 3* (E/1998/23), chap. II, sect. A.

[8] E/CN.4/2006/26.

[9] A/57/304, annex.

[10] See E/CN.4/2005/WG.18/TF/3.

[11] E/CN.4/2002/28/Rev.1, sect. VIII.A.

[12] Resolution 60/262, annex.

[13] Resolution 58/4, annex.

Resolution 61/170

[on the report of the Third Committee (A/61/443/Add.2 and Corr.1)]

61/170. Human rights and unilateral coercive measures

The General Assembly,

Recalling all its previous resolutions on this subject, the most recent of which was resolution 60/155 of 16 December 2005, and Commission on Human Rights resolution 2005/14 of 14 April 2005,[1]

Reaffirming the pertinent principles and provisions contained in the Charter of Economic Rights and Duties of States proclaimed by the General Assembly in its resolution 3281 (XXIX) of 12 December 1974, in particular article 32 thereof, in which it declared that no State may use or encourage the use of economic, political or any other type of measures to coerce another State in order to obtain from it the subordination of the exercise of its sovereign rights,

Taking note of the report of the Secretary-General,[2] submitted pursuant to Commission on Human Rights resolution 1999/21 of 23 April 1999,[3] and the reports of the Secretary-General on the implementation of resolutions 52/120 of 12 December 1997[4] and 55/110 of 4 December 2000,[5]

Recognizing the universal, indivisible, interdependent and interrelated character of all human rights, and, in this regard, reaffirming the right to development as an integral part of all human rights,

Recalling that the World Conference on Human Rights, held at Vienna from 14 to 25 June 1993, called upon States to refrain from any unilateral coercive measure not in accordance with international law and the Charter of the United Nations that creates obstacles to trade relations among States and impedes the full realization of all human rights,[6]

Bearing in mind all the references to this question in the Copenhagen Declaration on Social Development adopted by the World Summit for Social Development on 12 March 1995,[7] the Beijing Declaration and Platform for Action adopted by the Fourth World Conference on Women on 15 September 1995,[8] the Istanbul Declaration on Human Settlements and the Habitat Agenda adopted by the second United Nations Conference on Human Settlements (Habitat II) on 14 June 1996,[9] and their five-year reviews,

Expressing its concern about the negative impact of unilateral coercive measures on international relations, trade, investment and cooperation,

Expressing its grave concern that, in some countries, the situation of children is adversely affected by unilateral coercive measures not in accordance with international law and the Charter that create obstacles to trade relations among States, impede the full realization of social and economic development and hinder the well-being of the population in the affected countries, with particular consequences for women and children, including adolescents,

Deeply concerned that, despite the recommendations adopted on this question by the General Assembly and recent major United Nations conferences, and contrary to general international law and the Charter, unilateral coercive measures continue to be promulgated and implemented with all their negative implications for the social-humanitarian activities and economic and social development of developing countries, including their extraterritorial effects, thereby creating additional obstacles to the full enjoyment of all human rights by peoples and individuals under the jurisdiction of other States,

Bearing in mind all the extraterritorial effects of any unilateral legislative, administrative and economic measures, policies and practices of a coercive nature against the development process and the enhancement of human rights in developing countries, which create obstacles to the full realization of all human rights,

Noting the continuing efforts of the open-ended Working Group on the Right to Development of the Commission on Human Rights, and reaffirming in particular its criteria, according to which unilateral coercive measures are one of the obstacles to the implementation of the Declaration on the Right to Development,[10]

1. *Urges* all States to refrain from adopting or implementing any unilateral measures not in accordance with international law and the Charter of the United Nations, in particular those of a coercive nature with all their extraterritorial effects, which create obstacles to trade relations among States, thus impeding the full realization of the rights set forth in the Universal Declaration of Human Rights[11] and other international human rights instruments, in particular the right of individuals and peoples to development;

2. *Also urges* all States to take steps to avoid and to refrain from adopting any unilateral measures not in accordance with international law and the Charter that impede the full achievement of economic and social development by the population of the affected countries, in particular children and women, that hinder their well-being and that create obstacles to the full enjoyment of their human rights, including the right of everyone to a standard of living adequate for their health and well-being and their right to food, medical care and the necessary social services, as well as to ensure that food and medicine are not used as tools for political pressure;

3. *Invites* all States to consider adopting administrative or legislative measures, as appropriate, to counteract the extraterritorial applications or effects of unilateral coercive measures;

4. *Rejects* unilateral coercive measures with all their extraterritorial effects as tools for political or economic pressure against any country, in particular against developing countries, because of their negative effects on the realization of all the human rights of vast sectors of their populations, in particular children, women and the elderly;

5. *Calls upon* Member States that have initiated such measures to commit themselves to their obligations and responsibilities arising from the international human rights instruments to which they are party by revoking such measures at the earliest possible time;

6. *Reaffirms*, in this context, the right of all peoples to self-determination, by virtue of which they freely determine their political status and freely pursue their economic, social and cultural development;

7. *Urges* the Human Rights Council to take fully into account the negative impact of unilateral coercive measures, including the enactment of national laws and their extraterritorial application, in its task concerning the implementation of the right to development;

8. *Requests* the United Nations High Commissioner for Human Rights, in discharging her functions relating to the promotion, realization and protection of the right to development and bearing in mind the continuing impact of unilateral coercive measures on the population of developing countries, to give priority to the present resolution in her annual report to the General Assembly;

9. *Requests* the Secretary-General to bring the present resolution to the attention of all Member States, to continue to collect their views and information on the implications and negative effects of unilateral coercive measures on their populations and to submit an analytical report thereon to the General Assembly at its sixty-second session, while reiterating once again the need to highlight the practical and preventive measures in this respect;

10. *Decides* to examine the question on a priority basis at its sixty-second session under the sub-item entitled "Human rights questions, including alternative approaches for improving the effective enjoyment of human rights and fundamental freedoms".

81st plenary meeting
19 December 2006

[1] See *Official Records of the Economic and Social Council, 2005, Supplement No. 3* and corrigendum (E/2005/23 and Corr.1), chap. II, sect. A.

[2] E/CN.4/2000/46 and Add.1.

[3] See *Official Records of the Economic and Social Council, 1999, Supplement No. 3* (E/1999/23), chap. II, sect. A.

[4] A/53/293 and Add.1.

[5] A/56/207 and Add.1.

[6] See A/CONF.157/24 (Part I), chap. III, sect. I, para. 31.

[7] *Report of the World Summit for Social Development, Copenhagen, 6–12 March 1995* (United Nations publication, Sales No. E.96.IV.8), chap. I, resolution 1, annex I.

[8] *Report of the Fourth World Conference on Women, Beijing, 4–15 September 1995* (United Nations publication, Sales No. E.96.IV.13), chap. I, resolution 1, annexes I and II.

[9] *Report of the United Nations Conference on Human Settlements (Habitat II), Istanbul, 3–14 June 1996* (United Nations publication, Sales No. E.97.IV.6), chap. I, resolution 1, annexes I and II.

[10] Resolution 41/128, annex.

[11] Resolution 217 A (III).

Resolution 61/171

[on the report of the Third Committee (A/61/443/Add.2 and Corr.1)]

61/171. Protection of human rights and fundamental freedoms while countering terrorism

The General Assembly,

Reaffirming the purposes and principles of the Charter of the United Nations,

Reaffirming also the fundamental importance, including in response to terrorism and the fear of terrorism, of respecting all human rights and fundamental freedoms and the rule of law,

Recalling its resolutions 57/219 of 18 December 2002, 58/187 of 22 December 2003, 59/191 of 20 December 2004 and 60/158 of 16 December 2005, Commission on Human Rights resolutions 2003/68 of 25 April 2003,[1] 2004/87 of 21 April 2004[2] and 2005/80 of 21 April 2005[3] and other relevant resolutions of the General Assembly and the Commission on Human Rights,

Reaffirming that States are under the obligation to protect all human rights and fundamental freedoms of all persons,

Reiterating the important contribution of measures taken at all levels against terrorism, consistent with international law, in particular international human rights law and refugee and humanitarian law, to the functioning of democratic institutions and the maintenance of peace and security and thereby to the full enjoyment of human rights, as well as the need to continue this fight, including through international cooperation and the strengthening of the role of the United Nations in this respect,

Deeply deploring the occurrence of violations of human rights and fundamental freedoms in the context of the fight against terrorism, as well as violations of international refugee law and international humanitarian law,

Recalling the establishment by the Commission on Human Rights, in its resolution 2005/08, of the mandate of the Special Rapporteur on the promotion and protection of human rights and fundamental freedoms while countering terrorism,

Recalling also its resolution 48/141 of 20 December 1993 and, inter alia, the responsibility of the United Nations High Commissioner for Human Rights to promote and protect the effective enjoyment of all human rights,

Welcoming the establishment of the Human Rights Council, which is responsible for promoting universal respect for the protection of all human rights and fundamental freedoms for all, without distinction of any kind and in a fair and equal manner,

Recognizing the importance of the United Nations Global Counter-Terrorism Strategy adopted by the General Assembly on 8 September 2006,[4] and reaffirming its relevant clauses on the measures to ensure respect for human rights for all, international humanitarian law and the rule of law as the fundamental basis for the fight against terrorism,

Reaffirming that acts, methods and practices of terrorism in all its forms and manifestations are activities aimed at the destruction of human rights, fundamental freedoms and democracy, threatening the territorial integrity and security of States and destabilizing legitimately constituted Governments, and that the international community should take the necessary steps to enhance cooperation to prevent and combat terrorism,[5]

Reaffirming its unequivocal condemnation of all acts, methods and practices of terrorism in all its forms and manifestations, wherever and by whomsoever committed, regardless of their motivation, as criminal and unjustifiable, and renewing its commitment to strengthen international cooperation to prevent and combat terrorism,

Reaffirming that terrorism cannot and should not be associated with any religion, nationality, civilization or ethnic group,

Recognizing that the respect for all human rights, the respect for democracy and the respect for the rule of law are interrelated and mutually reinforcing,

Noting the declarations, statements and recommendations of a number of human rights treaty monitoring bodies and special procedures on the question of the compatibility of counter-terrorism measures with human rights obligations,

Recalling Human Rights Council decision 1/102 of 30 June 2006,[6]

1. *Reaffirms* that States must ensure that any measure taken to combat terrorism complies with their obligations under international law, in particular international human rights, refugee and humanitarian law;

2. *Deplores* the suffering caused by terrorism to the victims and their families, and expresses its profound solidarity with them;

3. *Reaffirms* the obligation of States, in accordance with article 4 of the International Covenant on Civil and Political Rights,[7] to respect certain rights as non-derogable in any circumstances, recalls, in regard to all other Covenant rights, that any measures derogating from the provisions of the Covenant must be in accordance with that article in all cases, and underlines the exceptional and temporary nature of any such derogations;[8]

4. *Calls upon* States to raise awareness about the importance of these obligations among national authorities involved in combating terrorism;

5. *Reaffirms* that counter-terrorism measures should be implemented in full consideration of minority rights and must not be discriminatory on the grounds of race, colour, sex, language, religion or social origin;

6. *Urges* States to fully respect non-refoulement obligations under international refugee and human rights law and, at the same time, to review, with full respect for these obligations and other legal safeguards, the validity of a refugee status decision in an individual case if credible and relevant evidence comes to light that indicates that the person in question has committed any criminal acts, including terrorist acts, falling under the exclusion clauses under international refugee law;

7. *Also urges* States, while countering terrorism, to ensure due process guarantees, consistent with all relevant provisions of the Universal Declaration of Human Rights,[9] the International Covenant on Civil and Political Rights and the Geneva Conventions of 1949,[10] in their respective fields of applicability;

8. *Opposes* any form of deprivation of liberty that amounts to placing a detained person outside the protection of the law, and urges States to respect the safeguards concerning the liberty, security and dignity of the person and to treat all prisoners in all places of detention in accordance with international law, including human rights law and international humanitarian law;

9. *Reaffirms* that it is imperative that all States work to uphold and protect the dignity of individuals and their fundamental freedoms, as well as democratic practices and the rule of law, while countering terrorism;

10. *Encourages* States, while countering terrorism, to take into account relevant United Nations resolutions and decisions on human rights, and encourages them to give due consideration to the recommendations of the special procedures and mechanisms and the relevant comments and views of United Nations human rights treaty bodies;

11. *Takes note with interest* of the report of the Secretary-General submitted pursuant to resolution 60/158;[11]

12. *Welcomes* the ongoing dialogue established in the context of the fight against terrorism between the Security Council and its Counter-Terrorism Committee and the relevant bodies for the promotion and protection of human rights, and encourages the Security Council and its Counter-Terrorism Committee to strengthen the links and to continue to develop cooperation with relevant human rights bodies, in particular with the Office of the United Nations High Commissioner for Human Rights, the Special Rapporteur on the promotion and protection of human rights and fundamental freedoms while countering terrorism and other relevant special procedures and mechanisms of the Human Rights Council, giving due regard to the promotion and protection of human rights in the ongoing work pursuant to relevant Security Council resolutions relating to terrorism;

13. *Takes note with appreciation* of the report of the Special Rapporteur submitted pursuant to Commission on Human Rights resolution 2005/80;[12]

14. *Acknowledges with appreciation* the cooperation between the Special Rapporteur and all relevant procedures and mechanisms of the Human Rights Council as well as the United Nations human rights treaty bodies, and urges them to continue their cooperation, in accordance

with their mandates, and to coordinate their efforts, where appropriate, in order to promote a consistent approach on this subject;

15. *Requests* all Governments to cooperate fully with the Special Rapporteur in the performance of the tasks and duties mandated, including by reacting promptly to the urgent appeals of the Special Rapporteur and providing the information requested;

16. *Welcomes* the work done by the United Nations High Commissioner for Human Rights to implement the mandate given to her in resolution 60/158, and requests the High Commissioner to continue her efforts in this regard;

17. *Requests* the Secretary-General to submit a report on the implementation of the present resolution to the Human Rights Council and to the General Assembly at its sixty-second session;

18. *Decides* to consider at its sixty-second session the report of the Special Rapporteur on the promotion and protection of human rights and fundamental freedoms while countering terrorism.

81st plenary meeting
19 December 2006

---

[1] See *Official Records of the Economic and Social Council, 2003, Supplement No. 3* (E/2003/23), chap. II, sect. A.

[2] Ibid., *2004, Supplement No. 3* (E/2004/23), chap. II, sect. A.

[3] Ibid., *2005, Supplement No. 3* and corrigendum (E/2005/23 and Corr.1), chap. II, sect. A.

[4] Resolution 60/288.

[5] See sect. I, para. 17, of the Vienna Declaration and Programme of Action adopted by the World Conference on Human Rights on 25 June 1993 (A/CONF.157/24 (Part I), chap. III).

[6] See *Official Records of the General Assembly, Sixty-first Session, Supplement No. 53* (A/61/53), part one, chap. II, sect. B.

[7] See resolution 2200 A (XXI), annex.

[8] See, for example, General Comment No. 29 on states of emergency adopted by the Human Rights Committee on 24 July 2001.

[9] Resolution 217 A (III).

[10] United Nations, *Treaty Series*, vol. 75, Nos. 970–973.

[11] A/61/353.

[12] See A/61/267.

Resolution 61/172

[on the report of the Third Committee (A/61/443/Add.2 and Corr.1)]

61/172. Hostage-taking

The General Assembly,

Reaffirming the purposes and principles of the Charter of the United Nations,

Recalling the Universal Declaration of Human Rights,[1] which guarantees, inter alia, the right to life, liberty and security of person, freedom from torture and other cruel, inhuman or degrading treatment, freedom of movement and protection from arbitrary detention,

Recalling also the Vienna Declaration and Programme of Action, adopted on 25 June 1993 by the World Conference on Human Rights,[2]

Taking into account the International Convention against the Taking of Hostages, adopted by the General Assembly in its resolution 34/146 of 17 December 1979, which recognizes that everyone has the right to life, liberty and security of person and considers the taking of hostages to be an offence of grave concern to the international community, as well as the Convention on the Prevention and Punishment of Crimes against Internationally Protected Persons, including Diplomatic Agents, adopted by the Assembly in its resolution 3166 (XXVIII) of 14 December 1973,

Bearing in mind the relevant Security Council resolutions condemning all cases of terrorism, including those of hostage-taking, in particular resolution 1440 (2002) of 24 October 2002,

Mindful of the fact that hostage-taking constitutes a war crime under the Rome Statute of the International Criminal Court[3] and is also a grave breach of the Geneva Conventions of 12 August 1949 for the protection of victims of war,[4]

Reaffirming its relevant resolutions, including the most recent, resolution 57/220 of 18 December 2002,

Recalling all relevant resolutions of the Commission on Human Rights on the subject, including its most recent, resolution 2005/31 of 19 April 2005,[5] in which it condemned the taking of any person as a hostage, as well as the statement by the President of the Human Rights Council of 30 June 2006 on the same subject,[6]

Concerned that, despite the efforts of the international community, acts of hostage-taking in different forms and manifestations, including, inter alia, those committed by terrorists and armed groups, continue to take place and have even increased in many regions of the world,

Appealing for the humanitarian action of humanitarian organizations, in particular the International Committee of the Red Cross and its delegates, to be respected, in accordance with the Geneva Conventions of 12 August 1949 and the Additional Protocols thereto of 1977,[7]

Recognizing that hostage-taking calls for resolute, firm and concerted efforts on the part of the international community in order, in strict conformity with international human rights standards, to bring such abhorrent practices to an end,

1. *Reaffirms* that hostage-taking, wherever and by whomever committed, is a serious crime aimed at the destruction of human rights and is, under any circumstances, unjustifiable;

2. *Condemns* all acts of hostage-taking, anywhere in the world;

3. *Demands* that all hostages be released immediately and without any preconditions, and expresses its solidarity with the victims of hostage-taking;

4. *Calls upon* States to take all necessary measures, in accordance with relevant provisions of international humanitarian law and international human rights standards, to prevent, combat and punish acts of hostage-taking, including by strengthening international cooperation in this field;

5. *Decides* to remain seized of the matter.

81st plenary meeting
19 December 2006

---

[1] Resolution 217 A (III).

[2] A/CONF.157/24 (Part I), chap. III.

[3] United Nations, *Treaty Series*, vol. 2187, No. 38544.

[4] Ibid., vol. 75, Nos. 970–973.

[5] See *Official Records of the Economic and Social Council, 2005, Supplement No. 3* and corrigendum (E/2005/23 and Corr.1), chap. II, sect. A.

[6] See *Official Records of the General Assembly, Sixty-first Session, Supplement No. 53* (A/61/53), part one, chap. II, sect. C.

[7] United Nations, *Treaty Series*, vol. 1125, Nos. 17512 and 17513.

Resolution 61/173

[on the report of the Third Committee (A/61/443/Add.2 and Corr.1)]

61/173. Extrajudicial, summary or arbitrary executions

The General Assembly,

Recalling the Universal Declaration of Human Rights,[1] which guarantees the right to life, liberty and security of person, the relevant provisions of the International Covenant on Civil and Political Rights[2] and other relevant human rights conventions,

Having regard to the legal framework of the mandate of the Special Rapporteur of the Human Rights Council on extrajudicial, summary or arbitrary executions,

Welcoming the universal ratification of the Geneva Conventions of 12 August 1949,[3] which alongside human rights law provide an important framework of accountability in relation to extrajudicial, summary or arbitrary executions during armed conflict,

Mindful of all its resolutions on the subject of extrajudicial, summary or arbitrary executions and the resolutions of the Commission on Human Rights on the subject,

Noting with deep concern that impunity continues to be a major cause of the perpetuation of violations of human rights, including extrajudicial, summary or arbitrary executions,

Acknowledging that international human rights law and international humanitarian law are complementary and not mutually exclusive,

Noting with deep concern the growing number of civilians and persons *hors de combat* killed in situations of armed conflict and internal strife,

Acknowledging that extrajudicial, summary or arbitrary executions may under certain circumstances amount to genocide, crimes against humanity or war crimes, as defined in international law, including in the Rome Statute of the International Criminal Court,[4]

Affirming the obligation of State to prevent the abuse of persons deprived of their liberty and to investigate and respond to deaths in custody,

Convinced of the need for effective action to prevent, combat and eliminate the abhorrent practice of extrajudicial, summary or arbitrary executions, which represent a flagrant violation of the right to life,

1. *Strongly condemns once again* all the extrajudicial, summary or arbitrary executions that continue to occur throughout the world;

2. *Demands* that all States ensure that the practice of extrajudicial, summary or arbitrary executions is brought to an end and that they take effective action to prevent, combat and eliminate the phenomenon in all its forms;

3. *Reiterates* the obligation of all States to conduct exhaustive and impartial investigations into all suspected cases of extrajudicial, summary or arbitrary executions, to identify and bring to justice those responsible, while ensuring the right of every person to a fair and public hearing by a competent, independent and impartial tribunal established by law, to grant adequate compensation within a reasonable time to the victims or their families, and to adopt all necessary measures, including legal and judicial measures, to put an end to impunity and to prevent the further occurrence of such executions, as recommended in the Principles on the Effective Prevention and Investigation of Extralegal, Arbitrary and Summary Executions;[5]

4. *Calls upon* all States in which the death penalty has not been abolished to comply with their obligations under relevant provisions of international human rights instruments, including in particular articles 6, 7 and 14 of the International Covenant on Civil and Political Rights[2] and articles 37 and 40 of the Convention on the Rights of the Child,[6] bearing in mind the safeguards and guarantees set out in Economic and Social Council resolutions 1984/50 of 25 May 1984 and 1989/64 of 24 May 1989;

5. *Urges* all States:

(*a*) To take all necessary and possible measures, in conformity with international human rights law and international humanitarian law, to prevent loss of life, in particular that of children, during public demonstrations, internal and communal violence, civil unrest, public emergencies or armed conflicts, and to ensure that the police, law enforcement agents, armed forces and other agents acting on behalf of or with the consent or acquiescence of the State act with restraint and in conformity with international humanitarian law and international human rights law, including the principles of proportionality and necessity, and in this regard to ensure that police and law enforcement officials are guided by the Code of Conduct for Law Enforcement Officials[7] and the Basic Principles on the Use of Force and Firearms by Law Enforcement Officials;[8]

(*b*) To ensure the effective protection of the right to life of all persons under their jurisdiction and to investigate promptly and thoroughly all killings, including those targeted at specific groups of persons, such as racially motivated violence leading to the death of the victim, killings of members of national, ethnic, religious or linguistic minorities, of refugees, internally displaced persons, migrants, street children or members of indigenous communities, killings of persons for reasons related to their activities as human rights defenders, lawyers, journalists or demonstrators, killings committed in the name of passion or in the name of honour, all killings committed for any discriminatory reason, including sexual orientation, as well as all other cases where a person's right to life has been violated, and to bring those responsible to justice before a competent, independent and impartial judiciary at the national or, where appropriate, international level, and to ensure that such killings, including those committed by security forces, police and law enforcement agents, paramilitary groups or private forces, are neither condoned nor sanctioned by State officials or personnel;

6. *Also urges* all States to ensure that persons deprived of their liberty are treated humanely and with full respect for their human rights and to ensure that their treatment, including judicial guarantees, and conditions conform to the Standard Minimum Rules for the Treatment of Prisoners[9] and, where applicable, to the Geneva Conventions of 12 August 1949[3] and the Additional Protocols thereto of 8 June 1977[10] in relation to all persons detained in armed conflict, as well as to other pertinent international instruments;

7. *Welcomes* the International Criminal Court as an important contribution to ending impunity concerning extrajudicial, summary or arbitrary executions and the fact that one hundred and four States have already ratified or acceded to and a further forty-one States have signed the Rome Statute of the Court,[4] and calls upon all those States that have not ratified or acceded to the Rome Statute to consider doing so;

8. *Encourages* Governments and intergovernmental and non-governmental organizations to organize training programmes and to support projects with a view to training or educating military forces, law enforcement officers and government officials in human rights and humanitarian law issues connected with their work and to include a gender and child rights perspective in such training, and appeals to the international community and requests the Office of the United Nations High Commissioner for Human Rights to support endeavours to that end;

9. *Takes note* of the interim report of the Special Rapporteur of the Human Rights Council on extrajudicial, summary or arbitrary executions to the General Assembly;[11]

10. *Commends* the important role that the Special Rapporteur plays towards the elimination of extrajudicial, summary or arbitrary executions, and encourages the Special Rapporteur to continue, within his mandate, to collect information from all concerned, to respond effectively to reliable information that comes before him, to follow up on communications and country visits and to seek the views and comments of Governments and to reflect them, as appropriate, in his reports;

11. *Acknowledges* the important role of the Special Rapporteur in identifying cases where extrajudicial, summary and arbitrary executions could amount to genocide and crimes against humanity or war crimes, and urges him to collaborate with the United Nations High Commissioner for Human Rights and, as appropriate, the Special Adviser to the Secretary-General on the Prevention of Genocide, in addressing situations of extrajudicial, summary or arbitrary executions that are of particularly serious concern or in which early action might prevent further deterioration;

12. *Welcomes* the cooperation established between the Special Rapporteur and other United Nations mechanisms and procedures in the field of human rights, and encourages the Special Rapporteur to continue efforts in that regard;

13. *Urges* all States, in particular those that have not done so, to cooperate with the Special Rapporteur so that his mandate can be carried out effectively, including by favourably and rapidly responding to requests for visits, mindful that country visits are one of the tools for the fulfilment of the mandate of the Special Rapporteur, and by responding in a timely

manner to communications and other requests transmitted to them by the Special Rapporteur;

14. *Expresses its appreciation* to those States that have received the Special Rapporteur and asks them to examine his recommendations carefully, invites them to inform him of the actions taken on those recommendations, and requests other States to cooperate in a similar way;

15. *Again requests* the Secretary-General to continue to use his best endeavours in cases where the minimum standards of legal safeguards provided for in articles 6, 9, 14 and 15 of the International Covenant on Civil and Political Rights appear not to have been respected;

16. *Requests* the Secretary-General to provide the Special Rapporteur with adequate human, financial and material resources to enable him to carry out his mandate effectively, including through country visits;

17. *Also requests* the Secretary-General to continue, in close collaboration with the High Commissioner, in conformity with the mandate of the High Commissioner established by the General Assembly in its resolution 48/141 of 20 December 1993, to ensure that personnel specialized in human rights and humanitarian law issues form part of United Nations missions, where appropriate, in order to deal with serious violations of human rights, such as extrajudicial, summary or arbitrary executions;

18. *Requests* the Special Rapporteur to submit to the General Assembly at its sixty-second session a report on the situation worldwide in regard to extrajudicial, summary or arbitrary executions and his recommendations for more effective action to combat this phenomenon.

81st plenary meeting
19 December 2006

---

[1] Resolution 217 A (III).

[2] See resolution 2200 A (XXI), annex.

[3] United Nations, *Treaty Series*, vol. 75, Nos. 970–973.

[4] Ibid., vol. 2187, No. 38544.

[5] Economic and Social Council resolution 1989/65, annex.

[6] United Nations, *Treaty Series*, vol. 1577, No. 27531.

[7] Resolution 34/169, annex.

[8] See *Eighth United Nations Congress on the Prevention of Crime and the Treatment of Offenders, Havana, 27 August–7 September 1990: report prepared by the Secretariat* (United Nations publication, Sales No. E.91.IV.2), chap. I, sect. B.

[9] *Human Rights: A Compilation of International Instruments*, Volume I (First Part): *Universal Instruments* (United Nations publication, Sales No. E.02.XIV.4 (Vol. I, Part 1)), sect. J, No. 34.

[10] United Nations, *Treaty Series*, vol. 1125, Nos. 17512 and 17513.

[11] See A/61/311.

Resolution 61/174

[on the report of the Third Committee (A/61/443/Add.3)]

61/174. Situation of human rights in the Democratic People's Republic of Korea

The General Assembly,

Reaffirming that States Members of the United Nations have an obligation to promote and protect human rights and fundamental freedoms and to fulfil the obligations that they have undertaken under the various international instruments,

Mindful that the Democratic People's Republic of Korea is a party to the International Covenant on Civil and Political Rights,[1] the International Covenant on Economic, Social and Cultural Rights,[1] the Convention on the Rights of the Child[2] and the Convention on the Elimination of All Forms of Discrimination against Women,[3]

Noting the submission by the Democratic People's Republic of Korea of its second periodic report concerning the implementation of the International Covenant on Economic, Social and Cultural Rights,[4] its second periodic report on the implementation of the Convention on the Rights of the Child[5] and its initial report on the implementation of the Convention on the Elimination of All Forms of Discrimination against Women,[6] as a sign of engagement in international cooperative efforts in the field of human rights,

Taking note of the concluding observations of the treaty monitoring bodies under the four treaties, the most recent of which were given by the Committee on the Elimination of Discrimination against Women in July 2005,[7]

Recalling its resolution 60/173 of 16 December 2005 and Commission on Human Rights resolutions 2003/10 of 16 April 2003,[8] 2004/13 of 15 April 2004[9] and 2005/11 of 14 April 2005,[10] and mindful of the need for the international community to strengthen its coordinated efforts aimed at urging the implementation of those resolutions,

Taking note of the report of the Special Rapporteur on the situation of human rights in the Democratic People's Republic of Korea,[11] including the specific concerns relating to women's rights, the rights of the child, the rights of the elderly, the rights of persons with disabilities and refugee rights addressed therein,

1. *Expresses its very serious concern* at:

   (*a*) The continued refusal of the Government of the Democratic People's Republic of Korea to recognize the mandate of the Special Rapporteur on the situation of human rights in the Democratic People's Republic of Korea or to extend cooperation to him;

   (*b*) Continuing reports of systemic, widespread and grave violations of human rights in the Democratic People's Republic of Korea, including:

      (i) Torture and other cruel, inhuman or degrading treatment or punishment, public executions, extrajudicial and arbitrary detention, the absence of due process and the rule of law, the imposition of the death penalty for political reasons, the existence of a large number of prison camps and the extensive use of forced labour;

      (ii) The situation of refugees expelled or returned to the Democratic People's Republic of Korea and sanctions imposed on citizens of the Democratic People's Republic of Korea who have been repatriated from abroad, such as treating their departure as treason, leading to punishments of internment, torture, cruel, inhuman or degrading treatment or the death penalty, and urges all States to ensure respect for the fundamental principle of non-refoulement;

(iii) All-pervasive and severe restrictions on the freedoms of thought, conscience, religion, opinion and expression, peaceful assembly and association, and on equal access to information and limitations imposed on every person who wishes to move freely within the country and travel abroad;

(iv) Continuing violation of the human rights and fundamental freedoms of women, in particular the trafficking of women for the purpose of prostitution or forced marriage, forced abortions, and infanticide of children of repatriated mothers, including in police detention centres and camps;

(v) Unresolved questions of international concern relating to the abduction of foreigners in the form of enforced disappearance, which violates the human rights of the nationals of other sovereign countries;

(vi) The violations of economic, social and cultural rights, which have led to severe malnutrition and hardship for the population in the Democratic People's Republic of Korea;

(vii) Continuing reports of violations of the human rights and fundamental freedoms of persons with disabilities, especially on the use of collective camps and of coercive measures that target the rights of persons with disabilities to decide freely and responsibly on the number and spacing of their children;

2. *Expresses its strong concern* that the Government of the Democratic People's Republic of Korea has not engaged in technical cooperation activities with the United Nations High Commissioner for Human Rights and her Office, despite efforts by the High Commissioner to engage in a dialogue with the authorities of the Democratic People's Republic of Korea in this regard;

3. *Expresses its very deep concern* at the precarious humanitarian situation in the country, compounded by the mismanagement on the part of the authorities, in particular the prevalence of infant malnutrition, which, despite recent progress, continues to affect the physical and mental development of a significant proportion of children, and urges the Government of the Democratic People's Republic of Korea, in this regard, to facilitate the continued presence of humanitarian organizations to ensure that humanitarian assistance is delivered impartially to all parts of the country on the basis of need in accordance with humanitarian principles;

4. *Strongly urges* the Government of the Democratic People's Republic of Korea to respect fully all human rights and fundamental freedoms and, in this regard, to implement fully the measures set out in the above-mentioned resolutions of the General Assembly and the Commission on Human Rights, and the recommendations addressed to the Democratic People's Republic of Korea by the United Nations special procedures and treaty bodies, and to extend its full cooperation to the Special Rapporteur, including by granting him full, free and unimpeded access to the Democratic People's Republic of Korea, and to other United Nations human rights mechanisms;

5. *Decides* to continue its examination of the situation of human rights in the Democratic People's Republic of Korea at its sixty-second session, and to this end requests the Secretary-General to submit a comprehensive report on the situation in the Democratic People's

Republic of Korea and the Special Rapporteur to report his findings and recommendations.

81st plenary meeting
19 December 2006

[1] See resolution 2200 A (XXI), annex.

[2] United Nations, *Treaty Series*, vol. 1577, No. 27531.

[3] Ibid., vol. 1249, No. 20378.

[4] E/1990/6/Add.35.

[5] CRC/C/65/Add.24.

[6] CEDAW/C/PRK/1.

[7] See *Official Records of the General Assembly, Sixtieth Session, Supplement No. 38* (A/60/38), part two, paras. 26–76.

[8] See *Official Records of the Economic and Social Council, 2003, Supplement No. 3* (E/2003/23), chap. II, sect. A.

[9] Ibid., *2004, Supplement No. 3* (E/2004/23), chap. II, sect. A.

[10] Ibid., *2005, Supplement No. 3* and corrigendum (E/2005/23 and Corr.1), chap. II, sect. A.

[11] See A/61/349.

Resolution 61/175

[on the report of the Third Committee (A/61/443/Add.3)]

61/175. Situation of human rights in Belarus

The General Assembly,

Guided by the purposes and principles of the Charter of the United Nations, the provisions of the Universal Declaration of Human Rights,[1] the International Covenants on Human Rights[2] and other applicable human rights instruments,

Reaffirming that all States have an obligation to promote and protect human rights and fundamental freedoms and to fulfil their international obligations,

Mindful that Belarus is a party to the International Covenant on Civil and Political Rights[2] and the Optional Protocols thereto,[3] the International Covenant on Economic, Social and Cultural Rights,[2] the International Convention on the Elimination of All Forms of Racial Discrimination,[4] the Convention against Torture and Other Cruel, Inhuman or Degrading Treatment or Punishment,[5] the Convention on the Elimination of All Forms of Discrimination against Women[6] and the Optional Protocol thereto,[7] and the Convention on the Rights of the Child[8] and the Optional Protocol thereto on the sale of children, child prostitution and child pornography,[9]

Recalling Commission on Human Rights resolutions 2003/14 of 17 April 2003,[10] 2004/14 of 15 April 2004[11] and 2005/13 of 14 April 2005,[12] and Human Rights Council decision 1/102 of 30 June 2006,[13]

Concerned that the presidential election of 19 March 2006 was severely flawed and fell significantly short of the commitments of Belarus to the Organization for Security and Cooperation in Europe to hold a free and fair election, and that the situation of human rights in Belarus in 2005 was steadily deteriorating, as documented in the final report of the Office for Democratic Institutions and Human Rights of the Organization for Security and Cooperation in Europe and in the report of the Special Rapporteur on the situation of human rights in Belarus,[14]

Noting that the Belarusian authorities have decided to hold local elections on 14 January 2007, and expressing its hope that those will be free and fair, in full respect of international electoral standards,

1. *Expresses deep concern:*

(*a*) About the failure of the Government of Belarus to cooperate fully with all the mechanisms of the Human Rights Council, in particular with the special rapporteurs on the situation of human rights in Belarus, while noting the serious concern relating to the deterioration of the human rights situation in Belarus expressed by seven independent human rights experts of the United Nations in a statement issued on 29 March 2006;

(*b*) That in spite of detailed recommendations by the Organization for Security and Cooperation in Europe and dialogue between the Government and the Organization for Security and Cooperation in Europe following previous elections, Belarus again failed to meet its commitments to hold free and fair elections, including through the arbitrary use of State power against opposition candidates, routine harassment, the detention and arrest of political and civil society activists, the obstruction of the access of opposition candidates to State media, the negative portrayal in the State media of opposition candidates and activists, including human rights defenders, and the serious shortcomings of the vote count, which lacked minimum transparency;

(*c*) About continuing reports of harassment, arbitrary arrest and detention of up to one thousand persons, including opposition candidates, before and after the election of 19 March 2006;

(*d*) About the continuing and expanding criminal prosecutions, lack of due process and closed political trials of leading opposition figures and human rights defenders;

(*e*) About the continuing harassment and detention of Belarusian journalists covering local opposition demonstrations, and that senior officials of the Government of Belarus were implicated in the enforced disappearance and/or summary execution of three political opponents of the incumbent authorities in 1999 and of a journalist in 2000 and in the continuing investigatory cover-up, as documented in the report adopted in resolution 1371 (2004) of 28 April 2004 by the Parliamentary Assembly of the Council of Europe;[15]

(*f*) About the decision of the Belarusian authorities to revoke the teaching licence of the European Humanities University in Minsk and to terminate the lease of its buildings, forcing the University in Belarus to close down;

(*g*) About persistent reports of harassment and closure of non-governmental organizations, national minority organizations, independent media outlets, religious groups, opposition political parties, independent trade unions and independent youth and student organizations, and the harassment and prosecution of individuals, including students engaged in the promotion and protection of human rights, the rule of law and democracy;

2. *Urges* the Government of Belarus:

(*a*) To bring the electoral process and legislative framework into line with international standards, especially those of the Organization for Security and Cooperation in Europe, demonstrate such commitment through the upcoming local elections in January 2007 and rectify the shortcomings of the electoral process, identified by the Office for Democratic Institutions and Human Rights in its report of 7 June 2006, including, inter alia, election laws and practices that restrict campaigning opportunities for de facto opposition candidates, arbitrary application of electoral laws, including on registration of candidates, obstruction of the right of access to the media, biased presentation of the issues by the State media and falsification of vote counts;

(*b*) To cease politically motivated prosecution, harassment and intimidation of political opponents, pro-democracy activists and human rights defenders, students, independent media, religious organizations, educational institutions and civil society actors; and to cease the harassment of students and to create the conditions whereby they can continue their studies in Belarus;

(*c*) To respect the rights to freedom of speech, assembly and association and to release immediately all political prisoners and other individuals detained for exercising those rights;

(*d*) To suspend from their duties officials implicated in any case of enforced disappearance, summary execution and torture and other cruel, inhuman or degrading treatment or punishment, pending investigation of those cases, and to ensure that all necessary measures are taken to investigate fully and impartially such cases and to bring the alleged perpetrators to justice before an independent tribunal, and, if found guilty, to ensure that they are punished in accordance with the international human rights obligations of Belarus;

(*e*) To investigate and hold accountable those responsible for the mistreatment and detention of domestic and foreign journalists in connection with the election of 19 March 2006 and post-election demonstrations;

(*f*) To uphold the right to freedom of religion or belief, including the ability to maintain communications with individuals and communities in matters of religion and belief at the national and international levels;

(*g*) To investigate and hold accountable those responsible for the mistreatment, arbitrary arrest and incarceration of civic and political activists leading up to and following the presidential election of March 2006 and to release immediately and unconditionally all political prisoners;

(*h*) To carry out all other steps called for by the Commission on Human Rights in its resolution 2005/13;[12]

3. *Insists* that the Government of Belarus cooperate fully with all the mechanisms of the Human Rights Council, in particular with the Special Rapporteur appointed pursuant to Commission on Human Rights resolution 2004/14[11] and whose mandate was extended in

Commission resolution 2005/13, as well as with the Representative of the Organization for Security and Cooperation in Europe on freedom of the media.

81st plenary meeting
19 December 2006

[1] Resolution 217 A (III).

[2] Resolution 2200 A (XXI), annex.

[3] See resolution 2200 A (XXI), annex, and resolution 44/128, annex.

[4] United Nations, *Treaty Series*, vol. 660, No. 9464.

[5] Ibid., vol. 1465, No. 24841.

[6] Ibid., vol. 1249, No. 20378.

[7] Ibid., vol. 2131, No. 20378.

[8] Ibid., vol. 1577, No. 27531.

[9] Ibid., vol. 2171, No. 27531.

[10] See *Official Records of the Economic and Social Council, 2003, Supplement No. 3* (E/2003/23), chap. II, sect. A.

[11] Ibid., *2004, Supplement No. 3* (E/2004/23), chap. II, sect. A.

[12] Ibid., *2005, Supplement No. 3* and corrigendum (E/2005/23 and Corr.1), chap. II, sect. A.

[13] See *Official Records of the General Assembly, Sixty-first Session, Supplement No. 53* (A/61/53), part one, chap. II, sect. B.

[14] E/CN.4/2006/36.

[15] See Council of Europe, Parliamentary Assembly, document 10062.

Resolution 61/176

[on the report of the Third Committee (A/61/443/Add.3)]

61/176. Situation of human rights in the Islamic Republic of Iran

The General Assembly,

Guided by the Charter of the United Nations, the Universal Declaration of Human Rights,[1] the International Covenants on Human Rights[2] and other international human rights instruments,

Reaffirming that all Member States have an obligation to promote and protect human rights and fundamental freedoms and to fulfil the obligations they have undertaken under the various international instruments in this field,

Mindful that the Islamic Republic of Iran is a party to the International Covenant on Civil and Political Rights,[2] the International Covenant on Economic, Social and Cultural Rights,[2] the International Convention on the Elimination of All Forms of Racial Discrimination[3] and the Convention on the Rights of the Child,[4]

Recalling its previous resolutions on the subject, the most recent of which is resolution 60/171 of 16 December 2005, and recalling also Commission on Human Rights resolution 2001/17 of 20 April 2001,[5]

Noting the submission by the Islamic Republic of Iran of voluntary pledges and commitments on human rights in accordance with General Assembly resolution 60/251 of 15 March 2006,[6]

Noting also the statements made by the Government of the Islamic Republic of Iran on strengthening respect for human rights in the country and promoting the rule of law, and noting further the relevant provisions of its Constitution,

1. *Welcomes:*

(*a*) The standing invitation extended by the Government of the Islamic Republic of Iran to all human rights thematic monitoring mechanisms in April 2002 and the cooperation extended to the special procedures during their visits, while regretting that no special procedure has been able to visit the Islamic Republic of Iran since July 2005 and expressing its hope that special procedures of the Human Rights Council will be able to visit in the near future;

(*b*) The report of the Special Rapporteur on violence against women, its causes and consequences on her visit to the Islamic Republic of Iran from 29 January to 6 February 2005;[7]

(*c*) The report of the Special Rapporteur on adequate housing as a component of the right to an adequate standard of living on his visit to the Islamic Republic of Iran from 19 to 31 July 2005;[8]

(*d*) The statement by the head of the judiciary of the Islamic Republic of Iran in October 2006 in which he expressed his hope that judges will choose alternative punishments for minors instead of long jail terms for some offences;

(*e*) The announcement by the head of the judiciary in April 2004 of the ban on torture and the subsequent passage of related legislation by the parliament, which was approved by the Guardian Council in May 2004;

(*f*) The human rights dialogues between the Islamic Republic of Iran and a number of countries, while urging the Islamic Republic of Iran to intensify those dialogues and ensure that they are held regularly;

(*g*) The release of some prisoners held without due process of law;

(*h*) The cooperation with United Nations agencies in developing programmes in the fields of human rights, good governance and the rule of law;

2. *Expresses its serious concern* at:

(*a*) The continuing harassment, intimidation and persecution of human rights defenders, non-governmental organizations, political opponents, religious dissenters, political reformists, journalists, parliamentarians, students, clerics, academics, webloggers, union members and labour organizers, including through undue restrictions on the freedoms of assembly, conscience, opinion and expression, the threat and use of arbitrary arrest and prolonged detention, targeted at both individuals and their family members, the ongoing unjustified closure of newspapers and blocking of Internet sites and restrictions on the activities of unions and other non-governmental organizations, as well as the absence of many conditions necessary for free and fair elections;

(*b*) The persistent failure to comply fully with international standards in the administration of justice and, in particular, the absence of due process of law, the refusal to provide fair and public hearings, the denial of the right to counsel and access to counsel by those detained, the use of national security laws to deny human rights, the prevalent atmosphere of impunity for officials who commit human rights abuses, the harassment, intimidation and persecution of defence lawyers and legal defenders, the adulteration of judicial files, the lack of respect for internationally recognized safeguards, inter alia, with respect to persons belonging to religious, ethnic or national minorities, officially recognized or otherwise, the application of arbitrary prison sentences and the violation of the rights of detainees, including the systematic and arbitrary use of prolonged solitary confinement, the failure to provide proper medical care to those imprisoned, the arbitrary denial of contact between detainees and their family members, and the death of detainees in unclear circumstances or resulting from general mistreatment while in custody;

(*c*) The continuing use of torture and cruel, inhuman or degrading treatment or punishment such as flogging and amputations;

(*d*) The continuing of public executions, including multiple public executions, and, on a large scale, of other executions, in the absence of respect for internationally recognized safeguards, and the issuing of sentences of stoning; and, in particular, deplores the execution of persons who were under the age of 18 at the time their offence was committed, contrary to the obligations of the Islamic Republic of Iran under article 37 of the Convention on the Rights of the Child[4] and article 6 of the International Covenant on Civil and Political Rights[2] and in spite of the announcement of a moratorium on juvenile executions;

(*e*) The continuing violence and discrimination against women and girls in law and in practice, the refusal of the Guardian Council to take steps to address this systemic discrimination and recent arrests of and violent crackdowns on women exercising their right of assembly;

(*f*) The increasing discrimination and other human rights violations against persons belonging to ethnic and religious minorities, recognized or otherwise, including Arabs, Azeris, Baluchis, Kurds, Christians, Jews, Sufis and Sunni Muslims; the escalation and increased frequency of discrimination and other human rights violations against members of the Baha'i faith, including reports of plans by the State to identify and monitor Baha'is, as noted by the Special Rapporteur on freedom of religion or belief; an increase in cases of arbitrary arrest and detention; the denial of freedom of religion or of publicly carrying out communal affairs; the disregard for property rights, including through de facto expropriation, as noted in the report of the Special Rapporteur on adequate housing as a component of the right to an adequate standard of living; the destruction of sites of religious importance; the suspension of social, educational and community-related activities and the denial of access to higher education, employment, pensions, adequate housing and other benefits; and recent violent crackdowns on Arabs, Azeris, Baha'is, Kurds and Sufis;

3. *Calls upon* the Government of the Islamic Republic of Iran:

(*a*) To ensure full respect for the rights to freedom of assembly, opinion and expression and for the right to take part in the conduct of public affairs, in accordance with its obligations under the International Covenant on Civil and Political Rights, and, in particular, to end the harassment, intimidation and persecution of political opponents and human rights defenders, including by releasing persons imprisoned arbitrarily or on the basis of their political views; and to increase actions to promote and facilitate human rights education at all levels and to ensure that all those responsible for training lawyers, law enforcement officers, the personnel of the armed forces and public officials include appropriate elements of human rights teaching in their training programme;

(*b*) To ensure full respect for the right to due process of law, including the right to counsel and access to counsel by those detained, in criminal justice proceedings and, in particular, to ensure a fair and public hearing by a competent, independent and impartial tribunal established by law, to end harassment, intimidation and persecution of defence lawyers and legal defenders and to ensure equality before the law and the equal protection of the law without any discrimination in all instances, including for members of religious, ethnic, linguistic or other minority groups, officially recognized or otherwise;

(*c*) To eliminate, in law and in practice, the use of torture and other cruel, inhuman or degrading treatment or punishment, such as amputations and flogging and, as previously proposed by the elected Iranian parliament, to accede to the Convention against Torture and Other Cruel, Inhuman or Degrading Treatment or Punishment;[9] and to end impunity for violations of human rights that constitute crimes by bringing the perpetrators to justice in accordance with international standards, noting in this regard, inter alia, the updated set of principles for the protection and promotion of human rights through action to combat impunity;[10]

(*d*) To abolish, in law and in practice, public executions and other executions carried out in the absence of respect for internationally recognized safeguards, in particular, as called for by the Committee on the Rights of the Child in its report of January 2005,[11] executions of persons who at the time of their offence were under the age of 18, and to uphold the moratoriums on juvenile executions and executions by stoning and to introduce these moratoriums as law in order to completely abolish this punishment;

(*e*) To eliminate, in law and in practice, all forms of discrimination and violence against women and girls and, as previously proposed by the elected Iranian parliament, to accede to the Convention on the Elimination of All Forms of Discrimination against Women;[12]

(*f*) To eliminate, in law and in practice, all forms of discrimination based on religious, ethnic or linguistic grounds and other human rights violations against persons belonging to minorities, including Arabs, Azeris, Baha'is, Baluchis, Kurds, Christians, Jews, Sufis and Sunni Muslims, to refrain from monitoring individuals on the basis of their religious beliefs, to ensure that minorities' access to education is on a par with that of all Iranians and to address these matters in an open manner, with the full participation of the minorities themselves, to otherwise ensure full respect for the right to freedom of thought, conscience, religion or belief of all persons, and to implement the 1996 report of the Special Rapporteur on religious intolerance,[13] which recommended ways in which the Islamic Republic of Iran could emancipate the Baha'i community;

4. *Encourages* the thematic procedures of the Human Rights Council, inter alia, the Special Rapporteur on extrajudicial, summary or arbitrary executions, the Special Rapporteur on torture and other cruel, inhuman or degrading treatment or punishment, the Special Rapporteur on the independence of judges and lawyers, the Special Rapporteur on freedom of religion or belief, the Special Rapporteur on the promotion and protection of the right to freedom of opinion and expression, the Special Representative of the Secretary-General on the situation of human rights defenders, the Working Group on Arbitrary Detention and the Working Group on Enforced or Involuntary Disappearances, to visit or otherwise continue their work to improve the situation of human rights in the Islamic Republic of Iran, and urges the Government of the Islamic Republic of Iran to live up to the commitment it made when it issued a standing invitation to special procedures by cooperating with them, and to illustrate how their subsequent recommendations have been addressed, including the recommendations of special procedures that have previously visited the country;

5. *Decides* to continue its examination of the situation of human rights in the Islamic Republic of Iran at its sixty-second session under the item entitled "Promotion and protection of human rights".

81st plenary meeting
19 December 2006

---

[1] Resolution 217 A (III).

[2] Resolution 2200 A (XXI), annex.

[3] United Nations, *Treaty Series*, vol. 660, No. 9464.

[4] Ibid., vol. 1577, No. 27531.

[5] See *Official Records of the Economic and Social Council, 2001, Supplement No. 3* (E/2001/23), chap. II, sect. A.

[6] A/60/770/Add.1, annex.

[7] E/CN.4/2006/61/Add.3.

[8] E/CN.4/2006/41/Add.2.

[9] United Nations, *Treaty Series*, vol. 1465, No. 24841.

[10] See E/CN.4/2005/102 and Add.1.

[11] See CRC/C/146.

[12] United Nations, *Treaty Series*, vol. 1249, No. 20378.

[13] See E/CN.4/1996/95/Add.2.

Resolution 61/177

[on the report of the Third Committee (A/61/448 and Corr.2)]

61/177. International Convention for the Protection of All Persons from Enforced Disappearance

The General Assembly,

Taking note of Human Rights Council resolution 1/1 of 29 June 2006,[1] by which the Council adopted the International Convention for the Protection of All Persons from Enforced Disappearance,

1. *Acknowledges* the adoption by the Human Rights Council of the International Convention for the Protection of All Persons from Enforced Disappearance;

2. *Adopts* and opens for signature, ratification and accession the International Convention for the Protection of All Persons from Enforced Disappearance, the text of which is annexed to the present resolution;

3. *Recommends* that the Convention be opened for signature at a signing ceremony in Paris.

82nd plenary meeting
20 December 2006

Annex
International Convention for the Protection of All Persons from Enforced Disappearance

Preamble

The States Parties to this Convention,

Considering the obligation of States under the Charter of the United Nations to promote universal respect for, and observance of, human rights and fundamental freedoms,

Having regard to the Universal Declaration of Human Rights,

Recalling the International Covenant on Economic, Social and Cultural Rights, the International Covenant on Civil and Political Rights and the other relevant international instruments in the fields of human rights, humanitarian law and international criminal law,

Also recalling the Declaration on the Protection of All Persons from Enforced Disappearance adopted by the General Assembly of the United Nations in its resolution 47/133 of 18 December 1992,

Aware of the extreme seriousness of enforced disappearance, which constitutes a crime and, in certain circumstances defined in international law, a crime against humanity,

Determined to prevent enforced disappearances and to combat impunity for the crime of enforced disappearance,

Considering the right of any person not to be subjected to enforced disappearance, the right of victims to justice and to reparation,

Affirming the right of any victim to know the truth about the circumstances of an enforced disappearance and the fate of the disappeared person, and the right to freedom to seek, receive and impart information to this end,

Have agreed on the following articles:

Part I

Article 1

1. No one shall be subjected to enforced disappearance.

2. No exceptional circumstances whatsoever, whether a state of war or a threat of war, internal political instability or any other public emergency, may be invoked as a justification for enforced disappearance.

Article 2

For the purposes of this Convention, "enforced disappearance" is considered to be the arrest, detention, abduction or any other form of deprivation of liberty by agents of the State or by persons or groups of persons acting with the authorization, support or acquiescence of the State, followed by a refusal to acknowledge the deprivation of liberty or by concealment of the fate or whereabouts of the disappeared person, which place such a person outside the protection of the law.

Article 3

Each State Party shall take appropriate measures to investigate acts defined in article 2 committed by persons or groups of persons acting without the authorization, support or acquiescence of the State and to bring those responsible to justice.

Article 4

Each State Party shall take the necessary measures to ensure that enforced disappearance constitutes an offence under its criminal law.

Article 5

The widespread or systematic practice of enforced disappearance constitutes a crime against humanity as defined in applicable international law and shall attract the consequences provided for under such applicable international law.

Article 6

1. Each State Party shall take the necessary measures to hold criminally responsible at least:

(*a*) Any person who commits, orders, solicits or induces the commission of, attempts to commit, is an accomplice to or participates in an enforced disappearance;

(*b*) A superior who:

(i) Knew, or consciously disregarded information which clearly indicated, that subordinates under his or her effective authority and control were committing or about to commit a crime of enforced disappearance;

(ii) Exercised effective responsibility for and control over activities which were concerned with the crime of enforced disappearance; and

(iii) Failed to take all necessary and reasonable measures within his or her power to prevent or repress the commission of an enforced disappearance or to submit the matter to the competent authorities for investigation and prosecution;

(*c*) Subparagraph (*b*) above is without prejudice to the higher standards of responsibility applicable under relevant international law to a military commander or to a person effectively acting as a military commander.

2. No order or instruction from any public authority, civilian, military or other, may be invoked to justify an offence of enforced disappearance.

Article 7

1. Each State Party shall make the offence of enforced disappearance punishable by appropriate penalties which take into account its extreme seriousness.

2. Each State Party may establish:

(*a*) Mitigating circumstances, in particular for persons who, having been implicated in the commission of an enforced disappearance, effectively contribute to bringing the disappeared person forward alive or make it possible to clarify cases of enforced disappearance or to identify the perpetrators of an enforced disappearance;

(*b*) Without prejudice to other criminal procedures, aggravating circumstances, in particular in the event of the death of the disappeared person or the commission of an enforced disappearance in respect of pregnant women, minors, persons with disabilities or other particularly vulnerable persons.

Article 8

Without prejudice to article 5,

1. A State Party which applies a statute of limitations in respect of enforced disappearance shall take the necessary measures to ensure that the term of limitation for criminal proceedings:

(*a*) Is of long duration and is proportionate to the extreme seriousness of this offence;

(*b*) Commences from the moment when the offence of enforced disappearance ceases, taking into account its continuous nature.

2. Each State Party shall guarantee the right of victims of enforced disappearance to an effective remedy during the term of limitation.

Article 9

1. Each State Party shall take the necessary measures to establish its competence to exercise jurisdiction over the offence of enforced disappearance:

(*a*) When the offence is committed in any territory under its jurisdiction or on board a ship or aircraft registered in that State;

(*b*) When the alleged offender is one of its nationals;

(*c*) When the disappeared person is one of its nationals and the State Party considers it appropriate.

2. Each State Party shall likewise take such measures as may be necessary to establish its competence to exercise jurisdiction over the offence of enforced disappearance when the alleged offender is present in any territory under its jurisdiction, unless it extradites or surrenders him or her to another State in accordance with its international obligations or surrenders him or her to an international criminal tribunal whose jurisdiction it has recognized.

3. This Convention does not exclude any additional criminal jurisdiction exercised in accordance with national law.

Article 10

1. Upon being satisfied, after an examination of the information available to it, that the circumstances so warrant, any State Party in whose territory a person suspected of having committed an offence of enforced disappearance is present shall take him or her into custody or take such other legal measures as are necessary to ensure his or her presence. The custody and other legal measures shall be as provided for in the law of that State Party but may be maintained only for such time as is necessary to ensure the person's presence at criminal, surrender or extradition proceedings.

2. A State Party which has taken the measures referred to in paragraph 1 of this article shall immediately carry out a preliminary inquiry or investigations to establish the facts. It shall notify the States Parties referred to in article 9, paragraph 1, of the measures it has taken in pursuance of paragraph 1 of this article, including detention and the circumstances warranting detention, and of the findings of its preliminary inquiry or its investigations, indicating whether it intends to exercise its jurisdiction.

3. Any person in custody pursuant to paragraph 1 of this article may communicate immediately with the nearest appropriate representative of the State of which he or she is a national, or, if he or she is a stateless person, with the representative of the State where he or she usually resides.

Article 11

1. The State Party in the territory under whose jurisdiction a person alleged to have committed an offence of enforced disappearance is found shall, if it does not extradite that person or surrender him or her to another State in accordance with its international obligations or surrender him or her to an international criminal tribunal whose jurisdiction it has recognized, submit the case to its competent authorities for the purpose of prosecution.

2. These authorities shall take their decision in the same manner as in the case of any ordinary offence of a serious nature under the law of that State Party. In the cases referred to in article 9, paragraph 2, the standards of evidence required for prosecution and conviction shall in no way be less stringent than those which apply in the cases referred to in article 9, paragraph 1.

3. Any person against whom proceedings are brought in connection with an offence of enforced disappearance shall be guaranteed fair treatment at all stages of the proceedings. Any person tried for an offence of enforced disappearance shall benefit from a fair trial before a competent, independent and impartial court or tribunal established by law.

Article 12

1. Each State Party shall ensure that any individual who alleges that a person has been subjected to enforced disappearance has the right to report the facts to the competent authorities, which shall examine the allegation promptly and impartially and, where necessary, undertake without delay a thorough and impartial investigation. Appropriate steps shall be taken, where necessary, to ensure that the complainant, witnesses, relatives of the disappeared person and their defence counsel, as well as persons participating in the investigation, are protected against all ill-treatment or intimidation as a consequence of the complaint or any evidence given.

2. Where there are reasonable grounds for believing that a person has been subjected to enforced disappearance, the authorities referred to in paragraph 1 of this article shall undertake an investigation, even if there has been no formal complaint.

3. Each State Party shall ensure that the authorities referred to in paragraph 1 of this article:

(*a*) Have the necessary powers and resources to conduct the investigation effectively, including access to the documentation and other information relevant to their investigation;

(*b*) Have access, if necessary with the prior authorization of a judicial authority, which shall rule promptly on the matter, to any place of detention or any other place where there are reasonable grounds to believe that the disappeared person may be present.

4. Each State Party shall take the necessary measures to prevent and sanction acts that hinder the conduct of an investigation. It shall ensure in particular that persons suspected of having committed an offence of enforced disappearance are not in a position to influence the progress of an investigation by means of pressure or acts of intimidation or reprisal aimed at the complainant, witnesses, relatives of the disappeared person or their defence counsel, or at persons participating in the investigation.

Article 13

1. For the purposes of extradition between States Parties, the offence of enforced disappearance shall not be regarded as a political offence or as an offence connected with a political offence or as an offence inspired by political motives. Accordingly, a request for extradition based on such an offence may not be refused on these grounds alone.

2. The offence of enforced disappearance shall be deemed to be included as an extraditable offence in any extradition treaty existing between States Parties before the entry into force of this Convention.

3. States Parties undertake to include the offence of enforced disappearance as an extraditable offence in any extradition treaty subsequently to be concluded between them.

4. If a State Party which makes extradition conditional on the existence of a treaty receives a request for extradition from another State Party with which it has no extradition treaty, it may consider this Convention as the necessary legal basis for extradition in respect of the offence of enforced disappearance.

5. States Parties which do not make extradition conditional on the existence of a treaty shall recognize the offence of enforced disappearance as an extraditable offence between themselves.

6. Extradition shall, in all cases, be subject to the conditions provided for by the law of the requested State Party or by applicable extradition treaties, including, in particular, conditions relating to the minimum penalty requirement for extradition and the grounds upon which the requested State Party may refuse extradition or make it subject to certain conditions.

7. Nothing in this Convention shall be interpreted as imposing an obligation to extradite if the requested State Party has substantial grounds for believing that the request has been made for the purpose of prosecuting or punishing a person on account of that person's sex, race, religion, nationality, ethnic origin, political opinions or membership of a particular social group, or that compliance with the request would cause harm to that person for any one of these reasons.

Article 14

1. States Parties shall afford one another the greatest measure of mutual legal assistance in connection with criminal proceedings brought in respect of an offence of enforced disappearance, including the supply of all evidence at their disposal that is necessary for the proceedings.

2. Such mutual legal assistance shall be subject to the conditions provided for by the domestic law of the requested State Party or by applicable treaties on mutual legal assistance, including, in particular, the conditions in relation to the grounds upon which the requested State Party may refuse to grant mutual legal assistance or may make it subject to conditions.

Article 15

States Parties shall cooperate with each other and shall afford one another the greatest measure of mutual assistance with a view to assisting victims of enforced disappearance, and in searching for, locating and releasing disappeared persons and, in the event of death, in exhuming and identifying them and returning their remains.

1. No State Party shall expel, return ("refouler"), surrender or extradite a person to another State where there are substantial grounds for believing that he or she would be in danger of being subjected to enforced disappearance.

2. For the purpose of determining whether there are such grounds, the competent authorities shall take into account all relevant considerations, including, where applicable, the existence in the State concerned of a consistent pattern of gross, flagrant or mass violations of human rights or of serious violations of international humanitarian law.

Article 17

1. No one shall be held in secret detention.

2. Without prejudice to other international obligations of the State Party with regard to the deprivation of liberty, each State Party shall, in its legislation:

(*a*) Establish the conditions under which orders of deprivation of liberty may be given;

(*b*) Indicate those authorities authorized to order the deprivation of liberty;

(*c*) Guarantee that any person deprived of liberty shall be held solely in officially recognized and supervised places of deprivation of liberty;

(*d*) Guarantee that any person deprived of liberty shall be authorized to communicate with and be visited by his or her family, counsel or any other person of his or her choice, subject only to the conditions established by law, or, if he or she is a foreigner, to communicate with his or her consular authorities, in accordance with applicable international law;

(*e*) Guarantee access by the competent and legally authorized authorities and institutions to the places where persons are deprived of liberty, if necessary with prior authorization from a judicial authority;

(*f*) Guarantee that any person deprived of liberty or, in the case of a suspected enforced disappearance, since the person deprived of liberty is not able to exercise this right, any persons with a legitimate interest, such as relatives of the person deprived of liberty, their representatives or their counsel, shall, in all circumstances, be entitled to take proceedings before a court, in order that the court may decide without delay on the lawfulness of the deprivation of liberty and order the person's release if such deprivation of liberty is not lawful.

3. Each State Party shall assure the compilation and maintenance of one or more up-to-date official registers and/or records of persons deprived of liberty, which shall be made promptly available, upon request, to any judicial or other competent authority or institution authorized for that purpose by the law of the State Party concerned or any relevant international legal instrument to which the State concerned is a party. The information contained therein shall include, as a minimum:

(*a*) The identity of the person deprived of liberty;

(*b*) The date, time and place where the person was deprived of liberty and the identity of the authority that deprived the person of liberty;

(*c*) The authority that ordered the deprivation of liberty and the grounds for the deprivation of liberty;

(*d*) The authority responsible for supervising the deprivation of liberty;

(*e*) The place of deprivation of liberty, the date and time of admission to the place of deprivation of liberty and the authority responsible for the place of deprivation of liberty;

(*f*) Elements relating to the state of health of the person deprived of liberty;

(*g*) In the event of death during the deprivation of liberty, the circumstances and cause of death and the destination of the remains;

(*h*) The date and time of release or transfer to another place of detention, the destination and the authority responsible for the transfer.

Article 18

1. Subject to articles 19 and 20, each State Party shall guarantee to any person with a legitimate interest in this information, such as relatives of the person deprived of liberty, their representatives or their counsel, access to at least the following information:

(*a*) The authority that ordered the deprivation of liberty;

(*b*) The date, time and place where the person was deprived of liberty and admitted to the place of deprivation of liberty;

(*c*) The authority responsible for supervising the deprivation of liberty;

(*d*) The whereabouts of the person deprived of liberty, including, in the event of a transfer to another place of deprivation of liberty, the destination and the authority responsible for the transfer;

(*e*) The date, time and place of release;

(*f*) Elements relating to the state of health of the person deprived of liberty;

(*g*) In the event of death during the deprivation of liberty, the circumstances and cause of death and the destination of the remains.

2. Appropriate measures shall be taken, where necessary, to protect the persons referred to in paragraph 1 of this article, as well as persons participating in the investigation, from any

ill-treatment, intimidation or sanction as a result of the search for information concerning a person deprived of liberty.

Article 19

1. Personal information, including medical and genetic data, which is collected and/or transmitted within the framework of the search for a disappeared person shall not be used or made available for purposes other than the search for the disappeared person. This is without prejudice to the use of such information in criminal proceedings relating to an offence of enforced disappearance or the exercise of the right to obtain reparation.

2. The collection, processing, use and storage of personal information, including medical and genetic data, shall not infringe or have the effect of infringing the human rights, fundamental freedoms or human dignity of an individual.

Article 20

1. Only where a person is under the protection of the law and the deprivation of liberty is subject to judicial control may the right to information referred to in article 18 be restricted, on an exceptional basis, where strictly necessary and where provided for by law, and if the transmission of the information would adversely affect the privacy or safety of the person, hinder a criminal investigation, or for other equivalent reasons in accordance with the law, and in conformity with applicable international law and with the objectives of this Convention. In no case shall there be restrictions on the right to information referred to in article 18 that could constitute conduct defined in article 2 or be in violation of article 17, paragraph 1.

2. Without prejudice to consideration of the lawfulness of the deprivation of a person's liberty, States Parties shall guarantee to the persons referred to in article 18, paragraph 1, the right to a prompt and effective judicial remedy as a means of obtaining without delay the information referred to in article 18, paragraph 1. This right to a remedy may not be suspended or restricted in any circumstances.

Article 21

Each State Party shall take the necessary measures to ensure that persons deprived of liberty are released in a manner permitting reliable verification that they have actually been released. Each State Party shall also take the necessary measures to assure the physical integrity of such persons and their ability to exercise fully their rights at the time of release, without prejudice to any obligations to which such persons may be subject under national law.

Article 22

Without prejudice to article 6, each State Party shall take the necessary measures to prevent and impose sanctions for the following conduct:

(*a*) Delaying or obstructing the remedies referred to in article 17, paragraph 2 (*f*), and article 20, paragraph 2;

(*b*) Failure to record the deprivation of liberty of any person, or the recording of any information which the official responsible for the official register knew or should have known to be inaccurate;

(*c*) Refusal to provide information on the deprivation of liberty of a person, or the provision of inaccurate information, even though the legal requirements for providing such information have been met.

Article 23

1. Each State Party shall ensure that the training of law enforcement personnel, civil or military, medical personnel, public officials and other persons who may be involved in the custody or treatment of any person deprived of liberty includes the necessary education and information regarding the relevant provisions of this Convention, in order to:

(*a*) Prevent the involvement of such officials in enforced disappearances;

(*b*) Emphasize the importance of prevention and investigations in relation to enforced disappearances;

(*c*) Ensure that the urgent need to resolve cases of enforced disappearance is recognized.

2. Each State Party shall ensure that orders or instructions prescribing, authorizing or encouraging enforced disappearance are prohibited. Each State Party shall guarantee that a person who refuses to obey such an order will not be punished.

3. Each State Party shall take the necessary measures to ensure that the persons referred to in paragraph 1 of this article who have reason to believe that an enforced disappearance has occurred or is planned report the matter to their superiors and, where necessary, to the appropriate authorities or bodies vested with powers of review or remedy.

Article 24

1. For the purposes of this Convention, "victim" means the disappeared person and any individual who has suffered harm as the direct result of an enforced disappearance.

2. Each victim has the right to know the truth regarding the circumstances of the enforced disappearance, the progress and results of the investigation and the fate of the disappeared person. Each State Party shall take appropriate measures in this regard.

3. Each State Party shall take all appropriate measures to search for, locate and release disappeared persons and, in the event of death, to locate, respect and return their remains.

4. Each State Party shall ensure in its legal system that the victims of enforced disappearance have the right to obtain reparation and prompt, fair and adequate compensation.

5. The right to obtain reparation referred to in paragraph 4 of this article covers material and moral damages and, where appropriate, other forms of reparation such as:

(*a*) Restitution;

(*b*) Rehabilitation;

(*c*) Satisfaction, including restoration of dignity and reputation;

(*d*) Guarantees of non-repetition.

6. Without prejudice to the obligation to continue the investigation until the fate of the disappeared person has been clarified, each State Party shall take the appropriate steps with regard to the legal situation of disappeared persons whose fate has not been clarified and

that of their relatives, in fields such as social welfare, financial matters, family law and property rights.

7. Each State Party shall guarantee the right to form and participate freely in organizations and associations concerned with attempting to establish the circumstances of enforced disappearances and the fate of disappeared persons, and to assist victims of enforced disappearance.

Article 25

1. Each State Party shall take the necessary measures to prevent and punish under its criminal law:

(*a*) The wrongful removal of children who are subjected to enforced disappearance, children whose father, mother or legal guardian is subjected to enforced disappearance or children born during the captivity of a mother subjected to enforced disappearance;

(*b*) The falsification, concealment or destruction of documents attesting to the true identity of the children referred to in subparagraph (*a*) above.

2. Each State Party shall take the necessary measures to search for and identify the children referred to in paragraph 1 (*a*) of this article and to return them to their families of origin, in accordance with legal procedures and applicable international agreements.

3. States Parties shall assist one another in searching for, identifying and locating the children referred to in paragraph 1 (*a*) of this article.

4. Given the need to protect the best interests of the children referred to in paragraph 1 (*a*) of this article and their right to preserve, or to have re-established, their identity, including their nationality, name and family relations as recognized by law, States Parties which recognize a system of adoption or other form of placement of children shall have legal procedures in place to review the adoption or placement procedure, and, where appropriate, to annul any adoption or placement of children that originated in an enforced disappearance.

5. In all cases, and in particular in all matters relating to this article, the best interests of the child shall be a primary consideration, and a child who is capable of forming his or her own views shall have the right to express those views freely, the views of the child being given due weight in accordance with the age and maturity of the child.

Part II

Article 26

1. A Committee on Enforced Disappearances (hereinafter referred to as "the Committee") shall be established to carry out the functions provided for under this Convention. The Committee shall consist of ten experts of high moral character and recognized competence in the field of human rights, who shall serve in their personal capacity and be independent and impartial. The members of the Committee shall be elected by the States Parties according to equitable geographical distribution. Due account shall be taken of the usefulness of the participation in the work of the Committee of persons having relevant legal experience and of balanced gender representation.

2. The members of the Committee shall be elected by secret ballot from a list of persons nominated by States Parties from among their nationals, at biennial meetings of the States

Parties convened by the Secretary-General of the United Nations for this purpose. At those meetings, for which two thirds of the States Parties shall constitute a quorum, the persons elected to the Committee shall be those who obtain the largest number of votes and an absolute majority of the votes of the representatives of States Parties present and voting.

3. The initial election shall be held no later than six months after the date of entry into force of this Convention. Four months before the date of each election, the Secretary-General of the United Nations shall address a letter to the States Parties inviting them to submit nominations within three months. The Secretary-General shall prepare a list in alphabetical order of all persons thus nominated, indicating the State Party which nominated each candidate, and shall submit this list to all States Parties.

4. The members of the Committee shall be elected for a term of four years. They shall be eligible for re-election once. However, the term of five of the members elected at the first election shall expire at the end of two years; immediately after the first election, the names of these five members shall be chosen by lot by the chairman of the meeting referred to in paragraph 2 of this article.

5. If a member of the Committee dies or resigns or for any other reason can no longer perform his or her Committee duties, the State Party which nominated him or her shall, in accordance with the criteria set out in paragraph 1 of this article, appoint another candidate from among its nationals to serve out his or her term, subject to the approval of the majority of the States Parties. Such approval shall be considered to have been obtained unless half or more of the States Parties respond negatively within six weeks of having been informed by the Secretary-General of the United Nations of the proposed appointment.

6. The Committee shall establish its own rules of procedure.

7. The Secretary-General of the United Nations shall provide the Committee with the necessary means, staff and facilities for the effective performance of its functions. The Secretary-General of the United Nations shall convene the initial meeting of the Committee.

8. The members of the Committee shall be entitled to the facilities, privileges and immunities of experts on mission for the United Nations, as laid down in the relevant sections of the Convention on the Privileges and Immunities of the United Nations.

9. Each State Party shall cooperate with the Committee and assist its members in the fulfilment of their mandate, to the extent of the Committee's functions that the State Party has accepted.

Article 27

A Conference of the States Parties will take place at the earliest four years and at the latest six years following the entry into force of this Convention to evaluate the functioning of the Committee and to decide, in accordance with the procedure described in article 44, paragraph 2, whether it is appropriate to transfer to another body—without excluding any possibility—the monitoring of this Convention, in accordance with the functions defined in articles 28 to 36.

Article 28

1. In the framework of the competencies granted by this Convention, the Committee shall cooperate with all relevant organs, offices and specialized agencies and funds of the

United Nations, with the treaty bodies instituted by international instruments, with the special procedures of the United Nations and with the relevant regional intergovernmental organizations or bodies, as well as with all relevant State institutions, agencies or offices working towards the protection of all persons against enforced disappearances.

2. As it discharges its mandate, the Committee shall consult other treaty bodies instituted by relevant international human rights instruments, in particular the Human Rights Committee instituted by the International Covenant on Civil and Political Rights, with a view to ensuring the consistency of their respective observations and recommendations.

Article 29

1. Each State Party shall submit to the Committee, through the Secretary-General of the United Nations, a report on the measures taken to give effect to its obligations under this Convention, within two years after the entry into force of this Convention for the State Party concerned.

2. The Secretary-General of the United Nations shall make this report available to all States Parties.

3. Each report shall be considered by the Committee, which shall issue such comments, observations or recommendations as it may deem appropriate. The comments, observations or recommendations shall be communicated to the State Party concerned, which may respond to them, on its own initiative or at the request of the Committee.

4. The Committee may also request States Parties to provide additional information on the implementation of this Convention.

Article 30

1. A request that a disappeared person should be sought and found may be submitted to the Committee, as a matter of urgency, by relatives of the disappeared person or their legal representatives, their counsel or any person authorized by them, as well as by any other person having a legitimate interest.

2. If the Committee considers that a request for urgent action submitted in pursuance of paragraph 1 of this article:

(*a*) Is not manifestly unfounded;

(*b*) Does not constitute an abuse of the right of submission of such requests;

(*c*) Has already been duly presented to the competent bodies of the State Party concerned, such as those authorized to undertake investigations, where such a possibility exists;

(*d*) Is not incompatible with the provisions of this Convention; and

(*e*) The same matter is not being examined under another procedure of international investigation or settlement of the same nature; it shall request the State Party concerned to provide it with information on the situation of the persons sought, within a time limit set by the Committee.

3. In the light of the information provided by the State Party concerned in accordance with paragraph 2 of this article, the Committee may transmit recommendations to the

State Party, including a request that the State Party should take all the necessary measures, including interim measures, to locate and protect the person concerned in accordance with this Convention and to inform the Committee, within a specified period of time, of measures taken, taking into account the urgency of the situation. The Committee shall inform the person submitting the urgent action request of its recommendations and of the information provided to it by the State as it becomes available.

4. The Committee shall continue its efforts to work with the State Party concerned for as long as the fate of the person sought remains unresolved. The person presenting the request shall be kept informed.

Article 31

1. A State Party may at the time of ratification of this Convention or at any time afterwards declare that it recognizes the competence of the Committee to receive and consider communications from or on behalf of individuals subject to its jurisdiction claiming to be victims of a violation by this State Party of provisions of this Convention. The Committee shall not admit any communication concerning a State Party which has not made such a declaration.

2. The Committee shall consider a communication inadmissible where:

(*a*) The communication is anonymous;

(*b*) The communication constitutes an abuse of the right of submission of such communications or is incompatible with the provisions of this Convention;

(*c*) The same matter is being examined under another procedure of international investigation or settlement of the same nature; or where

(*d*) All effective available domestic remedies have not been exhausted. This rule shall not apply where the application of the remedies is unreasonably prolonged.

3. If the Committee considers that the communication meets the requirements set out in paragraph 2 of this article, it shall transmit the communication to the State Party concerned, requesting it to provide observations and comments within a time limit set by the Committee.

4. At any time after the receipt of a communication and before a determination on the merits has been reached, the Committee may transmit to the State Party concerned for its urgent consideration a request that the State Party will take such interim measures as may be necessary to avoid possible irreparable damage to the victims of the alleged violation. Where the Committee exercises its discretion, this does not imply a determination on admissibility or on the merits of the communication.

5. The Committee shall hold closed meetings when examining communications under the present article. It shall inform the author of a communication of the responses provided by the State Party concerned. When the Committee decides to finalize the procedure, it shall communicate its views to the State Party and to the author of the communication.

Article 32

A State Party to this Convention may at any time declare that it recognizes the competence of the Committee to receive and consider communications in which a State Party claims that another State Party is not fulfilling its obligations under this Convention. The Committee shall not receive communications concerning a State Party which has not made such a declaration, nor communications from a State Party which has not made such a declaration.

Article 33

1. If the Committee receives reliable information indicating that a State Party is seriously violating the provisions of this Convention, it may, after consultation with the State Party concerned, request one or more of its members to undertake a visit and report back to it without delay.

2. The Committee shall notify the State Party concerned, in writing, of its intention to organize a visit, indicating the composition of the delegation and the purpose of the visit. The State Party shall answer the Committee within a reasonable time.

3. Upon a substantiated request by the State Party, the Committee may decide to postpone or cancel its visit.

4. If the State Party agrees to the visit, the Committee and the State Party concerned shall work together to define the modalities of the visit and the State Party shall provide the Committee with all the facilities needed for the successful completion of the visit.

5. Following its visit, the Committee shall communicate to the State Party concerned its observations and recommendations.

Article 34

If the Committee receives information which appears to it to contain well-founded indications that enforced disappearance is being practised on a widespread or systematic basis in the territory under the jurisdiction of a State Party, it may, after seeking from the State Party concerned all relevant information on the situation, urgently bring the matter to the attention of the General Assembly of the United Nations, through the Secretary-General of the United Nations.

Article 35

1. The Committee shall have competence solely in respect of enforced disappearances which commenced after the entry into force of this Convention.

2. If a State becomes a party to this Convention after its entry into force, the obligations of that State vis-à-vis the Committee shall relate only to enforced disappearances which commenced after the entry into force of this Convention for the State concerned.

Article 36

1. The Committee shall submit an annual report on its activities under this Convention to the States Parties and to the General Assembly of the United Nations.

2. Before an observation on a State Party is published in the annual report, the State Party concerned shall be informed in advance and shall be given reasonable time to answer. This State Party may request the publication of its comments or observations in the report.

Part III

Article 37

Nothing in this Convention shall affect any provisions which are more conducive to the protection of all persons from enforced disappearance and which may be contained in:

(*a*) The law of a State Party;

(*b*) International law in force for that State.

Article 38

1. This Convention is open for signature by all Member States of the United Nations.

2. This Convention is subject to ratification by all Member States of the United Nations. Instruments of ratification shall be deposited with the Secretary-General of the United Nations.

3. This Convention is open to accession by all Member States of the United Nations. Accession shall be effected by the deposit of an instrument of accession with the Secretary-General.

Article 39

1. This Convention shall enter into force on the thirtieth day after the date of deposit with the Secretary-General of the United Nations of the twentieth instrument of ratification or accession.

2. For each State ratifying or acceding to this Convention after the deposit of the twentieth instrument of ratification or accession, this Convention shall enter into force on the thirtieth day after the date of the deposit of that State's instrument of ratification or accession.

Article 40

The Secretary-General of the United Nations shall notify all States Members of the United Nations and all States which have signed or acceded to this Convention of the following:

(*a*) Signatures, ratifications and accessions under article 38;

(*b*) The date of entry into force of this Convention under article 39.

Article 41

The provisions of this Convention shall apply to all parts of federal States without any limitations or exceptions.

Article 42

1. Any dispute between two or more States Parties concerning the interpretation or application of this Convention which cannot be settled through negotiation or by the procedures expressly provided for in this Convention shall, at the request of one of them, be submitted to arbitration. If within six months from the date of the request for arbitration the Parties are unable to agree on the organization of the arbitration, any one of those Parties may refer the dispute to the International Court of Justice by request in conformity with the Statute of the Court.

2. A State may, at the time of signature or ratification of this Convention or accession thereto, declare that it does not consider itself bound by paragraph 1 of this article. The other States Parties shall not be bound by paragraph 1 of this article with respect to any State Party having made such a declaration.

3. Any State Party having made a declaration in accordance with the provisions of paragraph 2 of this article may at any time withdraw this declaration by notification to the Secretary-General of the United Nations.

Article 43

This Convention is without prejudice to the provisions of international humanitarian law, including the obligations of the High Contracting Parties to the four Geneva Conventions of 12 August 1949 and the two Additional Protocols thereto of 8 June 1977, or to the opportunity available to any State Party to authorize the International Committee of the Red Cross to visit places of detention in situations not covered by international humanitarian law.

Article 44

1. Any State Party to this Convention may propose an amendment and file it with the Secretary-General of the United Nations. The Secretary-General shall thereupon communicate the proposed amendment to the States Parties to this Convention with a request that they indicate whether they favour a conference of States Parties for the purpose of considering and voting upon the proposal. In the event that within four months from the date of such communication at least one third of the States Parties favour such a conference, the Secretary-General shall convene the conference under the auspices of the United Nations.

2. Any amendment adopted by a majority of two thirds of the States Parties present and voting at the conference shall be submitted by the Secretary-General of the United Nations to all the States Parties for acceptance.

3. An amendment adopted in accordance with paragraph 1 of this article shall enter into force when two thirds of the States Parties to this Convention have accepted it in accordance with their respective constitutional processes.

4. When amendments enter into force, they shall be binding on those States Parties which have accepted them, other States Parties still being bound by the provisions of this Convention and any earlier amendment which they have accepted.

Article 45

1. This Convention, of which the Arabic, Chinese, English, French, Russian and Spanish texts are equally authentic, shall be deposited with the Secretary-General of the United Nations.

2. The Secretary-General of the United Nations shall transmit certified copies of this Convention to all States referred to in article 38.

The manufacturer's authorised representative in the EU for product safety is Oxford University Press España S.A. of El Parque Empresarial San Fernando de Henares, Avenida de Castilla, 2 - 28830 Madrid (www.oup.es/en or product.safety@oup.com). OUP España S.A. also acts as importer into Spain of products made by the manufacturer.
Printed and bound by CPI Group (UK) Ltd, Croydon, CR0 4YY
14/09/2026
02216290-0020